Richard Strauss, July 1949: The last photograph

(Portrait study by Karsh of Ottawa)

RICHARD STRAUSS

A CRITICAL COMMENTARY
ON HIS LIFE AND WORKS
BY
NORMAN DEL MAR

VOLUME THREE

BARRIE & JENKINS
LONDON

PRINTED IN GREAT BRITAIN
BY W & J MACKAY LIMITED, CHATHAM
ISBN 214.65158.4

CONTENTS

CONTENTS

ILLUSTRATIONS

FOREWORD

IT is hard to realize that all of twelve years have passed since, spurred by the wise and encouraging hand of Geoffrey Robinson, the music editor of Barrie and Rockliff at that time, I set out on what has proved a far more extended journey than either of us foresaw.

Since then the international field of Strauss scholarship has borne much unexpected fruit, and knowledge which in the early 1960s could only be obtained from a single source has been expanded and corrected by reference to others published more recently.

In particular, therefore, much of the data in my appendices has been rendered obsolete and these have accordingly had to be rewritten; the necessity, however, kills two birds with one stone as it was always my intention that they should ultimately be moved from the first volume to the last, where they now reappear in their new and—I hope—definitive form.

I said in my Preface that I was conscious of a certain inexactness in my subtitle and this remains true: my scheme has continued to be primarily focussed on Strauss's output which I have aimed to comment upon in as complete a form as possible.

At the same time the biographical side has been incorporated at least to the extent of a framing commentary which, although making no claims to usurp the position to be filled by Dr Willi Schuh, Strauss's official biographer, does to the best of my belief cover all the essential facts.

I have also tried to deal as fairly as I could with that still acrimonious period of Strauss's life in which world events subjected him to so sharp a test of character and personal conduct. It is an interesting occupation to conjecture which of his predecessors in the ranks of the great composers, faced with a parallel situation at the same time of life, would have emerged with greater credit.

At any rate I would like to think that I have helped to avoid any recurrence of the kind of loaded distortion which was presented in a widely discussed television production.

As before, my grateful thanks are due to the many friends who have helped me in so many different ways—to Mr Klaus Schloessingk-Paul, who right up to the last page was a tower of strength with his wonderful clear-thinking and bi-lingual advice, to Mr Alan Jefferson with his enthusiasm for tracking down elusive details of knowledge and scholarship, to Mr Paul Reding for his passionate interest in accumulating and sharing *trouvailles* amongst the lesser-known works and Lieder, to Mr Michael Rose for invaluable assistance in the operatic chapters, to Mr Eric Sams for his encyclopaedic knowledge and keen perceptive help with the Lieder, to the late Dr Roth for many friendly and informative letters as well as for kind permission to quote from his splendid book, to Mr Barrie Iliffe for many highly enjoyable hours together clearing up points of language and detail, to Mr John Thomson for so much expert and friendly guidance in preparing the text of this and previous volumes for the press, and to all my friends at Boosey and Hawkes, at the BBC, and at the Hendon Public Libraries, who have made my researches so painless and enjoyable.

Nor must I neglect my publishers whose courtesy and generous co-operation has made possible the gradual progress of this enormous project which inevitably had to take its place against the background of my conducting assignments. And once again I must express my warmest affection and admiration for John and Alix Farrell, those more-than-Indexers, with whom collaboration has been a joy in itself.

I am indebted to the following for their permission to quote from copyright works: Boosey & Hawkes, Fürstner Ltd. and Oertel; Rahter; Universal Edition (Alfred A. Kalmus Ltd.); Henmar Press, New York; Bote und Bock; Forberg Verlag; Hinrichsen Edition (C. F. Peters); Leuckart; Challier; Dr Franz Strauss; Atlantis Verlag, Zurich; Beck, Munich; S. Fischer, Frankfurt; Victor Gollancz Ltd; Oxford University Press; Dent; Blackwood.

Millook Haven
January 1971   N.R.D.M.

LIST OF WORKS DISCUSSED IN VOLUME III

LIST OF WORKS DISCUSSED IN VOLUME III

ALPHABETICAL LIST OF SONGS

CHAPTER XVIII

A GAY PASTICHE

THE death of Hofmannsthal in 1929 caught Strauss on the verge of old age. He had for some time begun to feel that the creative impulse was threatening to dry up in him and that he had increasingly little desire to write any music other than for the stage. Since Hofmannsthal had been ten years his junior Strauss had reckoned on an indefinite period of collaboration to keep him supplied with operas for his regular mornings of composition. Now at one fell swoop the situation was utterly changed and it was of paramount importance that a successor be found forthwith.

With Kippenburg's suggestion of Stefan Zweig eagerly embraced,[1] Strauss pursued the contact assiduously even during the composition of *Arabella*. Although the halting progress of his work on Hofmannsthal's last libretto was one reason for this, there is no doubt that Strauss was anxious to maintain continuity in the sequence of his operas, almost as if he were frightened that an interruption might be fatal.

The choice of Zweig was certainly an interesting one. Although at the present time Zweig's work is suffering something of a recession, during his life he enjoyed enormous success and popularity both in Germany and abroad, and it would be no overstatement to say that he still occupies a place of esteem and affection in the field of German literature. Apart from his Novelettes, much of his best writing consists of biographical studies, whether of other literary figures (Verlaine, Verhaeren, Balzac and many more) or of fascinating historical charac-

[1] See Vol. II, p. 397.

ters (Mary Stuart, Marie Antoinette, etc.). A great humanist, he was absorbed by persons suffering as the result of some strong foible or obsession, many such appearing in his various books.

The humanistic aspect of his work emerged during the first World War at which time he exchanged many ideas with Romain Rolland. The importance of this will transpire a little later.

Zweig was a fervent believer in the universality of the theatre. If he had any criticism of his predecessor Hofmannsthal, for whom he had indeed an enormous admiration, it was that Hofmannsthal's stage works of the last years were too narrow in their appeal for his own views on the function of the theatre. In one of Zweig's first letters to Strauss he wrote:

> If I may speak openly, I find the last Hofmannsthal texts too heavily overladen with searching after a style, too greatly pressed into symbolism for the sharpness of any normal person's perception, so that it can no longer get across to a spectator who is not equipped with spy-glasses and a copy of the libretto. You must not misunderstand me over this. I am fully aware of the breadth of vision which Hofmannsthal had, which can only be gauged by the vibrant power of his language. But I fear that this impulse into, as it were, another dimension has harmed its transportable effectiveness—the validity of a work of art for each and all is not a prerequisite of its worth, but it is its last and decisive test.

When he saw that Strauss's approaches were in earnest, therefore, Zweig resolved to find some subject with good possibilities of wide appreciation. Two subjects came to hand as the result of turning over his files and these he outlined to Strauss without delay at the beginning of November 1931.

The first was a kind of Balletic Pantomime in the grand manner. Zweig seems to have set considerable store by this project which had, he said, been lying in his desk for the past ten years awaiting only the chance to be shown to Strauss, though out of courtesy to Hofmannsthal the plunge had never been taken. It was apparently to have been concerned less with choreographic possibilities than with the specific problem of bringing music to the people through the medium of the other arts. The scenic background was to be highly impressive, on the lines perhaps of Elektra. In particular it was to be so all-embracing, from deep tragedy to the lightest comedy, from the Apollonian to the Dionysiac, and yet crystal-clear in its expression, although wordless, that it would present no problems should it be played anywhere throughout the world.

It is tantalizing that the sketches for so comprehensive a scheme do not survive, for Zweig left nothing behind him on this scale of conception which, if truth be told, seems to have little in common with his work as we know it. It must have been something of a disappointment when Strauss shied away from it in favour of the second and more modest of his proposals.

2

It was whilst on a visit to Marseilles during the mid-1920's that Zweig inadvertently became interested in the writings of Ben Jonson. As he was searching for sources on a French subject in the Marseilles library he happened to come across Jusserand's *Histoire littéraire du peuple anglais* in which not only is Jonson prominently discussed but an unusually detailed synopsis is given of Jonson's play *Volpone*. Zweig was so taken with the plot of this that without even seeing the original text he at once wrote a free adaptation, completing the whole of his own *Volpone* at a single sitting.

He intended at first that what he had done should serve as no more than the prose sketch for a fully versified drama, but he was persuaded by the Dresden Court Theatre—to whom he showed the draft—that it would be a mistake to change a single word. The success it subsequently enjoyed encouraged Zweig to look more closely at the work of this remarkable Elizabethan poet and playwright.

Ben Jonson began life as a bricklayer before indulging in adventures as a soldier and actor, only to die in poverty after a period of outstanding success with his comedies. In German theatres Jonson's work had since become almost entirely unknown despite a collection of translations by Ludwig Tieck dating from the close of the eighteenth century.

Zweig's researches into Jonson naturally led him to Tieck, amongst whose collected writings he found one play of which Tieck had made no less than two transcriptions entitled respectively *Das Stumme Mädchen* and *Das Stille Frauenzimmer*. Here undoubtedly, in *Epicoene or The Silent Woman*, was one of the most important and amusing of Jonson's comedies, and Zweig duly earmarked it for future use. The opportunity he sought showed itself only a few years later with Strauss's quest for a subject and, the Pantomime rejected, Zweig successfully interested the composer in this second of his ventures into Elizabethan pastiche.

The subject of *Epicoene* was in no sense an original idea of Jonson's. The word itself, derived from both Latin (epicoenus) and Greek (ἐπίκοινος), denotes one who shares the characteristics of both sexes. The central feature of the plot is that of a foolish old man who marries, only to discover—to his intense relief—that the marriage is invalid since the supposed bride is a young man. The earliest example of this theme can be found as far back as the comedy *Casina* by the Roman dramatist Plautus (251–184 B.C.).

At the same time *The Silent Woman* hinges on the concept of a noise-hating misanthrope united to a mouse-like girl who immediately after the ceremony is transformed into a virago. This in its turn can be traced back to the *Declamatio sexta* by the Greek sophist Libanius (A.D. 314–393) which was printed in a Latin translation in 1606. Here we meet for the first time the name Morosus for the old misanthrope whose allergy to noise becomes the kernel of Jonson's drama of 1609.

Epicoene was subsequently used as the basis of Salieri's opera *Angiolina, ossia Il Matrimonio per susurro,* composed in 1800, while the mouse-turned-shrew aspect of the plot was also used for a comic opera by Pavesi produced in Milan in 1810, *Ser Marcantonius,* the libretto of which was by a certain Angelo Anelli.[2] It was from Anelli's comedy that Donizetti took the plot for his last opera *Don Pasquale*[3] which in this respect bears so strong a resemblance to Strauss's and Zweig's *Schweigsame Frau.*

Ben Jonson's comedy is a skilful combination of these two dramatic ideas in which Mistress Epicoene, at first all but voiceless, has plenty of time and scope to play the termagant before being unfrocked to reveal Ned Clerimont's Page-boy. Clerimont is a friend of Morose's nephew Sir Dauphine Eugenie, with whose connivance he is the inventor of the masquerade. Two further conspirators lend their support to the smooth course of the deception—another friend, Truewit, and Morose's barber who, in keeping with the descriptive names of so many characters in this as in other plays of the time, is called Cutbeard. Various comic side

---

[2] Anelli's script also contains one of the main ideas on which Puccini's *Gianni Schicchi* is based.

[3] Although not always recognized as such, the text of *Don Pasquale* was in fact the work of Donizetti himself (albeit with the aid of Giacomo Ruffini, who wrote under the *nom de plume* of Michele Accursi).

plots are provided by a collection of ridiculous figures such as Sir Jack Daw, Sir Amorous La-Foole, and a retired Land and Sea Captain, Thomas Otter, while the general noise and furore is heightened during the post-wedding débâcle by a grotesque group of advanced thinking Lady Collegiates.

By a curious chance, unknown to Zweig, this riotous comedy was at much the same time attracting other composers. Mark Lothar, a now forgotten German operatic composer had his *Lord Spleen,* specifically based on Jonson's *Epicoene,* produced in Dresden in November 1930; while of all composers, Elgar toyed for a time with ideas put to him by his friend Sir Barry Jackson for an opera based either on *Epicoene* or Jonson's *The Devil is an Ass.* Although nothing came of any creative projects during these last years of his life, Elgar seems to have been serious enough to have his nose put out of joint on reading in the newspaper early in 1933 of Strauss's plans for a Jonson opera.

3

Zweig decided to make a number of radical changes and simplifications to Jonson's play. The first and most far-reaching replaced Mistress Epicoene by a woman, and she none other than the actual wife of Morose's nephew. The effect of this was, perhaps a little unwisely, to increase the similarity with Donizetti's scenario in which Norina is specifically introduced as the inamorata of the nephew Ernesto.

The nephew himself was originally Sir Dauphine Eugenie, but Zweig, in order to emphasize to the utmost the clash with the noise-hating uncle, made him a member of a visiting Italian opera company. He was accordingly demoted from his knighthood, which Zweig conferred instead upon the uncle who became (with the typically continental misapplication of English titles—cf. Sir Churchill, Sir Beecham, etc.) Sir Morosus. The nephew became Henry Morosus, which appellation shows an unfortunate lack of understanding on Zweig's part of the function of the period character-names: the nephew in no way shares his uncle's misanthropic nature and therefore should not bear his name.

Zweig next pruned the action of all Jonson's subsidiary plots with the result that not only have the various comic figures (Jack Daw, La-Foole, Captain Otter, etc.) disappeared, but also the nephew's friends,

Clerimont and Truewit. The authorship of the deception therefore devolves upon the barber who accordingly grows enormously in stature from a mere accomplice to a Figaro personality, especially in the first act. His functional name, Cutbeard, Zweig translated literally as Schneidebart. The idea of Captain Otter was partially retained, however, by making Sir Morosus a retired sea captain. This has the virtue of justifying the old man's phobia, never explained but simply postulated in Jonson, which Zweig attributes to his experience of being blown up during a naval engagement.

Such an explanation certainly earns Sir Morosus a sympathy which, while no part of Jonson's design, was on the contrary very much in keeping with Zweig's humanitarian outlook; hence, through the humanizing of the central figure, the deepening of the whole drama quickly follows, an endearing asset despite some loss in verisimilitude at certain points.

Far from raising any objections to Zweig's redrafting of the action on either practical or artistic grounds, Strauss appears to have been uniformly delighted with his work at every stage. It had been his intention that Zweig should stay a few days with him *en famille* in the Garmisch villa, but although Zweig was more than ready to come to some modest Gasthaus in the neighbourhood, he repeatedly evaded the invitation to become a guest in the house. In excusing himself he reiterated his fear of being a disturbance to his hosts but there is small doubt that his shyness, his withdrawn personality, shunned the potential embarrassments from which any guest in Frau Pauline's establishment was likely to suffer, embarrassments which Hofmannsthal before him had so frequently taken pains to avoid. Seeing the red light therefore, Strauss abruptly abandoned his persuasions and, instead of leisurely discussions spread over a period in peaceful country surroundings, had a brief meeting or two with Zweig in a Munich hotel between various rehearsals and performances during November 1931. Zweig has written most interestingly of these early discussions:

> . . . it was a pleasant surprise to see how quickly, how clear-sightedly Strauss responded to my suggestions. I had not suspected in him so alert an understanding of art, so astounding a knowledge of dramaturgy. While the nature of the material was being explained to him he was already shaping it dramatically and adjusting it astonishingly to the limits of his own abilities of which he was uncannily cognisant. I have met many great artists in my life but never one

who knew how to maintain such abstract and unerring objectivity towards himself. Thus Strauss frankly admitted to me in the first hour of our meeting that he well knew that at seventy the composer's musical inspiration no longer possesses its pristine power. He could hardly succeed in composing symphonic works like *Till Eulenspiegel* and *Death and Transfiguration,* because just pure music requires an extreme measure of creative freshness. But the word could still inspire him. Something tangible, a substance already scaffolded, appealed to him for full dramatic realization, because musical themes sprang to him spontaneously out of situations and words, hence he had been devoting himself to operas in his later years. He knew well indeed, he said, that as an art form opera was dead. Wagner was so gigantic a peak that nobody could rise higher. 'But', he added, with a broad Bavarian grin, 'I solved the problem by making a detour around it.'

After we had agreed on outlines, he gave me a few minor instructions. He wished me to write unrestrictedly because he never was inspired by a ready-made book after the manner of a Verdi libretto, but only by a work conceived poetically. But it would suit him well if I were able to work in some complicated effects which would afford special possibilities for the employment of colour. 'I am not one to compose long melodies as did Mozart. I can't get beyond short themes. But what I can do, is to utilize such a theme, paraphrase it and extract everything that is in it, and I don't think there's anybody today who can match me at that'.[4]

At first Zweig's progress was not fast enough for Strauss. The full score of *Arabella* was nearing completion and he had wanted something fresh to work on for his summer composition period. But Zweig was not yet quite free and it was not until mid-August 1932 that the last pages of his great biography *Marie Antoinette* were sent off to the publishers and he was able to give his undivided attention to Strauss's libretto.

Nevertheless during June Zweig had managed to send Strauss a few pages of the opening scenes: 'This is only the first section—molto vivace—' he wrote, 'the lyrical passage in which Morosus laments his loneliness will follow at once, then comes the barber's canzona concerning women, and a duet. You will have all that at the end of the week at the latest . . . It goes without saying', he added diffidently, 'that all

[4] *The World of Yesterday.* Cassell, London, 1943.

this is merely a basis for work and if you want changes I will revise everything.'

But Strauss was not in any critical frame of mind. 'Enthusiastically I repeat that it is delightful,' he replied, 'the born comic opera—a buffo idea to be set beside the best examples of its kind—more suited to music than either *Figaro* or *The Barber of Seville*. I beg you to complete the first act as quickly as your other important work allows—I am burning to get started on it in earnest—I am always a little slow getting started until I get inside it and find the appropriate style. Once half an act is sketched out the feeling comes by itself.'

So, despite his many commitments, Zweig did his utmost to comply and the first half of Act 1 (up to Henry's entrance) was in the composer's hands by 14th September with the remainder of the act following exactly a month later. Strauss was delighted: '"Bravi, bravi, ganz ausgezeichnet" as it goes in *Così fan tutte*', he wrote.[5] The second act followed after an interval of only three months and again Strauss hailed it enthusiastically with an operatic quotation: 'Auch der zweite Bar gelang', from *Meistersinger*.[6]

This time there were a few comments to make, mostly in respect of compression. As Strauss pointed out: 'You wouldn't believe how setting to music elongates the most concise text'. It took Zweig only a single month more to make the required revisions and to polish off Act 3 which he sent to Strauss on 17th January 1933, this time with a quotation of his own: 'Plaudite amici, commedia finita est'—reputedly Beet-

---

[5] 'Bravo, simply excellent'. In point of fact Strauss not only misquoted the passage but dashing his letter off in the excitement of the moment he attributed the quotation to the wrong Mozart opera. I append the passage as it occurs in Act 1 Scene 15 of *Don Giovanni*.

In Strauss's defence however there are near parallels in *Così*.

[6] 'The second stanza is fine, too'; another inexact reference. What Wagner actually wrote was:

Perhaps Strauss was mixing it up with the earlier passage from the same scene of Act 3: 'Seht wie der ganze Bar gelang!'

hoven's words on his death-bed, though this time applied (as Zweig said) to happier circumstances. Strauss duly retaliated with a self-quotation with words and music, from one of the songs ('Ich trage meine Minne' op. 32 no. 1—it is amusing that even this is slightly misquoted) in which he twists the meaning of the poem to express his joy at having successfully found a true librettist.

The rapidity with which the work progressed at first was fantastic. It was as if, finding himself freed from the heart-searchings and arguments of working with Hofmannsthal, Strauss was indulging in the luxury of a straightforward text to the extent (as he later boasted indeed) of accepting it almost exactly as it stood. By the middle of February he had finished Act 1 and was making the fair copy. The opera was complete in particell (short score) by November 1933 and despite the gradual impinging of the sinister political situation the full score made excellent headway. Strauss gaily told Zweig that Act 1 was done in a letter of 21st January 1934, a similar letter for Act 2 followed on 24th August, and the whole opera was neatly copied out in score by 20th October, an extraordinary accomplishment of creative fluency for a seventy-year-old composer.

Finally, almost by way of an afterthought, Strauss added a little overture the following January, combining many of the best ideas from the opera in a single short burst of symphonic polyphony. The score of this was complete on 17th January and, tongue in cheek, he named it neither *Ouvertüre* nor *Vorspiel* but *Potpourri,* a derisory term once widely used to denote the medleys of opera or operetta cooked up for use by bands and café orchestras.

Its employment here is strictly speaking a misnomer since the predominant feature of such a piece was essentially that the tunes were strung end on end, often with no more than a simple modulation between them. The first musician to employ the word (which originally referred to a jar of dried petals mixed with perfumed spices) is said to be Johann Baptist Cramer, the composer pianist and publisher who worked in London during the first half of the nineteenth century. Chopin and Brahms were two of the composers who referred to works of theirs as Potpourris (the *Fantasia on Polish Airs,* op. 13 and the *Academic Festival Overture* respectively) but rather as a deprecating show of modesty than in earnest. Strauss's intention was hardly more serious though he went to the length of having the title printed at the head of the score.

The motif of Schneidebart's scheming is first heard as an ostinato on

the horn. This is a theme which Strauss had already employed as a
timpani figure for the last Interlude in the opera *Intermezzo*:[7]

Ex. 1

With Ex. 1 as background Strauss at once introduces a collection of
motifs which are associated with Timidia, Zweig's substitute for
Mistress Epicoene:

Ex. 2

Ex. 3

Ex. 4

Ex. 5

Before long Ex. 5, which in the opera accompanies Timidia's tantrums,
is replaced by the chordal motif of Morosus himself:

Ex. 6

[7] See Vol. II, p. 259. Its treatment here, however, strongly recalls the 'Carillon'
from Bizet's *L'Arlésienne*.

The cadence of the first group of subjects in this symphonic potpourri is then provided by the pathetic figure of Morosus' desire for peace:

Ex. 7

A transition section follows which uses a figure from Morosus' 'Noise' monologue in Act 1 (Ex. 8) and the motif of the garrulous Housekeeper (Ex. 9) to build quickly up to one of Timidia's more furious outbursts (Ex. 10):

Ex. 8

Ex. 9

Ex. 10

The music then passes directly to the conventional second subject for which Strauss employs the melody of Morosus' wedding to his supposed 'Silent Woman':

Ex. 11

Ex. 11 breaks off abruptly and the exposition is completed with two
further subjects belonging to the second group:

Ex. 12

Ex. 13

Ex. 12 is hardly more than an elaboration of the little figure ⌐ x ⌐
which is prominent during most of the busier ensembles, but Ex. 13 is
of particular significance since it reveals Timidia's true identity as
Aminta, the sweet devoted wife of Morosus' nephew Henry.

A development section follows which in its cataclysms of sound gives
a premonition of the ordeals in store for the poor old man (in this respect Strauss could certainly draw on personal experience). The recapitulation, although severely condensed, manages surreptitiously to
introduce a few more of the opera's motifs. The first of these derives
from Timidia's fury music but, transformed in various augmentations,
plays an important part in the character sketch of Aminta herself.

Ex. 14

Next, after an ingenious combination of Exx. 11 and 13, comes the
calm melody to which Morosus sings wistfully of his dreams of a companion in his lonely old age:

Ex. 15

The light staccato accompaniment to this theme is also motivic, being
the music to which Schneidebart and the opera troupe hatch their plot:

Ex. 16

Finally the return of Exx. 12 and 13 (also combined) leads to a melodic extension which originates in the duet for Aminta and Henry in the last scene of Act 2:

Ex. 17

The so-called Potpourri ends brilliantly with a *Stretta* in quicker tempo based largely on Exx. 1 and 2 but with the figures Exx. 12 and 14 reiterated to add to the general boisterousness of the closing bars. Short as it is, it makes an extremely effective overture not only in the opera house but for concert purposes, the repertoire of such pieces by Strauss being all too slender.

4

Zweig's decision to make Henry a member of a visiting opera troupe necessitated a change of period, since no such company existed in Jonson's day. The new date for the action was at first fixed for 1760 but this was moved forward a further twenty years to 1780 after the publication of the score (requiring little slips to be pasted over in each copy) perhaps since it was only by this later date that the Haymarket Theatre —in which the troupe was to play—had entered into its great period of prosperity under George Colman and could have undertaken the presentation of a season of Italian Opera.

At all events Zweig wrote to the designer Leonard Fanto that it was Handel's England at the time of George III which he had in mind, with especial reference to the costumes shown in Rowlandson's picture 'Vauxhall Gardens'.

Now that Jonson's Morose, the 'Gentleman who loves no noise' has become Sir Morosus, it is necessary that his nautical way of life should be firmly established at the outset. This is accordingly effected by the very appearance of his room, in which moreover the entire action of the opera is to take place. Every conceivable treasured possession of an erstwhile naval commander is to be seen crowding the stage—models of ships, anchors, flags, tackle, etc., not to mention firearms and the skeletons of giant fish.

The manservant Mute, with whom in Jonson's play Morose communicates only at a distance through a monstrous speaking-tube, is replaced by a garrulous Housekeeper. It is her themes which dominate the first pages of Scene 2 as she fusses about; Ex. 9 which has already appeared in the Potpourri is followed soon after by Exx. 18 and 19.

Ex. 18

Ex. 19

There is a knock at the door and she opens it to admit Schneidebart, infusing her welcome with interminable ingratiating remarks. At his entrance the motif of this factotum-Figaro-personality is unostentatiously slipped into the scurrying texture of the music:

Ex. 20

The barber's only concern is that the Housekeeper should announce his arrival but she cannot bear to waste the precious minutes when, her tyrannical master being asleep, she can be noisy with impunity.

During the course of her prattling it emerges that she has designs upon marrying Sir Morosus whom she has, after all, served faithfully for all of seventeen years, and that she looks to Schneidebart for assistance in her scheming. But the barber, already maddened by her ceaseless chatter, is outraged. He turns on her in fury and a violent quarrel ensues which is interrupted by the enraged figure of Morosus himself.

Ex. 21

It is quickly apparent that, unlike his Jonsonian prototype, Sir Morosus is prone to making more noise in his choleric outbursts than his disturbers were guilty of in the first place. He abuses the wretched Housekeeper in violent language full of colouristic nautical allusions and terrified she vanishes. The barber however, he clearly regards as an ally and Schneidebart soothes him with repetitions of the Peace motif Ex. 7.

But this evokes another outburst from Morosus whose one complaint in life is the impossibility of getting away from noise. In an extended monologue he describes the innumerable torments he endures from clamours of every kind. When he speaks of the world of entertainment and music Strauss enjoys himself by incorporating into the accompaniment quotations from one opera after another—*Faust, Freischütz, Tannhäuser, Meistersinger, Zauberflöte,* Nessler's *Der Trompeter von Säckingen* (aptly quoted on the trumpet)—all are intermingled in one great hotch-potch as if to justify Morosus' complaint.

The barber agrees that by day London is intolerable but suggests that at least during the night one might find peace. At this point he breaks for the first time into spoken dialogue, a form which Strauss uses largely (though not quite exclusively) for Schneidebart's more voluble moments.

Strauss was for some time undecided about the musical style of this new and very different opera. He wrote to Zweig at a quite early stage: 'I keep wondering if recitativo secco or spoken dialogue would be better for the many rapidly spoken scenes (especially for the barber). I'm worried that I won't be successful in recitativo secco which is not much in my line; its diatonic and harmonic Mozartian simplicity hardly fits in with the style of my music! What do you think?'

Zweig replied, trying to be helpful, but found it hard to express his views in clear-cut concise terms:

> I believe that full *Durchcomponierung* is the thing for a heroic subject (*Orpheus, Elektra*) or a lyrical one (*Tristan*). But in a gay opera which presents moreover a lively mixture

of different moods, and here in addition an incessant scenic and dramatic excitement, some relief from singing and from a full orchestration would be welcomed by the listener and would let him savour more fully the atmosphere of Comedy. Only I'm not in favour of having the accompaniment played on the harpsichord as in Mozart—that gives rather a scent of lavender, of historifying—I dream up, on the contrary, some quite light setting forth of underpainting with individual instruments—sharper in character than the harpsichord, such as flute, saxophone, drum, fife, violin, some kind of *modern* scansion; I believe something quite new could come from this, which lies very close to your personal art of short illustrative phonetics, a new form, *of our time,* of underpainting old recitative which could even have a lightly ironic tone as if during this recitative one was only playing about with music. I don't know whether I can make myself clear to you over my dreamings, but I have the feeling that it is just you who could show the young gentlemen how to bring up-to-date such an old technique as Recitative which, for example, the pathos of the barber parodies at the same time as it illustrates it—in short I wonder if one couldn't succeed in releasing the enthusiasm of the musician and make it bubble like champagne with the sparkling tones (but only very lightly, quite thinly between the individual movements) so that during the prose sections of the music one feels oneself now and then sharply excited but not satisfied . . .

Concerned lest he had still failed to make himself understood Zweig followed this exposé with a post-card emphasizing that the music should not actually stop for the dialogue lest each new entry would sound like an aria.

In many respects Zweig was on much the right track. A feather-weight continuous orchestral commentary as a background to spoken dialogue was often very effective and had for a long time been employed in *opéra comique*; witness, for example, Massenet's *Manon*. Strauss himself had used it—apart from his handling of melodrama—in *Intermezzo*. But this was a far cry from the idea that it could serve as a rejuvenation of an old technique for the benefit of the rising generation.

5

Schneidebart's suggestion that nightfall might bring to Morosus the peace he craves stimulates the old man to embark on a further jeremiad as he describes the tolling which emanates from the thousand belfries of old London during all and every night. This part of Morosus' monologue naturally gives Strauss the opportunity to join Moussorgsky and Rachmaninoff in the orchestral evocation of bells.

While he shaves his employer Schneidebart pursues the argument. Why does not Morosus replace his noisy dragon of a housekeeper by a sweet young 'silent woman'?

Ex. 22

At first Morosus scoffs at the idea but the barber, in another section of accompanied dialogue, prattles on as he warms to his idea. Instead of finding his talkativeness as tiresome as that of the old housekeeper, Morosus listens to Schneidebart who gradually returns to song for a vignette in which he describes the blessings and comfort a young wife can bring to an old man on a cold winter's evening. An inverted form of Ex. 22(x) becomes a dainty new theme suggestive of a happy marriage with some bright creature:

Ex. 23[8]

Morosus answers in a sombre but moving ariette based on Ex. 15. Certainly a beloved companion would give purpose to his old age, but when Schneidebart tries to take advantage of his softening mood he turns from him, recognizing that it would not do to impose age on youth. His bitterness finds expression in a theme of anguish.

[8] Cf. Dorimène's theme from the *Bourgeois Gentilhomme* music:

Ex. 24

But the barber is not to be discouraged. In a little Canzona, thus specifically labelled in the score, he expounds his thesis that there are sensible as well as silly girls in the world, girls who instead of being attracted by callow youths value the dignity and maturity of an elderly husband. Morosus tries to interrupt the progress of the song with re-iterations of his conviction that he is too old, but Schneidebart is irrepressible and the Canzona completes its formal scheme as a duet. The music of this pretty little set piece, skilful as it is, is extremely ingenuous and is more closely related to some of Strauss's lighter Lieder than to the music he had hitherto written for the stage. Nor, as will be seen, is this the only sign that Strauss was deliberately choosing a different style for what he regarded as a new direction in his operatic output.

Ex. 25

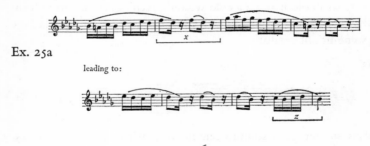

Ex. 25a

leading to:

6

There is a hubbub outside at the front door and Morosus springs up in a towering rage. In between his violent outbursts the voice of a visitor can be heard expostulating with the Housekeeper who is trying to prevent him from entering. She is, however, unsuccessful and suddenly Henry bursts in. At the sight of his nephew Morosus' anger evaporates instantly; through his expressions of amazement we learn that Henry had disappeared from university, where he was studying law, and had been given up for dead. He explains that the work was so tedious that he ran away, and the old captain—who himself ran away to sea as a boy—is delighted, welcoming him as a prodigal son. His repeated cries of 'A real Morosus' are supported by Ex. 21 on the heavy brass. Henry himself is introduced by a number of new motifs, alternately rhythmic and flowing, but Strauss refers to few of them during the course of the opera. The role was inescapably one for a tenor voice, never a favourite with Strauss, and Henry's character remains to the end the least clearly defined.

At once all ideas of marriage with a young 'silent woman' (Exx. 22(z) and 23) are banished. Morosus pronounces Henry his heir; he shall be shaved and generally cared for by Schneidebart (Ex. 20), nothing is too good for him (Ex. 6), he must make himself at home, eat, drink and have a bath (various watery noises on clarinet and strings).

But Henry has become decidedly uncomfortable. With the utmost nervousness he stammers out that he is not alone, that his troupe awaits him downstairs. Morosus, the retired commander, naturally connects the word 'troupe' with soldiers and to Henry's consternation enthusiastically calls out of the window, inviting them all into the house, as the music breaks into a spirited march based on the kind of material Strauss used for his Military Marches op. 57. Morosus himself struts about with galumphing figures on trombones and tuba which return periodically to depict his more gawkily dignified moments. The origin of such passages is to be found in the music which Strauss invented to describe Baron Ochs' similar antics.

Morosus is thunderstruck, however, when the military music gives way to a *Kleiner humoristischer Marsch*[9] and, in place of the platoon he had envisaged, a poorly clad troupe of opera singers gravely steps into the room.

Ex. 26

Of this composite theme, ⌐ x ⌐ characterizes the company as a whole, ⌐ y ⌐ is one of Henry's themes (it was indeed one of the motifs introduced at his first entry) and identifies him as one of their

⁹ 'Little humorous march'. Again the words appear as a title at the head of the page of score.

number, while ⌈ z ⌉ is concerned with the ladies of the troupe: Aminta, Isotta and Carlotta. Henry ignores the gathering storm of his uncle's wrath and introduces the company to him, beginning with Vanuzzi their leader, Morbio and the bass Farfallo, following up almost in the same breath with the three girls.

Morosus' objections are clearly based more on prejudice than actual hardship, for the prospect of having singers in his house infuriates him whereas he had viewed with pleasure the intrusion of a body of rowdy soldiers. Here the text departs entirely from Jonson's scheme; in addition to putting the action forward 150 years Zweig had also given Henry a profession which was wholly disreputable. As Professor Dent wrote: 'In the eighteenth century most opera singers were supposed to lead immoral lives, and in England it was something worse than that, for they were Italians and Papists and therefore in all probability secret agents of the Pretender.'

The thought that any member of his family should sing in public and for money outrages Morosus who can least of all understand why Henry should have dragged them over to England. Henry's account of Vanuzzi's prestige and the honour of presenting a season of opera at the Haymarket (accompanied by more operatic quotations, this time of 'La Donna è mobile' and of 'Mir anvertraut' from Die Frau ohne Schatten) only adds fuel to the fire and his own hopes of the leading role in the opera Orlando[10] make no impression upon the old man who rants about the shame to the house of Morosus. In addition to Exx. 7 and 15(x), the little descending figure Ex. 25(y) is strongly in evidence. Although this emanates from the barber's Canzone, it also harks back to Morosus' tirade against the noise of bells and it is clear that a battle is being waged in the mind of the old man between his desire for peace and his disappointment over the collapse of his plans for a happy re-tirement in congenial company.

The final straw comes when Henry confesses that he is married to one of the opera singers. He tries to introduce Aminta to his uncle but the

---

[10] Presumably Handel's, although Morosus tantalizingly interrupts Henry before he can utter the composer's name. Strauss and Zweig ignore the fact that Orlando was actually written for the castrato Senesino. Similarly Henry tells his uncle that Morbio, the baritone of the company, is celebrated for his performance in the role of Orfeo. Since this must surely be Gluck's opera there may be here a further clue in the matter of the opera's change of date from 1760 to 1780, since in 1760 Orfeo had not yet been composed, a fact likely to be familiar to Strauss, indifferent as he was to accuracy of circumstantial detail.

latter explodes. As Exx. 21 and 25(y) combine in a violent molto allegro Morosus disinherits Henry and an ensemble builds up quickly, every character on the stage (except Aminta and the barber) expressing the most furious indignation. There is even a little chorus of two tenors and two basses, representing the remainder of Vanuzzi's troupe.

In a towering rage Morosus hammers with his stick on the table and announces to the astonished company his decision to regard Henry as dead (more galumphing trombones). He then turns to Schneidebart (Ex. 20) and instructs him to proceed with his plan to produce a silent woman (Ex. 22(z)), complete with parson and notary; his marriage will take place the very next day. To a bevy of expostulations he reaffirms his intentions—any workhouse girl will do so long as she is quiet— wishes them all to the gallows and storms out slamming the door behind him.

7

In the *Letzte Scene* the stunned singers collect themselves. Apart from the lovers they are all indignant over the insult to their profession, but Aminta—who as the act progresses is more and more characterized by the figure ⌐ y ⌐ from the Silent Woman theme Ex. 22—is deeply concerned at the threat to Henry's background and inheritance. An ensemble develops based largely on Ex. 26(x) but embodying many of the relevant motifs of the situation such as Morosus' Ex. 6 and the marriage theme Ex. 23. The five remaining members of the company (Isotta, Carlotta, Morbio, Vanuzzi and Farfallo) vow to plague Morosus with every conceivable noise until he capitulates.

As their anger mounts Schneidebart steps between them and interrupts (Ex. 20), insisting that they are doing Sir Morosus an injustice (Ex. 21). They naturally reject such an idea out of hand but he persists, dropping into rapid speech as he explains the old man's intolerance of any noise 'other than what he himself makes'. The story of the powder magazine of his ship exploding and blowing him skyhigh is a little tall, especially his rescue unharmed but for his shattered eardrums. Nevertheless it all adds to the prevailing mood of light comedy which Strauss's spasmodic orchestral interpolations go far to enhance.

Above all, Schneidebart's (and Zweig's) main concern is to establish Morosus as a much maligned sweet old gentleman and Aminta as a softhearted sympathetic character who reacts to the tale with an instinctive show of pity and remorse at their behaviour to him.

The barber continues with an aria (non-motivic apart from the introductory bars of his Ex. 20) in which he warns Henry to act with discretion on account of the enormous extent of Morosus' wealth (and Henry's expectations) if only he can play his cards skilfully. The assembled company join in during the latter part of this elegant number with astonished repetitions of the sums involved.

This is followed by a duet for Aminta and Henry, once again markedly in the style of Strauss's Lieder rather than that of his previous compositions for the stage. As he worked he must have often said to himself 'I wonder what poor Hofmannsthal would have thought of this.' For here he certainly stripped off his Wagnerian armour and came closer to the spirit of classical opera than ever before or than he ever was to again.

Aminta begs Henry to sacrifice her freely rather than risk losing such wealth, and he for his part rejects any idea of money coming before his love. The music is again basically non-motivic, though little soaring phrases suggestive of Ex. 4 are ingeniously woven into both melody and accompaniment:

Ex. 27

The other members of the troupe add their approbation of this noble show of mutual self-sacrifice.

But Schneidebart is not satisfied. The ensemble breaks off in mid-air as he interrupts in order to point out that altruism driven too far with such a fortune at stake is indistinguishable from mere stupidity. Besides it is his responsibility to unearth some silent woman for the old man by the following morning. He addresses Isotta and Carlotta asking whether either of them are not attracted by the prospect of marrying sixty thousand pounds at the sole cost of being henceforth demure and silent.

Each replies in a little set piece, Isotta that she would laugh all day, and Carlotta that she would sing from morning to night. Strauss became somewhat oppressed by this succession of tiny numbers and asked Zweig for a few lines with which Aminta—and possibly Schneidebart—might join Carlotta. Zweig readily obliged and accordingly Aminta joins the others in a short trio which adds variety in rounding off

Carlotta's aria. Schneidebart's contributions consist of his self-evident convictions that none of this will do at all for Morosus (Ex. 6).

Suddenly the barber stops in his tracks: he has had an idea. In very stylized fashion the company echo his words and call for silence with a couple of foolish little unaccompanied choruses. Then Ex. 1 starts up and Schneidebart expounds his plan. Since it is with a stage company that he has to deal, it will be no problem for them to perform a mock wedding and one contrived in such a way that Morosus will be only too glad to discover subsequently that it is not valid.

At first the opera singers are bewildered but are gradually won over as Schneidebart fills in the details. Vanuzzi is to play the parson (Strauss supplies a short stretch of appropriately ecclesiastical harmony), Morbio and Farfallo notaries[11] (Ex. 26(x)), Carlotta a raw country wench and Isotta an elegant minx. Aminta is to be the sweet silent woman, full of charm and modesty—in fact she has no need to be other than herself. As a result Morosus is to be cured not only of his taste for marriage but, strange as it may seem, of his whole misanthropy at one fell swoop. Henry will regain his inheritance, a portion of which Schneidebart expects to come his way as a reward for his ingenuity.

The finale follows, a gay movement like an elaborate—and very extended—modernization of a Rossini finale. Each of the characters mimics the role indicated by Schneidebart whose praises they all unite in singing. There are three main musical sections, a dancing $\frac{6}{8}$ in which a version of the scheming motif Ex. 16 soon makes its appearance, an allegro $\frac{4}{4}$ largely concerned with the theme of the troupe Ex. 26, and lastly the Stretta:

Ex. 28

TUTTI: Die - sen_ O - heim zu_ ku - rie - ren, wird_ ein Spass be - son - de-rer Art_____
(to cure this uncle takes a special kind of joke)

leading via Ex. 16 to:

Ex. 28a

noch rascher

---

[11] In the event Farfallo is allotted a different role, but one so irrelevant to the situation that Zweig probably thought it wise not to confuse the issue at this stage.

The music waxes faster and ever more rumbustious, and the act ends with the entire company shouting 'Vivat Schneidebart'.

8

At the opening of the second act Morosus is shown dressing up for his wedding. It is the following afternoon and although he has not yet met the bride-to-be he is in no doubt that Schneidebart will be able to produce someone suitable. The Housekeeper is fussing round, making no secret of her opinion that they are making a fool of him (Ex. 18). The music in *Minuetto galante* style (again recalling the Act 2 introduction of the *Bourgeois Gentilhomme*) contains copious references to the marriage theme Ex. 23.

Morosus becomes increasingly irritable under the Housekeeper's taunts (Ex. 21) and eventually loses his temper with her. But she is a woman of spirit and although she quails under the outburst she reveals that her suspicions are based on plots she has overheard being hatched by the barber and his new accomplices (Exx. 20 and 16). Instead of appreciating the trouble she has taken on his behalf, Morosus turns on her for eavesdropping and chases her out of the room as Schneidebart enters.

The barber is very pleased with himself and his music is suave and ingratiating. Exx. 25a and 22(z) (the theme of his Canzone and the 'Silent Woman' motif) contrast sharply with the brusque interpolations of Ex. 21 which betray Morosus' anxiety and impatience. Schneidebart extols the virtues of the three candidates he has brought with him and assures Morosus that both priest and notary are standing by to officiate as soon as he has made his choice.

Within the normal conventions of opera it is now time for an aria and the barber accordingly has another little Canzone in which he prepares Morosus for the shy, ingenuous creatures soon to be submitted for his approval. The music contains no new material but incorporates the relevant motifs in the course of one of Strauss's typical pieces of neoclassicism. The instrumentation is delicately carried out in quasi-chamber music style, as Strauss was at pains to point out in a footnote (oddly, perhaps, for there is nothing different here from what he had already done many times before).

The girls now enter to music suggestive of the humorous march Ex. 26 and array themselves for inspection. Schneidebart goes through elaborate mock instructions telling them how to behave, what an honour it is for them to meet so important a personage as Admiral Sir Morosus, and so on, while the girls duly play up to him, exaggerating the naïveté of their adopted characters. The first to be introduced is Carlotta who, however, brashly delivers herself of a short tirade, spoken unaccompanied in the broadest country dialect, and is thus quickly disposed of. Next comes Isotta who, instead of the elegant minx projected in Act 1, is given the character of a prodigy of learning. Schneidebart begins the endless list of her accomplishments as the violins begin a rapid $\frac{6}{8}$ perpetuum mobile (her reputed skill in music causes a near crisis hastily averted when Schneidebart assures Morosus that it is purely theoretical knowledge) and she herself continues the account in a torrent of words. Morosus is soon breathlessly eager to have this babbler removed, and the coast is clear for Aminta to be presented. Schneidebart introduces her as Timidia, a descriptive name given (he says) by the Sisters at her convent school on account of her modest and retiring nature.

Timidia begins with a long monologue consisting of an extended self-display of virtue and piety, the slow tempo of which makes her improbable loquacity seem even more drawn out than the rapid chatter of her predecessor. Matters have of course, been so arranged that after the two previous candidates, Aminta–alias–Timidia has no competition and her success is a foregone conclusion. Nevertheless Zweig was unwise to give her so long a speech on her very first encounter with Morosus. It is surprising too that Strauss decided to make no excisions on his own account; not that he was unable to recognize the weakness of the section, for he wrote to Zweig asking him to reconsider it, as well as a number of other places, with a view to making the drama tighter.

Certainly if taken on its musical qualities much of the passage can be made to sound ravishing in the hands of a consummate coloratura artist. The texture, while primarily an elaborate development of Exx. 3 and 4, also introduces a new warmly melodic effusion:

Ex. 29

Morosus is entirely captivated and it now becomes Schneidebart's

role as go-between (Ex. 25a) to acquaint the girl with his marital intentions. This he does in a gentle Allegretto still based on the same music
though with the addition of a gently skipping triplet figure.[12] Timidia
pretends to be aghast at the idea of her being worthy of such an honour;
surely everyone must be making fun of her. Her show of humility is
illustrated by a new motivic phrase:

Ex. 30

At last Morosus speaks for himself and formally proposes. Carlotta and
Isotta march out of the room in mock rage at Timidia's having succeeded where they failed, Schneidebart goes to fetch notary and priest,
and the prospective bride and bridegroom enjoy a long melodic dialogue. Strauss knew that here too was a weak corner of the drama and
urged Zweig to compress it substantially. From the correspondence it
would appear that Zweig readily agreed and undertook to rewrite the
offending scenes in an altogether more concise form. Unless he somehow failed to keep this promise the conclusion seems to be that the
original was even more diffuse and long-winded.

Sir Morosus with gentle sympathy expresses his fears and doubts
concerning their disproportionate ages (Ex. 24), but Timidia reassures
him of her determination to overcome her unworthiness (Ex. 30); she
will love him as a father and do what she can to make him happy. The
climax comes with a glowing return of the Old-Age-Companion
motif Ex. 15, and the scene ends as the barber re-enters to announce the
dignitaries—in reality Vanuzzi and Morbio in disguise.

9

Here Strauss, a little at a loss to find suitable music to match this ponderous burlesque, was struck by a whim. Bearing in mind the Elizabethan origin of the Morosus drama it occurred to him that since he had
already amused himself by filling the score with quotations, a little

[12] The similarity of one of the permutations of this figure to Tchaikovsky's
Capriccio Italien has sometimes caused it to be taken as another deliberate quotation.
However, both the irrelevant context and the musical effect of the passage tell
against the suggestion.

music from Ben Jonson's own time might fit in very nicely. The fact that the action had been transferred to so much later a period was no disadvantage since scholarship or realism had never taken any part in the scheme, which is indeed such a hotch-potch that it scarcely bears serious investigation at any point.

So Strauss began to delve into the *Fitzwilliam Virginal Book*. It was really immaterial which piece he used and thumbing through the first volume his fancy lighted upon an anonymous Alman No. XIV.[13] So down it went verbatim.

Ex. 31

Schneidebart formally introduces the newcomers in rapid speech as the Alman runs its course, and Vanuzzi answers in unctuous tones accompanied by a passage underlining his ecclesiastical calling with the use of parallel fifths. It is Morbio's turn next to establish his presence in a legal capacity and Strauss sets his contribution to another quotation from the Virginal Book, an Alman by Martin Pearson, No. XC. Rather than reproduce a further piece unchanged, however, Strauss set about finding ways to embroider and adapt this new *trouvaille*. To begin with he transposed it down a tone,[15] added a rising counterpoint on the horn, and omitted the florid variations. These would clearly be unsuitable for the ensemble of brass and wind which he had decided would make an attractive contrast to his string instrumentation of the preceding Alman.

The two rogues strengthen the deception with a spoken dialogue of mock learning after which the marriage ceremony begins in earnest.

[13] The Alman (or Almain) was the old English term for the *allemande*, a slow dance in duple time. As Krause points out, it was unfortunate that Strauss mistook the word 'Anon' for the name of a composer.

[14] In transcribing this for strings Strauss interpreted the notation at its face value in the modern sense and ignored the editor's preface on the subject of ornaments. There it is explained that the double-strokes to the notes indicate 'Pralltriller' or 'Mordants' and not tremolos at all. However, it could be readily argued that even if he had noticed Strauss would not have been very interested.

[15] He achieved this by transcribing the opening bars exactly as he found them but for the trumpet in B flat, the sound emitted by this instrument being a tone lower than written.

The barber and the housekeeper act as witnesses and as a result they are required to reveal their full identity. Zweig obviously relished finding colourful names for them, settling upon Theodosia Zimmerlein and Pankrazius Schneidebart in defiance of Ben Jonson's habit of only adding first names to his type figures if these also contributed to their function or character (Sir Amorous La-Foole, for example).

Ex. 31 is repeated on the lower strings as Vanuzzi solemnizes the union, so far forgetting his presence in a Protestant community by pronouncing the crucial words in Latin (an alarming practice in 1780, the year of the Gordon riots). He then congratulates the happy couple and Morosus invites his guests to a drink in celebration of the occasion. The music builds up in Straussian manner once more, to an extended ensemble[16] which blossoms into the melody Ex. 11 now heard for the first time in the opera itself. The scene is one of unalloyed happiness and as the glasses clink Morosus expresses his emotion at so much peace and joy 'as if an angel were passing'.

Abruptly the peace is shattered. That it should be so was entirely to be expected, being part of the basic plot which at this juncture is at its nearest to *Don Pasquale*. But it should of course be Timidia who breaks the spell; her transformation into a virago the second she finds herself safely married is the moment for which everyone is waiting. The drama is specifically geared to this in the original Jonson as it is equally for Norina's transformation in Donizetti's comedy. So direct an approach was not in Zweig's timescale however, and Timidia's eruption has to take second place to another and wholly unexpected furore.

There is an appalling commotion downstairs and, as the noise approaches, the doors are flung open. Farfallo appears disguised as a seaman, leading a body of rough sailors who pour into the room. The music has broken off and amidst the commotion on stage Farfallo shouts at the top of his voice that here are Sir Morosus' old shipmates, come to celebrate the splendid news of his marriage.[17]

It is in vain that Morosus swears that he has never seen them before in his life. Farfallo strikes up a riotous drinking song which the chorus echoes with enthusiasm.

[16] Here again is a section which was originally even longer, but made more concise by Zweig at Strauss's request.

[17] It is to be understood, the stage directions instruct us, that these are all members of Vanuzzi's troupe dressed up, although it is the first time we have seen them in such numbers. It is also to be assumed that all these Italians are linguists enough to pass for rough British seamen who sailed under Sir Morosus in the British Navy.

Since they sing 'Vivat Sir Morosus' much as 'Vivat Schneidebart' in the Stretta of the Act 1 Finale, Strauss builds this section on largely the same material (especially Exx. 16 and 28a) though held together by a new collection of boisterous themes:

Ex. 32

Morosus, soon beside himself with rage (Ex. 21) is pressed on all sides to calm himself (Ex. 7) while Farfallo embarks on a second verse of his song in which, pretending to have taken offence, he flings open the window and calls to the entire neighbourhood to witness the ungracious way in which their well-meant display of congratulations has been received by the old man. A cataclysm ensues with the stage filled to capacity with people antagonistic to Morosus for one reason or another.

This chorus shows Strauss's technical skill at its best and with a change of tempo to a rapid ¾ he writes a development section on the lines of the comparable débâcle in the second act of *Rosenkavalier*. Ex. 32, the figure Ex. 12(x), Morosus' Ex. 21, the Companion theme Ex. 15 and Aminta's Ex. 27, all combine as the neighbours berate Morosus, the avowed woman-hater, for dishonesty, deceit, insincerity and so on. Henry enters disguised as the leader of the chorus and starts up a third verse of Farfallo's song in which everyone joins ironically singing 'Hollahoh to the old boy and his young bride'. They are instructed to bellow, shriek, laugh, blare, pummel and gesticulate, while Strauss does all these things in his orchestra as well, with eight percussion players pounding away for all they are worth.

When Morosus is practically at his last gasp Schneidebart makes a speech hypocritically thanking everyone on the old man's behalf and inviting them, equally on his account, to take a drink at the local pub. This calls for yet a fourth verse of Ex. 32 by Farfallo and the shipmates as they pour out of the house, leaving poor Morosus sighing with relief at their departure (Ex. 7). Somewhat artificial as the scene has been, Zweig might well have claimed that its justification lay in the parallel 'softening up' scene in Jonson where the conspirators arrange for Sir John (Jack) Daw and La-Foole to hold their party in Morose's house with all the noisy Lady Collegiates in attendance. This, however, comes *after* the shock of Mistress Epicoene's change from a silent into a very noisy woman, and Zweig's redrafting of the action is dramatically unsound since the pandemonium of Farfallo and his sailors cannot fail to steal a good deal of Timidia's thunder.

The stage empties and the principal actors each whisper encouragement to Aminta in turn as they also leave, in order that Morosus may be wholly at her mercy. But she is dreading her approaching ordeal for she has come to pity and respect the old man (a series of pathetic variants of Ex. 29 accompanies her lament) and the barber's assurance that 'it will take vinegar and salt to cure his folly' is cold comfort. The music dies right away, the door closes and silence reigns for a moment once more.

Aminta's actual dejection on finding herself alone with Morosus enables her to begin her play-acting with sincerity by sitting down and sighing heavily. Naturally the good old man at once becomes solicitous (Ex. 15) and he presses her to confide in him if anything has made her unhappy. The more she protests the more importunate he becomes, until suddenly she can stand it no longer and, having planned her moment, breaks out with a furious top C. Her long-delayed outburst has come at last.

10

The music of the next section was liberally drawn on by Strauss for the Potpourri and it is Exx. 2(x), 3(x), 4, 5, 10, and 12 which form the backbone to Timidia's tantrums. At first Zweig has enabled her volteface to be sparked off by Morosus' irritating importunity, but she quickly passes far beyond all reasonableness. Warming to her task she insists that she will require independence of thought and actions, that being young she must be free to laugh, sing, dance, buy new clothes, and fill the house with servants, lackeys, parrots and musicians, she will take singing lessons and so on. Morosus is again thrown into despair and bitterly regrets his folly in putting his head in the noose (Exx. 6 and 21).[18] The music grows ever faster and Aminta throws herself with mounting abandon into her role, in so doing heartlessly smashing all the poor man's valuable nautical treasures (his compass,

---

[18] Morosus' furious reaction misses the fine comedy of Pasquale's perplexed 'Dottore! È un altra!'

astronomical instruments, skeletons and the rest) an action surely out of character with the sweet person whom we have been led to believe Aminta to be. Stick in hand she even threatens Morosus' own person if he dares to cross her as she strips the place from top to bottom.

In the middle of this holocaust Henry appears, now dressed as himself, and Morosus is so demoralized that he throws himself on his knees before the nephew he has only just disinherited, begging to be saved from this Satanas. Here is just the situation Henry hoped for and he is able to play the magnanimous saviour of his tormented uncle in whose favour he is thereby sure to be restored. He quickly overcomes the protesting Timidia who allows herself to be reduced from ranting to whimpering and is finally driven howling from the room by the strong, resolute champion who has come to protect Morosus.

The old man's gratitude knows no bounds. He has never been a coward but nothing in all his naval experience approached this last battle in which he has been wholly routed. He cannot possibly go on like this, he says to many a return of the bitter motif Ex. 24, and Henry promises to put divorce proceedings in hand at once (scurrying sequences of the wedding theme Ex. 23). Under Henry's soothing influence the intensely relieved Morosus sinks into a soporific stupor, Ex. 7 reappearing more and more often as he moans about the quiet he needs, how tired he feels. Henry tells him to go straight to bed, guaranteeing that there will be no further plaguing from Timidia that evening, and dismally the old man drifts off, thanking Henry as he goes, his voice sinking into his boots (low C) as he repeats the word 'schlafen' ('sleep'). A long and difficult horn solo with soft brass accompaniment provides an interlude based on the two basic Naturthemen of the opera Exx. 21 and 2(x); potentially this should have been a moment full of magic of the kind Strauss was expert at conjuring up. This time, however, his inspiration deserted him and the passage sounds oddly lame and gauche. Morosus is heard locking himself into his bedroom and as soon as the coast is clear Henry runs to the other door and softly calls to Aminta (Ex. 4).

She rushes into his embrace and the Act ends with a lyrical duet in Allegretto $\frac{6}{8}$ the ritornello of which links together in a single flowing cantilena many of the the themes of the preceding scenes, while the verse introduces a new melodic idea which will acquire a double-edged significance in Act 3:

Ex. 33

Henry is overjoyed at the way things are going but Aminta has pangs of conscience—as well she may have—and wishes it were all over. Ex. 8 returns, and the melodic line rises and swells until the orchestra takes over the first statement of Ex. 13 complete with its full continuation as in Ex. 17.

The sepulchral tones of Morosus can be heard from within seeking reassurance from Henry that all is well, and he, holding the culprit tight in his arms, sings over her head that she is indeed silent. Again and yet again Morosus' voice growls his anxieties and each time Henry twists his answer so as to satisfy his uncle and at the same time comfort his adoring wife. At last Ex. 17 returns and Morosus falls asleep with re-iterated thanks to Henry on a low D flat supported and coloured by an off-stage organ pedal-note, while Aminta adds her own thanks in notes that rise to her top D flat. As the two 'thanks' alternate, the one high, the other low, the orchestra builds up a soft but glowing chord with repetitions of Ex. 4 across five octaves and the curtain falls, in contrast with Act 1, on a mood of absolute peace.

II

With Act 3 the furore begins again. Before the curtain rises there is a brief orchestral introduction in the form of an extremely busy fugato. The theme on which it is built, though partially new, is ingeniously con-trived to incorporate various motifs relating to Timidia's tantrums:

19 'You sweetest angel, how wonderfully you have played the devil. He is already as weak as wax . . .'

Ex. 34

As the fugato develops it is joined by other themes such as those of the Housekeeper (Ex. 9) and Morosus (Ex. 6), until at the climax Ex. 2 enters jubilantly in full, played by—amongst others—the three trumpets.

A new and highly dissonant chordal theme breaks in, soon to be associated with the awful parrot which is amongst Aminta's junk with which poor Morosus' parlour is being filled. When the curtain rises the confusion is seen to be absolute. Workmen are knocking nails into the wall while others continue to cram the stage with the most unlikely articles, all making as much noise as possible in their various tasks. It is again a day later and Morosus, after a wretched night, is remaining in the background until news can be brought to him that the divorce proceedings are ready to begin.

Aminta is rushing about, shrilly giving instructions right and left, the parrot is carried on shrieking 'Kora, Kora, Kakadu' to its earsplitting chords, and cruelly Aminta commands that it be set down in Morosus' bedroom. The Housekeeper runs in, imploring her new mistress to relent (Ex. 18) but it is to no avail, and with despairing gestures she vanishes once more.

A harpsichord is now brought in with Henry and Farfallo in attendance as music master and accompanist respectively (Ex. 13 with its extension of Ex. 17 against a continuing background of Timidia's Exx. 2 and 4). The instrument is set down, the noisy workmen banished with many winks and nods, and a singing lesson ensues exactly as in the corresponding place in—not *Don Pasquale*, but *The Barber of Seville*.

Yet, whereas Rossini makes Almaviva give Rosina her pretend lesson in a contemporary idiom, Strauss uses the scene as an opportunity for more of his time travelling. Handing Aminta a roll of manuscript, Henry improbably announces the first study piece as an aria from Monteverdi's *Incoronazione di Poppea*. However, not only is the chosen song hardly an aria, being the opening section of Valetto's duet with

Damigella in Act 2 Scene 4 of that opera, but the original bears only superficial resemblance to what Strauss made of it:

Ex. 35

This quickly reveals itself as a mere starting point for Strauss's fantasy in which only the words remain from Monteverdi's masterpiece.

Ex. 36

It is not long before the voice line reminds one more of Zerbinetta than of Valetto, and after Henry has complimented 'Timidia' on her performance (demanding only greater passion and movement in her execution) Ex. 35 returns, now a vehicle for a dazzling coloratura display in which Henry himself joins her.

A brief interlude is provided by the appearance of Morosus whose ears are fully muffled with a kind of turban, but his protests are unavailing and the lesson continues with an avowed Duett from an entirely different source. This time the music belongs neither to Jonson's day nor to the period of the opera itself, but somewhere in between. Strauss had long had on his shelves a copy of Riemann's *History of Music in Examples*,[20] a curious collection of snippets ranging from the thirteenth to the eighteenth century and all condensed uniformly onto two staves.

[20] Dr Hugo Riemann, *Musikgeschichte in Beispielen*. Leipzig, 1912.

His whim lighted upon a transcription of a duet from the opera *Eteocle e Polinice* composed in 1675 by the Venetian composer Giovanni Legrenzi.

Ex. 37

Once again, nothing but the words remained by the time Strauss had finished with it:

Ex. 38

This duet develops into a quartet when Morosus and the House-keeper (who had entered behind him) add their complaints—she repeating 'I told you so' with maddening insistence.

Farfallo now joins in and as the tempo quickens he and Henry applaud Aminta's prowess and call for an encore to which she readily agrees (Ex. 4). Beneath the thickened harmonies and polyphonic additions of Exx. 3 and 38, this più mosso has at first an almost Purcellian flavour. Greatly developed and elaborated though they are, such passages are clearly descended from Strauss's experiments in neo-classicism—as well as from his arrangements of Lully and Couperin in the *Bourgeois Gentilhomme* and the *Tanzsuite* respectively.

As a climax quickly builds up, all archaisms are however soon swamped by the opposing factions. The parrot adds its shrieks in a violently cacophonic passage of four bars (instructed to be repeated) be-

---

[21] So wild and extravagant is the coloratura part in these two duets that even Strauss wondered whether he was asking too much from his Aminta. Accordingly he made provision in the vocal (though not in the full) score, for both to be taken over by the singer taking the role of Isotta (in this case the lesson would of course become a concert). In practice, however, the Aminta usually retains the part with the aid of enormous cuts.

neath which Morosus' agonized moans (Ex. 7) are barely discernible. Then the ensemble comes to an abrupt end, the door opens and the barber enters breezily (Ex. 1). The time has arrived to prepare for the pantomime of the divorce proceedings and it is necessary therefore that Henry and Farfallo should withdraw at speed, especially as the latter is to change roles (and costume) from accompanist to one of the lawyers in attendance. With great show of courtesy Schneidebart begs them to postpone the music-making for the time being in anticipation of the imminent arrival of no less a personage than the Lord Chief Justice.

Morosus pounces on Schneidebart who elaborates on the briefing he has given to the legal representatives, both argumentative and financial. The barber's reference to money evokes from Strauss an allusion to the music of Schneidebart's aria on the subject, in the last scene of Act 1, with its glittering off-beat chords. The old man is desperately anxious nevertheless that a mere suggestion of the proceedings will be enough to cause a further bout of tantrums which would be more than his sanity could withstand. Pitifully (Strauss uses a pathetic little chromatic figure for poor Morosus' pleas) he begs Schneidebart to broach the matter with her in advance, using the very utmost tact.

Ex. 1 gives way to an elegant Minuet as the barber and Aminta carry out this mock conversation. Aminta scornfully (Ex. 2) rejects the suggestion that their connubial tiffs prove the marriage a failure (Ex. 23 and the 'Silent Woman' motif Ex. 22(z)). The tempo changes to Presto when panic sets in and Morosus offers her—through the barber's mediation—thousands upon thousands of guineas to release him. The busy fugato figuration Ex. 34(x) (treated generally in inversion) combines with the 'Ruhe' motif Ex. 7, with Morosus' Ex. 6, Timidia's Exx. 2, 3, 4 etc. and with the chinking money chords as the argument waxes more and more heated. Aminta's mockery finally breaks into a grotesque stanza of doggerel which Strauss sets as a folk song parody, an embarrassingly weak moment, alas, especially when one recalls how brilliantly Strauss had treated this kind of caricature thirty years before in *Don Quixote*.

At last the Housekeeper bursts into the room to announce the arrival of the legal gentlemen who have apparently driven up in two carriages. The conspiracy is nothing if not thorough. Morosus goes off quickly to make himself respectable (Ex. 15(x)) and Vanuzzi enters dressed as the Lord Chief Justice together with Morbio and Farfallo disguised as advocates. The stage is set for the divorce scene.

12

The music is suitably grave in character; in the same way as during
Vanuzzi's masquerade as a priest in Act 2, Strauss now accompanies him
with a further quotation from the Fitzwilliam Virginal Book. On this
occasion his choice fell on an *In Nomine* by Doctor John Bull (No.
XXXVII, also from Volume I):

Ex. 39

Strauss's transcription of this dignified piece for bassoons, horns and
trombones is at first very close to the original (although transposed
down a third), but varies more and more as it proceeds, never actually
reaching the beginning of the florid passage-work. The key-board right
hand line is given in octaves on the trombones which emphasizes its
cantus firmus character although at the same time Strauss soon departs
from the actual outline of the plainsong melody on which the traditional *In Nomine* is generally based.

But no sooner has Vanuzzi announced his presence and called for the
appellants than there is an interruption in the form of a long and irrelevant ensemble for the conspirators which seriously slackens the dramatic
tension. In a rapid scherzo movement based on the Finale to Act 1 and
strongly featuring a dancing version of Ex. 11, Aminta, Schneidebart
and the actors chortle at the brilliance of their plan and the triumphal
success just round the corner.

Only when this has run its course does Morosus re-enter now dressed
formally, the Housekeeper behind him, and Strauss recapitulates the
galante music with which, at the opening of Act 2, the old man's sartorial
preparations for his ill-starred wedding had been made. Dr Bull's Ex.
39 in diminution serves repeatedly as a motif for the fake lawyers who
lose no time in starting the bogus divorce rigmarole.

At this point Zweig to a great extent reverts back to Jonson, wading
through the cumbersome *duodecim impedimenta* with which Captain
Otter, disguised as a divine, and Cutbeard himself, parading as a canon
lawyer, plague the wretched Morose. The old man is however spared

the humiliation of publicly disclosing (uselessly as it transpires) his impotence[22] for which Zweig substitutes an alternative red herring in the shape of Aminta's adultery citing Henry as co-respondent. This allows for the joke of turning Epicoene's protest ('This is such a wrong as never was offered to poor bride before; upon her marriage-day to have her husband conspire against her' etc.) into Aminta's truthful declaration, perfectly substantiated through its hidden meaning, that she has never at any time been unfaithful in her marriage.

It is in the clarity and conciseness of the denouement that Jonson's Act 5 has the advantage over Zweig and Strauss, whose succession of ensembles punctuated by snatches of dialogue, arias and the rest, make their last act dangerously shapeless.

The first ground for divorce Vanuzzi puts forward for consideration is that the petitioner has married *in statu ignorantiae,* corresponding to Jonson's *error personae* (—as Otter puts it 'If you contract yourself to one person thinking her another'). Morosus jumps at this, for he had thought he was marrying a silent woman (Ex. 22(z)) and she turned out a Satana (Exx. 2 and 3). Jonson allows this as a true *impedimentum* though with the fatal proviso that it must be *ante copulam,* but Zweig maliciously throws it out on the grounds that it is an everyday occurrence.

Next Farfallo outlines the *impedimenta erroris* culminating in the *error qualitatis.* (Otter: 'If she be found *corrupta,* that is vitiated or broken up, that was *pro virgine desponsa,* espoused for a maid—') This is Schneidebart's cue and he leaps forward, denouncing Aminta and producing Carlotta and Isotta as witnesses (Ex. 16 in a jaunty variation). Both his testimony and Aminta's affirmation that she has consorted with no-one but her husband are accompanied by the constant incorporation into the music of Ex. 33(x) from the connubial love-duet at the end of Act 2, which accordingly points out the double edge in her plea of innocence. Vanuzzi's part in the plot is hinted at when (to the horn figure Ex. 1) he now questions the witnesses. The two girls maintain their poses as established in Act 2 and vitriolically bear false witness against their successful competitor, in which they are staunchly upheld by Schneidebart (Ex. 20).

Aminta answers back no less spitefully (Ex. 27) and a quarrelsome ensemble·develops which even includes the Housekeeper (Ex. 18). At its climax Aminta throws herself on her knees imploring the judges to pro-

---

[22] The word 'impotentia' is just slipped into the text *en passant* by way of lip-service.

tect her honour (as a true *Schweigsame Frau,* vehement repetitions of Ex. 22(z) on the woodwind and violins seem ironically to protest).

This ensemble also comes to a formal end and the *In Nomine* (Ex. 39) resumes, though this time with Ex. 28 superimposed on the horns: Schneidebart has called upon Henry as his next witness and the latter, in a grotesque disguise complete with false beard, at once enters to answer his summons.

The love music Ex. 13 floats in on the violins (whose low F sharp Strauss as usual takes for granted) and Vanuzzi cross-examines Henry regarding his association with Aminta (Exx. 4 and 33(x)). Even when the lawyers specify a carnal relationship Henry assents quite casually. Aminta at first simply repeats her equivocal defence (again Ex. 33, though continuing into the melodic expansion ⌐ y ⌐) but then tries to reject Henry. This gives him the opportunity for an aria, a fully-fledged love-song on the lines of a recapitulation of the Act 2 duet in Strauss's warmest and most lyrical vein.

Despite Aminta's continued disavowals (which however are so phrased as to amount to an acknowledgement of guilt) the case is considered to be proved and Morosus receives congratulations on every side. The *In Nomine* Ex. 39, the marriage motif Ex. 23, now treated somewhat as an ostinato, Ex. 18 (the Housekeeper almost faints with relief), Morosus' Ex. 6 in every form of augmentation and diminution, the 'Ruhe' motif Ex. 7, and the chromatic gasps which previously accompanied Morosus' despair, all these themes combine with Ex. 4, the theme of the defeated 'Timidia', as Morosus gratefully shakes hands with the entire company. It only remains for the marriage to be formally declared null and void. The trombones enunciate the *In Nomine* yet once more and Vanuzzi looks round at his legal confrères for their approbation.

13

But Farfallo dissents and it all begins again. Each of the characters repeats the words 'Er opponiert' ('he opposes') in turn, rather like the 'Tua madre' in the *Figaro* sextet. Strauss had really embraced the stylization of classical opera to a degree which could never have been foreseen in the days of *Salome* or even *Rosenkavalier*.

Farfallo's objection is, of course, both necessary to the plot and fully furnished with precedent in Jonson's comedy in which both Sir John

Daw's and La-Foole's idiotic claims that they have had carnal relations with 'Mistress Epicoene' are invalidated at the eleventh hour.

> Cutbeard: But, gentlemen, you have not known her since *matrimonium*?
> Daw: Not today, master doctor.
> La-Foole: No sir, not today.
> Cutbeard. Why, then I say, for any act before the *matrimonium* is good and perfect; unless the worshipful bridegroom did precisely before witness, demand, if she were *virgo ante nuptias*.
> Epicoene: No, that he did not, I assure you, master doctor.
> Cutbeard: If he cannot prove that, it is *ratum conjugium,* notwithstanding the premisses; and they do no way *impedire*. And this is my sentence, this I pronounce.

Zweig retains this legal argument exactly as it stands, with Vanuzzi supporting Farfallo's reasoning as Otter does Cutbeard's in Jonson's text. Schneidebart breaks the bad news to Morosus, who has understood nothing of all this learned quibbling and after arguing the point for a time at last gives way to despair, the sympathetic but helpless company around him promising all the while to think of a way out. Another huge ensemble builds up punctuated at its peak with the little rhythmic figure Ex. 12. The noise and tumult has once more become overpowering and, throwing himself onto the bed Morosus, stopping up his ears, buries himself under the blankets.

The time is ripe for the denouement, which in Jonson comes logically enough: the nephew, Sir Dauphine, promises his demoralized uncle to work the miracle of rescuing him from his seemingly inextricable marriage on receipt of a written promise of reinstatement as his heir, to which Morose replies:

> Where is the writing? I will seal to it, that, or to a blank, and write thine own conditions. . . . (Returns the writings.)
> Dauphine: Then here is your release, sir. (Takes off Epicoene's peruke and other disguises.) You have married a boy, a gentleman's son . . . What say you, master doctor? This is *justum impedimentum,* I hope, *error personae*?
> Otter: Yes sir, *in primo gradu.*
> Cut.: *In primo gradu.*
> Dauphine: I thank you, good doctor Cutbeard, and parson Otter. (Pulls their false beards and gowns off.)

Perhaps Zweig felt that the revelation that Aminta was a married woman would be too weak a substitute climax for Epicoene's disclosure as a boy. Perhaps he considered Henry too soft and affectionate a character, in spite of everything, to extract the written document of reinheritance so heartlessly under torture. At all events he rejected this wholly credible ending in favour of a Finale so unlikely and contrived as to leave one bewildered and open-mouthed.

At the height of the turmoil Schneidebart as chief conspirator holds up his hand. Instantly there is total silence. Henry and Aminta remove their disguises, gently go to the bed and kneel beside the groaning Morosus. A bassoon hesitantly enunciates the Stretta theme from Act 1 (Ex. 28) while Henry addresses his uncle in the tenderest tones. In music indistinguishable from his previous love-song he assures the old man that the terror and martyrdom is over, that Morosus is amongst friends, and that he himself is none other than his nephew, his adopted son.

Morosus slowly comes to himself, though he recoils when he sees Timidia, as he thinks, also kneeling by his side. Aminta now adds her song of affection; she too loves him and desires nothing more than to be his adopted daughter. Strauss would have liked her to have added something to the effect that she was 'within a hairsbreadth of becoming unfaithful to Henry' and Morosus: 'And I, old ass, was on the verge of really falling in love'. Zweig thought not, however: 'One should *never*' he wrote, 'introduce *new* elements into a last act, but simply resolve those already postulated. It would hardly be plausible for Aminta to show inclination for the strongly comically coloured Morosus. I believe that a strong *sympathy* born of pity, such as I am trying to portray in her, will suffice.'

The disrobing of the other comedians follows and the conspiracy is laid bare before Sir Morosus, who is naturally almost apoplectic with anger. Suddenly the orchestra explodes; cymbals and bass drum crash, the brass and timpani hammer out fanfares and the woodwind trills shrilly. From one second to another Morosus' fury has turned to uncontrollable laughter. He roars, bellows and guffaws as he savours with extravagant joy the joke which has been played upon him in, he says, so masterly a fashion. He compliments them all on their skill in characterization, promises them each a gift of fifty guineas, addresses sweet words to the girls, and calls to the Housekeeper to bring in drinks while he prepares to declaim the moral of the opera (which Strauss sets inexplicably to his continuation of the Monteverdi 'aria' Ex. 36): 'He who has once had a silent woman can endure all the noise in the world.' He encourages the actors to make all the music they desire, then sits at the table with Henry and Aminta to watch the others dance and sing a little tableau in his honour.

First comes a dance:

Ex. 40

and then a song:

Ex. 41

Finally the entire company joins in a paean of praise and good wishes to the old man (Ex. 13) after which one at a time they take their leave of him, tripping out to echoes of Ex. 40 very much in the manner of the Commedia dell'Arte figures in *Ariadne auf Naxos*. Only Henry and Aminta remain behind with the deeply-moved Morosus, whose transformation into a model of benignity is complete.

14

At the end of Act 1 the Letzte Scene was naturally succeeded by the Finale. Now the reverse takes place; the Finale is over and we have, more as a postlude one might say, the Letzte Scene which, however, caused its authors a few pangs. Zweig expressed his doubts as early as January 1933 when he wrote to Strauss:

> I leave it to your musical judgement whether, as I indicate in the text, we may in the end wish to bring forward the *Last* Scene, so that the opera would close with the barber's words 'und nun sind wir endlich fort' or in the version as it stands with Morosus' monologue. Here it should be entirely your feelings which decide the matter; perhaps the decision will only arrive out of the composition.

Strauss however, was in no mood for independent decisions. Certainly the ending presented a problem since without the conventional Jonsonian Envoi (spoken by Truewit) there would seem to be no escape from some wholly formalized ending, with for example dance and song, if an anticlimax were to be avoided. From this point of view it was possibly a good and daring idea to make a virtue out of that very anticlimax. For the last scene consists exclusively of an extended soliloquy for Morosus in which the good old man sighs with deepest contentment as he sits puffing his pipe, Aminta and Henry on either side of him, cured at last of his neurosis and at peace with the world. Zweig was sure that with all its implicit dangers it could make a very moving end; but it is a highly artificial situation and would only succeed if Strauss could be stirred into creating music for it on a par with, for example, the meditative closing pages of *Don Quixote* or *Heldenleben*.

At an earlier, or for that matter at a later, period Strauss might have succeeded. His idea of basing the music entirely on Ex. 15 was perfectly justified in principle. Yet although he marked the passage *innig,* Mahler's favourite indication for any deceptively simple music which speaks of profoundest feelings, it actually plumbs no depths, merely pursuing its easy-going path in the course of which the previously anguished Exx. 7 ('Nur ruhe') and 24 are equally smoothed into the prevailing stream of bland mellifluous E flat major. At last the warm placid flow comes to rest and the curtain falls; as Morosus says with maddening complacency, 'Wie schön ist doch die Musik—aber wie schön erst, wenn sie vorbei ist!'—'how beautiful music is, but especially when it is over.'

It is often said that Strauss identified himself with Morosus, and one may perhaps concede that grain of truth behind Strauss's wish to see himself as the good-natured old man whose bark (and he too had a formidable bark) was worse than his bite. Nevertheless this can hardly

be accepted as justification for his uncritical approach to so much artificiality in the final development of the central character. One is led to
wonder how his dramatic sense, normally so keen, came to be stifled
whilst setting to music the closing pages of the drama. His claim that
here was the unique example of a libretto which he was able to compose
virtually intact as he received it begins to savour of wishful thinking.
Nothing indeed was nearer to his heart than to establish a really close
liaison of a kind that had never been possible with Hofmannsthal. Had
he done so his initial encouraging expressions of undiluted praise could
gradually have been leavened with tactful criticism. Yet once again he
was baulked because it proved impossible for him to hold working
meetings and discussions at every stage with his new collaborator in
person.

For it was just as the draft libretto was complete and composition
was beginning in earnest that the Nazi party gained control of Germany.
Within a matter of weeks came the first strict edicts against 'non-
Aryans'. Zweig, the modest and retiring Jew, saw this as the end of his
work with Strauss, since theatres were peremptorily forbidden to produce any works in which the least participation by a Jew could be
traced. Moreover in order to make it clear that the matter had not escaped official notice, Goebbels caused to be announced on the radio the
scandalous news that Strauss was actually at work on an opera by a
Jewish librettist, adding insult to injury by giving the poet's name as
Arnold Zweig, the name of another and far inferior author.

These events had exactly contrary effects on Stefan Zweig and
Strauss. Zweig's diffidence now became obsessive whereas Strauss developed an increasing conviction that here, slipping foolishly and unnecessarily from his grasp, was the librettist of his dreams and the only
writer in the world to whom he could ever entrust the works of his
declining years. It was not possible that the outside world, which he had
all his life consistently ignored—even despised—could seriously interfere with him and his work. There was no doubt whatever that a few
words in the right quarter would remove these tiresome niggles. After
all, it was for precisely such a contingency that he had agreed passively
when, without his being consulted, the announcement had been made
on 15th November 1933 nominating him President of the Reichsmusikkammer.

In the same way he had already in March 1933 allowed himself to be
persuaded, however unwillingly, to take over the last Bruno Walter

abonnement concert with the Berlin Philharmonic Orchestra.[23] Strauss never understood why so much fuss was made in the world at large over his acquiescence in these matters. It had always been necessary to pay at least a token lip-service to the controlling regime of the time, whether some Arch-duke, the Kaiser, Hitler or whoever (and none of them ever lasted for long) if one wanted to be left in peace.

Nor could anyone deny his unselfish act in saving the concert and insisting that his handsome honorarium be donated to the orchestra's funds! Weakly perhaps, but all too understandably he thought he might more readily be able to exert a benevolent influence in German music and theatre by remaining in the Nazis' good books than by making protests which must be useless and could even be perilous to the many vulnerable people who were dependent upon him. Zweig wrote most touchingly in his autobiography on this tender subject:

> To be particularly co-operative with the National Socialists was furthermore of vital interest to him, because in the National Socialist sense he was very much in the red. His son had married a Jewess and thus he feared that his grand-children whom he loved above everything else would be excluded as scum from the schools; his new opera was tainted through me, his earlier operas through the half-Jew Hugo von Hofmannsthal, his publisher was a Jew. Therefore it seemed to him more and more imperative to create some support and security for himself and he did it most per-severingly.

The view has often been expressed since that this represented an immense betrayal—Strauss was the one German who could have acted with courage and resolution since it was on the contrary the Nazis who needed the collaboration of such a great man for the weight his opinion would carry abroad. Yet Strauss by no means saw himself in that light. Contemporary reports indicate that the crafty new hierarchy of officials had quickly perceived the soft core of the famous composer: here was rather a useful puppet figure-head over whom there need be no diffi-culty; he could be led on by any pretence of good faith which would satisfy him for the moment.

The unhappy septuagenarian actually felt it prudent to pay Goebbels a personal call early in 1934 which Goebbels returned on the occasion

[23] To be fair to Strauss, extreme pressure was put upon him to conduct from every possible quarter, from the Jewish impresarios themselves to Nazi threats.

of Strauss's visit to Bayreuth in order to conduct *Parsifal*. After an uncomfortable discussion Goebbels warned him that there might be
demonstrations including stink-bombs if he persisted in going ahead
with his plans to compose a non-Aryan opera. The next day, however,
Goebbels told Strauss that he had persuaded Hitler to withdraw his
objections pending an examination of Zweig's libretto. Strauss was now
convinced that he had secured not only indemnity for the new opera,
but an assurance of Stefan Zweig's absolute acceptance by the authorities. 'Finally', wrote Zweig, '[he] was summoned before the all-power-
ful and Hitler in person told him that he would permit the performance
as an exception although it was an offence against the laws of the new
Germany.' Zweig wisely put no credence whatever in these smooth
promises, while secretly deploring the loss of face such a contretemps
must certainly have cost Strauss.

Yet Strauss believed Goebbels, just as he believed Hitler himself.
After the performance of *Parsifal* at Bayreuth, the Führer had personally
assented to a number of demands on other professional matters which
Strauss was emboldened to raise. It suited him to believe, and believe he
really did. Dr Ernst Roth has written with justice and insight:[24]

> Strauss's complete detachment from all political and national
> affairs was truly monumental. It was no aversion, for any
> such aversion springs from an act of judgement. Politics
> simply had no entry whatever into his world . . . Already in
> 1914 he was the only prominent German artist who refused
> to sign the manifesto against England, and even then there
> was talk of treason. He made no effort to justify himself
> because he was convinced that he needed no justification
> . . . he took war, inflation, shortages, as a personal insult
> and felt himself in no way either involved or answerable
> . . . For certainly the times were evil, the decisions more
> fateful, the resolutions more unavoidable. Before he could
> look round, Strauss found himself in the middle of a dispute
> of principles, of challenges over human and political moral-
> ity. It was said that Strauss should have emigrated like
> Thomas Mann, he would have been honoured in many
> triumphs and could have lived in luxury. But to emigrate
> of one's own free will presupposes political convictions and
> these were foreign to him. Opinion never went so far as
> actually to attribute to him sympathies with the Nazi move-
> ment, but a culpable opportunism was found in his be-

[24] *Musik als Kunst und Ware*, Atlantis Verlag, Zurich, 1966.

haviour, a willingness to make a pact with the devil himself as long as it was profitable to him. But even in the first bewildering years of the new regime Strauss did the most contradictory things without seeking or obtaining profit for himself . . . In a time of heroes and scoundrels everything falls outside the rules and corresponds to the code of neither one nor another. Only few musicians emigrated who did not have to. In Germany there was Hindemith, in Italy Toscanini,[25] the shining symbol of the artist who climbs the barricades. Strauss was not made for this. He neither entered into open arguments with the regime, nor did he make peace with it like Furtwängler who, after a heroic beginning, ended by accepting the official Prussian title of Staatsrat. Strauss defended himself, his music and his family, and this brought him into conflict with the authorities and with his friends but never with himself. Such egotism cannot be spoken of with reverence, but it is more an indication that art exerted its despotic rule over Strauss's middle-class life than superficial judges could recognize.

The plea, affectionately presented, is a strong one. But Strauss's reputation as a shrewd man of the world, so far from that of an artist with his head in the clouds, plays into the hands of the many people who strongly believe that on the contrary he knew exactly what was going on. The bitter accusations of his enemies are voiced by George Marek in such highly subjective passages as the following:[26]

> . . . He not only read about the burning of the Reichstag and the subsequent trial, which made a mockery of court procedure; he also saw and heard the parade of Bavarian Brownshirts who roamed the streets of Munich with noisy rowdyism, looking, in their short pants, knobbly knees and paunches, like boy scouts gone berserk. He witnessed the vandalism of Jewish property . . . Close to home he learned what was happening to fellow musicians. Bestiality was all around the man who had set to music the words 'Music is a holy art'. When Goebbels attacked Hindemith—and Furtwängler, who had taken Hindemith's part—Strauss is said to have sent Goebbels an approving telegram.

[25] It was at this time that Toscanini made his well-known remark: 'To Strauss the composer I take off my hat; to Strauss the man I put it on again.' Zweig wrote to Strauss that he could not believe that Toscanini had really said it.

[26] *Richard Strauss, the life of a Non-hero*, George Marek. Gollancz, London, 1967.

However well-founded one may choose to regard such conjectures of what Strauss must have seen, read and done, much of this passage is clearly the purest speculation, and the last unauthenticated sentence appears almost scurrilous. Strauss's actual behaviour, as work on *Die Schweigsame Frau* gathered pace, shows rather that wrapped up in his own affairs he successfully minimized to himself the significance, above all the threat to his friends and colleagues, of what was happening around him in 1934.

With apparent recklessness or unconscious lack of tact Strauss repeatedly pressed Zweig with invitations to return to Germany for this or that performance of one or other of the operas. Zweig's patient, good-humoured replies are very endearing as are his quiet refusals to commit himself to further collaboration for the time being, although he presented Strauss *gratis* with several extremely promising schemes which could perhaps be worked out by some other poet acceptable to them both; he himself would always be more than ready to remain in the background in an advisory capacity.

Once this idea took hold of Zweig's mind it blossomed into a serious proposition. He took the step of arranging approaches from two such deputy-librettists, Lernet-Holenia and Josef Gregor—the latter a Viennese art-historian and theatrical archivist of some standing, already known to Strauss. But Strauss was scathing in his rejection of both even though the one took the trouble to send two prospective draft-libretti, and the other came in person armed with a potential reworking of poor Hofmannsthal's *Semiramis—Tochter der Luft* Calderón sketches. Gregor had been put up to this by Zweig, to whom Strauss had let out the secret that he had never stopped pining for that ill-fated text.

15

By now the full score of *Die Schweigsame Frau* was nearing completion and Strauss still had no new schemes in view. In January 1935 he added the little *Potpourri* and also filled in time by applying himself to some of his tedious duties as Reichsmusikkammerpräsident, including the composition of a Hymn for the Olympic Games to be held in Berlin in August 1936. (As he wrote to Zweig: 'I pass the boring time of Advent composing an Olympic Hymn for this common lot, I, the outspoken enemy and despiser of all sport! Yes, idleness is the start of all depravity.')

Again and again he tried to make Zweig change his mind; only he could bring *Semiramis* to life, only he could produce the texts he needed, as it were his own life-blood. Even if it meant writing works to put them away in a drawer it would still be worth while. At least they would both enjoy themselves and better days would be bound to come sooner or later. He became desperate at Zweig's incomprehensible obstinacy; on 17th June 1935 he wrote:

Your letter. . . drives me to despair! This Jewish obstinacy! It drives one into antisemitism! This racial pride, this feeling of solidarity—even I feel a difference. Do you imagine I have ever been led in the course of a single action by the thought that I am Germanic (perhaps, *qui le sait*)? Do you suppose that Mozart was consciously 'Aryan' in his composing? For me there are only two sorts of people; those who have talent and those who haven't, and for me the People only begin to exist when they become the Audience. It's all the same to me if they come from China, Upper Bavaria, New Zealand or Berlin, so long as they have paid full price at the box office . . . who has told you then that I have exposed myself *so far politically*? Because I conducted a concert for . . . Bruno Walter? That I did for the sake of the orchestra —because I stood in for that other 'non-Aryan' Toscanini— that I did for the sake of Bayreuth. It had nothing to do with politics . . . because I mime out this Presidency of the Reichsmusikkammer? In order to do good and prevent greater mischief. Simply because I know where my artistic duty lies! Under any regime I would have taken on these pestiferous honorary positions, but neither Kaiser Wilhelm nor Herr Rathenau have ever dictated to me. So be a good fellow, for a few weeks forget the Messrs Moses and the other Apostles and get to work . . .

Little did Strauss suspect that he was being watched. He had never given a thought to being careful what he said or did. As the most famous living German musician, and Reichsmusikkammerpräsident to boot, he took it for granted that he was inviolate. For example his eye caught the deliberate omission of Zweig's name from the theatre billing on 22nd June, two days before the first performance of *Die Schweigsame Frau*. Purple with anger he announced that unless the matter was put right then and there he would take the next train home and the opera could go on without him. The omission was rectified but such behaviour did not endear him to the Nazis and they were not slow to seize any opening to discredit him. This last letter to Zweig gave ample pretext. It was intercepted and sent to Hitler himself on 1st July with a covering letter by the Gauleiter, one Martin Mutzchmann,[27] which spoke deprecatingly of the première of the new opera. This had in fact taken place amidst scenes of enthusiasm in the Dresden Staatstheater on 24th June with Maria Cebotari in the title role, conducted by Karl Böhm and produced by Josef Gielen. Hitler had given indications that he would come to one of the performances but the covering letter represented that tickets for the opening nights were largely given away and that 'the third performance was so poorly attended that it had to be cancelled'. Without waiting for Hitler's reaction, the Nazis had struck.

16

Strauss fell from the clouds. On the eve of the first performance he had written to Zweig in high excitement of how well everything was going, and that Dr Goebbels was coming on Monday with his wife 'to give it a real Reichs-bonus. You see the wicked Third Reich has also got its good side'. Now after the second performance[28] the opera was publicly banned and its further production, which had been widely planned, forbidden throughout Germany. On 6th July two high-ranking Nazi officials suddenly appeared at Strauss's house to demand his resignation from the Reichsmusikkammer 'on grounds of ill-health'. But they held out the offending letter with whole sections underlined in red, and for the first time it began to dawn on Strauss what a volcano he had been sitting on. The loss of the presidency certainly gave him no heartache; but the humiliation of his new position left him shaken. His first act was to write an abject letter of exculpation to 'his Führer', which makes sad reading:

> My whole life belongs to German music and to an indefatigable effort to elevate German culture. I have never been active politically nor even expressed myself in politics. Therefore I believe that I will find understanding from you, the great architect of German social life, particularly when, with deep emotion and with deep respect, I assure you that even after my dismissal as president of the Reichsmusik-

[27] The whole letter is quoted in the Strauss–Zweig *Briefwechsel*, S. Fischer, Frankfurt, 1957.
[28] Authorities disagree over the number of performances which actually took place before the axe dropped.

kammer I will devote the few years still granted to me only to the purest and most ideal goals.

Confident of your high sense of justice, I beg you, my Führer, most humbly to receive me for a personal discussion, to give me the opportunity to justify myself in person.[29]

Yet even now he tried to sort out his ideas logically and make the recent events into some kind of sense. Purely for his own peace of mind he jotted down a couple of lengthy memoranda (which were not published until long after his death) in which he once more set forth all the old protestations of good faith, his inexplicable treatment at the hands of the authorities ('things have come to a sorry pass when an artist of my standing has to ask a puppy of a minister what he is permitted to compose or perform'), his utter inability to make head or tail of their Aryan policy when applied to the arts. This last sentiment, which he elaborated endlessly with reference to Bach and Mozart, gives the clue to Strauss's pathetic encounter with the Nazis. He was constitutionally unable to grasp that there *was* no logic in their arguments— that honesty and courtesy had never played any part in the political double-talk with which they had fobbed him off all these months.

But one thing he saw very well at long last; the collaboration with Zweig was over. In retrospect one wonders whether this need have been the disaster for Strauss that he made it, throwing himself on the rebound into the arms of an inadequate substitute. Certainly it was a veritable tragedy for Zweig, and the last in a whole succession of bitter disappointments and blows of fate which he had suffered all his professional life. Yet if Gregor was no Zweig, Zweig for all his sweetness and humanity was no Hofmannsthal. *Die Schweigsame Frau* suffers from much lameness of words and action and Strauss's gay music is hardly inspired enough to rescue it; despite an early resurrection in Munich shortly after the fall of the Nazis the work has enjoyed only sporadic revivals. Strauss's one excursion into traditional *opera buffa* thus remains at best a curiosity and was to have no successor. After his most whole-hearted attempt to achieve lightness of style he was pitchforked by circumstances and by his own determination to save what he could of Zweig's dramatic proposals for their future, into one of the most Wagnerian and high-minded of all his stage works.

[29] George Marek quotes Strauss's letter in full.

CHAPTER XIX

ON THE REBOUND

'MY life-work seems to have definitely come to a full close with the *Schweigsame Frau*. I might otherwise have still been able to create a few more not entirely worthless things. Pity!' The gloom into which Strauss was plunged when he wrote those words at the beginning of July 1935 probably led him seriously to believe them. It was unendurable that the plans and ideas he had been toying with for the past twelve months must be put aside, one and all. There had been endless possibilities; the discussions with Zweig had been so very promising. At first Strauss had slyly put forward for Zweig's consideration a few of his suggestions to Hofmannsthal which had provoked such scorn years before. But Zweig had quietly steered clear of these with a proposal for something on the lines of a two act version of *The Pied Piper of Hamelin*. Strauss had then retaliated in his turn with a potential one act partner to *Feuersnot,* based on an old Italian Renaissance comedy *Calandria* which he had found in a rather fine *World History of the Theatre* by Joseph Gregor. It would make a pretty contrast and could even have a comedy overture.

Zweig was none too sure about the re-creation of Renaissance theatre in terms of contemporary production, especially operatic, and came back with two further ideas. The first was Kleist's *Amphitryon* of which he spoke enthusiastically, while the second sounded a bit intangible: it seems that he had come across a promising little comedy by the Abbé Casti, the librettist who with Salieri had formed a rival partnership to Mozart and Da Ponte. But the text, when he read it, turned out to be hardly workable as it stood, although the title, *Prima la Musica, poi le Parole* greatly took his fancy, as it did Strauss's when he received Zweig's postcard describing it as 'magical'.

The Kleist idea Strauss rejected out of hand; he himself had been pondering over some medieval subject. Perhaps some sort of one act festival piece could be made out of the Saxon King Henry III and his famous Peace of Constanz in 1043.[1] Here was something which could not fail to stimulate Zweig's interest. A close literary friend of Romain Rolland whose humanist views he shared, Zweig had already during the 1914–1918 war so filled his great play *Jeremias* with pacifist expressionism that it had fallen foul of the censorship. In the last years of the war he had managed to visit and remain in neutral Switzerland, in which detached and unbiased surroundings his philosophical attitude against war continued to stiffen.

He forced himself to return to the hardships of defeated Austria after the armistice with an unshakeable resolution to work for peace wherever possible. Hence he was, during the uneasy months of 1934, working at a monograph on Erasmus whom he presented as the first great European cosmopolitan and humanist. He told Strauss that the little book would soon be on its way to him '. . . a calm song in praise of the anti-fanatic human being to whom artistic achievement and inner peace are the most important things on earth—with it I have sealed in a symbol my own attitude to life.'

That Strauss too should have hit on a pacifist subject was gratifying. Which historical peace meeting should form the basis was immaterial and could easily be discussed when they met at the forthcoming Salzburg Festival.

The Salzburg meeting did in fact take place though in different circumstances and later than Strauss had intended; for, despite the fact that the 1934 Festival had been planned to celebrate his recent seventieth birthday, the Nazis summarily refused to allow him to conduct on the grounds that two enemies of the Third Reich, Bruno Walter and Toscanini, would be taking part. Nevertheless, after a tussle Strauss managed at least to pay a short visit to Salzburg where he made the much appreciated gesture of a personal appearance at Krauss's performance of *Elektra*. As a result he was able to hold a cordial meeting with Zweig which allowed their plans to develop considerably.

[1] Strauss's history seems to have been a little shaky. The Peace of Constanz was signed by Frederick Barbarossa in 1183.

Zweig had remembered something about Henry III's predecessor, Henry II, having built Bamberg Cathedral as a specific gesture towards world peace, but this snippet of historical information proved less productive than another work on the subject of peace which Strauss had again picked out of Gregor's *World History of the Theatre*. This was a play *La Redención de Breda,* once more by Calderón, based on the great Spanish victory of 1625 at which, after an eight-month siege, the Dutch Commander Justin of Nassau surrendered the key of the city to Spinola. The outstanding feature of this victory was the courtesy and magnanimity with which Spinola treated the defeated army and its leader. The inspiring scene was also depicted by Velasquez who, like Calderón, was at the Court of Philip IV and was commissioned by that monarch to portray the victory as one of a series of such events which had taken place during his reign. The painting, known as *Las Lanzas* and completed in 1635, is one of Velasquez' most famous works and was well-known to Strauss and Zweig;[2] Strauss had indeed composed a piece based upon it some forty years before, as part of his contribution to the Saxe-Weimar golden wedding celebrations in 1892.[3]

Spinola's impressive human gesture was for Zweig exactly on the right lines; as in Calderón's drama, the opposing commanders 'meet one another on such a high plane of humanity that it would be impossible to speak of victors and vanquished'. At the same time, there were elements about the occasion itself which did not quite fit in with his and Strauss's ideas. Strauss had really been looking for a subject in medieval German history whereas Zweig was concerned with something altogether more universal. The peace which formed the climax to their drama needed to come after a conflict of almost unimaginable length and horror. If the Breda scene could be transferred to the Thirty Years War and the Peace of Osnabrück, this might come nearest to their ideas. The opera would be in a single act, more of a pageant in many ways, and might even be called *24 October 1648*, the date of the Peace of Westphalia, a treaty concluded by the Holy Roman Empire with France at Münster, and with Sweden and the Protestant estates of the Empire at Osnabrück, thus bringing the Thirty Years War to an end.

Zweig now began to have a clearer vision of how the action might

[2] A curiously similar picture by Rubens (also completed in 1635) shows the two Ferdinands shaking hands in front of their troops before the battle of Nördlingen.
[3] See Vol. II, p. 267.

develop and on 21st August, only a few days after their meeting, wrote to Strauss in such interesting detail that it must be quoted in full:

> I have been thinking a great deal and would like to submit to you a plan in basic outline. In it I want to embrace three elements: the tragic, the heroic, and the humane, merging into that Hymn to the Reconciliation of the People, to the Grace of the work of Reconstruction; only I would like to leave emperors and kings right out of the action which I would put into anonymity. Let me recount my plan to you scene by scene.
>
> Time: the thirtieth year of the Thirty Years War. Place: the interior of a citadel. A German fortress has been besieged by the Swedes. The Commandant has sworn to show no mercy. Terrible deprivation reigns in the lower town beneath the citadel. The burgomaster begs the Commandant to surrender the fortress; the people press in, different voices are heard personifying distress, anguish and hunger (single voices, others intermingled, crowd scenes). The Commandant does not yield. He orders the people, who curse him, to be pushed out by force. Alone with his officers and soldiers he explains that he can no longer hold the citadel. But rather than surrender it he will blow it sky-high. He allows each the freedom to go down into the town and beg for pardon from the enemy; he himself would accept none. Now single scenes (concise but each one sharply accentuated). Some go, some stay (according to the different characters).
>
> Those who remain behind: mood of tragic heroism. Religious scene. The wife of the Commandant appears. He orders her to go, without telling her of his intention. She divines his purpose. Strong scene. She makes no attempt to dissuade him, for she knows of his oath. But she does not go. And stays with him (this as lyrical element) in order to die with him.
>
> Preparations for the blowing up of the citadel. Last farewells. All embrace. The fuse is set and lit. Complete stillness.
>
> Then, a cannonshot. Everyone jumps up. The Commandant expects an assault. The fuse is extinguished. They are happier to die in open battle. But there is no second cannonshot. They all wait. Bewildered. Uneasy.
>
> Moment of new and strong suspense.
>
> Into the silence from far off out of a neighbouring village a bell (very distant). Then a second from another. Then (still very far away) a third. A trumpet call. Someone reports the approach of an officer carrying a white flag. Then more and more bells. And suddenly from below a cry: Peace,

Peace is concluded. The bells peal more and more and
mingle with the jubilation of the (invisible) people.

The truce-bearing officer appears. Peace has been concluded in Osnabrück. The enemy Commandant begs to be
allowed to offer his greetings. Consent. Scene of awakening.
Ever and again the bells, which stream through the whole
scene like an organ.

The enemy Commandant appears. Both look darkly at
one another. They have both vowed to annihilate each
other. Gradual change of heart. They step nearer. They
stretch out their hands. They embrace.

The people pour in jubilant, praising the Commandant.
He makes a speech: now everyone must set to work. Reconstruction and reconciliation. All for all. Individual
answers of agreement. One group after another takes the
word. And out of all this the big chorus builds itself step by
step, in which all tasks and achievements of peoples at peace
can be celebrated as befits each walk of life, and which can
expand with a mighty surge into the Finale: the Hymn to
the Community.

That would be my plan. Now one could, if one wanted
to, contemptuously call such an idea of peace between
peoples 'pacifism', but here it seems to me altogether bound
up with the heroic. I would leave everything in anonymity,
giving no names either to the town or to the Commandants;
everything would merely be the form, the symbol, and not
the once-only individual . . .

2

All this looked very encouraging in itself, but unfortunately the same
letter also marked the beginning of Zweig's personal withdrawal.
Strauss's most urgent pleas could not get him to start actually setting
down some pages of text he could use, although any discussion on
general lines created no problems. For instance, Strauss had a few ideas
of his own on how this peace pageant might be pepped up.

Still turning over in my mind your *24 October 1648,* I have
today—I think—had a good idea! The draft you put to me
(excellent in its build-up) seems a little bit too simple and
straight, lacking a spiritual conflict which would give
deeper interest.

How would you react to a love affair between the wife,
who could be some 20 years younger (than the 50 or so
year old Commandant of the fortress), and one of these

lieutenants under his command, slipped in on something like the following lines:

Beginning of the opera: Flirtation scene between the wife, who is in love with the Lieutenant without having become aware of it herself, and the Lieutenant who has not yet confessed to her his own love, simultaneously setting out the whole tragic situation of the fortress and its inmates.

The scene would come to an end with the entry of the Commandant, on whom the first realization begins to dawn how it is with the pair of them. Then could follow the scene with the burgomaster and the people, the Commandant's decision on no account to surrender the fortress and to allow anyone who does not want to stay to depart without hindrance.

The wife suspects that her husband intends to destroy himself. Hereupon a big scene between the wife and the Lieutenant during which she urges him to leave the fortress, thereby also betraying her love, but after a passionate outburst and stormy embrace she decides to remain and die with her husband if only her lover can be saved.

Urgently she entreats him to flee, he leaves her without having taken a definite decision, vacillating between love for her, whom he will not abandon, his honour as a soldier, desire to live—this seems to me a very fine glittering situation.

Next follows the scene between Commandant and wife, in which she tells him of her resolve to remain at his side—there is a great refinement here, now that the Commandant is ever more aware of the love between wife and Lieutenant and is moved by her doubly magnificent sacrifice.

From here on the action runs exactly as in your draft until the end, where amidst the general atmosphere of rejoicing the love between wife and Lieutenant will become apparent in some way or other (also to the Commandant), perhaps in the moment of exaltation the Lieutenant kneels down before the wife and kisses the hem of her dress.

The Commandant shoots himself and thereby now makes the sacrifice, that he had originally meant to dedicate to his honour as an officer, as an act of human renunciation towards his loved and honoured spouse, for by so doing he leaves the way free for union with her beloved.

This briefly puts my idea forward roughly for your friendly criticism . . .

Zweig was perfectly prepared to consider seriously this new elaboration of his scheme although to superimpose a conventional love-triangle upon his ideological parable went against the grain.

. . . I have thought about your plan a great deal, but I find
the connecting of the heroic with a love episode too operatic
in the worst sense; for my taste it springs here from a particular sort of conventional romanticism, which involun-
tarily also influences the music. I always feel a little distressed
when men who have been presented as heroes suddenly
break into love arias—probably it is, as so often proved,
the ideal mixture for the public. But I have an instinct
inside me which builds up a resistance against it . . .
I'll risk making a sketch in December: I see more that is
stirring in the tragi-heroic stuff than the simple telling can
put over. Even the wife has quite a big role beyond the
erotic . . . I don't think that the bare outline of contents can
give here any idea of the tension possibilities, but I can
already see most clearly that the stuff would contain the
utmost tension: revolt, despair, determination . . .

In principal Strauss was bound to agree although he could foresee
the danger which was likely to arise for himself:

You are absolutely right: the stuff, as you depict it, is certainly cleaner and bigger—but don't forget that I've also got
to compose it and that the feelings contained in it must
come to an expression which will awake in me corresponding feelings in music: despair, heroism, weaknesses, hate,
reconciliation, etc.—I am afraid lest I can't summon up
enough melody which will really touch the heart. What I
proposed to you is, naturally enough, operatic—but where
does Kitsch stop and opera begin? Naturally I mustn't over-
press you, but I have the feeling that it is a bit too straightforward and lacks contrast—even that of eroticism . . .
Perhaps if you have another look at it something else will
come to you, better and less Kitschy, which will fit in with
my qualms and wishes.

But this was as far as Zweig had been prepared to take the matter as
the political threat grew month by month. Strauss's idea of writing for
posterity, each new work to go quietly into a drawer to wait for better
times, was to Zweig unworthy of an artist of Strauss's stature. One
after another came the suggestions for alternative librettists—Robert
Faesi, Lernet-Holenia: Strauss's heart sank. There were even new ideas
for opera subjects which Zweig made clear he would not actually
write himself—Kleist's *Amphitryon* (already proposed but now urged on
Strauss yet again by Zweig), *Celestina* (an old Spanish drama-novel),[4]

4 See Chapter XX, p. 120.

Zweig was ready to discuss anything rather than carry forward the two one act dramas for which Strauss had firmly convinced himself he was waiting: *1648* and the Abbé Casti piece, *Prima la Musica, poi le Parole*.

It was in answer to Zweig's multifarious counterproposals that Strauss had brought up again poor Hofmannsthal's *Tochter der Luft,* but by April 1935 even this had been deposited firmly into the lap of Joseph Gregor, leading within a month to the depressing and embarrassing interview when Gregor had brought sheaves of reworkings of the material which Strauss had no intention of using. Gregor might be a first-rate scholar and historian, but he was not a poet nor himself a sufficient man of the theatre to qualify for this assignment.

Utterly unsettled and wretched, Strauss had pressed for another meeting and on 2nd June he and Zweig did manage to see each other at Bregenz in Austria. But all that emerged was Strauss's renewed interest in Zweig's *1648* and Zweig's determination that Gregor was the man to write it. Overwhelmed with the arrangements for the *Schweigsame Frau* première Strauss reluctantly gave Gregor another appointment for 7th July in the hopes that by that time, with *Schweigsame Frau* safely launched, things would look different. Instead, the Nazi axe had dropped, he himself was—incredibly—in disgrace, and (as he wrote in the Memorandum) his life work was apparently once and for all at a full stop.

3

Yet there remained that infernal interview with Gregor which could hardly be cancelled, and grimly Strauss steeled himself to go through with it. Gregor was not the man to waste such an opportunity and arrived armed with a bundle of prospective libretti. Luckily he was so gratified by the occasion that he wholly mistook Strauss's dejected impatience while the great man carelessly skimmed through the wad of six sketch scenarios:

> I remember with the greatest clarity (wrote Gregor) that he never lingered over any of the sheets for more than a couple of minutes, nor did he go back and peruse any of them a second time. Rather did he, even as he read, put three on one side which he then handed back to me with the remark that they would interest him as dramatic material. Within a brief quarter of an hour was the working programme of up to four years laid down.

Strauss's quick decision to accept two of these drafts is easily explained since one was *1648* (Gregor was certainly no slow worker) while the other, *Daphne*, must have caught Strauss's eye as corresponding very closely to an old Hofmannsthal project for a Greek bucolic drama.[5] The third draft, however, remains something of a mystery. Many authorities follow Asow's example in accepting Gregor's word that it was *Die Liebe der Danae*. But although by chance there was a Danae sketch amongst the scenarios Gregor submitted to Strauss, there seems little question of it having been one of those positively accepted at this time. Had he even spotted it, Strauss would certainly have been reminded of Hofmannsthal's draft, whereas, on the contrary, when this did come into the picture he was unable to recall the very existence of Gregor's, loath as that worthy would be to admit it.[6]

With Zweig now wholly in the background (such very few letters as he and Strauss still exchanged were signed cautiously 'Morosus' and 'Robert Storch') there was no longer the least hope of infusing any new contrasting matter into *1648*, whether on the lines of his own love interest or any other. It was as much as Strauss could do to get a tolerable text even keeping strictly to Zweig's original draft scheme. At first he was so downright rude to Gregor that he felt it safest to apologize afterwards:

'. . . Your entire dialogue is still developed on far too literary and untheatrical lines. Do you understand me? . . .' he wrote, and then a few days later:

> . . . I don't think I can ever find music for it. These are none of them real people . . . the dialogue of the two Commandants is wholly undramatic: this is how two schoolmasters would hold a conversation on a given subject: '30 Years War' . . . won't you try to rework the whole thing over again in *elevated prose*, but just like *real* people speak—no theatrical figures out of the 30 Years War. *And then* we must plough through the whole thing once again thoroughly *and then* we must submit it to our friend for the most merciless criticism, for the most fundamental superrevision . . . before you come back here to me.
> I hope you were not too offended by yesterday's letter.

However, whether he was or was not offended Gregor had no intention of showing it and risking the loss of such an important collabora-

[5] See Vol. II, p. 299.
[6] See also Chapter XX, p. 126.

tion. His replies were pure honey and conciliation as he tried to meet Strauss's demands. It was at this time, October 1935, that the name of the work was changed to *Friedenstag,* as being more in keeping with Zweig's plan of universality.

It was, moreover, historically a wise precaution in view of the sentiments put into the mouths of the soldiers, for the facts were not on the side of Zweig's idealism. As H. A. L. Fisher puts it:

> The peace of Westphalia, which closed this long war, was [not] the result . . . of any inclination of the rival armies in Germany to force a military decision, for of such inclination —war being a most profitable calling—they had none . . . there must be no mistake about the undiminished gusto with which the soldiers . . . carried on their trade to the end. Fighting and pillaging was the breath of their nostrils; and if the diplomatists had not come to an accord . . . [they] might have fought on until the time came for them to bequeath their war game to yet another generation . . .

Zweig was able up to a point to supervise the work and even took an active part in the revision of the scene between the two Commandants. But bearing in mind his natural diffidence, as well as his loyalty to Gregor, it is unlikely that he allowed himself to interfere to any substantial extent. Nevertheless Strauss could not resist sending one last direct letter of appreciation to Zweig:

> I thank you warmly for the trouble you have taken over *Friedenstag.* Your version is more theatrical and concise than that of our friend Gr., but even today I would be unable to say what I shall decide, all the more since the whole ending still hasn't got the shape I asked from its author! . . . I have now been busying myself for a few weeks with the composition, but it won't turn into the sort of music I must expect from myself. The whole material is after all a bit too everyday—soldiers—war—hunger—medieval heroism— people all dying together—it doesn't really suit me—with the best will in the world . . . I would have liked still a little joy in my work for the last years of my life . . . *Friedenstag* is too wearisome a task—Gr.'s verses have no depth, they are nothing but nicely ringing surface tones without music!

However, Strauss persevered; he had, after all, little else to do. Gregor, unlike his predecessors, did not hesitate to allow himself to be installed in a nice room in the tower of the famous Garmisch villa and there, interrupted only by Strauss's few brief conducting trips abroad, the two worked side by side through the autumn. By February Strauss was able to play the Particell through to Gregor on the piano, and by the middle of June 1936 the full score was complete. Less than a year after he had thought never to compose another note he had completed a new opera, for which, moreover, a companion piece was already far advanced. It was simply not in Strauss's nature to go into retirement, whatever the circumstances.

4

Friedenstag divides into three clear sections; the desperate situation, the Commandant's Wife, and the arrival of peace. All three are clearly separated and contrasted in style. There is no Prelude and the curtain rises after the woodwind have baldly declaimed the bleak motif which depicts the stark, gaunt citadel:

Ex. 1

The military atmosphere is then established by a theme in martial character:

Ex. 2

(cf. Parsifal Graalszene)

Despite the suggestion of a march the scene is one of silence amidst desperate fatigue and a prevailing sense of hopelessness. Soldiers of the Guard are sitting around motionless in the grey dawn. The Wacht-meister, their commanding N.C.O., an old grizzled soldier, stops on his round of inspection and interrogates one of the soldiers who is keeping watch at an embrasure. This soldier is described as a Schütze, a low-ranking rifle-man, and was one of the first characters to be clearly envisaged by both Strauss and Gregor. He was actually intended to be more significant than in the end he became. Gregor wrote of him: 'that pacifist who, amongst the extremely varied types of service-men and mercenaries surrounding the Commandant, in the face of death, for the first time experiences to the full the meaning of the idea of duty'. His replies to the Wachtmeister go far to conjure up the surrounding desolation, the burning farms, the fleeing peasants numb with misery, the total lack of food and drink, and so forth; above all, the prevailing scale of values in which the ghastly fate of the local people is reckoned to be of no consequence.

The gloomy Ex. 3 suggests something of their passive despair:

Ex. 3

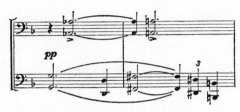

In answer to the hopeless cry of the young soldier, 'where can it all end?' the Wachtmeister reminds him of their dedicated Commandant, whose music, built over the *Parsifal*-like Ex. 2(x), becomes increasingly reminiscent of that opera:

Ex. 4

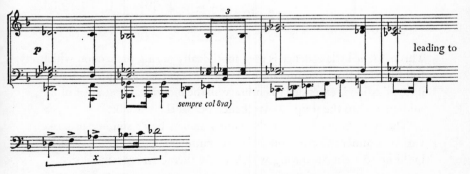

The rising figure ⌈ x ⌉, given at first to the trombones, is used increasingly during the opera to denote the Commandant's heroic loyalty and unswerving devotion to duty.

At this point there is a change of colour in the orchestra, and to a gentle G major allegretto an Italian tenor sings a simple folk-song. It is

a young Piedmontese youth who during the night has brought a letter
from the Kaiser to the Commandant, braving the enemy hordes through
which he had to pass unseen in order to reach the citadel. The words for
this ditty had been noted by Gregor in the South Tyrol during the first
World War and are used here very effectively. Strauss's music for the
verses have the typical bitter-sweet quality he was always able to impart to such pastiches:

Ex. 5

Ex. 5a

This pathetic little cadence is used motivically during the section which
follows, and the rhythmic figure ⌐ x ⌐ is particularly prominent as
its application is extended to embrace all the individual nostalgias of the
soldiers whom the song has awakened out of their stupor.

The numerous verses of the young Italian boy's singing provoke
varied comments, some rough, some sentimental, and these gradually
build up to a chorus during which a new theme emerges:

Ex. 6

Ex. 6 is only the first of a series of different forms through which this motif passes in its application to the various characters of the drama as it symbolizes each of the creeds by which they live. To the soldiers, thoughts of flowers, gardens, women, peace itself, seem infinitely far away and their code of existence is dominated rather by the more immediate realities of pay and plunder. Hence the stern even brutal energy shown by their version of this many-sided theme.

The chorus subsides and leaves behind a desolate, whimpering repetition of his refrain Ex. 5a by the Piedmontese boy. This opens up fresh discussions amongst the soldiers leading by way of humming to a new chorus, now in more popular, half blasphemous character. It is, moreover, punctuated by references to the Lutheran hymn 'Ein' feste Burg ist unser Gott',[7] establishing the religious origin of this seemingly endless war.

Once again the chorus breaks off as distant but threatening voices of the townsfolk are heard approaching the citadel. Over a grumbling ground-bass new cries of despair are heard, though similar in character to Ex. 3:

Ex. 7

Ex. 8

Driven nearly crazy with hunger, the townspeople have swarmed towards the fortress; at the climax of this powerful ensemble the outer gates give way with a crash. Soldiers rush to and fro and an officer tells the protesting Wachtmeister that a deputation headed by the Burgomaster has entered the citadel (Ex. 1).

The music changes to a *Trauermarsch* as the pitiable body enters looking 'like a group of ghosts'. They are headed not only by the Burgo-

---

[7] This well-known Chorale had already been used by Mendelssohn in his *Reformation* Symphony and by Meyerbeer in *Les Huguenots*, to exemplify the struggle of the different Protestant sects against Catholic oppression.

master but by the aged and venerable Prelate of the town. Strauss uses suitably dismal chromatic phrases to underline the lamentable condition of the deputies who include some other dignitaries and also a few women representatives, all woebegone to the last degree, while the Prelate has literally to be supported. As they look round bewildered at the rows of soldiers surrounding them, the voices of the massed townspeople (offstage) can be heard strongly now, and very near as they reiterate their shouts of 'Hunger' and 'Bread' (Exx. 7 and 8).

At this moment the Commandant makes a dramatic entrance at the top of the stairs, affording the greatest possible contrast to the group huddled below. His peremptory motif shows neither tolerance nor understanding but merely impatience, even irritability:

Ex. 9

He addresses them sternly: he is authorized to hear what they have to say but any attempt on their part to force his hand will receive merciless treatment; he sends a musket clattering down at their feet to a violent declamation of Ex. 6, for the Commandant is first and foremost a soldier.

There is a moment's pause and then the Burgomaster, acting as spokesman, briefly begs for the city to be opened to the enemy. He speaks softly with great deference and his words are accompanied by the motif of distress (Ex. 3). But after his servility has provoked a savage reply from the Commandant, the Burgomaster is sufficiently incensed to expostulate: this enemy whom they are resisting so bitterly—all he can see beyond the city walls are men no different from themselves, with identical needs and sufferings, and who even believe in the same God. Here, deliberately oversimplified, is the first expression of the opera's main purpose, its crusade against the tragic futility of war.

The constant repetitions of Ex. 3 gain in intensity throughout the Burgomaster's altercation with the Commandant, whose answers continue to incorporate vehement interjections of the motif typifying his outlook as a soldier, Ex. 6. A terse reference to his own personal motif Ex. 4, also enters however, when he speaks of his role as their protector who shares, when all is said and done, a hunger no different from their own. He turns to the Prelate and with a touch of mockery expresses surprise that an old man so near to the Judgement Seat is prepared to advocate the surrender of his altar to the opposing faith.

A softened version of Ex. 6 can be heard within the gentle texture of the accompaniment as the venerable ancient confesses that he will indeed do just this for the sake of his flock. He has assuaged his conscience with the thought that according to the scriptures only the meek can truly win through to victory.

Indignation now pours from the lips of the outraged Commandant to whom the word 'Victory' can have only one meaning. So feeble an interpretation in the mouths of weaklings is to him the sacrilegious betrayal of a heaven-born concept.

During this tirade the predominating Exx. 4 and 6 are joined by a lyrical theme which, already hinted at during the Prelate's words, will develop during the course of the work into the motif representing the eventual happy resolution of the drama (see below, Ex. 11). The Commandant can at present visualize this resolution only in terms of a military triumph. Despite his ruthless attitude, there is something horribly admirable about his unflinching heroism—unimaginative as such heroism always is—in the face of the impossible odds which are rising against him.

A new and frantic ensemble develops, at the climax of which a bugle call announces the arrival of a desperately wounded officer from the front line who bursts onto the scene with the news that the situation is hopeless and can only be abandoned. Ex. 1 is given in violent diminution as the disastrous report unfolds with its imminent threat to the citadel. The deputation numbly reasserts the uselessness of the Commandant's attitude, while the officer from the front begs for the ammunition to be released which, he reveals, is known to be hoarded in the vaults. But here also, for reasons which are all too soon to become apparent, the Commandant is adamant, even when the officer falls to his knees in supplication. Forcing the wretched man to his feet, the Commandant produces the letter which, as we have heard earlier, the Piedmontese boy has succeeded in bringing through the enemy lines. To an impressive chordal background of heavy brass he reads aloud to the assembled soldiers and townsfolk the sacred words of the Emperor, commanding that the town be held regardless of the odds or sacrifices in human life.

A woman now steps forward from the crowd and, deathly pale, addresses the Commandant. Gregor saw this feminine member of the cast as the war-victim counterpart to Maria, the Commandant's wife; but as we have not yet seen that all-important lady, nor has there been any reference to her in the text so far, the concept can have little reality.

The peasant-woman's view of her sovereign's decree is diametrically opposed to that of the Commandant. It is a soldier's métier to be killed, but by no means that of the civilian population. As she sees it, the Kaiser is exceeding his province with such a decree.

She follows up this convenient view of professional warfare with a description of the havoc wrought over the past thirty years. She is quickly supported by voices from the crowd shouting of the miseries they have endured, the houses shot to pieces, the children killed or dead from starvation, the universal hatred and suspicion. A new chromatic theme adds pathos to their cries:

Ex. 10

With united voices they call to the Commandant to murder them all on the spot and so end their sufferings. The woman turns on him again, daring him to cry out for victory. As if to pinpoint the savagery of the scene, the sun has risen and shines blood-red through the embrasures. The Commandant's Ex. 9 is hammered out fortissimo and breaks off for a breathless pause.

5

But the Commandant knows he can go no further. Visibly shaken on observing even his own soldiers kneeling in support of the townspeople, he relents—or makes a show of relenting. In a moving passage based on the ascending motif of his heroism, Ex. 4(x), he instructs the Burgomaster to take his people back to their work in the town, to await, with the striking of noon, an unmistakable signal. Only when that signal comes may the city gates be opened.

When he speaks of this great signal which will mark the end of the siege a flowing theme appears, premonitions of which have been heard earlier:

Ex. 11

Ex. 11 now dominates the chorus of relief and gratitude which greets the Commandant's pronouncement. Gradually the deputation leaves the scene and the crowd of townspeople can be heard withdrawing, their cries of 'Bread' and 'Hunger' changing to 'Hope', 'Life' and 'Courage' as the purport of the Commandant's words is passed on to them.

The Commandant looks scornfully after their retreating backs and comments bitterly on the joy they have derived from his apparent lapse into cowardice. He turns to his soldiers and reassures them that he has no intention of betraying their trust or of becoming a traitor. The music combines the military theme Ex. 4 and the diminution form of Ex. 1 with a new motif, the chromatic opening of which had been hinted at when the Commandant was reading the Kaiser's letter:

Ex. 12

This motif of loyalty, which represents equally that of the men to their commanding officer and his own to the Kaiser, becomes increasingly in evidence during the development of the scene. A further motif also appears as the Commandant unfolds his plans:

Ex. 13

or Ex. 13a

Ex. 13, which represents Despair, also appears later in other forms, viz:

Ex. 13b

(cf. Tod und Verklärung)

or Ex. 13c

Although the Commandant speaks in oblique terms, his meaning quickly dawns on the soldiers who, as he calls for the fuse (i.e. to blow them all up) cry out in horror. A terse drum figure, Ex. 14 later associated with the ultimate command for self-destruction, is heard softly during descending phrases of Ex. 13c and there is a stunned silence.

This was the place for Zweig's 'singly contrasted and sharply accentuated' scenes in which the various soldiers were to emerge as different in character while making their several decisions whether to stay in the citadel or take the opportunity of deserting and flee to the town. In principle this seemed a good scheme, but, left to themselves, Gregor and Strauss failed to accomplish it satisfactorily. There was little enough time for the characters of the soldiers to emerge even in Zweig's scenario, but Gregor's libretto leaves most of the talking to the Commandant.

In a group of quatrains he turns first to the Wachtmeister describing how the latter saved his life at the battle of Magdeburg. He offers to repay this debt of honour now, but in a concluding quatrain the Wachtmeister replies that as in the past he will stand by his commander.

The two embrace (Ex. 13c) and the Commandant addresses the Konstabel (a gunner's rank) to whom he also sings a song in quatrains revealing a similar debt of honour. Like the Wachtmeister, the Konstabel rounds off the song with a final quatrain in which he swears that he will never abandon the officer whose life he was once privileged to save. The Commandant presses his hand (Ex. 12) before turning to the Schütze (rifle-man). This time the quatrains are sung by the Schütze as he affirms that, much as he hates war and longs for his loved ones, he would not forsake the officer he admires so much. His rather tragic song has a theme of its own, very much in *Rosenkavalier* style:

Ex. 15

The orchestra strikes up a little Pomp and Circumstance March as the Commandant praises the loyal rifleman, and indeed the whole section has become stilted and unnatural. Gregor's use of naïve quatrains gives a change of style which, hardly on the lines of characterization Zweig had intended, is also not redeemed by Strauss's artificial device of setting the Commandant's addresses to the Wachtmeister and the Konstabel in the manner of an old German Ritterlied (knightly song) and Jägerlied (Huntsman's song) respectively.

Now the Commandant questions the professional soldiers; his tone of voice as he speaks to them collectively is far from reassuring and they for their part are by no means unanimous in their allegiance. Contemptuously, though with great dignity, he dismisses them and, seeing the young Piedmontese still in their midst, thanks him warmly for the Kaiser's letter which has provided the inspiration for this ultimate deed of military sacrifice. Another impressive theme makes its appearance in this passage, descriptive once again of the Commandant's devotion to his royal master:

Ex. 16

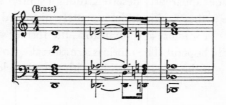

The Loyalty motif (Ex. 12), interspersed with those of Despair (Ex. 13c) and of the Commandant's devoted heroism (Exx. 4(x) and 16), is nobly developed here, culminating in a mighty rising statement on six horns. The drum figure Ex. 14 has now been transferred to brass and strings fortissimo (sounding unfortunately very like Tchaikovsky's *Capriccio Italien*) and the Commandant ascends the stairs; peremptorily he gives the order to prepare the explosives in the vaults for detonation and there is a feverish outburst of motifs—Despair (Ex. 13b), Commandant (Ex. 9), Fuse (Ex. 14), Soldiers (Ex. 4)—which quickly dies down as the stage is deserted. The sun now shines brightly onto the scene, which is set for the entry of Maria, the Commandant's wife.[8]

6

Maria's appearance marks the beginning of the second phase of the drama. Here is not only the best, but also the simplest scene of the whole work. It consists of an extended aria for Maria, followed by a duet between her and the Commandant, either or both of which are worthy of independent existence in the concert hall. If not the best of their kind, these are big pieces in the true tradition of Strauss's lyrical scenas for soprano voice.

It is easy to understand that Strauss's heart lay nearer to so human a part of the score. Where Gregor was concerned however, this revival of interest created difficulties, since Strauss became proportionately more demanding. Whole pages of the text had to be rewritten according to his specific instructions in order that it should correspond with a predetermined sequence of thought, the musical scheme for which was already clear in the composer's mind.[9] In the case of the aria Strauss planned the form in three sections, although the second and central of these is composite in tempo and mood.

The first section is to some extent introductory in character. It describes the astonishment and perplexity of the Commandant's Wife at finding the citadel apparently deserted, though sinister sounds seem to come from the nether regions. She is acutely disturbed at the unusual behaviour of both soldiers and townsfolk, the former sullen and grey, the latter weirdly hopeful. The music is a restless allegro which skilfully combines many of the relevant motifs with a new melody relating to Maria herself.

Ex. 17

It can be seen that this feminine theme embodies a phrase from the

    [8] She is the only member of the cast to be given a name, in accordance with Zweig's wishes for anonymous universality.

    [9] Gregor in his book *Richard Strauss, Der Meister der Oper*, R. Piper Verlag, Munich, 1939, quotes these changes in detail.

motif of the siege's end (Ex. 11), a resolution of their troubles so near to the heart of the woman, if not to that of the man she loves.

The second section is marked by a change of pulse in the music. A sombre variant of Ex. 6 leads to Ex. 16 as Maria's thoughts turn to her grim, unsmiling husband who—as she sees it—is eternally haunted by the dictates of an implacable duty. She cannot pretend to understand the philosophy which dominates his existence, and his singleminded pursuance of his military calling has led her to feel that she is indeed wedded to the very war itself which has from the first day overshadowed her married life.

With the description of her marriage not to a husband but only to a soldier, the music breaks into a quicker section built upon the Commandant's impatient Ex. 9. This in turn gives way to a mysterious passage in which shifting harmonies form beneath the constantly repeating outline of Ex. 1, above which a sinister meandering violin figuration weaves uneasily to and fro. Maria, from the vantage-point of her unhomelike refuge in the citadel, has watched the desolation war has cast over town and country alike. In contrast she invokes the streaming rays of the sun and abruptly the aria bursts upon its climactic closing section, beginning immediately with the motif of the Sun which to Maria is symbolic of joy and hope:

Ex. 18

From this point the aria rises ecstatically to its end with only a momentary drop to pianissimo when Maria fervently desires that her man may yet smile again, a theatrical idea which Strauss insisted that Gregor insert in order that the final cadence could be approached in a passionate crescendo.

7

The radiant end of the aria collapses abruptly as the stern figure of the Commandant appears above. Maria sees at once all too clearly that her hopes were illusion and his expression as sombre as ever. The scene which follows pursues the lyricism of this central portion of the opera, the Commandant chiding Maria for remaining in the citadel, while she urges him to tell her the truth about their predicament. At first their music is contrasted, his unrelentingly gloomy, based largely on the

heavy chordal Ex. 16 (so reminiscent—remarkably—of the Bund motif
from *Guntram*), whilst Maria's exhortations build easily into new glowing phrases such as Ex. 19:

Ex. 19

The motif of Despair, Ex. 13, also becomes prominent, especially when,
in answer to Maria's expression of confident hope that their darkness
will one day be turned to light (Sun motif, Ex. 18), the Commandant
at last reveals his plans for self-destruction together with the annihilation
of the entire citadel and all its occupants.

He urges her to flee and in so doing reveals his tenderness for her, a
softer side to his nature which she has not seen for many a year. Their
voices blend for the first time as she, so far from obeying his urgent
injunctions, determines to die with the lover whom she perceives still
lives within that harsh exterior. In this duet the theme of the Commandant's nobility of soul (Ex. 4(x)) is combined with Exx. 11 and 18
which continually alternate to form the basis of Maria's outburst.

But as the music surges to a climax, she is misled into believing that
they are wholly reunited and presses him to flee with her. At once he
stiffens; pompously he reminds her once more of his oath to the Kaiser
(the brass re-enter with Ex. 16) and she shrinks back appalled.

Thus when the duet resumes, the words of Maria and the Commandant are directly in opposition, viz:

Maria	Commandant
Fearful is the dictate of honour	Glorious is the dictate of honour
The dictate of love is worth nothing!	There is nothing higher on this earth!
Fearful is the oath you have sworn—	Glorious is the oath I have sworn—
No one hears the prayers from deep within the heart!	It raises itself up mightily to to divine heights!
War, fearful strangler . . . etc.	War, glorious thought . . . etc.

The whole passage, in which the two voices defiantly parody each other's phrases, recalls the parallel duet in the first act of *Die Aegyptische Helena*;[10] and like Hofmannsthal, Gregor felt obliged to supply a heavy justification for the perhaps somewhat artificial but typically operatic device:

> The evocation of war, affirmative on the part of the Commandant: 'I was only a soldier!', negative on the part of Maria: 'accursed art thou, War!', I consider to be the highpoint of the work. Strauss who was still saying at the outset that he did not believe that people in the Thirty Years War spoke like that, suddenly accepted this formulation born of the present day. It is linked with the duet: despite the diametrically contrary meaning of their words, the music has the power to establish the higher unity in the same way as these two human beings are united in love . . . it is not a 'recognition', such as that between Orest and Elektra, it is the recognition of true being and feeling. The woman is the *stronger,* the man it is who now stands in awe. It is consequently not correct to see the outcome of *Friedenstag* as a 'miracle' . . . because it is already present in the soul of this woman. . . .

In the closing lines of the duet Maria's and the Commandant's words merge. The Commandant, touched at last by Maria's idealism and devotion, is forced to accept her self-sacrifice. There is a long embrace signifying his assent that they should die in each other's arms. A tremendous orchestral peroration sublimates their mutual heroism with Ex. 4(x) and Ex. 16 (for the Commandant) alternating and combining with Ex. 18 (for Maria). The soaring polyphony builds to yet a further climax in which the motifs of Despair and the Fuse enter (Exx. 13 and 14). In the fading light the soldiers are reappearing from the vaults, their dreaded tasks of preparation completed. They have come to assemble for that last fatal word of command, in anticipation of which the Wachtmeister approaches, the lighted fuse in his hand. Gradually the music subsides with repeated statements of the citadel theme (Ex. 1) until, after a linking drawn-out version of the Despair motif Ex. 13, only the terse figure connected with the Fuse itself (Ex. 14) is left. The Commandant tears himself from Maria and gives the order with a sharp gesture before returning to her embrace. The soldiers kneel and in the profound stillness many are seen to have covered their faces.

[10] See Vol. II, p. 322.

8

A cannon shot is heard in the distance; then a second and a third. The Commandant starts violently, seizes the fuse and treads it out. In the belief that this is the sign for the long-awaited battle he orders the soldiers brusquely to their posts (violent ejaculations of Ex. 9). But instead of the sounds of battle there is a renewed silence. The Wachtmeister, who has rushed to the look-out, stammers in perplexity that there is no assault to be seen, and the soldiers confirm that the battlefield is empty and covered by a sea of dense mist (a striking pictorial image initiated by Strauss).

Into this eerie waiting, which has been punctuated by soft reiterations of the drum-figure Ex. 14, from infinitely far away comes a new ostinato—the sound of bells. We are on the threshold of the final section of the work and as further bells add their different tollings one by one a new theme rises up from the bass in constant repetition, much as the Transfiguration motif in the final section of *Tod und Verklärung*, although the theme itself is more akin to the Kaiserin motif from *Die Frau ohne Schatten*.

Ex. 20

The soldiers are dumbfounded by the unfamiliar sound of the bells but Maria senses the truth and softly hails the dawning glimpse of light and hope (Ex. 18). The Wachtmeister, Konstabel and Schütze, their hearts filled with wonder, in turn identify the different bells, all of which have been silent for so many weary years, but their awestruck excitement is not shared by the Commandant who can think of nothing but the enemy and the onslaught which he is expecting to burst over them at any moment.

Yet to his impetuous interrogation (Ex. 9) the Schütze answers with incredible news. Long columns of enemy infantry are advancing upon the town in unopposed parade formation and bearing white flags of truce. This fantastic account is accompanied by the first strains of the Parademarsch by which the Holsteiners (the enemy in question) are identified. It is quoted as it shortly appears in full—and disconcertingly vulgar—panoply at the entry of the Holsteiner troops:

Ex. 21

With such shrill brutality does the violent intrusion of this common-place march jar upon the listener's sensibilities that one wonders at Strauss's purpose. For it is music comparable only with those dreadful military marches with which he had long ago so perfunctorily fulfilled his obligations to Kaiser Wilhelm. It may indeed now have a satirical purpose and the garish return of 'Ein' feste Burg' by way of bass to the Parademarsch supports the idea that we may be intended to hear the music and see the Protestant newcomers through the ears and eyes of an anti-religious, anti-militarist Richard Strauss as well as through those of the desperate Commandant.

The scene is now one of the wildest emotional conflict. The Com-mandant has been frenziedly exhorting his men to armed resistance, Maria has long since fallen to her knees, the Burgomaster and the deputation of townsfolk have crowded once more onto the stage, their heartfelt cries of welcome to the Day of Peace ('O Tag des Friedens!') mingling with those of the soldiers themselves.

And still the Commandant closes his mind to any such idea. The Burgomaster's effusion on the evergreen brotherhood of man, on the miracle of such a day when joyful shouts are ringing out in every valley in the land, is meaningless to the dedicated soldier.

Above all, the figure of the Holsteiner, the enemy commander himself, whose off-stage voice and subsequent appearance marks the climax of this section, is to the Commandant pure anathema. In vain may the youthful Holsteiner courteously doff his hat and, addressing the Commandant as a 'mighty hero', relate the story of the Münster peace negotiations which have ended the war. He is received with the coldest hostility.

The Holsteiner's recital, at first based on continued repetitions of Ex. 20, leads to a further motif of this great and joyful occasion:

Ex. 22

Against the shimmering sounds of Ex. 22 distant cries of 'Friede! Friede!' are heard, while Maria breaks excitedly into a paean of praise of the sun (Ex. 18). This evokes from the Commandant a vicious rebuke upon which the Holsteiner, perceiving the situation, reproaches the Commandant and renews his assurances of succour and friendship in the new reversal of circumstances (Ex. 22). He then steps forward and holds out his hand.

The duet which follows is the passage which Strauss insisted should be referred back to Zweig on the grounds that Gregor had made the two commanders talk like university lecturers in history. The final version is certainly better and more powerful; but the dramatic problem remains almost insurmountable. Army leaders, who up to barely half an hour before have been committed to wholesale destruction and slaughter on account of their irreconcilable creeds, do not indulge in dialectical niceties nor instantly become staunch friends as a result of a truce concluded by some unknown body countless miles away. As his troops invade the citadel the seemingly humane and friendly demeanour of the Holsteiner savours of hypocrisy, in the light of his irrevocably victorious appearance.

The Holsteiner is at last stung by the Commandant's antagonism, and his words of reconciliation turn to impassioned religious dispute which intensifies until the two men draw swords. The music of this vehement duet is based partly on Ex. 6 and partly on a new gawky figure:

Ex. 23

Just as the Commandant is about to hurl himself upon the Holsteiner, the hated tones of 'Ein' feste Burg' on his lips, Maria wildly interposes herself. The short but impressively emphatic aria, in which she implores her beloved husband to see reason, contains the opera's philosophic kernel, reviling the power of words to instil hatred, and conjuring up 'the spirit of Peace as a Prince above Princes, a Lord above Emperors'.

Itself climactic, this creates the climax of the work. Maria's outburst, its emotional power replacing logical argument, breaks down her husband's bitter resistance. It was, of course, essential for Zweig's very concept that it should be so. Yet Strauss, the experience of a similar last-minute volte-face in the action of *Die Schweigsame Frau* fresh in his memory, had sensed the undramatic nature of what Zweig was prescribing. ('Gradual change of heart. They step nearer. They reach out their hands. They embrace' etc.) Seen from this point of view Strauss's proposition that the Commandant should shoot himself for the sake of love would undoubtedly have made a more immediate impact in the theatre, for all its banal conventionality. But Zweig was quite clear in his mind that no irrelevance in the action should obscure his message and in the end Strauss remained faithful to his friend's ideals.

At the time when the work was still formulating, Strauss had made out for Gregor a résumé of the concluding action as he now saw it:

> Dispatches! Following straight on: short dramatic dialogue up to the duel, and then the embrace. Then gradual pressing in of the townsfolk. The official proclamation of the Kaiser's message. Solemn silence. Then Maria begins . . . Song of Peace, in which everyone gradually joins in, building up to the highest jubilation.

'This framework' wrote Gregor in retrospect, 'was retained; I only took out the Kaiser's message'. However, as we have seen even so far, the finished work differs in many important particulars from Strauss's rough outline. Certainly no solemn silence marks this juncture. In particular, during the supreme moment when the Commandant throws away his sword and embraces the Holsteiner, people are flooding into the citadel, all the townsfolk and soldiers of both opposing armies, as the orchestra pours out a mighty peroration, built entirely upon soaring repetitions of the Commandant's Ex. 4(x), together with Exx. 6 and 11. We are to accept that the Commandant has at last seen the light and hence found his way to reconcile within himself the lifting of the siege with a future unstained by dishonour.

9

The remainder of the opera is pure pageant—a cantata on the prevailing subject of Peace and the Brotherhood of Man. Ex. 22 returns as the accompaniment to a hymn for women and tenor voices saluting the Holsteiner as their new ruler:

Ex. 24

The bells then return (Ex. 20) and are greeted ecstatically by Maria and a chorus of basses, comprising members of the deputation from the town reinforced by soldiers and, in due course, the Burgomaster and the Prelate.[11]

Next the two Commanders sing a stanza in unison, rejecting their earlier conflict based on hatred in favour of the new creed (return of 'Ein' feste Burg'). Maria joins them and a cheerful trio leads to a fortissimo restatement of Ex. 24 for double chorus sounding like a combination of *Tannhäuser* and Mahler's 8th Symphony; the walls part, the tower of the citadel sinks into the ground and the stage is filled (according to the stage directions) with sunlight and a surging sea of humanity. So unrealistic a climax is justified, explained Gregor, through the transition at this point away from Music Drama towards the pure spirit of music itself. The final all-embracing chorus thus carries the work beyond the limits of possibility prescribed even by opera, that complete personification of the theatre.

---

[11] During the rehearsals for the opening performance Strauss prescribed a 16-bar cut in this section, commenting ruefully that one can never tell for sure that the proportions are right until the work has actually been brought to the stage.

But for Strauss the loss of dramatic verisimilitude in favour of an idealized symbolic cantata on a static stage, became crippling. Until now the music had at least been reasonably representative of his operatic manner. The next verse of Ex. 24, however, can only be compared with the Hymn Strauss had just written under pressure for the Berlin Olympic Games which, in fact, it resembles very closely. It is set in block chords for full chorus and orchestra with all the violins running about over the top in ceaseless triplet figuration. Moreover, the key has changed—significantly—to C major, in which (apart from brief passing modulations) it remains until the end. Perhaps Strauss felt that the lofty idealism of the closing paean demanded precisely this key to which, whether in *Tod und Verklärung* and *Guntram,* or *Zarathustra, Salome* and *Frau ohne Schatten,* he had always turned whenever his aim was the expression of the divine or of sublimity. Indeed, analogies have been made with the finale to Beethoven's *Fidelio,* also in C major and centring about the subject of the Brotherhood of Man.

But such an idea lay at the root of Beethoven's innermost being and into it, often in this very same key, he poured his greatness as artist and as man. It would be hard to claim so much for Strauss, or for music such as Ex. 25, on which phrase the closing pages are largely built.

Ex. 25

Ex. 25 is handed over to the solo voices dominated by Maria's high soprano which encompasses a succession of top C's, the chorus enters antiphonally, and the work ends with a short orchestral postlude of drums and fanfares.

10

Gregor's enthusiasm on hearing Strauss play through the completed
score was so extravagant as to raise doubts over his sincerity:

> The great simplicity and monumental nature of *Friedenstag*
> will make this work everlastingly shine out from amongst all
> your works . . . this consummation, to which you have
> attained in your closing chorus, will be compared with
> the greatest examples of their kind. The only real compari-
> son I can find is the closing of the Ninth [Symphony], but the
> closing of *Friedenstag* is still simpler, more monumental,
> more dome-like, whereas for my taste the close of the Ninth
> becomes restless through the prominent sound of the solo
> quartet. In *Friedenstag* everything is simple, monumental,
> truly pure dome-like C major, not even broken up by the B,
> as in *Zarathustra*.
>
> Unprecedented the effect of the choruses as they stream
> together, so that the tower is dissolved, dematerialized,
> disintegrated! But what a different disintegration from that
> by gunpowder!! This ideal effect of two choruses streaming
> together (St. Matthew Passion, opening) I have always
> wanted to *see also on the stage*—to you belongs this sublime
> success! . . .

One can imagine the smile on Strauss's face as he wrote in reply:
'. . . I hope in your enthusiasm of authorship you do not overrate me'.
For it had always been one of Strauss's most endearing qualities that
just as he knew and accepted his own stature and worth, he never had
the slightest illusion concerning his limitations, as his various remarks to
Zweig had illustrated.[12]

In normal circumstances Strauss would have had the plans all laid
for the première of his new opera long before the score was ready. But
the circumstances were far from normal and in any case as it happened
there was always to have been a companion piece for *Friedenstag,* the
subject for which Strauss had settled in that curt quarter of an hour's
browse through Gregor's portfolio. Until this other one-act piece was a
good deal further advanced, the question of having another sniff at the
political atmosphere could be tactfully postponed.

Gregor's industry was formidable. By 10th October (1935) he had
already taken Strauss at his word and completed two elaborate and

[12] See pp. 6–7 above, and Vol. II, p. 346.

verbose libretti on the legend of Daphne. In principle Strauss could scarcely find fault here: Greek drama and mythology, as Gregor well knew, had provided the subject-matter for no less than three of Strauss's earlier operas. There had even been a time when Hofmannsthal had urged Strauss to concentrate specifically on music drama based on mythology (see the letter quoted in Volume II, p. 312—'Let us write mythological operas, it is the truest of all forms, believe me').

One is inclined to think that these words of his dead friend, together perhaps with the memory of that thrown-out idea of Hofmannsthal's for 'some rustic bucolic opera . . . pagan-mythological . . . a peasant wedding . . . the whole a ceremony . . .' were more influential in making up Strauss's mind than a study of classical representations of the legend in the Uffizi Gallery and the Villa Borghese with Gregor, as the latter would have us believe.[13] For his part Gregor claimed to have derived his own initial impetus from a lithograph 'Apollo and Daphne' by the nineteenth century French painter Théodore Chassériau.

The Daphne myth is relatively simple: a mountain nymph, daughter of Peneius—a Thessalian river-god—and Gaea, or Mother Earth, whom she also served as priestess, Daphne was so beautiful that she excited the admiration of none other than Apollo himself. This is not to say, however, that she did not have mortal lovers and chief amongst these was Leucippus, son of Oenomaus. Apollo was jealous of Leucippus and plotted his destruction by the ingenious device of advising the mountain nymphs to bathe naked. As Leucippus had been in the habit of joining Daphne's mountain revels disguised as a girl, he could now no longer conceal his manhood and on his discovery he was torn to pieces by the nymphs.[14]

But Apollo's craftiness did not lead to the attainment of his desires, for no sooner did he pursue Daphne in the certainty of conquest than the nymph in her distress cried out to Gaea. Coming instantly to Daphne's rescue, Gaea transported her to Crete leaving a laurel tree in Apollo's arms. Out of the laurel Apollo made a wreath in Daphne's memory which has thereafter remained the highest emblem of distinction in combat or the muses.[15]

[13] Nevertheless, Strauss later hit on the idea of using Bernini's sculpture in a medallion for the cover of the vocal score and text book.

[14] There is a curious mixture of legends here, since another Leucippus, a young Cretan, was actually turned miraculously from a boy to a girl by the Titan, Leto.

[15] Robert Graves cites a fascinating account of the myth's origin in the Hellenic

In order to emphasize the character of the story as a nature myth, some versions make Daphne actually turn into the tree by her own request, the physical transformation taking place at the moment of capture at the hands of the god. It is this better-known ending which Gregor makes the climax of his adaptation. He also retains the names Peneius and Gaea for Daphne's parents, though reducing their status to that of mere fisher-folk. Leucippus becomes a shepherd and Daphne's childhood companion, although he has since come to love her to distraction.

These altered roles were at first intended by Gregor in some subtle, rather intangible way to be commensurate with their original identity in the myth. The draft summary of the action which he submitted to Strauss on that July day of 1935 reads:

> Daphne. One act of tragedy with dances and choruses—
> wonderful Grecian landscape. Mankind identified both with
> nature and with the gods!—Old Peneios is at once the river
> and the singing fisherman who lives by the river. Gää[16] is
> his wife and at the same time the lovely green earth by the
> Peneios. Their daughter Daphne in the deepest state of emo-
> tional unawakening . . . sport with the waves of the Peneios
> which are choruses of nymphs. Two suitors: Apollo as cow-
> herd, wise, baritone-like, surrounded by his servant-
> priestesses, and the young tenorish shepherd Leukippos.
> Daphne remains enigmatic, even when the cow-herd on one
> occasion confronts her with lightning . . . Leukippos, perse-
> cuted by the jealous Apollo, hits on the idea of dressing up
> as a girl. This entirely changes Daphne's manner, she now
> inclining towards him as one girl to another. Through this
> deception he comes to attain his desire. Now Daphne is
> throughly upset and opens her heart to the cow-herd!—
> Apollo reacts both as god and as man, and slays Leukippos
> with a thunder-storm. Peneios begs Zeus, amidst funeral
> choruses for Leukippos, to change mankind back into its
> primeval state. This Zeus grants and amidst the play of the
> water-nymphs and in front of Leukippos' flaming pyre the
> tree Daphne grows aloft.

---

capture of Tempe with its cult of 'orgiastic laurel-chewing Maenads' annually tearing apart the 'sacred king of the local horse cult' (Leucippus = white horse). See *The Greek Myths*, Vol. I. Penguin Books, London, 1955.

[16] The full score uses variably the two methods of spelling Gaea and Gää, which latter was that used by Strauss and Gregor in their correspondence.

Gregor visualized this nature-drama as linked with *Friedenstag* in more than just its mere joint performance in a double bill. *Daphne* was to be representative of Peace in Nature as was *Friedenstag* of Peace among Men, and both works were to end with static choral cantatas on their respective aspects of the common subject. Such a concept was bound to appeal to Zweig, to whom Gregor paid the courtesy of sending his first verse sketches even before Strauss saw them. Zweig, the soul of loyal friendship, expressed his delighted ('entzückend') approval in a letter which Gregor passed straight on to Strauss. Not that all this manoeuvring in any way affected Strauss's judgement. Sadly he risked Nazi censorship and wrote directly to Zweig at the end of October:

> No doubt our dear friend is very gifted—but what is lacking is superior force and ideas, which lie somewhat apart from the dramatic mainstream—as also, what is most perturbing, the quite distinct atmosphere of the theatre. That becomes especially noticeable in *Daphne*, the very pretty basic idea of which is simply not 'formulated' at all. Words upon words —schoolmaster banalities and no concentration to a focal point. There is no interesting spiritual conflict. Daphne (especially colourless), Apollo and Leukippos should clash in some scene in the manner of Kleist;[17] instead of remaining that boring virgin, she should fall in love with them both, the god and the man. . . .

Perhaps an account of his simultaneous work on *Perikles* (a substantial historical book on Ancient Greek Culture and History), Gregor seems really to have spread himself in the versified second draft, with Zeus as well as other additional legendary characters floating in and out, for Strauss continues:

> . . . moreover, that Zeus-Wotan with his sermons on world-wisdom is really impossible; the Medusa pantomime would have a simply laughable effect on the stage. . . .

The idea of Zeus appearing in person seems to have occupied an important place in Gregor's mind, and he continued to elaborate on it in a considerable sketch. According to this, when Apollo makes his entry he is accompanied by 'an old old Homer-like swine-herd, who at the end of the piece reveals himself to be Zeus'. As the action develops,

[17] Zweig had continued to press Strauss not to reject the idea of Kleist's *Amphitryon*.

Hermes is also introduced and made the instrument by which Leukippos' deception is uncovered; in fact, Gregor was beginning to picture an altogether 'more personal, richer part to be played by the world of gods, amongst whom particularly Zeus was an attractive figure'. In the closing scene whilst still incognito he was 'calmly to drink of the sacrificial wine—to the general horror; in the end no grudge is borne against the ancient and half-deaf swine-herd. But finally on hearing Peneios' prayer to Zeus that Daphne be transformed, he manifests himself, rising up powerfully in his rags. Faced with Leukippos' death at Apollo's hands, he explains significantly that since Prometheus' deed, the boundaries between gods and men had fallen in any case; and that he felt happier as a swine-herd than as shaker of the heavens.'

So much last-scene moralizing by some venerable old character conjures up memories of Friar Laurence or the Hermit in *Freischütz*, and it is not surprising that Strauss jibbed at it. Ultimately Zeus disappeared entirely from the scenario although Gregor's spirits must have risen when he found the opportunity to re-introduce the god as Jupiter in *Die Liebe der Danae*.

II

As Strauss progressed with the full score of *Friedenstag*, so Gregor, wholly undeterred by the composer's cruelly frank rebuffs, worked and reworked his scholarly little classical verse-drama until, by the summer of 1936, Strauss was prepared majestically to concede that it was in tolerable shape and could be composed. Only Gregor's favourite cantata ending still seemed utterly artificial and untheatrical. Strauss had, in fact, been giving the subject a good deal of thought on and off, especially during a journey to Italy in February and March. It is fascinating to discover in the published correspondence the degree to which Strauss felt it necessary to concern himself with the psychological meanderings of the situations, proposing, criticizing (often the verses themselves), and rejecting with a ruthlessness which contrasts sharply with his relationship to previous librettists.

His way of sending poor Gregor off to seek help from other men, whether Zweig, Lothar Wallerstein, or whoever, must have been humiliating; for if Zweig had been deferential Gregor was almost sickeningly humble. Time and again he willingly accepted interference

from Strauss's numerous professional colleagues amongst whom the
conductor Clemens Krauss was quickly emerging as the most influential
and opinionated. It was Krauss who ultimately, nearly a year later,
solved the opera's closing scene to Strauss's satisfaction, Gregor having
to submit to the final indignity of seeing his own elaborate conclusion
jettisoned *in toto*.

It was some measure of the man that he was able not only to swallow
such treatment but actually refer in glowing terms to its results in his
study of Strauss's operas published only a few years later.[18]

Such a relationship sounds distinctly unpromising and yet, not for
the first time in the illogical world of opera, it produced a work of substantial quality. In some unforeseeable way the serenity of the legend
subject was in tune with the ageing Strauss's need for peaceful music-
making. Already the first notes set the mood of the gentle Nature-
drama.

Ex. 26

The pastoral spirit of the work is emphasized by the exclusive use of a
small woodwind group for the instrumental introduction, which also
presents a succession of additional themes such as:

Ex. 27

Ex. 28

[18] One of the most ingenious features of this book is its total suppression of
Zweig's name. It stands to reason, of course, that permission would not otherwise
have been granted for its publication.

Ex. 29

All these melodic ideas refer in one way or another to Daphne her-self—her chaste purity (Ex. 26), her bewitching loveliness (Ex. 27), her innocent love for Apollo in his identification with light and the sun (Ex. 28), her yearning to be at one with all nature (Ex. 29). The whole tiny prelude can thus stand as a portrait of the semi-creature who is so faint and elusive as to appear unreal, already less than human, even though her mythical status as a mountain-nymph forms no part of Gregor's scheme.

The curtain rises as an alphorn sounds on stage, surely the first or-chestral use of this splendid if unwieldy instrument.[19]

Ex. 30

Ex. 30 later turns out to be an augmentation of the motif of the Diony-sian Feast to which the alphorn is summoning a group of shepherds.

Dionysus (or our old friend Bacchus) is not in any way involved in the Daphne myth except, perhaps, in so far as he was the god not only of wine but of trees; nor is he actually to be introduced in person during the opera although he is frequently invoked. But Strauss had wisely felt that the Apollonian aspect of the myth would be too monochromatic by itself and the opera would end up by becoming wearisome. 'Couldn't Daphne', he wrote to Gregor, 'represent the human embodiment of nature itself touched upon by the two divinities Apollo and Dionysus, the contrasting elements of art?' Accordingly the climax of the action was now planned to take place against just such a background as the Dionysiac revels would provide.

As a result, some motivation for these revels would need to be estab-lished as early as possible. Gregor had originally planned for the opera

---

[19] Good specimens often measure nearly eight feet in length. The only instance I know of an alphorn taking part in a concert hall was during one of the London Festivals of the late Gerard Hoffnung, cartoonist and musical humorist.

to begin with a frolicsome ensemble for a group of water-nymphs. Peneios, at that time still half river-god, was then to make an early entrance playfully rebuking these latter-day Rhine Maidens who were then to resume their carolling.

All this was thrown out and in its place a scene inserted in which the shepherds of the surrounding neighbourhood should discuss and clarify the forthcoming celebrations. There were in fact a number of such feasts dedicated to Dionysus by the Ancients, occurring at widely varied times of the year ranging from October to March. For dramatic reasons Gregor exercised considerable poetic licence in choosing the 'feast of the blossoming vine', and setting it on Midsummer's Day as a Festival of Fertility (the latter essentially an independent Spring Festival).

The scene is set amidst olive groves between a stony bank of the river Peneios and the slopes of Mount Olympus. The sun is on the point of setting and the shepherds have been driving their flocks down to the river. Strauss depicts the busy situation with music wild enough to suggest a violent storm, and which later in the work is actually reintroduced for that and similar purposes, although for the time being nothing more alarming than the sounds of large numbers of sheep in motion is intended. Surging chromatic string passages form the background to sundry dramatic figurations:

Ex. 31   Ex. 32   Ex. 33

The alphorn sounds again (Ex. 30 'very loudly') and the tempestuous noises die away in order to allow for the shepherds' discussion. Gregor made use of the convention by which an older and fatherly shepherd tells a young one (who for reasons not given has somehow remained ignorant of the whole affair) that the summons of the alphorn is of all-consuming importance. Peneios himself is giving the feast in celebration of the young god Dionysus' annual rebirth. The elder shepherd's explanation, which lays stress on this as a mating season for beasts and men alike, is built on a number of new musical ideas which sway and surge in anticipation of the dancing to come:

Ex. 34

leading to:

Ex. 34a

Although many of the figures contained within this flowing melos are developed symphonically during the scene, it is predominantly those contained within Ex. 34a which emerge as motifs of the Dionysiac feast, ⌐ x ⌐ in particular being pre-eminent (hence, of course, its use as part of the alphorn summons, Ex. 30).

As the shepherd concludes he is hailed by other shepherds whose greetings he returns. The alphorn then repeats its summons and the noises (Exx. 31–33) resume as before though with the addition of the melodic strand ⌐ z ⌐ from Ex. 34a. When the shufflings and confusion have yet again died away it is this theme which re-emerges as the lyrical background for a song of farewell to the dying day, sung in unison by the retreating shepherds.

12

Daphne herself now enters and at once embarks on the first of her two big solo scenes. Unjustified by the dramatic action though it is, an immediate exposition of the central character was planned in exactly this way from the very first. Certainly it constitutes the principal expression of the whole work, the aspect which had initially caught Strauss's interest and for which accordingly he conjured up the right music without difficulty. Whatever faults he had to find with the libretto, this section of Gregor's poem was acceptable as it stood for he found it to contain a subtle (albeit unintended) analogy with his own life.

Daphne outlines her dependence on light in order that she may see the manifestations of nature to which she feels herself intimately related. To her mankind is clumsy, alien, even destructive to all she holds dear. She can find nothing but reproach for her father Peneios who is summoning these hateful beings into savage assembly. Her refuge in these threatening circumstances is her beloved tree to which she will turn in the darkness, the boughs and branches singing to her once again of the day, of the warm sunlight, whose god—Phoebus Apollo—her song apostrophizes.

It was in just so abstract a conception that the tired, disgraced Strauss could find an absorbing escapism from a sour, inhuman reality in which there was no part he cared to play. The score breathes an undisturbed peace of a kind unprecedented in his work so far. Against a kaleidoscope of orchestral colour, the soprano voice floats in endless melisma. Beautiful, translucent, its serenity is as unreal as the character it portrays.

The scena falls into two main sections. In the first the different themes follow one another in pursuance of Daphne's thought. Ex. 26(x) is expanded to form the invocation with which the solo begins and ends:

Ex. 35

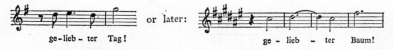

Exx. 28(x) and 29 follow as Daphne sings of daylight, the source of life itself. She enumerates her many 'brothers and sisters'—trees, flowers, springs, butterflies—while Strauss toys with gentle woodwind turns and string trills, a pattern which is soon to reappear flitting across the canvas at the mention of butterflies:

Ex. 36

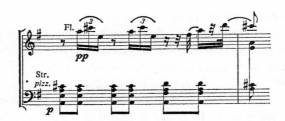

Daphne's reference to the lovely emptiness of night brings with it a moment of gloom from which Ex. 30 twists upwards through the woodwind. She has remembered her father's summons to the feast and as she sings rhetorically to Peneios in sad reproach his theme is given on the horn:

Ex. 37

followed by a few short Dionysiac phrases suggestive of the hateful celebrants and the havoc soon to be wrought. A solo violin ascending with Ex. 29 then leads to the second and main section.

Here we get a foretaste of what Strauss was later to make into the great Verwandlung (transformation) scene which ultimately formed the opera's finale. The strings, divided into some fifteen parts, sing, twitter or rustle magically while the melodic lines drawn from Daphne's numerous themes are shared between the solo wind and stringed instruments in addition to the long soprano cantilena. Moreover, hidden in the texture in diminution are two further ideas:

Ex. 38

Ex. 39

Ex. 38 is the first of Apollo's motifs while Ex. 39 represents the laurel, symbol of Daphne's actual and total unification with the trees she loves so much, that physical transformation which can be her only fulfilment. Although these themes are only hinted at for the present, they are so important in the opera's later stages that their first appearances should not be overlooked. One further phrase needs to be quoted, for not only is it one of the main strands of Daphne's ecstatic paean to her tree but is also woven into the concluding cadence of the whole radiant outburst:

Ex. 40

There is a downward swoop and the spell is broken.

13

Leukippos has jumped out from behind the tree, where he has been hiding all along.[20]

At once the style of the music changes, the thick textures being replaced by the lightest conversational accompaniments of the type Strauss had perfected in his every-day opera *Intermezzo*. The horn and bassoon give Leukippos' motif in a gay canon:

[20] He actually says 'Ich war der Baum!' (I was the tree), surely an unnecessarily confusing piece of deception in these peculiar circumstances.

Ex. 41

Leukippos' function is described as that of 'play-mate', a role which his music consistently emphasizes; some of it indeed is so insubstantial that he appears quite characterless. At first Daphne scarcely even acknowledges his presence, much to his consternation.

Ex. 42

Like all good Ancient Greeks, whether gods or shepherds, from Pan to Daphnis or Damon, Leukippos has done his wooing on the flute and it now becomes apparent that the somewhat commonplace Ex. 36 referred not only to butterflies but to Leukippos, of whose music-making it is eminently typical. Daphne in fact has always thought of him in a disembodied way, his girlish red cheeks (which are to have their use in due course) as the springtime blossoms, his flute as the wind or the flowing of water and so on. He is understandably jealous of the tree towards which she turns so affectionately, and he fails entirely to understand how she alone has missed what has been so plain to everyone, his growing passion.

Daphne's descriptions of her favourite nature phenomena (the wind kissing the blossoms, etc.) draw from Strauss his most delicate tone-painting reminiscent of the coloratura song 'Amor' from the *Brentano Lieder* with the addition of the gold-dust violin slithers from *Josephs-legende*.

But Leukippos' impetuosity grows, Exx. 41 and 42 being joined by Ex. 27 which is to become increasingly symbolical of the desire Daphne arouses, whether in Leukippos or (as later) Apollo. Yet Daphne does feel some sympathetic rapport with so dear a companion of her childhood days. She tries with gentle kindness to explain this as the music develops into a more generously flowing passage based not only on Exx. 26–29 but a new little phrase suggesting that she is aware of his sufferings, Platonic as her affection may be.

Ex. 43

die   eig – ne Trä – ne [21]

Naturally, however, none of this satisfies Leukippos who angrily smashes his flute and tries for the first time to break down Daphne's resistance by force. He feels the Dionysiac influence at work within him and, likening her to the goddess Diana (not the only time this comparison is made), embraces her.

All in vain: the impending feast which has emboldened him is to her repellent, and she shakes him off so vehemently that he tears himself away in despair just as Daphne's mother Gaea enters.

A kind of Erda, Gaea was brought on by Gregor in this short scene in order to supply Strauss with an otherwise lacking contralto voice. It was also the intention that this primeval mother-symbol 'would later add meaning to her daughter's destiny' but this idea came to nothing; Gregor was no Hofmannsthal.

Nevertheless Strauss took advantage of the opportunity for a deep voice, carrying Gaea's tessitura down to the low E flat, an extreme range for any contralto, while giving the slow moving accompaniment to predominantly deep-sounding instruments.

Gaea has come to call the reluctant Daphne to the festivities. But on approaching she has overheard Daphne's rejections of Leukippos and this has caused her anxiety which she gently tries to express to her daughter who remains uninvolved. Daphne at first shows herself obedient to her mother although certain limitations quickly become apparent.

She will be present at the feast if she is so bidden, but only in the same way as the trees and meadows are present. Hence she is unwilling to dress up attractively according to the purpose of the occasion. At Gaea's command, two maids ceremoniously hold out garments and jewels for

[21] ('my own tears', i.e. those which Daphne sheds on seeing tears in the eyes of one for whom she has so much sisterly devotion.)

her, but abruptly she runs off into the house, leaving Gaea to utter a short prophetic soliloquy before following her.[22]

The maids, now abandoned by mother and daughter alike, break into a formal duet in which they apostrophize the clothes and jewelry: 'never will they know the beauty they were intended to adorn', and so on. This artificial sentiment is elaborated amidst much carolling and gaiety in a scherzando section which contrasts well after the austerity of Gaea's music.

Leukippos' voice is heard bewailing his plight. He has been listening to the maids' chatter and identifies himself with the cast-off garments. The anguish his hopeless love for Daphne causes him is symbolized by Ex. 27 which repeatedly threads its way upwards in alternation with the gay phrases of the maids. They chide him with being so late for the feast, and mockingly taunt him with their own access to Daphne's person. A sugary duet in Straussian thirds and sixths follows as they tell how, so far from being merely servant-girls, they have the power to gratify his most ardent dreams. They offer him the rejected feminine attire, in which disguise they assure him he will have no difficulty in winning his love. At first he is outraged, then incredulous, but gradually, remembering how Daphne spoke of his red cheeks and his tears, the idea becomes less preposterous and finally, joining in the hilarity, he runs off with the two girls to effect the transformation. Leukippos' masquerade, one of the strongest features of the original myth, has thus been successfully incorporated, if with a certain heavy ingenuity which has necessitated a change of time-scale. Nevertheless Strauss always regarded it as the merest side-issue on the grounds that the omniscient Apollo was bound to see through it in an instant.

There is a short orchestral interlude in which Daphne's Ex. 26 and Leukippos' Ex. 41 are combined with peals of rippling laughter on the flutes and the music then settles down to a graver tone as Peneios enters, impressively bearded and accompanied by Gaea together with all the shepherds.

The early scene for Peneios having been thrown out, this becomes his first appearance and Strauss began to have a few justifiable pangs that he had caused this rather important father-figure to be under-stressed. He wrote over Gregor's sketch:

---

[22] Strauss made no musical allowance to enable this ponderous character to get off the stage and it has become the custom to make a 3-bar repeat not marked in the score.

Peneios should now be somewhat more prominent—not too much evocation of nature—Peneios' vision from the first draft, the gods who have fled—could be used in part.

Ever obedient, therefore, Gregor restored some of his original ideas although with confusing results, and it is amusing to see him saddling Strauss with the ultimate responsibility:

With the Peneios scene tragic accents impinge for the first time upon the idyll; wholly untroubled in mind the fisherman actually allows his thoughts to wander off into Apollonion spheres on the evening of the Dionysiac festival—this fermentation I created at the desire of the composer; Peneios had to be a 'creative human being'.

The 'vision' to which Strauss refers in his letter is a particularly enigmatic conception, and it is of this that Peneios sings immediately upon his entrance (Ex. 37 in broad tones on horns and cellos). The shepherds are a little puzzled, as well they might be, and even Gaea his wife calls him an 'everlasting dreamer'. The gist of his prophetic utterances is that Phoebus Apollo is approaching, that the gods are shortly to return from their Olympian retreat to their one-time home on earth. He calls to the shepherds to look at the summit of Mount Olympus, all red in the setting sun 'and not yet hidden behind the rising vapours of the vine-branches'. He anticipates a visit from none other than Apollo (Ex. 38 as well as an anticipatory entry of Apollo's majestic second motif, Ex. 45) and he refers to himself mysteriously as 'the abandoned brother, once a god like them', an isolated semi-reference to his true mythological status.

Gaea and the shepherds begin to fear that Peneios is being too provoking and a glowing ensemble builds up. Peneios waxes ever more enthusiastic over the preparations for the banquet of roast meats and wine which he believes the gods are coming to share, although he never mentions the name of Dionysus, in whose honour the feast is really being given. The Dionysiac motif Ex. 34(x) begins to appear in the polyphony, dance rhythms are added to the texture, and as the climax approaches a new figure appears on the trombones:

Ex. 44

Ex. 44 is symbolic of godly merriment. Peneios has become so excited that he is imagining a company of divine guests all laughing as they sit at his table and he sings of this laughter against the rising voices of Gaea and the shepherds, Ex. 44 constantly returning in ever closer repetition. At last he himself bursts into real laughter which is echoed uncannily from all around, much to the alarm of the shepherds who cluster for protection like children round the maternal Gaea. Moreover there are flashes of lightning and Strauss adds a violent orchestral storm based not only on the echoing laughter motif Ex. 44, but on those stormy motifs Exx. 31–33 which, at first only sheep noises, now seem really to come into their own.

There are also, however, entries of a new fanfare motif which shows these manifestations to be the work of Apollo, whose second theme it is. I quote it in its later fully harmonized form:

Ex. 45

But whereas Peneios had expected a group of gods to come to his banquet, the only newcomer to appear out of all this cataclysm is a very human-looking cow-herd. In fact it is, of course, Apollo but no one recognizes him, not even Peneios in spite of all his preamble. After all, it was quite normal for the gods to appear amongst men in mortal guise, so that it seems very slow-witted of Gaea and the shepherds when they taunt Peneios with his disappointing guest.

With engaging bonhomie Apollo addresses Peneios and Gaea by name. Peneios civilly returns his greeting upon which he tells his story, which is that his herd, after being rounded up for the night on the slopes of Olympus, caught the stimulating aroma of Peneios' feast and immediately broke into a mass stampede. They have only just been reassembled and as for him—he adds with fortunately unchallenged logic —Peneios can see him standing there in his presence!

The unlikely tale makes an agreeable monologue with a nicely contrasted middle section when Strauss describes the antics of the legendary cows.[23] The more bestial aspect of the Dionysiac feast here grows a new and important figure:

Ex. 46

while Apollo's geniality is portrayed by a melodic line recalling Sir Morosus in one of his more relaxed moods in *Die Schweigsame Frau:*

Ex. 47

Ex. 47 becomes the dominating motif during the closing part of the scene, the shepherds singing to it their last mocking phrases. Peneios cuts short this show of incivility to the unexpected guest, lowly though he may be, and instructs Gaea to send their daughter to wait upon him as they all go towards the house, Gaea and the shepherds still laughing at the cows (Ex. 46) and their keeper (Ex. 47), Peneios following thoughtfully behind. Night has fallen.

14

Left alone for the moment, Apollo has a short soliloquy in which he reproaches himself with so debasing his divinity by lies and deception. As Strauss explained to Gregor after a discussion with Wallerstein: 'Apollo transgresses against his godhead by approaching Daphne with the feelings of Dionysus'. The later repercussions of the drama are to spring from this realization which Strauss marks by a new motif in the brass:

[23] The possibility must be borne in mind that Strauss took these cows seriously and intended the return of Exx. 31–33 not so much as an Apollonian storm as to illustrate their mass motion much like that of the sheep at the beginning of the opera. There is notably, however, no such corresponding indication in the stage directions.

[24] Cf. Ex. 15 in Chapter XVIII.

Ex. 48

Apollo then sees the radiant form of Daphne approaching and all self-recriminations are set aside. A variant of Ex. 27 combined with a hesitating rising phrase (see Ex. 49 below) becomes the motif of the effect her breathtaking beauty has upon him, (until now Ex. 27 has been largely concerned with its impact on Leukippos) and again and again it rises up in various warm keys through the orchestra together with other motifs of both Apollo and Daphne, Exx. 26 and 38, as well as a new seductive melody:

Ex. 49

At first Daphne moves with hieratical gestures; she is followed by a group of maidens and in the light of the rising full moon she can be seen holding out with both hands a cup of pure water.[25] The maidens then withdraw as Apollo apostrophizes the vision before him. Like Leukippos, he compares her with Artemis (an alternative name for Diana), but calls her 'sister', a piece of inspired psychology, as he kneels before her. The word stirs an immediate response in her, bewildered as she is by this remarkable stranger whom she finds in apparent homage before her. She explains that she is to serve him as bidden by her father (Peneios' Ex. 37 mingled with the constant repetitions of Ex. 49) but gladly responds to the sisterly idea.

Apollo thereupon leaps up. To the ringing tones of Ex. 45, now for the first time in all its glory, he quickly takes advantage of the opening in her defences. Stretching out his hands he establishes this primary step

[25] The analogy with Arabella is so close that it cannot possibly have escaped both Strauss's and Gregor's notice.

in their relationship and begs for refreshment after 'the longest summer day's journey', an allusion to his heavenly calling she cannot possibly follow. Nevertheless with the motif of her love for the sun, Ex. 28, floating to and fro in violins and flutes she pours water from the cup over his hands and then hangs a blue mantle about his shoulders.

A manifestation of divinity suddenly emanates from him: the cloak billows about him majestically and he seems to glow with an unearthly radiance (Exx. 28 and 45 are combined in a beautiful piece of iridescent orchestration). Still Daphne does not guess the truth although she begins to suspect that this cow-herd is more than he seemed.

Apollo now describes how during his solar orbit round the sky his attention was riveted by her gaze and by her words of adoration to the day and the sun. He quotes her aria 'O bleib, geliebter Tag' while she wonders at the mystery of her new-found brother who seems to have probed her innermost thoughts.

This duet is the opera's centre-piece and of a genre in which Strauss could scarcely go wrong. In such circumstances, and with the bulk of his thematic material to hand, his flow of symphonic lyricism was still virtually inexhaustible. Here any indications that the composer is a tired and disillusioned septuagenarian retreat to vanishing point: the passion and energy are indeed extraordinary and are maintained for page after page as one ecstatic climax succeeds another.

In the construction of these climaxes Strauss introduces the motif of fulfilment the significance of which is to become clear only in the final scene of the opera:

Ex. 50

Its initial entry is at a moment of deep feeling when Daphne, sensing at last that she is in the presence of that personification of light and sun which in child-like innocence she loves with all her being, sinks into his arms.

Jubilantly Apollo promises that she shall join him in his heavenly chariot and, ignoring her cries of 'brother, brother', embraces and kisses her in the fullness of his desire. The atmosphere is one of sudden stillness dominated by the heavy brass masses of Ex. 48.

15

Daphne is dumbfounded. Psychologically this should be a crucial moment for the convincing motivation of all that follows and Strauss struggled hard to stimulate Gregor into some flash of insight which would bring it all to life:

> Please don't grudge the labour and go on thinking about it. Above all it is too cheap for Daphne's feelings to turn to hate immediately after Apollo's kiss. Even if she has no knowledge of human love-desire or abhors it, the kiss of the god must awaken in her other feelings than simply those of hate . . . a nature-being like Daphne must be supremely incapable of hatred. The feelings Apollo's kiss conjures up in her can only be fear, astonishment or anguish . . . (she) senses the falsehood in his kiss and since she is a pure creature of nature and instinct she recoils from the unclean god even while in her trembling she senses who he is, though without full recognition . . . and if Apollo presents himself as a cowherd this is in no sense a deception, but merely one of the shapes in which the god can present himself to mankind. So also the 'brother' in which guise he gives her that opening kiss, don't invest it with too much significance: in any case no primary motif. . . .

One feels that Strauss was trying to take over Hofmannsthal's role of symbolic philosopher, while bullying poor Gregor to make revision after revision whether or not he really understood what solution he was looking for.

All this was in any case largely subservient to Strauss's sound musical instinct in the handling of the gradual transition from the duet to the succeeding festival scene. The kiss itself is a very extended and beautiful passage, which however notably lacks the quality of ecstasy. There is a gloom in the thick, warm harmonies as they outline not only Apollo's themes but an undulating chordal motif derived from the Dionysiac Ex. 34(x). Daphne does not at first appreciate the pervading eroticism although it causes her to break away from the embrace of her false brother (various of her motifs in scurrying form on basset-horn and oboe) just when he has at last dared openly to declare his love.

Suddenly however these same undulating harmonies form the basis, together with fragments of Ex. 34, for an off-stage chorus of the shepherds as they invoke Dionysus, and with the slow dawning of unwilling comprehension (Ex. 50 in drooping inversion) Daphne knows she has been betrayed. Unmoved by Apollo's fervent protestations, she miserably expresses her remoteness from everything and everybody around her, and above all—she cries out in despair—from him, that is, her vainly importunate divine lover, the god for whom she had hopefully felt so strong an affinity.

For long, the moon having tactfully hidden behind a cloud, only the shapes of Apollo and Daphne have been discernible in the darkness, but suddenly the red light of torches flares up as a procession of shepherds enters headed by Peneios. The Dionysiac feast has arrived.

A corresponding procession of women led by Gaea comes from the opposite side and the scene as they dance is suggested by rearing horn passages of Ex. 34(y) though transformed into the rhythmic pattern of Ex. 46.

Apollo, who had laid his bow and arrows aside, now arms himself again and retreats to await developments while Daphne seeks refuge with her mother.

The ritualistic dances follow and, if not the greatest of Strauss, are by no means without their interest, falling easily into a number of short characteristic sections which succeed one another though never actually breaking the flow of the music. At first the mood is one of broad jubilation; Peneios calls out in a mighty voice as he dedicates the wine to Dionysus. He is echoed enthusiastically by the chorus as Gaea assists him in the sacrificial pouring.

Ex. 34 here naturally finds its true place, the constituent motifs all intermingling in a swirling orchestral texture. A primitive form of Ex. 50 can also be discerned rising or falling amongst the cauldron of themes. Daphne is not alone in seeking fulfilment in this great annual mating feast.

From amongst the hordes of feasting revellers a savage dance develops, executed by shepherds wearing ram's masks and sheepskins. Gregor found the idea for this in the remarkable scenes which are perpetuated as decoration around ancient Greek vases.

The furious $\frac{6}{8}$ movement with which Strauss matches the evocation of pagan revelry is not far removed in its musical language from the equally wild and surging $\frac{6}{8}$ of the Knallbonbons' dance in *Schlagobers*. Yet he knew how to intensify the effect of violence with abrupt intrusive figurations, as well as by curtailing its progress after a surprisingly short time with frenzied interruptions of Ex. 34(y) in its broken rhyth-

mic form and a further stamping pattern which is strongly featured
throughout these dances:

Ex. 51

The wine-drinking, which has been deliberately held back until this
moment, is now begun in earnest and a group of men call out in jocular
tones to the women to beware the inevitable consequences.

As if in answer, a women's dance ensues, sharply contrasted with the
preceding in its gentle stylization. The music softly trips and trills in alternation with repeated quotations from the passage-work in thirds and
sixths of the two maids whom we have met earlier. (There is more than
a hint of *Rosenkavalier* in this pretty section of the score.) The maids
themselves are in fact taking part in the dance and so, heavily disguised
as one of the thyrsus-bearers,[26] is Leukippos.

There is another short burst of violence during which the ritual of
rape is enacted and Leukippos seizes the opportunity to approach Daphne
(Ex. 41 vigorously on the horn). It seems almost as if Gaea is party to the
deception for she now intercedes, pressing Daphne to accept wine from
the cup Leukippos offers her. The music takes on a suave Sarabande-
like character as Leukippos follows up his advantage and presses Daphne
to dance with him. All the actions are extremely stylized throughout
and Strauss even labels the score at this point: 'slow hieratic dance'. The
maids slyly rejoice over the success of their plan and various shepherds
even comment on the likeness between Daphne and her new 'partner'
whom none can remember seeing before. Daphne's and Leukippos'
motifs alternate against a background of Dionysiac themes until gradually Ex. 50 comes to prominence. Everyone from Gaea her mother to

---

[26] The thyrsus was a staff symbolically tipped with some phallic ornament and
swathed in vine-branches.

the many onlookers hopes and believes that the natural conventional fulfilment of Daphne's womanhood is at hand.

She herself, however, only agrees to partner the disguised Leukippos because she too can recognize in him a sisterly mirror-image of herself. Yet even so, and especially in her acceptance of the wine of Dionysus at the hands of Leukippos, she jeopardizes her very future existence by participating in a way fundamentally alien to her true nature.[27] As an indication of the significance of her action, the theme of Daphne's life fulfilment (Ex. 50) leads continually to broadened versions of Dionysus' Ex. 34(y).

Nevertheless, the dance remaining purely ritualistic, Daphne seems in no immediate danger from Leukippos' amorous intentions (Strauss: 'Leukippos must in no circumstances kiss Daphne!') despite the approving praises to Dionysus murmured by the shepherds as they watch the dancing.

To the divine onlooker, on the other hand, the situation is nothing short of intolerable. In his omniscience Apollo has at once seen through Leukippos' disguise and furiously he exclaims that the ritual dance is simply a fraud, much to the consternation of the shepherds who still have no inkling of his identity. Angry at his disruption of the proceedings they set about him (Ex. 33) and shout that since he seems to think himself so clever he had better offer some sign of his power (Ex. 45).

This is a challenge Apollo is unable to resist and at once with a swing of his bow he conjures up a violent thunderstorm (harp glissandi, piccolo flashes and growlings of Ex. 38). All is now confusion. The shepherds rush hither and thither crying that the pens have opened and all the animals are escaping (Ex. 32). They appeal to Peneios and Gaea who

[27] Strauss was never very happy about this highly obscure piece of psychology and would gladly have shelved the whole business. He wrote vehemently from Monte Carlo: 'So let's have no more deception! Perhaps not even that of Leukippos! . . . Couldn't the catastrophe be brought about by making the two divine elements Apollo and Dionysus encounter one another at the festival, so that Daphne in terror of the god virtually flees to Leukippos whom by all means she may soon *recognize through the disguise*, perhaps allow herself to join with him in a dance which grows ever more intense with the joy of the wine—which all goes to show that Dionysus continues to stand nearer to *Daphne the human being* than the unapproachable sun-god. Hence Apollo becomes jealous of Dionysus. . . .' But this was getting further and further away from the existing framework with which Strauss quickly saw he would have to rest content. The final version as we have it owes much to conversations Strauss had on the subject with Clemens Krauss, the fruits of which he communicated forthwith to Gregor (see the detailed letter from Paris dated 1.4.36, *Briefwechsel*, pp. 60–61; Otto Mühler, Salzburg, 1955).

can however give no help, and all rush off—none to be seen again throughout the opera. At one time Peneios was to have had a few lines by way of transition to Gregor's cantata-finale but these were sacrificed with the choral verses. Gaea's role however, seems always to have been truncated in this unsatisfactory way. Encouraged by Wallerstein, Strauss tried to press that at least Daphne be given some closing duet with her mother on some basis such as Gaea's identification with the earth into which the roots of the tree Daphne will ultimately descend. But Gregor could see no practical way to reintroduce her and so, fragmentary as their roles are, both Daphne's parents disappear with all the other minor characters, the closing scenes being played out entirely by the three main protagonists.

16

Apollo turns in the utmost rage upon Leukippos reviling him for so base a masquerade in which he not only insulted Dionysus but aimed to rob him, Apollo, of the glorious Daphne. The impetuous flow of the music builds up widely-strung cumulative sequences of the Dionysus themes (Ex. 34(x) and (z)) with vehement repetitions of Apollo's and Leukippos' motifs (Exx. 38 and 41), while flickering flutes and piccolo continue to show the progress of the storm. The sky is still a weird and ominous colour.

With remarkable courage Leukippos flings aside his disguise in full intuitive knowledge of whom he is facing. In reply to the accusation of disrespect he invokes Dionysus directly whose power he feels he has imbibed with the wine and in whose name he now pleads for Daphne. His song is heroic and convincing in its passionate appeal, but it falls on hostile ears. Daphne possesses no Dionysiac feelings whatever with which to respond; she now considers herself doubly betrayed, in Apollo by a false brother, in Leukippos by a false sister;[28] any hope of fulfilment (Ex. 50) seems doomed. The rivalry between her two suitors, human

[28] After Leukippos' partnership in the hieratical dance it is quite logical for Daphne to think of the effeminate Leukippos as a quasi-sister. Gregor even wondered whether Strauss might not have fancied him for one of his travesti roles as this would have had the additional advantage of helping with the deception scene. Strauss realized, however, that such a step would fatally weaken the all-important confrontation with Apollo and the 'catastrophe' of his death. The word 'sister' in the present context was accordingly avoided in favour of 'playmate' as in earlier scenes.

and divine, can only be hypothetical since both desire her carnally and she is devoid of sexuality.

Yet the argument rages on. Leukippos justifiably throws Apollo's taunt of deception back in his teeth. He, a god (Ex. 45), masquerading as a cow-herd (Ex. 47) amongst the mortals he despises!—Leukippos incites the immortal into revealing himself. Apollo, realizing the danger of such a course, appeals to Daphne but she too wants the truth in requital of the fulfilment (Ex. 50) he promised her during his deceitful courtship.

Apollo therefore has no option but to disclose who he is. In a fine extended solo he portrays himself on his daily journey through the sky in his sun chariot.[29] Essentially this is a proud account of his position as the god of sun and light, but at one point it contains an unmistakable threat. He sings of his arrow-shots and as he raises his bow in illustration, his majestic themes are clearly set in apposition to Leukippos' motif, Ex. 41. Strauss further introduces a new idea suggestive of the god in all his glory:

Ex. 52

Daphne's soul is torn apart. She knows she is in the presence of the god of her innermost yearning (Exx. 29 and 40) yet she cannot yield to his desires. She falls on her knees and to Apollo's perplexity prays for help to nature, to radiance,—that is to say, to Apollo, yet not to the incarnation of Apollo which stands before her. Leukippos, still desperately defiant in spite of the peril in which he is placed, takes heart at Daphne's seeming rejection of the god and calls to her for protection. The final paradox is now reached. She cannot follow or help Leukippos much as she may wish to, as her heart is wholly possessed by light; Apollo is that light and yet she cannot follow him either. She is thus ultimately trapped and Leukippos, realizing her predicament, curses Apollo.

There is a blinding flash and Leukippos falls to the ground (Ex. 41 fragmented on the horns). Daphne, at first immobilized, comes to herself and groping, still dazzled, through the waning storm (Exx. 38 and

[29] Strauss used a similar staccato violin figuration to Saint-Saëns' symphonic poem *Phaëton*, which also describes the progress of the sun chariot drawn by its fiery horses.

45) throws herself on the stricken Leukippos. The theme of her fatal beauty, Ex. 27, is answered by that of Apollo's desire Ex. 48. A suggestion of her blighted fulfilment Ex. 50 tails away and leaves a long silence.

Leukippos' death scene follows, a touching little solo though barely more than a dozen bars in length. With failing breath he calls to his playmate Daphne acknowledging that by falling in love with her he has brought divine retribution upon himself. The music wistfully recalls motifs of Dionysus (Ex. 34(y)), Daphne (Exx. 26 and 27) and Apollo, whose Ex. 45 breaks the spell with three peremptory assertions on full brass and timpani.

Daphne is broken-hearted and over his dead body sings a lament which is one of the great passages of the opera. Through his death she has learnt the meaning of suffering and now for the first time recognizes her responsibility for all that has happened. At the same time she still cannot perceive that the cause lies deep in the very substance of her being, that in no circumstances could she ever have acted otherwise.

She recalls their early scene together (Ex. 36, though the pizzicato accompaniment has given way to a soft undulation of violins) and understands at last what the flute of her childhood companion was trying to express. If only she had followed him, instead of seeking the god at whose feet she should have begged that he leave poor mortals alone. Above all, she bitterly regrets her failure to protect Leukippos by sacrificing herself and her chastity to the will of Apollo.

Through these last sentiments the ever growing intensity of Ex. 50 has shown that a real process of maturing is taking place within Daphne. But still in all her recriminations she fails to experience the sense of fulfilment for which she yearns. That lies ahead and in a way she cannot possibly foresee.

With the simplicity which is her essence she makes precisely the one sacrifice to Leukippos' memory consistent with her remoteness, her unreality—the sacrifice of total renunciation. In a passage of delicate filigree work she formally dedicates to him all the things of nature in which she has hitherto delighted.

A passionate orchestral interlude follows, a section so dramatic and full of sincere lamentation that it seems almost too extravagant for the fragile half-being whose feelings it describes. Particularly moving are the repeated phrases of Ex. 40(x) which in this new context and treatment have much in common with Elektra's mourning for Orest. The music then subsides once more to Daphne's last threnody over her dead lover, beside whose grave she intends to remain in eternal sorrow and deepest humility, waiting—ever waiting, until she is summoned by those higher beings who bestowed love upon her, but death upon Leukippos.

Apollo has stood by silent and motionless ever since he struck down his human rival. But now has come the time for his own act of expiation, of self-purification as, in Strauss's words, 'he has in Leukippos killed the Dionysiac element *in himself*'.

At first he is shocked, and then spellbound by the beauty of Daphne's song of farewell to which, being an immortal, he would have expected himself to be impervious. Accordingly his last scena begins infinitely softly with more than a suggestion of wonder in the quiet intermingling of Daphne's Ex. 49, Apollo's Ex. 38 and the haunting echoes of Daphne's last pitiful stanza 'ich aber, armsel'ge Daphne' given *ppp* in chorale style on a trombone.

Apollo then pulls himself together. He is a god and must settle his account with his fellow immortals. He addresses himself to them directly, declaring his guilt by killing in his uncontrollable desire (Ex. 48) not only that one poor wretch but also in effect the blameless maiden herself who is the incarnation of the brightest purity.

The gods are brought to mind with an impressive fanfare as Apollo calls out to them:

Ex. 53

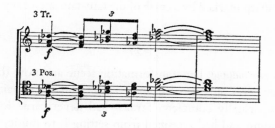

Now Apollo speaks specifically to Dionysus whose feast he has desecrated (Ex. 34(y) and (z) in broad lines on massed woodwind together with Apollo's own Ex. 38). He not only begs forgiveness, but generously asks that Dionysus take Leukippos into his service in the spheres of immortality, promising quaintly that he will enjoy his flute-playing.

Most important of all, however, is Apollo's address to Zeus himself (Ex. 53 in even more commanding tones), referring to him somewhat

unusually as Zeus Kronion—i.e. son of Kronos.[30] To the father of creation Apollo acknowledges the crime of interference: he knows that it
was unforgiveable to step outside his own pre-ordained circle in heaven.
He now beseeches that Daphne be granted to him, not in her forbidden
beauty as a human being, but in the personification of nature which she
herself so ardently desires. Transformed into a laurel tree she will find
her true fulfilment (Ex. 50 together with her other motifs) while for his
part Apollo can thus bestow upon her the highest honour of which he is
capable. Ex. 45 peals out and he pronounces her destiny as if taking the
most solemn oath.

As priestess she is to serve Phoebus Apollo, who will thereby indeed
be her brother in the love he bears her through all time, past and future.
In token of this her branches will supply the laurel wreaths of the
Apollonian crown, the greatest reward for valour and prowess in peace
or combat.

He vanishes amidst gathering darkness and the orchestra carries forward the stirring peroration with unyielding impetus, lower strings
playing energetic arpeggiando figures in accompaniment to the motivic
polyphony and sweeping counterpoints which, imbibed with his
mother's milk, as Strauss used to say, still poured from his pen with
undiminished vigour and inventiveness.

Daphne suddenly tries to rush after the vanished god and is as
abruptly rooted to the spot. Ex. 26 parallels this hectic movement with a
rush up from the bottom to the top of the orchestra and a plunge to the
deepest C sharp marked by a crash of the tam-tam and heavy drumrolls.

17

Daphnes Verwandlung, her transformation scene and now the epilogue
of the opera, was only decided upon a year after the remainder of the
work was virtually complete. Strauss had never cared for Gregor's
cantata ending and had refrained from setting it to music, though six
years later he resurrected it as an entirely independent concert piece.

Ironically the altered finale is now the best-known part of all and has
often been performed and recorded by itself. But the brainwave came

---

[30] This is in fact technically correct but not perhaps something of which Zeus
would care to be reminded. Kronos was in the amiable habit of swallowing his
children whole, lest they dethrone him. Zeus' mother saved him by substituting a
stone which Kronos successfully swallowed in his stead.

from Clemens Krauss to whom Strauss turned one day in despair. Krauss himself recounted the incident:

> Strauss said to me: 'Just read it through once, I can't get on with the ending'. I told him quite simply that the idea of bringing people onto the stage to sing to the tree after the transformation was absurd. The moment people are brought together with the transformed tree it has nothing to do with *Daphne* but is just a theatrical device; I advised him to close the piece with the visible transformation and the gradual transition of human language into the voice of nature . . . I said, 'We don't understand trees when they rustle but they are certainly saying something'. Strauss found that very pretty. . . .

So on 12th May 1937 Strauss wrote to Gregor from Garmisch:

> On Sunday Clemens Krauss was here and we have both come to the opinion that after Apollo's *Abgesang*, no human being other than Daphne can appear any more on the stage, no Peneios, no solo voices—no chorus—in short no oratorio: all this would have a weakening effect. During Apollo's last singing, Daphne, who has been looking at him in amazement, slowly rises from Leukippos' corpse and when Apollo has gone wants to follow him, but after a few steps suddenly remains standing as if rooted to the spot; and now—in the moonlight, but fully visible, the miracle of transformation is slowly worked upon her—*only with the orchestra alone!* At most Daphne could during the transformation still speak a few words, which then merge into stammering and *wordless* melody! Perhaps not even that! At all events right at the end, when the tree stands there complete she should sing without words—only as a voice of nature, eight more bars of the Laurel-motif! . . .

This substantially is the version we have today. From the deep sustained C sharp the theme of Daphne's fulfilment (Ex. 50) slowly rises, ebbing and flowing with the motif of her yearning to be at one with nature (Ex. 29) also growing out of the heavy texture exactly like some great plant from the thick life-giving earth. Amidst the strange sounds Daphne's voice can be heard with broken phrases calling at first to her verdant brothers and then to her brother Apollo whom she can now freely call by that name (Ex. 38).

The orchestration steadily if imperceptibly grows richer and more detailed, blossoming as she is blossoming, with endlessly divided string and woodwind parts trilling and shimmering polyphonically. When all her themes have been incorporated and the melos has come to a climax on a chord six octaves deep, the orchestra draws as it were a deep breath and softly pours out the great slow-moving cantilena which is the song of the laurel-tree presaged in the concluding stanzas of Daphne's aria at the beginning of the opera. As then, so now the many bars of ecstatic melodizing develop towards Ex. 40, but here the soaring phrases go beyond and find their true goal in Ex. 28, Daphne's love of Apollo whose own Ex. 38 is also constantly reintroduced.

At last the mass of radiant sound floats upwards leaving only a chirruping on flutes and violins against which the disembodied voice of Daphne shares with a single oboe alternate phrases of the Laurel and Chaste Daphne motifs, Exx. 26 and 39. Daphne's last words had been a prayer that with birds living amidst her branches she may remain a symbol of undying love and this Apollo has granted. As the twittering gently slows, the curtain falls on the laurel tree standing alone in bright moonlight.

18

Even Pauline's heart had been touched. Karl Böhm who conducted the première tells that at the end of the Generalprobe she leant forward from her isolated seat in the front row and kissed him before the whole audience, although characteristically adding that he wouldn't get another as he was too sweaty. To the end she considered *Daphne* to be her favourite amongst her husband's operas and whatever allowances and reservations may have to be made, this is an opinion which cannot be ignored.

The score was finished on Christmas Eve 1937 in Taormina and as Strauss worked on the magical closing pages he must certainly have derived much atmosphere and inspiration from that wonderful scene with the Greek amphitheatre set against the background of Etna, in itself the perfect setting for *Daphne*.

He seems to have had so clear an impression of how the opera was to appear scenically that he formed strong views over the costumes. When the designer Leonard Fanto later told him that Gregor had expressed a desire for the work to be set in the sixth century he wrote peremptorily to the wretched poet:

> . . . I regard this as quite impossible. The Daphne you have indicated, bound up with nature as she is, to run around like some Artemis of antiquity! Rather Botticelli: Primavera or

a Rubensian Apollo (or Hermes?) as a cow-herd and Rubensian fauns! . . . I can't bring myself to see eye to eye with
you about your Greek costumes! They are magnificent on
those early sculptures and vase-paintings of marble and
terracotta, but dreadful in the theatre; not a singer can wear
them; they can't move or act in them! Hardly perhaps even
a genius of a Russian ballerina.

I am absolutely set on fantasy costumes; for all I care, of
any century, suggestive of Grecian style—but they must be
becoming and wearable by German singers. I know these
Greek garments, how lifelessly they hang on the body . . .
Once more then, for Daphne Botticelli, the others Rubens.
Keep your mind on the stage and let's have no lectures on
archaeology. . . .

For now that the question of performance had become relevant Strauss
had no compunction about taking the whip-hand all along the line.
Again, Gregor had never doubted that *Daphne* and *Friedenstag* were
intended for each other and would receive a double première. It had
therefore been a shock when Strauss suddenly wrote asking whether
Gregor knew of a short classical ballet suitable to precede *Friedenstag* at
the 1938 Munich Festival. 'Did Gluck write other ballets besides *Don
Juan*? (Gothic—not baroque) lasting 40 minutes. Would you have a look
in the Nationalbibliothek? I think Cherubini wrote some ballets but
they might be too humdrum (philiströs). Gluck would be better.'

Gregor was very vexed, but it quickly became apparent that over
the matter of the first performance Strauss had been subjected to some
outside influence. Perhaps because of a guilty conscience he reacted extremely sharply to Gregor's remonstrances that the joint première had
long been promised to Böhm and Dresden. Strauss wrote irritably that
Munich was quite an exceptional situation and arrangements would
have to be made to obtain the necessary concession from Dresden. There
was nothing he could do to extricate himself and the double-bill would
have to follow later. He hoped Gregor had not been opening his mouth
wide to all and sundry in Vienna. Gregor should kindly curb his poet's
aspirations and let Strauss handle the theatres alone without meddling
or there would soon be row after row.

Clearly Clemens Krauss, to whom together with his wife Viorica
Ursuleac *Friedenstag* was dedicated, had exerted pressure over the
première which he was determined to secure for himself.

In this he was successful and as a result, moreover, it followed naturally that Ursuleac should create the role of Marie. The performance

took place on 24th July 1938 in the Munich State Opera and was, as it finally turned out, preceded by a performance of Beethoven's ballet, *Prometheus*. It is perhaps significant that in settling on Beethoven Strauss did not consider reviving for the purpose the version he and Hofmannsthal had concocted of *Die Ruinen von Athen*, which had long fallen by the wayside and into which he had inserted considerable portions of the *Prometheus* score.[31]

The double bill first performance, of which the première of *Daphne* formed a part, followed on 15th October the same year in the Dresden opera house, under the conductorship of Karl Böhm who in his turn became the proud recipient of the dedication of *Daphne*.

It was not to be expected that *Friedenstag* would have much impact at that particular time and place. It is perhaps a wonder rather, that the performance of what is broadly speaking a pageant on the subject of pacifism was sanctioned at all by the Nazi authorities. Nor, for dramatic as well as musical reasons, have there been many post-war revivals and it has perforce to rank with *Guntram* and *Die Aegyptische Helena* as one of Strauss's least-performed operas.

Daphne is a different matter, however, and Strauss was undoubtedly well advised to let the two one-acters go their different ways rather than insisting on an indissoluble partnership which would certainly have retarded the progress of the stronger member.

For short as it is, *Daphne* stands as hardly less considerable a work, though immeasurably less powerful of course, than the great stage tone-poems, *Salome* and *Elektra*. In some ways it is indeed over-compressed, as if Gregor grew so frightened of Strauss's endless rebukes at his schoolmasterly verbose poetics that he shrivelled up altogether. The opening scene of the shepherds, the Daphne-Leukippos duet, Gaea's tiny appearance, even the Dionysian festivities are all so concise that one is surprised at the end to realize how substantial the work is as a whole, lasting only a little less than two hours. Clemens Krauss even thought it a possibility that *Daphne* might be extended to a full-length opera.

On the other hand for a Berlin performance Krauss thought the work might profit by the total excision of the opening scene with the shepherds. Krauss seems always to have been full of ideas for the improvement of Strauss's works from *Die Frau ohne Schatten* (in which he took the responsibility of devising a major compression and re-staging of the second act) until in the later operas his contributions to their final

[31] See Vol. II, p. 308.

shape grew to the point where he became the actual librettist of *Capriccio*. In connexion with the latter, his last idea for *Daphne* was to link it with *Capriccio* very much in the manner of the *Bourgeois/Ariadne* scheme.[32]

None of these proposals received any encouragement from Strauss, however, and *Daphne* has, without revisions or improvements of any kind, nevertheless won a place of especial affection amongst Strauss's works of the second rank. There are undoubtedly faults and uneven qualities which have to be considered in making such an assessment: the perfunctory nature of many of the scenes; the unconvincing character portrayals of all the lesser parts; the wide gap in inspiration between the scenes for Daphne herself and the remainder of the score; in particular, the odd trap Strauss set for himself in allocating both Apollo and Leukippos to tenors, a voice he had always found uncongenial for anything but character parts, and for which as a result he experienced difficulty in finding appropriate music. Even Gregor had taken it for granted that Apollo would be a baritone, a colour oddly missing from the major roles.

Yet *Daphne* contains passages which are the quintessence of what the ageing Strauss had to say, of that rich nostalgic mellifluousness which found its ultimate expression in the *Vier letzte Lieder*.

It seems also that Strauss knew he had found something valuable in the peaceful beauty of Daphne's transformation into pure nature; in 1943, his operatic work finally behind him, he came back once more to the subject and scanned through the discarded cantata ending which his ever-regretted and now dead friend Stefan Zweig[33] had helped to mould. Rejecting the lines for Peneios and Gaea (they were to have re-entered to apostrophize in hymn-like tones their transformed daughter) Strauss took up again the final chorus which, corresponding to the apotheosis in *Friedenstag*, Gregor had intended as the unifying link between the two works—the one symbolizing Peace amongst Men, the other Peace amidst Nature.

This he asked Gregor to reshape for him as a separate work which, after some minor vicissitudes, he set to music for an unaccompanied chorus in nine parts under the title *An den Baum Daphne* (*Epilog zu Daphne*).[34] The chorus is distributed as a conventional double chorus

[32] See below, Chapter XXI, p. 195.

[33] Zweig, after finding asylum in Brazil, committed suicide on 23 February 1942.

[34] See Chapter XXIII, p. 420, for a fuller account of the commissioning, composition and performance.

with the addition of an upper part for boys' chorus, one of the prides of Vienna (for whose State Opera Chorus it was written) and it is clear that the use of the word *Epilog* is in no way intended to suggest its use in connexion with the parent opera, of which indeed it forms no part.

Although *An den Baum Daphne* gives an illusion of continuous formless melody, it is in fact built in a number of clear symphonic sections with an Introduction and an extended coda. The opening introductory bars invoke the Tree-Daphne with the same music and words that Daphne herself had used, Ex. 35, linked immediately with her own motif Ex. 26. Strauss sets the music, however, in that warm soft key of F sharp major of the Verwandlung in which the opera had ended.

The first main section then begins with the second chorus outlining in block harmonies how Daphne's feelings as sister and playmate towards the manifestations of nature have ended with her transformation into a complete physical unity with them at the hands of a god who loved her.

While the second chorus is hymning, the first adds, strand by strand, various apostrophes or a fragment of wordless melody with Ex. 29. The two choirs also reverse these roles after a few bars.

They then join together in describing Apollo's prayer to Zeus with music in unison or block formation which not only quotes Apollo's Ex. 38 but also a melodic phrase from his great closing aria. The voices drop to a pianissimo pause at the end of Apollo's prayer, and then re-enter forte as they exclaim at how Daphne's feet are rooted to the ground. The boys' chorus enters here for the first time in the work, though for the moment only to reinforce the ejaculatory phrase 'Und sieh' ('and look').

This leads to the second section, a kind of little Verwandlung scene. The choruses roughly follow the thread of the operatic version's opening pages with Exx. 50 and 39 additionally featured, singing to a wordless vocalise.[35] Against this the boys, making their first sizeable contribution, sing the next few lines of the poem. They sing in unison throughout the work, thus supplying the ninth part as well as an important variation of colour. The section ends with a general call to 'Daphne, göttlicher Baum!' based on a phrase from Ex. 40.

In the third and central section the boys are again silent. Here the choruses extol Daphne's new role of crowning the brows of the finest

---

[35] Strauss adds a footnote in which he leaves the manner of execution (mouths open or closed, etc.) entirely to the taste of the conductor.

and most valiant amongst all mankind. The flowing lines are drawn together in a dramatic climax at the centre-point of this section giving a much-needed contrast of texture.

There have been wide modulations, but as the boys re-enter at the beginning of the fourth section after a pianissimo linking pivot-note we are back amidst the many sharps of the home key. As before, the two choruses accompany the boys with humming though they are now primarily concerned with Ex. 39.

This section is subdivided into two parts as the choruses break off their vocalise in order to take over from the boys the concluding lines of the hymn. These tell of the song which Daphne can now sing in her transformed guise under the influence of the morning sun, when Apollo kisses her topmost branches, 'a stronger song than the song of men; the song of love, of eternity, the song of Daphne'. The lines give the clue not only to the succeeding section in which all the voices, including the boys, take part, but to the closing passage of the Verwandlung itself, the ending of the opera *Daphne*. As there the orchestra, so here the voices join in a wordless outpouring of melody, which culminates in an ethereal duet in which the alternating voices of Daphne and the solo oboe are replaced by a boy's treble voice and a solo soprano from the second chorus. But unlike the opera, *An den Baum Daphne* ends with an abrupt return of Ex. 35 ('Geliebter Baum') delivered in full-blooded tones by the assembled voices. Theatrical atmosphere has given place to effectiveness of formal design in the concert hall.

An den Baum Daphne is fully in line of descent from the earlier Rückert choral works, the Op. 34 *Hymnus* and the *Deutsche Motette*, with which it is linked by a small collection of pieces for *a cappella* chorus all to words by Rückert, which occupied Strauss as a side-line during 1935. Three of these, 'Vor den Türen', 'Traumlicht' and 'Fröhlich im Maien', form a group for male voices alone and are of minor importance; far more considerable however, completed in February, is a setting for double mixed chorus of *Die Göttin im Putz-zimmer*.

Here Rückert's gay profusion of words describing a multiplicity of confused effects ('welches erotische Tausenderlei! Alle die Nischen, alle die Tischen' etc.) stimulated Strauss into a lively exhibition of choral virtuosity, which is humorously transformed into unanimity of expression quite abruptly at the word 'Plötzlich!' when order is brought out of chaos by the extraordinary housekeeper; 'surely she must be a mighty magician', in the words of the poem (an allegory on the function of the artist). This jolly p˙ece stands alone in Strauss's choral output for its concise directness and enchanting end.

One other work remains to be mentioned, a setting again for male voices *a cappella* but to words by Wildgans, the author of the Österreiches Lied.[36] Entitled *Durch Einsamkeiten* it was composed in 1938 for the seventy-fifth anniversary celebrations of the Vienna Schubert-Bund, the organization for whom Strauss had—just over ten years before—composed *Die Tageszeiten*, and who gave the new offering its first performance under Keldorfer's successor, Otto Nurrer, on 1st April 1939.

But this too was only a relaxation from Strauss's work in the theatre, for by that time the indefatigable veteran was once more immersed in a full scale operatic venture, *Die Liebe der Danae*.

[36] See Vol. II, p. 374.

CHAPTER XX

DIE LIEBE DER DANAE

C OLLABORATION with Gregor on a permanent basis—this was not at all the road Strauss had wanted; yet he seemed to be inescapably committed. By the middle of 1936, with 'No. 1' complete and 'No. 2' (as he referred to their pair of one-acters in his letters to Gregor) virtually ready for orchestration, he would soon be casting about for a new subject. Strauss had carefully given Gregor no indication or encouragement that he was proposing to pursue their collaboration a stage further but still the eager little historian jumped in to show his readiness to be of service—*Semiramis? Celestina?* anything Strauss liked.

Shrewdly enough, and doubtless having come to realize that Strauss had few illusions over his qualities as an original librettist, Gregor made as yet no suggestions emanating from ideas of his own. Both *Semiramis* and *Celestina* were the products of his predecessors, the former from Hofmannsthal, the other from Zweig.

Semiramis we have indeed encountered at intervals from the earliest days of Hofmannsthal's association with Strauss. First mooted before *Elektra*, held by Hofmannsthal to be 'no longer possible' in 1911, reconsidered and elaborated in 1919, it was soon dropped again and for the last time—at least as far as Hofmannsthal was concerned. When after Hofmannsthal's death Zweig refused to handle it and it fell into Gregor's lap it had swollen in Strauss's mind to the proportions of *Les Troyens*, a two-evening affair. The first evening would consist of a Vorspiel played by the immortals together with the Menon tragedy, while the second evening would give the Semiramis drama in a further full three acts.

For his part Gregor saw no reason why it should not be workable on the scale of *Götterdämmerung*.

In view of such wild thinking, it is perhaps less surprising that Strauss ultimately set his mind firmly against entering into such a project with a Gregor as collaborator. He was in any case in no very good humour with Gregor whom he strongly suspected of indiscreet talk to the press. Hence even when he had mastered his annoyance enough to profess at least a token acceptance of Gregor's assurances of innocence, he still rejected *Semiramis* outright. There remained *Celestina*.

This had been an idea of Zweig's dating from as recently as March 1935, only a few months before the débâcle with the Nazis. *La Celestina, Commedia de Calisto y Melibea*, is according to Zweig 'the oldest drama in all Spanish literature, long before Calderón and Lope, and as a result particularly worthy of attention'.

Although cast in dialogue form, *La Celestina* is more properly a novel—the first European novel, Gerald Brenan calls it in his admirable account of the work.[1] In its later edition of 1502 it was expanded into some twenty-one 'acts', many of which seem to have been the work of Fernando de Rojas, the original text having been published anonymously in 1499. Rojas further entitled it a tragicomedia, which appellation seems amply justified since virtually all the principal characters die or are slaughtered before the piece is over.

Zweig had thought it promising enough material to write to Strauss in considerable and attractive detail: the romantic Romeo and Juliet-like central love drama, the coarse underworld against which this is pitted, and between these the figure of Celestina—intriguante, procuress, arch-priestess of sexual love, through whose machinations the entire action evolves, although she herself falls a victim to her own minions in the closing pages. Brenan goes so far as to describe her as 'one of the most vivid and splendid creations of all literature'.

It is perhaps more than usually regrettable that Strauss was not won over sufficiently to take up *Celestina* as a workable project. One suspects that it might have stirred once again the vein of wit and romanticism which called the great music of *Don Quixote* into being. But he found the lovers conventional, the piece as a whole 'even weaker than the

[1] Gerald Brenan, *The Literature of the Spanish People*. Cambridge University Press, 1951.

Merry Wives' although conceding the glittering nature of the title-role.

So *Celestina* lapsed and did not endear itself any the more to him when, thumbing through the pages just before Gregor mentioned it to him again, he discovered on reaching the end for the first time that the lovers come to grief: '*Calisto falls down a ladder* and Melibea throws herself from a *high tower*', wrote Strauss in discouragement, 'after *Daphne* I should really like to do something cheerful! I've had enough of tragedy!'

At this point Strauss had an idea.

2

It was during December 1919 that Hofmannsthal had begun work on a comic opera which he hoped might be to Strauss's liking after the severity of their last joint enterprise, *Die Frau ohne Schatten*. In telling Strauss the following February that he was at work, he described the new venture as 'a light piece in three acts, closely related to operetta and very near to the world of Lucian. Perhaps,' he continued with a touch of whimsy, 'you will once more see before you the necessary waters on which to sail your beautiful little ship.'

On 23rd April the draft duly arrived, together with the letter in which he indicated how the new comedy was to continue the line of Strauss's previous lighter stage-works (*Rosenkavalier, Ariadne-Vorspiel, Bürger als Edelmann*[2]). 'It calls', he added, 'for light witty music such as only you can write, and you only at this phase of your life. It is a mythological subject of early antiquity. . . .'

As always with Hofmannsthal's light operetta ideas, this new example was considerably more complex than his remarks would seem to indicate. The conception hinged on the subtle combining of two Greek myths, entirely separate and distinct from each other excepting only for their common use of gold as motivating agent. In the one, Danae, daughter of Acrisius, is locked in a tower by her father but nevertheless is successfully seduced by Zeus in the guise of a shower of gold, the fruit of their union being the hero, Perseus.

The other legend concerns Midas, King of Macedoniom Bromiom. As a reward for entertaining the old satyr Silenus, Midas is granted a wish by the grateful Dionysus, whose pedagogue Silenus had been.

---

[2] See Vol. II, p. 300.

Without a moment's hesitation he chose that all he touched might be turned to gold, not realizing that this would also apply to his food and drink. Highly amused, Dionysus released the starving and parched king from his golden touch by telling him to wash in the river Pactolus whose sands remain bright gold to this day.

Hofmannsthal saw in this gold motif the means to create an attractive dramatic situation uniting Danae and Midas. In addition he quickly saw capital to be made in bringing Zeus' manifestation as golden rain into conjunction with his other disguises as lover. This entailed introducing into his scheme the various fair objects of Zeus' affections such as Europa, whom Zeus visited as a snow-white bull; Leda, Zeus as a swan; Io, Zeus as woodpecker; Semele, Zeus as thunderstorm; or Alkmene, Zeus as Amphitryon. In some way Hofmannsthal intended, already in the first sketches, working all or some of these princesses into the action although they would lose their mythological identity in every respect other than their association with Zeus.

However, the ladies keep these liaisons a jealous secret with the result that no one suspects anything for, as Hofmannsthal quaintly says: 'mythology is not known'. Zeus' function in the drama was accordingly to be that of an invisible influence over the whole, much as Kaikobad in *Die Frau ohne Schatten* though Zeus' godhead would apply more specifically to love and life, and the protection of all Secrets.

Danae, having also suffered a divine visitation, is regarded by the princesses (or queens: Hofmannsthal dithered over their rank) as one of themselves. The purpose of their visit lies in her impending marriage.

Marriage has been forced upon Danae by her old father, whose kingdom is ruined. While she had hitherto always dreaded that suitors would seek her hand for the sake of her fortune, now it is she who has to find a rich husband. Hofmannsthal was greatly preoccupied with Danae's psychology at the early stage of the drama, for its metamorphosis was to be the central thesis until at the end she would realize that all monetary considerations must be swept aside for the sake of love.

In order to strengthen the initial emphasis on the importance of riches Hofmannsthal decided to make the princesses homeless as the result of an all-enveloping war. Their royal husbands might also come into the picture, their hopeless dependence on slaves, cooks, dancing girls etc., symbolized by various forms of music, ceremonial or ballet. This little group of poverty-stricken royalty seems always to have been in the nature of light relief. Hofmannsthal wrote of them:

The three queens, bird-like, vain, forgetful, gossiping about everything, even religious matters. The three kings vain, gamblers, running after the dancing-girls. . . .

Later Hofmannsthal settled on four queens who would go through the action like a little semi-chorus.

As for Danae's rich betrothed who would solve all their financial problems overnight, he is to be heralded by an off-stage march. Hofmannsthal envisaged that Danae's father might send her portrait to King Midas,[3] receiving in exchange Midas' likeness in a golden miniature together with a cortège of loaded camels; there would be hunting parties, and so on; the opportunities for Strauss seemed immense.

Now an elaborate stage deception came into Hofmannsthal's mind. When at last the much-heralded golden ship enters the harbour it proves to bear a richly-clad figure who announces that he is not King Midas but only Midas' confidant, his cup-bearer in chief, his shade-bearer—Hofmannsthal racked his brains for some suitable menial before deciding to make him Midas' tailor. Once fixed upon, he became a focal point—the tailor as philosopher . . . the tailor as psychoanalyst(!) . . . the tailor as Master of Ceremonies, surrounded by page-boys, eunuchs, body-guards, singing children, a troupe of dumb mannequins dancing a little ballet.

In due course it transpires that the so-called tailor, who has always behaved in a suspiciously regal manner, is none other than Midas himself. The masquerade was purely in order to have the chance of finding out in good time whether the prospective bride would be in good enough taste ('these islanders are such a provincial lot') for the Lydian king.

So Hofmannsthal's scheme gradually took shape. A duet between Danae and her father would establish the conviction of both, though in their different ways, that nothing in the world is as important as gold. When a medallion arrives ostensibly bearing the portrait of Midas, but so heavily encrusted with gold as to be unrecognizable, they accept it eagerly and without question, thus enabling that richest of all men to carry out his masquerade with impunity. Hofmannsthal then planned a great conversation-duet between Danae and the tailor-Midas for the kernel of Act I containing a narration concerning Midas and his protector Zeus, to be cast in the form of a Romanze.

According to this, Midas was once no more than a poverty-striken

[3] Cf. Count Waldner and Arabella's portrait sent to Mandryka. Many facets of the action are strongly reminiscent of *Arabella*.

prince, but raised by Zeus to his present riches with the specific purpose of wooing Danae on the god's behalf. Should he at any time betray his divine mentor, the golden gift would be instantly revoked. Hofmannsthal intended the 'wonderful old man' (i.e. Zeus in disguise—who appeared to Midas with the proposal) to be identified musically by a horn or some such instrument. The old man would then play a predetermined motif to indicate to Midas if and when his riches must be yielded up (an idea Hofmannsthal deliberately borrowed from Victor Hugo's *Hernani*). In the course of the narration the tailor-Midas also tells Danae of Zeus' previous exploits with the other princesses, and expresses his own fears of the marriage-bond and its inevitable consequences.

Danae is perplexed, but greatly taken by the tailor whom she quickly senses to be more than he seems. She is further bewildered when he conjures from the air a cloak of flowing gold which recalls her earlier secret girlhood experience with Zeus. This brings the duet to a climax upon which the old king, Danae's father, re-enters and dances for joy at the sight of the golden cloak. The Finale to Act I then follows as he is joined by the other kings and queens, mannequins and the rest, all dancing and singing in a 'very pellucid, cheerful finale in the manner of Mozart'.

Hofmannsthal next planned the second act to open with the bridal feast on a scale, as he described it, 'fit for the Olympic gods'. There would be fanfares for the entry of Midas' retinue followed by a short ballet with veiled dancing girls, negroes, dwarfs and so on. Only the bridegroom's place remains vacant, and indeed, so far as anyone knows, he has not yet shown his face at all.

With enormous ceremony a letter is brought in and read first, oddly enough, by the full company and only afterwards by Danae to whom it is addressed. In it Midas exhorts Danae to leave her unworthy entourage, put on the miraculous golden cloak and join him in an underground grotto. Amidst general consternation she obeys the instructions, her departure giving the opportunity for a long slow march followed by a dance of the queens with their husbands as they too leave the stage.

The remainder of the act was to consist entirely of an extended duet between Midas and Danae, played in the grotto which towards the end becomes transparent, revealing a sumptuous bed-chamber.

Midas, having first appeared as the tailor and then dramatically disclosing his true identity, now woos Danae in his own right, whereupon she significantly tells him that riches will always be the first consideration, for as an integral part of her present poverty it is not in her nature to give, only to receive. The spirit of Zeus, to be symbolized by the horn call, hovers ominously over the duet and various miraculous occurrences enliven the lonely subterranean wedding feast. Golden slaves vanish and reappear like Ifrits, very much as in *Die Frau ohne Schatten* of which Hofmannsthal had only recently completed the Erzählung.

The duet, repeatedly described in Hofmannsthal's note-book as *Grosse Szene*, is full of various supernatural and psychological implications which he never entirely sorted out, while the third act is by his own admission only roughly indicated.

The marriage has been consummated (without, oddly enough, Danae being herself turned to gold: this was an inconsistency Gregor was quick to observe) and the pair awaken in the bed-chamber which turns out to be in Midas' enchanted palace. Midas uneasily recognizes Zeus' motif coming from the orchestra and in fact the dreaded retribution soon overtakes him and Midas witnesses with despair the evaporation of all his wealth into a sea of mist. Not realizing that Danae has undergone a transformation, repudiating the love of gold in her new-found maturity, he accordingly steels himself to her loss also. In the closing scene, therefore, he is once more the destitute prince with one tethered donkey and a single ragged slave as he had described himself to Danae in the first act Romanze. The palace has utterly disappeared and as they lie on the bare earth the sun reveals the plight of the lovers in all its wretchedness.

However, Danae's love overrides the shattering blow. She is now the stronger partner and under her leadership they rise above their new hardships. After first kneeling to Zeus in gratitude for their new-found happiness, they saddle the donkey and ride off together singing, the gayest beggars alive: '. . . from a *marriage de convenance* (Vernunftheirat) has come a love-marriage, gold has been conquered'.

3

Such in brief was the plan which Hofmannsthal had submitted to Strauss in April 1920. As it stands, its theatrical shortcomings are clear enough: the first half has too much scenic complexity, the second too little, consisting exclusively of uninterrupted duet for Danae and Midas. This is not to say, nevertheless, that it could not have been hammered into shape had Strauss and Hofmannsthal had a mind to do so. Possibly Strauss was a little put off by Hofmannsthal's admonition:

The more 'French' you are in your handling of this, the
better; the German quintessence, the deeper and graver element, will remain at the core anyway, just like in my case
the kernel of lyricism, beneath which the symbolism and
metaphysics remain hidden.

On the other hand it may simply not have been strong enough to
win Strauss over at a time when he did not particularly need a new
libretto from Hofmannsthal regardless of whether it was his meat or
not. He was, after all, unusually busy at this time with his administrative
work at the Vienna Opera, his South American conducting tours and
two major stage compositions which he was working on by himself,
Schlagobers and *Intermezzo*. And Hofmannsthal too, though still inclin-
ing to classical mythology, soon turned his attention to the Helen saga,
with the result that *Danae, oder die Vernunftheirat* was dropped in favour
of *Die Aegyptische Helena*. Forgotten, it lay in Strauss's drawer until 1933
when he allowed Herbert Steiner, the publisher of Hofmannsthal's collected works, to take it away and print it in a periodical, *Corona*. Even
then he thought nothing of it and only three years later again was his
interest at last aroused. For, just as his two Gregor one-act operas were
sufficiently far advanced for him to be wondering what to work on
next, Willi Schuh unexpectedly brought the *Corona* printing to his attention by sending him a copy from Zurich.

Strauss was delighted. Completely forgetting that there had been a
Danae sketch amongst the drafts Gregor had brought to him that July
day in 1935, and which he had barely had the patience to thumb
through, Strauss abruptly changed the subject during a letter on the
Celestina project to ask Gregor whether he had seen the posthumous
publication of Hofmannsthal's scenario.

No, Gregor had not. But he quickly remedied the omission, though
taking care to remind Strauss that he had already produced one of his
own on very much the same lines. After all it could not have been very
flattering to see the prospect looming of being saddled yet again with the
reheating of someone else's cabbage.

For a time he still tried to fan the dying embers of Strauss's enthusiasm for *Celestina,* and on 23rd July a completed *Celestina* scenario was
on its way to Strauss together with Gregor's own *Danae* sketch of which
Strauss had unashamedly confessed to having not the least recollection.

But all these machinations were unavailing. As far as Gregor's own
work was concerned Strauss frankly preferred *Celestina* to *Danae*. But

it was still the Hofmannsthal *Danae* draft for which the composer now yearned. So, despite one last attempt to turn the scales by setting quickly to work on an actual *Celestina* libretto from the scenario, Gregor became increasingly aware that it was no good. Strauss's mind was made up. Gregor's next concern, having temporarily reconciled himself to working on Hofmannsthal's sketches, was to see whether he might not be able to keep in hand some of his own ideas, if indeed he could not find some ingenious compromise which might allow for their positive incorporation. At first, however, every time he attempted to swerve from the beaten track Strauss brought him relentlessly back, sternly criticising one after another of his personal contributions as either too heavy, too scholastic for this elegant mythological farce, or alternatively too grotesque and tasteless, in any case not at all what he wanted. No doubt Strauss was unfair, especially when one recalls the ill-fated evolution of *Helena* from its similar 'light operetta' beginnings. But perhaps it was on that very account that he was anxious lest *Danae* should suffer the same pitfalls. Auber—*Fra Diavolo*—*that,* said Strauss, was to be Gregor's model, strange and unrealistic as it may seem.

The principal alteration Gregor sought to make was the actual appearance of Jupiter[4] in person on the stage, not merely a pervading influence as in Hofmannsthal's conception. Whether a survival from his neglected sketch, or a rankling disappointment that he had been unable to retain Zeus in the action of *Daphne,* here was a character which Gregor decided positively to insinuate into the drama, however many rebuffs he would have to endure before Strauss's resistance was gradually worn down.

Gregor's first idea was that Jupiter should be visible in the guise of a magician during Danae's vision of the golden rain, but this was quite unacceptable to Strauss who determined to keep that picturesque scene for himself in a purely orchestral interlude. So Gregor next turned to Hofmannsthal's masquerade of Midas as the tailor which was already so complicated that Strauss acknowledged that he was foreseeing difficulties over how it should be handled in its later stages. 'How on earth can one arrange it that Midas remains unknown to Danae until the very end of the love scene in the cave?' he wrote.

Gregor saw the opportunity to cut the knot by substituting a new

---

[4] For some reason the Roman counterpart of Zeus (used by Hofmannsthal in only one of his sketches—a slip?) is grafted onto the basically Greek background. It seems odd for Gregor, a classical scholar, to commit such a solecism.

tangle of his own. Instead of Midas impersonating his tailor in order to have a first view of Danae on his own account, how much better to have Midas impersonate the bearer of his gold as precursor to Jupiter impersonating Midas.

Now Strauss was really bewildered, to a point beyond any simple out-of-hand rejection. In vain his repeated protestations that all these awful problems were arising because the Hofmannsthal script had been left too far behind; by Strauss's own admission this itself had presented conundrums.

Yet perhaps some solution might still be found through the four queens; after all, Hofmannsthal's basic conception had postulated the background figure of Jupiter as a kind of divine Don Juan. The chief difference was that now, instead of having succeeded in his seduction of Danae during her vision of the golden rain, Jupiter's advances in disguise were to be a mere prelude to his courtship in the flesh which was to form a new and culminating theme of the opera.

What was needed, therefore, was some reason for Jupiter's use of a catspaw Midas, whose rank was to be reduced from that of a penniless prince to a beggarly donkey-drover. In the first place there was Danae's preoccupation with gold to the exclusion of all interest in love and accordingly the hopelessness for any suitor, divine or otherwise, to use a direct approach. Secondly, Jupiter for his part had to be exceedingly circumspect on account of Juno, his jealous spouse. Strauss correctly analysed the new problem in letter after letter during the early months of 1938:

> Best thanks for the despatch; it contains a lot of good things but is nowhere near light enough for me. Also it must be still much gayer and there are several obscurities. Why in the case of Danae, who is poor and so much in love with gold, does Jupiter *not come straightforwardly to her in the form of the gold-giving Midas,* just as he came to his other darlings as bull, swan, etc.? It must be clearly stated that Jupiter, in all other matters the Almighty, is so hellishly frightened only of his stronger spouse Hera (just like Wotan) that he comes to his beloved ones so transformed that Hera[5] doesn't at once notice. And when she notices it, Jupiter with Mercury's help has already married off the girls with the result that the stern guardian of wedlock is each time reconciled anew

[5] Hera was Zeus' consort and twin sister, whom Gregor also gave the Roman name Juno. Hence when in due course Mercury was added to the action at least the divine characters became consistently Roman.

(some sparkling aria in couplets must be found for this!)—
Then why this time does he send Midas ahead and risk that
the latter really manages to snatch Danae away from him,
instead of substituting him as prince-consort only after
Jupiter's seduction of Danae is over, like the other princes?
And even if he does, then he must clearly have expressed it
in the pact with Midas that he reserves the *jus primae noctis*
with Danae in exchange for the gift of the golden touch, and
that the poor donkey-drover is content to serve thereafter
as deputy bridegroom.

Jupiter thus plays around with the lives of men as well as
women, and never considers that his wishes could ever encounter any serious opposition. So the idea simply doesn't
occur to him that between Midas and Danae love should
come in earnest, pure and enduring enough that it could
cause them to renounce all the treasures of this world! . . .
And when Jupiter wants actually to win Danae for himself—
what form does he take? His own as Jupiter? Or as Midas? . . .

Gregor's lengthy answers of self-justification tried in vain to persuade Strauss that everything was quite all right and so much better than
Hofmannsthal's version which, he added, was only good for a novelette
and quite untheatrical.

Displeased, Strauss turned once again to the colleagues who had
helped him so much before, Krauss and Wallerstein. Unfortunately this
time they had no immediate answer and to make matters worse Wallerstein even suggested that there might be a double impersonation act
with Danae's maid Xanthe falling in love with the real Midas, leaving
Danae herself free to work out her intricate schizophrenic entanglement
with gold, Jupiter disguised as gold, Jupiter disguised as Midas, or what
not.

The confusion being now absolute Strauss took what seemed to him
the only possible step: he began to compose. This at least brought him
face to face with the simpler problem of Gregor's poetic gifts. Either the
language was laboriously weighty or unbearably commonplace. Nor
could Strauss ever manage to convey to the poor struggling, over-
willing history professor what was needed to put it right. For Strauss
himself with all his experience had never been a master of words and
his exhortations were rarely of a practical or constructive nature: 'It's
all too much like popular ballads! . . . It's still, none of it, in the style I
have in mind! Some of it's too bombastic, like the first draft—and now
these poetics in elevated speech tempt one all too readily into hollow

phrases, and padding which doesn't say anything and empty rhyming jingles!'

To every devastating letter Gregor wrote back saying how much he *did* agree with every word of criticism, how he had thought it all along but believed he had understood and that this was what Strauss wanted. Hopeless. At Strauss's insistence he recast whole scenes in the baldest prose, only to be made to change it straight back to verse the moment Strauss took one glance at the result. Such as they were, the rhymes would have to do.

4

So by the middle of June 1938 Strauss had made a good start at the introductory scene of Act I in spite of his realization that Gregor's verses remain the merest doggerel:

> König: Nehmt den Palast!
>   Nehmt alles was er fasst!
> Gläubiger: Ist eitler Fadenschein!
>   Kein Nagel mehr ist dein!
> König: Nehmt Münze, Weiderechte, Fischerei!
> Gläubiger: Verpfändet alles! Nichts dabei!
>   —O König Pollux, sag uns an:
>   Wo hast du alles hingetan?
>   Nimm unsern Fluch! Nimm unsern Spott!
>   Die Insel Eos ist—bankrott![6]

Despite the differences to come during the course of the action, the situation is basically that postulated by Hofmannsthal: Danae's aged father, ruler of a small provincial island, has mortgaged his entire kingdom to the hilt and is now besieged by his creditors. Gregor calls the island Eos, the king Pollux, these names being chosen purely at random and in no way referring to their real bearers. Gregor's allusion to bankruptcy, however, with its seemingly incongruous whiff of modern life

---

[6] A literal translation might perhaps be:

> King: Take the palace!
>   Take its entire contents!
> Creditors: It's all threadbare!
>   You haven't got a nail left!
> King: Take the coins, the pasture and the fishing!
> Creditors: All mortgaged! Nothing left!
>   —O King Pollux, tell us:
>   What have you done with it all?
>   Take our curse! Take our mockery!
>   The island Eos is—bankrupt!

may well be authentic. Banking as we know it was already firmly established in Ancient Greece. Whatever his failings, Gregor was a reliable historian.

Pollux tries to play for time by telling the ravening creditors first of the four kings (Pollux's nephews—they are mere cyphers and never graced with names) and their queens, Alkmene, Semele, Europa and Leda. All have been sent out as ambassadors on behalf of the beautiful Danae whose portrait they have been carrying in the hope of attracting a rich suitor. Since these royal emissaries are also penniless, they arouse no interest in the creditors, who are not even placated by news of the possible arrival of Midas, the richest king in the world. Pollux expresses his pious belief that Midas will discharge every debt in full if they will but be patient, but in vain. The crowd storms the throne and the curtain falls.

The scene is hardly more than a single short tableau, like many such in *Danae*, which is in this respect closely related to *Intermezzo* despite the utter contrast in subject matter.

Strauss employed a simple and direct musical style in this opening section which is a self-contained symphonic structure for solo tenor (Pollux), male-voice chorus and orchestra. It might perhaps be thought surprising that he did not occupy himself in writing an overture while Gregor hacked away in the background. But it was far from his normal practice and he was as always impatient to start the task of setting the text itself to music. Moreover, although this was to be belied again and again in the years to come, he reckoned, as he had explained to Zweig, that ideas no longer came to him without the stimulus of words. Even the Potpourri of *Die Schweigsame Frau* was only brought to life on the spur of the moment to fill in an idle period after the opera was complete, the material therefore already created and ready to hand.

The motif of the creditors is announced in the very first bars and is rarely absent in one form or another throughout the section:

Ex. 1

Another little theme, applicable to the ruined and wretched king Pollux, quickly emerges from the mass of figurations with which Strauss builds the texture of the music:

Ex. 2

The characteristic consecutive fifths of Ex. 2 add a welcome spice to the heavily ornamented score, which the uniform mass of men's voices in close position tends to render opaque. This is not to say that the scene and its music are uneventful: there is a passage in attractive four-part imitation at one point, whereas Pollux's reference to the mission on which he has sent his four royal nephews and their beautiful queens brings new textures in the form of the relevant theme, later to be exploited more fully when these personages appear on the stage:

Ex. 3

(cf. Lohengrin)

As the scene develops, Pollux's announcement of Midas' name also produces a corresponding motif:

Ex. 4

'Mi-das   von   Ly. - dien !

Repetitions of Ex. 4 in diminution are combined with Exx. 1(x) and 2 in a hectic orchestral climax as the curtain falls. The music then dies away in preparation for the 'Golden Rain' Interlude which Strauss inserts at this juncture although Jupiter's visitation of Danae has surely taken place some time previously.

It was not for nothing that Strauss had resolved upon a purely orchestral treatment, for he handled it with not only his customary virtuosity of colour and technique but considerable insight. This

'Orchester-Vorspiel', as he described it in a letter, establishes Jupiter's relationship with Danae in addition to laying the foundation of her character and outlook.

At first Strauss had meant to go even further and set the passage against a principal motif of an oracular pronouncement. The intention of this would have been to fix the solemn warning which hangs over poor Midas '. . . that he will remain rich only until he comes into conflict with higher rivals. Jupiter must snatch the gold away from him again out of simple jealousy when he notices that Midas has won his own former beloved whom [the god] could only approach in the form of golden rain.'

Although this remains the substance of the drama Strauss realized that it was far too much to present to the audience in bulk at the beginning, let alone by mere implication during an orchestral interlude. So, leaving Midas out of the picture for the present, he concentrated on Danae and the reason for her obsession with gold. '. . . Danae sees in the golden rain the augury or prophecy that her yearning for gold may yet reach fulfilment. "Who brings me gold, be he god or man, he shall be my suitor!"'

Ex. 5

Ex. 5a

later appearing as: (cf. Saint-Saëns: *Le Cygne*)

Yet there is more to it than that: '. . . why does Danae love gold so exclusively? Precisely because hitherto she has found no mortal who has appeared worthy to her! So, must there not be some small indication given that already in the golden rain she has had a premonition of something more exalted—the god? . . . This is *all* very delicate and must be presented with the utmost finesse!'[7]

Strauss accordingly took it upon himself to give this 'fine delicate indication' in the orchestra. When the golden rain has gathered strength with the gradual addition of harps, piano, flutes and muted strings, Jupiter's motifs surreptitiously make their appearance.

Ex. 6

Ex. 7

Ex. 8

The golden rain is, of course, simply one of Jupiter's many disguises and Ex. 8 is the retrograde form of Ex. 5(x), a subtlety which should not be overlooked. Moreover Ex. 8 differs from Jupiter's other themes in that it refers less to the personality of the god than to his amorous attachment to Danae; at times it is even made to reflect the love-inspiring figure of Danae, and its development during the opera, especially in the closing scene of Act 3, is one of the most striking features of the overall musical design. Subtly the god envelops the entranced Danae, whose theme follows directly upon Ex. 8:

Ex. 9

[7] It is noteworthy that all these fragments come from Strauss's letters to Gregor and not the reverse.

The score becoming increasingly sonorous, Jupiter's impressive motif of
Godhead, Ex. 6, is transferred to the trumpets and trombones and as a
glittering climax is reached it is clear that the divine seduction is triumphantly accomplished. The curtain rises and through the streaming rain
of gold the form of Danae becomes more and more perceptible. She is
reclining on her bed and as she awakens the gold quickly dies away although echoes of its sound linger for some time.

5

The new scene is again static and consists of a discussion between Danae
and her maid Xanthe.[8] This is Xanthe's only appearance in the work
since Wallerstein's abortive attempt to give her a more positive dramatic
function and hence she possesses no musical themes of her own. Her
isolated scene is thus based for the greater part on Danae's and Jupiter's
motifs, to which latter are added two new themes, epitomizing Jupiter
in the role of seducer:

Ex. 10

Ex. 11

Danae is still under the spell of her golden experience which she describes to Xanthe who, however, cannot understand since the golden
rain is not visible to her. Danae's ecstatic outpourings ('glittering weight
upon shoulders and arms, golden kiss upon my lips', etc.) are sung to
repetitions of Exx. 6, 7 and 11, as well as the flowing lines of Ex. 10 in
cumulative imitation. Xanthe can only think that Danae has had another
dream brought on partly by her love of gold and partly by its dearth in

[8] Xanthe is not a mythological character. Her name, chosen for its aptness,
simply means 'yellow' or 'golden'.

her father's island (Exx. 1 and 2). Strauss was insistent that this should all be heavily emphasized:

x before Juno notices! (added Strauss in the margin)

. . . the more I write, the more strongly I feel that *Danae until now has only loved gold* and was *inaccessible to any other love.* During the discussion with Xanthe in Act 1 it must be stated plainly that (to her father's dismay) she has turned away every suitor. This is also *known by the omniscient Jupiter.* But he wants to possess Danae and as an *actual lover.* That's why he has endowed the handsome fellow with the gold magic and has sent him on ahead as bridal wooer—*so that Danae should fall in love with him.* Once this has happened, he intends to change into his shape and enjoy a human love with her[x] at least as the human-being-Midas (not as some swan or bull). And Midas does fulfil this mission—only he provides a flaw in Jupiter's reckoning by himself falling in love with Danae . . . Yet if Jupiter stands in need of Midas the basis for this must seem to lie in Danae's character . . . night and day she dreams of nothing but gold, so that this time too Xanthe won't believe in the golden rain. . . .

The climax of the short, again tableau-like scene is the radiant out-pouring of Ex. 5a set for the two women, both high sopranos, in the style of the duet 'Aber der Richtige' from *Arabella*, though inevitably lacking the touching quality of that great passage in the absence of a comparably convincing dramatic situation.

A little march in $\frac{5}{4}$ time (unusual for Strauss) strikes up in the wind instruments, heralding the approach of some ceremonial procession.

Ex. 12

leading to:

Xanthe energetically tries to arouse enthusiasm in Danae at the prospect of a new suitor, but her efforts are misguided and as the curtain falls Danae renews her vows never to accept any but a gold-bearing wooer.

During the tiny Entr'acte which follows, the march grows rapidly stronger, Ex. 12 alternating with Ex. 3, the motif established in Scene 1 to represent the mission of the royal nephews and nieces. Success has crowned their efforts and in the third tableau, upon which the curtain quickly rises, they make an impressive entry before an eagerly-awaiting court and recount their adventures.

It is not easy to understand the logic behind the action here, for so many things are artificial stipulations. In accordance with Hofmannsthal's draft, for example, the four queens appear purely on account of their previous liaisons with Jupiter, and their common status as the wives of Pollux's four nephews becomes a coincidence not only out of line with actual mythology but inconceivable in terms of dramatic plausibility. Then again, their mission could not fail to have this one specific successful outcome since Jupiter had already initiated his scheme for the seduction of Danae and the future is accordingly predetermined. One cannot know how Hofmannsthal would have handled what he saw as the lightest possible farce, but in Gregor and Strauss's 'Heitere Mythologie'[9] these conflicts continually arise between pageant, in which verisimilitude is immaterial, and the attempt to create some reasonable cause and effect.

At all events the passage worked out quite nicely for Strauss as an elaborate vocal ensemble including full chorus—the creditors—and two independent semi-choruses—the four kings and the four queens, the latter tying up very prettily with Hofmannsthal's wishes (see p. 123 above).

The royal envoys describe how they took Danae's picture from one country to another until they arrived at Lydia and found themselves confronted by Midas' miraculous golden palace. When they tell of how King Midas himself is coming to take Danae for his bride an appropriately majestic motif is introduced:

Ex. 13

9 'Cheerful mythology.'

The creditors are at last impressed by the tale of ubiquitous gold; the
four kings emphasize the mighty, godlike appearance of King Midas
and the queens carry the revelation a stage further.

For in actual fact it was not Midas who greeted them in the golden
palace, but Jupiter in disguise—as the queens at once perceived to their
surprise, for they know nothing of the complicated deception. This is
all very difficult to bring across to the audience and Strauss wrote to
Gregor:

> You keep writing about Jupiter *transformed* into Midas?
> What this really means is that he gives it out that he is Midas
> so that no one knows him!
> Then how do his four former loves recognize him now,
> when he had only approached them as bull, cloud, Amphi-
> tryon? Simply at sight? . . . He has never appeared to any
> of them in his own likeness! There must be some indication
> already in the first narrative of how the four pairs are on their
> travels and suddenly come face to face with Midas; how the
> very sight of him arouses in them significant thoughts and
> premonitions right from the start. . . .

Accordingly during the ensemble the queens tell how Jupiter's
glance fell on them as that of a cloud, a swan, or as Amphitryon (Ex. 11).
A little figure also emerges during their recollections which is to be
featured in the scene of the queens and Jupiter at the beginning of Act 2.

Ex. 14

At the same time the stage directions faithfully incorporate into the
action Hofmannsthal's suggested dance for the pages (during which they
mime the adventures of the emissaries) and a ceremonial ballet. This
puts a heavy burden on the intricate scene, especially since Strauss decided against any special music for the purpose. On the contrary, the $\frac{5}{4}$
march continues relentlessly throughout, although taking some of the
appropriate motifs in its stride. Indeed, if it were not for the headings in

the score it would be impossible to tell from internal evidence at what point the dances were intended to take place, a strange omission of the formalized treatment indicated in Hofmannsthal's draft.[10] Strauss seems, however, to have been determined to keep this part of the work as concise as possible, and anything so expansive as set numbers for ballet (as for example in Act 1 of Berlioz' *Les Troyens à Carthage*) was altogether outside his timescale.

An enormous bouquet in pure gold is unveiled to the general astonishment and enraptured delight of Danae who had entered unobserved (Ex. 5a). The four queens tell her of the spell by which everything Midas touches turns instantly to gold and a premonition is heard of the motif which later marks the telling of how the Golden Touch came to be bestowed.

Ex. 15 gives the subsequent full version of this interesting theme, Strauss's counterpart in somewhat lusher harmonies to Wagner's magic Tarnhelm motif:

Ex. 15

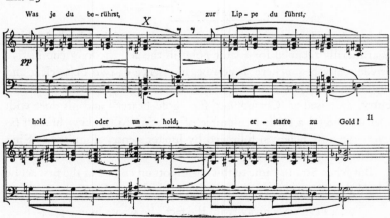

[10] During the rehearsals for the première the producer, Rudolf Hartmann, found the situation getting increasingly out of hand and ended by jettisoning the complicated ballet *in toto*.

[11]   'Whatever you touch, or carry to your lips,
            fair or ugly, will stiffen to gold!'

Strauss complained to Gregor that this meant Midas would be unable to eat (as in the legend), but Gregor pointed out that in Act 2 it was Midas' kiss and not his touch which was going to turn Danae into gold. In any case, one should not interpret the opera too literally, he added; none of the details would bear so naturalistic a scrutiny.

The relationship between the undulating harmonies of this theme and those of Ex. 1(x) is plain, and logical enough since the one concerns the creation of the gold lacking in the other. At times Strauss so juxtaposes the undulations as to make it doubtful which theme is being recalled.

Although Midas' golden bouquet is a love-pledge to Danae, it is seized by the creditors as the only form of repayment in sight; and when Danae tries to insist that the golden sprig is rightfully hers, they start to seize her as well. A disaster is averted just in time by shouts that Midas' ship is in sight approaching the harbour.

The tempo changes and Strauss builds up a new and exhilarating ensemble based on a rising figure.

Ex. 16

Although the last scene-change to the actual site of the island's harbour is artificially retained for a later point in the act, the long cumulative Finale really begins here. It consists in essence of two quite clear and distinct parts: (1) the ensemble of greeting to Midas, followed by Midas' entry, disguised as 'Chrysopher' (i.e. 'gold-bearer') and his duet with Danae; and (2) a further ensemble of greeting to the king himself (as everyone now believes) followed by Jupiter's entry disguised as King Midas.

But when Strauss came to this all-important climax of the first act he found that it still remained a stumbling-block:

> '. . . I can't get away from the fact', he wrote in exasperation, 'that the relationship between Jupiter and Midas is utterly unclear . . . How can Jupiter make a visible appearance as Jupiter-Midas at the end of Act 1, because all the world can see that he is Jupiter and *not* Midas? . . .'

Gregor obligingly tried yet again to explain at some length but it would be hard to claim that he succeeded in making matters crystal clear:

> Of course Jupiter will profit by Midas' enquiries in the guise of Chrysopher, since he is looking for adventure. Therefore he takes the form of Midas just as he had taken the form of

Amphitryon. If the bridal courtship runs smoothly, if Danae still continues to show herself well-disposed towards gold *and* towards the man, then Jupiter will come forward as Midas (Finale Act 1) and all will be well for him.

Where Jupiter is trapped by fate is that the bridal courtship goes too well and Danae and Midas are enveloped by a simple human passion. But Jupiter goes on remaining in the shape of Midas for *everyone* right to the finish, by which time all his hopes are at an end and even Chrysopher has been recognized as Midas . . . only the queens recognize him as a result of their old relationships . . . otherwise in the first act *no one* knows him.

Strauss saw therefore that it was essential to clothe the situation in the most direct musical and dramatic form possible, and this he strove to do, attaining at least reasonable success, even if at the sacrifice of probability. Thus at the end of the $\frac{6}{8}$ ensemble (Ex. 16) the entire company rushes off to the harbour with the sole exception of Danae herself (Ex. 5a). It is in isolation, therefore, that she welcomes the equally lonely figure of Midas/Chrysopher who, as the stage directions acknowledge, makes a surprising entry. After a few words of courtesy to 'Midas' bride', he quickly disillusions her over his identity:

Ex. 17

Danae sadly echoes his confession that he is 'only Chrysopher' and this pathetic little phrase recurs at intervals during the scene in the manner of a refrain. For Midas himself it signifies his sadness at having to woo this beautiful princess merely in the role of intermediary; for Danae it expresses her disappointment that the handsome newcomer is not Midas after all. The violins' melodic fragment Ex. 17(x) reflects Midas' humility as he stands before Danae.

Midas puts on a brave front as he prepares Danae for her coming encounter. Since gold is the basic idea behind the entire courtship, in gold she herself must appear. Making miraculous use of his Golden Touch he conjures up three beings[12] carrying golden garments with which they adorn Danae. The artificial panache is cleverly evoked by a superficially cheerful phrase later used motivically to recall the Golden Cloak:

Ex. 18

Danae is greatly confused and recalls her dream of golden rain while the self-assurance melts away from Ex. 18 which mixes with fragments of Ex. 5. Midas' real feelings quickly emerge in a restless passage which reveals his anxiety that Danae will be influenced in her actions more by golden glitter than by the promptings of her heart. He has in fact begun to fall in love with her:

Ex. 19

[12] The visual conception of the golden figures framed by arcades was suggested to Strauss and Gregor by Pompeiian frescoes.

[13] In Dolf Lindner's otherwise excellent little monograph on the opera, published for the première at the 1952 Salzburg Festival, this theme is cited rather misleadingly as the Midas motif.

He recalls his oath to Jupiter (the Magic Touch motif, Ex. 15, flits by) and restrains his ardour with the thought that he has repudiated thereby the right even to his own name. His ruminations contain a derivative of Exx. 17 and 18 which becomes so important later in the drama that it must be quoted as a motif in its own right.

Ex. 20

From [x] is to develop the theme of Midas' love for Danae to the exclusion of all other considerations; from [y] that of her equally sacrificial love for him. The way in which the latter grows from this duet is extremely interesting. It ultimately becomes the title theme of the whole opera, *Die Liebe der Danae*, and the very adoption of this title in preference to Hofmannsthal's *Danae, oder die Vernunftheirat,* a comparatively late decision, emphasizes the importance acquired by the motif which is therefore quoted here in its later definitive form.

Ex. 21

The sounds of the assembled people off-stage shouting welcome to 'King Midas' (Exx. 4 and 16) bring the entranced pair back to reality, and Danae with dignity asks to be led to the King (Ex. 13). Poor Midas/Chrysopher is obliged to comply although he cannot restrain himself from warning her against the god, knowing as he does all about Jupiter's previous liaisons. The music features Exx. 5 and 11, as well as a further Jupiter motif, a meandering chromatic theme symbolical of the god's flightiness.

Ex. 22

Danae ignores Midas' incomprehensible forebodings of her impending desertion (Ex. 22(x)), his references to dark secrets (Ex. 15) and to his own woeful future. She believes still that her lot is inextricably bound up with gold, and so to her mighty suitor she must go. The golden attendants (they are now called 'genies') reappear to accompany her and, the music building up in ever richer colours, Midas leads the way. Exx. 4, 5, 7, 8 and 11 are welded into a surging symphonic development to which Ex. 2 and the little figure Ex. 14(x) add a running accompaniment as the scene is transformed to the harbour where Pollux and all his people await their saviour.

The orchestral texture is accordingly soon joined by all the voices in an extended chorus; this is the counterpart—or continuation in a sense —of the chorus of welcome which preceded the unexpected appearance of Midas/Chrysopher. Now, however, all expectations are fulfilled. As the huge musical structure reaches its climax with pealing repetitions of Ex. 6, Jupiter/Midas steps forth regally from the golden ship.

Impressively he greets Eos and its inhabitants, and then turns to deliver a personal, softer greeting to Danae:

Ex. 23

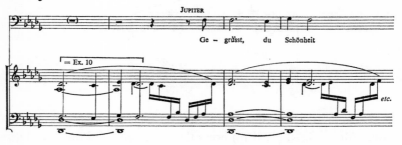

Strauss composed the role of Jupiter as a high baritone, so high indeed that it creates enormous problems in casting, and the compromise has generally been adopted, ever since Krauss established the precedent, of transposing whole sections of the score down a tone.[14] The music suffers,

[14] The passages to be so transposed are indicated in the full score though not in the score for voice and piano.

needless to say, a considerable loss of brilliance by such a practice.

Filled with awe Danae stands before the resplendent newcomer, for some instinct within her seems to connect him with her golden rain. Nevertheless she replies to his greeting in a slow poetic monologue addressing him as 'Midas, great king'. At first she is wholly submissive and the music is based on Jupiter's numerous motifs; but suddenly Midas/Chrysopher's Ex. 17(x) breaks into the melodic line. At the very moment when Danae's obsession with gold is on the point of fulfilment she has become aware that her heart belongs instead to the handsome young intermediary. The little descending figure Ex. 17(z) accompanies her collapse as she sinks unconscious into the arms of her attendants.

It had been Gregor's scheme for Danae to faint into Midas' arms and much of what follows still springs from this. But, as Strauss half-humorously pointed out, it would mean putting Midas into gloves if she were not to be turned prematurely to gold.

This is, however, the explanation for Jupiter's sudden angry reaction. He stamps his foot and, as with the Wanderer/Wotan in *Siegfried*, there is a roll of thunder. No one seems to notice, however; the scene is —yet again—pure tableau. Almost like an echo from Danae's heart, Midas/Chrysopher's Ex. 17(x) sings out passionately in the full orchestra and, unexpectedly enough on a pregnant situation, the curtain falls.

6

Gregor had planned to open the second act with a scene between Jupiter and Danae but, although this was the obvious next step, Strauss somehow did not care for it. Instead he proposed bringing forward a passage originally intended for Act 1 in which the four queens recall the different qualities of Jupiter as they remember him. This led Strauss to a further idea. 'How would it be', he wrote, 'if at the beginning of the second act we insert a pretty scene between Jupiter and the four women, who could perhaps be adorning the bridal chamber and could each in turn pay court to Jupiter—only sensing, but not knowing for sure, that he was the swan, the cloud, etc.? Four sweet little episodic roles could emerge from this before Danae's entrance.'

And so it became. First the queens are seen singing as they bedeck the bridal chamber with wreaths of roses like so many Lohengrin bridesmaids, and then Jupiter enters dressed entirely in gold to receive their various advances, with the only difference that they address him as

Jupiter/Midas thus making it instantly clear that they know exactly who he is. Jupiter thereupon behaves just like a naughty schoolboy caught out in some foolish prank and begs the women shamefacedly not to give him away.

The music begins with fragments of Exx. 12 and 14, the first hesitant phrases before the rise of the curtain once more anticipating the opening bars of the Oboe Concerto, just as the *Schlagobers* Waltz had done:

Ex. 24

After a delicate orchestral introduction, the queens sing a set-piece of envious praise to Danae and admiration for her divine lover. Although largely making use of the relevant motifs from Act 1 (Exx. 4, 7, 8, etc.), their song contains some new thematic material:

Ex. 25

Jupiter's jaunty music, based on Ex. 7, seems designed to emphasize the grotesque figure he is cutting. The ladies address him ironically as 'Jupiter-Midas, Midas-Jupiter' (Ex. 4), upon which he quickly hushes them. They start a new verse of Ex. 25, but in dejected tones he interrupts, asking why they address him so, since they have penetrated his disguise.

The queens now emerge more as individuals; alternately they mock and woo Jupiter, though larding their banter with some pertinent questions regarding his unconventional approach to their successor, the fortunate Danae.

Like Strauss, the queens find it hard to grasp the necessity for so many contrivances. Jupiter explains, perhaps tactlessly, that Danae is a special case needing oblique handling and to their understandably hostile ears he extols her pride and chastity (Ex. 9). Not being mortal himself, he has found the winning of her love a difficult problem (Ex. 21).

Unperturbed by the palpable chagrin of his discarded mistresses Jupiter expands the subject in a section which Strauss appropriately uses to develop the Flightiness motif Ex. 22. The queens confess to each other that they have never before heard so intense an effusion over what is simply another *affaire du coeur,* and wisely change the subject by asking why Jupiter has kept Midas in attendance.

It now emerges that there is another side to his predicament. As Wotan is hen-pecked by Fricka, so is Jupiter by Juno. A good deal of genuine classical mythology is mixed in here, if the listener can but catch and recognize it, including the sad plights of Io (turned by Juno into a white cow) and Callisto (similarly turned into a bear). Who knows what Danae might not be turned into should Jupiter fail to take adequate precautions? The four queens can really consider themselves lucky to have survived with nothing worse than having to marry old Pollux's nephews (Ex. 2).

Jupiter's latest contrivance, thin as it might seem, has been to protect Danae by disguising himself as Midas; in an emergency the real Midas can thus take his place literally at a moment's notice.

This entertaining scherzando section finally returns to the amorous entreatings of the four queens by way of reprise, and Jupiter seems on the point of succumbing to their importunities out of nostalgia for bygone pleasures when, inconsequentially, Midas enters.

The purpose of his interruption is never explained, but he is self-possessed enough to be wryly amused rather than discomforted by the foolish charade upon which he has intruded. With mocking laughter the women run off and Midas is left alone with a thoroughly embarrassed Jupiter, who tries to set himself at his ease by shedding all the heavy golden clothes he has presumably just put on for the forthcoming bridal night with the gold-infatuated Danae.

So much at a disadvantage is Jupiter that Midas fearlessly mocks his gallivanting, and the god is stung into an outburst of self-justification in which he irritably affirms that his interest in the ageing queens is a thing of the past now that he has seen the beautiful Danae. In a glowing solo full of romantic ardour built on his love-themes (though significantly including that of his inconstancy) Jupiter declares his intention of possessing her that very night, though lamenting her continued coldness towards him.

Midas quietly points out that Danae is so mystified that she has even forgotten her desire for gold (Ex. 15). Jupiter, however, had noticed how at their first encounter Danae's eyes instinctively sought those of Midas and the god suspects that he has already been betrayed. He cross-examines Midas on the course of his mission as Chrysopher and Jupiter's mood gradually passes from relaxed informality to that of a violent and tyrannical master.

Still quietly unperturbed, Midas obediently gives a resumé of his conversation with Danae in Act 1, the music confirming his statement that he had been careful not to exceed his province. But Jupiter has quickly become implacable and begins to threaten, as the result of which we learn for the first time of Midas' true status as a mere donkey-drover. Now indignant, Midas protests against Jupiter's impetuosity which, he claims, is as much at fault now as when he raised him from abject poverty in the first place, and he delivers a little homily to the god on the mysteries of a maiden's heart.

Jupiter is momentarily nonplussed. Then quite suddenly he switches the entire plan, on the verge of fruition as it is, to a new and tortuous course of action. The wretched Midas is to continue deputizing for Jupiter during the whole of the coming night, but taking care to preserve the god's exclusive claim to Danae. On this outrageous scheme, designed solely to test Midas' loyalty, is to hang his reward, the gold and riches which hitherto he has only enjoyed nominally, the golden throne of 'King Midas' having been occupied all along by Jupiter, as we know from the narration of the queens in Act 1.

Sternly Jupiter reminds Midas of their understanding and portentously reiterates the Magic of the Golden Touch, the 'Goldzauber' Ex. 15, with its implied threat to Danae's own person which, 'overlooked' by Hofmannsthal, was now to supply the focal point of the opera.[15]

Although unsought by Midas, and bestowed by Jupiter only to further his own seduction plans, the god represents the gift of gold as a favour so priceless that its betrayal becomes a sin beyond telling, past all forgiveness.

---

[15] Curiously enough neither librettist took into account the aspect of the original legend whereby Midas' food and drink also turn to gold with almost fatal consequences.

Ex. 26

later with a chordal motif superimposed:

Ex. 26a

Time and again Jupiter warns Midas, the rhyming couplets being here interspersed with the phrase 'Wäge, Midas, wäge!' despite its overpowering similarity to Wagner's famous 'Weiche, Wotan, weiche!' in *Rheingold*. Indeed Gregor may well have been conscious of it, for he uses the identical formula later in the same act and yet a third time in Act 3 (see 'Wähle, Danae, wähle!' and 'Warte, Jupiter, warte!' pp. 153 and 164).

Jupiter, improbably enough, then storms out of his own bridal chamber, abandoning his hard-earned Danae on her wedding night, together with the golden suit and helmet which Midas dons while awaiting the approaching Bridal Procession, irresolute and perplexed, as well he might be.

7

Strauss clearly realized the dramatic weakness of the second act up to this point, for he wrote: 'I think that with myths and legends one really can't be too concerned with motivation and roundabout subtleties of explaining.'

Nevertheless the Jupiter/Midas duet had built into a very satisfactory musical structure centring around the 'Goldzauber' Ex. 15, itself a fine and haunting motif. The tension created by Jupiter's mounting anger had allowed the music to work towards a true Wagnerian climax at the point where the god rages off, and Strauss now allowed himself the luxury of writing a furious orchestral interlude, laced by flashes of lightning, thundering brass gestures, soaring horns and tempestuous strings. Short as it is, this section remains one of the purple passages of the opera, providing a magnificent synthesis of Jupiter's many motifs before gradually subsiding into growling undulations of the menacing Goldzauber.

With an abrupt switch of tonality the Bridal Procession follows, looking remarkably like a parody of *Lohengrin*. Danae's predicament is, however, considerably greater than Elsa's. Although she is accompanied by a group of golden attendants the singing is left to the semi-chorus of the four queens who spitefully tell the bride not to preen herself too much, as each of them has at some time in the past enjoyed a turn with the bridegroom, and at last Danae, sensing their malice though she cannot know what they mean, recoils from them. All this time Midas, not wishing to disclose himself, has been standing with his back turned raging inwardly at the song, the purport of which he for his part understands only too well.

The music is to a large extent a reprise of the queens' scene from the opening of the act (Exx. 24 and 25) but various King Midas motifs are also superimposed: Ex. 13—at first with almost ostinato-like persistence —Ex. 4 and Ex. 18, which latter, deriving from the Chrysopher scene, hints at the new deception of which the queens themselves are so far unaware. The golden glitter of the scene is further emphasized by a return of Ex. 5(x), also in ostinato style picked out by staccato flutes, harps and celeste.

When the queens have drawn quite near, Midas turns round violently and, realizing that matters have gone unexpectedly awry, they flee in disorder (followed presumably—although the stage directions neglect to say so—by Danae's bridal attendants). After a shrill outburst of Ex. 25(x) the orchestra dies down to a murmur (Ex. 24(x)), there is a brief silence and Danae turns to face her lover.

But which lover? To the best of her belief Danae has just been wedded to King Midas and she is therefore utterly perplexed when, after her first words, in which she expresses confident trust in her golden dream

(Ex. 21 hesitantly on cor anglais and oboe), she is answered by a being who speaks with the voice of Chrysopher (Ex. 20(x)), while asserting that he is indeed Midas (Ex. 4).

Moreover the very gold has become so entangled that she cannot distinguish dream from reality, a conflict which the latest impersonation, itself no part of the original plan, has intensified. Jupiter's and Midas' love themes (Exx. 8 and 18) are here set against constant repetitions of Danae's own Ex. 21, as if voicing the conflict of her heart.

Nor is her plight relieved when Midas declares his own love for her and tries to lay bare the god's duplicity. Hitherto Danae's every action, her very philosophy of life has been dominated by the memory of her traumatic Golden Rain visitation. Since she has met her divine suitor, however, her wonder has turned to awe at his hard powerful appearance. Instead it is now the messenger who is arousing her love; she begs Midas to give her some sign which will make the truth clear to her.

Here Gregor had indicated a long breathless pause, still to be found in the published libretto, but Strauss ignoring this immediately plunges into a surging, passionate movement as Danae, carried away by rapture she has never before experienced with a mortal, embarks upon a love duet with Midas.

Two new themes are introduced at once:

Ex. 27

Ex. 28

Although Ex. 27 is presented by itself it soon becomes largely inseparable from Ex. 28. Both themes alternate with the Goldzauber Ex. 15, for Midas not only convinces Danae of his power by quoting the spell in its complete original form, but illustrates its effect by turning first a single rose to gold and then, in an overwhelming gesture, the entire chamber.[16]

---

[16] Strauss illustrates the glitter of this moment with a complicated section in composite tempi whereby the broad $\frac{3}{4}$ of Ex. 28 is straddled across two bars at a

Throughout this duet the spirit of Jupiter seems to be hovering about, as if eavesdropping, with Ex. 8 in the opening bars and then the little ornamental phrase from the scene with the queens Ex. 25(x) which becomes omnipresent, even when Midas is quoting Jupiter's own declamation of the Goldzauber.

Danae is ecstatic at the sight of so much gold and joins Midas in a big unison song culminating in a top C sharp,[17] upon which the lovers throw all to the winds and fall into each other's arms.

There is a violent clap of thunder and the scene is plunged into darkness.

8

It is perhaps an ingenuous complaint that Midas had been told endlessly in the famous slogan 'You have been warned', and that his despairing cries of 'Danae, Danae' coming out of the pitch black over the *fff* enunciation of the Betrayal motif Ex. 26(x) are fruitless. It was in fact clear from the beginning of his scene with Danae that he was heading towards catastrophe with his eyes open.

One needs rather to remember that it was precisely in order to make possible the particular catastrophe of Danae herself being turned to gold that Gregor twisted the previous action into such contortions. And it undoubtedly makes a very striking and dramatic centre-point as well as a perfectly logical climax to any drama based on the Golden Touch. Perhaps it was for this very reason that the over-subtle mind of Hofmannsthal never at any time took into account this surely obvious cause and effect, rather than that he committed an incredible oversight as Gregor naïvely supposed.

Sternly the heavy brass declaims Ex. 23 in the minor key, and as sight gradually returns with a cold pale light the golden statue can be discerned, which is all that is left of Danae. In broken phrases Midas sings a short soliloquy of bitter self-recrimination in which themes from

---

time of $\frac{2}{4}$ (Ex. 27) or $\frac{6}{8}$ (Ex. 25(x)). This proved wholly beyond the ingenuity of Ernst Klussmann, the arranger of the vocal score, who simplified the passage out of all recognition both with respect to tempo relationships (with what precedes and follows it) and character.

[17] Taking advantage of the precedent he had allowed himself in no fewer than five of Jupiter's passages, Clemens Krauss avoided the task of finding in particular a tenor with so high a range by transposing this further section down a tone.

his two scenes with Danae (Exx. 17(x), 28, etc.) appear over the ever-threatening Betrayal theme Ex. 26.

Jupiter then becomes suddenly visible in a ghostly luminance and confronts Midas. To a dramatically transformed version of Ex. 23 the angry god represents that although Danae is now dead as far as Midas is concerned, she still lives in the realms of divinity and henceforth belongs to him, Jupiter.

But instead of a contrite and mortified adversary Jupiter finds himself facing Midas who, full of righteous indignation, berates him for a murderer, and asserts that, on the contrary, if Danae is to live it will be for Midas whom she loves (Ex. 20), and not at all for the god. The scene develops into a duet in which the two rivals for her love approach Danae's golden statue and offer her various enticements. Danae's Ex. 9 is alternated with, in turn, Ex. 20—as Midas offers her a life of human love—and Jupiter's Exx. 13 and 22—as the god gives her the option between golden dreams and a life of poverty with a donkey-boy.

The climax of the duet comes with repetitions of the once more plagiaristic phrase 'Wähle, Danae, wähle!' ('Choose, Danae, choose!') delivered to Ex. 23 which in the quicker tempo becomes uncomfortably like a bowdlerized version of Mendelssohn's *Ruy Blas* Overture. The final phrase is declaimed fortissimo by Jupiter and Midas in an unaccompanied unison confirming one's anxieties that more distinguished invention both of words and music was needed to rescue the spectacle of the king of all the gods competing on such equal terms with a mere mortal for Danae's favour.

A violent enunciation of Ex. 26 on the full wind is followed by a succession of spaced-out questioning phrases. Muted brass then provides an eerie background for Danae's reply, a tiny distant voice which, with the moral support of her love theme Ex. 21 on a solo violin, calls unequivocally for Midas, and repudiates her dream finally and for ever in favour of love.

There is a new cataclysmic outburst of thunder and lightning, by the light of which Danae can be discerned restored to life. She rushes to Midas and both vanish into the renewed darkness. Ex. 26a peals out in the full orchestra and Jupiter reappears framed by an isolated circle of light to deliver a closing oration. He apostrophizes the departed Danae and laments her betrayal of himself and her golden visions in favour of a life of poverty and suffering. In a fervent rhapsody he outlines the future he had prepared for her, a mountain seat in a golden temple high above the clouds, to be worshipped by all mankind as the goddess of gold (though one wonders what Juno would have to say to this deification of her royal husband's paramour).

Strauss paints the scene in suitably glowing colours with Danae's Ex. 9 singing out on all the violins against Jupiter's Ex. 8, with soft majestic brass chordal passages, and with the golden rain recalled by Ex. 5 on flutes, celeste and harps. The chromatic motif of Jupiter's flightiness in matters of love Ex. 22 can also be heard sinuously winding its way through the texture. Lastly come the Goldzauber Ex. 15, Ex. 7 and, as Jupiter visualizes the exalted position Danae might have held as a gold deity, Ex. 6 in fanfare style on the full brass. But she has thrown in her lot with mankind and his face will henceforth be turned from her. (As Act 3 will show, however, he lacks the strength to carry out this resolution.) There is a savage postlude (the Betrayal theme, Ex. 26a, and Ex. 7 in a defiant gesture on trumpets and trombones) and with Jupiter also vanishing into the impenetrable gloom the curtain falls.

Strauss struggled hard to get this last dramatic section to his liking, not only outlining to Gregor the shape the verses were to take, but even throwing in some of the keys he had in mind for the various passages in the hope that they might awaken corresponding contrasted moods.

'Fühlt Ihr den Gott?' 'Blieb mir die Macht?' are empty phrases! I suggest you begin straightaway:

> Treulose Danae
> du hast gewählt!

And then the angry description of the fate which awaits her at the side of the donkey-drover, in a wretched hut, on a bed of straw, in poverty and want! (stormy G minor). Then as soon as his fury has abated, straight on without transition.

> Ein goldglänzender Tempel
> (broad D flat major)
> Danae war er geweiht . . .' and so on.

Strauss realized, nevertheless, that the Act 2 curtain was as lame as that of Act 1. But he also knew that it would be unfair to lay the responsibility solely on Gregor's shoulders, when he was simply obeying the most specific instructions. In fact, just as Strauss had feared from the start, the whole second act never recovered after Hofmannsthal's draft had been abandoned. It had now virtually lost all recognizable connexion with that admittedly imperfect but fascinating document.

9

The drama is over for all intents and purposes. Hofmannsthal himself had found difficulty in finding enough action to fill out the scenario for a third act. Yet in Strauss's and Gregor's completed opera it is by far the longest of the three.

The answer to this paradox is threefold. For whereas Hofmannsthal had conceived any potential third act purely in terms of the resolution of Danae's transformation from a gold-struck girl to a woman, Gregor added a finale containing two additional facets: the outcome of Pollux's financial predicament and Jupiter's last farewell to the defaulting couple, whom he would encounter on their wanderings. The opera should end with Jupiter accepting his failure to win Danae in a mood of cheerful resignation.

These three independent situations all carried their own problems causing each in turn to swell into a scene of considerable proportions. The first, which reveals Danae and Midas impoverished though happy in their mutual love, comprises in itself the whole of Hofmannsthal's postulated resolution to the drama. But since Clemens Krauss pointed out to Strauss that the opera lacked any aria for the principal tenor it seemed a good idea to interpolate one here which might spring from the need to explain how Midas had originally become involved with the old man who subsequently turned out to be Jupiter.

In the second half of the act Gregor planned to round off the sub-plot of the four queens with a supper ensemble, followed by a crowd scene forming the climax of the Pollux episode which Jupiter would bring to a satisfactory end by throwing handfuls of gold to the assembled people. It had always been hard to know how to place the god convincingly into either of these rather artificial dénouements and the figure of Hermes (or Mercury as he was afterwards called) had at a very early stage come into question as a kind of aide-de-camp, perhaps for the actual seduction of Danae or for hoodwinking Juno. In the end Mercury was not required until this point in Act 3 where, however, he proved indispensable.

But how to link the action to any valedictory episode of Jupiter with the lovers remained a serious concern, the solution to which was again produced by the ever-resourceful Clemens Krauss. What was needed, he felt, was yet another closing scene in which, on Mercury's advice, Jupiter would actually pay a visit to Midas' and Danae's desert hut. This would not only tie up with the figure of the mysterious old man out-lined in Midas' new narration aria from the first scene, but provide the opportunity for a soprano aria as well, the other most serious omission in the opera as it stood. Here too would be the scope for a full-scale working out of Jupiter's last unsuccessful bid for Danae followed by his ultimate renunciation and blessing. The opera might even, thought Strauss, be called *Jupiters letzte Liebe*.

Of course some details remained to be decided: Krauss's plan differs from the final version in a number of points (principally the presence of at first Mercury and later Midas in this further closing scene). But the basic conception, and especially the curtain-fall, is present in all essentials:

> 'Here', wrote Strauss to Gregor, 'is Cl. Krauss's idea: Hermes: Dear Jupiter, you can easily convince yourself about this! *Get yourself up in disguise* and let us pay a visit *incognito* to her wretched hut. Final tableau: Danae *alone* in her hut busying herself with household affairs, cooking, clearing up, mending clothes etc. Expression of absolute contentment with her lot *or else* happy memories of the golden rain, of Jupiter, or thoughts over the change in her fate, sincere avowal of the love with which she has sur-rendered herself to Midas: *Danae's Aria*!
>
> When this comes to an end, enter the disguised Jupiter (either *with startling effect* like the Flying Dutchman, with Midas and Hermes behind him,—or else led on by Midas as a *beggar* seeking aid and shelter). Pretty dialogue between the three of them: their hospitality to Jupiter who at the end takes his leave as a guest with some gift (perhaps a last golden bracelet, or a clasp of gold, which Jupiter had left her as a last memento after the transformation, or some other charming thing might occur to you); and he has convinced himself how the two of them are completely happy in their present condition (you could add their beauti-ful memories!!) and desire nothing more! In addition a half accidental, half conscious sidelong glance by Danae towards the *undisguisable* eye of the god, the similarity of the voice— the dialogue could give rise to splendid subtleties and at the end, when Jupiter has gone, would be posed the question: 'Was it he? Or wasn't it? In any case all thanks and praise be to him for what he has done to us!' Then embraces: Danae! Midas! Curtain!

Since a prominent role for Jupiter had always been Gregor's brain-child, this emphasis in the closing scene of the opera obviously delighted him with the result that he replied enthusiastically and, setting cheerfully to work, produced some of the best material in the opera. He was therefore the more mortified when Strauss sent it all back insisting that it would have to be rethought from start to finish excepting only a new narrative section for Jupiter which he, Strauss himself, had just concocted (this, the 'Majaerzählung' as it became, was an important afterthought and will be explained at the proper time).

For once, Gregor allowed himself to reveal the reason for a lengthy breakdown in his progress; this time Strauss's blunt rejection had upset him to a point at which all his poetic ideas had shrivelled away.

So hurt was he that he did not even travel from Rome (where he was spending some weeks with a literary delegation) to Dresden for the first performance of *Daphne*.

Now Strauss had to eat humble pie with Gregor, which magnanimously he did, though with expressions of wide-eyed innocence—he had thought Gregor had undertaken never to take offence over anything connected with the job; of course he hadn't meant to injure his feelings; what about some nice new ballet project to go with *Daphne* or *Friedenstag* for the occasions when they might be given separately?

Mollified, Gregor happily took up his pen again. A friendly meeting in Salzburg followed and gradually the mood and shape of the final scene approached the version as it stands today. But it was again Clemens Krauss who thought of the Act 3 curtain, in which Midas does not actually reappear—the last bars merely showing Danae as she rushes to meet him. In this way he is not seen again after the duet at the beginning of Act 3, a solution which Strauss felt to be 'much more refined, more French' as well as allowing the beautiful mood of Jupiter's last farewell to Danae to be kept right through to the end. As a result Strauss was enabled to conjure up the corresponding musical atmosphere of tender resignation which, typified by warmly glowing melodic lines, remains the outstanding feature of the whole opera although this had in no way been foreseen when the work was first undertaken.

The whole ending was now clear to Strauss, so that he could easily evade Gregor's various ideas for a more conventional finale on Baroque opera lines—a closing ensemble, a ballet sequence à la Gluck, and so on. It can scarcely have been flattering to Gregor that for a second time his ideas for an operatic coda were set aside *in toto* through the interference of Clemens Krauss; but he did not risk another major protest, even when Strauss cut out an entire scene for Jupiter in favour of an orchestral interlude. He did, however, pay a special visit to Berlin where he not only met Clemens Krauss in person but found to his surprise Strauss's wife and son at the hotel.

Krauss took advantage of the situation to bully Gregor not only into agreeing with all his proposals, but to suggest many more, embodying new psychological implications such as would require yet another entire redrafting of the closing scene.[18] Dismally Gregor wrote to Strauss for confirmation of these lamentable new instructions, but to his relief Strauss wrote back in high good humour that he need not bother; it was all set to music and there would be no trouble in seeing that it met with Clemens Krauss's approval. So Gregor could, if he wished, busy himself instead with the next opera.

10

The short orchestral introduction to Act 3 is very unexpected in character and its purpose at first seems far from obvious. It consists of a full statement of Ex. 5a, Danae's expression of her gold fixation taken intact from her scene with Xanthe in Act 1, followed by alternations of Jupiter's and Midas' motifs. These lead into a précis of the love duet from Act 2 which itself culminates in a dramatic recreation of the opera's climax when Danae is turned to gold. The music then subsides, as in the parallel place in Act 2, into sombre statements of Ex. 23 in the minor key as the curtain rises. It is as if before showing the last stage of Danae's history Strauss wishes to remind us of all that has led up to it by means of a concise resumé.

The characteristic dissonance 'X' from the Goldzauber Ex. 15 lends poignance to the scene which is disclosed. By a dersert road in an oriental wilderness, under a clump of withered palm-trees, lie Midas and Danae. Slowly they wake to bleak reality as the strings play broken fragments of their love music. Danae at first appears unable to recall anything—she cannot even remember who Midas is, or what has happened to all the gold, to her golden cloak (Ex. 18). Patiently, tenderly Midas tries to comfort her and when she cries bitterly on mistaking sunshine on a stone for some fragment of the vanished gold he reminds her of her own recent transformation into that lifeless metal.

---

[18] It was at this time also that Krauss tried to force Gregor to agree to the suppression of the opening scene of *Daphne*. This move caused a minor political crisis in the Berlin Opera House when the unhappy Gregor successfully elicited Strauss's support.

This raises the confusing question of how it came about that Jupiter's curse of gold was implemented through its mere bearer, the one-time Chrysopher, and Strauss introduces against the love themes the motifs of the god as gold and as lover simultaneously, the one being the inversion of the other (cf. Exx. 5 and 8).

Midas now answers Danae's mystification with his narrative: this is the aria for which Clemens Krauss had rightly seen the necessity, and Strauss found a natural opportunity here for its insertion. He was, however, a little unrealistic in asking Gregor for something on the lines of 'Una furtiva lagrima', the famous tenor aria from Donizetti's L'Elisir d'Amore. As it turned out, Gregor's knowledge of Italian opera proved unequal to the suggestion, but even had it been otherwise Gregor might have found such static pieces of bygone operatic conventionality at odds with the style in which he and Strauss were working.

Gregor therefore used the aria as an opportunity for Midas to narrate how once, when in Syria with his donkey, he had encountered an old man in a burnous (Ex. 7 transformed into a serious, deep-toned melodic phrase) who promised him untold wealth as part of a strict compact to be made between them. Midas repeats yet again the Goldzauber Ex. 15 in full, and then goes on to explain the attendant conditions—absolute obedience and readiness to change places at a moment's notice, the least betrayal to carry instant revoking of the gift (Ex. 26).

Thus it came about that Jupiter occupied Midas' throne in Lydia (Ex. 13) and became the enamoured recipient of Danae's picture. Midas omits to say, since indeed he does not know it, that this was the very raison d'être of the whole enterprise, but Strauss makes it clear by accompanying this last explanation by the motif of Jupiter's philandering, Ex. 22.

The aria then passes to its closing lyrical phrase, Midas telling how his resultant role as Chrysopher led him to come face to face with Danae's beauty and her love (Ex. 21), through which he gained the strength needed to break the odious bargain with impunity. Midas ends with fervent repetitions of the words 'Danaes Liebe' as the orchestra surges up with an advance statement of Ex. 29, the melody of the duet which is shortly to close the scene.[19]

Danae now acknowledges that from the first she had been touched to the heart not by the golden cloak he brought her (Ex. 18) but by the

[19] With a paternal eye on the success of his tenor aria Krauss shamelessly interpolated a two-bar cadence into the score to allow for potential applause.

emissary himself. This is the first time she has expressed in words the change which has taken place within her, and Ex. 21 continues to grow in prominence with constant repetitions.

Midas lifts her gently onto a donkey and as they set off down the road the lovers sing a little duet, the words proclaiming that love is more important than gold, the basic theme of the opera as a whole:

Ex. 29

The air of artless simplicity recalls the ingenuous sublimity of 'Ist ein Traum, kann nicht wirklich sein' from the closing scene of *Rosenkavalier* but alas, the comparison serves to show how Strauss had, at least for the time being, lost the art of fashioning immortal melodies. Ex. 29 never recovers from the disappointingly banal cadence in the fourth bar, a weakness which Strauss curiously makes no attempt to disguise even when the orchestra recapitulates the duet as an interlude after the curtain has fallen. However, the melodic line then branches out into a rich extended arch, taking in other motifs before finally coming peacefully to rest with another full cadence.

Suddenly, with an abrupt change of tonality, Jupiter's themes re-enter and we are transported into an entirely different world.

II

The scene is described as 'a Southern wooded landscape in the mountains', although this has little relevance to the action. Perhaps Gregor was hard pressed to find a common site for the different sub-plots which are all in turn to be tied up like so many loose threads.

At first Jupiter enters alone pondering on his disappointment over Danae. The gloomy, ominous treatment of his various themes echoes the bitter nature of his thoughts. Ex. 8(x) in particular is treated by the basses, tuba and bassoons in an eerie serpentine manner like the Amme motif from *Die Frau ohne Schatten*:

Ex. 30

The theme of Midas' betrayal Ex. 26a becomes prominent and Jupiter's anger rises as the intensity of the music builds up with Exx. 6 and 7 on the lines of the closing bars of Act 2.

Suddenly there is a break and the massive threatening sounds are replaced by a darting scherzando movement. Mercury leaps in front of Jupiter, having just flown down from Olympus:

Ex. 31

Cruelly he tells Jupiter how the reverberations of Danae's choice have caused high hilarity amongst the immortals,[20] even Juno herself laughing until she cried at Jupiter's comical discomfiture. Mercury then rubs salt into the wound by warning Jupiter of the approaching people of Eos (Exx. 1 and 2). With the disappearance of Midas and Danae their hopes of redemption from insolvency have also vanished into thin air. Jupiter ignominiously proposes immediate flight back to Olympus but Mercury restrains him, saying that at least he must not disappoint the advance guard consisting of the four queens.

With disgruntled reluctance Jupiter receives the affectionate group of his discarded mistresses whose music from the opening scene of Act 2

[20] The recital of names led Gregor into trouble in the matter of consistency. Mercury tells Jupiter about Ares (Mars in Roman mythology), Vulcan and Ganymede, before switching over to Venus and Juno.

is recapitulated in the lengthy ensemble which follows. It is best to regard the section in a purely formal light since the dramatic substance could scarcely be more tenuous and contrived.

After their opening greeting (a parody of the scene in Act 2 now that his disguise as Midas has been set aside), the queens reveal that they have been invited to leave the ruined palace of Eos (Ex. 2) and rejoin Jupiter who, as Mercury would have them believe, has merely been using Danae as a cover to provide the opportunity for renewing his liaison with them.

Jupiter greets them with ill-humour, but his retorts pass them harmlessly by and in a formal canon based on Ex. 6, they try to wheedle him. The set piece reaches its peak as they laugh maliciously at Danae's lot with her donkey-drover (in this connexion it should be observed that the colour of the characteristic dissonance from the Goldzauber, Ex. 15(x), is used increasingly to symbolize Midas' reversion to his former penniless condition).

Jupiter is placated and instructs Mercury to conjure up a supper table at which the queens take their places. Together they toast their divine lover who, however, warns them that their day is irrevocably past. The queens then in turn try to detain Jupiter by evoking memories of his assumed shape when engaged upon their several seductions, but he replies to each with an appropriate farewell. The ensemble ends with a last quartet for the queens and an extended song of parting for Jupiter in which he takes leave for ever not only of his past loves but of the Earth itself and his philandering therein. It is here that the phrase occurs:

> Wo der heisse Wunsch
> Ihm Erneuerung bot
> Der schönsten Verwandlung
> Der letzten Liebe!

which suggested to Strauss the alternative title for the opera, *Jupiter's letzte Liebe,* based on the idea of Danae representing Jupiter's last experience of earthly love.[21] The music accordingly rises (by means of Exx. 5a, 8 and 23) to a climax of passionate intensity. Strauss set some store by this monologue for which he was determined to provide Jupiter with a really 'grateful lyrical phrase'. In striving for this he actually gave the music a yearning quality which recalls the nostalgic idiom of Rachmaninoff's symphonic music:

[21] See above, p. 156.

Ex. 32

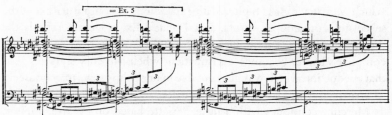

As he composed Strauss left far behind him the text Gregor had supplied and the necessity arose for extra lines to fit the music.[22] Strauss showed in his demands that, despite earlier fears, Jupiter was in fact turning more and more into a Wotan-like figure. He even insisted the monologue should end with the words 'Ich—der Gott' but here Gregor did not comply (fortunately, or the analogy with Wotan's Farewell from *Die Walküre* would have been inescapable).

There is a black-out in which the queens retreat and Pollux, the four kings, the creditors together with all the people of Eos rush towards Jupiter. As previously with the queen's musical material so now the music of Act 1 Scene 1 receives its formal recapitulation.

The kings realize they have been cuckolded, while Pollux and the others claim compensation from the being they now suspect to be no Midas at all (Ex. 4). In some way never explained, they know all the details of Danae's fate after her disappearance from their midst although she has been whisked to the Oriental desert many hundreds of miles away. Furiously, they deride Jupiter as a swindler and insist on full payment in restitution of her loss.

Helplessly, Jupiter turns to Mercury much as Wotan leans on Loge in *Rheingold*, and Mercury at once provides the obvious answer. In this beautiful world, he says caustically, money will solve most things. So a second and more materialistic Rain of Gold ensues, giving Strauss the opportunity for a further onomatopoeic exhibition based, naturally enough, once more on Ex. 5. Gleefully scrabbling for the showers of gold pieces, the entire company of islanders depart leaving Mercury and Jupiter alone for Clemens Krauss's motivation of the final scene.

This is to be found in a duet in which Mercury persuades Jupiter that all may not yet be lost where Danae is concerned. The duet is skilfully

[22] The published correspondence reproduces a most interesting page of Strauss's sketch-book illustrating this point. (See *Richard Strauss und Josef Gregor Briefwechsel*: opp. p. 161.)

contrived to emerge out of the previous Rain of Gold chorus, during which Mercury mocks Jupiter with expressions of congratulation at the successful outcome of events. But Danae's Ex. 9 clearly reveals the direction of Jupiter's thoughts, and the god who irritably rejects his accomplice's banter becomes less impatient when Mercury slyly suggests that a seduction which was inacceptable in her palmy days may not seem so unattractive in Danae's present squalor.

Mercury continues with a little $\frac{6}{8}$ ariette based on 'Warte, Jupiter, Warte!'; the stylistic link with the previous examples in Act 2 can only have been intentional, however misguided. On the other hand it is worked together with a great many of the opera's motifs into a scherzo, which is especially welcome in view of the predominantly serious and slow-moving finale which succeeds it.

12

The change of idiom is instantaneous, so abrupt indeed that the sight of Jupiter craftily stretching out his hand to Mercury, in approval of the invidious scheme to entice Danae from her loving Midas, is incongruously accompanied by the beautiful melodic flow which is to characterize the deeply-benevolent Jupiter of the closing scene. The Interlude, played to a curtain-drop, is in fact one of the most inspired passages of the opera,[23] and in its sustained nobility of utterance looks forward to the renewal of Strauss's genius for which his extreme old age was remarkable. It consists of a single huge span, containing within its contours repeated use of Exx. 5 and 7 though so broadened and imbued with warmth as to be almost unrecognizable.

At last the line comes to rest, though on the Goldzauber dissonance, twice struck and resolved in full brass and wind before the massive orchestration melts away to an isolated line of violins linking the music to the closing scene, and to themes recalling Danae's and Midas' love, Exx. 17 and 29. The curtain has risen to reveal the poverty-stricken hut of a donkey-drover. Great stress is laid on the general appearance of order and cleanliness, despite its meagre simplicity.

Danae is alone and the scene begins with her aria which, deliberately of an artless simplicity, is a self-contained song in ternary form. The outer sections dwell on Danae's happiness, and repeat in the manner of a

---

[23] Strauss was himself particularly fond of this interlude which he called 'Jupiters Verzicht' ('Jupiter's renunciation').

refrain the line 'Midas Hütte, Danaes Reich!' ('Midas' hut, Danae's empire!') Melodically these main portions are freely based on the Chrysopher theme Ex. 17(x) and ideas derived from the duet Ex. 29. The contrasted middle section refers to the curious experience Danae has undergone—'an enigmatic approach of a strange being' she calls her adventure, as the music changes to the Goldzauber (Ex. 15) and the Golden Seducer (Ex. 5 followed by Ex. 22 and 7). But through his anger (Ex. 26) came the blessing of Midas' love (Ex. 28)—and so comes the return of the lyrical music in which she again extols her new life. Although it could be said to lack the effusive sweep of passages such as, for example, the monologue from *Die Aegyptische Helena*, the aria has a calm beauty of its own which should not be underestimated.

A quiet statement of Ex. 7 on the horn then accompanies Jupiter's entrance and the closing duet follows, arguably the finest part of the work, and the shaping of which owes so much to Clemens Krauss as well as to Strauss himself. Yet several weaknesses remain, the first of which concerns Jupiter's appearance in Midas' hut for, as was agreed with Krauss, Jupiter now comes alone without either Mercury or Midas. In consequence the gist of the opening dialogue is peculiarly irrelevant to the subsequent action.

Jupiter speaks of some servant whom he had commanded to precede him hither; Danae replies that he has gone ahead to Ispara (*sic*),[24] and Jupiter prepares to follow without further ado. She stops him, however, on the grounds that Midas will shortly return (Ex. 29) and sighing heavily Jupiter sits down.

His strange appearance, his voice—his eye, arouse in Danae a chord of memory (Exx. 4 and 23)—and she is also struck by his similarity to the old man in a burnous Midas described in his aria, the music of which now echoes the melodically transformed Jupiter motif Ex. 7. He is smitten to the heart by her reference to his age but, veering away from her growing realization of his identity, the god under whose curse she now lives, he accepts her offer of a cooling drink.

There is a moment's gap in the flow of the music and with the entry of the broadened form of Ex. 8 the true substance of the duet begins, both Jupiter and Danae abandoning all pretence thereafter. Here at last is the full statement of the metamorphosis towards which Ex. 8 has been tending during its development throughout the opera, and its significance is integral to Strauss's whole conception.

[24] ? Isparta, a village in Turkish Asia Minor.

Ex. 33

Jupiter's love for Danae has deepened far beyond his initial desire to add her to his list of seductions, while for her part she too has matured to the point where seduction by gold no longer fulfils her understanding of what love can mean.

Jupiter therefore blesses Danae in her happiness whilst, in a last attempt to win her love, simultaneously revealing the torment in his own breast.

With gentle simplicity she acknowledges his blessing but says that in Midas' poor hut she has found peace and sufficiency (Exx. 17 and 29). She contrasts the extremes of wealth which Jupiter had offered, with the immunity from divine retribution (Ex. 26a) which happiness with Midas has brought her. Although Jupiter understands her well enough he deplores the barren poverty to which so radiant a creature has been reduced. Danae's answer to his deeply-felt outburst contains the first statement of the phrase, now to be repeated many times as the kernel of the opera: 'Siehe, ich liebe' ('but see, I am in love!') quoted as Ex. 21 already on p. 143 above.

This then, is *Die Liebe der Danae*, and its repetition as a refrain was Strauss's idea, seeing it as a study on the meaning of happiness and its relation to the opera's message. Danae was originally intended to ask Jupiter: 'Stranger, are you happy?' but, as Strauss wrote to Gregor:

> . . . one thing is denied to the all-powerful god, creator of the world: the happiness to be found in human love, the self-sacrificing fusion into one another of two people really in love!
>
> And so to begin with: who is happy? A creator, a modeller—so then a god—an artist. But both are egoists (I'm afraid I express myself very superficially): in the urge of creation, in being wholly lost in one's work—that it benefits the community—the feelings of love as of sex to sex are *not* contained.
>
> Who is happy? Whoever desires and still hopes. Hence Danae in her yearning towards gold, in her wishing-dreams where the god draws near to her in the form of golden rain. During Act 2 the dream of gold is extinguished in her when

Chrysopher wakens her human feelings and when she sacrifices the fulfilment of her ambition—to be enthroned as a golden statue amongst the gods—for the sake of a destiny amidst poverty and the loyal fulfilment of duty at the side of a true lover. Thus the question arises within her: '*who then could that have been, who had the power to procure for me this exalted destiny?*'

This uncertainty, who the old man in the burnous was, and who the false Midas (of the first act), must give her much cause for thought: 'who was it for whom Chrysopher was to lay courtship, who could promise me the temple, who has now turned us into donkey-drovers, who also seemed to feel human love although it was not the kind of love which led me to Midas?' This specific erotic moment, which Danae experienced once so vividly during the first Golden Rain scene, must also shine out in her moving encounter with the god when he is making his final renunciation . . . Now he is returning to his own proper sphere of activity, once again to direct the affairs of the world which he has created in all its beauty, and to rejoice that he has succeeded in fashioning *one jewel* in the hearts of men which cannot even enter into his own dreams, and before which all, all his might, all the magic of gold, is powerless . . .

The phrase 'Sieh, ich liebe' can stay in the same way as—if you remember Salome's refrain 'ich will den Kopf des Jochanaan!' Things like that always work well in opera!

In the last scene, which really gives the point to the whole, you need not restrict yourself for space. If it contains genuine wisdom and beautiful poetry, then however much more there is of it, I will still be able to cope! And in a posthumous work everything is allowed!

A posthumous work—herein lies the secret of this last scene and of the depth of feeling with which many of its pages are imbued. For, based posthumously on Hofmannsthal's fragment as it is, *Danae* also appeared to Strauss more and more as one of his own posthumous works. With the political scene beyond the windows of his Garmisch home rapidly darkening Strauss became convinced that not only would *Danae* be his swan-song but that he would never hear it performed (though in the event his premonition proved over-pessimistic).

Be this as it may, there seems to have been more than a little self-identification on Strauss's part with the Jupiter of these closing pages, a character who bears little resemblance to the parodied figure of the earlier scenes of the opera, but who like Strauss himself is the creator of a world of beauty to which he is obliged, in a mood of the saddest resignation, soon to say farewell.

So it is that Strauss was able to guide Gregor more precisely than ever before over the succeeding passages in which the god appeals with the greatest pathos to a woman whose seduction now represents the pursuit of pure beauty. The god's words are directed to be sung as a restless and ghostly invocation, and Strauss's accompanying music (based on, in order of importance, Exx. 32, 8, 22, 7 and 6, thus comprising a symphonic synthesis of Jupiter's themes) is appropriately full of chromatically shifting passage-work. Jupiter sings of the golden nights in which he once visited Danae (Ex. 5 in full on flutes and celeste) at which she joins him in an ecstatic duet until suddenly an incautious word recalls her to her senses, and with Exx. 6 and 11 she impresses on Jupiter the chasm which must always gape between them.

The repetition of the refrain Ex. 21 brings Jupiter sharply up against the impotence of his might where human love is concerned (as in Strauss's letter), and his despair is proclaimed over passionate reiterations of the Chrysopher theme Ex. 17(x).

Yet love too is Jupiter's creation, like human fulfilment and human happiness, and with soft but ringing fanfares based on the godhead theme Ex. 6 the music sinks gently down again, the descending phrases recalling the little duet Ex. 29. Again Danae answers the god with her refrain and Jupiter bids her listen as he embarks upon the Majaerzählung —the story of yet another and earlier love.

13

Maia, in Greek mythology, was an Earth goddess and the mother of Hermes by Zeus. The Romans on the other hand associated her with the fire-god Vulcanus, whose acolytes made sacrifices to her on the first day of May, to which month she gives her name.

Strauss combined the legends of the ancient world, Greek and Roman, to produce this additional nostalgic experience for Jupiter, who is left desolate after the ravished Maia had been transformed into the annual floral manifestation of spring-time which follows the barrenness of the earth in winter.

There is a dual purpose in this apparently irrelevant eleventh-hour interpolation. As an adjunct to the deepening personality of a new and noble-hearted Jupiter during this closing scene, the Majaerzählung sub-

limates the god's practice of earthly seductions, which hitherto have
been shown as a series of somewhat sordid escapades. Moreover, the
episode provides a fine musical landmark in a duet which may have
threatened to become too diffuse for an operatic finale. In this respect
the similar duet finales in *Guntram* and *Ariadne II* make interesting
comparison, especially as both contain interruptions—different in kind
(by the Fool and by Zerbinetta respectively) but identical in formal
dramatic intention.

Some such purpose is served here, if in yet a different way, by the
colourful orchestration and the change from rhetoric to lyricism of the
Majaerzählung, for which Strauss invents new motivic patterns:

Ex. 34

Ex. 35

Over this gorgeous orchestral carpet Jupiter pours out his plea that
through the memory of his love for Maja the whole world has benefited.
But as his outburst blossoms into a duet Danae reminds him that Maja's
gift to the world was spring and flowers; whilst if she were to submit to
his love her offering would be cold and feelingless gold, far inferior to
the happiness of human love, as she and Midas have found (Ex. 21 in
glowing augmentation).

Jupiter now knows that he has lost her, and deploring his poverty in
being denied the love enjoyed by mortals, he prepares to take his leave.
And here another part of Krauss's plan is incorporated (see Strauss's

letter above, p. 156); Danae detains Jupiter at the very threshold and begs him to accept as keepsake a clasp which she has preserved through the whole débâcle, hidden in her golden hair.

Thus in the reversal of their roles, through her bestowal of her last golden trophy upon the gold-giver himself, Danae's drama completes itself. So she begs to be remembered, expressing her gratitude to the god for having raised her from the darkness of night to the day of love. This her last song welds into a single line the hitherto opposed motifs of her love-experience with Jupiter (Exx. 5, 8 and 9) and with Midas (Exx. 21, 28 and 29).

With great tenderness and mounting intensity Jupiter answers her with his final monologue of resignation and farewell. In accepting back from her this one golden survival from the curse he had cast over Midas and Danae he repudiates the very curse itself. With touching sincerity he sings to a continuation of the same fusion of love motifs, his own and Midas'. But Jupiter goes further: as the Majaerzählung music returns (Ex. 35) in alternation with the sublimated melody of his love for Danae (Ex. 33) he substitutes a blessing. Instead of pain and hardship, she and Midas will enjoy the earthly beauty which was the fruit of Jupiter's love for Maja. Although he must for ever remain distant from them, his blessings and his gratitude perpetually shine upon them.

During a most beautiful orchestral peroration he quickly takes his leave, Danae remaining motionless as she looks for a long time at the door through which he has vanished. His motifs of divinity (Exx. 6 and 7) as seducer (Ex. 11) and as Golden Rain (Ex. 5) are at first underlaid by the gloomy Ex. 30, but this gives way to brighter themes, the Majaerzählung melody Ex. 35 combining again with Ex. 33. Yet again, Ex. 30 returns but is carried up to the heights by the violins as the 'Liebe der Danae' theme Ex. 21 enters to round off this symphonic portrayal of Jupiter's renunciation.

The remainder is mere epilogue. The melody of the little duo Ex. 29 enters on four horns as Danae sights the returning Midas. There is a surge on the orchestra as she rushes towards him (Exx. 20 and 21) . . . and the curtain falls without our seeing Midas. The music broadens and, with phrases again from the duo, descends to the final cadence in tones of calmness and confidence.[25] Danae's love has triumphed.

[25] The trombones and tuba which have been associated predominantly with Jupiter in the final scene are omitted from the closing pages including the last chords of the opera, a nice psychological touch.

14

By the time the full score of Act 1 was complete Germany was at war. With sunken spirits Strauss continued to press on with the task, as he later did with its successor, but he believed he saw the close of his life-work clearly mapped out. *Danae* was to be his last true opera, only to be followed by a small-scale stage work which he regarded purely in the nature of an epilogue. Still persuaded that the fate of *Die Frau ohne Schatten* was due to conditions in a Europe at war or immediately post-war, he made up his mind that *Danae* should not be performed until at least two years after the cessation of all hostilities, '. . . that is to say,' he wrote to Gregor, 'it will take place after my death. So that's how long you will have to preserve your soul in patience.'

But he reckoned without Clemens Krauss with whom he worked ever more closely as the months passed. Once the full score of *Danae* was complete—the last page is inscribed 28 June 1940—it was impossible to withhold the news from Krauss, especially since he had played no in-considerable part in fashioning much of the action. Never slow on the uptake Krauss immediately requested, and obtained, from Strauss a ver-bal undertaking that he was to conduct the first performance, whenever that should ultimately take place.

But as time went on Krauss saw very clearly that such a promise could prove hard to implement. Strauss might well not outlive the war which was becoming daily more serious and was certainly not likely to be over for many a year. With life in Germany worsening all the time Strauss was certain to be subjected, before it became too late, to pres-sures from the opera houses in Dresden or Berlin—two obvious possi-bilities and both of them localities in which Krauss had no position or influence. Rumours of a new Strauss opera were already filtering all over Germany and competition would be keen. However steadfast Strauss remained, if he died before war was over Krauss might well find it im-possible to establish his claim.

Accordingly in mid-September 1941, barely more than a year after the completed score had been sadly put away, Krauss himself laid siege to Strauss's position, begging to be allowed to present *Danae* at a Salz-burg Festival. He made no secret of his personal reasons for wanting to overcome Strauss's strictures, but gave emphasis to his argument by describing the effect such a première would have in ensuring for Strauss's

music a place of honour for all time in Salzburg, the home and birthplace of his beloved Mozart.

As it happened, Strauss had meantime quietly allowed Oertel (the
junior manager who under the Nazis had taken over as Strauss's publisher from the Jewish Fürstner) to begin the task of printing the full
score, and a proof copy had recently appeared on his desk. On spotting
a host of mistakes (some misprints but some his own errors) he thought
he might as well let Krauss have the score for a while on the pretext that
he could do a useful job of additional proof-reader. As to Krauss's request, that was not likely to be granted overnight. Strauss reaffirmed
his views while also voicing other qualms:

> . . . do you really think that *Danae,* which is so hard and so
> demanding, could be at all adequately presented scenically or
> acoustically in that riding-school barn of a Festspielhaus?
> The old well-known operas can stand up to even a tempor-
> ary set-up like that, but a new work whose whole future
> hangs on the way it is given at the first performance?
> You will yourself be the best judge of this when you have
> had a look at the enclosed score, and provisionally the
> première of *Danae* can come into your programme to intro-
> duce you. But over the date I would really ask that the pre-
> vious agreement stands: at least 2 years after the conclusion
> of peace-talks—that is to say, when the other stages are
> half-way to the point when they can guarantee a satisfactory
> production. For the *Frau ohne Schatten* still suffers today from
> having to be put on in German theatres too soon after the
> last war. Even the second Dresden performance (at that
> time) was a disaster. And you will see for yourself from the
> new score how hard the work is. . . .

Even so, it took Krauss no more than one further year actually to
attain his object. In a letter of 5th November 1942 we find him thanking
Strauss profusely '. . . for having during your recent personal visit
assigned the première of *Die Liebe der Danae* to me for Salzburg. I shall
then bring the work to its first performance at the 1944 Salzburg Festival, as a festival performance in celebration of your 80th birthday.'

Much had, of course, happened during that past year to bring
Clemens Krauss so close to Strauss that the composer felt himself under
an obligation to Krauss to the point where he was prepared to grant
even this favour against all his most determined resolutions. His growing dependence upon Krauss's professionalism in the theatre had cul-

minated only the week before the above letter was written in the first performance of Strauss's operatic epilogue, *Capriccio*, the libretto of which was, once Gregor had been satisfactorily deposed, written by none other than Clemens Krauss himself in direct collaboration with Strauss.[26]

Krauss's position had in fact become unassailable and triumphantly he wrote to Goebbels giving the good news and invoking the Minister's protection on the important occasion of this much-coveted première.

But if 1942 had been profitable for Krauss, 1943 and 1944 were bad years for Germany. Both the mounting reversals on the Russian front after Stalingrad and the entry of America into the war took their inevitable toll on morale and conditions in the German home-land. In the course of the ever-increasing and indiscriminate bombing of German cities, one opera house after another paid the ultimate penalty. By the summer of 1944 the Allies had opened the Second Front in Europe and the state of emergency could no longer be disguised: on 20th July a decree from Goebbels himself expressly banned all festivals. Simultaneously came the discovery of the famous von Stauffenberg plot of top-line German generals against Hitler's life.

By this time the preparations for the *Liebe der Danae* première were far advanced although there had been continual set-backs such as the destruction through air-raids of both the scenery and, indeed, the complete first printing of the musical material. Travel and communications, as important in their way for the mounting of an opera as for any war effort, were also greatly hampered.

Krauss had written to Strauss that a short postponement of the opening night could not be avoided and that, instead of 5th August, it would now take place on 15th August with a Generalprobe two days earlier. Then on 29th July Goebbels issued a further statement specifically cancelling the *Salzburger Theater und Musiksommer,* as it was to have been called; but Krauss added to his letter that he still hoped nevertheless to be able to keep to his revised schedule. Krauss's optimism was based on the local Gauleiter's expressed desire to allow at least one of the completed productions to see the light of day so that all the hard work of preparation would not be wasted.

This Gauleiter, Dr Scheel by name, seems to have been unusually well-disposed towards Strauss, who was on far from cordial terms with the Nazis. A peremptory edict had even been circulated to the effect

[26] See Chapter XXI, p. 185.

that his eightieth birthday should be allowed to pass without formal recognition. (See also pp. 420 and 424.)

It must therefore have been an act of some courage for Dr Scheel to arrange that the plans for the *Danae* première, if no more, would be permitted to proceed. Yet even this gesture was only partially successful as events turned out.

Strauss travelled to Salzburg on 7th August in order to attend the final rehearsals. Three days later a further decree was issued by Goebbels to the effect that owing to the serious turn of military events 'the cultural life of the Reich would have to be severely restricted' and that employees in the film and theatre world would shortly be directed to munition factories. The Josefstadt Theatre in Vienna was given a week in which to close, and a notice was posted in Salzburg allowing the *Danae* production to continue only as far as the Generalprobe, which was to take place on 16th August. However, the Berlin Philharmonic Orchestra which was already in Salzburg would be allowed to give one of its two projected concerts under Furtwängler, a performance of Bruckner's 8th Symphony, on 14th August.

Moving accounts are given by contemporary observers of Strauss's behaviour in the opera house during these gloomy yet hectic days. He knew that this was to be his last operatic première and believed moreover that neither his own nor Germany's death could be long delayed. When he arrived in Salzburg Krauss's orchestral rehearsals had just reached the third act. The producer Rudolf Hartmann (who had also produced the première of *Friedenstag*) has written a long letter to Willi Schuh[27] in which he described in detail not only the problems he encountered in trying to make any consistent and plausible presentation of the complicated action but his memories of the last days when the depressed Strauss hovered quietly and seriously over the intense work of devoted preparation amidst the turmoil of war for a performance which, it was becoming more and more clear, would never be given. There is no mention of Pauline being present and Strauss himself merely made a few side comments of approval or correction as Krauss worked. A particularly deep impression was made on the artists present when Strauss got up from his seat and went to the orchestra pit to watch as well as listen to the Interlude before the last scene, his especially dear 'Jupiter's renunciation' music. At the end he merely raised his hands in

[27] The letter is reproduced in full in the *Richard Strauss Jahrbuch 1954*, Boosey & Hawkes, Bonn.

thanks to the orchestra and sadly said: 'Perhaps we will see each other again in a better world', words far more affecting in such circumstances than any conventional expressions of appreciation could have been.

Then, accepting Hartmann's arm for support back to his hotel, he said: 'Come on, let's go round by my beloved Mozart!'

It is perhaps a miracle in itself that the so-called General probe of 16th August took place. For it became in every way the true première, and was recognized as such by the artists as well as by the invited audience who were privileged to be present. Even when the official première took place at the 1952 Salzburg Festival, also under Krauss and produced by Hartmann, there was no doubt in anyone's mind that the actual first performance had taken place eight years earlier.[28]

There was an ovation and Strauss had to appear many, many times, but he made no further speech. Gregor was not present, and bearing in mind his abstention from the première of *Daphne* this may have been deliberate—he had suffered too many humiliations (and there were more ahead). His reverence for Strauss was so great that he could never refuse to come running when the master crooked his little finger, but these public occasions were a bitter-sweet experience for him.

15

After it was all over Strauss was found in his dressing room poring over the full score. Pointing upwards, he said: 'When I make my way up there I hope I'll be forgiven if I bring this along too.' There are many indications that he had a strong, if not entirely uncritical attachment to this last full-scale of his fifteen operas. He wrote to Willi Schuh in glowing terms both of the unique occasion of that isolated performance (Schuh had been unable to be present) and of the sterling quality of Krauss's and Hartmann's collaboration. He was also pleased, even relieved in places, at the effect of the opera from his own point of view, and his letter lists the passages which interested him particularly:

> . . . the beginning: very lively, supple choral scenes in grey-brown colouring, leading with strong contrast to the Magic Gold with Jupiter's shining trumpet and trombone . . . very happy duet for the two women flowing into the highly original 5-in-a-bar march-like entrance of the four queens

[28] In his Foreword to Dolf Lindner's little book on the opera, Krauss refers to the 1944 occasion as the '*Uraufführung*'.

and their consorts in which the oscillating rhythm of the
horns hardly allows the listener to come to his senses until
the appearance of the ship—all very well constructed dramatically and with nice contrast, fresh in tempo and expression.
Then something of a recession after Midas' entry—perhaps
the scene is necessary for the action and as an exposition of
new themes later to become important, but with the exception of the passage where the gold dress is introduced I myself did not feel very contented with it. Perhaps the rather
dry text was to blame, Hofmannsthal would most probably
have given me a more exciting basis . . . the end of the act,
almost contrary to my worst fears, once again works very
well. . . .

He was, as we have already seen, especially pleased with the third
act, believing it to contain some of the best music he had ever written.
That it was the achievement of a 75-year-old veteran was another cause
of pride.

In view of the sad nature of his declining years, it should give one
pleasure that Strauss was at least able to view his recent work with satisfaction. But this need not blind one retrospectively to its true quality
relative to his output as a whole, and in this respect the truth has to be
faced that *Die Liebe der Danae* does not rate a very high place, despite
some beautiful moments, especially in the last scene.

In 1920 Hofmannsthal wrote that the subject would be very suitable
for Strauss 'at that phase of his life'. Whether it was still so twenty years
later was quite another matter. Hofmannsthal thought of it in terms of
operetta; Gregor described it as a 'Cheerful mythology';[29] in the end
(not unlike *Die Aegyptische Helena*) it suffered increasingly from
Strauss's heavier Wagnerian manner despite the tableau-like nature of
the first act. There is a forced quality about much of the music and
Strauss was not being entirely unjust when he considered that the shortcomings of the text had to take their share of the blame for his own
lack of inspiration 'trotz "Zwangvoller Müh und Plage"' (despite 'enforced toil and drudgery'), as he wrote to Schuh, quoting Mime's first
despairing words in the opening scene of *Siegfried*.

Yet there are some fascinating pages, as always in Strauss: the Golden
Rain interlude, the little march in $\frac{5}{4}$ time, the stormy exit of Jupiter in

---

[29] *Heitere Mythologie in drei Akten* says the full score, adding at Strauss's insistence: 'mit Benützung eines Entwurfes von Hugo von Hofmannsthal'. Inexplicably
this important line is missing from the voice and piano copy.

Act 2 and, of course, the music of Jupiter's renunciation. Remembering Strauss's affection for the latter Clemens Krauss arranged from it a short Symphonic Fragment shortly after the 'first' performance at the 1952 Salzburg Festival, that is to say, three years after Strauss's death.

With the exception of the opening section, Jupiter's stormy exit in Act 2, and the eight bars of the Goldzauber, the music he chose all comes from the final scene and is therefore somewhat uniform in character. The Fragment can thus easily give a misleading impression of the opera as a whole with its many sharply-contrasted textures. The passages of which it is comprised are so organized that they run consecutively, without pause or break, as follows:

Act 2: Fig. 59–62
Act 3: 9 bars after Fig. 82—10 bars before 86
Act 2: 8 bars before Fig. 56—Fig. 56 itself
Act 3: Fig 99–102
Act 3: Fig 138–139 (this passage is transposed up a minor 3rd)
Act 3: Fig 144—8 bars before 145
Act 3: 8 bars before Fig. 147–153

(the last two bars are then repeated in augmentation and the Fragment ends with an added final chord).[30]

Krauss agreed to allow the publication of the Fragment but modestly insisted that his own name should be suppressed in connexion with its preparation. It had been a labour of love, and he always regretted that his efforts to bring the opera back to the stage during Strauss's lifetime had been unsuccessful—a production in a small theatre in Geneva under the auspices of the Red Cross was one proposal. But Krauss was at first hampered by his own need to be officially de-nazified and in any case Strauss had returned to his own former strictures against immediate post-war productions: '. . . the time for it is still not yet ripe,' he wrote to Krauss, 'and painful though this renunciation is to me, for the sake of the work's future I must resist the temptation. The right thing for *Danae* is therefore to wait patiently and if I do not live to see the première in five or ten years' time, I can at least close my eyes in peace with the thought that I am leaving the work in the best hands. A pity! But one must be sensible!'

[30] The editors of the posthumous volume of Asow's *Thematisches Verzeichnis* try to supply this list but unfortunately fail to identify two of the passages. They also accept at face value Boosey & Hawkes' incorrect details of the slightly-reduced instrumentation.

Krauss tried once more but received a brusque refusal: '*As I wrote to you*, the *Danae* première postponed to the Greek Calends. Perhaps in five or ten years the new Vienna Opera can open with it. Mercury can then personally deliver my greetings telegram'. And that was that.

Nevertheless it was possibly a good thing that Strauss himself never again heard the music of *Danae*. For incredible as it may seem, the octogenarian master had actually progressed beyond the tired, stale quality which is the most disappointing feature of so many of its scenes—the Xanthe/Danae duet (for all Strauss's praise), the Chrysopher entrance, the music of the four queens in both the second and third acts, the Mercury scene and so on. With his face sternly set against opera, yet another phase of his long life had begun.

When on 1st September 1944 Goebbels finally shut down every theatre in Germany Strauss formally declared his life at an end: it would have been far the best, so he said, could he then have been summoned to Olympus. It is indeed fortunate that he was not, for he still had some of his greatest and most beautiful music to write.

CHAPTER XXI

THE INDIAN SUMMER (I):
AN OPERATIC TESTAMENT

STRAUSS'S position during the last years before the second World War was more doubtful and delicate than he had ever experienced. Tolerated for the sake of his world-wide eminence, yet frowned upon by the German authorities whom he made no efforts to placate although he had learnt to fear them, he was driven almost to become a recluse.

Deprived forcibly of Zweig, the colleague he had chosen, he found himself pursued with indefatigable importunity by Gregor for whom he had little respect not only on account of the inferior quality of his poetic gifts and theatrical sense but because of his irritating servility of manner.

So Strauss allowed himself the luxury of indulging in a cat and mouse game instead of revealing that he had little inclination to follow up Gregor's multifold schemes. Sometimes these were born of some hint thrown out by Strauss himself such as a thirty-minute ballet to replace *Daphne* in the double bill with *Friedenstag*, but more often extensive sketches would arrive unsolicited on the irascible composer's breakfast table.

Yet the anxiety remained that if Strauss rejected Gregor he would no longer be able to find any acceptable substitute. Thus while some of Gregor's manuscripts were dismissed outright, two at a time maybe, others might receive acclaim which sent Gregor into raptures: 'This', Strauss would write, 'is exactly what I need; just what I have been waiting for. Congratulations!'

Nevertheless all were to suffer the same relentless fate: *Nausikaa* (two-act opera or ballet), *Zenobia* (ballet-pantomime after, once again, Calderón), *Nephretete* (ballet but too near to *Aïda* for Strauss to stomach), a ballet based on the subject of the French eighteenth century prima ballerina Maria Camargo (Strauss initiated this suggestion himself), and many others including, of course, the endlessly reappearing *Semiramis*, this time drastically abbreviated to a maximum of forty-five minutes.

Had these proposals been dropped in favour of some startling project, all would have been understandable. But Gregor must have wondered whether he was dreaming when Strauss suddenly returned to the Abbé Casti miniature, a subject so fragile that—as Gregor remarked helplessly —he could see nothing whatever to draw from it excepting only the title: *Prima la Musica e poi le parole*.

But there was clearly more to Strauss's decision than superficial logic, let alone literary distinction. His reactions were largely emotional; Gregor's suggestions were antipathetic precisely because they came from Gregor, while the Casti had become dear to him since it was the last project to stem from his bitterly-regretted lost colleague, Stefan Zweig. That out of Strauss's affection was to emerge his operatic epilogue, a little masterpiece of unconventionality, was naturally far beyond Gregor's perception.

2

Zweig himself never thought of the Casti as anything other than a trifle but it had caught his eye at a time when, his work on the libretto of *Die Schweigsame Frau* being virtually at an end, Strauss was particularly eager to hear what ideas Zweig might have for their future collaboration.

It so happened that towards the end of 1933 Zweig spent a little time in London in search of material for a companion to his biography of Marie Antoinette. His chosen subject was to be Mary Stuart and with this in mind he carried out researches in the British Museum. It was there that he spotted some old Italian opera libretti which at first glance seemed at least to have possibilities: 'Enchanting characters and situations side by side with feeble ones' was how he described them to Strauss. During a return visit in February his eye at last settled upon two volumes of libretti by the Abbé Giovanni Battista Casti, a contemporary and rival of Da Ponte. The music is not contained in these old printings and when Zweig picked out the fascinating title ('Prima la Musica e poi le parole') he mistakenly believed that it had been written for Pergolesi, 'a musician', as he wrote to Strauss, 'of the second class'. In fact it was Salieri (an even lesser master) who set the text to music, the first performance being given in 1786 at Schönbrunn in a double-bill with Mozart's parallel but infinitely more important theatrical *divertissement, Der Schauspieldirektor* (*The Impresario*).

Prima la Musica e poi le parole is a short one-act comedy occupying some thirty pages of the 1821 edition of Casti's works. Its four characters include a Maestro di Cappella and a Poet who are required by their patron (a Count who does not appear) to produce together and forthwith an example of their joint art in the shape of a Scena for two singers, one of whom is the Count's mistress. The machinations and intrigues both artistic and personal which surround this endeavour provide the action which ends happily with an ensemble.

After taking some trouble to study this slender plot Zweig came to the conclusion that 'the little piece was not *in itself* usable' but that it could easily be reshaped. The enchanting title and a few individual features could then be taken over in fashioning a light comedy on the subject of opera.

Strauss, who had by now completed no less than thirteen operas of great variety and scope, was acutely interested in the enormous practical problems posed by this most far-reaching of all art-forms, as the two lengthy Forewords to his experimental *Intermezzo* had shown. Accordingly he jumped at the idea, ignoring Zweig's warnings about the value of Casti's work which he rightly saw to be irrelevant. With Zweig at his side the idea alone might be made to bear fruit. Eagerly he drew Zweig's attention to two remarkably appropriate essays by E. T. A. Hoffmann entitled respectively 'Poet and Composer' and 'Sufferings of a Theatre Manager'.

But it quickly became clear that Zweig would not be at Strauss's side to help bring to fruition a fascinating but decidedly tricky proposition. It was Zweig's intention before starting detailed work to show Strauss a rough sketch. By October 1934 this was complete but before the opportunity came to present it he had reached his decision that it would be wiser to continue working for Strauss only indirectly while remaining discreetly in the background. As part of this plan therefore, Zweig now arranged a little holiday with Gregor in June 1935 by the lake of Zurich during which they could discuss the Casti draft with the fixed intention of turning it into a workable proposition. According to Gregor:

> Strauss had expressed the desire for a sort of discourse set in dialogue after the manner of Plato over the old argument: is it the music or the text which in opera is the more important? Zweig came along with a bag full of history, with the little comedy of the Abbé de Casti,[1] *Prima le parole, dopo la Musica* but neither of us knew what to do with it. A few radiant summer days changed our mood to one of wild dionysiac poetics. We became obsessed with an idea: a group of comedians come upon a feudal castle; they fall headlong into a delicate situation; a poet and a musician both sue for the hand of the lady of the castle; she herself does not know which to choose[2]. . . we were at once of the same mind that such a band of players must have a magniloquent director, a blunt caricature of that so much revered Max Reinhardt, full of his art, full of the theatre. As we laughed and sang on a wooden bench in a Gasthaus we found the original concept of the director La Roche. . . .

Industrious as ever, Gregor then put together a scenario with alacrity and despatched it to Strauss with a covering note in which Zweig bowed himself out of the scheme with characteristically self-effacing modesty. It was indeed this very note, as well as the disappointment at receiving Gregor's draft instead of one by Zweig, which exasperated Strauss into writing the fatal letter which fell into the hands of the Nazis[3]—and from which so many of his troubles sprang.

The fact that Strauss rejected the piece (which lay dormant for nearly four years) purely because of Gregor's role in its preparation cannot have endeared it to the poor historian and it is hardly surprising that when in March 1939 Strauss suddenly came back to it Gregor replied coldly that he found it quite faded and distant. Nevertheless, within four days he had obediently cooked up another draft and sent it along. This he described as 'a little comedy in the manner of Eichendorff; to a

---

[1] The origin of the 'de' in Casti's title with which Strauss and his librettists persist in investing him seems doubtful.

[2] The similarity of this situation with Hofmannsthal's original setting for the *Ariadne divertissement* (see Vol. II, p. 4) is unmistakable. Moreover, there is a further parallel, this time between Casti's libretto and Ariadne II, in the patron nobleman who remains in the background and never actually appears. Yet if Gregor's account is to be credited this is all purely fortuitous.

[3] See above, p. 49.

remote and unworldly castle comes a little opera troupe; at first they
cause confusion; but then the true feelings of the inmates becomes
apparent; the great Diva is already there with her good appetite; the
colleague who encourages her . . .' and so on.

But Gregor failed to realize that such dramatic situations were pure
irrelevance. All that interested Strauss were the Abbé Casti and his title,
that *ben trovato* title which he was for ever muddling up and getting
wrong. His variants had now reached the very opposite of the original,
viz: *Prima le parole, doppo* (sic) *la Musica*,[4] but this gives the key to
Strauss's preoccupation: which of the two—words or music—should
in fact take precedence over the other, a problem which lies at the root
of the whole nature of opera as an art-form.

For his part, Strauss was still to learn that only a musician can really
be absorbed by such a conflict which has always had to be solved anew
by each composer in every era, in his own way and according to his
own technique. It is doubtful whether Zweig himself could have produced the closely-reasoned text Strauss had in mind. But clearly Gregor
was a non-starter, although it took Strauss (with Clemens Krauss's
moral support) over six months to establish the fact once and for all.
Strauss reminds us of Siegfried shattering one after another of poor
Mime's swords as he rejects outright each of Gregor's attempts. But his
letters of rebuff make such interesting reading that one at least must be
quoted:

> Your de Casti draft was a disappointment . . . nothing like
> what I had in mind: an ingenious dramatic paraphrase on
> the subject of
>
>   First the words, then the music (Wagner)
> or First the music, then the words (Verdi)   to jot down
> or Only words, no music (Goethe)   only a few
> or Only music, no words (Mozart)   headings!
>
> In between there are naturally many half-tones and ways of
> playing it! These all presented in various cheerful figures,
> which overlap and are projected into cheerful comedy
> figures—that's what I have in mind!. . . Take for example,
> the love duet in the second act of *Tristan*: the beginning: 'O
> sink hernieder Nacht der Liebe' doesn't need any words,
> here the music says all there is to express, and so too does the

---

[4] When Strauss, at Clemens Krauss's request, reorchestrated a short section of
the third act of *Die Frau ohne Schatten* in the cause of greater textural audibility he
caustically headed the first page of the revision with this version of Casti's title.

B major finale! Only from 'Lausch, Geliebter' do the words naturally take on a necessary function and add depth—yet take the words away and the whole central part of the love scene would be incomprehensible. Do I make myself clear? In Italian opera the Prima Donna and the Tenor regard the words as unnecessary, as long as the cantilena is nicely executed and the notes themselves bewitch the ear! Now accepting that the arias are also very important in opera and nearly decisive; in an opera, which even half makes sense— if for whole stretches you don't hear a word of the singer's part—this is also impossible. Three hours long only notes —unendurable! Conflict between performer and poet! First the producer—then the conductor! First the conductor —then the producer, here you've got a theme just like First the poet, then the composer . . . For the representation of this alone you need at least 8 to 10 performers and singers! These all worked into a pretty and graceful action—a task worthy of a Beaumarchais, Scribe and Hofmannsthal! . . .

In a later letter Strauss amusingly carried the argument forward to the *reductio ad absurdum* in a footnote:

'The point could perhaps be made: the finest of all then is ballet; there you get *neither* words *nor* music, a drum and a tambourine are enough for accompaniment. So *neither* words *nor* music, only rhythm!'

3

At last by September 1939 the action was beginning to take something of the shape we know today, yet where the style of the text was concerned composer and poet were still no further than they had been the previous March, and both were frankly coming to their wits' end. For whenever Gregor tried to get to grips with the task of putting flesh on the bones of the structure he betrayed his fatal insensitivity to Strauss's thought. He was for ever adding detail—new action, new psychology, new poetic effusiveness, causing Strauss to explode time and time again until poor Gregor found himself wondering how to build any sort of dramatic structure at all through the constriction of Strauss's strait-jacket.

And all the time Clemens Krauss was in the background, putting his finger with unerring instinct on the weaknesses of Gregor's laborious drafts and even gradually volunteering some very positive views of his own. The climax came when Krauss, together with his friend and colleague the producer Rudolf Hartmann, spent a day in Garmisch thrashing out the problem. This resulted in Krauss himself contributing a complete new scenario which Strauss received at the same time as yet another from Gregor.

Although Strauss felt that a third and similar draft of his own was neater, 'more precise' as he put it, he was inclined to be grudgingly tolerant of Gregor's latest effort, a draft of the first scene drawn up in dialogue form. But Clemens Krauss was scathing. The only hope now was that he and Strauss put their heads together over the work and either keep Gregor merely trailing alongside (just in case he came up with any useful thoughts) or, perhaps better still, get rid of him altogether. The obvious pretext would be that Strauss had decided to write the piece by himself as he had ultimately done in the case of *Intermezzo*.

Strauss entirely agreed and on 28th October wrote to Gregor formally thanking him for all the trouble he had taken, but instructing him to cease work. The situation could hardly have been more delicate: Gregor had already expressed his resentment at some mocking remarks Krauss had let fall on his attempts, and Strauss was still in the midst of an active collaboration with Gregor over *Danae* which he by no means wished to bring to an end. However, the letter of congé was well expressed, with reference (just as Krauss suggested) to *Intermezzo*, Hermann Bahr, and the parallel situation which had arisen twenty years before (see Vol II p. 242), and thus the act of diplomatic withdrawal was successfully effected. Clemens Krauss had at last attained to the coveted position of Strauss's artistic right-hand man.

4

In starting work on their own, Strauss and Clemens Krauss were confronted with a mass of heterogeneous drafts and ideas. Gregor had wanted to put the setting in a German castle where a piece was to be performed by a touring theatrical group. As he reminded Strauss, Goethe's *Wilhelm Meister* contains analogous situations; references to Mozart, Beethoven, even the young Romantics, would easily arise in such a milieu.

None of this suited Strauss however. In any case, he clearly saw that the first essential was to sketch out some sort of overall plan. The dialogue would be in prose, the songs in verse; parts would be spoken without music. After a purely musical introduction there might very well be a rehearsal of a play—this would represent the *prima le parole* section which would be gradually encroached upon by music until in the end musical expression would take over *in toto*. The leading characters would be the Countess together with the musician and the poet who were competing for her favour.

Strauss particularly emphasized the importance of the culminating moment when poet and musician determine to collaborate in the improvisation of a new piece, a play within the play, forming a kind of *Gesamtkunstwerk* (Wagner's favourite conception of a work combining each of the fine arts). All the artists, creative and interpretative, would join in this collective offering.

Quite naturally, Strauss assumed that the dominant role would be that of the musician. Nevertheless he was insistent that the action be kept on a strictly dialectical level; in fact he really wanted the opera as a whole to amount to hardly more than an abstract theoretical discussion. (This was particularly remarkable when one recalls the arguments with Hofmannsthal over such a concept in the days of *Die Aegyptische Helena*.[5])

Above all there must be no Beethoven and Goethe personalities, the style to be far removed from poetry and modelled more on Molière and Oscar Wilde. The castle was now to be in the hands of a young Count and Countess—perhaps twins just like 'word and tone'. The work could be cast as a single act of five scenes, the first scene featuring the spoken recitation of a short single act sketch, the offering of the poet, and which must already contain the all-important verses around which the drama revolves; the second scene would introduce the Reinhardt-like theatre-director together with a pair of Italian opera singers who would perform a stylized piece of music. As a contrast on the musical level, the musician would produce as his offering a piece of absolute music.

Strauss now began to visualize the chief central scene with the Director, the Italian singers, the instrumentalists—a quartet of string players—an actress and the young Count (a liaison here would be in keeping, as the Count could take part as an amateur in the rehearsal of a scene from some short play in which his courtship of the actress would be furthered), and of course the Countess with her poet and musician. The debate might easily arise out of this situation, each character con-

<hr>

[5] See Vol. II, p. 311.

Strauss orchestrating
Die Schweigsame Frau

A draft being submitted:
Strauss and Gregor

hear what the Countess, somewhat moved, will say; then the butler gives a sign to four young waiters to serve tea during which the five servants are able to overhear snatches of the theoretical discussion which follows.

First the Countess begins by confessing that she is stirred by music, but at the same time perturbed by emotions she does not understand . . . hence she is not wholly satisfied by absolute music.

The poet takes the musician's side and emphasizes his inclination towards music as it could be found in Goethe. . . .

The Count chips in with praise of the spoken word so that everyone knows at once 'where they are'.

He recites the poet's verses . . . 'Isn't that beautiful?' he says, 'you see with words one can express one's feelings better than through the indefinite medium of notes'. The Countess *very much likes the poem* but, as with music alone, she is not wholly satisfied.

Now the director could put in his oar with the trite outlook of the pure man of the stage as regards the subordinate role of poet and musician alike when compared with the scenery, décor, the exhibiting of pretty girls and costumes and nice voices . . . something like: 'The most important thing is that the librettist gets hold of some good hits and that the musician couples them with music easily grasped and full of tunes one can whistle on leaving the theatre.'

This sort of exposé in easy conversational style I regard as necessary already in the first scene, as the basis for the outbreak of more serious argument in the coming ensemble. Here also is laid the foundation stone for the later discussion of the five servants who should represent the broad public, that is, embracing the entire spiritual proletariat from the lowest to the highest strata of class-society . . . as Carl Maria von Weber said of the public: 'Each individual is an ass, but the whole is the voice of God. . . .'

The old butler could perhaps . . . right at the very end, listen unnoticed as the Countess sings the song over to herself before he quietly withdraws—wiping a tear from his eye—leaving her alone and confronted by the final question mark. . . .' ('Would that be too *Kitsch*?' asked Strauss naïvely.)

The great quarrel ensemble should begin with the introducing of the Italians' duet, criticism of which sparks off the debates. The Countess finds all this too quite pretty in its way and admires the fine voices! The director explains that these are the deciding factor in all opera . . .

The Countess asks what the words are about. Director:

'That really could not matter less, no one troubles about them.'

The musician praises the singing but, he says, for such technical virtuosity it seems to me a clarinet is more perfect. No, says the Director, there is not a single instrument which can come near to the physical effect of the beautiful high notes of the human voice.

This could lead to the recitation scene between the Count and the actress so as to prove that spoken drama actually makes quite a different spiritual impression from the Italian sing-song with a wholly meaningless stupid subject as pretext. Out of the gradually developing quarrel comes the decision by poet and musician to write the real opera; they form a group on the right.

On the left another group: the Count and the actress whose dramatic recitation imperceptibly turns into a love-scene.

In the centre: the Countess in front, the Director and the Italian artiste in the background, who in the end dominate the whole in the manner of a Canto Firmo—the musician and poet could gradually and modestly introduce their courtship of the Countess until in the end the peak is reached: we both want to write the real opera in which word and tone are equal.

The Director shouts at them: 'Nonsense, one can never understand the text enough, the main thing is the fine voices'. Poet: 'If the public cannot understand the text for three hours they will be bored by the most beautiful music . . .'

In the end conciliatory resolutions: all three one-acters will be played[6] and the Countess will then give the ultimate judgement!

Whether the scene of the servants, where they quarrel over which of the principles (that they have overheard) they should follow in knocking up their satire-play, comes next —that will emerge later. Each of them could suggest something different!
The whole perhaps a whispered dialogue. When the Countess comes back they vanish!

After the meeting with Krauss and Hartmann, Strauss decided to change the location to a French château in the vicinity of Paris and the time to 1770–89 (the period, he said, of Gluck, Diderot and Rousseau).

---

[6] Strauss's meaning lies in his original plans for the presentation of the opera. See below, p. 195.

The Countess would be 'no pale German girl, but an enlightened 27-year-old Frenchwoman with a correspondingly liberal outlook in matters of love and more serious aesthetic concepts than her brother, the *philosophical* friend of the theatre and dilettante.'

The meeting had also served to clarify Strauss's mind with respect to the psychological purpose of the work as a whole: 'Here too', he wrote, 'springs the inner meaning of the little piece's action and the content which will interest the public to such an extent that they willingly swallow the theoretical discussions . . . that is to say, the *love issue* concerning the Countess must run side by side with the artistic question of Word *and* Tone, Word *or* Tone; that she experiences the same sympathetic feelings for the poet as for the musician but in a different way. . . .'

The contrasted characters of the two creative personalities were thus beginning to come alive in Strauss's mind: the musician a handsome elegant fellow who naturally appeals to the woman in the Countess: the poet a more serious, sharper intellect, arousing feelings more of friendship although these could at times awaken to something deeper. The symbolism is clear: a satisfactory situation only exists when the Countess's two lovers (= art forms) are united—Strauss hastened to add that no question of marriage with either could ever exist in any case at the period under consideration, because of the difference in social standing.

Krauss's own scenario is extremely interesting[7] and reflects at every turn the unusually clear-sighted theatrical instinct of this remarkable man. He describes the opening tableau with a wealth of charming detail—the view through the french windows to a snow-covered park, the recital in the off-stage music-room which is lit in such a way that the actions are reflected by shadows in the more dimly-illuminated salon on the stage itself, and so on. The music is being played to the Count and Countess who are therefore present in the inner room and not on stage as in Strauss's outline. The quartet has also grown (so far) to a quintet.

Krauss felt that spoken dialogue, although—or perhaps because—it is specifically under discussion, should not in fact be used, but rather that the text should be delivered in rapid concise recitative-like singing over 'an orchestra which makes music alongside'. One of Krauss's ideas was that the poet should, on the spur of the moment, recite a prose

[7] It is to be found complete in the Strauss/Clemens Krauss *Briefwechsel*, pp. 44–9. C. H. Beck, Munich, 1963.

sketch of his poem against a background of a passionate finale of his rival's quintet still being played in the music-room within. This would suggest the simultaneous meeting of the two arts, though not as yet mated.

Krauss also proposed a symmetrical trilogy of scenes in which the courtships of, respectively, the poet and composer are separated by an *entretien* between the Countess and her brother concerning the nature of their love-affairs—she with her two admirers between whom she cannot choose; he, taking altogether a more light-hearted view, with his enchanting actress. Krauss reveals considerable perception in his handling of the different personalities, their actions as they enter or leave the stage being again described very fully and with ample justification for their movements.

Strauss had not yet really considered how the Italian singers were to be introduced but Krauss proposed that great capital be derived from the comedy of their accompanying dogs, trunks, costumes and so on. The whole scene was to be irrepressively gay with singers and instrumentalists all rushing off to try their parts. The action could then pass directly to the conflict between the two rivals culminating in their decision to combine their arts, and so (on the return of the assembled company to the stage) to the central discussion, or quarrel ensemble, with the theoretical exposés of music, tone, action and dance (mustn't forget that! added Krauss).

Krauss greatly reduced the theatre director in importance though he does here make a positive contribution, citing the coloratura of the Italians in support of his arguments. Ingeniously this is made the pretext for a spinet to be brought on stage (in preparation for the last scenes). But all ends in discord; as Krauss jovially put it, '. . . everyone is right, everyone is wrong. The conflict causes everyone to be in more or less of a fury . . . the only consequence on the credit side is that the Count manages to arrange a definite rendezvous with the actress. . . .'

For the ensemble of the five servants Krauss carefully allocated to each Diener a personal favourite amongst the artistic elements under survey (including one Diener who does not care for any of them).

The Composer only plays his completed song to the Countess after the exit of the servants thus causing an undramatic delay to her final scene. This was a weakness of form in Krauss's scenario. The intention was to allow the infatuated musician to arrange a further private meeting with the Countess for the following day, perhaps through the mediation of the butler. The curious fact could then emerge that the poet has also arranged a rendezvous with her for the next day and at the identical time. The enigmatic conclusion would thus be posed on both a personal and an artistic basis as the Countess tries out the words and melody of her new song, now separately, now together.

Possibly recalling the magical ending of *Rosenkavalier,* Krauss suggested that the butler might be the last character to be seen; in closing the spinet after the Countess has thoughtfully left the stage, he could pick up the sheet of manuscript and examine it with the keenest interest as the curtain falls.

Quickly realizing the failing of his closing sequence however, Krauss deftly switched the action round, bringing the scenario several degrees closer to the final version. In particular, this change brought into being the supremely moving moment of the opera in which the Countess makes her magical entrance after the darkened stage has been vacated by the servants. She is dressed at her most elegant as she is expecting to have supper with the Count her brother; but as we know, he has other irons in the fire. Her decision to eat alone, ordered as it is, thus still makes allowance for the butler's reappearance near the end, i.e. after the Countess's monologue, to announce that the meal is served, and so to tie up with as much of the original plan as Strauss cared to use.

5

There had been enough juggling with scenarios and both Krauss and Strauss now applied themselves in earnest to the actual libretto. It stands to reason that Krauss, coming with a fresh mind to the task, was able to take Strauss's sketches and clear up any literary troubles while preserving intact all his wishes with respect to content and conversational style. At the same time no new problems arose since the minds of both men were on an identical wave-length. Clemens Krauss was no poet but Strauss had by and large no desire for a poet. Only for the two or three set pieces might any such need arise and as this was a period drama it would be quite legitimate to choose suitable extracts from the literature of the time.

The first and most important poetic requirement was the verse passage which was to form the basis of the combined offering to the Countess by her two rival admirers—the kernel of the whole opera. It so happens that Krauss had been responsible for bringing to Berlin a subconductor by the name of Hans Swarowsky. Swarowsky, who has since become a well-known conductor in his own right, was in those disturbed times at the outset of his career, but had had the misfortune of falling under suspicion of the Nazi authorities. In addition however to his musical accomplishments he was something of a linguist so that when after the outbreak of war he had to leave Berlin on political grounds Krauss pressed successfully for permission to retain his services in Munich if only as dramaturgist, and there he did sterling work in composing operatic translations such as a complete new German version of Verdi's *Simone Boccanegra* as well as a revision of the previously inadequate translation of the closing fugue 'Tutto nel mondo . . .' from *Falstaff*.

At Krauss's behest Swarowsky undertook researches into French literature of the eighteenth century. With unbelievable thoroughness Swarowsky combed the poetry of the period only to discover that after the sonnets of the older masters little was written in the way of love-lyrics other than those of the revolutionary André Chénier. French poets of the time were for the greater part occupied in writing either patriotic or satirical verses.

Accordingly it seemed more sensible to waive strictness of period and settle for some poem more specifically suitable for inspiring good music. Swarowsky accordingly picked out the following sonnet by a writer from an earlier century, Ronsard:

> Je ne sçaurois aimer que vous,
> Non, Dame, non, je ne sçaurois le fair:
> Autre que vous ne me sçaurois complaire,
> Et fust Venus descendue entre nous. etc.[8]

Pierre de Ronsard, the best known poet of the French Renaissance, was born in 1524 (Krauss actually mistook the date when writing about him to Strauss). He was the leader of the school known as La Pléiade, a group of high-minded writers dedicated to raising the stature of French poetry through a reversion to classical forms and traditions. His precepts for versification exerted considerable influence and he came to enjoy an enormous reputation especially for his *Odes* and *Amours*, which were intended to be sung with string accompaniment. The sonnet chosen by Swarowsky, one of the *Amours*, celebrated the beauty of a

---

[8] The whole sonnet is printed in an article by Tenschert published in the Boosey & Hawkes periodical *Tempo*, No. 47, Spring, 1958.

Florentine lady, a certain Cassandre Salviati who was of a notably chaste disposition and represented an inspiration of idealized love.

It is clear therefore on all counts why this poem should have appeared outstandingly apt for the present purpose and Strauss was delighted. His first action was to set it to music in Swarowsky's own well-wrought translation, giving it for the time being a conventional piano accompaniment. The song was finished on 22nd November and a few days later Strauss made a fair copy which he sent to Swarowsky with a grateful dedication to 'the faithful discoverer and excellent translator'.

Of the remaining set pieces, the dramatic excerpt to be declaimed by the Count and the actress was now planned immediately to precede the Sonnet and so naturally fell into Swarowsky's province. On the other hand the duet for the Italians had essentially to be a piece of stylization. Strauss was no longer sure that the idea was such a good one; what he would have preferred was something nearer to Vaudeville. But with a formidable display of erudition Krauss persuaded him to the contrary in a long letter containing a fascinating history of opera and operetta during the past three centuries.

In a way the problem of finding the right Italian text was that it had to be typically conventional and yet not of such inanity that it would throw the very subject into disrepute. The natural source thus seemed to Krauss to lie amongst the countless libretti of that inveterate supplier of the *genre*, Metastasio.

Metastasio, whose real name was Pietro Trapassi, lived from 1698 to 1792. It has been said of him that the foremost composers turned to him for their books as unerringly as we today go to the post office for telephone service. Hundreds of operas were composed to his librettos, some of which were set more than once by the same composer. His dramas are logical and well written but lack dramatic intensity, while the characters are the merest sketches of men and women; hence the stories themselves hardly seem life-like but are more in the nature of courtly charades or, at worst, sermons.

Here then, is the epitome of the versifier used by composers as the clothes-peg on which to hang their music. He was, moreover, one of the chief targets of Gluck's reforms, although Gluck had in his earlier years set to music a host of Metastasio's books. Krauss had no need to be particularly subtle over his choice although he expressed himself willing to continue the search for a complete edition of Metastasio amongst the second-hand shops. His first thoughts were perfectly adequate, however, a simple song of farewell of a youth who has to part from his beloved. The lines are so typical that they are almost a caricature of themselves. As Krauss pointed out:

> Addio, mia vita, addio,
> Non piangere il mio fato;
> Misero non son'io:

and so on, can be understood by anyone.

6

All the major problems were sufficiently resolved for work to progress, and great headway was made during the New Year and spring of 1940 with ideas and revisions for text and scenario passing to and fro, day after day, in the astonishingly fertile correspondence. The characters had at first been thought of as the purest symbols—'the poet, the theatre director, the Countess' etc. as for example the type figures in *Intermezzo*, but they quickly acquired unmistakable personalities and thence splendidly suitable names. The poet and composer became Olivier and Flamande respectively; the Countess, Madeleine; the theatre director, La Roche; the actress, Clairon, after the distinguished actress of the time Claire Legris de Latude, who was in fact widely known as Mlle Clairon. Even the poor little *Souffleur* (prompt) received the delightful appellation of Monsieur Taupe. Krauss said that the idea of adding this endearing if shadowy figure came to him quite suddenly while driving back to Munich in a torrential rain-storm, the picture clear in his mind of 'the deserted dark empty stage onto which the prompt would emerge, he too a symbol, in opposition to the main acting figures. . . .'

One uncertainty over the practical function of the work remained an anxiety. Strauss had originally thought of it as a discussion on the theory of opera to last no more than three-quarters of an hour. It would then form a single evening's entertainment together with the other two contrasted one-acters *Daphne* and *Friedenstag* to which it would be in the nature of an Introduction piece. The intention was that the audience, identifying itself with the Countess (for whose benefit the other two operas were understood to have been given), would make the final evaluation in her name, as it were.

Even when it became clear that the new opera was growing to proportions which made this rather far-fetched proposal quite unreasonable,

Daphne was still retained by itself as the opera supposedly composed by Olivier and Flamand, and presented to Countess and audience alike after the interval. With this purpose in view Strauss had sketched some appropriate lines linking the two works, such as:

> Countess: It rises up above the ruins of battle,
> a proud Phoenix—my opera!
> The beautiful legend, the poem of Ovid,
> The charming tale of Daphne,
> Working united you will build it
> Into an opera for me . . . etc.

But Krauss had serious doubts; the work had developed far beyond the point where it was no more than the Prelude to another opera. Moreover, apart from the unwieldy nature of the composite scheme, experience had taught him that in such cases difficulties over one opera could jeopardize the frequency with which performances would be given of the other. Opera houses might well end by dropping both.

For long Strauss cherished the idea; he had even composed music containing thematic references to *Daphne*. But at last he wisely allowed himself to be persuaded, upon which he had a positive brainwave: why not have the characters decide to make the opera re-enact the events in which they had all just been taking part? The intriguing effect is thus given as of a set of endlessly reflecting mirrors. The lack of any true ending is entirely faithful to the work's philosophy, while preserving the light spirit of comedy.

Although Strauss was all this time still occupied with *Die Liebe der Danae*, it in no way prevented him from giving the new work his full attention and by June matters were so far advanced that he had actually composed music for the Introduction and opening scene up to the first words of La Roche. Each week during the past months Krauss had produced whole new sections completed to Strauss's entire satisfaction and the veteran composer's glee was like that of a child with a new and long-coveted toy. This psychological rejuvenation could not have been more fortunate for it impacted directly upon his creative powers, opening up springs of a freshness which had not risen to the surface for many years and had seemed to be buried for ever. With the beautiful string sextet (the addition of yet one further player is characteristic) which forms the Introduction to the new opera, Strauss's marvellous Indian Summer period was triumphantly launched.

7

The beginning of the string sextet comprising the Einleitung is actually played in the orchestra pit. The opening sentence contains all the basic material consisting of a group of phrases which are so homogeneous in character that they flow in and out of each other with the utmost ease.

Ex. 1

Ex. 2

Ex. 3

Ex. 4

Ex. 5

Ex. 6

From this collection of thematic fragments Strauss builds a miniature sonatina comprising in embryo a classical exposition, development and recapitulation. The exposition is entirely self-contained and comes punctually to a full close in the dominant key. In fact the music switches to the dominant already in the second bar, a daring stroke which owes its success to Strauss's instinctive mastery of form.

The development begins with a dramatic passage based on Ex. 3(x) with exciting tremolo effects and rushing solos for the first violin and first viola. This leads to a long fantasia which can be regarded as the prototype of the many stretches of the kind to be found in the works of Strauss's Indian Summer period. The accusation levelled all too easily is that of note-spinning, but when indulged in as beautifully as here, and with such an unfailing flow of ideas, the word acquires a new and less prejudicial meaning.

At last the exquisite meandering comes to rest on the home chord and the recapitulation follows, this time remaining appropriately in the tonic key. Moreover the curtain has risen and this recapitulation has been taken over by a sextet on stage.

The scene is the salon of a French rococo château exactly as described in Krauss's scenario with the sole exception that the snow-covered park seen through the french windows is in the full bloom of maytime. This was at Strauss's earnest request; his love of the sun lasted his life. Olivier and Flamand are standing near the door leading to the Countess's salon off-stage and we see her through their eyes, watching her as she sits listening to the music played in her honour. In a subdued exchange against the last phrases the two establish their relationship of friendly rivalry both as men and artists, ending with Casti's title quoted by each in appropriately its original and reversed forms. Thus the thesis of the opera is presented at once together with an anticipation of the only possible resolution, viz:

'Tone *and* word are brother and sister.'

Near to the rivals in an armchair sits La Roche, the theatre director. To their amusement the music has sent him to sleep, and only when the last chord has died away does he abruptly wake up; his remark that there is nothing like soft music for a good snooze starts the discussion without ado, because the other two very naturally deplore that their brain children should be at the mercy of such a confirmed Philistine.

Clemens Krauss and Strauss, in their intention of modelling La Roche on Max Reinhardt, made of him an anachronistic figure, and he is far nearer to our present-day producer (or director as the Americans call him) than, for example, the manager-type 'Direktor' of the *Vorspiel auf dem Theater* in Goethe's *Faust*. The position he holds, in which he 'produces' the speech and movements of the actors as well as being responsible for scenery and costumes, has no reality in terms of the period of the action. For only during the past century has play-production evolved as a profession in itself, with the producer acquiring such pre-eminence in the theatre. At the time in question the play would have been directed by Olivier, who might also have been the chief actor, like Molière. Strauss and Krauss, however, needed their Reinhardt-personality as a kind of counsel for the prosecution, and this role La Roche[9] assumes with his very first words.

His contention is the all-too-familiar one that the sole purpose of art is entertainment. No matter how high-minded the authors, if the public fails to respond their work is in vain. He, La Roche, in his capacity of intermediary, knows exactly the relative merits of the various artistic contributions which make up a theatrical undertaking, and if his views seem cynical they are at least born of wide professional experience.

Since the opera is set in the latter half of the eighteenth century the dispute is conducted in the light of the *Guerre des Bouffons* and of Gluck's reforms, which latter are staunchly upheld by Flamand and Olivier. La Roche brushes aside their claims of popular support as mere fashion and affirms that all Gluck's heavy-handed attempts to raise artistic standards only result in the swamping of the words by the 'tumultuous orchestra' and in so starving the music of melodic content that the arias all sound like recitative. He cites as fellow-sympathizer a prominent librettist of the time, Count Carlo Goldoni, a contemporary of Metastasio and specialist in Venetian buffo operas.

It is easy to see the hand of Strauss in forging the good-humoured argument and he clearly enjoyed setting it to music. The references to Gluck are accompanied by quotations from the Overture *Iphigénie en Aulide* and those to Italian opera and *opera buffa* by passages strongly savouring of Rossini and Donizetti although the composer in question is naturally enough Gluck's rival Piccinni. But when La Roche speaks of his own aim of gratifying the public's natural desire for stage charac-

---

[9] Significantly La Roche's part is labelled 'Direktor' throughout the score although his name is as firmly established as those of Flamand and Olivier. This is because his role is always that of the professional; we learn nothing of his private life.

ters they can believe in as real people, a noble theme enters which later describes the essential greatness of his character. Thinking of Reinhardt, Strauss composed here with true affection:

Ex. 7

An allusion to the beautiful Clairon brings with it a gracious thematic phrase:

Ex. 8

La Roche makes the bantering suggestion that Olivier is not impervious to charming actresses, and the talk passes to the Count's intention to play opposite Clairon in a dramatic scene written by Olivier and due to be rehearsed this very day.

At last La Roche warns the two artists that the Countess, although still visibly under the spell of the music, has risen from her chair. So now her motif is also introduced as they watch her with ardent admiration:

Ex. 9

A varied form of Ex. 9 contains thematic phrases later to prove of psychological significance:

Ex. 9a

The onlookers perceive with conflicting emotions that the Countess has
been deeply stirred and it is these true promptings of her heart which the
additional motivic strands ⌐ x ┐ and ⌐ y ┐ portray. In vain Flam-
and and Olivier seek to fathom her enigmatic smile as Ex. 9a is added
by a solo violin to echoes of the sextet (Exx. 3 and 4). The Director then
suddenly interrupts with a return to more practical matters; if the Countess is coming it is high time to repair to the theatre and make ready for
rehearsal. Now is the turn for his métier—stage production—the overriding importance of which he extols to a pompous motif, vigorously
announced by the orchestra:

Ex. 10

La Roche then whisks his two authors off with him, leaving the stage
bare and free for the entrance of the Count and Countess.

8

Scene 2 is a self-contained duet for the noble brother and sister and
presents an exposition of their opposed points of view. The trouble is
largely one of temperament; she is moved by the music, which unfortunately leaves him cold. This puts him, as she expresses it, into the
role of the dreaded critic:

Ex. 11

In fact throughout the opera the Count is to a great extent represented
motivically by elegant twists in diminution of Ex. 11.

But the Count's dispute with his sister is also coloured by speculation
on how far love for an art may be stimulated by attraction to the artist,
symbolized in the present instance by the Countess's feelings of sympathy for Flamand and, as she is quick to retaliate, his for Clairon.

The Countess acknowledges that she is influenced by the character
of the composer when listening to his music. Couperin's playing she
finds too superficial (Strauss quotes a particularly tinkly example) and
while Rameau is undoubtedly a genius, his ill-mannered behaviour
spoils her enjoyment of an often-recalled air:

Ex. 12

It is hard to know what factual basis the Countess's comments on
Rameau's conduct may have, but the air she quotes is not only genuine
but of considerable interest, being possibly the only Italian aria in
Rameau's stage works, although at the time of Lully it was not unusual
to find interpolations of the kind. Specifically entitled 'Air Italien', it
occurs in an appendix to Rameau's *Les Indes Galantes* of 1735, but there
is no contemporary evidence that it was ever sung during performances,
and one might wonder how the Countess came to know it so well. For
Strauss's purpose, however, it had a very positive significance, being a
rare example in Rameau where the words are the merest pretext for a
piece of pretty music.

The music changes back to reminiscences of the Sextet (Exx. 5 and
6) alternating with Ex. 8 as the banter of brother and sister fluctuates, he
deliberating over which of her artistic admirers she will end by choosing, she retorting that his infatuation with Clairon will lead him beyond
a simple predilection for drama. The contretemps turns into an operetta-
like duet recalling something of the manner of Lehár or Kalmán though
inevitably coloured by Strauss's harmonic ingenuity.

It comes to a formal close with a cadence in which the two sing in
unison, followed by a miniature orchestral ritornello leading to Scene
3. The Director has returned with Flamand and Oliver to tell their
patrons that all is now ready and rehearsals may begin for the birthday
celebration. He begins by outlining the proposals which are organized
around contributions from all three of them, but goes on to expound
his own grandiose share—a *Huldigungsfestspiel*, that is to say, a 'festival
play of homage' (Strauss accompanies his pompous announcement with
impressive chordal motifs, see below, Exx. 23 and 24). This is greeted

by expressions of derision from the other two. The quarrel which springs up is, however, quickly interrupted by Clairon's arrival and the Count hurries to meet her.

The first part of Scene 4 centres round the exposition of Drama—i.e. words without music. Clairon's entrance evokes admiration from one and all (even Flamand concedes that she would be irresistible if only she could sing) while the orchestra elaborates appropriately on Ex. 8 together with a new and gaily tripping little theme also connected with the figure of the actress in her lighter mood:

Ex. 13

Clairon receives their compliments with elegance and humour and at once addresses herself to the purpose which has brought her. She is to interpret—together with the Count—the new lines Olivier has written which consist of a poetic love-scene in dialogue culminating in a Sonnet. The inspiration has only come to Olivier that very morning. Strauss's orchestra quietly sinking to rest, Clairon and the Count read aloud from their parts in unaccompanied poetic declamation.

There is no question over the effect produced by the beautiful words (of which due acknowledgement is made to Ronsard at the appropriate place in the score) and Clairon in high good-humour praises the Count's diction and professional style (Ex. 13). She then turns to the Director and in mock melodrama instructs him to apply his skill to producing their dramatic fragment on the stage (Ex. 10).

Nothing loath, he takes her and the Count off to the adjacent theatre leaving the Countess with Flamand and Olivier[10] to compare their differing reactions to the recital they have just heard. The Countess is impressed by the sincerity of the fervent words Olivier has put in the mouth of his lover but he is not satisfied with the way they were rendered. In particular he had intended the verses as a eulogy on the beauty of the Countess herself, and with great intensity Olivier declaims the Sonnet once more, now directly to her face.

[10] La Roche's insistence that Olivier remain behind, saying that he cannot allow the author to be present at the staging of his work, underlines the anachronism of his role.

The adoration she inspires in Olivier is reflected by a motif of typical
Straussian eroticism which makes its appearance here for the first time.

Ex. 14

In remarkable contrast, however, to Ex. 14 with its romanticism stands
the period formality of the music which, as Olivier recites, Flamand improvises on the harpsichord.

Ex. 15

Flamand has been enormously taken with the poem and, seizing the
sheet of verses, rushes off to the music room with it much to Olivier's
alarm. In the fifth scene the poet, addressing the Countess as Madeleine
for the first time, reveals his torment at the thought that a composer is
tampering with the verses in which he has been trying to express his
devotion.

The problem is one of fundamental ethics and extremely complex.
It had, moreover, an especial relevance to Strauss not only in relationship to his operatic but also to his vast Lieder output. There is a strong
argument that at its best poetry contains its own music and can only
suffer if actual music is added since this inevitably swamps the music of
the words. (Strauss's own support of this view is quoted at the beginning of the next chapter, see p. 247.)

To present a logical thesis in terms of dramatic dialogue is never an
easy matter and it is doubtful whether Olivier's passionate scene does
more than touch the fringe. Yet it poses the question attractively:
Olivier is challenged by the Countess to express his feelings for her in
simple prose, and this he is constitutionally unable to do. But from
where she sits the Countess can watch Flamand at work composing in
the adjoining room. She restrains Olivier from going to disturb him

and tries to persuade him that, so far from doing harm, composition may give a new and more enduring life to the words even though the music represents the courtship of a rival.

Here is the first real opportunity for Strauss to allow the music of the opera itself a freer rein. For, beneath its dialectics, the duet is a miniature love-scene and develops the Countess's Ex. 9 and Olivier's surging Ex. 14 in a fine piece of symphonic effusion to which fragments of the Sextet representing Flamand's music provide an undercurrent. Moreover, when the Countess gives it as her opinion that, much as one may treasure the words of a poet, they may not plumb all the hidden depths, Strauss illustrates the argument by relating one of the phrases from Olivier's outburst to the well-known descending phrase from the 'Lausch, Geliebter' melody in the *Tristan* love-duet, references to which are integrated into the texture. This passage links up, therefore, with the point Strauss made in his letter quoted above (p. 183).

9

The duet ends as Olivier, full of confidence in the justice of his cause, entreats the Countess to make her choice and crown the victor. Hearing these last words Flamand comes running in and, flourishing his completed manuscript, claims the prize for himself. Quietly the Countess assures him that he has her close attention and in Scene 6 the Sonnet, now fully assembled with music matched to the words, is presented for her (and our) consideration by Flamand who sings to his own accompaniment on the harpsichord.

There is an analogy here, of which Strauss must certainly have been conscious, with *Die Meistersinger* where the power of music added to words is also proclaimed even though Wagner, despite his avowed intentions, ended up by begging the question. For however much he believed in the quality and importance of his verses in conveying Walther's poetic vision, there is no doubt in the listener's mind that it is purely his overriding genius as a musician which ultimately wins Walther the laurel wreath.

Admittedly Strauss seems not to have set out to give his Preislied that irresistible quality which sweeps all before it; nevertheless one cannot repress a certain disappointment at the degree to which Flamand's setting has changed the character of Olivier's passionate love-song. The music is tender but coolly self-possessed, and also more than a little mannered in its combination of stiff period formality and sophisticated Straussian harmonies; so that when the Countess, just like Eva and the people of Nürnberg, is carried away by what she hears, one witnesses her enthusiasm with interest, rather than heartfelt agreement.

Yet Strauss clearly realized that Flamand should not score a conclusive victory at such an early point in the opera, and seen in this light the exquisite little setting could be said to serve its purpose very well.

Ex. 16[11]

(An interesting feature of the song is its five-fold bar-structure which Strauss, determined that it should not go unobserved, indicates in the score.)

Throughout Flamand's performance very soft strings have been supporting the harpsichord. The last cadence being reached, the melody is given in full for a second time though now in the orchestra (with the addition of woodwind) as background to Olivier's and the Countess's reactions. While Flamand is hard at work making last minute corrections, Olivier mutters gloomily that it is all just as he feared, and he refuses to share the Countess's joy which he interprets as a victory for Flamand.

Impervious to the combined effect of words and music, Olivier is only conscious of the disruption of his carefully wrought symmetry and the submerging of the rhymes which now go for nothing. He speaks scathingly of the musician's technique and complains not without justification that, in a setting of this kind, the meaning of the music is

---

[11] In addition to being transposed down a third from the original and over-exacting key (which gave too many very high notes for the tenor), the sonnet differs in a number of particulars from the first version which Strauss had sent to Swarowsky with a grateful dedication. These differences are discussed in great detail by Tenschert in the *Tempo* article (see p. 193, footnote).

more readily communicated than that of the words to which no one really listens. As a result he now no longer knows whether the Sonnet is his or Flamand's. With a twist of his meaning the Countess declares that now it is hers and she seizes the manuscript from the delighted Flamand. However much Olivier may resist, he and Flamand are herewith united, she says, through her Sonnet.

At this moment the Director reappears with the purpose, he explains apologetically to the Countess, of taking Olivier away for rehearsal: he, La Roche, has made some excellent cuts for which he wants Olivier's sanction. There is some brief, good-humoured by-play over the propriety of this kind of amputation and Olivier runs off laughing with the Director leaving this time Flamand alone with the Countess.

Scene 7 accordingly gives the antithesis to the preceding duet, a fervent outburst in which Flamand—like his colleague—pours out his love.

As sure of his success as Olivier was before, Flamand in his turn also beseeches the Countess for a decision between them. A new phrase is now added to Ex. 14; Exx. 17 and 17a give its initial and basic form as well as one of its many developments. Oddly enough both versions are reminiscent of motifs from earlier Strauss operas, Ex. 17(x) recalling the phrase 'Mein Elemer' from *Arabella* and Ex. 17a—with particular relevance—to one of the themes of the young Composer from the Vorspiel to *Ariadne II*.

Ex. 17

(cf Ex. 21 ⌐x⌐ Chapter XVIII)

Ex. 17a

(cf Ex. 51b Chapter X)

Naturally themes from the Sextet are also indigenous to the scene, since they represent Flamand's creative spirit which has been stimulated by his passion for the Countess.

But plead as he may, he is unable to sway the Countess in his favour,
moved as she acknowledges she has been by the vivid way his music
has brought Olivier's bare words to life. This success of the musician is
integral to the message of the opera and therefore the Countess's words
of encouragement to Flamand, which contain a premonition of her
ultimately insoluble dilemma, are sung against a soaring version of the
sonnet melody which is to become the central motif of her closing
scene.

Ex. 18

In an ardent outburst Flamand tells of how he came to fall in love,
silently watching the Countess from a secluded corner of her library as
she sat reading a volume of Pascal on the philosophy of love; when she
left the room, still in ignorance that she was being watched, he too
studied the book which had so engrossed her.

Ex. 19

The Countess is touched by his account, but surprised that a musician should have been so affected by the power of the word, properly
the province of his rival. She and Flamand quote Pascal to each other in
support of their arguments, and Flamand receives a promise that the
Countess will give her answer at eleven the following day in the library
where his love was born.

Overcome with excited anticipation he impetuously plants a kiss on her arm and rushes off, leaving her greatly troubled in mind.

10

There is an extended orchestral interlude while the Countess struggles to compose herself; falling thoughtfully back into an armchair, she considers Flamand and all that has just happened. Ex. 19 re-enters and together with Exx. 17a and 18 mingles with phrases drawn from the Sextet material in a warm flowing line.

During the latter part of the interlude, sounds have been heard from the adjacent theatre; Clairon and the Count are declaiming amidst critical comments from the Director. An incident is then caused (not reflected in the beautiful curve of Strauss's orchestral cantilena) by the prompter being found to be fast asleep—thus establishing for future reference the presence of this semi-comical figure. The outburst of general hilarity disturbs the Countess's reverie and, rising from her chair, she rings for her Major-domo to bring the chocolate, as the interlude music tails away into silence.

The Count now rejoins the Countess, full of gay enthusiasm from his exhilarating rehearsal with Clairon, and in Scene 8 they continue the argument that had begun in Scene 2, a more diffuse and complicated lay-out of the action than Krauss's original plan to limit their entretien to a single dialogue sandwiched between the parallel love-scenes of Poet and Composer (see above, p. 191).

Nevertheless the revised scenic juxtaposition allows the Countess to tell her brother of the two declarations she has received, and so enables them to discuss what logical outcome might result. He hears with some surprise how Flamand has set the Sonnet to music, so touching her heart which the words alone had failed to do. To his query where this can lead to, she answers 'perhaps, to opera', the first mention of this term, which is the thesis of the work.

One might perhaps have expected Strauss to accord some vital motif to so important a new idea, but this he hardly does. At times of point-blank interrogation over which art, poetry or music, is to receive the victory Strauss had introduced a quasi-theme consisting of a to-and-fro alternation of chords, the contrasting tonalities of which stand each for one of the competitors. Since opera is to be postulated as a way in which *both* are victorious, this same quasi-motif serves here too, viz:

Ex. 20

(a)

(Flamand, Olivier to whom do you hold out the prize?)

(b)

(an opera!)

Bearing in mind that the composition of *Capriccio* overlapped with work on the orchestration of *Die Liebe der Danae* it may not be too fanciful to comment, amongst the deliberate plethora of allusions, on the similarity of this idea—representing 'opera'—to the Goldzauber motif from this newest of Strauss's own operas.

With the reappearance of the other characters the ninth scene, the centre-piece, begins. Clairon, Olivier and the Director have come from the theatre, their rehearsal finished, and Flamand also returns.

All are thus reunited both for the main discussion, which is the *raison d'être* of the opera, and for a series of set pieces, which will spark off the different aspects of the argument as well as preventing the work from turning into a static display of dialectics.

The scene is long and complex, but is subdivided into sharply differentiated sections, viz:

(a) Short conversation leading to
(b) Ballet: Three Dances
(c) Fugal debate
(d) Italian opera: Duet of the Italian singers
(e) Conversation leading to La Roche's Great Plan Part 1
(f) Laughter ensemble
(g) La Roche's Great Plan Part 2
(h) Quarrel ensemble
(i) La Roche's Speech and Apologia
(j) Lyrical ensemble leading to decision to write opera and choice of subject.

From this resumé it is clear that the pith of the work lies here, without comprehension of which most of Strauss's purpose in writing the opera must go for nothing, despite the enchantment of the music.

The opening conversation not only establishes an atmosphere of relaxation, but also plants one or two necessary details of the later action. A brief post-mortem on the rehearsal and its comic incident leads to talk about the prompter while Clairon, being pressed by the Count to stay to supper, refuses as she will have to memorize a new part in a Voltaire production. As the company sit down and are waited upon by lackeys with refreshments the Director then presents a dancer, one of his protégées. Accompanied by three musicians (violin, cello and harpsichord) she enters and performs a Passepied, Gigue and Gavotte.

The music (which is performed entirely on stage, the orchestra remaining silent) is a pastiche of Couperin, a composer with whose style Strauss was at this time preoccupied. For it was precisely during the composition of *Capriccio* during 1940–1 that Clemens Krauss brought Strauss's attention back to his earlier arrangements of Couperin's clavecin *Pièces* and persuaded him to add new movements both for the ballet *Verklungene Feste* and for the subsequently published orchestral *Divertimento* op. 86.[12]

Strauss found, therefore, no difficulty in supplying three appropriately stylized little movements, though allowing himself a certain

[12] See Vol. II, pp. 275 et seq.

latitude in the course of their progress. Yet, original as they are, and very Straussian in treatment, they often recall the genuine models on which they are based and which Strauss was busily transcribing. (Cf. the Gigue, for example, with La Linotte Effarouchée from the 14ème Ordre, incorporated by Strauss into the fifth movement of his *Divertimento*.)

During the Passepied the Director tells the fascinated Count how he found this entrancing artist and enticed her away from some aristocratic protector; the Gigue, on the other hand, becomes the background for an unhappy exchange between Olivier and Clairon, showing that at some time in the recent past they have been lovers. Clairon firmly snubs him and the Director, having noticed the incident, comments to Olivier that he seems unlikely to feature in Clairon's memoirs, thereby alluding to Clairon's place in real life, for a volume of her *Memoires et réflexions sur l'art dramatique* did in fact appear in 1799 bringing a much needed income to her old age.

II

In the introductory Sextet we had an instance of music serving nothing but its own ends, i.e. absolute music. In the Sonnet we were shown music in its capacity of enhancing words, serving their meaning while also supplying a further significance of its own. Lastly we have just had an illustration of music providing the rhythm for a choreographic display, an additional facet emphasized by Strauss at a very early point in the work's gestation (see p. 184) and endorsed by Krauss when he took over from Gregor.

Now is clearly the moment for the debate to begin and so, no sooner are the dancer's and musicians' backs turned than the Director comments that in this case at least Flamand's music (Ex. 1) is merely a vehicle, an accessory, to another entirely different art. Flamand naturally disagrees and the argument is in full swing.

Strauss and Krauss originally saw the debate as an entirely independent vignette from which would spring the title of the whole work, as for instance:

'The Language of Tones'
Theatrical Fugue in 1 Act

Even when this plan was changed something of the fundamental idea remained and the fugue itself is now headed:

Ex. 21

Fuge (Diskussion über das Thema : Wort oder Ton)
Allegro moderato
OLIVIER

Tanz und Musik   stehn im Bann des Rhythmus, ihm un - ter - wor-fen seit e - wi - ger Zeit.
(Dance and music stand in thrall to rhythm, subjected to it since eternity....)

Despite so formal a statement, Strauss is only faithful to the concept of fugal design in so far as the section contains entries of Ex. 21 in fair profusion in the midst of other matters. In this respect it is far less of a true ensemble fugue than, for example, the famous Finale of Verdi's *Falstaff*. To begin with there is no intention of treating the words of the discussion fugally together with the musical theme. The argument flows naturally as in real life and Strauss's purpose in setting it to music is to keep the texture alive and clear so that the listener's interest is never lost even though the conversation revolves around ideas instead of dramatic action.

The first strand in the exchange of views concerns, then, the relative dependence of verse and music on rhythm. Flamand, to whose art rhythm is admittedly indigenous, makes the point that poetic metre is, on the contrary, an artificial restriction, so striking at the root of the very nature of poetry, of which it could be argued that the stronger the sense of rhythm the closer it moves towards song and hence to music. In so doing, it is able to extend its meaning beyond the mere apparent significance of the words which constitute its being, and achieves that communication of thought normally the sole province of music. Who can say what music is 'about'? Olivier's claim that this quality of indefinability makes music inferior to the precise meaning of word-images presupposes a lack of sensibility not only to the inexplicable depths of which music is capable but equally to the similar potential of poetry itself. Moreover it must not be overlooked that the two arts are capable of the most extraordinary *rapprochement* as when, in Edith Sitwell's *Façade* for example, words are used for their qualities of sound and associations rather than their intrinsic meaning.

Nevertheless, however much poetry is generally representational in a way that music need not be, both can be made to serve theatrical ends. When this happens, the pre-eminence of the one over the other becomes academic in the eyes of the La Roches of this world. The conversation accordingly swings now to the integrity of the theatre in trying to impose ethics of showmanship upon the twin ideologies of the poet and musician, in whatever capacities.

'Showmanship', 'theatricality', are coloured words implying a sacrifice of artistry to effect which is not necessarily consistent with their best aspects. Flamand's outburst, extolling the sublimity of music in the abstract and rejecting subservience to such base purposes, is a purely emotional reaction and it is significant that although his passionate words 'Musik ist eine erhabene Kunst!' inevitably recall the parallel phrase of the young Composer in the Vorspiel to *Ariadne II*, Strauss carefully refrains from pursuing the allusion with a musical reference.

The truth is rather that music in the theatre makes a human contribution of inestimable value. For at the highest level drama can provide one of the most vital experiences of a civilized society. To view this with Flamand as no more than a trick is a failure in perception as serious as any lack of artistic appreciation. Strauss and Clemens Krauss express their convictions through the Countess's retort that the stage reveals to us the secret of reality by means of a gripping symbol of life. 'We see ourselves', she says, 'as if through a magic mirror'.

But the simile of a *Zauberspiegel* set Strauss's mind working in another direction. Twice before had 'Spiegel' (a mirror) featured in his output and the first, *Eulenspiegel*, had been quoted both as word and music in the second, the song-cycle *Krämerspiegel*. The ramifications of this most remarkable piece of satire are described later.[13] It suffices here to isolate the extended melody which Strauss introduced into two of the songs, given in the relevant chapter as Ex. 88. Its place in *Krämerspiegel* is at no time part of the settings, but serves as Interlude or Postlude in a symbolic capacity, representing the unsullied nature of musical inspiration in contrast with the materialistic world, all too eager to derive profit from genius.

Strauss's purpose in extracting this melody with its symbolic overtones was two-fold, as he explained to an enthusiastic Clemens Krauss when seeking his colleague's opinion on such self-borrowing: firstly to break the monotony of too much recitative during the discussion, and secondly to rescue a really very beautiful melody from guaranteed obscurity in its original, somewhat risqué setting. Whether for these reasons or for other more personal ones which he did not choose to reveal it was certainly close to his heart, for it is not simply referred to *en passant* here, but returns at length on several subsequent occasions

[13] See p. 355.

during the opera culminating in the famous moonlight interlude before the Countess's final scene.

Each of the contestants, Director, Poet, Musician, now overstating his case for supremacy, the Countess (Ex. 9) invokes Gluck as the genius who has established the existence of music drama (Ex. 20). Her remark is immediately challenged by the Count; for although she as a music-lover sees opera to be the culminating art-form which triumphantly combines all the others, there is an opposing point of view which is extremely wide-spread.

Appreciation of opera relies on the absolute acceptance of a number of conventions, without which it can only appear as a monstrous and intolerable absurdity. Opera is normally carried on in song regardless of the various dramatic requirements. Any lapse into the spoken voice requires a violent adjustment in the listener which amounts to a drama-tic effect in itself, as does the return to singing. In the *Singspiel* this to and fro between song and speech is part of the form and thus produces its own problems since the abruptness of transition does not in any way become minimized through frequency. Here is, of course, one of the main reasons for the various misguided attempts to short-circuit the difficulty by adding recitatives to works like *Carmen* and *Freischütz*. Acute as the hazards of spoken dialogue may be, it is part of the constitu-tion and intention of these works, which are damaged instead of im-proved by interference.

The reverse would be equally true were the much despised recitative to be jettisoned in favour of spoken dialogue, thus inserting a series of jolts for which the composer had made no allowance. The Count echoes the sentiments of innumerable followers when he groans aloud at the idea of recitative. Yet recitative has the basic advantage of continuity, minimizing the jolts in fact, and indeed beautifully constructed recita-tives such as Mozart's in the Da Ponte operas are far easier for opera singers to make dramatically convincing than the superficially natural-istic speech of *Zauberflöte* or *Fidelio*. Although apparently stylized and illogical, recitative is no more so when intelligently performed than the entire operatic convention of which it forms a part.

Once accepted, instead of barely tolerated or even debunked, it can be made to merge imperceptibly in and out of the 'through-composed' sections, as Mozart initiated so brilliantly, leading to the flexibility of Wagner and Strauss himself. The stepping-stone was the accompanied recitative, where the continuo is replaced by the orchestra, a device which Gluck played so vital a role in developing (as Flamand reminds the company, who make no attempt to belittle it).

But if the music is to be continuous, then there is no limit to the *coups de théâtre* which have to be executed within its context. To complain, as the Count does, that commands, political meetings or death scenes are carried on willy-nilly within the frame-work of song is to misunderstand the part played by music in opera. In return for a sacrifice of actual verisimilitude, this musical emphasis offers an intensification of emotional and spiritual experience unrivalled in the history of spectacle—but on the one condition that certain questions are never asked.

To protest that by the time the fugitives have finished singing 'We must fly' while standing motionless upon the stage they will long have been caught; that Hunding could never sleep soundly through the overwhelming noise of Siegmund and Sieglinde singing against Wagner's mammoth orchestra however strong his sleeping draught, and so on; this is merely to collapse the balloon which can carry the listener to a world of intense emotional participation such as only poetry and music can create. In terms of real life the third scene of *Walküre* Act 1 lasts far less than the half-hour it takes in performance and would have made hardly any sound. The operatic time and sound scales take place in totally different dimensions from those of reality and are answerable only to artistic formal requirements. To find opera absurd (as the Count claims in the famous passage: 'Eine Oper ist ein absurdes Ding' to the accompaniment of the first long return of the *Krämerspiegel* melody) is for ever to miss that sympathetic dramatic participation which is the unequalled splendour of opera.

There is, however, a more practical objection to the sheer decibels of the Wagnerian (or Straussian) orchestra: unless it be judiciously curbed it simply drowns the singers who may be driven to screaming at the total expense of words and voices alike; the Director's complaint has obvious reason on its side. Yet, if on the contrary unduly restrained, much of the orchestra's own intrinsic glory, no inconsiderable part of the whole, is sadly sacrificed. How important, then, is clarity of words? Indeed, will they possibly be really understood when listened to for the first time unless the music be coldly and methodically relegated to subsidiary importance? The Count ruthlessly takes it for granted that they never can be heard, and that in any case they are not worth hearing.

The probability is that no ideal compromise will ever be found and that for true enjoyment of opera some pre-knowledge of the words will remain a *sine qua non*. Hofmannsthal already recognized this when he insisted so vehemently on the circularization of his libretti. By *Aegyptishe Helena* he had even become such a realist that he begged for the libretto to be distributed with the programmes and the house lights left up so that his text could be read and followed during the performance.

Well may the Count say that he and his companions are in the middle of the chief bone of contention of their time. As Strauss and Clemens Krauss realized all too clearly, it has remained so until the present day. What they purposely do not take into account, however, is the basic pre-eminence of music in the partnership; i.e. that an opera with music of sufficient genius will live regardless of the merits of its libretto. Their reasons were two-fold. Firstly, total acceptance of any such consideration would make nonsense of their opera; and secondly over the last decades the axiom that music must always take priority has itself come strongly into disrepute. Yet, loath though one may be to admit it, once music loses its lead the dangerous situation arises which is threatening many an operatic scene today and has led to the decline of opera itself in contemporary music, namely the tendency for composers so to subordinate their contribution to the clarity of the words that the music risks becoming the merest overlay. This has the additional effect of throwing an unprecedented spotlight upon the quality of the libretto which as a result can easily become embarrassing if anything short of a literary masterpiece. Hence, instead of a composer or conductor, it is the La Roches of our world who are emerging pre-eminent in the opera house as formerly they were in the theatre. It follows naturally that they must in turn become more sympathetic to music as well as more knowledgeable, so that it is quite in character that it should be La Roche himself who nostalgically recalls the original function of opera as a vehicle for beautiful singing; the classical *bel canto* now, he says, is all but dead. Clairon makes fun of his edict which Olivier calls exaggerated, but the Countess hails it as an excuse to ask that La Roche allow them to hear an example before it is too late. He therefore introduces the two Italians and the Fugue is over.

12

Strauss's pangs over the Metastasio excerpt were to a large extent prompted by an instinct that it would damage their thesis to poke fun at Italian opera.

But Clemens Krauss managed ultimately to convince him that there was no need to incur this danger. 'On the contrary', he wrote, 'the piece which the Italian singers perform must be an excellent piece of music excepting only in its total disregard of the words: it could consist, then, of a glorious effusion of *bel canto* melody which might perhaps be in direct contradiction to the sense of the words. Coloratura doesn't need to play any part in it; the utility operas of Rossini and Donizetti belong to a much later period while the songs of the *castrati* were at the time of Gluck for the greater part purest Solfeggi.'[14]

There is, therefore, little attempt to imitate a specifically Italian style in the setting of the Metastasio text, and much of the Duet is reminiscent, if anything, of Strauss's neo-classic manner of the scenes between Henry and Aminta from *Die Schweigsame Frau*.

Ex. 22

[14] *Solfeggi* were exhibitions of vocal technique based on exercise formuli. Rossini wrote a most amusing parody of them in a little piece more recently popularized in Britten's transcription *Matinées Musicales*.

The Countess observes that the melody does not fit the words, a criticism which could with equal justification be applied to innumerable genuine operatic examples of the kind. This is the point. Such pieces of vocal music used the words as the merest pretext, making no effort to retain either their scansion or mood. As the Count says (to his characteristic Ex. 11), so long as the cantilena is beautiful it does not matter what the words mean. Hence there is no need for them to be understood for the broad progress of the drama to be followed. Equally logically they can be in a foreign language. Much of the colour of Ex. 21 derives not from the meaning of the text but from its Italianate flavour. Wagner sung in French can sound oddly like Massenet, Puccini in German like d'Albert. The sacrifice—bearing in mind how much an audience not already conversant with words and action may expect to learn during the performance—is often very considerable. Performances of, for example, *Boris Godounov* in Russian, *Katya Kabanova* in Czech, *Bluebeard's Castle* in Hungarian, become incomparably rewarding for the well-prepared devotee who does not speak one word of the languages but who knows the *sound* of both text and music, the wedding of which is at best an integral part of the whole conception. For him a transcribed version adapted to his own tongue may be hardly more than a study for the real thing, similar to a print of an oil painting.

This thorny question has, of course, especial relevance to *Prima le Parole*. On the surface the present opera seems to lose all *raison d'être* unless every word is understood as much as if it were spoken drama. Presumably no performance should be allowed other than in the language of the country. Perhaps Strauss took it for granted since in German-speaking countries, as elsewhere in Europe, this is in any case the regular custom and which led to Stravinsky's experiment in *Oedipus Rex*, where the opera is sung in Latin and explained at intervals during the drama by a commentator *speaking* in the vernacular.

But the fact remains that Strauss's work is loved today, a quarter of a century after its creation, less for the lucidity of its arguments than for its beautiful and captivating music.

The Italians warble a second verse of their duet but the Count has lost interest and can be heard beneath the closing cadence asking Clairon whether she will allow him to take her home. The party breaks up and the Countess rises to thank and congratulate the singers. As they sit down at her gracious invitation to partake of the refreshments, the Director tells her that they are to contribute, if only in minor degree, to his immense plans for her birthday celebration programme. She accordingly presses him to divulge at long last this closely guarded secret and, as the attention of the others is caught, he obliges.

Strauss had already in Scene 3 made reference to the stately themes which portray La Roche's project, and here they are appropriately reintroduced and developed. A short but impressive motif presents the many-sided scheme as a whole, a 'grandiose *Azione teatrale*' as La Roche calls it:

Ex. 23

while the first part, an allegorical representation, is described by:

Ex. 24

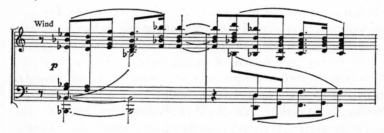

The subject of the allegory is to be 'The Birth of Pallas Athene', and La Roche tells his fascinated listeners something of the grotesque myth on which it is to be based. They give vent to various expressions of incredulity and amusement as they hear the preposterous details—this is one of the more extravagantly lurid of the Greek legends—of how Athene's father Zeus, following in his own father's footsteps,[15] swallowed her mother whole. In authentic mythology this was Zeus' first wife, Metis, and he performed the horrid deed lest the child should turn out to be a boy who would supplant him; upon which Athene sprang from the head of her father, Hephaestus having conveniently cracked it open with an axe for the purpose.

Strauss was obviously revelling in all this although, with Danae and

[15] See above, p. 110 footnote.

Jupiter still in the foreground of his mind, he and Krauss mixed their sources, introducing from the other opera the god's fear of Juno's jealous vengeance against his mistresses.

It is all by the by, however, and the laughter of the party soon merges into hilarious ridicule of La Roche himself for his choice of such a subject. With the utmost skill Strauss turned the ribaldry into an elaborate ensemble, and actually so labelled it, viz.: 'Oktett (Erster Teil: Lachensemble)', like the fugal discussion which was similarly entitled, a curiously self-conscious suggestion of formality through set numbers in an opera which, like its predecessors, is in all essentials *durchcomponiert*.

With engaging gaiety the different characters pursue their individual lines of thought, many of which are reflected as occasion warrants in the orchestral texture binding the whole together. Naturally the strongest motivic element comes from themes concerning the Director and his professional theatricality, Exx. 10, 23 and 24, to which must be added a further motif linked with La Roche's vision of his Athene saga;

Ex. 25

Ex. 25(x) first arises together with the chordal passage Ex. 24 to which it acts both as introduction and continuation before rapidly acquiring individual life on its own.

La Roche is obviously somewhat offended at the jovial reception of his cherished brain-child, a reaction which the Countess quickly observes although even she cannot prevent herself chuckling at the ingenuous side here revealed by the Grand Old Man of the theatre who has retained his youth through his enthusiasms.

Olivier and Flamand hold up to scorn the idea of the allegory, both dwelling on Hephaestus' act of splitting open Zeus' skull which they view anachronistically as the potential centre-piece of some Elektra-like spectacle with chorus and a welter of percussion effects in the orchestra (the latter introduced by Strauss in reality as Flamand shouts 'Tschin, tschin, Bum-bum').

Even the Count, drama-lover though he is, finds the idea hopelessly head-in-air and only Clairon can find words of praise for La Roche's courage and forward-looking approach to his métier.

The Octet is completed by the voices of the two Italians. The soprano (true to the composer of *Schlagobers*) waxes ecstatic over the quality of the Torte she is guzzling, much to the disgust of her companion whose rather unworthy worry is lest their hosts should forget to pay them the promised honorarium in the heat of the argument.

At last the Countess, seeing the Director's discomfiture, goes up to him with words of conciliation. Gently apologizing for their amateurish behaviour, she asks him about the second part of his scheme.

But this turns out to be even more colossal, a representation of the Fall of Carthage on a scale only comparable with our present-day million-dollar motion picture epics, and La Roche is soon interrupted in his effusive descriptions by the outraged Olivier and Flamand. At once the second part of Strauss's Octet breaks out, formally headed in the score just like its forerunner:

Ex. 26

Oktett (Zweiter Teil : Streitensemble)

This time, however, instead of an ensemble of laughter it is one of quarrelling and is carried forward with the utmost vivacity. The Countess is very upset that her innocent question has only made matters worse, her lament providing the first contrasting element to Ex. 26.

Ex. 27

O   weh!.. Jetzt fallen sie   ü-ber ihn her. Mein Rettungsversuch ist gründlich missglückt Die Situation ist für ihn.
(cf the Countess' Ex. 9 with its initial descending ninth)

Both the figures ⌐ x ⌐ and ⌐ y ⌐ in the above example play a substantial role in the musical development of this much longer and more elaborate of the two examples.

Unlike the *Lachensemble*, however, the actual quarrelling of the title only concerns Olivier, Flamand and the Director, which latter is himself soon reduced to silence by the unlooked-for vehemence of the two artists. As far as they can see, it is no longer a question of 'Words or Music' but instead, as they put it, 'Flying machines or Trap-doors', and, pouring indignation upon ridicule, they dissociate themselves from any such hare-brained project.

Meanwhile the Count has become perturbed to see La Roche thus apparently torn to pieces, although Clairon assures him that the Director knows very well how to look after himself (repetitions of Ex. 23). The whole mêlée of opinions is combined into the excitable Allegro based on Exx. 26 and 27 upon which are superimposed the voices of the two Italians singing the melody of their duet to words satirically adapted to express a farewell, not to each other, but to their beloved honorarium, which they will never see. The general hullabaloo is strongly reminiscent of the noisy scenes from *Die Schweigsame Frau*.

13

Suddenly the ensemble is cut short at its height by La Roche who, losing his temper, thunders forth to the amazement—but admiration—of everyone. His tirade is justly one of the most famous passages in the opera although opinions are divided about its merits. The case for the prosecution of that school of thought which finds it tedious and offensive has its spokesman in George Marek who belittled it bluntly as a 'conceited lecture'. But this so dismally understates its monumental egocentricity, that it is as well to examine Clemens Krauss's expressed purpose when first he drafted it. He wrote to Strauss:

> . . . [La Roche] should justify himself as the specialist of the theatre whose duties even embrace light music, but only where it is on an artistic level, Singspiel, or good comic operas and ballets . . . [he] should nevertheless remain a sympathetic advocate for practical thinking in the theatre, which also supports great art out of its proceeds and so has made it possible for many a talent to come forward. His speech should finish comically and bombastically, perhaps so that he blows his own trumpet and crowns himself with the halo of the Art Patron . . . The Director is the one whose mission it is from his own experience to chastise all that is bad in the theatre . . . As a result he somehow remains a sympathetic figure and never sinks to the level of a provincial hack. Such a man would scarcely have been invited by the Countess to her château to make arrangements for her birthday celebrations, and under the production of such a one Clairon would also not play her role in the poet's piece—It is in this way, I believe, that the scene of the Director's plans and of his self-justification should roughly unfold.

It is readily seen that the portrayal of La Roche still remains sur-rounded with immense dignity even if he is allowed at times to become overwhelmingly pompous. After all, Krauss was himself an acknow-ledged master of the stage who undoubtedly knew many analo-gous figures amongst his professional colleagues. This was no place for false modesty and it must finally be remembered that if, when speaking of himself, La Roche takes it for granted that he is really a very great man, he represents the embodiment of Strauss's supreme gesture of homage to that much loved doyen of the theatre, Max Reinhardt.

In rounding, therefore, upon his accusers La Roche, while conceding their artistic gifts, sternly challenges their presumption; how dare they stand in judgement where he is king and they the purest beginners? Turning first to Olivier, he reminds the poet that however well his verses may have sounded when declaimed by Clairon (Exx. 8 and 15) his sense of dramatic construction had proved decidedly fallible. Passing to Flamand, he is prepared to give him the benefit of the doubt where the creation of a pretty piece of chamber music was concerned (Exx. 2 and 3(x))—he is no connoisseur in that field and was in any case fast asleep whilst it was being played—but in the wider scope of music drama (Ex. 20) Flamand has still to make his mark.

He then tirades against the appalling slough into which taste has fallen in the capital, i.e. Paris, as one needs to remind oneself; La Roche is now Strauss's mouthpiece and the theme of the Commedia dell'Arte figures from *Ariadne* (Ex. 24 from Chapter X) is introduced as La Roche talks of the sad state in which Comedy finds itself. So far from being himself the enemy, he is a very saviour to the artist when Philistinism rears its head. With a vehement return of his Ex. 10 he hurls their ac-cusation back in the teeth of the two young men whom, he says, are equally guilty by their silence. It is the real adversary they should attack instead of him.

This takes him to his panegyric upon his own function. Initially introduced by Ex. 23, it is predominantly built upon an extended exposition of the noble-hearted Ex. 7. And certainly La Roche has no illusions about the exalted position he occupies, for it is he alone who preserves all that is fine and durable in art.

But it is again Strauss who is speaking when the Director, taking advantage of the opportunity specifically given him here by Clemens Krauss, says with the present day in mind:

Full of piety I guard the old
patiently awaiting the fruitful new,
expecting the works of genius of our time!
Where are the works which speak to the heart of the
    people?
which mirror their soul?
where are they?—I cannot find them, however hard I seek.
Only pale aesthetes look me in the face;
they ridicule the old and create nothing new. . . .

These are indeed the words of the ageing composer who in good faith once asked Hindemith, 'Why do you compose like that? You don't need to, you have talent.'

As in the theatre, so in opera: shadowy ghosts of phrases from earlier Strauss stage works stalk the music while gloomily he recalls some of the improbable, unlife-like characters he as well as others have misguidedly placed behind the foot-lights. Now his only concern is to conjure up real people, and La Roche reiterates this sentiment which was already expressed in Scene 1, at the first entry in the opera of Ex. 7, though the melodic range of that fine theme is here extended to far higher flights of declamation.

Ex. 28

With stern formality he challenges Olivier and Flamand—and this is the focal point of his harangue—to write the masterwork he and his stage are looking for. If they are unable to do this they forfeit the right to criticize men of his stature who, at the peak of their careers as he is, are the inspiration without which theatre itself could hardly survive. He speaks of but one of the many examples of great talent which he has brought to the fore and then, carried on the wings of his own grandiloquence, he pronounces once and for all the integrity of his aims and those of the theatre he represents.

Clemens Krauss had said that he should 'finish comically and bombastically' and so indeed he does. In a monstrous display of self-importance he pronounces his own epitaph: 'Here rests La Roche, the unforgettable, the immortal . . . beloved of the gods, held in wonder by mankind! Amen.'

There is general applause, capped by Clairon's enthusiastic but endearingly shrewd 'La Roche, you are monumental!' Flamand and Olivier sarcastically continue the Amens and the Italian Soprano, who has allowed too much wine to influence her emotional susceptibility, bursts into loud sobbing and has to be led off by her partner. Curiously enough, the Tenor's furious chiding suddenly changes from Italian to German just as the two singers disappear, suggesting perhaps that they are bogus and not of Italian origin at all.

It is, at best, an awkward moment and the Countess quickly takes the centre of the stage in order to seize on the one point in La Roche's monologue which is of the greatest practical value to the present discussion. If the theatre is threatened, as he says, then his invitation to the two young authors should at once be acted upon in the highly appropriate circumstances.

Alarmed, the Count groans to Clairon that he can see an opera being commissioned (Ex. 21), but the Countess knows what she is about. In a glowing solo she enlarges her theme: after dispute comes reconciliation in a combining of the arts under one roof. Clairon then takes up the thread and leading Olivier and Flamand to where the Countess stands, urges them to receive her in a symbolic role, that of goddess of Harmony in its broadest sense.

This is a purely lyrical episode, analogous possibly to the great Quintet from *Meistersinger*, and with the voices of the Poet, the Musician, and also La Roche joining in, it develops into an ensemble of homage to the Countess, a *Huldigungsquartett*, as it is described in the score. Musically it falls warmly and gracefully upon the ear with its predominantly lilting ⁶⁄₄ motion within which a number of relevant motifs are recalled and intertwined. The Countess's phrases arise from Ex. 27 which, in its many repetitions, blossoms in a variety of different directions. The *Krämerspiegel* melody is revived first by implication and then more directly, though still elegantly transformed in the prevailing rhythm, when she speaks to Flamand of his heaven-sent gift. Her reference to Olivier's poetic muse brings not only his Ex. 14 but the Tristan-like phrase which had featured so strongly in the scene where he had declared himself to her. Clairon's contribution easily incorporates her Ex. 8 to which this particular swinging pulse is already indigenous.

Only the Count has remained silent and at last he bursts out with his protest. He is clearly to be the victim of what he begins to view as a conspiracy. But the die is cast. His sister apologizes to the others that the only music he likes is marches (Ex. 11) and in high good humour they address themselves to the new practical problems which now confront them. Gaily, the Director gives his young collaborators a few words of advice, axioms which Strauss selected to head his lengthy preface (or *Geleitwort*,[16] as he called it) to the opera in the guise of a 'motto':

> To the Aria its due!
> Consideration for the singers!
> Not too loud the orchestra. . . .

and although Olivier and Flamand clearly regard La Roche as an old fogey nothing any more can upset the happy atmosphere.

The chief question is the subject on which the opera is to be based. Perhaps a little obviously, Olivier suggests *Ariadne auf Naxos* which Flamand dismisses on the grounds that it has been done too often before (quotation of Ariadne's Monologue Ex. 23 from Chapter X). Flamand then proposes *Daphne*, a suggestion which Strauss had originally intended to lead up to the actual performance of that opera, as we have seen (p. 195). Whereas that project had been set aside it amused Strauss to keep the idea of *Daphne* in discussion even though it would mean finding some plausible reason for throwing it out. So we find that Flamand is very keen (repeated entries of Exx. 26 and 39 from Chapter XIX) but Olivier points out the difficulties of mounting the Verwandlung scene on the stage (surprisingly since this is surely La Roche's province and we have just been hearing how little experience of the

---

[16] Literally: 'accompanying word'.

theatre the young poet has). La Roche on the other hand, is discouraged
at the prospect of going back again to classical legend, against which he
thought they had all set their minds.

14

Ironically it is the Count who comes up with the brain-wave (Ex. 11
strongly featured). Undoubtedly to make an opera out of themselves
and all that had just been happening would satisfy La Roche's wish to
portray real people (Exx. 10 and 23). But it would also pose a whole
host of new and intriguing problems particularly, Olivier hazards, in
view of the inescapable paucity of dramatic action.

At first wisps of their themes have been reflecting the instinctive
shock of the different characters at the astoundingly daring proposal,
but as each in turn is suddenly struck by its felicity they express their
delight in a new motif, henceforward to be associated with the Countess's opera itself:

Ex. 29

La Roche is the hardest to convince. He is not blind and in view of
what is going on he fears that the result could well prove more than a
little indiscreet.

However, despite the Countess's wry dig at her brother for being
malicious, she puts a bold face on the situation; it will depend, she
assures La Roche, on the delicacy of his production. Olivier is by now
entirely won over and can hardly wait to begin work, but Clairon
senses that it is time for the party to break up. She begins to make the
courtesies of departure in the course of which she improvises an elegant
little mock-canzonetta in praise of the Countess's Salons. The music is
based predominantly on Ex. 8, although the Count's part in making her
enjoyment complete is slyly suggested by a pair of interpolated entries
of his Ex. 11. The Countess, acting in traditionally regal manner, bids
farewell to her guests and herself withdraws, bringing to an end this
long central scene.

By contrast Scene 10 is brief and is concerned purely with the departure of the others. Olivier and Flamand have remained deeply under the spell of the Countess and hover round the door through which she has passed. Her exit has taken the form of a richly orchestrated return of the *Krämerspiegel* melody against which other motifs are contrapuntally interwoven: Exx. 1 (Flamand), 14 (Olivier), 8 (Clairon) and 27 (the Countess herself).

The Director then comes to life (Ex. 10) and rescues the two Italians, who have been lurking in the off-stage theatre. He waves aside their attempts to speak with reassurances that their money will not be forgotten. The Count escorts Clairon to her carriage, the music giving them a fine parting sweep of their Exx. 8 and 11, leaving Olivier and Flamand still disputing the Countess's favours. As at the beginning of the opera they quote Casti's title, though now in mock *galanterie* each to his opponent's advantage. At the same time each mutters to himself his real confidence in his own ultimate success.

Suddenly the Director returns, ostensibly to hurry the two young artists along as he is taking them back to Paris. They can talk plans as they go, he says; the important thing is that he himself should be made the central figure of their opera and that he is given a well planned and successful exit at the end. Since this *is* in truth his exit, one is suddenly reminded that *Capriccio* itself is supposed to be the product of Olivier's pen and that by a contrivance he has in his capacity of librettist actually managed to give La Roche the featured ending for which the Director is asking. Illogically one cannot help hoping he was pleased with it even though Olivier did not manage to include, as La Roche insists, a scene showing him in rehearsal, 'a veritable Field-marshal of the stage'. The little vignette is filled with La Roche's motifs which fade away as the stage is left momentarily empty. His last words tail into inaudibility and a memory of the fugal discussion Ex. 21 makes a subdued appearance on the basses, linking the music to the eleventh scene, the scene of the servants.

15

The part played in opera and drama by groups of servants makes a fascinating study, especially when they have scenes to themselves in which they comment, often with insight and wisdom lacking in their masters and mistresses, on the events of the drama. Perhaps the most famous, if weirdest, instance of the role of servants in modern theatre is that of Maeterlinck's *Pelléas et Mélisande*,[17] while Hofmannsthal's (and Strauss's own) *Elektra* naturally comes to mind in this context.

Strauss had always thought some commentary by the servants to be a good idea for this new opera about opera, giving the unsophisticated point of view of the Man in the Street. On the other hand, Krauss's proposal to particularize their roles each with a clearly differentiated character and artistic preference, seemed rather too complicated. Something more in the nature of a small chorus was nearer to Strauss's ideas, (when discussing the possibilities with Gregor he had cited as a model Verdi's pianissimo choruses in, for example, *Macbeth*) providing a nice contrast after the hurly-burly of the central argument.

In the end a compromise was reached based on a group of eight Diener. As Krauss said: '. . . but you will need a double-quartet, so that this scene will be to some extent chorally worked out. Eight lackeys are in any case not too many in such a château. . . .' Hence, although in the main they are treated as two antiphonal groups with four each of tenors and basses, they also contribute here and there as individuals. The first Diener, for example, is a particularly bucolic type who is principally concerned that the Italian Soprano has wolfed all the cake (Strauss accompanies his remark with the theme of that classic bucolic servant Sancho Panza from *Don Quixote*). Again, the Fifth Diener is singled out as an older man, who has understood something of La Roche's monologue which they have overheard and explains, as far as he can, the gist of it to the others. They, however, are scornful. No doubt, says one with an entertaining twist of the situation, they will write parts for the servants in their operas.

They have watched their master and mistress play-acting, and philosophize on how they, standing in the wings, can see through the foolishness of the world, the Count's intrigue with Clairon, the Countess's with her two artists (each is underlined by relevant motifs). Scathingly they dismiss the idea of the Countess causing an opera to be written in order to help make up her mind (entries of the Sonnet melody).

The whole mêlée is welded musically into a cogent entity by a new theme which both begins the ensemble and returns at regular intervals throughout its length:

[17] Not so much, however, Debussy's opera, which omits their two most important scenes.

Ex. 30

Various themes connected with the writing of the opera are prominent (Exx. 29 and the Count's critical Ex. 11) especially when the servants add their weight to the argument (Ex. 21) that opera serves only to clothe the incomprehensible in song. They then pass on to a discussion of other forms of entertainment one of which might possibly be suitable for their own contribution to the birthday pageant. One of the servants claims acquaintance with the Brighella of a touring troupe of Italian comedians and Strauss again quotes the *Ariadne* Commedia dell'Arte theme which had made a fleeting appearance during La Roche's monologue (see p. 224), though this time adding to it a little phrase from Rossini's Overture *L'Italiana in Algeri*.

The Countess's Major-domo now enters and bids them hurry with the supper preparations. Strauss actually provides a supper-motif:

Ex. 31

The ensemble ends with a little pianissimo $^6_8$ coda in which the servants rejoice at the prospect of a quiet evening without hordes of guests and reiterate their remarks about the Count's and Countess's love affairs. The metamorphosis of many of the motifs (including Ex. 31) into the graceful pattern of the $^6_8$ Allegretto rounds off the episode with great delicacy.

The servants have vanished into the gloom of the now wholly-darkened salon leaving the Major-domo busying himself with last minute details. The stage is actually set for the Countess's finale but Krauss's idea for an extra scene featuring the prompter was irresistible. Accordingly a voice is heard calling and the Major-domo stops in astonishment, unable to fathom who the intruder can possibly be.

Clemens Krauss's Monsieur Taupe is a fey shadowy creature of fantasy and atmosphere, and his scene breaks away momentarily from the dramatized real-life which has been the prevailing speciality of this unique opera. Strauss matches the concept of a dream-like interpolation by muting his entire orchestra. This involves muting some instruments which normally have no provision for doing so. It is especially unusual for some of the woodwind, and Strauss adds a footnote leaving the means of execution to the players' initiative. This twelfth and penultimate scene is also set in one of Strauss's comparatively rare instances of fluctuating bar-lengths which again add to the air of elusive unreality.[18]

After some mysterious and enigmatic replies, the Major-domo's increasingly exasperated questions are finally resolved. The strange newcomer announces that he is the *Souffleur*, and Krauss was whimsically determined that his identification should remain a secret until this moment, unrevealed even in the Dramatis Personae listed in the scores or the theatre programmes, where he is merely 'Monsieur Taupe, Tenor'.

Monsieur Taupe, having committed the one unthinkable, unforgivable sin of falling asleep at his post, has awakened to find the theatre deserted and himself abandoned. The poor little man, whom a subterranean and largely subliminal existence has rendered melancholic, is portrayed by a wistful pathetic motif:

Ex. 32

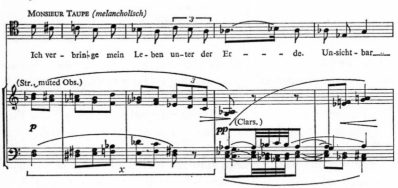

To the amused, though not unsympathetic Major-domo he explains with mingled pride and sadness his mysterious overlordship in a world

---

[18] Never entirely at his ease in an irregular metre, Strauss seems to have been undecided on the proper method of notation. As a result the vocal and full scores differ in their choice of time signatures, the $\frac{7}{8}$ in the full score being very unconventionally laid out.

of magic and illusion, (Ex. 10, for this is also essentially La Roche's domain). There is some pretty satire in the self-apologia of the troll-like creature who sits hidden in his tiny dark box watching a phantom-like mirror image of reality passing endlessly before his eyes, in the knowledge that he controls this wheel of fate; only when he sleeps is the thread broken, the public awakened and his own existence realized.

The Major-domo cuts short his querulous complaints of neglect with a few suggestions of practical common sense. What Monsieur Taupe needs is refreshment and transport back to Paris. It is within his province to supply both and he leads the way off, the little short-sighted *souffleur* groping his way after, wondering—to repeated fragments of Ex. 32(x) —whether he is not perhaps still dreaming. Horns toll repeated bell-like C's like some distant half-heard, half-imagined knell; the wisps of Ex. 32 fade away, the darkened stage is once more empty.

16

Into this moment of breathless enchantment the first horn softly plants the bell-like C's which are revealed as the opening notes of the *Krämer-spiegel* theme. During the song cycle itself this great melody is developed in different ways in the two songs where it appears. This last and most extended quotation links together the two major passages from the original work—that is to say, the first half of the introduction to No. 8 ('Von Händlern wird die Kunst bedroht'), which is reproduced identically in the same key of A flat, and, after a six-bar modulating passage, the whole of the epilogue of No. 12 ('O Schröpferschwarm, O Händler-kreis') transposed from D flat to A major although otherwise entirely complete and unaltered.

The first quotation and the modulatory link are set as a long horn solo with predominantly string accompaniment, but the remainder is given a full, warm treatment with elaborate parts for two harps which appear for the first time in the opera.

The Countess has re-entered elegantly dressed for supper and passing through the darkened salon has stood for a while on the balcony where, bathed in moonlight, she presents a magnificent tableau. The Major-domo has meanwhile lit the candles in the salon assisted by two servants who slip away as the Countess turns and addresses the Major-domo. She asks after her brother and is told of his departure for Paris with

Clairon (Exx. 8 and 11) leaving her, with due apologies, to sup by herself (Exx. 19 and 31, themes of the Countess's solitary meditations and of supper, and also less obviously Ex. 14, the eroticism of which tails away unfulfilled).

Her thoughts are on her brother and his philosophy of life, the easy pleasure-seeking ephemeral nature of which amuses her. She recalls his bantering words to her during their little Scene 2 duet, but Strauss subtly refrains from quoting from the music of the earlier passage and merely combines with a light hand themes contrasting their different emotional entanglements while, through it all, the Count's sardonic little figure Ex. 11 ripples ceaselessly.

She then realizes that the Major-domo is still standing before her, clearly with something more to say. Olivier has left a message that he will be attending the Countess's pleasure the following morning in the library at eleven o'clock in order to learn how the opera is to end.

The Major-domo bows himself out leaving the Countess in a turmoil of conflicting sensations. This is exactly the time and place she has unwisely allowed Flamand a rendezvous for the very same purpose. The thought of their consternation at finding only each other at the trysting-place instead of herself gives the Countess an unhappy twinge. Furthermore the ending of the opera is no foregone conclusion. Ex. 29 acquires a new bitter-sweet tang when she so much as considers its possibility:

Ex. 33

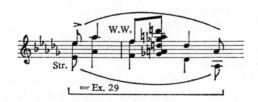

Comparison with the similarly sweet-and-sour Silver Rose music is inescapable (Chapter IX Ex. 45) and indeed the Countess now becomes ever more the symbolic impersonation of opera itself. When, very shortly, she is to study her expression in the mirror the analogy with the Marschallin becomes overwhelming. This whole magnificent final scene, Strauss's operatic farewell, is a very nostalgic and moving experience.

In her search for the impossible, her choice between words and music (Olivier's and Flamand's themes conflicting during the passionate outburst) she turns to the Sonnet, the manuscript of which is still lying on the spinet, and seating herself at her harp she sings it through to her own accompaniment.

The magical modulation at 'Leben oder Tod' ('Life or Death') causes her to break off for a moment to consider the hopelessness of her endeavour. The poem and its musical setting seem to her already to be so much parts of a single whole that it is hard to imagine either having ever existed separately.

The brief outburst, in which Strauss combines a whole host of relevant themes, subsides as the Countess takes the harp again and resumes her singing of the Sonnet which she now continues to the end before allowing her feelings once more to overwhelm her.

A surge of impassioned orchestral polyphony interrupts the final cadence of the Sonnet as she rises hastily from her harp and rushes across the salon in great distress. Olivier's and Flamand's motifs (Exx. 1, 14, 17 etc.) battle for supremacy over her Ex. 9, but when she sings, it is to the lyrical derivative of the Sonnet melody Ex. 18 which plunges along in alternation with repeated returns of Ex. 9, wisps of the introductory sextet forming rapid and restless figures of accompaniment. Poignantly conscious of their love for her, she conjures up the figures of her two lovers, both of whom stir her passionate admiration equally, so making it unbearable to reject either by choosing the other. The whole rhetorical outpouring ends in a gigantic question-mark in the form of the long-awaited phrase ⌈ x ⌉ from Ex. 9a which had sowed the seed in the very first scene of the opera. Against the importunate queries of this beautiful theme the Countess calls out to her own heart for its solution to the enigma.

But if the aristocratic Countess does not know the answer, no more does Madeleine, who is her romantic inner self. Strauss's orchestra glows and soars behind the yearning cantilena as the Countess's mind goes round and round the problem. She has played with fire and must pay the penalty. In matters of love there is always loss, whatever the gain.

The last axioms are declaimed in silent pauses between what has become separated bursts of orchestral fragments which ultimately come round yet again to the theme of Madeleine's heart, the touching curved phrase from Ex. 9a. It is in vain that she looks for some guidance from her face in the mirror; the face which looks back at her seems to be smiling ironically and for a brief moment she loses her temper. There *must* be an answer (Exx. 14 and 17).

Both the melodic fragments ⌐ x ⌐ and ⌐ y ⌐ from Ex. 9a have now combined and form the basis, together with Ex. 33 (the motif of the opera's non-end), of the long concluding peroration. At first this is purely orchestral, then for the last time Madeleine apostrophizes her reflection in the mirror. After all she has reached one inescapable conclusion—can there be an ending, she asks, which is not trivial?

So, as planned all along, the opera ends in the great question-mark of Ex. 9a, the soul of Madeleine, which is not in any way disturbed by the tiny epilogue. The Major-domo has returned silently to announce supper (Ex. 31). With gentle mockery the Countess taps her mirror reflection with her fan, curtseys to it, and gaily goes off into the dining room humming the Sonnet (Ex. 18).

The Major-domo is about to follow but is a little perplexed and during Strauss's graceful orchestral envoi, combining many of the motifs, looks after her with astonishment and then peers with puzzlement back at the mirror. Two statements of the opera's own motif Ex. 29 on the horn are punctuated by the infinitely gentle chords of the orchestra with its two harps, and the curtain has fallen. A more exquisite ending it would be hard to imagine.

17

For a long time the opera was referred to in correspondence and conversation by Casti's title. In fact, as Strauss pointed out, so much had this been the starting point for the whole venture that it seemed impossible to think of the work under any other name, let alone improve on it. After shelving the issue for a time Strauss came to the conclusion that something near to a translation of Casti would really simplify matters, such as:

> *Wort oder Ton?* with perhaps the subtitle:
> *Theatralische Fuge.*

At least this was to the point; more so than Clemens Krauss's suggestion 'Die Sprache der Töne' which together with the 'theatrical fugue' idea which also came from Krauss, seemed rather academic.

Then Clemens Krauss had a brainwave. On 6th December 1940 he suddenly wrote:

What would you say to:

Capriccio
Theatralische Diskussion in 1 Akt.
. . . the whole thing is exactly that, a caprice, just as it was a caprice on your part to get it into your head to write an opera on this of all themes.

It was really a clever thought, especially bearing in mind Strauss's previous use of a similar light Italian form-title, for the opera *Intermezzo*. Nevertheless Strauss, while acknowledging its felicity, did not altogether take to it at first. Although when telling Krauss on 24th February that the composition was finished he referred to it *pro tem* as *Capriccio*, by the time the full score was ready, on 3rd August, he had started toying again with other ideas such as:

Das Sonett der Gräfin
Ein rätselhaftes Theaterstück

Then just as he was writing to say that he continued to find *Capriccio* empty and banal he had a visit from Walther Thomas, the head of the Vienna Staatsbühne who assured him, with some knowledge of the work in question, that really *Capriccio* was the best solution. And so it was decided.

The subtitle also gave the authors heart-searchings. As late as March 1942 it was still fixed as:

Theoretische Komödie in einem Aufzug.

Once more it was Clemens Krauss who found the best way out with Strauss yielding a little unwillingly. It could not be called an opera; nor was it in truth a comedy. The work should be called precisely what it is:

Ein Konversationsstück für Musik.

'Don't you think that's right?' wrote Krauss, '. . . to the best of my knowledge, there has never before been a conversation piece for music. This subtitle would also disarm all possible objections that the piece has little apparent action, but in fact only consists of, as we believe, amusing and interesting dialogue, for it attests that there was the intention to write just such a piece.'

No sooner was the work complete than Strauss was suddenly smitten with a pang of conscience about Gregor whom he had remorselessly cast aside when it suited him and who had submitted to his fate with characteristic deference. There had in the meantime even been the possibility of renewed collaboration over a transcription of Spohr's *Jessonda* on the lines of Strauss's versions of *Iphigénie* and *Idomeneo*, though it was never more than the barest whim on Strauss's part, hardly worth the industry it instantly evoked from Gregor.

Now Strauss found it in his heart to write the very nicest letter enclosing a copy of the just completed libretto of *Capriccio* for Gregor's comments. But courteous and correct as was this action, it reopened the wound and Gregor's letters of thanks hardly disguise the offence which still rankled despite his anxiety to remain on the right side of Strauss. For his part, Strauss too saw the red light but was in a position to shrug his shoulders; he had made his gesture and the incident could be dropped.

18

As always, though with an even greater degree of thoroughness, Strauss concerned himself with the purely theatrical side of the new work's presentation. The illustrations on the opposite page show how faithfully Rudolf Hartmann, into whose hands the first production was entrusted, followed Strauss's wishes; the upper diagram is reproduced from a letter by Strauss to Clemens Krauss written shortly after the completion of the score, the lower diagram from the detailed production book published in 1943 by Oertel as a permanent documentation of the first performances.

The biggest anxiety was naturally the familiar one of where so specialized a work should be launched. 'Never forget', wrote Strauss, 'that our *Capriccio* is no piece for the broad public, any more than it should be played in a big house where only a third of the text can be understood.'

For this reason Strauss preferred some intimate milieu such as the Salzburg Festival would provide. There seemed an additional reason for this choice in that Clemens Krauss had just been appointed musical director for the festival, and a première of Strauss's last opera in which he himself had been co-author would be a very nice and appropriate beginning to his first season.

But unexpectedly enough Clemens Krauss had other ideas. Krauss was at this time riding the crest of the wave. The Nazis and the war having between them removed his potential rivals, posts which repre-

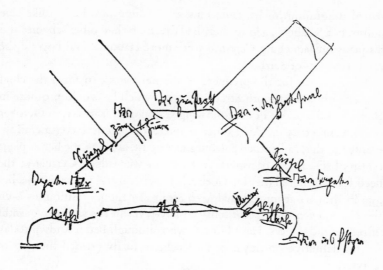

GRUNDRISS.
(Möbelstellung I bei Aufgehen des Vorhangs.)

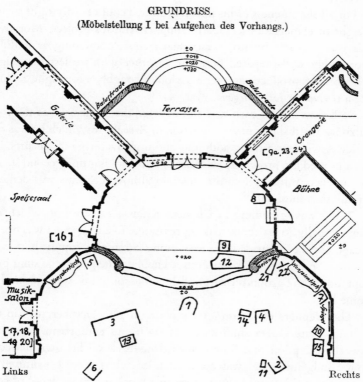

sented the summit of his ambitions were falling into his lap like ripe plums. For Salzburg, a long cherished dream, he had other schemes and his plans for launching *Capriccio* were more elaborate and beyond the resources even of Salzburg.

His idea was for the première of the new work to form the chief attraction in a mammoth Strauss Festival which he would promote in Munich at the outset of the following season, that is to say, in October or November 1942. An immense range of practical considerations pointed to this, rather than Salzburg in August, as being the better plan: rehearsal schedules; transport problems in war-ridden Germany; the need for ministerial (i.e. Dr Goebbels') approval and protection—a big gun in Krauss's argument owing to Strauss's delicate position vis-à-vis the Nazis; even the susceptibility to hay-fever in the summer months of one of the singers, Hans Hotter, who although better known today for his definitive portrayal of La Roche, actually created the role of Olivier.

For all the sureness of his instincts Strauss could hardly fight such a weight of evidence as seemed to support Krauss's project. Moreover this was in itself by no means unattractive, combining as it did a thoroughly well-prepared première together with no less than eight other Strauss productions over a period of roughly a fortnight, including a revival of *Josephslegende*.

So Krauss had his own way and devoted the Straussiana of the 1942 Salzburg Festival to a new production of *Arabella* for which he was full of ideas, with rewritings, additions and improvements of all sorts. He even pressed the producer, Hartmann, into cooking up a second stanza of the Fiakermilli's coloratura quatrain although Strauss was demonstrably unenthusiastic.

There was something in Clemens Krauss's constitution which led him eternally to set about making revisions. Even *Capriccio* was not to escape and he persuaded the easy-going Strauss to supply him with alternate sections for Clairon's music enabling the part to be sung by a soprano on the grounds that good-looking contraltos were so hard to come by.

The première of *Capriccio* took place on 28th October 1942 in the Munich State Opera amid scenes of enormous enthusiasm. So warm was the reception that Strauss turned his back on his own perfectly sound judgement and was quite offended when a critic ventured to suggest that this would always remain a work for an audience of connoisseurs. 'Will it really not speak to the heart of the people?' he wrote to Krauss in high indignation.

In the event his own previous verdict and that of the critic have proved to be well-founded; but within that limitation it has over the years gathered a considerable following based on real affection. Nor has the two-hours-or-more span of virtually action-less conversation proved an impediment to its appreciation. The iniquitous custom of inserting an interval after the interlude following the Countess's scene with Flamand is the merest device for the convenience of opera houses and has no artistic or popular justification. It was initiated by the conductor Joseph Keilberth together with Hartmann himself and necessitated the provision of some ten bars of curtain music. This division of the work into two very uneven portions, the interval coming after hardly more than a quarter of the opera has passed, has unfortunately had far too wide an acceptance.

Although forced to wait until the autumn to hear his new opera, Strauss saw no reason why he should not allow the opening Sextet to have an earlier airing. Accordingly he asked Clemens Krauss already in March whether it might be possible to arrange with Oertel to strike off the necessary copies of the parts for the appropriate string players from the Vienna Philharmonic. Krauss understood at once what was in Strauss's mind and quickly arranged for this to be done. The first reading of the Sextet was given at a gathering of the so-called 'Contemporary Circle' in the house of the Gauleiter Baldur von Schirach, who was then Nazi controller of Vienna. Surprising as this may seem it is at least understandable when one knows all the facts which led up to it.

When back in 1924 the city of Vienna had honoured Strauss on the occasion of his sixtieth birthday with the donation of a plot of ground, Strauss had built upon it at enormous personal expense a second villa. The piece of land was in a highly desirable neighbourhood and was adjacent to the botanical park called the Belvedere, from which indeed the large garden was partially borrowed.

Strauss and Pauline were never prone to think small, least of all where standards of living were concerned, and it was not for nothing that the new villa came to be described as a Schlösschen (little castle).

In recognition of the favour bestowed on him by the city authorities Strauss presented them with the manuscript full score of Rosenkavalier.

But, slightly in the manner of municipal councils, the land was not after all a gift outright of the freehold, but only a loan for sixty years.

And when ten of the sixty had elapsed, in 1935, Strauss began to feel more than a little concerned. By this time he had fallen into the regular routine of spending the winter months in Vienna as a base for his conducting activities, in between orchestrating the music he had composed during the summer months at Garmisch. He and Pauline occupied the upper storey of the Schlösschen while on the ground floor he had installed his son and daughter-in-law, who lived there all the year round.

Now Strauss wondered whether it was really necessary that this very sumptuous mansion would have to revert to the city in 1984 together with the ground it stood upon, instead of remaining as part of his inheritance to Franz and Alice and their family. He therefore approached the city once again and, shrewd business man that he was, succeeded in acquiring the desired freehold in return for the additional autograph score of *Aegyptische Helena* and a hundred free performances in the Philharmonie or the Staatsoper.

It was a highly satisfactory transaction and Strauss had every reason to be content. But he had reckoned without Hitler's *Anschluss* and the second World War, as a result of which it quickly became impracticable to run two such establishments. So whilst retaining their ownership of the Belvedere Schlösschen the Strauss family retreated *en bloc* to Garmisch.

Here, however, things were far from ideal. Tact had never been Strauss's strong point and his opinion of the Nazis was by now well known. Nor did Pauline lose any opportunity of making all too clear her contempt for the 'rabble' who were leading their beloved country to ruin and destruction.

The Nazi authorities in Garmisch accordingly retaliated swiftly with the result that life became less and less bearable. For they struck at Strauss not only in his private needs which, being considerable, afforded plenty of scope for persecution, but above all through his Jewish daughter-in-law who was publicly ostracised, and his grandsons, Richard and Christian, who had to run the gauntlet whenever they went to school.

It is therefore understandable that when Strauss saw a chance he seized it even though it meant swallowing his pride. Schirach had made it known, as soon as he was appointed, that his heart was set on restoring Vienna once more as the cultural centre of Europe, and to him Strauss therefore turned with the proposal that he and his family be allowed to return to his Belvedere home and so be in a position to contribute to this artistic revival.

Schirach could ask for nothing better, but even he had to tread warily. The famous composer was in such bad odour that even at times of military crisis Hitler, Goebbels and Himmler found the spare moment to issue peremptory directives ensuring that Strauss should not be publicly featured or honoured, whether in the press or in any other way.

To achieve the desired object, Schirach thus thought it safest to send first a deputy to Garmisch to fix the conditions with Strauss. In return for his collaboration Strauss and his family would be allowed to live in Vienna unmolested but permanently on parole, as it were, against his good behaviour and that of his sharp-tongued wife.

It was an uneasy truce but it worked, and Strauss had ample cause to be grateful to Schirach. The first performance of the *Capriccio* Sextet in Schirach's home was but one small token of this gratitude.

19

Inevitably *Capriccio's* strongest links are with Strauss's other conversational opera *Intermezzo*. At the time he had persuaded himself that he had formulated a new and successful vocal style which, carried to its logical conclusion, had solved once and for all the problem of, as he put it, 'the alternation between ordinary prose, *recitativo secco*, and *recitativo accompagnato*'.[19]

In the event this proved largely self-delusion and in most of the intervening operas he either returned to his normal *cantilena* style or deliberately accentuated the differences he had claimed to have ironed out so skilfully, as in the frequent snatches of spoken dialogue in *Die Schweigsame Frau*. Here too he often returned deliberately to a classically conventional demarcation of operatic forms such as recitative, ariettes, duettinos, ensembles and the rest.

In this respect *Capriccio* clearly owes much to *Die Schweigsame Frau* although naturally the purpose is largely illustrative, the main argument being carried on once again in precisely the style on which Strauss had so prided himself in *Intermezzo*.

But there are other ways in which *Capriccio* differs markedly from that earlier experiment in operatic style. Delicately as it is treated, the orchestra is a large one with five members of the clarinet family and full strings including sixteen each of first and second violins. Even so it

[19] See Vol. II, p. 261.

makes no attempt to pursue *Intermezzo's* precedent in relegating the chief musical interest to symphonic interludes in which the orchestra can have its head. Little can therefore be performed from the opera in the way of individual extracts other than the chamber music Einleitung (Introduction), the *Krämerspiegel* entr'acte, and the closing scene in which, the dialogue being at an end, Strauss's inveterate lyricism naturally reasserts itself. One further exception consists of the three pastiche ballet movements—Passepied, Gigue and Gavotte—which Strauss arranged in June 1944 for harpsichord solo with the addition of a short concert ending. The incentive for this had arisen out of the first Vienna performance of the opera on 1st February of that year in which the harpsichordist was the well-known player Isolde Ahlgrimm.

Strauss was so taken with her artistry that he went up to her and said 'Well now, how would it be if you played the ballet music in your recitals?' A little diffidently she replied that it would be hard to bring along the two string players specially, and that to play it alone was a fearsome prospect; it was already hard enough as it stood. 'Oh, you'll manage it alright' was Strauss's reply, and so she applied herself to the problem. A priceless interchange ensued when in April she wrote asking Strauss for the concert ending and Strauss replied asking whether she would prefer a loud or a soft coda.

Actually it was a loud end which reached her a couple of months later complete with dedication and date (5th June 1944). But it was not until after the war that Madame Ahlgrimm was able to fulfil Strauss's intention, giving the first performance on 7th November 1946 in the Mozart-Saal of the Vienna Konzerthaus. She made up for the delay however by following the première with many subsequent performances.

One further link with *Intermezzo* remains to be considered. This is the long prose preamble with which *Capriccio* is also prefaced and to which reference was made above in connexion with its opening quotation of La Roche's dicta (See above p. 227). Although demonstrably less significant than its sister-preface, it is undeniably entertaining for the insight it affords into the workings of the veteran composer's mind—his views on rehearsal technique and the opera orchestra; his conviction that Wagner is the supreme pinnacle in the history of music; his consciousness of the problems of balance raised by his own work, etc. And the somewhat loosely strung-together thoughts and anecdotes are nicely introduced and rounded off by means of linking references to the thesis of the whole work contained in Casti's title and the remark of Flamand and Olivier uniting music to words as brother and sister.

Strauss had, from the first, thought of *Capriccio* more as a treatise than as an opera in its own right, and although it ultimately became finer and greater than so modest an appellation would suggest he still thought of it in the nature of an appendix to his output for the stage. The preface, with its handful of reflexions and recollections,[20] is thus hardly different in kind from the opera itself to which it belongs as an integral part.

Capriccio brings to an end the huge cycle of fifteen operas which had begun with *Guntram* half a century before. This second of the inter-locking curves of Strauss's life work thus links both in style and quality with the third and last, that of the Indian Summer, the advent of which it heralds with its sudden freshness and light-handed inspiration. According to all the rules the very antithesis of a successful opera, it has won its ardent devotees through the return to genius of its octogenarian composer, a revivification virtually unparalleled in music or indeed any art, together with the wholly unexpected qualities of Clemens Krauss as a creative as well as an interpretative master. It forms indeed, and Strauss made no error of judgement in recognizing this, a worthy con-clusion to his magnificent gamut of stage works and he wisely resisted the efforts of Krauss to tempt him into making *Capriccio* the first of a new series of conversational music-dramas. Very kindly but quite firmly he shut the door on any such idea. 'Isn't this D flat major', he wrote, 'the best winding up of my theatrical life-work? One can only leave one testament behind!'

And to this resolution, born of a sure artistic instinct, Strauss held fast, through Krauss's inevitable disappointment and Gregor's tireless importunity which continued through the post-war years almost to the day of Strauss's death. The one semi-product, the fragment *Des Esels Schatten*, will be considered in a later chapter but is wholly unimportant and occupied so small a corner of Strauss's heart that it in no way alters the overall picture. With *Capriccio* one of the main threads of this saga has reached its beautiful and well-timed end.

[20] i.e. *Betrachtungen und Erinnerungen*, the title of the whole collection of such jottings which Strauss subsequently allowed to be published, and which includes the prefaces to both *Intermezzo* and *Capriccio*.

CHAPTER XXII

A LIFETIME OF LIEDER WRITING

C*APRICCIO* was the aptest possible last opera of a composer
whose long life had been filled with constant preoccupation
over the problems of setting words to music. For it tackles and analyses
this eternally fascinating task in ways which must have been uppermost
in Strauss's mind for as far back as he could remember.

When Olivier cries out 'Er componiert mich!' on hearing Flamand's
first tentative essays at fitting music to his beloved sonnet, his protest
has every justification. Sir Michael Tippett admirably laid bare the
meaning of this scene, the very point Strauss and Clemens Krauss were
trying to illustrate, when he wrote:[1]

> The moment the composer begins to create the musical
> verses of his song he destroys our appreciation of the poem
> as poetry, and substitutes an appreciation of his music as
> song . . . As soon as we sing any poetry to a recognizable
> melody we have at that instant left the art of poetry for the
> art of music . . . we might even demonstrate by experi-
> ment the moment when chanted recitation of poetry hovers
> perhaps on the border-line between the two arts; the poetic
> listener still trying to appreciate the poetry, the musical
> listener already appreciating the chanting as music. Once the
> chanting has gone over into song, then our appreciation of
> the words virtually ceases. If the poem is very fine in its own
> right, and very well known, then we *imagine* sometimes that

[1] 'Conclusion' from *A History of Song,* edited by Denis Stevens. Hutchinson,
London, 1960.

we are still appreciating the poetry when it has become a song, but I think this is illusion.

When we hear a good song we are rarely if ever disturbed by the quite possible fact that the poetry is poor. We may discover this later on, as many people have done concerning many Schubert songs. But . . . it is only a discrepancy to someone who holds to the illusion that we can appreciate a poem as poetry in the act of appreciating the song a composer has made of it . . . The music of a song destroys the verbal music of a poem utterly.

The same point is made by Susanne Langer:[2]

Consider for instance a good poem successfully set to music. The result is a good song. One would naturally expect the excellence of the song to depend as much on the quality of the poem as on the musical handling. But this is not the case. Schubert has made beautiful songs out of great lyrics by Heine, Shakespeare and Goethe, and equally beautiful songs out of the commonplace, sometimes maudlin lyrics of Müller. The poetic creation counts only in a song in exciting the composer to compose it. After that, the poem as a work of art is broken up. Its words, sounds and sense alike, its phrases, all become musical material. In a well-wrought song the text is swallowed hide and hair. This does not mean that the words do not count, that other words would have done as well; but the words have been musically exploited, they have entered into a new composition and the poem as a poem has disappeared into the song.

Although Strauss tried hard to make his Countess Madeleine find a solution more favourable to Olivier, he himself clearly recognized the validity of this view. He wrote to Gregor:

. . . for example, a perfect Goethe poem doesn't need any music; precisely in the case of Goethe, music weakens and flattens out the word. A Mozart String Quintet says everything profound with more beauty of sentiment than any words . . . Many songs owe their origin to the circumstance that the composer looks for a poem which will match a fine melodic idea and the poetically musical atmosphere; Brahmsian songs! If he *can't* find a poem you get a Song *without* Words (Mendelssohn). Or the *modern* Lied; the verse gives birth to the vocal melody—not as happens so often, even in Schubert, that the melody is poured over the verse without getting the cadence of the poem quite right! . . .

[2] *Problems of Art.* Routledge, London, 1957.

Much is made clear here, both in Strauss's choice of poetry (like Schubert and Brahms, only rarely from the truly great poets) and in his manner of song composition. In a letter written as a young man in 1893 to the eminent Austrian historian and musical theorist, Friedrich von Hausegger, he described himself as having perhaps for some time no impulse to compose at all; then one evening he may be turning the leaves of a volume of poetry; a poem will strike his eye, he reads it through, it agrees with the mood he is in, and at once the appropriate music is instinctively fitted to it. He is in a musical frame of mind, and all he wants is the right poetic vessel into which to pour his ideas. If good luck throws this in his way, a satisfactory song results. But often the poem that presents itself is not the right one; then he has to bend his musical mood to fit it the best way he can; he works laboriously and without the right kind of enthusiasm at it. The song, in fact, is made not born.

This revealing self-analysis exposes both Strauss's strength and his weakness; his weakness because he was capable of pursuing a composition even when his heart and imagination were not involved, merely in order to occupy himself; his strength because he possessed that invaluable quality of instinctive response to situation which, to quote Tippett once more, is the primal gift of the song writer.

2

Strauss seems always to have had this gift, from the very tenderest years. In the enormous list of his childhood compositions the songs constitute a major proportion and number no less than forty-two:

1*	Weihnachtslied	Schubart	Dec. 1870
2*	Einkehr	Uhland	21 Aug. 1871
3*	Winterreise	Uhland	1871
4	Waldkonzert	Vogel	1871
5	Der weisse Hirsch	Uhland	1871
6†	Des Alpenhirten Abschied	Schiller	1871
7	Der Böhmische Musikant	Pletzsch	1871
8(†)	Herz, mein Herz	Geibel	1871
9*	Der müde Wanderer	Hoffman v. Fallersleben	1873
10*	Husarenlied	Hoffman v. Fallersleben	1873
11*	Der Fischer	Goethe	
12*	Die Drossel	Uhland	
13*	Lass ruhn die Toten	Chimasso	1877
14*	Lust und Qual	Goethe	

15* Spielmann und Zither	Körner	Jan. 1878
16* Wiegenlied	Hoffman v. Fallersleben	early 1878
17* Abend- und Morgenrot	Hoffman v. Fallersleben	early 1878
18* Im Walde	Geibel	early 1878
19 Arie der Almaide (from 'Lila') ORCH	Goethe	early 1878
20 Der Spielmann und sein Kind ORCH	Hoffmann v. Fallersleben	28 Feb. 1878
21* Nebel	Lenau	1878
22* Soldatenlied	Hoffmann v. Fallersleben	1878
23* Ein Röslein zog ich mir im Garten	Hoffmann v. Fallersleben	1878
24* Alphorn (with horn obbligato)	Kerner	1878
25† Für Musik	Geibel	7 Apr. 1879
26* Waldesgesang	Geibel	9 Apr. 1879
27† O schneller mein Ross	Geibel	10 Apr. 1879
28† Die Lilien glühn in Düften	Geibel	12 Apr. 1879
29† Es rauscht das Laub zu meinen Füssen	Geibel	May 1879
30† Frühlingsanfang	Geibel	24 May 1879
31† Die drei Lieder	Uhland	18 Dec. 1879
32 In Vaters Garten heimlich steht	Heine	24 Dec. 1879
33† Der Morgen	Sallet	10 Jan. 1880
34* Die erwachte Rose	Sallet	12 Jan. 1880
35† Immer leiser wird mein Schlummer	Lingg	17 Dec. 1880
36* Begegnung	Gruppe	18 Dec. 1880
37† Mutter, O sing mich zur Ruh	Hemans	29 Dec. 1880
38 John Anderson, mein Lieb	Burns	31 Dec. 1880
39† Geheiligte Stätte	Fischer	24 Dec. 1881
40† Jung Friedel wallte am Rheinesstrand	Becker	Dec. 1882
41† Waldesgang	Stieler	10 Dec. 1882
42* Rote Rosen	Stieler	11 Sept. 1883

The songs above designated with an asterisk (*) are included in the collected edition of Strauss's songs,[3] whereas those with a dagger (†) still seem to be lost at the time of writing. The last that is known of them is that they were in the possession of Strauss's aunt, Johanna Pschorr, who some years before the first World War allowed them to be examined by Max Steinitzer, since when they have vanished without a trace.

Of the earliest song No. 1, Strauss himself wrote:

[3] Boosey and Hawkes, 1964. They are to be found in Volume III which contains a section at the end devoted to *Jugendlieder*.

> My first attempts at composition (at the age of six) consisted
> of a Christmas Carol, for which I 'painted' the notes myself
> but my mother wrote the words below the notes since I
> could not then myself write small enough, and the so-called
> *Schneiderpolka*.

The words, of which three more verses are printed in the Revisions-
bericht of the Complete Edition, are by the eighteenth century poet
and musician Christian Friedrich Daniel Schubart, who is best known
today for *Die Forelle* immortalized by Franz Schubert. The song was
originally entitled *Der Hirten Lied am Kripplein* (The Song of the Shepherds at the Manger) but the little Strauss and his amanuensis mother
abandoned this for the shorter and more direct *Weihnachtslied*.[4] The
setting could hardly be simpler, of course, with the piano accompaniment amounting to just a straightforward harmonization of the four-
square tune.

In No. 2 the piano still spends most of its time running along together with the voice, but the melody itself is more assured and there is
an attractive plunge onto the so-called German 6th at its climax:

Ex. 1

This song, *Einkehr*, is of particular interest in that the mature Strauss
returned to Uhland's poem, making a new setting as part of the group
op. 47. It is amusing to put the imaginative and delicate music of the
thirty-six year old master alongside the child's naïve but well-wrought
ditty. Ludwig Uhland was a much-loved German poet of the early
nineteenth century and Strauss drew on him for several works culminating in the choral ballad *Taillefer* (see Vol. II, p. 363).

Most of the early songs were written for Aunt Johanna to sing, but
Einkehr was especially dedicated to her on her name-day and Richard
was now able to write out for her both words and music without
parental assistance, apart from a few minor corrections from Papa.

[4] A facsimile of the autograph appeared in the first edition of Steinitzer's
biography.

A further song to Uhland words No. 3 at once shows an advance, with far greater freedom of line and considerable use of dramatic effect. The C minor tremolos in the introduction and coda suggest that Strauss's enthusiasm was aroused by going with his parents to a performance of *Der Freischütz*, always thereafter one of his favourite operas.

Nos. 4 to 8 were originally in a book containing another copy of No. 1, some small piano pieces and even a song by Strauss's sister Johanna. The volume has not survived but luckily sketches of the songs still exist[5] with the exception of No. 6, Strauss's only song to a text by Schiller.[6] *Der weisse Hirsch* No. 5 is again Uhland, but Nos. 4 and 7 are by minor poets, Johann Nepomuk Vogel and Oskar Pletzsch. Still simple enough in style these settings are more particularly remarkable for the variety and resourcefulness they show when compared with each other. *Waldkonzert*, for example, makes pretty play with the contributions from various birds and animals (including a cadenza for nightingale with echo effects), and the sketches for *Der weisse Hirsch* show suggestions for dividing up the vocal part between no less than three singers (alto, tenor and bass) taking the roles of different huntsmen.

Of No. 8 only a sketch of the voice line remains in a copy partly in Strauss's but mostly in his father's hand. The poem is by Emanuel Geibel, the author to whom, with Paul Heyse, Hugo Wolf was indebted for his *Spanisches Liederbuch*, while Schumann and Brahms also made settings of his verses. Writing in the middle of the nineteenth century, Geibel was the epitome of the popular lyric poet and it was natural that the young Strauss was attracted to his writings, soon afterwards composing a group of six songs in addition to the one or two of the early period.

Nos. 9 and 10 come after an interval of some two years, by which time Strauss was nine years old. They consist of a pair of settings to poems by the patriotic writer August Heinrich Hoffmann von Fallersleben, the author of Germany's National Anthem, *Deutschland, Deutschland über Alles*. This is not to say, however, that Hoffmann von Fallersleben's entire output is jingoistic, even though it is by his political poetry that he is best remembered. Much of his work is extremely scholarly on the one hand, and frankly romantic on the other.

Certainly *Der müde Wanderer* falls into the latter category with its

---

[5] They can be found in the *Nachlese* which Willi Schuh prepared for Boosey & Hawkes in 1968. This also includes for the first time Nos. 20, 32 and 38.

[6] The text of *Hymnus* (No. 100) ascribed to Schiller, is of doubtful authenticity.

portrayal of the weary nomad; bewildered by the pealing of distant bells, he is plunged from his horse into a gorge where he finds his last resting place. The succession of different images allowed Strauss his first opportunity for an episodic Lied-form, handled with notable success. By contrast, *Husarenlied* is a straightforward strophic air in gay popular style punctuated by little mock fanfares.

3

Again there is a gap, this time of four years during which Strauss worked principally at instrumental composition, both chamber and orchestral (including the *Festmarsch* subsequently published through his Uncle George's generosity as his op. 1) before turning to Lieder writing once more, beginning with none other than the great Goethe himself. *Der Fischer* is one of the best-known ballads, standing in most collected editions between *Erlkönig* and *Der König in Thule*. Strauss was by no means first in the field here, Schubert, Loewe, Reichardt and the young Schumann having all composed settings. Schubert, like Reichardt before him, treats the poem strophically making no attempt to bring out its dramatic potential.

Strauss however, who was by this time studying with Wilhelm Friedrich Meyer, the Munich Hofkapellmeister, was ready to spread his wings a little and built the song into a veritable Scena. The exciting middle section with its quasi-operatic climax divides the restless first and last strophes which, in keeping with the parallel nature of the verses, Strauss set to the same music including his ingeniously interpolated repeat of their last two lines, though adapted to allow for the tragic little coda.

None of the other three songs Nos. 12 to 14, which together with No. 11 form a group (as he proudly wrote to his friend Ludwig Thuille), are on a comparable scale. *Die Drossel*, to another Uhland poem, has for prelude a burst of bird-song transcribed as a cadenza for the piano right hand, after which the almost Schubertian simplicity of the air itself comes as something of a surprise.

Lass ruhn die Toten is quite different in character. The eerie title intrigued Strauss who drew Thuille's attention to it with hardly concealed enthusiasm. The poem is by Adalbert von Chamisso, properly Louis Charles Adelaide de Chamisso, a Frenchman of noble birth whose family fled to Berlin at the time of the Revolution when he was still a boy. All Chamisso's poetry is in his adopted tongue and the degree to which he was successful in entering into the prevalent spirit of German Romanticism may be gauged by the fact that he was the author of the verses which form Schumann's cycle *Frauen-Liebe und Leben*.

The poem on which Strauss's choice fell is a mood picture of awe and fear surrounding a man who by night treads the gravestones of an ancient fortress. The tiptoeing introduction and weirdly meandering bass-line growling around the depths are new elements in the work of the future master in the sphere of the grotesque.

The last song in the group, No. 14, is a second Goethe setting. *Lust und Qual* is hardly perhaps one of the greatest of Goethe's lyric poems, with its naïve representation of a fisherboy comparing himself with one of his own fish which, caught in his net, swims helplessly amongst the rest of the catch. So the boy too, caught by some flirtatious shepherdess, struggles in vain to free himself from amongst the throng of her numerous admirers. The tone is on the whole frivolous and Strauss treated it with appropriate lightness of touch although in choosing a wholly strophic setting—that is to say, with all three verses sung to the same music laid out within repeat signs—he lost the one possible opportunity of introducing the element of *Qual* (torment) into the final stanza.

No. 15, composed the following year, is a much more ambitious undertaking. Like Hoffmann von Fallersleben, Theodor Körner is largely remembered for his patriotic songs and it was in fact as a soldier that he met his death in 1813 at the age of twenty-two. *Spielmann und Zither* is, however, a thoroughly romantic conception of a minstrel whose zither is swept into the sea as he sits dreaming on a crag, and on discovering his loss himself plunges into the water to perish alongside his beloved instrument.

There was plenty of scope here for the budding musical pictorialist and the way the roar of the breakers is imitated in the opening bars calls to mind the similar effect Strauss was to create in *Enoch Arden*. But the particularly interesting feature of the song is its alternation of two different melodic settings for the contrasted dramatic and lyrical verses, culminating in a catastrophe of almost operatic intensity.

The next two (Nos. 16 and 17), again to poems by Hoffmann von Fallersleben, are much simpler but by no means devoid of interest. *Wiegenlied* gives the impression of being a Schubertian strophic setting but is most ingeniously varied by starting the second verse with the continuation instead of the beginning of the melody. This matches the corresponding device of the poem in which 'weary flowers look around' in the second line of the opening verse and are recalled at the outset of the balancing stanza.

The second of these little Fallersleben Lieder, *Abend- und Morgenrot*, also has a strong Schubertian flavour, not only in the deceptively in-genuous folk-song flavour of its melody but in the constant to-and-fro between major and minor. This, one of Schubert's favourite and best-known devices is introduced by Strauss to contrast the care-free play-fulness of the gnat (Mücke) in the warm evening sunshine and the silent corpse of a young girl revealed as the fresh sunlight shines through the window the next morning. The song ends gaily in the major, no tinge of sympathy colouring its portrayal of the insect's lack of concern as the girl's body is borne away to its funeral.

Im Walde (No. 18) is another isolated Geibel song from a group of poems entitled *Lieder als Intermezzo*, the opening words of which recall Heine's *Dichterliebe*, so memorably set by Schumann:

Im Wald, in hellen Sonnenschein   Im wunderschönen Monat Mai,
wenn alle Knospen springen,   als alle Knospen sprangen

Strauss, however, treats Geibel's less magical version brightly. Rather, his jaunty ⁶⁄₈ strain brings to mind Brahms's well-known *Botschaft*, especially in the choice of piano figuration:

Ex. 2

The coda, on the other hand, contains a pretty surprise with its minia-ture vocal cadenza interpolated before the simple cadential ending.

4

At this point the thirteen-year-old Strauss tried his hand at a couple of orchestral Lieder. He had by this time several fully-scored pieces for orchestra to his credit and to work orchestrally with his regular vocal composition was thus a natural development. The choice of Goethe's *Arie der Almaide* was part of a more ambitious plan to set to music the whole of the Singspiel *Lila*, in the second act of which this aria occurs. *Lila* is a fascinating play with its songs and dances, its ogre and demon and its choruses of children, fairies and prisoners in chains. It had already been set to music twice, though admittedly by minor composers (Reichardt in 1790 and Seidel nearly thirty years later) and its musical and dramatic opportunities were obviously very tempting.

Nevertheless the scale of the undertaking proved altogether beyond Strauss's powers at this time even though he wrote to Thuille enthusiastically of his progress. But in the end he only completed two numbers, a chorus with Tenor solo from the fourth act and the Almaide aria 'Sei nicht beklommen', the orchestration of which latter was also never finished. He was left with wistful memories of the project however, and returned to it as late as 1895 on the advice of Cosima Wagner, under whose influence he made a large number of sketches before finally abandoning it for ever.

The second orchestral song, composed within the month, is a setting of another Fallersleben poem and thus, in its capacity as Lied pure and simple, qualifies as the first of Strauss's important contributions in this controversial field.

For reasons rarely stated explicitly but none the less real, accompaniments for orchestra or even for any instrumental group other than the single pianoforte are held in stern disfavour by all true connoisseurs of the art of song. Many scholars when discussing in detail the songs of composers such as Schubert, Wolf or Duparc, prefer to dismiss orchestrations even when they are the work of the composer himself.

Thus in Eric Sams's admirable study of Hugo Wolf[7] there is no indication anywhere to show which songs were instrumentated, and the only reference to the orchestra at all is under *Prometheus*, where it is grudgingly conceded that 'He orchestrated several of his songs, but only of this one can it be said that it is better so arranged'.

Even such an exhaustive survey as *A History of Song*, edited by Denis Stevens, fails to recognize and discuss the orchestral Lied as a subject with its own ethos and historical background dating from Berlioz's orchestration of Schubert's *Erlkönig* and his own *Nuits d'été* during 1843–60 (although an interesting case might be made for some of Mozart's concert arias standing in direct line of ancestry).

[7] Eric Sams, *The Songs of Hugo Wolf*. Methuen, London, 1961.

At its purest, the Lied is an intimate form analogous to chamber music. Weingartner and Schönberg made full orchestral versions of a Beethoven Piano Sonata and a Brahms Piano Quartet, but both take away more than they impart and the results are hybrid monstrosities—intriguing or interesting maybe, but hardly more than that. So, it might seem, must be the parallel effects of treating Lieder in the same way.

Yet this need not be so, for the voice-and-orchestra Scena is a form in its own right, perfectly satisfactory in its concert-hall presentation and making no pretence of being more or less than it is. Admittedly it stands at a faintly uncomfortable midway point between concert versions of dramatic excerpts on the one hand and Lieder, whose intimacy it has inevitably sacrificed, on the other. Moreover there is a fundamental difference between an orchestrated Lied and a song originally cast for voice and orchestra. The Germans mark a differentiation between Lieder and Gesänge, the latter being larger in conception and so incorporating the orchestral Lied, but the point is a nice one and is easily obscured. As in every art form there is no hard and fast rule and every kind of exception or borderline instance abounds. Some songs expand naturally into orchestral Gesänge, even becoming masterpieces in the process; others cannot sustain the new varieties of colour and weight given them by instrumentation however sensitively carried out. The answer may perhaps lie in the composer's own approach to the piano and to the orchestra; contrast, for example, the conductor Mahler and Brahms the pianist. It is, in this connexion, significant that Brahms never orchestrated any of his songs (though strangely he did so arrange some of Schubert's) and that orchestral versions of the *Vier ernste Gesänge*, seemingly the most obvious candidates, have all been still-born.

Although a more than competent pianist, Strauss wrote little for the piano outside his Lieder accompaniments, whereas he was to become one of the world's greatest orchestrators. The only surprise is, therefore, that *Der Spielmann und sein Kind* should have remained for over fifteen years the isolated precursor of a long line of masterworks in the genre. That it was to open up the boy's vivid imagination was only to be expected; as Steinitzer wrote of it, '. . . the music (has) strongly dramatic accentuation, to some extent in an entirely different style from anything so far'. This is particularly true of the exciting opening and closing sections, although the operatic-style recitative which precedes the central andante makes a new and significant point of departure.

Like *Im Walde*, this ambitious Scena was composed for one of the senior singers at the Munich Court, Caroline von Mangstl, and very respectfully dedicated to her on the fortieth anniversary of her appointment to the Hofkapelle.

5

Four more songs belong to 1878 (Nos. 21–24), the first being a remarkable little tone-painting on a poem by Lenau, who was to inspire Strauss to his first unqualified world-wide success, *Don Juan*. *Nebel* is one of a set of verses entitled *Erinnerung* although in some editions it is included amongst the collection inscribed with the name of Bertha, a beautiful if somewhat naïve Viennese girl with whom Lenau had a passionate love affair.

Despite an opening disarmingly reminiscent of the first bars of Haydn's *Clock Symphony* the song matches the poem's evocation of mist and fog with its chromatically meandering harmonies in the gloomy minor key of six flats.

Ex. 3

By comparison the first of two more Fallersleben songs *Soldatenlied* (No. 22) strikes a relatively conventional note although this masks some quite interesting subtleties in suggesting the infantryman who is less inured to a soldier's lot than he wishes to show.

Soldatenlied is also the first song specifically to be written in the bass clef for a male voice. Even the parallel earlier military song *Husarenlied* (No. 10) being in the treble, can theoretically be sung by either a man or a woman.

It is a curious part of Lieder tradition that indications of gender in the poem are no guide in the matter of interpretation. Such masculine sentiments as Mahler's *Lieder eines fahrenden Gesellen* were for many years only sung by contraltos with disconcerting anomaly in phrases like:

. . . seh' ich von Fern das blonde Haar
im Winde weh'n! O weh!

Wenn ich aus dem Traum auf-fahr'
und höre klingen ihr silbern Lachen. . . .[8]

Nor does the practice necessarily go against the wishes of composers who rarely indicate their intention (merely marking the voice part 'Gesang', 'chant', etc.) and have moreover frequently been known to give performances themselves accompanying singers of either sex.

Ein Röslein zog ich mir im Garten (No. 23), Strauss's last Fallersleben song, is nearer in character to *Abend- und Morgenrot* with even a similar slip into the minor as sadness clouds the joy of the poet whose rose has been plucked by another hand, never to be seen again. Perhaps the song suffers a little from Hoffmann von Fallersleben's misfortune in hitting upon a poetic phrase so reminiscent of the sublimely poignant *Gretchen am Spinnrad* from Goethe's *Faust* (See Ex. 4 below). Strauss, however, with sure instinct treated with the lightest touch this doubtful piece of sentimentality. Certainly the Mendelssohn-like coda is quite winning:

Ex. 4

[8] '. . . seeing from afar the fair hair
wafting in the wind! O what pain!

When I start up from dreaming
and hear her silvery laughter. . . .'

No. 24 *Alphorn*, opens up yet further possibilities though, strangely, ones which Strauss hardly ever exploited again—that of the Lied with piano accompaniment but with the addition of a further concertante instrument. Schubert provided the best-known precedents in his *Auf dem Strom* and *Der Hirt auf dem Felsen* with obbligato horn and clarinet respectively.

Strauss composed *Alphorn*, of course, as a clear act of homage to his father, to whom the song is dedicated and who must have delighted in the well-contrived and grateful solo horn writing, the precursor of his son's splendid handling of the instrument's possibilities which was soon to follow in the Concerto op. 11. The song formed one of a pair of works Strauss wrote for his father in 1878, the other being an Introduction, Theme and Variations for horn and piano.[9]

The song is ternary in design with a dramatic andante interrupting the easy-going pastoral flow of the outer allegretto sections. Andreas Justinus Kerner, who wrote the text, was an intimate colleague of Uhland, together with whom he founded an important school of romantic poetry. Slight as this particular example of his art may be, it is highly characteristic with its indefinable regret called up by the tones of the horn resounding through mountain and valley, and much of this is charmingly captured in the music. For all the patent immaturity of its composer *Alphorn* is by no means negligible and deserves a place in the scanty repertoire of such works.

In the Spring of 1879 Strauss returned to Geibel for the last time, composing no less than six settings. Of these only one survives, *Waldesgesang* No. 26, which was originally planned and carefully revised as one of a set together with Nos. 27 and 28. They were written for Cornelia Meysenheim, another singer at the Munich Court Opera, who first presented them in the Museumsaal on 16th March 1881. Strauss's sister Johanna, towards the end of her life, recalled the occasion tenderly:

> . . . two days later three of his Lieder were sung with great success in the Museumsaal by Frau Kammersängerin Meysenheim. Mother and I were full of anxiety and excitement, but were then overjoyed and proud when Richard took his bow, shyly smiling, on the podium hand in hand with the

[9] In after years Strauss dated the song 1876 and the editors of the posthumous Vol. 3 of Asow's *Thematisches Verzeichnis* accordingly felt obliged to list it amongst the earlier compositions. Nevertheless, as they readily concede, internal evidence as well as sheer probability indicates that 1878 is more likely to be the true date and that the two horn works were conceived together.

singer. The next day there came for him from the friends
and relations of the family his first little laurel-wreath, the
size of a plate, with a blue bow and golden inscription: 'on
the most memorable day of your life! Dedicated on March
16 1881'. I have kept this relic until the present day. He received as well a golden signet ring with a black oval stone
impressed with his monogram R.S. which Richard has
worn ever since until he presented it to his elder grandson
Richard on his eighteenth birthday.

Waldesgesang[10] begins and ends with a simple Schubertian strain recalling *Die Drossel* (No. 12), but what occurs in between shows how
important the past two years have been to the boy's development.
Indeed, still more might have been shown had not the song been rewritten, severely cutting back the more extravagant modulations, to
the satisfaction of his father as he wrote to Thuille. But much remains
with foretastes of the true Straussian manner.

Ex. 5

In addition to the missing Geibel Lieder, six other songs of this and
the next couple of years are lost, as can be seen from the list above

[10] Strauss supplied the title, the poem coming once more from the collection
Lieder als Intermezzo.

(p. 249). Of these one most regrets, perhaps, the *Immer leiser* of Lingg
which would have been so interesting to compare with Brahms's
famous setting, and a song with the unexpected choice of a poem by
Felicia Hemans,[11] best known as the authoress of *The Boy Stood on the
Burning Deck*. Nos. 33 and 41 are each one of a pair by their respective
poets, Sallet and Stieler, the companion songs of which still survive.
But of the other two lost songs, to words by Uhland and Becker, we
no longer have any clue to the style or content.

Three songs long considered missing have come to light in a fair
copy which resides in the Deutsche Staatsbibliothek, the original manuscripts being amongst those formerly in the possession of Johanna
Pschorr: No. 32, an isolated Heine song, No. 38, an equally unexpected
setting of a Robert Burns love song composed two days after the Felicia
Hemans song (perhaps Strauss stumbled upon a volume of British
verses) and No. 36, again an isolated song to romantic verses by the
normally somewhat academic Otto Friedrich Gruppe.

The Heine setting, which like the Burns has recently been published
in the *Nachlese* volume, is something of a *trouvaille* amongst the Jugendlieder. The poem itself is a haunting allegory with its deathly pale secret
flower in Father's garden, the plucking of which—at its own insistent
behest—bestows angelic peace to the troubled heart. Strauss's imaginative treatment alternates between melancholy and an ethereal calm
which at times approaches the sublime simplicity of Mahler in his
Knaben Wunderhorn Lieder. Particularly interesting is the development
of the two contrasted motifs:

Ex. 6

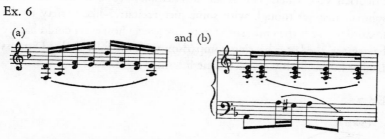

culminating in a dramatic outburst and collapse on (b) as the flower is
actually plucked, followed by an extended lyrical coda in the major in

[11] Steinitzer amusingly mistook Miss Hemans's Christian name for the title of
her poem. At the same time, he did leave us some small indication of the character
of Nos. 35 and 39 by quoting their opening bars.

which (a) floats about gently in the upper register depicting the resultant 'stille Engelslust' ('calm angelic happiness').

By comparison the Robert Burns song (the poem is composed in translation) is inconsiderable, a straightforward strophic setting the main interest of which lies in the imitative touches and rich harmonies of the accompaniment. The coda too is not without merit, appearing to be plunging onwards into an abortive third verse before tailing away in the absence of encouragement from the voice.

Begegnung (No. 36) not only reappeared in the Berlin manuscript but in a further copy together with Nos. 34 and 42. It would seem that when Strauss was on holiday at Bad Heilbrunn during the summer of 1883 he made the acquaintance of Lotti Speyer, a granddaughter of a once well-known song composer Wilhelm Speyer (1790–1878). Although the flirtation was short-lived it lasted long enough for Strauss to take the trouble to compose a song especially for her and to copy out two older ones to keep it company. The three songs were then sent off with a charming accompanying letter of dedication not to be heard of again until the manuscripts were discovered by Otto Albrecht in the possession of Lotti Speyer's niece and, in 1958, published for the first time. The new edition takes the step of describing the songs collectively as *Drei Liebeslieder* and incorrectly ascribes all three to 1883 which is only true of *Rote Rosen* (No. 42), the one song Strauss actually composed for Fräulein Speyer.

The earliest of the three is *Die erwachte Rose* (No. 34) the survivor of a pair of Lieder to words by the early nineteenth century theologist Friedrich von Sallet. This is an unremarkable song in the Mendelssohnian manner though with some nice recitative-like variety to the texture towards the end. The step to *Begegnung* however, could hardly be greater, the latter bearing comparison with the fully-fledged Strauss Lied as in this highly characteristic interlude figuration:

Ex. 7

or the gay *Meistersinger*-like strain:

Ex. 8

It was most likely the reference to roses in the above example which prompted Strauss to include it in his offering to Lotti Speyer since it is roses which are common to all three Lieder rather than their character as love songs. In any case *Begegnung* provided an excellent element of contrast to the predominantly dreamy mood of the other two.

Strauss came upon the Stieler poem *Rote Rosen* in an anthology by Paul Heyse, *Münchner Liederbuch*; he had in fact already used some verses by the Munich poet Karl Stieler for the missing *Waldesgesang* (No. 41). He was greatly taken by the poem and yet, when he came to set the lines to music he found them inflexible (spröde), as he wrote to Lotti apologizing that the promised song had not turned out better. He considered it, he said, hardly suitable for any but the very smallest audiences, and he would have been staggered to have witnessed its first performance, together with those of its two companions, in Carnegie Hall before a crowd of nearly three thousand people by Elisabeth Schwarzkopf on 30th November 1958.

One may perhaps feel that he was a little cavalier in his treatment of the young lady, knowing as he did that he was capable of better music than this rather pale lyric. For by 1883 the nineteen-year old Strauss was on the threshold of his career; several major works had already been printed and he was just completing and preparing for publication his first truly representative set of Lieder, the op. 10 group of eight songs to verses by the Tyrolean poet Hermann von Gilm.

6

43	**Zueignung** ORCH 1940 (also orch.			
44	**Nichts**	Heger)		
45	**Die Nacht**			
46	**Die Georgine**		Gilm	1882–3
47	**Geduld**		aus *Letzte Blätter*	op. 10
48	**Die Verschwiegenen**			
49	**Die Zeitlose**			
50	**Allerseelen** (orch. Heger)			

Strauss owed his discovery of Gilm's poems to Thuille who brought back a copy after a visit to Innsbruck. This copy was a collected edition published in 1864, the year of Gilm's death, and the later verses were grouped together under the title *Letzte Blätter*, no longer adhered to in subsequent editions.[12] Actually, despite Strauss's blanket description of his op. 10 set, the first song does not come from *Letzte Blätter*, and moreover is not called *Zueignung* by Gilm who gave this title to two different poems. But it was with sure instinct that Strauss chose and so labelled this particular poem to open his first group of songs to appear in print.

With its refrain 'Habe Dank' (Gilm's own original title) and prevailing air of ceremonious dedication, it plunges the listener headlong into that brand of enthusiastic *Schwung* which was henceforth to be Strauss's speciality. His genius was now galloping forward at a spectacular rate and with it his grasp of standards. It shows a keen sense of responsibility that with no less than forty-two songs to his credit he withheld even the most recent from publication, preferring to wait until he knew he could present a group more assured and personal in style and accomplishment.

Under its acquired title *Zueignung* has become one of Strauss's best known songs, a tribute in itself to his patience and judgement. In 1932 an orchestral version of the song was published by the conductor Robert Heger, and on 19th June 1940 Strauss himself completed an orchestration which he dedicated to Viorica Ursuleac. Unfortunately however, he took the opportunity of altering the end in order to incorporate a tribute to Ursuleac on her performance of the title role in *Die Aegypt-*

---

[12] In the 1894 Gesamtausgabe of Gilm's works, *Die Georgine, Geduld* and *Allerseelen* belong to a collection entitled *Sophie,* and *Die Zeitlose* to *Sommerfrische in Natters.*

ische Helena. As a result his authentic orchestration is now hardly performable without emendation, not an easy task as, in order to accommodate the extra words 'du wunderschöne Helena' before the final 'Habe Dank', Strauss greatly altered the latter part of his composition. This has left the Heger version in full possession of the field which is regrettable not only since it is greatly inferior to the composer's own colourful score but because Strauss made a number of important other revisions whilst he was about it (changes of vocal line, bar-lengths etc.). Perhaps an official performing score should be put in hand by the publishers, unimpeachably correct as they were in the first place to print the manuscript exactly as Strauss left it.

Nichts is a gay, vivacious song based, in the best Lieder tradition, for the greater part on a single figure:

Ex. 9

f (mit Laune)

Its exuberant good humour and boisterous ending are nicely balanced with moments of broad lyricism as well as fragments of recitative which are eminently suitable for such colloquialisms as:

Ex. 10

aptly expressing the poet's exasperation at being expected to portray in song a mistress of whom in truth he knows virtually nothing.

Die Nacht is another well-known song and justifiably so, for its maturity is remarkable despite moments of seeming plagiarism from sources as widely disparate as Walther's *Preislied* and the Love Duet from Gounod's *Faust*. But perhaps its most famous feature is the opening phrase which cannot fail to recall the wonderful oboe solo from Strauss's own *Don Juan* to be composed five years later.

Ex. 11

Aus dem Wal - - de tritt die Nacht,
(cf Vol. I, Chapter III, Ex, 14)

Although far more rarely performed and less obviously popular, *Die Georgine* is the centre-piece of the group and in many ways its most interesting song. The harmonic freedom, especially of the opening, anticipates Wolf's manner whilst the imaginative variation of a basically strophic structure is hardly less than masterly.

Geduld is again an impetuous song though the deceptive flippancy of its $\frac{6}{8}$ rhythmic pattern hides tragic undertones which blossom into full-blown drama before the end. The lover who can no longer endure being told to exercise patience ends by tearing himself away in despair, for he knows that youth and springtime know no return. The sudden burst of poignancy in the last bar after the long tragic die-away is brilliantly conceived.

In *Die Verschwiegenen* Strauss exploits a freer, more declamatory idiom only hinted at in *Nichts* and which was again to become a salient characteristic of Wolf's Lieder style. This is a short, terse song as is also *Die Zeitlose*. The title of the latter has nothing to do with timelessness but signifies the saffron, a flower which contains a poisonous element just like—so the poem says—the deceptive beauty of a last love. A simple little song, it is interestingly harmonized and has shades of Brahms in its coda.

Lastly comes the ever-popular *Allerseelen*, like the opening song, *Zueignung*, a broad effusion in Strauss's glowing lyricism. *Allerseelen* (All Souls' Day) which falls on 2nd November is the day consecrated to the dead. The poem is, however, a love song set against a background

of graveside flowers and memories of May-time love. This song too
was orchestrated by Heger though not by its creator.

It would be no overstatement to say that the set as a whole is a
magnificent achievement. The selection and ordering of the songs is
organized with the greatest care and skill to show their extraordinary
range and variety to best effect: the expansive outer songs; the alternately gay and dreamy *Nichts* and *Die Nacht* leading to the central *Die
Georgine*; the dramatic *Geduld* followed by two brief songs, themselves
nicely contrasted, all make the group into an unusually satisfying whole,
the key relationships of which are also sensitively handled.

Particularly irksome, therefore, is the seemingly irresponsible tradition in the matter of Lieder publication which splits up the songs
higgledy-piggledy with those of other groups into Lieder albums[13] in
three different vocal transpositions without even stating the original keys.

Indeed the way in which the Lied as a genre is treated with equanimity in the matter of pitch and tonality is quite extraordinary. No one
would dream of performing an instrumental composition in any but
the original key; yet Lieder are freely subjected to virtually unlimited
tonal juggling in order to bring them into the repertoire of every and any
singer regardless of vocal range and character. For the first time since
the early years of their life the songs can only now be readily studied,
appreciated and even performed as they were written, through the
splendid Complete Edition of all Strauss's Lieder.

Furthermore, Strauss expressly stated that with these songs he had
the tenor voice in mind and this led him into a little family trouble. His
father had been particularly anxious that Richard's first published songs
should be dedicated to Aunt Johanna who had been such a source of
encouragement during the years of childhood composing. But when it
came to the point two years later the principal tenor of the Munich
Court Opera Heinrich Vogl expressed a warm admiration for them
and formally requested the young composer that they might be his.
Strauss was greatly flattered and wrote with great anxiety to his father
to pacify Aunt Johanna, as he could not possibly go back on such a
commitment. He would write the next set of songs for a contralto and
they could be for her.

But how far he fulfilled this undertaking will shortly emerge.

---

[13] Universal Edition publishes all the songs of op. 10, 19, 21, 26, 27, 29, 32, 36
and 37 thrown together into a meaningless jumble in four books and for high,
medium and low voice.

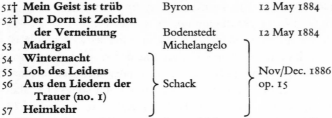

51†	**Mein Geist ist trüb**	Byron	12 May 1884
52†	**Der Dorn ist Zeichen**		
	der Verneinung	Bodenstedt	12 May 1884
53	**Madrigal**	Michelangelo	
54	**Winternacht**		
55	**Lob des Leidens**		Nov/Dec. 1886
56	**Aus den Liedern der**	Schack	op. 15
	Trauer (no. 1)		
57	**Heimkehr**		

The two songs Nos. 51 and 52 which separate op. 10 from Strauss's next published group are again unfortunately lost. The Byron text 'My soul is dark' comes from the famous set of *Hebrew melodies* which includes *The Destruction of Sennacherib*, while the Bodenstedt poem forms part of his once fantastically popular volume of imitation oriental poetry *Die Lieder des Mirza Schaffy* published in 1851. Both songs were written in a single day in May 1884 for Aunt Johanna (who kept them) and it is difficult to understand why they were not used as the starting point for a further group to follow up the success of the Gilm settings. Perhaps Strauss did not think highly enough of them or, being deeply involved with the tremendous spurt of instrumental composition which produced all the early symphonic and chamber works, was not so much in the mood for song writing. At all events, the promised new set was not put in hand until the late autumn of 1886, six months after the family upset.

And a slightly odd group it turned out to be. The first song is a translation of the Michelangelo madrigal 'Porgo umilmente all'aspro giogo il collo', an entirely new departure for Strauss. His attention had, no doubt, been drawn to Michelangelo as a poet during his holiday in Italy, the visit to which we owe the Symphonic Fantasie *Aus Italien*, and one may wonder how it is that having found an adequate volume in Sophie Hasenclever's translations of 1875 he did not select more of them. This is a finely-shaped song but the formality of the poem's mode of expression drew from Strauss more elegance of manner than true spontaneity.

The remaining songs of the group are all settings of poems by Schack. Graf Adolf Friedrich von Schack was a great patron of the arts and his mansion in Munich not only housed a noteworthy collection of modern German paintings but became the active centre of Bavarian literary life. He himself contributed in no mean measure, writing novels, plays, translations from Iberian literature and a quantity of verses, which were published in 1867.

Strauss was clearly more on home ground when he applied himself to Schack's poems and in *Winternacht* he quickly got into his stride. The raging of the storm is suitably graphic, with rearing phrases across the entire range of the keyboard and a happy moment of contrasting lyricism when the poet speaks of the spring which love has awakened in his heart despite the winter night.

Rich harmonic colouring characterizes the central song, *Lob des Leidens* (In praise of suffering), the theme of which is that suffering brings with it beauty of an especial poignancy. Some curious features in this otherwise straightforward if warmly romantic setting cannot go unmentioned, such as the irrelevant preluding piano arpeggios in the opening bar, and a sudden fanfare figure towards the end, wholly unrelated to anything which comes before or after.

The next song is one of two taken from a collection of ten poems entitled *Lieder der Trauer*, the second appearing in a later group. It is a highly dramatic outpouring but with most of its interest lying in the piano accompaniment which makes excellent motivic use of the recognizably Straussian figure:

Ex. 12

Heimkehr with which the group ends is certainly the best known and is amongst the more popular of Strauss's Lieder as a whole.[14] A gentle, rather sentimental miniature, it gives an early example of the rows of consecutive thirds which became an increasing feature of Strauss's mature style.

Ex. 13

[14] An orchestration of *Heimkehr* by one Leopold Weninger exists but is rarely heard.

zu dir ____   kehrt heim ___ mein Herz

There is an undeniably comparable symmetry in the juxtaposition of these five songs and yet they form less of a balanced unit than did the Gilm settings. The single Michelangelo text, alongside the remainder all by Schack, would make it harder to consider them as an entity. It would appear too that Strauss himself viewed them more individually, at least to the extent of dedicating only the second and last, *Winternacht* and *Heimkehr* to Aunt Johanna in partial acquittance of his promise. The others are inscribed to Victoria Blank, the contralto of the Munich Court Opera and Strauss, with perhaps a touch of opportunism, may well have tried to kill two birds with one stone, for when the songs were published two of them were transposed a tone lower and the complete set described as being for 'mittlere Stimme'.

Although Aunt Johanna only received two of the five op. 15 songs it could be said that she had the best. For, with the possible exception of *Heimkehr*, none of them quite compares for distinction of melody and vocal line with their predecessors from op. 10. It is possibly unfair however to assess them wholly apart from the songs of the next and sister set with which they were published simultaneously.

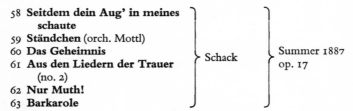

58 **Seitdem dein Aug' in meines schaute**		
59 **Ständchen** (orch. Mottl)		
60 **Das Geheimnis**	Schack	Summer 1887
61 **Aus den Liedern der Trauer** (no. 2)		op. 17
62 **Nur Muth!**		
63 **Barkarole**		

Here all the poems are by Schack, and the settings are once again for high voice, though this time they lack any dedication. Strauss was now back in the swing of Lieder composition; these six further settings of Schack's verses were written close upon each other's heels the following summer and were quickly followed by others. Moreover his imagination had been restimulated and the variety of style and mood in this new group is again fascinating.

The first, *Seitdem dein Aug'*, is short and almost introductory in character. A single arch of love music, it starts abruptly with voice and piano together. Already in *Heimkehr* the voice had entered at the first note but here the impetuousness is heightened by making the song start in the middle of a bar.

In seeking fervour of expression Strauss uses wide intervals and range in the vocal line and, anxious to send the voice into a soarting tessitura, he adds a footnote asking high tenors to transpose the song up a whole tone.

With No. 59 *Ständchen* we come face to face with the most popular of all Strauss's songs. So familiar is it, indeed, that it is hard to put it into context as one of a group and perceive it in relationship to its lesser known companions. So often too has it been heard in its orchestral form that it is easy to forget that the instrumentation is not by Strauss at all but by Felix Mottl,[15] the Wagnerian conductor who also made the orchestrations of four of Wagner's Wesendonck Lieder. A transcription for piano solo (without voice) was also made by the famous pianist Gieseking who, while he was about it, made a similar transcription of *Heimkehr*. Other arrangements for piano duet, salon orchestra, etc. quickly followed, and the song could well claim to have made Strauss's name into a household word single-handed.

That it is a masterpiece there can be little doubt, and only the fact of its being unbearably hackneyed, which Strauss himself deplored, can be blamed for its relegation by some critics to the realms of vulgar trash. ('Populär-Schmissig', even the normally adulatory Ernst Krause labels it.) The featherweight accompaniment to its light and beautifully shaped melody sets the song apart from anything in the young Strauss's Lieder output up to this time, while the surges of lyricism both in the refrain and at the climax of the song are the essence of that glowing ecstasy which is the particular quality of Strauss's art at its best.

In later years he expressed dissatisfaction at, of all things, the handling of the text and some commentators have since taken their cue from this. But at the time he had no such qualms and wrote home with excited pride after performing the song at Weimar (on 28th October 1889,

---

[15] Mottl extended the climax by adding an extra bar at the point where the voice takes the high A sharp, a liberty which Strauss afterwards sanctioned even for performances with piano.

just after his appointment there as conductor) telling how Heinrich
Zeller the tenor had had to repeat it.

The tendency to think of *Ständchen* as an isolated song rather than as
part of a group is heightened by the degree to which it differs stylistically
from its immediate neighbours. With *Das Geheimnis* the music returns
to Strauss's more usual manner in the songs of this period. Not that this
should be understood in a derogatory sense, for *Das Geheimnis* has
many very attractive qualities. The naïve questions on the meaning of
Nature by the unawakened girl are set against gentle, somewhat sugary
phrases and curving arpeggios which come to a bald halt when the all
too adult recipient of the queries turns to her in mock chiding with the
phrase familiar to every child: 'What a silly question!' delivered
against a sudden silence from the accompaniment.

Ex. 14

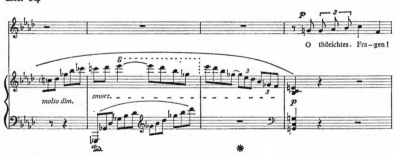

But it is not unkindly meant and the music melts into a soft and
distant key for the final *clou* lines—that love, not words, will teach her
the answers—leaving the piano postlude to twist the music back to the
home key for the final arpeggio.

The second song which Strauss chose from the *Lieder der Trauer* is
entirely different from its predecessor in op. 15, being short and very
gloomy. The poem is mystic and obscure so that even if Strauss's music
adds little but a general atmosphere of oppressed foreboding it serves a
purpose by way of interlude before the big *Nur Muth!*

This, though in no sense a rival to *Ständchen* in sheer immediate appeal, is in many ways the most beautiful of the set. The music expands
from the fine introductory bars with a sure appreciation of the considerable proportions they imply. New motifs are gathered on the way,
building to impressive climaxes in the voice before at last subsiding to
the long Brahmsian postlude. The words with their exhortation to

endure long suffering with courage, for relief will surely follow, find sympathetic expression in the warmth and confidence of the setting.

After such a large-scale song, the concluding *Barkarole* has very much the air of an *envoi* though in a new genre. The music never rises above a *piano*; the water lapping against the little boat is suggested by the ceaseless barcarolle movement of the left-hand accompaniment, and the rocking of the boat by the alternate threes and twos of the bar-lengths in the opening section:

Ex. 15

The recurrent Straussian thirds and sixths will not pass unnoticed, while the figure anticipates to a marked degree one of the principal motifs from *Lied der Frauen*, the great closing song from the Brentano Lieder op. 68. Slight and fragile as it is, this *Barkarole* has considerable enchantment and deserves to be better known.

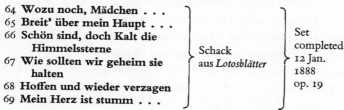

64 **Wozu noch, Mädchen** . . .		
65 **Breit' über mein Haupt** . . .		Set
66 **Schön sind, doch Kalt die Himmelssterne**	Schack aus *Lotosblätter*	completed 12 Jan.
67 **Wie sollten wir geheim sie halten**		1888 op. 19
68 **Hoffen und wieder verzagen**		
69 **Mein Herz ist stumm** . . .		

Lotosblätter is an enormous assemblage of poems divided into five sections, two of which are described as *Verwehte Blätter* (Windswept

Leaves). It is from these that the songs are taken, with the exception of *Hoffen und wieder verzagen* which comes from an entirely different collection of *Liebesgedichte* (Love Poems).

With this set Strauss came to the end of his preoccupation with Schack's poetry which had, when all is said and done, served him well. Moreover, these Schack songs contain—to a greater extent than the last sets—much that is most typical of Strauss's individual style.

Wozu noch, Mädchen has that element of light conversational banter which is often to recur in the best of the coming Lieder, but mixed with accompaniments suggesting the mature operas such as *Rosenkavalier:*

Ex. 16

or Ex. 17 which anticipates quite unmistakably the Falcon's theme from *Die Frau ohne Schatten:*

Ex. 17

The song ends coyly with a rising question-mark on a dominant seventh which resolves down to the deep G flat harmonies of *Breit' über mein Haupt,* a dramatic effect which is ill-sacrificed when one or other of the songs is transposed or performed out of context.

Yet this second song is of a kind at which Strauss found it harder to excel, as comparison with Wolf's analogous examples will quickly show. (For instance *Und willst du deinen Liebsten sterben sehen* uses a similar simplicity of means to create far greater heart-felt response.) Yet *Breit' über mein Haupt* has many points of interest, especially in the growing awareness it shows of the singer's technical skill, even mannerisms, in expressive moments:

Ex. 18

Schön sind, doch kalt die Himmelssterne is overshadowed by the similar and far more melodically memorable love-song *Du meines Herzens Krönelein* from the next group of Lieder op. 21. There are nonetheless some lovely touches such as the softening of the thick harmonies and the delicacy of the piano's echoing phrase at the metaphorical transmutation of the loved one's charms into a sweet shower of rain.

But it is well placed to precede *Wie sollten wir geheim sie halten,* a thrilling song, full of breathless fervour suggestive at times of *Lohengrin* as well as Strauss's own *Feuersnot.* Perhaps Strauss allowed his enthusiasm to get the upper hand at the expense of taste in his over-use of vocal portamenti, as if he were so excited by his discovery of the device that he could not restrain himself from calling upon it at every turn. But the élan carries all before it, giving this central song a climactic quality different in character from any of the corresponding songs in the previous sets.

From this high point the mood of optimism subsides quickly. *Hoffen und wieder verzagen,* though relatively seldom performed, has great intensity and an almost symphonic variety of invention. Key relationship between the Lieder is again exploited and to an even greater degree, this song starting with a chord of A, the tonality of the jubilant *Wie sollten wir geheim sie halten,* before descending to its own gloomier but still related F sharp minor. The alternation of mood which this produces born of the song's title ('to hope and again to despair') returns in the piano postlude.

The last song *Mein Herz ist stumm . . .* is concerned with the winter of old age and affords a fascinating contrast between what the young composer visualized in 1888 and what the octogenarian Strauss actually felt as expressed in his last songs of exactly sixty years later.

The protagonist of Schack's verses regrets with poignant bitterness that the blossoming of nature is no longer able to awaken and rejuvenate his aged heart. Horncalls are heard floating over the spring breezes giving Strauss specific justification for phrases which are by now a very hall-mark of his musical thinking. At length with agonized chord progressions the bleak numbness of the opening gradually returns for the last bars, a device similar in manner to the coda of the preceding song though Strauss goes further in allowing the voice to repeat the opening words in a monotone against the piano's recollections of the initial phrases.

It makes a depressing ending to a set which had begun gaily, but the feeling of unity within the group as a whole is once again remarkably strong and well balanced. Of the three Schack groups this must certainly rank as the finest even though each of the other two contains songs which individually are far better known than any in the *Lotusblätter* settings, namely *Heimkehr* and *Ständchen*. There is some evidence moreover, that Strauss thought of the op. 15 and op. 17 sets as complementary: the placing of one plum in each, of one Trauerlied in each, the use of the unusual Barkarole to bring—in effect—both groups to an interesting end, not to mention Strauss's offer of these sets together and uniquely to the Hamburg publisher Daniel Rahter.

For his op. 19 *Lotosblätter* songs Strauss returned to his true publisher of that period, Spitzweg of Joseph Aibl Verlag, who had taken all his major works since the String Quartet op. 2. The question of dedication also arose once more and Strauss, with what may well have been a personal reason, selected another member of the Munich Opera, Emilie Herzog. For Fräulein Herzog had at Strauss's request undertaken to give advanced lessons in vocal technique to the young and promising soprano Pauline de Ahna.

The songs are dated significantly enough, for 1888 is the year of *Don Juan*, and although many of them must date from the latter months of 1887 this is the time when Strauss's genius was flowering. It is also well over two years since Strauss's historic meetings with Ritter, the Meiningen violinist and composer whose influence in directing Strauss towards the Liszt-Wagner camp had been so far-reaching. It is not idly that one finds oneself continually seeing traces of Strauss's future operas. With op. 19 Strauss the composer of vocal music truly comes of age.

7

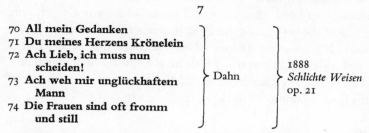

70 **All mein Gedanken**
71 **Du meines Herzens Krönelein**
72 **Ach Lieb, ich muss nun
    scheiden!**
73 **Ach weh mir unglückhaftem
    Mann**
74 **Die Frauen sind oft fromm
    und still**

Dahn

1888
Schlichte Weisen
op. 21

Felix Dahn, to whose verses Strauss next turned, was a poet-historian who had for many years held a professorship in Munich University. A man of wide scholarship, Dahn is remembered today more by his historical works than by his poetry, but in the 1880s his reputation as a creative lyrical writer was at its height as a result of the appearance of a third volume entitled *Balladen und Lieder*.

Strauss's attention was most likely drawn to Dahn by Alexander Ritter, who had himself based his opera *Der faule Hans* on a story by Dahn. The poems Strauss chose belong to a collection called *Schlichte Weisen*—that is to say 'Simple ditties' although the verses are less naïve than this would suggest. The light-hearted title, however, may have contributed towards popularizing the songs which, with the exception of the last, are among Strauss's better known Lieder. Reger in particular, who arranged the first two for piano solo[16] was so taken that he also used Dahn's title *Schlichte Weisen* for his op. 76 which characteristically comprises no fewer than sixty songs in six volumes. In addition he placed at the head his own setting of Dahn's *Du meines Herzens Krönelein* though the remaining fifty-nine texts are by a variety of known or unknown authors.

Dahn's *Schlichte Weisen* is a group of forty poems which, as he described in a footnote, derive from a list of first words of ancient folk songs which he came upon in a museum. Nothing more than these openings was to be found and Dahn amused himself by grafting on continuations while knowing nothing of how any of them went originally.

[16] In addition Reger also made piano solo arrangements of Strauss's op. 10 No. 8, op. 19 No. 2, op. 27 Nos. 2, 3 and 4, op. 29 Nos. 1 and 3, op. 32 No. 1 and op. 37 Nos. 1 and 3. (The twelve arrangements were published in two volumes in 1899.) It was no doubt an outcome of Reger's work in this field that he was led to make a considerable number of his own settings of poems already composed by Strauss.

The resultant poems are generally most successful and Strauss clearly found them gay and stimulating. *All mein Gedanken* is a captivating song, one of the very best in his lightest manner. The delicate humour with which he matches Dahn's whimsical conception of the lover's thoughts travelling like so many little birds to the loved one's window and clamouring for admission, would stand comparison with any of Wolf's finest examples of the kind:

Ex. 19

Nor did Strauss fail to realize that he had hit on rather a splendid idea for he repeated it at the end, the piano taking over the embroidered figure ⌐ x ⌐ by way of postlude. The effect is entrancing.

The justly popular love song *Du meines Herzens Krönelein* is more finely wrought than the apparent naïveté of its opening melody would suggest. Endearing as it is in its straightforward presentation with conventional accompaniment, Strauss had too sophisticated a mind merely to repeat it as, for example, Beethoven does with profoundly heart-warming effect in the Rondo of his E minor Piano Sonata op. 90. Strauss uses the two balancing phrases motivically in a variety of different ways,

[17] 'Pick out your window from all the others, and knock, and call out "open up, let us in, we come from your best beloved with fine greetings".'

even to playing them simultaneously in the piano's tiny coda. But the charming song is perfectly shaped and its ingenuity is not unduly obtrusive.

Much simpler is the affecting *Ach Lieb* No. 72, with its opening and closing refrain so reminiscent of the César Franck Symphony, composed the same year. Here too, however, Strauss's sense of contrast and proportion was unerring when planning the set. The following song bursts in with great panache.

It would have been intriguing to know how the original folk song followed up that wry explosion of self-pity; *Ach weh mir unglückhaftem Mann* ('O Lord, what an unlucky fellow I am'), yet Dahn's continuation catches a light-hearted vein which seems exactly right and Strauss too responded with a deft touch of wit and wry jauntiness. The coach and four in which the hero of the song reckons he would carry off his beloved if only he had a cent to his name is musically the same equipage which the Marschallin sees in her mind's eye when the crowd will watch her drive past in old age as 'die alte Fürstin Resi'—even to the cracks of the whip.

There is also many a harmonic twist and flourish which herald the future master of caricature, while the return to the opening key phrase ('Ach weh' etc.) is dictated by a splendid dramatic instinct, bringing the dreamer back to earth with a jolt, his precious coach and four (now very much in the minor key) receding into the gloom of his imagination.

The last song *Die Frauen sind oft fromm und still* is strange, even enigmatic, and Strauss showed some courage in ending the group with it. Dahn's pious women with their heavenward glances may have been intended with child-like sincerity. But despite the solemnity of Strauss's interesting harmonic chordal setting, it is hard to suppress the feeling that his notoriously anti-religious tongue is in his cheek, especially when at the end, instead of returning to the home key of the song, the piano goes off at a tangent with rising chords of A major, for all the world as if he sees these sanctimonious women like so many Lohengrins each searching the sky for her own pet dove of the Holy Ghost. Understandably the song is rarely heard and yet in its way it ranks as one of the most curious and interesting amongst Strauss's earlier Lieder.

75 **Kornblumen**		28 Mar. 1888	
76 **Mohnblumen**	Dahn	29 Mar. 1888	*Mädchenblumen*
77 **Epheu**		1888	op. 22
78 **Wasserrose**		1888	

A second set of Dahn settings proved less successful. *Mädchenblumen* ('Girl-flowers') is a song cycle in which Dahn sentimentally rhapsodizes over different sorts of girls in terms of their botanical equivalents. Such heavily-laden romanticism would stand in danger of dating irretrievably even in the hands of a great poet and this, for all his eminence as historian, Dahn was surely not.

Yet to damn these songs out of hand through distaste for the verses, as do commentators like Gysi and Muschler, is to beg the question a little hastily. The sole issue is whether or not Strauss's imagination was captured. The idea of the cycle undoubtedly amused him, for he set all four of the poems, retaining Dahn's sequence which suggested nicely contrasted musical moods—a gently flowing lyricism for the cornflower, vivacious trilling and intriguing harmonic flourishes for the blood-red poppy, relaxed sentimentality for the ivy, and ethereal delicacy for the water-rose (the far from obvious floral selection also affording an engaging opportunity for the designer of the very period front cover).[17a]

Kornblumen and *Wasserrose* both provide fascinating examples of how Strauss was able to find inspiration *en route* after at first merely drawing on his unfailing technical skill. Melodically both begin somewhat unmemorably but deepen in the touching way which is at the root of Strauss's mastery:

Ex. 20[18]

Similarly this passage from the closing pages of *Wasserrose* will not fail to affect all lovers of Strauss's peculiar brand of soaring nostalgia:

[17a] See opposite p. 354.

[18] I give the quotation from *Kornblumen* in the key (D major) in which it appears in the autograph. For some reason it was published a semi-tone lower (even for high voice). Nor is this an isolated case.

Ex. 21

He may have relied on it too often, but Strauss certainly understood the secret of the $\frac{6}{4}$ chord.

Fragile as they are, the prevailing danger to these songs is their sentimentality and here *Epheu* (Ivy) is the greatest sinner and accordingly the weakest of the set. By the same token *Mohnblumen* (Poppies), being the liveliest and most sparkling, is also the most accomplished and it is perhaps a sign that Strauss recognized its superiority that he made a special copy with dedication of just this one song to a young lady in Frankfurt, one Marie Fleisch-Prell, whereas the cycle as a whole is inscribed to Hans Giessen. Giessen was Strauss's principal tenor at the time of the composer's appointment to the Weimar Court Opera in 1889, and was to become a regular performer of Strauss's Lieder with Strauss himself at the piano, as well as a companion at Skat[19] together with the conductor Ernst von Schuch.

Strauss published *Mädchenblumen* in 1891 entrusting them to the Berlin house of Adolph Fürstner, this being the start of what was to be almost a life-long association.[20] Nevertheless it was a humble beginning

[19] Strauss's favourite card game. See Vol. II, p. 253.

[20] A confusing misconception by Asow has been perpetuated in the Boosey & Hawkes Complete Edition, that *Mädchenblumen* were first published in London by O. B. Boise. In fact the American Otis Bardwell Boise was a theorist and pedagogue who lived in Berlin between 1888 and 1901. During this time he supplemented his income from teaching by editing composers' manuscripts for

considering the far-reaching consequences, for the *Mädchenblumen* have remained until the present day amongst the least known and performed of all Strauss's Lieder, a neglect they hardly deserve, uneven as one must acknowledge them to be.

79 **Frühlingsgedränge** ⎫ Lenau ⎫ 2 Dec. 1891, op. 26
80 **O wärst du mein!** ⎭ ⎭

Strauss's period of office as conductor of the Weimar Hoftheater was not of a nature which enabled him to indulge in bursts of creative activity. Such time as he had for concentrated thought in the midst of a formidable programme went into the planning and consideration of his first opera *Guntram*, the actual composition of which was largely carried out during his Egyptian holiday after his health had broken down.

It is thus no coincidence that the only important products of these years are arrangements and revisions (Gluck's *Iphigenie auf Tauris* and Strauss's own tone poem *Macbeth*) other than a pair of Lenau settings which he wrote for his pupil Heinrich Zeller, the unfortunate tenor who against heavy odds undertook in due course the title role of *Guntram* at the première in 1894.[21]

Although generally classified as a German poet, Lenau was in fact a Hungarian (his full name was Nikolaus Franz Niembsch von Strehlenau) and his work is characteristically full of melancholy and disillusionment. Apart from the early song, *Nebel* No. 21, Strauss's preoccupation with Lenau had of course centred round the verse-drama *Don Juan*, but these two sharply-contrasted Lieder give a further indication of his fascination with Lenau's work and outlook.

The first song *Frühlingsgedränge* is an outpouring of eager questioning to the spirits of spring, one of a group of ten poems all devoted to different aspects of springtime. Strauss's treatment with its rapid, rippling Lisztian arpeggio figures is deliciously light-weight especially in the transparent ending, yet curiously fails to reflect the poem's wistful final note of interrogation.

If *Frühlingsgedränge* harks back to Liszt, *O wärst du mein!* might even be said to look ahead to early Schönberg with its daring and unconventional chromatic harmonies. Although the music carries a key signa-

---

publication, Brahms being amongst the other masters who profited by his work.

The original plate numbers of the *Mädchenblumen* provide further evidence refuting the statement of the Complete Edition that the association with Fürstner began only with the op. 31 Lieder.

[21] See Vol. I, p. 93, for Strauss's wry account of this event.

ture of three sharps it can hardly be said to be in any key at all, beginning as it does in F sharp major and in the absence of the final implied cadential bar, appearing to end on a $\frac{6}{4}$ chord of B flat minor with every kind of fluid modulatory progression in between.

The broken-hearted lament is one of two poems headed *An ★* from a group of verses entitled *Liebesklänge*, although they are sometimes inscribed *Sophie*, a young girl whom Lenau met when she was only eleven but who came to be one of the strongest influences upon his creative life. The poem's expression of yearning despair inspired Strauss to music of a new depth and intensity. Even whilst one recognizes that the broken and freely declamatory style may militate against its ever attaining the widest popularity, passages like Ex. 22 deserve a more than superficial admiration:

Ex. 22

One cannot but wonder how it is that Strauss was satisfied to publish these songs as a set of two, finding no more Lenau poems to spark an imagination which was making such strides in both technique and expression. Probably *Guntram* was beginning to obsess him to the exclusion of all else and when, with that mighty venture behind him, he turned next to the Lied, he struck gold at the first blow.

8

81	**Ruhe, meine Seele!**			
	ORCH 1948	Henckell	7 May 1894	
82	**Cäcilie** ORCH 1897	Hart	9 Sept. 1894	op. 27
83	**Heimliche Aufforderung**			
	(orch. Heger)	Mackay	22 May 1894	
84	**Morgen!** ORCH 1897	Mackay	21 May 1894	

The first performance of *Macbeth* was but one of many occasions which took Strauss to Berlin during these formative years and here in the great German capital he naturally associated with the advanced thinkers and poets of the day. He was plunging avidly into literature of all sorts at this time and his researches into philosophy on account of the problems connected with *Guntram* took him not only into the world of Nietzsche (leading ultimately to the tone poem *Also sprach Zarathustra*) but also into that of the anarchist-individualist Max Stirner.[22] More important, since Stirner was already long since dead, he fell in with Stirner's followers who, since the Franco-Prussian war, had been trying to establish themselves as a literary counter-movement of primary importance.

The reaction was against the soft-grained sentimental poetry of the mid-nineteenth century culminating in the verses of poets such as Geibel and Heyse (favoured by Hugo Wolf) and including mock medieval or folk poetry, such as the *Des Knaben Wunderhorn* collection, or the work of Rudolf Baumbach.[23]

[22] Stirner was a pseudonym for Kaspar Schmidt (1808–56) whose most famous and influential work was *Der Einzige und sein Eigenthum*. Although now all but forgotten he was at one time considered to be a red-hot radical compared with whom Karl Marx was the mildest of socialists.

[23] Baumbach wrote two volumes in 1877 and 1880 entitled *Lieder eines fahrenden Gesellen* and *Neue Lieder eines fahrenden Gesellen* respectively. Mahler's addiction to this class of poetry thus goes beyond his numerous settings of the *Knaben Wunderhorn* verses to this adoption of Baumbach's title for songs of his

The most virulent member of the new group was Stirner's arch-disciple, the Scottish-born John Henry Mackay who had, however, lived in Germany since early childhood. Karl Henckell was a vigorous hymnist of the new Socialist ideals whilst other prominent members of the movement, if perhaps leaning more towards individualism and the freeing of German poetry than political anarchy, are Liliencron, the brothers Hart, Busse, Falke, and especially Richard Dehmel, which are all names shortly to appear in Strauss's Lieder.

Perhaps these lively reformers saw in the young modernist composer a kindred spirit who would help to further their cause with the aid of his ever more widely accepted music. If so, they had sadly mistaken their man: Strauss's interest in politics or sociology was minimal. Certainly he composed several of their verses, but the ones he chose were for the most part their least radical effusions, poems ironically characterized by the very romanticism upon which they believed they had turned their backs.

Henckell is represented by a beautiful if sombre Lied from his controversial *Buch des Kampfes*. The title of the poem, *Ruhe, meine Seele!* is taken not from the opening words, but from an injunction which appears half in the manner of a refrain though at different points during the second and third stanzas. It comes like an introspective self-admonition to a sorely troubled spirit whose turmoils at last lie behind him, and there is profound significance in that Strauss returned to this Lied fifty-four years later, revising and orchestrating it immediately after completing *Im Abendrot*, the first to be composed of the *Vier letzte Lieder*.

This orchestral version, dated June 9 1948, two days before Strauss's 84th birthday, is of immense importance to the understanding and interpretation of the song. The seemingly simple block chords of the piano accompaniment are shown in the orchestration to have great weight and poignancy whilst in many places the natural inflexions of dramatic timing are stressed by the addition of a bar here or two bars there. The bell-like counter-motif is introduced already near the opening before the entry of the voice and the climax of the song is emphasized in a way which increases its whole stature. By far the hardest to grasp and therefore the least known of a very famous set, *Ruhe, meine Seele!* remains the most impressive.

---

own. In this connexion it is interesting to note that *Das Lied von der Erde* is the title of a volume of poems by Franz Evers which appeared in 1896.

It is followed by *Cäcilie*, which could lay claim to being the most patently Straussian of all the composer's many Lieder. Dashed off on the eve of his wedding, it is to the songs what *Don Juan* is to the orchestral works. The music pours out in a passionate and ceaseless flow of pure inspiration.

The poem by Heinrich Hart[24] takes its title from the poet's wife, the name never actually appearing in the text itself. Instead, great play is made with the phrase 'Wenn du es wüsstest' ('If you only knew'), the repetitions of which build up through the three verses into an ardent declaration of love. The whole song shows unmistakable signs of having been created at a single burst, the élan carrying it beyond the last soaring climax into the postlude, which Strauss varied and improved still further when orchestrating it in 1897 together with *Morgen*, for his Pauline to sing with him during his conducting assignments.[25]

That it was a natural subject for orchestral treatment is self-evident from a mere glance at the style and texture, and eye-witnesses of Strauss's own performances at the piano relate that he produced such a wealth of colour from the instrument that one could almost imagine one was listening to a full orchestra.

A similar *Schwung* characterizes the next song, *Heimliche Aufforderung*, the first of Strauss's Mackay settings, but there is a difference. The accompaniment is much more genuinely pianistic and it is far from idle chance that not only did Strauss refrain from orchestrating just this one of the set, but Heger's over-elaborate version is really no success and is hardly ever used.

Anything further from Mackay's anarchistic mission than this fervent love song it would be hard to find and the whole conception of the lovers' secret tryst amidst a group of merry-makers is happy in the extreme. As in *Cäcilie* the passionate impetus is maintained throughout the song though the much more varied and transparent texture and soft coda sometimes mislead performers to relax the tension.

Again we have an eye-witness account of Strauss's own interpretation. The Viennese musicologist Alfred Orel's[26] description of a Liederabend by Elisabeth Schumann with Strauss at the piano is fascinating:

[24] It is sometimes wrongly ascribed to Hart's brother, Julius.
[25] Strauss orchestrated five songs in all at that time which were afterwards published (in 1911) as a set of 5 *Orchesterlieder*. Apart from *Cäcilie* and *Morgen*, they are *Liebeshymnus* (No. 94), *Das Rosenband* (No. 102) and *Meinem Kinde* (No. 108).
[26] Alfred Orel, 'Richard Strauss als Begleiter seiner Lieder', *Schweizerische Musikzeitung*, Jahrgang 92, Vol. I, p. 13.

. . . I had been chosen to act in the capacity of 'page-turner'. To this day I remember with what trepidation I stepped behind Richard Strauss out of the artists' room and onto the platform of what is today the Brahms-saal and sat by him at the piano. When I opened the music of the first song Strauss said softly to me 'You mustn't look at the notes, for I play it quite differently'. And now I was able to savour an art of accompaniment at first hand such as I have never again experienced in the thirty years or so that have since passed. Such freedom and yet at the same time the highest precision in following the singer, whilst also guiding her interpretation, such support and then again the subtlest understanding of where she needed help, whether in allowing time for breathing, whether to avoid forcing her to exaggerate her own breath control, in short, such complete unity between singer and accompanist was probably never equalled. The printed notes were, in fact, repeatedly only an *aide memoire* for the composer, so to speak, vocal scores such as a singer might use when working with her repetiteur. Without actually becoming 'orchestral' he went far beyond the printed accompaniment and used the possibilities of the piano in an inimitable way. For instance I can remember that in *Heimliche Aufforderung* the well-known leaping runs of the piano began far lower down and therefore flowed in much quicker notes than as it is notated, most likely in order to bring out the contrast with the succeeding quiet quavers still more strongly. Doubling of the bass, enriching of the chords, all these Strauss employed on countless occasions. . . .

The last song in the group is the ever popular *Morgen!* again to a love poem by Mackay, though this time in a mood of deep rapture. A feature of the text is the manner in which it starts as if in the middle of a sentence, 'Und morgen wird die Sonne wieder scheinen' etc. ('And tomorrow the sun will shine again') and this gave Strauss the idea of giving the piano the whole of an opening span of melody, the voice remaining silent as if too moved to give expression to an emotion so full of enchantment.

Only during the closing phrase does the singer enter with seemingly the last, not the first line of the verse but continuing at once, now no longer tongue-tied, while the huge arch of melody repeats itself without interruption. Nor does the voice even now sing the actual melody but—still utterly rapt—rhapsodizes against it in tones of wonderment.

When at last the melody has subsided a second time the music passes into a coda of profound stillness in which the voice gives recitative-like a last blissful sentiment, though breaking off—as it began—in mid-sentence. The melody obediently begins to arch upwards a third time, but stops poised inconclusively on a $^6_4$ chord. The poem, and the song, is over.

So beautiful a curving cantilena all too naturally suggests the sweet tones of a solo violin and if Strauss had not supplied the obvious instrumentation someone else would surely soon have done so. There can be, however, a touch of banality in replacing the implied by the actual and in this instance the piano version presents the highly original if dangerously cloying song to better advantage. Strauss, according to Orel, was careful not to indulge himself in *Morgen!* but played the accompaniment strictly as he had set it down.

These four songs were his wedding present to Pauline; three of them were composed in May 1894 shortly before they left Weimar to return to Munich via Bayreuth, whilst *Cäcilie* was added at the eleventh hour on September 9th. They inaugurated a brilliant partnership of connubial music-making which lasted for many happy years and took them all over the world. Strauss had found not only his life partner but his ideal interpreter in one person, and during the next years the songs poured from his pen.

85	**Traum durch die Dämmerung** (orch. Heger)		
86	**Schlagende Herzen**	Bierbaum	7 June 1895 op. 29
87	**Nachtgang**		

Amongst the friends whom Strauss cultivated on his return to the Munich Court Opera as co-conductor with Levi, was the popular poet Otto Julius Bierbaum. It was Bierbaum who together with Wolzogen and Wedekind was later responsible for the Munich-born *Überbrettl* movement,[27] and Strauss who was at the time looking for a new opera libretto quickly struck up friendship with these lively literary figures. The collaboration with Wolzogen eventually bore fruit with *Feuersnot*, but neither Wedekind nor Bierbaum was able to provide Strauss with the operatic schemes he wanted. Bierbaum in particular offered a couple of texts called *Lobetanz* and *Gugeline* which quite tempted Strauss at first, and then instead of rejecting them outright he farmed them out,

---

[27] See Vol. I, p. 202 (footnote) for a brief account of this partly café, partly music-hall venture.

first to Max Schillings, who was not at all interested, and then successfully to his boyhood friend Ludwig Thuille.

Bierbaum, who was almost Strauss's own age, has been described as
the typical decadent, a frivolous writer of *chansons* and *chansonettes*, and
contemptuously labelled a *Trallalant*. Yet, whilst it is true that he aimed
at pleasing young people with an imitation folk-song idiom, his verses
are of a far higher quality than his detractors implied, and in their day
they enjoyed a genuinely well-deserved success.

Although the operatic schemes came to nothing Strauss was sufficiently drawn to Bierbaum's work to set three of the poems to music
there and then and others were to follow later. The first, *Traum durch
die Dämmerung* is an outstandingly beautiful little piece of nostalgic
nothingness which Strauss turned into one of his most haunting Lieder.
It was with a sure appreciation of its effect that he selected it to represent
him in the 'Works of Peace' section of *Heldenleben*. Passages such as the
following possess that quality of poignancy with which a Lotte Lehmann can summon tears to the eyes at their very recollection:

Ex. 23

A greater contrast than the following song *Schlagende Herzen* it would be difficult to imagine. Bierbaum's poem is exactly the kind of ditty which earned him his doubtful reputation but is carried off with such *joie-de-vivre* that it is indistinguishable from, for instance, the genuine *Knaben Wunderhorn* ballads.

The gay young fellow prancing along to meet his sweetheart, all nature in tune with the wild beating of his heart in anticipation of their meeting, this was an ideal subject for the composer who had just completed *Till Eulenspiegel*. Particularly happy is the way in which the lovers' hearts do not beat or pound but ring like little bells, an idea already present in the text.

Lastly comes a piece of real German nineteenth century romanticism of the Schumann/Heine variety. Such associations with the evergreen *Dichterliebe* must have so enveloped Strauss that his music reverts to something of his earliest Schumannesque style (though note the maturer deep purple of the flat supertonic, marked X in the example, which imbues the whole song with its recurrences):

Ex. 24

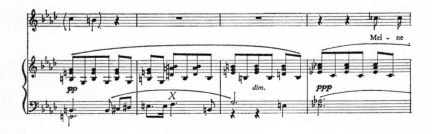

(*Warum?* from *Phantasie-Stücke*, Schumann)

88	**Blauer Sommer**		1 Jan. 1896[28]	
89	**Wenn . . .**	Busse	15 June 1895	op. 31
90	**Weisser Jasmin**		24 June 1895	
91	**Stiller Gang** (with viola obbligato)	Dehmel	30 Dec. 1895	op. 31 no. 4

Carl Busse, an ardent follower of Liliencron, aimed to use the new expressionist movement to bring the whole art of poetry away from an esoteric minority and nearer to the people. Unfortunately for all his desire to rank as a folk-poet he had too minor and too derivative a talent to make any lasting impression. Even the three texts which Strauss selected for his next group of songs are distinctly pale and Strauss never again explored his work.

The occasion for this new set of Lieder was the marriage of Strauss's sister Johanna. In July 1895 she married Otto Rauchenberger, an army

[28] From this point, where the dates of composition conflict with the sequence of opus numbers, to avoid confusion the enumeration preserves the latter.

officer of the real old school, and although Strauss was never a lover of the military he retained a lasting affection for Johanna.

The songs did not come easily and were by no means finished in time, so that the dedication had to be back-dated when they were printed the following year. The publisher was once again Fürstner, although the surrounding works, orchestral and Lieder alike, continued for another three years to be in the hands of his old friend Spitzweg.

The first of the set, *Blauer Sommer* was composed much later than the other two and moreover, improbably enough for the subject of the poem, in mid-winter. It is a strange song consisting of five virtually identical repetitions of a single five-bar strain. The opening chromatically descending phrase is used for modulation so that each of the five statements drops a minor third until at the last the original key is reached once again. Some melodic variety is introduced when the voice, after first enunciating the strain in unison with the piano, then goes its own way; but the thick unaltered texture of block chords moving in heavy quavers is mechanical and uninspired, however much it might be said to portray the torrid heat of a summer's day.

Wenn . . . aims at being an impetuous declaration of love *à la Cäcilie* though it lacks melodic distinction. The motto phrase, however, which opens and closes the song, as well as punctuating its verses, comes from the same vein of invention which was to create Octavian's leaping motif from *Der Rosenkavalier*.

Ex. 25

The song indulges in a great deal of Strauss's favourite plunges in and out of distant tonalities but, characteristic as it is, the music suffers from the fact that in this instance the device is used maliciously as a gibe against his die-hard critics. For in the closing stanza the piece jumps right out of key and never gets back, finishing in E major, a semitone higher than its basic key of E flat. And at the point where this last leap takes place Strauss added a facetious footnote to the effect that singers still performing in the nineteenth century would be well advised to transpose the last two bars down again and finish the song in its original key.

One might think from this that *Wenn . . .* was the first Lied in which Strauss attempted so daring a stroke of modernity, but as we have seen from time to time this is by no means the case. The point lay precisely in the sly way it is carried out, a mere change of key signature, the notes remaining essentially the right ones.

Wenn . . . , complete with its footnote, was first published by itself in a Munich magazine *Jugend* and duly caused the stir Strauss had hoped for. In particular his Intendant at the Munich Opera, Perfall, did not let the opportunity slip through his fingers of giving Strauss—for whom he bore little love—an official reprimand, saying that it was unseemly for a Court conductor to behave like that in public.

Strauss, of course, cared nothing for such rebukes and yet ironically his own trick ultimately misfired: both the E major ending and the twisted cadence by which he reaches it are actually less satisfying than if his jocular suggestion were adopted and the song concluded in its true home key.

Strangely Strauss repeated the very same trick though in reverse, on a bigger scale, and with serious intent in the closing pages of *Rosenkavalier* Act I.[29] There too it leaves a slightly unsatisfactory feeling especially as it is preceded by a long recapitulation of the opening music in the tonic E major before slipping into E flat for the coda. However, although something of formal symmetry is sacrificed, in the opera there is a real gain both in the beauty of the modulation by which the key of E flat is reached and in the soft colour of the tonality for so nostalgic and subdued a dramatic situation. The importance of *Wenn . . .* may well lie less in its intrinsic merits than in the ideas which Strauss was able to carry over into his most popular masterpiece.

Another extraordinary Schumann allusion marks the beginning of the fragile *Weisser Jasmin*, the third song of the triptych. The opening melody, given by the voice, is just like the subsidiary section of *Aufschwung*, one of the best known movements of once again the *Phantasiestücke*.

But there is little Schumannesque this time about the treatment, which in its delicacy and harmonic twists often looks forward to the

[29] See Vol. I, p. 377.

Strauss of the *Bourgeois Gentilhomme* music, such as the Act 3 Sicilienne. Insubstantial as it is, *Weisser Jasmin* is perhaps the most remarkable of the three Busse settings which were planned and published as a group to form Strauss's op. 31.

However, by the time they were completed and placed in Fürstner's hands Strauss had composed another song, and this too something of an oddity. *Stiller Gang*, a setting of words by Richard Dehmel, is for the first time since *Alphorn* (No. 24), a Lied with piano and an obbligato instrument.

The idea of adding a solo viola must have come to Strauss in conjunction with Brahms's two songs op. 91 for the same combination and it is indicative of his purpose that like the Brahms Gesänge, *Stiller Gang* is for low voice. It is dedicated, uniquely, to Marie Ritter, the younger daughter of Alexander Ritter, and may well have been intended for her to sing together with her father. Strauss's nice gesture was soon, however, to be tinged with sadness, for Ritter died on 12th April 1896, just over three months after the song was written. It was published, tacked on to the Busse Lieder, as op. 31 No. 4 with an entirely differently designed front cover and looking very much like an afterthought. But by its very nature it contained problems for the publisher as it does for the would-be performer, and it stands alone not only amidst the works of its time but in the whole of Strauss's output.[30]

If it were no more than an occasional piece, a casual throw-out, it could be conveniently forgotten; but it is on the contrary a most beautiful little song and in many ways superior to the three to which it forms so strange an appendix. It is also Strauss's first setting of words by Dehmel, a poet of particular importance in the new school and one to whom Strauss turned for some of his most beautiful songs in the years to come.[31]

The poem, from a volume entitled *Weib und Welt*, is more a mood painting than a coherent account of the wanderer passing through the burning fields in fast falling autumn twilight, a chafer buzzing past his ear. Strauss's response has the sure touch of immediate sympathetic understanding; the melancholy wail of the viola, the three unexpected

[30] The Complete Edition fails to include the rarely-found printing of the song for voice, viola and piano which it even refers to as a *Bearbeitung*. Moreover, the condensed version is incomplete and contains no reference to the altered voice line in the latter half of the song.

[31] Dehmel was also the author of the poem on which Schönberg based his *Verklärte Nacht* as well as some of his early songs.

pizzicato notes, against the weird undulations of chromatic triplets, all sketch the half-tones of the eerie scene to perfection whilst the resulting Tristanesque harmonies, as in *O wärst du mein* (No. 80), border on the stylistic developments of early Schönberg. There is a single brief outburst of anguish and the song then quickly returns to its former mood, dying away with reiterations of the word *vorbei*. The chafer has passed although we can still sense its buzzing in the ceaseless to-and-fro of the piano's chromatic triplets. This is a fine, and for Strauss most unusual, study in grey.

92	**Ich trage meine Minne**			
	(orch. Heger)	Henckell	26 Jan. 1896	
93	**Sehnsucht**	Liliencron	24 Jan. 1896	
94	**Liebeshymnus** ORCH 1897	Henckell	25 Feb. 1896	op. 32
95	**O süsser Mai!**	Henckell	28 Mar. 1896	
96	**Himmelsboten**	aus *Des Knaben Wunderhorn*	3 Jan. 1896	
97	**Wir beide wollen springen**	Bierbaum	7 June 1896	

The next group was again written for Pauline and contains three settings of poems from the *Buch der Liebe* by Henckell, with whose *Ruhe meine Seele* he had begun his wedding present set op. 27. *Ich trage meine Minne* (Strauss rejected Henckell's simpler title *Minnelied*) has all the artlessness of a folk song, an impression which is intensified by Strauss's repetition, at the end, of the first stanza intact to identical music which is in an equally ingenuous style. Only the central section darkens the gay light-hearted mood and Strauss, while keeping the symmetry of the lines, takes his theme into the minor and, repeating it imitatively in voice and piano, builds a warm climax before melting into the reprise of the opening.

It is a sweet song if a little sentimental especially when taken too lingeringly, and it has understandably become one of Strauss's better-known Lieder. But its true place is as an introduction to *Sehnsucht*, the largest and most important song of the group.

Strauss acted wisely in interrupting his Henckell settings in order to place at just this point so expansive and symphonic a Lied. For the poem is by Liliencron and it was the first time Strauss tackled the work of this extraordinary figure.

A Holsteiner of noble descent, Detlev von Liliencron grew up doing little else than hunting and soldiering. Only after he had lived through a dangerous and to some extent frustrating existence as an officer in the

Prussian army did his thoughts deepen and reveal an outstanding bent towards vivid and realistic poetry. Although his verses at first naturally reflected the military world he knew best, lyrical poems flowed in ever greater profusion until he found himself revered as a pioneer amongst the young naturalist poets of the new movement. It was not for nothing that Busse worshipped him and that Richard Dehmel edited and prepared for publication the first complete eight-volume edition of his works.

An interesting and unusual feature of these volumes is the occasional snatch of music interspersed in the text, a little march for fife and drum, or a line of melody for a gentle refrain showing that not only did the one-time Prussian officer hear his poems sung in his mind's ear, but was often able to pin-point the music itself.

Sehnsucht is remarkable for its complete change of mood midway in the poem and this, with its implicit musical possibilities, clearly fascinated Strauss. The lonely wanderer on the barren heath becomes obsessed with thoughts of his beloved to the point of seeing her hallucinatory image, cold in manner at first, but touched by his repeated declarations of love, ultimately with laughing, shining eyes.

Strauss paints the bleak scene with an extended series of arpeggiando discords which resolve with increasing Tristanesque poignance. At long last the yearning of the song's title evokes the actual image of the beloved:

Ex. 26

ff *molto espress.*

There is a passionate climax based on Ex. 26 amidst the last strophic repetitions of the favourite words 'ich liebe dich'. But towards the end the desolation of the earlier arpeggiando figure returns, giving the impression of the enraptured lover reawakening to an unwelcome awareness of his surroundings. In the last bars, however, he has a fleeting vision of the beloved and the sweet strains of Ex. 26 are recalled wistfully high up in the topmost register as if on a solo violin.

It is indeed strange that Strauss was never led to orchestrate this song, with its almost operatic middle section, rather than the next, *Liebeshymnus*, a much more straightforward piece of lyrical melodizing to a throbbing background of block harmonies, albeit with many an enchanting Straussian side-slip.

The poem, which is another idealistic paean of love ('Hail to the day in which thou wast born' etc.) ends with the phrase:

> Und flehend ruf' ich zum Geschicke:
> O Weile, weile wandellos[32]

So reminiscent is this of the key line from Goethe's *Faust*:

> Zum Augenblicke dürft ich sagen
> Verweile doch, du bist so schön![33]

that it seems to have conjured straight up in Strauss's mind the Gretchen melody from Liszt's *Faust Symphony*.

Ex. 27

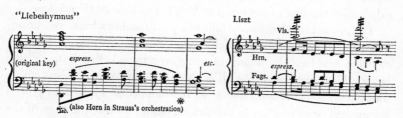

More interesting, though far less well known, is *O süsser Mai!* the last Henckell setting of the group. Here the would-be lover lacks a mistress towards whom to direct his spring-time yearnings and he implores the abstract figure of May to select for him some suitable maiden.

Slightly banal as the idea may seem, it is not untypical in its romantic effusiveness, and Strauss's easy-going setting flows with a sure and natural power of invention. The piano writing has, aptly enough, much of the delicacy (and indeed some markedly similar passagework) of Grieg's popular little Lyric Piece *Schmetterling* ('Butterfly'). At the same time the ingenuously engaging phrases in the closing section of the song are unmistakably Strauss's own.

[32] 'And imploring I cry out to fate: O stay, stay awhile unchanged!'
[33] 'Could I but say to the passing moment: "Ah still delay, thou art so fair!" '

Ex. 28

cf, for example, Ex. 41 of Sinfonia Domestica (Vol. I, p. 190)

It was in 1801 that Clemens Brentano met Achim von Arnim, who became his dearest friend and with whom, during the next few years, he collaborated in travelling up and down the Rhine, collecting and taking down hundreds of folk-songs much as Bartók and Kodály were to do in Hungary a hundred years later.

Brentano and Arnim, being primarily poets, did not concern themselves with the tunes of the songs but only the verses to which, moreover, they applied their own art in adapting and re-writing. The results which they published in 1806–8 as a three-volume anthology were entitled, after the first of the songs in Vol. I, *Des Knaben Wunderhorn.*

The poem *Das Wunderhorn* tells of a youth on horseback who brings to an empress a heavily-jewelled magic horn. If you rub the horn, he explains, you hear the sounds of many wondrous bells of unparalleled beauty. He leaves the horn with her before riding away. It is sometimes thought that the *Wunderhorn* is to be understood symbolically, as a cornucopia or otherwise. In the elegant design on the title page of the original 1806 edition, however, the youth on his cantering horse is shown flourishing the little ivory horn with its four golden bands.

The elaborate dedication was to none other than Goethe himself who, despite the liberties the authors had taken with their material, expressed his delight with their work which he pronounced indispensable to 'all lively-minded people'. It should be kept, he said, 'under the mirror, or wherever one keeps song books or cookery books, to be turned to at any time or in any mood'.

The many hundreds of verses are as varied in style and content as the multifold sources which are mostly given beneath the titles of the songs. So rich are they that it is surprising to find them virtually ignored by the nineteenth century Lieder composers until the advent of Mahler, whose first settings date from 1882. Mendelssohn, Schumann and Brahms had all admittedly drawn on the poems but only for a mere couple of songs or part-songs, and it throws an interesting light on the prevailing serious attitude to the Lied that folk-poems were normally considered as no more than a subsidiary source of material until the last decades of the century.

Strauss's first *Knaben Wunderhorn* setting is so much one of his gayest and most imaginative Lieder that its total neglect remains a mystery. *Himmelsboten zu Liebchens Himmelbett*, the complete original title of the poem, is a whimsical exhortation to the heavenly manifestations of dawn, natural and mythological alike, to awaken the beloved with kisses on this or that part of her delightful anatomy (the English translation is highly entertaining in its genteel avoidance of anything so embarrassing as a 'Brüstlein rund').

This is another song which is linked in its original tonality with the one before, *Himmelsboten* beginning in the A major of *O süsser Mai* and only reaching its own key of F by way of a truly Straussian detour. The lightness of touch and unfailing resourcefulness of the piano figuration anticipates Strauss's best operatic manner and it is particularly interesting to see him instructing the singer, when saying 'good morning' to the beloved, to make a gesture as of bowing before her, a visual histrionic effect which hardly belongs to the art of the Lied.

Wir beide wollen springen No. 97, does not form part of the op. 32 set and moreover was only published for the first time in 1964 when it was incorporated into Volume III of the Complete Edition. It is an isolated Bierbaum setting with the peculiarity that it was composed a year later to the day than the Bierbaum group op. 29.

That this was no error on Strauss's part when dating the autograph is borne out by the fact that Bierbaum's poem itself only appeared during the early half of 1896. Nor was it one of a collection of verses in the conventional sense but formed part of an illustrated almanack entitled *Der Bunte Vogel von Achtzehnhundertundsiebenundneunzig*. ('The Many-coloured Bird of 1897'). Strauss's setting may have originated in connexion with this elaborate publication as the manuscript was itself embodied into an extraordinary piece of decorative illustration by Julius Diez. Diez completely surrounded Strauss's neat calligraphy with an extravagant Art Nouveau design showing a huge personification of Aeolus, the wind god, his great black wings outstretched, in symbolic representation of the opening line 'Es geht ein Wind durch's weite Land'.[34] The landscape, complete with tiny village and loving couple, is in the lower part of the design beneath Strauss's manuscript.

[34] 'A wind drives through the wide land.'

The carefully executed page was completed too late for inclusion in the main scheme, but was reproduced in facsimile in the Oct. 17 1896 issue of *Jugend* (the Munich weekly magazine which had first published the Lied *Wenn*. . .). It then remained forgotten until long after Strauss's death. The song itself is curious, so full of Straussian mannerisms as to be almost a caricature and suggestive in many ways of an improvisation, with its super-dramatic opening flourish intended for the violent gust of wind and its devil-may-care abandonment of the home tonality after only four bars.

Actually this last feature remains its least satisfactory aspect as the music gets so firmly established in the distant key of G that when the voice reaches 'Wir beiden wollen springen' (in fact, the conclusion of the poem) this basic phrase of the title is introduced in that key with all the panache of a final home-coming. Thereafter, the wrench back to the true tonic of F sharp for the coda, however conventionally correct, never has a chance to be wholly convincing. Perhaps Strauss realized the song's impromptu character too clearly to make any efforts towards its preservation.

9

98 **Verführung**	Mackay	5 July 1896	Vier Gesänge
99 **Gesang der Apollo-**			für eine
priesterin	Bodman	end Sept. 1896	Singstimme
100 **Hymnus**	attr. Schiller	5 Jan. 1897	mit Orches-
101 **Pilgers Morgenlied**			terbegleitung
—An Lila	Goethe	25 Jan. 1897	op. 33

There has been some discussion above (with reference to No. 20) on the nature of the orchestral Lied but a little more needs to be added, for in this group of songs op. 33 Strauss boldly followed up Mahler's very recent pioneering with Lieder specifically planned and composed with orchestral accompaniment. Indeed Strauss went a stage further for so integral are his orchestral settings that the piano versions are the merest rehearsal *Klavierauszüge*. These were provided, in the case of Nos. 98 and 99, by Hermann Bischoff, one of Strauss's pupils, while Nos. 100 and 101 were arranged by the well-known Otto Singer who had already made the vocal score of *Guntram*. In this they differ from the *Lieder eines fahrenden Gesellen* and *Knaben Wunderhorn* songs in which the piano accompaniments are Mahler's own alternatives, whereas Strauss definitely made no allowance for performance at Lieder recitals, an uncompromising attitude not always to be found in this composer.

Moreover Strauss's first use of the term 'Gesänge' is also indicative of the entirely new scale of these pieces. *Verführung* in particular is an enormous canvas carried out symphonically with a multiplicity of themes and teeming with imaginative orchestral details recalling *Zarathustra* which was gestating at this time. A surging love song (the title means 'Seduction') it was sternly received by the critics at the first performance and the wretched singer accused of immodest behaviour.

The glowing, passionate texture is built on motivic themes exactly in the manner of the mature operas Strauss was soon to produce once his psychological blockage after the failure of *Guntram* was overcome.

Ex. 29

Ex. 30

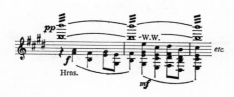

Ex. 31

Ex. 32

At the resplendent climax of the song Exx. 29 and 32 are combined with a rearing augmentation of Ex. 31, after which the mood gradually subsides over a yearning pedal point to the long and beautiful coda.

Hardly less expansive in conception is the fine and stately Song of the Apollo Priestess with its brass fanfares and richly harmonized opening melody.

Ex. 33

Ex. 34

Both these examples undergo elaborate thematic development during the course of the Gesang, together with a warm strand of melody which is built upon a series of perhaps somewhat scholastic imitations:

Ex. 35

It is, however, the opening phrase ⌐ x ⌐ of Ex. 34 which acquires especial interest for the way in which it foreshadows Salome's great motif 'Ich will den Kopf [des Jochanaan]'.[35]

Ex. 36

So lurid a prophetic allusion is, however, far from Bodman's portentous text.

Emanuel von und zu Bodman was, like Liliencron, of noble birth and with a military background. One of the younger members of the late-romantic literary circle, Bodman was in his early twenties when he wrote the verses chosen by Strauss. Although the poem treats of naked

[35] See Vol. I, p. 262, Ex. 25.

youths and maidens sporting amidst the beauties of nature, it maintains a detached view of such behaviour as befits a paean sung by an acolyte in adoration of the divinity she serves. Hence Strauss also preserves a certain distance which is oddly accentuated by the rhythmic throbbing figures of accompaniment and the use of swinging pizzicato chords. These, introduced at first during an intriguing central duet for solo violin and clarinet, return with greater emphasis in the grandiose postlude and conjure up a suggestion of the priestess's mighty harp.

The orchestral harp, having been ingeniously omitted from the *Gesang der Apollopriesterin*, is featured in the following song, *Hymnus*, which actually begins with a long harp solo[36] for all the world like Wolfram preluding at the Sängerkrieg in *Tannhäuser*.

The poem has given rise to much head-shaking since, although it appears in complete editions of Schiller's works, it is included amongst the poems of which his authorship remains doubtful. Entitled 'Im Oktober 1788' (*Hymnus* is Strauss's additional heading) it is, like the Bodman verses, addressed to a divinity though this time by the poet in gratitude to his muse.

Strauss takes as his cue the poet's reference to his *Saitenspiel*, the lyre with which, thanks to the goddess who has bestowed it, he can pour out his praise. But, although the idea is in principle a good one and the Gesang well contrasted with its neighbours, it suffers from the fact that the opening melody, from which most of the material is derived, lacks distinction. As a result, despite some attractive passages during its amiable flow and some fascinating detail, one is left with an unusually blank impression. *Hymnus* possesses the double-edged distinction of being at the same time the best known and the weakest of the set.

The last song is again vintage Strauss. Goethe's sub-title *An Lila* should not cause the Lied to be associated with Strauss's struggles to make something of Goethe's Singspiel of that name. This was a different Lila for the poem was one of two which Goethe wrote in May 1772 after spending Easter in Homburg where he met a young lady, Luise von Ziegler, who was also familiarly known as Lila. *Pilgers Morgenlied* was actually written on the morning Goethe left Homburg.

Strauss turns it into a wild impetuous tirade built on the striking initial figure:

---

[36] A curious misprint in the orchestral score adds to the first bars all the indications for sustaining pedal to be found in Otto Singer's piano arrangement. Needless to say, the harp has no sustaining pedal.

Ex. 37

The score prescribes a high baritone and this leads to the problem of the group as a whole. According to the scores, No. 98 is for soprano or tenor, No. 99 for soprano, No. 100 for baritone or mezzo-soprano and No. 101 for baritone, thus making it clear that there is no question of the four Gesänge being presented as an entity by a single singer. At the 1910 Munich Strauss Festival, when Strauss himself conducted, they were divided across two concerts, at one of which Edyth Walker sang the first two Gesänge and at the other Fritz Feinhals sang the third and fourth.

In fact *Verführung* does not lie well or sound satisfactory for a tenor and this is another instance of the composer condoning the use of a female artist to proclaim words unquestionably addressed by a man to a woman. Conversely *Hymnus* is quite certainly a male voice Gesang (the vocal line is even written in the bass clef which is itself not the invariable custom when writing for baritone) and would be quite unsuitable for mezzo-soprano. Moreover, it is by no means every baritone who could tackle both Nos. 100 and 101 as the former descends to while the latter goes up to the unusually high:

Practical considerations may thus have contributed to the unfortunate neglect of these important Gesänge which despite their uneven quality deserve a better fate, especially the magnificent No. 97.

10

102	**Das Rosenband** ORCH 1897	Klopstock	22 Sept. 1897	
103	**Für funfzehn Pfennige**	aus *Des Knaben Wunderhorn*	2 Sept. 1897	op. 36
104	**Hat gesagt—bleibt's nicht dabei**		31 May 1898	
105	**Anbetung**	Rückert	24 Mar. 1898	

On 30th March 1898 Strauss wrote to his mother 'I am being very industrious and have got eight new songs ready . . .' This was at the time of the first performance of *Don Quixote* and Strauss had also just entered into contractual arrangements to take over the Berlin Court Opera so that this was for him a fine period full of exciting prospects.

However, he did not publish the songs, the grouping of which did not yet satisfy him, until he had added a further seven which—as he told his father—Pauline was to present with him in Weimar on 30th January 1899. These fifteen Lieder he then reshuffled into three groups for publication, the first two sets being the last of all his works to be assigned to his old friend and sponsor Eugen Spitzweg of Joseph Aibl Verlag.

The op. 36 set consists of four songs, two love lyrics embracing a pair of lively *Knaben Wunderhorn* ditties. *Das Rosenband*, the opening love song, is one of Strauss's two Klopstock settings and is also one of the very few songs in which he chose a poem already set to music by a great predecessor, in this instance Schubert. It belongs to the vast collection of lyrics which form the most inspired part of Klopstock's enormous output and which the poet grouped together in 1771 under the rather misleading title of *Oden* (Odes). Klopstock had originally called it *Cidli* after the pet name of Meta Möller who was his wife for only four blissful years.

A gentle love-song, the poem describes how the lover ties up his beloved with rose-chains whilst she lies sleeping. Schubert had treated the two verses strophically, though varying the piano accompaniment to his essentially simple melody. It goes without saying that Strauss's version is far more sophisticated, but one needs to take into account the fact that, alone in this group, it was composed for orchestra. Moreover, the rarely heard orchestral accompaniment contains a mass of enchanting detail which Strauss ruthlessly put aside when this time he made his own piano transcription.

Interestingly enough Strauss followed Schubert, whose familiar song he will certainly have known, in building his new setting on a basically strophic plan, although his variations in the second verse are highly individual. A side by side comparison of the opening lines makes a fascinating study of the two composers' approaches to a single problem:

Ex. 38a

(Schubert)

Im Früh-lings-schatt-en fand ich sie; da band ich sie mit Ro-sen-bän-dern:

Ex. 38b

Their comparable use of melody is disguised, apart from Strauss's more elaborate piano figuration, by his distortions in order to throw the emphasis onto the word 'sie', and also by his typical side-slips to and from a distant tonality. It is this latter characteristic which then becomes the strongest feature of Strauss's strophic variations, for he slips so far away that the second verse actually starts in the wrong key and only finds its way back, with winning effect, at the return of the bar ⌐ x ⌐ in Ex. 38b.

This bar is also important for the precedent its curving melisma sets for a twist of pianissimo vocal cantilena on the final word 'Elysium'. The little postlude is based on the ascending phrase which has additionally served as second subject during each of the two verses of the song.

Ex. 39

Here too, in this broadly legato wide-spanned motif, is a further indication that Strauss conceived the song orchestrally, with Ex. 39 appearing first on clarinet and horn, then during the second stanza on violins and cellos, and in the coda an octave higher on a solo violin accompanied, with faultless sense of colour, by three flutes.

Das Rosenband has a separate dedication from the remainder of the op. 36 set, being inscribed to a cousin of Strauss, Marie Hörberger, though in her married name of Riemerschmid, still today a distinguished family of Munich architects.

The other three songs are dedicated to Strauss's colleague, the tenor Raoul Walter who was famous for his opera and Lieder performances. *Für funfzehn Pfennige* is undoubtedly the best known and rates amongst Strauss's more popular songs though its rather coy joviality offends some critics.

The English equivalent would, one supposes, be 'for twopence ha'penny', the folk-song telling of a girl who seeks a bridegroom for that sum. She falls in with a rich scribe who is more than willing to woo her but in the end she is rude to him and he sends her packing. The regular intrusions of the phrase 'Für funfzehn Pfennige' as the little tale unfolds are often apt, and Strauss varies their treatment with all the infinite skill and resourcefulness at his command, but the song's whimsy comes at times dangerously near to archness.

In finer taste, if less direct, is the other *Knaben Wunderhorn* setting *Hat gesagt—bleibt's nicht dabei*. The poem's asperity and humour reflects in every line the spontaneous wit of the country folk from whom Arnim and Brentano took it down by word of mouth. It is by turns sharp, sparkling, malicious, gay and Strauss gives many an indication of enjoyment in his setting, which is full of happy ideas.

Every verse is treated separately, each with a full close and fermata (pause) in a different key. In the first two the sly young girl disposes contemptuously of her parents' pie-crust promises. Those of her lover in the third verse are, however, a different matter and rapturously she reflects that in matters of love one thing has a way of leading to another (this is the 'bleibt's nicht dabei' of the title). The little turn:

Ex. 40

which only makes its appearance in this third verse, is exploited with the utmost charm as the girl's enthusiasm mounts, and the whole song looks forward to the felicities of the *Bourgeois Gentilhomme/Ariadne* music.

Anbetung is Strauss's first Rückert Lied, although he had the previous year, in 1897, made a choral setting of his verses. Friedrich Rückert has already been cited (in Vol. II, p. 368) as the author of Mahler's *Kindertotenlieder*. He is also the author of that best-loved of all Schumann's songs *Du meine Seele, du mein Herz*, which comes from the same collection of *Liebesfrühling* in which Strauss found the poem *Anbetung*. A far earlier literary figure than the fin-de-siècle poets of so many of Strauss's previous songs, Rückert belongs to the lyricists of the first part of the nineteenth century and his love poems have much in common with his contemporaries Heine and Eichendorff.

Strauss's craftmanship in the extensive *Anbetung* is of a high order, with a wealth of thematic material presented in the fervent opening bars:

Ex. 41

Unlike the first verse which is largely built from the piano's arpeggios, the second verse is a grazioso interlude which develops the light-hearted phrase ⌈ w ⌉. After a soft episode based on ⌈ v ⌉ the piano takes over the vocal themes ⌈ x ⌉ and ⌈ z ⌉ in a high register and devoid of ornamental elaboration. This is a well planned point of repose even though the voice line pursues its own recitative-like way through it.

Now the song's main climax is worked up, beginning with a resumption of the arpeggios which lead to the first return of the opening passionate phrase, combining and alternating with the warm cadence ⌈ y ⌉. The climax itself, at the words 'Wie soll ich danken?' ('How should I give thanks?') dissolves into a dramatic pause, and the soft coda then reiterates the key words 'wie schön' no less than eight times to repetitions of ⌈ y ⌉ and ⌈ u ⌉.

It can be seen that here is a considerable example of Strauss's symphonic Lieder construction and one would expect so much fine musical thinking to carry all before it. Yet the coda which ought to be especially moving fails in its effect, the very many 'wie schön's becoming at last almost embarrassing.[37] Rightly chosen in the first place as the large-scale culmination of an interesting set of songs, *Anbetung* has ironically come to be the only one to fall by the wayside.

106 **Glückes genug**	Liliencron	8 Feb. 1898	
107 **Ich liebe dich** ORCH 1943	Liliencron	7 Feb. 1898	
108 **Meinem Kinde** ORCH 1897	Falke	8 Feb. 1897	op. 37
109 **Mein Auge** ORCH 1933	Dehmel	16 Apr. 1898	
110 **Herr Lenz**	Bodman	9 June 1896	
111 **Hochzeitlich Lied**	Lindner	30 Mar. 1898	

Strauss chose two Liliencron Lieder to open the op. 37 group. Composed in quick succession, they could hardly be more strongly contrasted in style even though they are both love-songs. *Glückes genug* is a sugary-sweet rhapsody in the form of a pair of little verses each of which ends with the words of the title, set to a wide swooping phrase itself like a sigh of contentment. The principal theme, which dominates the song and also supplies the postlude, is characterized by Strauss's favourite rows of consecutive thirds. Sentimental as it certainly is, this is a very charming song.

[37] Strauss omits the last four lines in which the long poem descends into tragedy with the death of 'the fair Freimund'.

Ich liebe dich, on the other hand, is very far from what Liliencron's title suggests. Curiously enough, and especially after *Sehnsucht* (No. 93, see above p. 296) one searches in vain for these words in the new song which turns out to be heroic and stirring in expression. Here it is Liliencron the soldier-nobleman who, almost defiantly, lays at the feet of his beloved a coach-and-four, a castle, his unquestioning fidelity in adversity and, at the last, companionship in a self-inflicted death with his own dagger.

To Strauss, heroic gestures and the key of E flat had been linked once and for all by Beethoven, and just as he was at this very time building a major symphonic work in E flat on a heroic theme (*Ein Heldenleben*) so this song is full of comparable bravura firmly established in that same key and culminating in a flamboyant coda for the piano alone.

This was an obvious candidate for orchestration and is one of the songs Strauss turned to forty-five years later when, for the second time, a major world holocaust was to limit the outlook for large-scale compositions. As always, the composer's own orchestral version is valuable and revealing. In the first place, although this set of op. 37 Lieder is dedicated *en bloc* to Pauline in celebration of their little son Franz's first birthday (April 12th 1898), *Ich liebe dich* is above all a man's song and in the full score the vocal line is designated for a tenor and in the tenor clef. Then, instead of entrusting the unaccompanied voice with the establishing of a martial atmosphere as in the original piano version, he now precedes the entry with a fanfare of brass and drums which emphasizes even further the uncompromising nature of the nobleman's declaration of love.

Meinem Kinde which follows is again as utterly different as it is possible to be; a rapt cradle song, its composition (in February 1897) may well have been with the Strausses' expected new baby in mind. One of his most beautiful songs, it is especially so in its delicate setting for a chamber ensemble of ten solo instruments.

This is the only Lied Strauss composed to words by Gustav Falke, another prominent member of the Liliencron circle, and the mood of idyllic wonderment created by the poem is caught in sounds which look forward to the most affecting moments of the Marschallin's music in *Der Rosenkavalier.*

Ex. 42

(The key of G flat in which the instrumental original is set has a particularly apt velvety quality and is infinitely preferable to the generally
accepted transposed version for high voice.)

In the spring and summer of 1898 Strauss turned again and with more
determination to the poems of Richard Dehmel, selecting the first of the
resultant half dozen or more settings for inclusion here. Dehmel considered *Mein Auge* one of his weaker poems and even went so far as to
send Strauss a copy of his latest collection begging the composer to
throw away the early one lest he be tempted to set to music other im-
mature verses of the kind. But this verdict by its creator seems unwar-
rantably harsh and in any case the poem drew from Strauss another
attractive love-song though more in a lyrical mood of devotion than
of passion. The Schumannesque principal melody harks back to the
Strauss of *Zueignung* although the harmonies which persist throughout
the song in descending clusters of thick harp-like block chords, are very
much those of the mature composer.

Au fond a fine song, the unvaried accompaniment gives a rather

turgid effect; Strauss seems to have recognized this failing as his instrumentation shows some most interesting rethinking. This is one of
four songs[38] which, while taking a cure at Bad Wiessee in September
1933, he later orchestrated for Viorica Ursuleac who, together with her
husband Clemens Krauss, was enjoying the early days of their close
association with Strauss.

It would even appear that the orchestral version of *Mein Auge*, as we
have it, does not represent Strauss's last thoughts which for some reason
he may have forgotten to carry out. In his diaries he writes of his intention to add a seven-bar Vorspiel, but when the editor of the Complete Edition, Dr Franz Trenner, located the score amongst the Strauss
archives at Garmisch no trace of the promised Vorspiel was to be found.

Disappointing as the loss may be, for the idea had been excellent,
the score itself is interesting enough for it makes a big change in the
character of the song. This it achieves by concentrating on the melodic
aspects at the expense of those pounding chords which, so far from being on the harp (although there is a harp in the scoring) descend
smoothly on soft solo strings and thus for much of the time are submerged against the broad generous cantilena.

Herr Lenz is the second of Strauss's two Bodman settings and was
written in the same year as the *Gesang der Apollopriesterin*, that is, somewhat earlier than its companion songs of this group. A jaunty, even
hearty outburst, it sets out to portray the effervescence which the sudden
arrival of spring awakens in an extrovert young fellow.

In the last song *Hochzeitlich Lied* we are again back in the world of
soft undulations. The poem is by the Viennese author, Anton Lindner,
who afterwards tried to tempt Strauss with his translation of Oscar
Wilde's *Salome*. Its theme is one of seduction and Strauss includes a
quotation from the Venusberg scene in the first act of *Tannhäuser*:

Ex. 43

(= Venus' song: 'Geliebter, komm'. Sieh dort die Grotte' etc.) It is a

---

[38] The other three were *Befreit* No. 115, *Frühlingsfeier* No. 159 and *Lied der
Frauen* No. 184. (See below, pp. 317, 353 and 378.)

big and also difficult song, not only in its very wide vocal range and chromatic harmonies (the chromaticisms are often so deceptive that the transposed editions for lower voice contain some important wrong notes in the piano part) but for the pianist in establishing the right mood of swaying languor while maintaining a flowing tempo, the voice being instructed to remain soft-toned but extremely passionate throughout. In its role of concluding song it makes interesting comparison with *Anbetung*, the corresponding last of the preceding group op. 36. Although on an equally large scale, *Hochzeitlich Lied* aims less high and thus, as often with Strauss, is more successful.

112 **Leises Lied**	Dehmel	2 July 1898	
113 **Jung Hexenlied**	Bierbaum	31 May 1898	
114 **Der Arbeitsmann** ORCH 1941		12 June 1898	op. 39
115 **Befreit** ORCH 1933	Dehmel	2 June 1898	
116 **Lied an meinen Sohn**		8 July 1898	

Strauss now made up a group of almost entirely Dehmel settings including, for the first time, two sociologically important poems. Indeed the sprightly Bierbaum Lied seems almost out of place amidst such serious company except that it was most likely for the sake of light relief that Strauss interpolated it.

Dehmel has been called the most controversial poet of the expressionist movement and in the songs of this period Strauss presents a cross-section of his work. *Leises Lied* is a mood picture in half tones and Strauss actually comes close to the veiled mysticism of Debussy. The delicate treatment of the voice and the development of the tiny semiquaver figure (which only on four widely separated instances varies the pulsating rhythm) are the work of an almost Gallic sensitivity. Only his deeply rooted instinct to resolve the enigmatic harmonies into conventional cadences betrays the German romantic composer.

Jung Hexenlied is also technically fascinating though in a very different way and, if *Leises Lied* is the closest Strauss came to the French school, this daring song, as Strauss referred to it when writing to his parents, is nearer to the half-humorous, half whimsical character sketches of Hugo Wolf. Bierbaum's poem is a very strange ditty, full of jocular onomatopaeic refrain lines—'rack, schack' for the weird little witch-mother's pony as she rides home over the mountains in blackest night: 'kling-ling' for the curious ringing as of children in her ears, which stops dead as she espies her house deep in the valley below, its light shining to pick out her own expectant 'Bübchen'.

Strauss naturally makes the most of all the countless pictorial opportunities and ingeniously pinpoints the oddity of the vignette by setting it in two keys, so that one is never convinced that either is the real tonic, least of all the one on which the song suddenly ends. Amidst the many twists and turns, a lightly tender motif is featured as if to show that the feelings of the young witch for her offspring are genuine and even human.

Ex. 44

(Leicht bewegt)

ausdrucksvoll

It is one of the songs in which—according to Strauss himself—his Pauline used to excel, and this throws an interesting further light on her artistry and personality. For with all her sharpness of manner she clearly had an enchanting sense of fantasy and a liveliness of wit which never ceased to delight her admiring husband.

With *Der Arbeitsmann* ('The Workman'), however, we turn to sterner matters. Strauss was the last man to become involved in social reform but where his art was concerned he was equally fearless in his adoption of inflammatory subject-material. Hence when during his study of Dehmel his eye lighted upon this stirring poem of protest, he entertained no more thoughts of the disapproval it might arouse than he would, a few years later, over the sexual extravagances of Wilde's *Salome*. To him, here was a magnificent vehicle for music, and of it he made one of his very greatest songs, full of drama and pathos.

Its three fine motifs are developed on a symphonic scale, first the dignified labourer himself, grim representative of an under-privileged working class:

Ex. 45

Next an ominous gloomy theme which might be taken as the motif of Time that all-important ingredient of their life which is rapidly running out:

Ex. 46

wuchtig

As the song steadily intensifies, Ex. 46 (often together with the threatening ascending figure Ex. 45(x)) is given dramatic urgency by the use of diminution, viz:

Ex. 46a

and even double diminution:

Ex. 46b

drängend

The last, but most important of all, is the pathetic motif which, originally forming part of the opening statement of Ex. 45, quickly becomes identified with the workman's desire for freedom amidst the beauties of nature, and at the tearing climaxes of the song it epitomizes his sufferings:

Ex. 47

On 9th September 1941 Strauss wrote to the great bass-baritone Hans Hotter, who was shortly to create the role of Olivier in *Capriccio*,

> . . . I have—as also suitable for you—instrumentated *Der Arbeitsmann*, but it is in manuscript and is in Vienna, from where I would gladly send you the material.

No more suitable or desirable song for orchestral presentation can be imagined and it is tantalizing that up to the time of writing no trace

of score or parts has been found, or even evidence that the orchestral
version ever actually reached performance.

Befreit, the third of this particularly important group, is another of
Strauss's greatest songs although it failed to satisfy Dehmel, the author
of the text. The meaning of the words gave rise from the first to a considerable amount of discussion; although Dehmel used to say that no
poem was worth twopence unless it could be interpreted in at least half
a dozen different ways all equally good, he decided in this instance to
circulate his views and intentions, which were published in the May
1902 number of the Journal *Die Musik*. After criticising Strauss's approach, he went on to reveal that he had, while writing down the
poem, the picture before him of a man speaking to his dying wife,
though Dehmel took care to cover himself by saying that he would
have nothing against seeing it as some other kind of parting between
any pair of lovers ('after all, every farewell is related to death').

He became voluble over the way one should be affected by such a
poem ('the value of art in "feeling-tableaux" (Gefühlsbildern) lies in its
ability to uplift beyond the insipid state of being moved'), and scathing
over those people who have no idea how to read poetry. But it is hard
to find in his lofty explanations the grounds on which he rejected
Strauss's profoundly stirring rendering as being too soft-grained.

The title-word *Befreit* derives from the basic sentiment of the poem,
an ultimate devotion which has 'freed' the loving pair from suffering
to a point which not death itself can threaten. The firm serenity of the
music reflects the immortal quality of their love which is also emphasized
by a phrase recalling the so moving passage of Gretchen's ineffable
love in Liszt's *Faust Symphony*:

Ex. 48

This theme recurs at various key-points, but the true refrain lies in the
bitter-sweet phrase 'O Glück!' ('O happiness!', i.e. in the midst of
poignant sorrow) which crowns each verse of the song, and it is the

melodic line which accompanies this which Strauss extracted when he chose *Befreit* to join *Traum durch die Dämmerung* as representative of his Lieder output in the Works of Peace section of his new tone poem *Ein Heldenleben.*

Ex. 49

This is the second of the four songs which Strauss orchestrated for Viorica Ursuleac in September 1933. It is strange that the publishers, Robert Forberg of Leipzig, to whom the group op. 39 was entrusted, remain ignorant of this beautiful score, which is printed in Volume IV of the Collected Edition, and continue to issue a far inferior version by one Hans Stüber.

Lastly comes *Lied an meinen Sohn,* a violent stormy tirade of which Jethro Bithell writes:

> One of the first documents in the Sohn-Vater-Kampf which marks [the] period; the revolt of youth against parental authority and old-fashioned doctrines was part of the *Jugendbewegung* and was taken over as one of the main tenets of expressionism. Dehmel himself had given his father trouble.[39]

In fact the poem goes even further than this, for the young father actually implores his baby son not to heed him when he becomes a man but to remain true to himself.

The music makes great play with the storm which reminds the father of his own fearful childhood. So wild is the piano accompaniment that, as Strauss said himself after battling with it on tour, 'it takes the devil to play that!' Savage drumbeats, cascading chromatics, wailing motifs, rearing arpeggios, it goes through all the motions. As in the two previous groups Strauss strove to make a culmination of this closing song,

[39] *Anthology of German Poetry 1880–1940.* Methuen, London, 1941.

but somehow he was misled by the undoubted significance of the poem into seeing in it the wrong kind of climactic quality. Nowhere is there that sense of overwhelming triumph over adversity suggested by Strauss's C major peroration which accordingly ends by becoming banal. It is unfortunate especially as the remainder of this group is on such a consistently high level of achievement. Nevertheless op. 39 brought great success to Strauss and established him as a Lieder composer in addition to his already unassailable position as the leading symphonist of his time.

II

117 **Wiegenlied** ORCH 1900	Dehmel	22 Aug. 1899	
118 **In der Campagna**	Mackay	24 Aug. 1899	
119 **Am Ufer**	Dehmel	15 Aug. 1899	op. 41
120 **Bruder Liederlich**	Liliencron	16 Aug. 1899	
121 **Leise Lieder**	Morgenstern	4 June 1899	

The well-known *Wiegenlied*, which was also subsequently set by both Pfitzner and Reger, comes from an extremely long and involved complex of poems which Dehmel describes as an 'Erotic Rhapsody'. Entitled *Die Verwandlungen der Venus* ('The Transformations of Venus'), it consists of no less than thirty-two extended effusions with a so-called 'moralische Ouvertüre' and various linking sections. The main verses are all given appropriate sub-titles such as *Venus Creatrix, Venus Religio, Venus Metaphysica*, even *Venus Bestia* and *Venus Perversa*; one of the last in the cycle *Venus Consolatrix* actually exceeds the bounds of what was at the time considered decorous and the law insisted that the Complete Edition of Dehmel's works published in 1913 replace a substantial portion of the text with rows of dashes.

In this scheme of things the *Wiegenlied* constitutes the poem entitled *Venus Mater* (as opposed to the following disillusioned *Venus Mamma* with which it is connected by a couple of sardonic linking stanzas).

Here we are once again concerned with an especial popular favourite. Not only is the magical atmosphere maintained across a considerable canvas, but the simple melody itself is one of Strauss's most beautiful.

Within a few months the orchestral version followed, to make up a little group of *Mutterlieder* together with *Meinem Kind* (No. 108) and *Muttertändelei* (No. 123, the latter composed a week before *Wiegenlied* but published later as one of the set op. 43). These three 'Songs of a Mother' Pauline sang at several of Strauss's orchestral concerts during 1900 and 1901.

Exquisite as it is, the orchestration of *Wiegenlied* presented its problems and the composer had some second thoughts on how to transcribe the essentially pianistic arpeggiando figure which persists practically without interruption throughout the song. After some cogitation he took the unusual step of adding a footnote allowing for a variant of the figure, which is given to three solo violins (or later violas) on the grounds that

> since according to the singer's breath-control the tempo of this song is changeable like the favours of a woman (wie Frauengunst) yet these arpeggios are only possible in a certain tempo . . .[40]

Strauss was nothing if not experienced and *Wiegenlied* is still subject to the widest variations of speed in the hands of different performers who find the enormous spans of its melodic phrases taxing. Yet, unlike so many of his accompaniments, the basic texture is so transparent that the song suffers surprisingly little from this diversity of treatment.

In der Campagna is the last of Strauss's Mackay settings and also the least satisfactory, being out of scale for its content. It is not the length, for the song is relatively compact, but rather the extravagant manner which bursts the bounds of Lied form and almost suggests some mighty operatic Scena.

Moreover the piano clatters away at its very topmost octave until the music seems to cry out for the rich sheen of Strauss's soaring violins and warm background of wind and brass:

Ex. 50

[40] Elena Gerhardt, who had access to Strauss's own copy, saw the original and quoted it in the commemorative edition of *Tempo*, Boosey & Hawkes, London, Summer 1949. It is a pity that the original publishers saw fit to prune Strauss's footnote of its allusion to feminine caprice, no doubt finding it unbusinesslike in a professional conducting score.

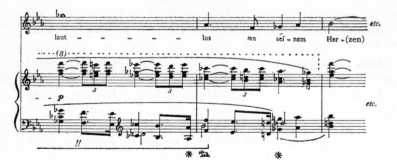

It is nevertheless remarkable for its tremendous élan as well as for some odd unexpected harmonic clashes and bald gawky polyphonic writing (as in the bracketed passage in Ex. 50). Motivically it looks forward to works such as the *Alpensinfonie* and even *Elektra*, the closing scene of which it anticipates in no small degree.

Mackay's verses are an enthusiastic outpouring of welcome to all nature, the poet hardly knowing how to contain his *joie de vivre*, and Strauss seems to have been trying for all he was worth to recapture the ecstasy of his own joyful paean *Aus Italien*.

But he was never throughout his long life able to put the clock back successfully. The time of the tone poems was passing and he was approaching one of the main turning points in his creative life. The songs which bridge the gap before he reasserted himself triumphantly in the opera house often reflect this uneasy moment of impasse.

After the wild exuberance of *In der Campagna, Am Ufer* is quite extraordinarily static. Dehmel's little poem is almost pure atmosphere and Strauss's interpretation, apart from the three gentle ripples lapping the shore, consists of soft slow block chords.

But the apparent simplicity is deceptive and the vocal line both subtle and extremely difficult.

Bruder Liederlich is one of Liliencron's best known poems though it represents the apogee of an early style that he himself longed should be forgotten—the disturbingly successful portrayal of that type of swashbuckling, over-bearing German youth which, after the poet's death, reached such a hideous glorification in the S.S. and Hitlerjugend.

In fact the bluster is to some extent a defence mechanism for in the course of his worthless gadding about (Liederlich means 'dissolute') the young rascal has played fast and loose with the girls, one of whom has fallen for him. Nothing loath he has seduced her and then, the fun over, 'gives her her chips' ('so rauh gab den Reisepass . . .'). But he finds he cannot get her bitter tears out of his mind and tries desperately to drown the image in drink and cards.

Every few words are punctuated by his flamboyant 'Halli und Hallo' which Strauss handles with as much ingenuity as he had used in *Für fünfzehn Pfennige* (No. 103), but *Bruder Liederlich* exchanges the arch manner of the earlier song for an uncomfortable heartiness.

Leise Lieder (No. 121) (not to be confused with Leises Lied) is Strauss's only song to words by Christian Morgenstern, a younger contemporary of Dehmel's and something of a mystic. This is certainly in keeping with the poet's concept of songs so soft that they are inaudible not only to the human ear but to the very moon and stars.

Though it contains some lovely harmonies, this is hardly one of Strauss's more inspired Lieder, especially as it conforms to the general rule that his attempts at pursuing mystical ideas were apt to degenerate into sentimentality.

For the dedication of these five songs Strauss turned again to the younger daughter of his old friend Ritter, for whom he had already written the song with viola obbligato, *Stiller Gang* (No. 91). In the meantime Marie had married Friedrich Rösch, an old school-mate of Strauss and with whom he had preserved a lively friendship. To him Strauss had already dedicated *Tod und Verklärung*, *Feuersnot* was soon to follow and, in particular, *Krämerspiegel* for reasons which will be discussed in their proper place. Rösch, that unusual and valuable combination of lawyer and musician, had recently been instrumental together with Strauss in forming a Composers' Guild.

The op. 41 Lieder were amongst the first Strauss composed after his move from Munich to Berlin in connexion with his appointment to the Berlin Court Opera, although only the last, *Leise Lieder*, was actually composed in his new home in the suburb of Charlottenburg, the others being the fruit of a summer holiday in the family mountain retreat at Marquartstein.

122 **An Sie**	Klopstock	14 Aug. 1899	
123 **Muttertändelei** ORCH 1900	Bürger	15 Aug. 1899	op. 43
124 **Die Ulme zu Hirsau**	Uhland	4 Sept. 1899	

These three songs are to poems by 'ältere deutsche Dichter' as Strauss entitled them.

An Sie is, like *Das Rosenband* No. 102, another of Klopstock's Odes also set by Schubert. This one, dated 1752, begins with an address to 'blessed Time, the bringer of all bliss'. (Here is a different aspect of the enigmatic figure of Time from the one seen by the Marschallin in 'Die Zeit, die ist ein sonderbar Ding'.)

It is, however, a little obscure in its expression, a quality hardly calculated to stir Strauss's most spontaneous invention. Beautifully moulded and with some lovely harmonies, the Lied remains too conventional, even formalized. The pianistic figuration weaving continuously over and around the melodic line has almost the manner of some Chopin Étude. Strauss's heart was not touched and *An Sie* is hardly more than a product of his craftsmanship.

In *Muttertändelei* however, composed the following day, Strauss was once more in his element. The poem is a delightful miniature by that great original, Gottfried August Bürger, best known for his dramatic ballads which inspired composers such as César Franck and Duparc in their *Le Chasseur Maudit* and *Lenore* respectively. Nor is this the ultimate significance of these splendid poems which have been compared with Goethe's *Werther* in their far-reaching effect on the romantic movement in Europe.

To Bürger 'Volkspoesie' was the only poetry that was true and living, a view amply illustrated in *Muttertändelei*, an effervescent little song of a young mother boasting of her paragon of a child to all her friends and neighbours. Strauss's setting is in his own gayest and most popular idiom:

Ex. 51

This is certainly Strauss's equivalent to Mahler's *Wer hat dies Liedel erdacht*. Here for comparison are the last few bars of that favourite amongst Mahler's *Knaben Wunderhorn* songs:

Ex. 52

(Voice with upper line)

The similarity is, of course, more a matter of genre than of melodic line (though compare the last bars) and both are in any case descendants of Schumann's *Das ist ein Flöten und Geigen* from the *Dichterliebe*. But the approach between Strauss and Mahler is brought the more to one's attention by the orchestrations of the two songs which make the most fascinating comparison.

Muttertändelei is undoubtedly one of the most winning of Strauss's Orchesterlieder, from the happy idea of the two new introductory bars for bassoons and clarinets rising in thirds, to the exclusion of double basses from the small and delicately handled instrumentation which was carried out, just over six months after the song was composed, to make the third of the little group of *Mutterlieder* mentioned above (p. 318).

Die Ulme zu Hirsau is indeed an unusual song. The choice of poem is itself curious, though it marks Strauss's return to Uhland who had been a source of texts several times in the Jugendlieder (See Nos. 2, 3, 5, 12 and 31) and within a year Strauss was to devote an entire group to Uhland settings.

This particular poem is however, a rather pretentious allegory. Hirsau is the site of an ancient Benedictine monastery and Uhland tells of an old elm pushing its way up from the restrictive darkness of the ruined walls to the light and freedom of the upper air. So, he says with rising fervour, did the liberating force of Protestantism which flourished in that other monastery at Wittenberg also press upwards with its giant boughs. (One is to remember that it was from Wittenberg that Martin Luther emerged to spread the word and spirit which led to the Reformation.)

Strauss's setting begins by putting into juxtaposition a simple folky, even Schumannesque strain with a decorative filigree suggestive of the elm's foliage fluttering in its search for light. Both undergo considerable development (including some quite strange and interesting harmonies) during this extensive song.

In due course the analogous idea is reached of Luther's Reformation spreading like the branches of a tree to become the illuminating spirit of the world, and here Strauss struggles manfully to match the exalted sentiments. The voice proclaims the majestic words in heroic strains, the piano thunders in rising octaves and ripples in high arpeggio flourishes reminiscent of the cadenza to Grieg's Concerto. At last, for the climax, Luther's own most famous Chorale *Ein' Feste Burg ist unser Gott* is intoned impressively after an exciting switch upwards to a new shining tonality.

But with unerring instinct Strauss causes the last chord of the chorale (which has led back to the home key of the song) to dissolve into the foliage figuration and the vision fades so that the end of the song reverts once again to the ancient elm amidst its ruined walls of the Hirsau monastery.

Although *Die Ulme zu Hirsau* is a less important song than it ought to be, reflecting Strauss's personal lack of religious conviction, it is of considerable interest in its anticipation of salient features in the two one-act operas of over thirty-five years later, *Daphne* and *Friedenstag*. Strauss certainly must have thought back to his earlier evocation of rustling leaves when creating the magical scene of Daphne's transformation.

Ex. 53

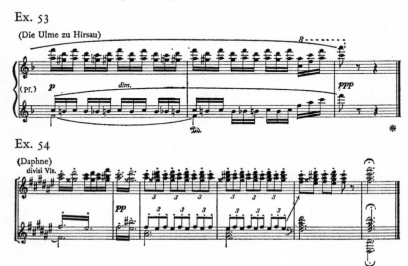

(Die Ulme zu Hirsau)

Ex. 54

(Daphne)

And where *Friedenstag* is concerned the palpable suitability of quoting *Ein' Feste Burg* in an opera based on the religious wars[41] which centred on the Reformation cannot fail to have reminded Strauss of his previous quotation of that Protestant hymn of defiance.

125 **Notturno**	Dehmel	16 Sept. 1899	Zwei grössere Gesänge
126 **Nächtlicher Gang**	Rückert	10 Nov. 1899	für tiefe Stimme mit Orchesterbegleitung op. 44

In letters to his parents Strauss referred to these two works as 'Baritongesänge' although in the first the vocal line is written in the treble clef whereas the second is in the bass. This betrays in the oddest way the song's chief difficulty since by converse *Notturno* takes the voice down to which is properly in the register of a bass-baritone if not a true bass singer, whereas *Nächtlicher Gang* goes right up to: and indeed spends much of the time in that exalted tessitura which is only possible for a very high baritone.

As a result both, although ranking amongst Strauss's finest as well as more ambitious vocal works, have been wholly neglected and are to this day quite unknown.

Dehmel's poem comes from the collection entitled *Aber der Liebe* and tells of the vision in a dream of Death in the shape of a much loved friend who appears in bright moonshine at deepest night playing a supplicating air on his violin. The title *Notturno* is Dehmel's own and the long poem one of great emotional intensity.

Strauss seems to have thought that the apparition being no more than a dream robs it of much of its impact, for he omitted the opening stanza and last line of all—that is, the framework which contains the idea of the poet's awakening thankfully to allow the solemn and gloomy song to recede from the memory of his dream and fade softly back into the night.

If the omissions render the meaning of the verses as a whole more obscure, they certainly add to the mystic unreality of the conception, a quality which attracted the young Schönberg to other such examples of Dehmel's work. Moreover, as with Schönberg, this side of Dehmel led Strauss to some quite remarkable harmonic thinking.

In the first place *Notturno* is in two keys (F sharp minor and G minor) and the way it slithers to and fro between these basically distant tonalities is at times even more subtle than the corresponding switches in Strauss's previous great bi-tonal work, *Also sprach Zarathustra*.

[41] See above, Chapter XIX, p. 65.

Such juxtapositions of tonal centres are established at once in the opening introductory section although the high woodwind chords seem to be searching for the right alternative to the persistent gloomy fifth on F sharp: . Strauss had already effectively introduced bare fifths in *Guntram* to depict bleakness not only of scenery but within the soul of a protagonist, and he was soon to achieve particularly striking results with them in *Elektra*. Indeed the latter opera is to be presaged in many ways in the course of these Gesänge.

The singer passes from the barren snowscape to his awareness of his dead friend's spectre and the solo violin, which true to the suggestion in the poem is a centre figure of Strauss's score, makes its appearance on the highest possible F sharp. Then meandering mournfully down, it leads to the principal themes which henceforward dominate the song.

Ex. 55

(wie   einst —   so   mild, —)
(as once so gentle)

Ex. 56

Apparently of the utmost simplicity, these motifs are worked and combined with ingenious and fruitful imagination. Ex. 56 begins life as a mere secondary bass-line to Ex. 55 but almost immediately takes over a principal role in forming one of those highly charged chromatic cadences such as the Russian miniaturist composer Liadov used so hauntingly in his tiny symphonic poem, *Kikimora*.

Ex. 57

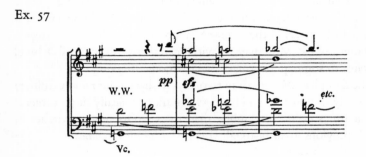

The arrival of Ex. 57 marks the first resting-point for the song's shifting Tristanesque harmonies in its other main key of G minor, but it is hardly allowed to linger there. Ex. 55—now transformed into an extended melody—not only moves into new and highly nostalgic regions but gives one or sometimes two little upward lurches of its entire harmonic apparatus at just the most poignant moments:

Ex. 58

This chromatic hoist becomes a salient characteristic of the score especially in the turbulent middle section, where it is combined with an elaborated form of the scrunch of Ex. 57 recurring again and again. Anguished climaxes are built up, at the peak of which the bare fifths of the opening now scream against the despairing moans of Ex. 58(x), viciously asserting F sharp in point-blank rejection of the wailing attempts to bring the music to a softer resolution in G.

At last the suffering is over and the song ends with a long shivering coda. The bleak fifths return as at the opening though sliding chromatically up and down against the groping woodwind chords, occasionally giving rise to polytonal effects. But Strauss was not ready, as in *Salome* and *Elektra*, to pose jammed-together tonalities for their own sake any more than he left his advanced chromatic harmonies unresolved in the way that Schönberg, faced with similar situations, was very soon to do. Yet for his day the Strauss of this period could be far from conventional: just as the song's first true stanza after the scene-setting introduction has gravitated almost naturally from one to the other of its main keys, so the final cadence of Ex. 57 (instead of remaining content in F sharp) goes through the same motion and twists itself to come to rest on a warm and grateful chord of G minor, giving rise at the time to much excited comment.

So interesting and colourful a score is it, that one finds it hard to realize that Strauss has dispensed entirely with horns, trumpets and all percussion; only the three trombones are preserved for their sombre quality.

He makes up for this economy, however, in the second song *Nächtlicher Gang* which is scored for an extravagant orchestra including six horns, six percussion players (as well as timpani) and two piccolos in addition to an already unusually large section of four flutes.

As before with other Strauss songs, similarity of title could lead to confusion, this time with *Nachtgang* (No. 87) and even perhaps with *Stiller Gang* (No. 91). But this is a very different proposition from either of those: the first of six Rückert settings which he composed between November 1899 and February 1900, it is based on an extraordinary and little-known poem of that great romantic author.

In common with Dehmel's *Notturno*, it is eerie and uncanny in expression, whilst its furious vivacity makes it an ideal foil even as it preserves some unity in forming a ghostly diptych. Moreover although nothing is lacking in the build-up of nocturnal horror, much is left to the reader's imagination—what might be these two fearful coal-black phantoms tearing through the night to the shriek of owls ('Uhu'—memories of *Der Freischütz*) past church-towers and grave-yards, hills and streams, through farms, in and out of kennels with red teeth gleaming, until their destination is reached—the window of the Beloved, the Bride, who lies in bed groaning in her dreams.

And every verse ends with the phrase 'Es muss doch zur Liebsten gehn!' ('Onwards, but onwards to the Beloved!') which Strauss makes into a more gently harmonized refrain:

Ex. 59

The stalking of the nightmares is also depicted through a recurring motif:

Ex. 60

which is often in direct conflict with the prevailing tonality.

The yearning Ex. 59 plays the double role of germinal theme amidst the frenzy of the main passage-work (with its graphic instrumentation and chromatic or even polytonal harmonies), and of softening melodic influence with harp arpeggios when it comes into its own at each refrain.

An additional significance of the Beloved's theme lies in its initial augmented triad ⌐ x ⌐ which enables it to increase the ambiguity of the harmonies as it ploughs through the rushing chromatic scales on horns, woodwind, piccolos, against birch, xylophone, castanets, rubbed tam-tam—piling entry upon entry in its feverish agony. A further even more desperate phrase is added as the terrible journey presses on towards its climax:

Ex. 61

At the end Strauss adds one extra 'Es muss doch zur Liebsten . . .' which is left unfinished with grisly intent swamped by the cataclysm in the orchestra. There is a long, long silence and the Gesang then closes with two slow and very soft statements of the Beloved's motif against alternating sustained chords, on horns and cellos, of E flat minor and C major.

Nächtlicher Gang is again one of the stepping stones on the road to *Elektra*, but no longer in the mere matter of general indications foreshadowing the idiom of that landmark in Strauss's development; clearly and directly it anticipates such supreme moments as the ghastly procession which precedes the entry of Klytemnestra or of the brutal hammering motif of the Tutor (Vol. I, p. 325 Ex. 39) who with inflexible purpose forces Orestes to achieve his fearful murders.

Even the last bars correspond, for it was precisely with the same two contrasted chords that Strauss chose to end the opera, though hurled savagely instead of, as here, dwelt upon with sinister implication. It is best not to think too much about what became of the wretched bride.

12

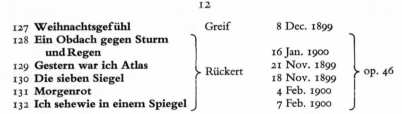

127	**Weihnachtsgefühl**	Greif	8 Dec. 1899	
128	**Ein Obdach gegen Sturm und Regen**		16 Jan. 1900	
129	**Gestern war ich Atlas**	Rückert	21 Nov. 1899	op. 46
130	**Die sieben Siegel**		18 Nov. 1899	
131	**Morgenrot**		4 Feb. 1900	
132	**Ich sehewie in einem Spiegel**		7 Feb. 1900	

Before continuing the survey of Strauss's Rückert Lieder of this period it is necessary to make a short digression in order to take in an isolated song which seems to have been completed in their midst.

Weihnachtsgefühl is something of a mystery. Steinitzer classed it amongst the childhood songs of 1879 but appears not to have seen the latest manuscript which is carefully dated and also bears the place-name Charlottenburg, Strauss's Berlin home only since the last few months of 1899. Moreover Steinitzer quotes the opening for baritone in the key of D flat whereas the manuscript, which was reproduced in facsimile in the Berlin journal *Woche* on December 23 1899, is a tone higher and makes no specification of voice.

It would seem likely that the version we now have is a recomposed Lied for, simple as it is, it has many touches which could not have been written by the boy Strauss.[42] Unfortunately the manuscript Steinitzer saw was in the possession of Uncle George Pschorr and, like those of Aunt Johanna, has disappeared.

Strauss's only setting to words by Martin Greif, it is rather a beautiful little song. Greif, whose real name was Friedrich Hermann Frey, was one of the more inspired lyric poets of the Geibel, Schack, Bodenstedt circle in Munich. He too, like Liliencron, was strangely enough a retired army officer, and yet his poetry—in company with some others of this epoch whom we have encountered—often has a strong folk-song flavour for which he is affectionately remembered. *Weihnachtsgefühl* is a very typically German expression of nostalgia at the approach of Christmas, of the lustre of childhood bliss which seems dream-like to weave about the Christmas tree though 'it will never again return'.

The music echoes these melancholy thoughts with some harmonic invention and also, though briefly, with strands of melody; the whole

---

[42] It is still included amongst the *Jugendlieder* in Vol. III of the Complete Edition whilst bearing the inscription under the last bars for all to see: 'Charlottenburg 8 December 1899'.

is directed to be performed as if in a dream. Although admittedly slight, it is by no means an unworthy addition to the already large and fast growing body of Lieder.

Strauss had intended his five Rückert settings op. 46 for his father's seventy-eighth birthday but, when offered the male-voice choruses op. 45 by way of alternative, the old man decided that those were nearer his style. It was not, however, too serious a loss that he suffered through his rather naïve choice as these sentimental songs are scarcely more successful than was Strauss's first attempt at composing Rückert's very stylized lyrics (cf. *Anbetung* No. 105).

These strangely unsuitable texts come partly, once again, from the *Liebesfrühling* volume and partly from some Persian quatrains. Rückert concocted well over a hundred quatrains and Strauss picked out a few that seemed as if they might fit together, as in No. 129 which is a combination of three.

Ein Obdach gegen Sturm und Regen is a love poem built around the proverb, quoted as a refrain, that 'he who seeks little finds much'. Thus when in the storms of winter the poet sought a haven, what he actually discovered was his heart's ultimate refuge.

Strauss, in his own easy-going manner, clothes the whole in an agreeable lilting $\frac{6}{8}$ movement, treating Rückert's naïve lyric with light-hearted abandon.

In the second song *Gestern war ich Atlas* he tried to come to grips with the content of the amorous verses (these are the Persian quatrains), yet not only the far-fetched opening line which gives the song its title ('Yesterday I was Atlas bearing the weight of heaven when my beloved's heart beat upon my breast') but such ding-dong rhymes as:

> . . . je länger, je lieber
> . . . je enger, je lieber,
> . . . je bänger, je lieber.

produce too stilted an expression to transmute convincingly into music. Strauss exercised much skill in contriving varied and interesting motivic subject-matter—one theme is intriguingly reminiscent of a phrase from *Zarathustra*—but despite some purple passages the song remains obstinately artificial.

Die Sieben Siegel, another of the *Liebesfrühling* collection, is again a trivial idea (the seals are kisses laid in seven places upon the beloved to preserve her chastity) but this time evoked a feather-weight response from Strauss. The style is admittedly of the kind which produced much spontaneous and good-humoured music from *Till* to *Feuersnot* and *Ariadne* but here its mannered perkiness becomes tiresome:

Ex. 62

Weil ich dich nicht le - gen kann   un- ter Schloss und Rie - - gel (etc.) [43]

and later:

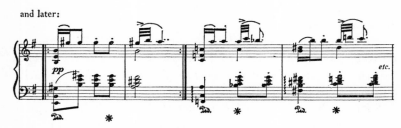

The fourth of the set, *Morgenrot* (as with *Die sieben Siegel*, Strauss supplied the obvious title), is in many ways the most captivating and surges along with typical *Schwung*. At the same time its principal theme is so closely derived in melodic outline, key and harmonization from the Trio section of the Scherzo of Brahms' op. 1 Piano Sonata that it almost makes one wonder whether Strauss had perhaps been idly strumming through the Brahms movement whilst at a loss for ideas, and still had it in his head when he finally applied himself to the task in hand.

If not then vintage Strauss, it is an infectiously enthusiastic love song with an extremely exacting vocal line. In this connexion one notes Strauss in later years recommending *Morgenrot* to Hans Hotter amongst others of his more rarely performed Lieder.

Lastly comes *Ich sehe wie in einem Spiegel* which seems to hark back to the early days of *Aus Italien* and the Violin Sonata. Of its kind, nevertheless, it is a beautifully made reverie formed out of two ideas, the opening melodic phrase and a gentle harmonic motif:

[43] 'Since I cannot put you under lock and key.'

Ex. 63

Ex. 64

Ex. 64 in particular leads the music through some delicate as well as more impassioned moments during the central developing section of the song.

These Rückert Lieder mark Strauss's decision to return for most of his future works to the Berlin publisher Adolf Fürstner, in celebration of which the songs were printed each with an elaborately designed front cover showing a lady and bearded gentleman in various postures of devotion or rapture. It is in the nature of illustrative art that these have so dated as to become hilarious period pieces,[44] but they have had the unfortunate effect of underlining the inherent sentimentality of what must, for all its well-balanced grouping, be classed as one of Strauss's weaker sets.

133 **Auf ein Kind**			5 May 1900		
134 **Des Dichters Abendgang**					
ORCH 1918			8 May 1900		
135 **Rückleben**	}	Uhland	23 May 1900	}	op. 47
136 **Einkehr**			30 May 1900		
137 **Von den sieben Zechbrü-**					
dern			11 June 1900		

The previous year Strauss had not only set Uhland's *Die Ulme zu Hirsau* (No. 124) but had chosen one of the poet's best ballads, *Das Schloss am Meere* for his companion melodrama to *Enoch Arden*. In this

---

[44] Two are shown in the illustration between pp. 354 and 355. Although, writing in 1924, Muschler described them as 'scheusslich' or 'entsetzlich', today they can be greeted with a more indulgent delight in the vagaries of past taste.

flat interim period when his creative powers were inclined to falter he may well have felt that to work on Uhland's poetry, for which he had had an affection since early childhood, would reawaken his imagination.

And so to some extent it did: *Auf ein Kind* is quite a remarkable little song in its way, being in two clear—though continuous—sections. The tortured first half subsides into serenity for the second, which consists of entirely different thematic material, as the mood changes; the poet's spiritual oppression has been dispelled by the angelic innocence of the child to whom the song is addressed. At the end the rising figure on which the whole closing section has been based drifts upwards to a cloudless C major and dies away in ethereal calm.

Like some previous groups, op. 47 thus begins with a miniature which serves as an introduction to weightier matters. *Des Dichters Abendgang* is a full scale heroic song and originally composed in Strauss's heroic key of E flat. It is particularly necessary to emphasize this because the relationships between the tonalities of these Uhland songs are important once again. Yet Strauss himself not only sanctioned the use of lower transpositions of *Des Dichters Abendgang* but subsequently orchestrated it in the soprano key of D flat (uniquely in the group this song was intended specifically for a tenor).[45]

In fact the deeper keys ill suit the texture and style which can all too easily become heavy and muddy. It is largely characterized by two strongly contrasted elements, the ostinato figure portraying the poet as he ambles along:

Ex. 65

together with a declamatory theme (its initial phrase suggesting the trumpets and trombones to whom Strauss later gave it) which depicts a sunset so majestic that its effect will endure to uplift the spirit in times of adversity to come.

Ex. 66

[45] The striking low tessitura of the voice's last bars had even to be abandoned in the orchestral version which gives only the previously second-best *ossia* upper line.

Des Dichters Abendgang is one of Strauss's more impressive Lieder, and yet it often seems to fall short of the high expectations it arouses. This may be partly due to the dangerously jaunty Ex. 65 which persists without interruption throughout the song in apparent conflict with the tempo direction 'sehr ruhig und feierlich' ('very quiet and solemn'). The orchestral version shows that on the contrary the ostinato, which is played legato by cellos and lower woodwind, should not be allowed to become too obtrusive and disturbing to the essential mood of wonder in the face of nature's beauty.

From such exultation, *Rückleben* plunges abruptly into the depths of sorrow. The words are thought to be in memory of a certain Wilhelmine Gmelin, a girl with whom Uhland was infatuated, though he never declared his love, and who died at a very early age. Uhland expressed his sorrow in a pair of linked poems, the first of which, *Ein Abend*, also describes (like *Des Dichters Abendgang*) the poet raising his eyes to a glorious sunset, and it may very well have been this which attracted Strauss's attention though he decided against the inclusion of *Ein Abend* itself for fear, perhaps, of repeating himself.

Rückleben begins in the most profound darkness as the poet kneels by the grave of his beloved. The reference to 'Totenreich' ('Realm of Death') must certainly have remained in Strauss's memory to be re-awakened when coming to Hofmannsthal's lines 'Es gibt ein Reich . . . Totenreich' in Ariadne's monologue from *Ariadne auf Naxos*, and which, as here, he set by sending the soprano down to her deepest chest notes.[46]

The strange word *Rückleben* which heads the song refers to the poet who in his grief imagines time reversing so that his loved one emerges from her bier. She rapidly regains her beauty, upon which they relive their life together backwards to the very first ecstatic kiss until at last they find themselves again in the radiant mornings of their shared childhood.

It is with this idea that the song takes wing, a wide spanned melody which begins in the new and bright key of D major (the gloomy opening had remained in the darkness of B flat minor). Not that it remains there long, for as it flows forward it modulates into warmer regions through 'flat' tonalities related to the introductory opening, thus preserving unity within the basic structure of the song, in the course of which it grows new and heart-felt melodic extensions.

---

[46] Despite the male connotations of the words the vocal line is, as so often in Strauss, composed for a woman's voice.

Ex. 67

The vision swells to radiant rhapsodic heights and finally falls away as if to close in the rich D flat we have come to expect (its sombre relative minor has been left far behind).

But with one of Strauss's deft harmonic switches the last meanderings of the arpeggio accompaniment, now extended upwards to the extreme limits of the piano, remain suspended in the far distant D major in which the mourner had first beheld the vision of the beloved.

Strauss had once before exploited the idea of reliving one's past childhood in *Tod und Verklärung* and it is not surprising that this song employs a stylistic approach comparable to the relevant episode of the tone-poem (one may recall the similarly wide-spanned violin solo against harp arpeggios).[47]

Rückleben is thus one more of those Strauss Lieder which end in a remote key. But in this instance its importance is more far-reaching, for the remaining songs of the group are both in 'sharp' keys, giving this central song a pivot function.

It is especially noticeable how *Einkehr* at once gaily takes the last held A of *Rückleben* for its home key, the little rippling motif with its subtle cross-rhythm introducing, and afterwards interluding, one of Strauss's more appealingly ingenuous melodies though with many a sophisticated turn of phrase.

This is the one and only example of Strauss returning to a poem he had already set as a child (No. 2, see p. 250). In that earliest attempt at putting a great poem into music he had quite naturally made it strophic with the sentences corresponding symmetrically to those of the words. This time he went to the other extreme and was so intent on avoiding any suggestion of a four-square treatment that the new setting comes at

[47] There is also an intriguing similarity with Rachmaninoff's handling of the Ex. 67 arpeggiando accompaniment in the slow movement of his Second Piano Concerto composed the following year in 1901. The influence of Liszt on both composers is, of course, decisive.

times perilously close to a formlessness which is out of keeping with the simplicity of both the poem and Strauss's own very attractive tune.

Nevertheless the lasting impression is of a delightful song which looks forward to the happiest writing for Zerbinetta or the coloratura Brentano Lieder. The verses make the analogy of a hospitable apple tree which rests and nourishes the traveller as an innkeeper might a welcome guest. It is purely a vignette and so contrasts splendidly with the last song for which Strauss chose one of Uhland's ballads.

Von den sieben Zechbrüdern describes how seven drinking companions hearing of a new tavern beyond the forest set out to investigate its possibilities. On the way they are beset with thirst in the beating sun but spurn with derision the waters of a near-by spring. The hot day changes to a torrential downpour and, soaked to the skin, they lose themselves in the woods. When finally they emerge, they see no tavern awaiting them, but instead having unwittingly gone round in a circle they are on the road back homewards.

The narration serves to explain the reason why (as we are informed in the opening of the ballad and reminded in an envoi-like coda) the companions have made a vow never in any circumstances to let the very word 'water' pass their lips. The whole faintly foolish but hilarious saga is whisked along racily in a flurry of scherzando *Till*-like motifs directed to be executed as fast as possible. There are a number of entertaining details such as the graphic storm (complete with lightning flash) and the subsiding of the flood water into an amiable but admonishing stream; but the most interesting feature of the song is Strauss's handling of a constantly interchanging pulse of $\frac{6}{8}$ and $\frac{3}{4}$. This gives the music a hectic manner which he later developed still further for the Jews' quarrel in *Salome*.

But here all is good humour and where the $\frac{3}{4}$ episodes have time to establish themselves they develop a Ländler quality which makes its appropriate reappearance in anticipation of *Feuersnot*.

Ex. 68

It is to be expected that a narrative ballad of this kind is on quite a different scale from the preceding songs and perhaps its very length is one reason why it is another of the more neglected Lieder. Yet with its subtle pianissimo end in the hands of artists of wit and imagination it should make a delicious effect. Although like others of this set it too is ascribed to either soprano or tenor voice, *Von den sieben Zechbrüdern* is both vocally and dramatically more suitable for the male singer, calling moreover for a wide range. It is in its way, therefore, an unusual song and forms the climax to a group which shows Strauss's creative powers once again in the ascendant.

138 **Freundliche Vision**			
ORCH 1918	Bierbaum	5 Oct. 1900	
139 **Ich schwebe**		25 Sept. 1900	
140 **Kling! . . . .**	Henckell	30 Sept. 1900	op. 48
141 **Winterweihe** ORCH 1918		23 Sept. 1900	
142 **Winterliebe** ORCH 1918		2 Oct. 1900	

Strauss had built his Uhland group on the principle he had so often adopted in the past, of aiming to make its final song the most ambitious. For this new set, composed only a few months later, he picked out the loveliest—indeed one of the most ingratiating of all his songs—to stand at the head. *Freundliche Vision* is, oddly in a collection otherwise devoted entirely to Henckell, another isolated Bierbaum setting. It was to be Strauss's last association with this popular poet. Soon after, the two men were estranged on account of the antipathy of the 'Dilettant Bierbaum' (as Strauss wrote to his parents) to his choral setting of Uhland's ballad *Taillefer*, Bierbaum having the temerity to attack the work in the press.

The quarrel is regrettable because Bierbaum's verses, of themselves often light-weight, were able to touch a vein of gold in Strauss's lyrical make-up. The mood and expression in *Freundliche Vision* has much in common with *Traum durch die Dämmerung* although the new song has a more sophisticated melodic outline and does not, therefore, imprint itself as indelibly on the memory as the earlier masterpiece.

Yet it is full of Strauss's most melting harmonies, matching Bierbaum's 'Friendly vision' with its inviting little white house. Half hidden in shrubs, it lies amidst a flowering meadow towards which 'I walk with one who loves me . . . in peace and beauty'. Strauss repeats these lines bringing them together at the end of his song as they give the clue to the musical atmosphere of the whole.

This, like No. 134 in the Uhland set, was one of five songs all of this period which Strauss orchestrated in 1918, shortly before the end of the war when, with *Die Frau ohne Schatten* completed and all the to-ing and fro-ing of the *Ariadne/Bourgeois Gentilhomme* revisions brought to an end once and for all, he found himself creatively in something of a quandary. Such turning points in his production of major works were often times when he would keep his hand in with Lieder, whether orchestrating or composing, and it is to the same hiatus that we owe the great Brentano Lieder.

One of the longest and most serious of these pauses has, of course, been the period at present under discussion, between the completion of *Ein Heldenleben* and Strauss's return to the stage with *Feuersnot*, a gap of three years—not in itself a very considerable span, but incorporating an unsettling change of direction and irksome for a man of such unremitting industry. In addition to his Lieder he had—as we have seen in Vol. I (p. 201)—been passing the time by toying with possible ballet schemes, the most promising of which had been the extensive drafts for *Kythere*.

Amongst the extraordinary range of music which emanated from the sketches for this exceedingly interesting fragment, (passages from *Feuersnot, Bourgeois Gentilhomme, Ariadne, Schlagobers,* etc.) is *Ich Schwebe*, the first of four songs to words by Henckell. Something of its balletic origin survives in the completed song which cavorts in a friskier way than even the light-hearted poem warrants, for all the 'ringing tones and sweet melody' of the beloved's farewell greeting.

The swift, tinkling waltz with its rows of sugary consecutive sixths accompanies a floating voice line which is vocally so grateful that it has endeared the song to countless artists, while the turn of phrase in the opening bars was emulated by Dohnányi for the enchanting Scherzo of his F sharp minor Suite.

Ex. 69

Perhaps the various allusions to 'klingen' also led Strauss to his next Henckell setting, which is of a poem actually called *Kling!* . . ., each of the three verses beginning with this isolated declamation, though in the middle stanza it is changed to 'Sing! . . .'. Strauss adds a few extra Sings and Klings in his ebullient setting especially at the end where the poet apostrophizing his soul is sent soaring up to a top C. It is a stimulating outburst with its chords in a swinging $\frac{6}{4}$ rhythm alternating with harp-like rising arpeggios, but hardly of any great depth.

For the last two songs of this group Strauss reverted to a more serious vein, choosing two of Henckell's four poems on the subject of winter. (The others are *Wintersonne* and *Wintermond*, neither of which have been set to music whereas *Winterweihe* was also composed seven years later by Schönberg as one of his two songs op. 14.) They are to a large extent complementary and when Strauss came to orchestrate them eighteen years later he worked on them together, completing the scores on adjacent days. Moreover, he made a note on the score of *Winterliebe* that the orchestral parts were to be transposed down a semitone into E flat, so bringing it to the same key as its precursor *Winterweihe*.[48]

A feature of both songs is the strong relationship each bears to a passage from one of the later operas, resemblances too marked to have been wholly fortuitous. Strauss reproduced the devout mood and manner of the melody of *Winterweihe* ('Consecration to Winter') in his adaptation of a Croatian folk-song for the moment of wonder when Arabella and Mandryka consecrate their love:

Ex. 70

In dies-en Win - ter- ta- gen, nun sich das Licht ver - hüllt,____ lass uns im Her - zen tra- gen,

[48] The unifying purpose behind this instruction was unfortunately obscured by the publication of the score and parts in no less than three different keys. Even the Complete Edition retains the original key of E for *Winterliebe*.

One of the composer's favourite devices to achieve an air of breathless calm was by a melting modulation a major third higher, and this he uses here, repeating it three times until he arrives at the key he started from, a mechanical yet undeniably beautiful procedure and similar (though in the opposite direction) to that which he had used in *Blauer Sommer* No. 88 (See p. 292).

Winterliebe is an impetuous love song though its emotion is abstract; the lover in winter has, so far as we are told, no specific object of his passion. This, however, causes Strauss no inhibitions, nor does the wintry subject of the poem call for a corresponding frigidity in his setting, which bursts upon us with full ardour:

Ex. 71

That this passage is patently the origin of the Kaiserin's great affirmation 'Was er leidet, will ich leiden' from Act 3 of *Die Frau ohne Schatten* (cf. Vol. II, p. 203, Ex. 48) is made still clearer in the orchestral version, especially when Strauss's desire for it to be transposed into E flat—the key of the *Frau ohne Schatten* excerpt—is observed. One is reminded that the orchestration was carried out not long after the completion of the opera, for Strauss also added a chattering woodwind triplet figure (featured in a new introductory bar) identical to that which accompanies the Kaiserin.

However seasonal they may or may not sound, these two winter songs make a stimulating conclusion to an important group which confirms that Strauss's genius if still unsure was on the ascent once more.

The next collection of no fewer than eight curiously miscellaneous settings, composed for the most part a year later, is to show a similar upward trend.

143 **Waldseligkeit** ORCH 1918	Dehmel	21 Sept. 1901	
144 **In goldener Fülle**	Remer	13 Sept. 1901	
145 **Wiegenliedchen**	Dehmel	20 Sept. 1901	
146 **Lied des Steinklopfers**	Henckell	24 Sept. 1901	op. 49
147 **Sie wissen's nicht**	Panizza	14 Sept. 1901	
148 **Junggesellenschwur**	aus *Des Knaben Wunderhorn*	11 May 1900	
149 **Wer lieben will, muss leiden**	aus *Elsässische Volkslieder*	23 Sept. 1901	
150 **Ach, was Kummer, Qual, und Schmerzen**			

As in the op. 48 group, Strauss here again led from strength. *Waldseligkeit* is one of two last settings of poems by Dehmel; a study of deep self-fulfilment in the face of nature's beauty, it has something of that serene loveliness which Strauss was to find again in the *Vier Letzte Lieder* at the very end of his life.

The poem comes from the collection entitled *Erlösungen* ('Redemptions') from which Strauss also picked *Leises Lied* (No. 112). Although seemingly concerned with the solitary night-time wanderer in the rustling woods, romantic fulfilment comes at the end with the lines:

> da bin ich ganz mein eigen
> ganz nur dein.[49]

which clearly influenced Strauss when selecting this particular song for dedication to his wife. The vocal line too has that sustained floating quality in which she excelled and in which on her account Strauss specialized more and more, even after she had long given up her career.

It is only natural with so magical a tone-painting that the elaborate orchestral version has a quality only hinted at in the piano original. Indeed this is one of the many songs which give the impression of being only temporarily set for piano until Strauss was able to find time to give them their true orchestral realization.

The author of the next song, Paul Remer, was a minor follower of Liliencron, on whom he published a study in 1904. For a few years editor of the journal *Woche* as well as of an anthology of verse *Die Dichtung*, Remer suddenly abandoned town-life and devoted himself to gardening in the far off countryside.

The title of the song Strauss chose, *In goldener Fülle*, seems to have been a favourite with Remer for he used it again to rename one of his

---

[49] 'There I am quite my own, only thine.'

dramas *Osterglocken* on the occasion of a new edition in 1906. The words
feature prominently during the course of the gay poem and Strauss
accentuates them by repeating at the end all the verses in which they
appear. The subject is a sense of unalloyed happiness in life and death
alike which Strauss interprets with a bouncing dancing $\frac{6}{8}$ movement derived unmistakably (despite the four flats in the key signature) from
Beethoven's Seventh Symphony:

Ex. 72

It is hard to know why *Wiegenliedchen,* the other Dehmel setting, is
so seldom heard as it is a delicious little song. Dehmel was an acknowledged master of children's poetry, many examples of which he grouped
together under the heading *Der Kindergarten.* Strauss's exquisite handling has much of the taste and subtlety of Hugo Wolf especially when
the rocking berceuse motion hesitates in order to allow for a series of
intriguing variants of this chromatic cadence:

Ex. 73

From a lullaby to the long-suffering proletariat—no stronger contrast
can be imagined than is shown by the next song, Henckell's startling
Lied des Steinklopfers, the very first poem from his *Buch des Kampfes.*

Strauss's detractors are fond of emphasizing his romantic choice of poetry and forget that his output does actually include two such inflammatory settings as Dehmel's *Der Arbeitsmann* (No. 114) and this bitter song of the stone-breaker who 'is no minister, no king, has no title or decorations and also no money'; who 'has eaten nothing today, to whom the All-merciful has sent nothing, who has dreamt of golden wine, and breaks stones for the fatherland'.

Here, in a poem whose savage irony looks forward to Brecht, Strauss for the first time gives us a glimpse of Henckell's primary role of social reformer, even of revolutionary prophet. The musical setting is also full of imagination and insight; it was hardly less than genius which led Strauss after the climax to repeat isolated phrases in a kind of bewildered muttering, as if the wretched Steinklopfer has reduced himself to a state of shock by his outburst of ironical enthusiasm for his fatherland. The song disintegrates in utter despair with numb repetitions of 'Für's Vaterland', the piano still hammering away as it has done throughout, often with very strange chordal progressions.

Remarkably enough one of the phrases in the vocal line anticipates exactly a motif Strauss used to characterize Barak in *Die Frau ohne Schatten*, (See Vol. II, p. 176, Ex. 28). Considering Barak's station in life this is not likely to have been accidental. Though *Das Lied des Steinklopfers* will probably never rival Strauss's most popular Lieder, it is beyond question one of his most important.

With *Sie wissen's nicht* we return to a gentler world. Oscar Panizza, a Moravian of Huguenot descent, was something of a schizophrenic, combining his more conventional literary work with uncontrolled tirades against Church and State in consequence of which he spent some months in prison. Although at first an inhabitant of Munich he had to flee to Zurich whence he was removed to an asylum.

In view of this lurid career it is quite a disappointment to find the only poem by which he is represented in Strauss's output to be of almost folk-song naïveté. A gallant, standing beneath the four-storey building at the top of which lives the local beauty, reflects that as the nightingale is oblivious of its supremacy, so the girl knows nothing of her charms; they are alike entirely ignorant of the sighs they arouse in the lonely watcher below.

It is a pretty enough whimsy and Strauss treats it in a corresponding folk idiom at times recalling Mahler's *Wunderhorn* manner. Both the bird and the maiden have their individual themes:

Ex. 74

Ex. 75

and the extremely simple harmonies take on an anguished chromaticism when the song refers to the broken-hearted admirer. The music ends happily however, with a postlude in the major featuring both Exx. 74 and 75, since the nightingale and the maiden continue to remain in contented unknowing (hence the title which also appears as a kind of refrain).

Once on the folk-song level Strauss stayed there for the remainder of this op. 49 set. *Junggesellenschwur*, the last of his own *Knaben Wunderhorn* settings, was actually composed at the time of the previous op. 48 songs but certainly fits in much better in these surroundings.

The title was added by Strauss (the poem being headed in the original by the words from the first line 'Weine nur nicht!') aptly, one may agree, as the three verses constitute a young fellow's attempts at reassuring his sweetheart with promises of all kinds of fidelity, although she really cannot expect him to tie himself down with marriage and suchlike. He has no idea what all the tears and fuss are about and is at times quite brusque with her.

For her part she is inconsolable and the song begins and ends with a petulant little phrase in a totally different key from the rest inscribed 'Des Mägdleins Klage'. The boy then alternately wheedles and blusters, presenting by and large a somewhat unattractive account of himself.

It thus remains a little unclear where the composer's sympathies lie—perhaps with neither party—and this may be why *Junggesellenschwur* remains the least captivating of Strauss's *Wunderhorn* Lieder for all the lively musical invention in which it abounds.[50]

---

[50] The *lebhaft* cadential figure featured in the interludes and coda anticipates the harmonic idiom of the young Bartók's Second Suite for Orchestra op. 4, composed some five years later.

Lastly come two settings from a collection of Alsatian folk-songs published at Strasbourg in 1884 by Curt Mündel, who devoted much time and energy to assembling traditional legends, sayings and verses from his native Alsace.

Mündel's anthology comprises 256 folk-songs given—like the *Knaben Wunderhorn* volumes—entirely without music. The two Strauss selected are Nos. 34 and 57 respectively and are both pathetic expressions of a maiden's disappointed love. In the first, *Wer lieben will, muss leiden,* the unhappy girl seeks comfort at her mother's grave only to be told that her one release from suffering lies in death.

Strauss turns this lamentable episode into a study in chromatic wailing which stood him in valuable stead when he came to write Octavian/ Mariandel's mock weeping in the scene with Ochs during the third act of *Rosenkavalier.*

Ex. 76

Like *Junggesellenschwur,* this is another song which can hardly be said to be in any particular key; Strauss darts in and out of a great many during its course and it is interesting to see from the key signature that he actually thought of it as being in E minor. Even the opening phrases slip away into other regions with such exaggerated woe that the Mariandel similarity serves rather to confirm one's suspicions: Strauss's tongue is firmly in his cheek.

At the end the song arrives sweetly in the key of six sharps for the pianissimo coda in which the spirit of the mother speaks from the grave and the music dies away with the tortured chromatics coming gently and peacefully to rest.

The companion Alsatian folk-song is also no more than half serious with its comically grief-stricken phrases of:

Ex. 77   Ex. 78

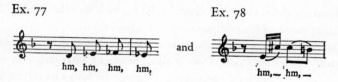

There are also, however, some lines of actual text in between, telling of the 'Kummer, Qual, und Schmerzen' (three words meaning between them virtually all the different forms of grief or woe) which lie on the maiden's 'Herz(en)'.

As with other Strauss Lieder which exploit gimmicky refrains (*Für funfzehn Pfennige*, *Bruder Liederlich* with its 'Halli, Hallo', *Schlagende Herzen* with 'Kling, klang', *Kling* with its own 'Kling' and 'Sing' and so on) there is always the danger that in the long run the catchwords (or sounds) become tiresome. Yet in the hands of a singer with a delicate, refined sense of comedy *Ach, was Kummer, Qual und Schmerzen* can be a most engaging song.

Thus in a mood of relaxation after sterner matters Strauss brought to an end what had been a long period of steady Lieder writing. In the past six years he had composed fifty-nine songs, many of them of the first rank. From his point of view they had served their purpose in providing an outlet for his urge to compose for the voice, denied him in the opera house since the failure of *Guntram*. With *Feuersnot* triumphantly launched he now stood on the brink of one of the most spectacular operatic careers vouchsafed to any composer. Accordingly his dependence on the Lied for self-expression was bound to be greatly reduced. It gives the measure of his affection that he never abandoned it altogether, even when his composition of all musical forms other than opera had virtually ceased.

13

151 **Das Thal**	Uhland	11 Dec. 1902	Zwei Lieder für eine tiefe Bass-stimme mit Orchesterbegleitung op. 51
152 **Der Einsame**	Heine	18 Feb. 1906	

As can be seen from the dates of composition, these two orchestral bass songs were not planned as a pair, *Der Einsame* following after an interval of over three years. Strauss came to the idea of setting Uhland's *Das Thal* ('as a kind of aria', he wrote to his parents) in the course of his

work on *Taillefer*, the great choral ballad which was the final and culminating point of his composition to Uhland texts.

Das Thal ('The Valley') is concerned with what is so often described
nowadays as 'getting away from it all'. The poet invokes a lovely valley
full of happy childhood memories, to which he longs to return when
the stresses and troubles of the world overwhelm him, and in which he
hopes to lie in ultimate peace when life is over.

It is an unsophisticated subject and Strauss's leisurely study in warm,
deep tones is well suited to its affectionate nostalgia. In this connexion
a feature of the score is that it marks the beginning of Strauss's adoption
of the basset-horn, an instrument which had fallen into abeyance since
Mozart. As he was soon to do in *Elektra*, Strauss actually uses two basset-
horns which, together with the by now customary bass clarinet, lend a
new and entirely appropriate colour to his wind palette.

Composing especially for the magnificent bass singer of the Berlin
opera Paul Knüpfer, he exploits the voice's deep range with fine appreciation of its richness, yet taking care that it is never obscured by the
orchestral accompaniment which is a model of carefully calculated
sonorities. The only times when the full resources of wind and strings
are allowed to combine are at the approaches to the two heart-felt
climaxes when, briefly, the voice has remained silent. The song is a fine
piece of beautifully sustained lyricism and should be in the repertoire of
every bass.

Its companion *Der Einsame* is on an altogether smaller scale and it is
arguable that when the two songs are given together it should precede
Das Thal in order of performance. The accompaniment is essentially for
an orchestra of divided strings although, assuming that the song would
never be programmed unless a full orchestra were already assembled on
the platform, Strauss introduces a number of wind parts just for the
final chords including the two basset horns which are required for *Das
Thal* and three trombones and tuba which are not.

Sensibly tacked on to *Das Thal* to form part of op. 51 (the publication of which Strauss held up for the purpose) *Der Einsame* derives from
a group of Heine settings composed in 1906 and the remainder of which
Strauss included in his next set, op. 56. The poem is taken from Heine's
Lyrisches Intermezzo, a collection of 65 poems and prologue written
between 1822–23, whose particular musical interest certainly lies in its
being the source of Schumann's *Dichterliebe*.

None of the poems have individual headings and the title *Der Ein-*

same was added by Strauss, who emphasized its suggestion of desolation by exploiting even further than he had in *Das Thal* the deep tones of his favourite basso profundo, Herr Knüpfer, to whom this song is also dedicated. The gloomy voice of Heine's Ritter describing the primeval night into which he has been plunged, deprived of the light of his beloved's eyes, brings to mind the grave tones of Gurnemanz telling Parsifal of the sad decline of knighthood.

Ex. 79

The little rising phrase bracketed in Ex. 79 dominates the whole song though it is extended tenderly to a ninth when the loved one is addressed:

Ex. 80

At the end Ex. 79 returns in ever deeper registers until the bass descends to a low F. The orchestra thereupon takes this as a suitable tonality on which to settle, and the song ends accordingly in this distant key as if wholly enveloped in blackest darkness.

Gloomy though it may sound in description, this too is a very affecting song and makes a good partner to the more substantial *Das Thal*. Strauss must certainly have had it in mind that these two Gesänge together make a grateful concert item which on purely practical grounds is easier to present than the other relatively ambitious pair of bass Gesänge op. 44.

53 **Liebesliedchen** Zwei Lieder aus ⎫
 4 **Lied der Chispa** *Der Richter von* ⎬Calderón ⎬16 Aug. 1904
                        Zalamea ⎭

155 **Gefunden**	Goethe	8 Aug. 1903	⎫
156 **Blindenklage**	Henckell	1903	
157 **Im Spätboot**	Meyer	1903	
158 **Mit deine blauen Augen**		1906	⎬ op. 56
159 **Frühlingsfeier** ORCH 1933	⎱ Heine	1906	
160 **Die heiligen drei Könige aus**	⎰		
Morgenland ORCH 1906		7 Oct. 1906	⎭

Although hardly Lieder in the accepted sense of the word, the two Calderón settings are included for the sake of completeness. At least their titles suggest that they might find a place here. They owe their origin to a Berlin production in September 1904 of Calderón's play *Alcalde de Zalamea* and are unique in Strauss's output for their guitar accompaniments.[51]

The play in which the verses appear is itself unusual amongst Calderón's works for its social criticism and lively character studies. The Alcalde in particular, who is elected to this exalted position during the course of the play, turns out to be a rough but prosperous peasant, half buffoon yet half worthy of admiration.

Since Strauss was persuaded to put pen to paper and produce these two songs, it seems a shame that he did not add further movements for such an occasion and on a subject which might well have attracted his sense of caricature. Even the songs are hardly more than trifles; the first is a soldier's song for solo tenor, whilst a chorus of soldiers also features in the second which is for mezzo-soprano.

With *Gefunden* however, we return to our muttons. It had at this time been Strauss's intention to compose a series of Goethe Lieder but in the end he only wrote the one, dedicating it to 'my beloved Pauline' on the date of his Heidelberg doctorate.[52] As we know from the letter to Gregor quoted at the beginning of this chapter, Strauss had always felt himself inhibited when confronted with great poetry such as Goethe's, and this obviously accounts for the relatively few authors of the first rank amongst his Lieder. Such Goethe texts as he did select are generally small-scale and less well-known, whereas Schubert and Wolf went straight to the finest and even the largest poems of the great master (*Erlkönig, Prometheus, Grenzen der Menschheit*, etc.).

---

[51] Strauss actually plays safe by doubling the guitar with a harp in No. 153 and with two harps in No. 154, though without indicating how the parts are to be distributed. Nor are there any records to show how (or even whether) the songs were in fact performed in the theatre.

[52] See Vol. II, p. 363.

The dedication of *Gefunden* gives perhaps the clue to its choice, for Goethe had written the verses for his own wife Christiane (shortly after their silver wedding). The poet wanders without aim or purpose and comes upon a lovely flower; instead of picking it as is his instinct, he preserves it from withering by gathering it by the roots and replanting it in his own home, where it thrives and blossoms anew. This symbolism on marriage is apt enough and Strauss contrives a composite idiom of quasi-classical folk-song melody leading to a more sophisticated but attractively contented vein such as he was currently using for passages in his *Sinfonia Domestica*. (Asow believed that an orchestral version existed but this has never come to light.)

All the other songs of op. 56 are dedicated to Strauss's mother, beginning with *Blindenklage*, the last of the Henckell settings. Like most of the group it is on a symphonic scale though almost entirely organized around a single motif, the lamenting quality of which is emphasized with many a poignant repetition:

Ex. 81

The afflicted in Henckell's bitter poem has none of Milton's philosophical calm in the face of his own blindness. The sense of deprivation is absolute and recollections of nature, colour or light bring despair.

Ex. 82

Im Spätboot is Strauss's only setting of words by the Swiss poet Conrad Ferdinand Meyer. Meyer was a contemporary of Gottfried Keller,

---

[53] 'Dead is my curse and dead alike my blessing.'

the author of *A Village Romeo and Juliet*, and while never rivalling Keller's international reputation, he was much admired in Germany and his native Zurich, especially for his dramatic poetry.

It is certainly a remarkable example Strauss chose, this weary, shadowy vision of a dark, wind-swept journey on the *Spätboot*, that is the last boat at the end of the day; it seems almost that we are on Charon's boat. Strauss once again turned to the basso profundo, giving the song an aptly sombre quality, though this is partially dissipated by harmonies and modulations which, if deep-toned, are full of true Straussian warmth. Perhaps the composer preferred not to stress the ambiguity of the eerie poem for he avoids any blank musical atmosphere to correspond with the 'pale ship's lantern by whose light a shade gets off but none gets on . . .' Indeed, the whole song centres round the rich key of D flat giving the singer a wonderful opportunity to display his deepest note in the closing bars.

The three-year gap which separates the remaining songs, three Heine settings, represents the composition and launching of *Salome*. With this behind him Strauss completed not only the present op. 56 group but also the preceding orchestral bass Lieder the second of which, *Der Einsame* (No. 152) is, as we have seen, also to a Heine poem. Strauss had not touched Heine's work since his isolated Jugendlied *In Vaters Garten heimlich steht* (No. 32) composed over a quarter of a century before, and he made a point of selecting poems which are striking not only in themselves but in the sharp contrast they present to one another.

Mit deinen blauen Augen is a simple love-song, similar in scale and naïvete to *Gefunden*, the first of the group, though the Schubertian turn of phrase now definitely looks forward to the pastiche classicism of the *Rosenkavalier* closing duet 'Ist ein Traum, kann nicht wirklich sein'.

Ex. 83

Nor was Strauss unconscious of the similarity; he was on at least one occasion, whilst accompanying his wife, heard to switch slyly across to the *Rosenkavalier* duet, an amusing trick which Alfred Orel also heard him play when introducing another of his Lieder, *Du meines Herzens Krönelein* (No. 71).

Strauss had found the poem *Mit deinen blauen Augen* in the later 1831 collections of Heine's love lyrics entitled *Neuer Frühling*. The next song *Frühlingsfeier*, however, belongs to the still later *Romanzen* of 1839–42. Startling and vivid, it depicts one of the wildest and most colourful of Spring rituals, the festival of Adonis which was in ancient times held annually in Greece and Western Asia. In addition to being the ideal of manly beauty, Adonis was the god of vegetation whose death and return to life represent the decay in winter and its revival in spring.

> . . . the death of the god was mourned, with a bitter wailing chiefly by women . . . At Alexandria images of Aphrodite and Adonis were displayed on couches; beside them were set ripe fruits of all kinds . . . the marriage of the lovers was celebrated one day, and on the morrow women attired as mourners, with streaming hair and bared breasts, bore the image of the dead Adonis to the sea-shore and committed it to the waves. Yet they sorrowed not without hope, for they sang that the lost one would come back again.[54]

But Heine does not complicate the impact with this hopeful sequel and the song is wholly one of passionate mourning which Strauss intensifies to the full with elaborate, tempestuous music. This, if any, was a song which needed the orchestra for its proper realization and it is fortunate that Strauss chose this as the third of the group he instrumentated in 1933 for Viorica Ursuleac.

Ernest Newman reckoned the welter of notes in the main body of the song to be disproportionate to its content, while Philip Radcliffe regarded the undeniably welcome oasis of elegiac calm in the centre of the turbulence ('Das wunderschöne Junglingsbild') as the more characteristic section 'with its combination of simple harmony and widely curving melody'. Yet despite an element of truth in these criticisms,

---

[54] Frazer, *The Golden Bough*. Macmillan, London, 1922. It is particularly interesting to find Gabriele d'Annunzio drawing a parallel in the third act of his *Le Martyre de Saint Sebastien* with the Adonis rites. The movement in which the Women of Byblos and the Coryphées bemoan 'Il est mort, le bel Adonis' is one of the most moving in Debussy's incidental music to d'Annunzio's *Mystère*.

Frühlingsfeier remains a very impressive outburst, and in its orchestral version one of the most passionately colourful of Strauss's Lieder.

Lastly comes a masterpiece, certainly one of the finest of all the songs. *Die heil'gen drei Kön'ge aus Morgenland* is one of Heine's comparatively few poems on a religious subject. Heine was of Jewish origin, a fact which was to create all sorts of problems during the Nazi regime in connexion with the countless acknowledged masterpieces set to his verses. He embraced Christianity in 1825 when he was 28 years of age, and this poem, belonging as it does to the collection *Die Heimkehr* written during the two previous years, shows that his faith and interest in the Christian myth had been growing for some time until he was actually converted.

The subject is of course Epiphany and the enchanting verses are, as it were, Heine's counterpart to Goethe's riotous poem *Epiphaniasfest* (which Hugo Wolf turned into one of his greatest Lieder). Strauss uses them as the centre-point of a large-scale symphonic design, so that there is not only a long and gloomy introduction for lower strings, describing the initial aimless wanderings of the three holy men of the East before the golden star guides their steps, but the song ends with a huge and glowing coda nearly as long again as the main vocal section of the work.

The song is pervaded by Natur motifs such as:

Ex. 84   Ex. 85

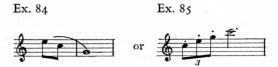

and, once the deep meanderings of the opening bars have dissolved into a glittering texture punctuated by celeste, harps and a large group of percussion treated with the utmost delicacy, the flow of the music is characterized by the generous warm-hearted C major tonality. There are moments of pictorialism when the poem refers to the appearance of the star, the ox lowing, the Child crying, but these are soon enveloped in the surge of melody the clue to which springs from the closing line 'die heil'gen drei Könige sangen', the orchestra carolling away long after the voice has stopped.

It is apparent that I have described the song entirely in terms of its orchestral setting and this gives the pointer to a curious conflict in Strauss's plans for the grouping and publication of these Heine Lieder. The orchestral *Der Einsame* (No. 152) was no problem; being for a deep

„Ein Obdach gegen Sturm und Regen."

(Fr. Rückert)

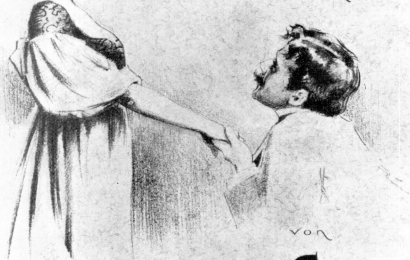

von

Richard Strauss.

OP. 46. Nº 1.

Nº 1.
Für Sopran oder Tenor
B dur.

Nº 2.
Für tiefe Stimme
G dur.

Pr. M 1.60 netto.

A 5142. 5147 F

„ Gestern war ich Atlas "

(FR. RÜCKERT)

von

Richard Strauss

Op. 46 № 2.

№ 1
Für Sopran oder Tenor.
(A dur)

FR. M. 1. 60 netto.

№ 2
Für tiefe Stimme.
(F dur)

A 5143   5148 F

Richard Strauss

OP 68   Nr. 4

Als mir dein Lied
erklang

(Clemens Brentano)

VERLAG UND EIGENTUM FÜR ALLE LÄNDER
ADOLPH FÜRSTNER, BERLIN W

Four cover designs for
the first editions of Lieder

bass it was naturally coupled with *Das Thal* even though this was to an Uhland text. But the new Epiphanias song was certainly for soprano and moreover made a splendid climax to the op. 56 collection which had been lying incomplete for three years. So Strauss decided to compromise and made a transcription for piano so that *Die Heiligen drei Könige aus Morgenland* could take its place with the other piano songs and be published as part of op. 56. Yet when he came to condense the great orchestral postlude he found himself in insoluble difficulties with the result that the ostensible piano version contains on the last page an extra stave which comes and goes, bearing cues specifically designated for trumpet. In fact the all too rare performances of this splendid song are always given with orchestra. It marks a climax not only to the group as part of which it was published, but to the great outpouring of Lieder which, begun in childhood, was to come to a temporary but extended halt for a number of complicated reasons.

14

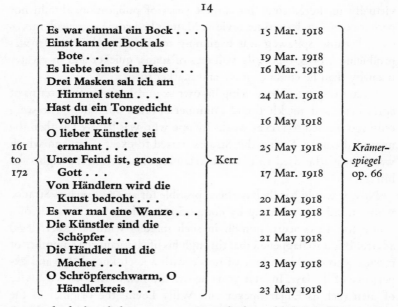

	Es war einmal ein Bock . . .		15 Mar. 1918	
	Einst kam der Bock als Bote . . .		19 Mar. 1918	
	Es liebte einst ein Hase . . .		16 Mar. 1918	
	Drei Masken sah ich am Himmel stehn . . .		24 Mar. 1918	
	Hast du ein Tongedicht vollbracht . . .		16 May 1918	
161	O lieber Künstler sei ermahnt . . .		25 May 1918	*Krämer-*
to	Unser Feind ist, grosser	Kerr		*spiegel*
172	Gott . . .		17 Mar. 1918	op. 66
	Von Händlern wird die Kunst bedroht . . .		20 May 1918	
	Es war mal eine Wanze . . .		21 May 1918	
	Die Künstler sind die Schöpfer . . .		21 May 1918	
	Die Händler und die Macher . . .		23 May 1918	
	O Schröpferschwarm, O Händlerkreis . . .		23 May 1918	

Strauss had placed the op. 56 songs with the publishers of his *Sinfonia Domestica*, the Berlin house of Bote & Bock, and in an unguarded moment allowed a seemingly innocent clause to be inserted in the contract giving them the rights to his next group of songs whenever this should appear. To understand how this was to become a veritable thorn in his side it is necessary to go back a few years.

The decision in 1898 to leave Spitzweg of Joseph Aibl Verlag, to whom Strauss had owed so much in the earliest days of his career, was no careless move of pique or temper. In those days performing rights such as composers now enjoy were entirely unknown. By contrast with the present time in which performances of contemporary works can only be given by means of hiring non-purchasable orchestral scores and material, it was then the very sale of that material which conveyed the right of performance. Furthermore all rights were held by the publishers, the composer reaping little in the way of royalties once he had parted with his work for an initial fee. The German copyright law left much to be desired, and despite the comparatively recently signed Berne Convention of 1886 the composer could expect scant protection against the various abuses or unauthorized handling of his scores.

By 1898 Strauss was already a very successful man and he began to wonder whether the arrangement with Spitzweg, which had continued virtually unaltered since his earliest years of publication, should not perhaps come under serious review. Matters had come to a head, moreover, because Spitzweg was beginning to complain that Strauss was producing works, especially volumes of songs, quicker and in greater quantity than he could engrave and market them.

Strauss responded by voicing his own complaints over their terms of agreement, and quickly found a number of other publishers who were only too pleased to accept works by one who was hardly less than the man of the hour. Seeing this Strauss started to exact a demand which was pioneer: he tried to insist on retaining the performing rights for himself.

Now it would hardly have been possible for an artist such as Strauss, whose mind was taken up by composition and the hectic career of a conductor, to concern himself in such matters without expert legal advice. But it so happened that through his life he acquired a number of friends who combined love of music with a keen knowledge and experience of the law. In later years he owed much to the shrewd advice of men such as Edgar Speyer and Willy Levin (the original of the Kommerzienrat in *Intermezzo*). At the present time his right-hand man was Friedrich Rösch.[55]

Together with a certain Zincke, who also composed under the nom-

[55] See above, p. 321.

de-plume of Hans Sommer, Strauss and Rösch founded that same year, 1898, the 'Genossenschaft deutscher Tonsetzer', a society with enlightened and far-reaching aims towards the betterment of conditions for composers.[56] As was to be expected, even the composers themselves were at loggerheads and only gave partial support to the scheme, while publishers and politicians fought it tooth and nail. It stands very much to Strauss's credit that he would accept no discouragement even when his plans were publicly defeated in the Reichstag. He saw all too clearly the weakness of his colleagues in business matters and was determined to establish an organisation for the collection of fees and royalties even if he had personally to pay for it as an advance against the future.

Over the years, thanks to 'Rösch's colossal energy', as he wrote to his parents, much ground was gained and it would be no exaggeration to say that the numerous organisations which exist today protecting the rights of composers in every country were decisively influenced by Strauss's efforts and dedication in those crucial early days.

Not that the path was ever smooth. One of the immediate consequences of the formation of the 'Genossenschaft deutscher Tonsetzer' was that many of the leading music publishers created a counter-organization for the protection of their own interests. This 'Genossenschaft zur Verwertung musikalischer Aufführungsrechte', or GEMA as it was called, not only became very powerful but naturally stood in direct opposition to many of the aims of Strauss's brain-child.

And one of the leading members of GEMA was the house of Bote & Bock.

Meantime after a certain amount of experimenting, Strauss had come more and more to a firm understanding with the publisher Adolf Fürstner who had long courted him and who readily acceded to his demands, including his personal retention of performing rights in all his works—that is to say including songs. Strauss's insistence on this, as he explained to Spitzweg at the time of their dispute over *Heldenleben*, was part of the lead he felt obliged to give as prime figure in the battle for German composers. 'This is', he wrote, 'the main point in our whole movement, and I as instigator cannot set a bad example.'

It was therefore particularly unfortunate that in the early 1900's, before he had realized how bitter a dispute was developing, Strauss had

[56] George Marek outlines the details very interestingly in his biography of Strauss.

placed himself under a contractual obligation to his chief opponents, and well he knew that Kommerzienrat Hugo Bock (his opposite number as none other than the founder of GEMA) would not give the least ground in his requirement for a song cycle on the old and now unacceptable terms. It was deadlock.

So Strauss's joy in song writing soured. Nor was it so necessary to him as a born vocal composer, for it was just this period which saw the blossoming of his great operatic curve. While masterpiece followed masterpiece—*Elektra, Rosenkavalier, Ariadne*—Strauss could reasonably claim the pressure of more important assignments, and so hold the enemy at bay. But the day came when, after no less than twelve years had passed, the issue could plainly no longer be postponed; with the coming of the first world war he was unable to avoid that period of marking time, and despite his periodic preoccupation with *Ariadne II* and *Die Frau ohne Schatten*, Bote & Bock decided to exert pressure.

Strauss delayed as long as he could, but when he found himself threatened with a court action he saw that he would have at last to make a move. But he was not one to give in easily or with good grace. Remembering a little book of satirical poems entitled *Die Harfe* which had been sent to him in 1913 by its author, a well-known Berlin literary critic Alfred Kerr, he conceived a malicious project by which he might find freedom from the contract and simultaneously get his own back. Much as he had proposed a revengeful libretto to Wolzogen in the days of *Feuersnot*, full of double meanings and spiteful word play, so now with that Eulenspiegel side of him uppermost once more, he turned to Kerr with a sharp-toothed scheme.

Alfred Kerr was born in Breslau in 1867; his real name Kempner he had shortened for professional reasons in 1911 when he was established in Berlin and making himself notorious as the lively author of articles, poems and reviews of every kind which appeared in the numerous Berlin journals of the day. By 1918 Kerr was in the unassailable position of critic of the largest and most prominent newspaper, the *Berliner Tageblatt*, and in the security of this position gleefully welcomed Strauss's idea, which he had no compunction in pursuing to the limit. He quickly concocted and sent to Strauss on 8th March 1918 a dozen scurrilous little verses on the subject of the composer's victimization, actually incorporating the names of several front-rank publishing houses and their owners or managers alike.

Strauss was simply delighted. Before the end of May all were set to music and he immediately started to talk terms with Kerr, although the writer had from the first said that he wanted nothing in the way of a fee. The fun of writing the poems and the cause which lay behind them were their own reward and moreover Kerr had it in mind that he might prevail on Strauss to set to music some of his more serious writings.[57]

But the business arrangements were not so simply disposed of; as Strauss obviously foresaw, such a fulfilment of his contract with Bote & Bock was simply unacceptable. The publishers, deeply offended, turned down the songs out of hand. What Strauss did not, perhaps, bargain for was that in pressing ahead even more vigorously with their legal action against him, they easily obtained an injunction that he discharge his liability forthwith.

There was now no question of further procrastination and seeing the red light Strauss capitulated, hastily sketching and sending off a further set of songs which were accepted and published as op. 67.

But all the same, Strauss was not finished with his work of protest. Despite its puckish character he had put a lot of real music into it and was determined to get it into print, ignoring the very real risk of further legal complications. Certainly no music publisher would ever accept such songs and they ultimately appeared three years later in 1921 as a collector's item. The art publisher Paul Cassirer was persuaded to produce a private de luxe limited edition of 120 copies, illustrated copiously by Michael Fingesten, and autographed by Fingesten and Strauss. It was a relieved Strauss who wrote to Cassirer from Vienna on 10th March 1921:

> I hear with great joy that you have decided to take the *Krämerspiegel* into your edition. At last there is a man who, even though a publisher himself, has the necessary humour to assess this work correctly. . . .[58]

The title *Krämerspiegel*, added for the publication, is a coloured word contemptuously signifying 'shop-keeper's mirror'. Fingesten's drawing shows a large looking-glass reflecting a monstrous pig over which a caricatured Strauss appears riding a winged horse on a tight-rope. (See illustration facing p. 410.)

[57] See Vol. II, p. 299.
[58] This letter is reproduced in facsimile after the title-page of the beautifully produced volume.

Naturally enough Strauss starts with an attack on Kommerzienrat Bock himself. 'Bock' is unfortunately the German for 'goat' and in the first song a goat is munching at a pot of flowers which symbolizes music. It is all clothed in a mock-innocent 'There was once upon a time . . .' style which Strauss emulates in the folky ingenuousness of his melody:

Ex. 86

In the second song the 'Bock' comes as 'Bote' (i.e. 'messenger', thus incorporating a pun on the other name of the publishing house) to the Rosenkavalier—i.e. Strauss, whose name actually appears in the next line in its meaning of a bunch of flowers. The Rosenstrauss jabs its thorns into the thick skin of the Botenbock, and the remainder of the poem consists of somewhat coarse admonitions to the Bock to jump backwards.

This is the most obviously direct allusion to the dispute and Strauss, after a mock-serious introduction, treats the matter with frivolous abandon in a waltz. The music accordingly combines themes from *Der*

[59] 'With deeply intimate feeling and good humour.' The indication is ironic to a degree.

Rosenkavalier (Ochs' most popular waltz-tune 'Mit mir, mit mir' and Sophie's melody which features in the Presentation of the Silver Rose) with the principal theme of the song-cycle now emerging into a more characterful phrase:

Ex. 87

Kerr now turns to the most eminent of all German music publishers Breitkopf & Härtel, whose proprietor was at this time Geheimrat Dr Oskar Hase. 'Hase' is the German for 'Hare'. Moreover 'Breitkopf' signifies a broad head, so that a phrase like 'sein Breitkopf hart und härter war' was virtually ready-made.

Strauss had no great affection for Breitkopf & Härtel who had rejected his early compositions once they were no longer backed by Uncle George's money, and this poem is not just spiteful but vicious with its insinuations of hypocrisy and 'sucking composers' blood'. To this day the great publishing house remains adamant in banning the text on, for example, programmes and record sleeves.

On the other hand it is musically one of the more attractive songs in the cycle, full of rich twisting phrases suggestive of Wagner, of *Hänsel und Gretel* or of Strauss himself, especially in the closing bars which descend in shifting harmonies recalling *Don Quixote*.

With the fourth song Strauss returns for the last time to his opening subject, building upon its version as Ex. 87 a weird chromatic fugue evoking the mystery of the Three Masks (Dreimasken-Verlag, a less familiar publishing house and now hardly known). The music builds to an awesome climax as the text reveals that behind the masks (O terror!) can be seen . . . Herr Friedmann (the managing director). Abruptly the mood collapses into extravagant hilarity with a boisterous postlude in the shape of a polka. Clearly Ludwig Friedmann was a less ferocious ogre than he wished to appear.

Kerr's menagerie continues: the German for Reynard the Fox is Reinecke and, incredible as it may seem, one of the publishing houses in the enemy camp was owned by the two brothers Karl and Franz of that name. One wonders indeed whether the whole idea of the work did not come from this fantastic circumstance of the different publishers' names. This poem exhorts the composer who has written a tone-poem to beware lest the foxes gobble it up. The verses are once again the merest doggerel but Strauss turned them into a gay enough Scherzo in $\frac{6}{8}$ hunting vein.

Two publishers are satirized in the next song 'O lieber Künstler': C. F. Kahnt of Leipzig and Robert Lienau of Berlin. 'Kahn' is the German for a small boat. (It is a 'Kahn' into which the Amme's cloak is transformed in *Die Frau ohne Schatten*.) Kerr ingeniously twists this into the required name by coining a verb: 'Wer in gewissen Kähnen Kahnt . . .' i.e. 'who boats in certain boats (is in the water up to his neck)' and underlining the operative word to make sure no one misses the point.[60]

From Lienau Kerr creates a plausible pleasure-ground advising the artist not to take a stroll there since 'Long Robert' is prone to haunt it.

The elegant Mazurka Strauss conjures out of all this nonsense would make a pretty little piano piece on its own without the foolish voice line, which curiously makes no independent musical contribution.

A far wittier as well as more successful song is the next, devoted to a gibe against the very well-known firm of B. Schott's Söhne in Mainz and its proprietor Kommerzienrat Dr Ludwig Strecker. The pun here dates the work: our enemy, says Kerr, is—like the Brite (Englishman)—so the Schott (Scotsman). It will be recalled that *Krämerspiegel* was written in 1918 when Great Britain was at war with Germany. As for Strecker himself, 'strecken' is 'to stretch', hence the idea that Schott is 'the enemy who puts many to the rack' ('streckbett', lit. 'stretch-bed'). But the stormy anger of the opening dissolves into a coda of high good humour in which the jagged principal theme reveals an unsuspected allegiance to Sancho Panza before dying away to nothing.

It is at this point (none too soon) that Strauss has a surprise up his sleeve. No. 8 of the cycle begins with a long romantic Schumannesque interlude for the piano:

---

[60] The stress is omitted in the 1959 Boosey & Hawkes edition, perhaps for reasons of tact.

Ex. 88

Here is the fine passage which Strauss ingeniously rescued nearly a quarter of a century later in the opera *Capriccio*. As described above (p. 214) it takes no part in the setting of Kerr's verses but pursues an existence of its own, unsullied by the mercenary forces around it, just like artistic inspiration amidst the commercial world.

The threatening businessmen are depicted by a rough figure which breaks in again and again upon the serene atmosphere and which bears the vocal line when this enters in due course. The burden of the song is a general one to the effect that the dealers 'bring Death to music and Transfiguration (i.e. the bliss of financial gain) to themselves'.

So naïve a sentiment has naturally only one purpose and Strauss could hardly do other than oblige with the Ideology motif from *Tod und Verklärung* (see Vol. I, p. 81, Ex. 22). This is then combined with the businessmen's theme in a skittish *scherzando* coda which at last subsides to a final drooping phrase from the Inspiration melody Ex. 88.

The ninth song 'Es war mal eine Wanze' ('There was once a bug') takes again an overall view of the dispute and of Strauss's success in organizing the Composer's Guild. In musical slang 'Wanzen und Flöhen' (bugs and fleas) is sometimes used to mean 'sharps and flats' but

Kerr also uses the colloquial sense of Wanze as a blood-sucker, likening the publishers to an evil-smelling insect 'which sucked and sucked'. But, he adds, the 'Musici' crushed it as a hymn of praise rose to the heavens.

Strauss uses the double meaning of 'sharps and flats' as the starting point for a mock-doleful chromatic theme which contains more than a touch of irony as does also the little kick in the last syllable of 'Wanze' and its rhyme 'Ganze', later reflected in the texture of the piano part. There is not, however, any jubilant flamboyance to the creature's demise but only a brief glow of lyricism to mark the heavenly Lobgesang.

Die Künstler sind die Schöpfer is another boisterous song. Calling on a string of colourful terms of abuse ('fleecers', 'guardians of the money-bags', 'stirrers-up of disputes', 'germ-carriers', etc.) its theme is that the publishers are in the end no more than so many uncouth Ochs von Lerchenau blundering about. Strauss accordingly bases the music once more on themes from Rosenkavalier, especially the little tag at the end of Faninal's motif which, referring to the poor old man's noble aspirations towards the house of Lerchenau, ends by being applied more and more to Ochs' boorishness (see Vol. I, p. 378, Ex. 40).

With the penultimate song the rancour takes on a personal note. These petty tradespeople, it says, with their profiteering are the HERO'S (Kerr's capitals) antagonists.

The music cue being again self-evident, Strauss builds the song on numerous motifs from Heldenleben. The HERO is represented by the opening phrase (Vol. 1, p. 167, Ex. 1a) as well as the figure Ex. 3a, while the adversaries confine themselves to their Ex. 7. At the same time, significantly enough, Strauss establishes his identity by combining his own theme from the Sinfonia Domestica at the word 'Helden' for, contrary to general belief, he never saw himself in the role of hero where Ein Heldenleben was concerned, but simply used elements of his life by way of illustration.

The end of the song suddenly changes to a Clerihew-like couplet:

> Der lässt ein Wort erklingen
> Wie Götz von Berlichingen.

which Strauss accompanies with repetitions of the famous opening figure of Beethoven's Fifth Symphony.

Götz von Berlichingen mit der eisernen Hand, Goethe's first and one of his most famous plays, is a historical drama about a feudal baron in the Peasants' Revolt. In the third act Götz is beleaguered in his castle by a troop of Imperial soldiers. Through an open window one hears a voice demanding Götz's surrender and Götz shouts back: 'I have all respect for His Imperial Majesty, *aber Er kann mich – – –.*' The obscene expression of disdain represented by the blanks was here hinted at for the first time in a literary work, but every German listener understood it then as he understands it now. Although the phrase is not finished, the first two bars of the Beethoven Fifth Symphony fit the rhythm of the sentence precisely so that just as many people imply the coarse retort by merely saying the one word 'Götz', so musicians would often simply hum the first two bars of the Fifth Symphony—which is of course what Strauss is doing in the latter part of this song.

The cycle closes with the apostrophizing 'O Schröpferschwarm, O Händlerkreis' ('O swarm of fleecers, O circle of tradesmen') which also acts as sign-off, the signature being, appropriately enough, *Till Eulenspiegel*. Till's horn motif (Vol. I, p. 125, Ex. 4) is elegantly transformed to fit the prevailing Ländler tempo, which thereupon gives way to an extended re-statement of the Inspiration melody, Ex. 88, and it is on this serious, even wistful note that surprisingly the whole malicious but impish practical joke comes to an end.

With its recent publication the claim has sometimes been made that *Krämerspiegel* far transcends its original purpose and has a strong claim for survival in the sheer quality of the music. This, however, is an overstatement to say the least. Despite many ingenious touches and some admirable moments the songs are far too closely allied to Kerr's words for these to be considered 'a mere pretext for some enchanting music' as Kerr himself once indicated.

In the event performances have been exceedingly few and far between, and the publishers' reluctance to encourage the propagation of the words is an additional impediment.

The première which took place in 1921, the year of publication, had to be held in private for fear of legal action. Kerr himself sent the invitations and the performance was given secretly in the Hotel Kaiserhof, Berlin. Even Strauss was absent as he was on tour abroad: it is improbable that he was greatly upset. The work had fulfilled its purpose and he had moreover actually secured a publisher for it. Its subsequent fate was hardly likely to be a happy one. The rescue operation on the one outstanding passage (Ex. 88) is thus very easy to understand and to commend, for it has served not only to familiarize the world with a very beautiful piece of music but also to arouse curiosity over its origin in one of the most extraordinary works in the whole field of song.

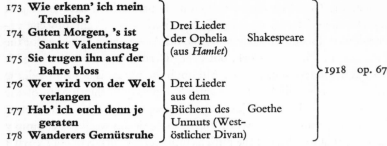

173 **Wie erkenn' ich mein Treulieb?**	Drei Lieder der Ophelia (aus *Hamlet*)	Shakespeare	
174 **Guten Morgen, 's ist Sankt Valentinstag**			
175 **Sie trugen ihn auf der Bahre bloss**			1918 op. 67
176 **Wer wird von der Welt verlangen**	Drei Lieder aus dem		
177 **Hab' ich euch denn je geraten**	Büchern des Unmuts (West-	Goethe	
178 **Wanderers Gemütsruhe**	östlicher Divan)		

With the prospect of his dispute with Bote & Bock being settled and the world of Lieder being once again open to him, Strauss had early in 1918 eagerly embarked on a collection of settings of Brentano, many of the songs actually pre-dating the *Krämerspiegel* group which was to have set him free.

When, however, he found himself still legally bound to supply his enemies with their stipulated six Lieder he did not for a moment consider letting them have the Brentano set which bade fair to be one of the best he had ever written. Instead he rapidly threw off a bundle of little sketches intended to make clear his irritability at being thus forced to capitulate. They consist in fact of three mad songs and three bad-tempered songs, the mad songs being settings of nonsense fragments chanted by the demented Ophelia in *Hamlet* Act 4 Scene 5.[61]

Strangely he used the more literal but stilted translation by Karl Simrock rather than the Schlegel and Tieck version (which is held in such high esteem that the Germans are said to claim Shakespeare as their greatest poet). One cannot but feel that Simrock's:

> Bei Sankt Niklas und Charitas
> ein unverschämt Geschlecht!
> Ein junger Mann tut's, wenn er kann,
> fürwahr, das ist nicht recht.'

misses the strong colour of:

> By Gis and by Saint Charity
> Alack, and fie for shame!
> Young men will do't, if they come to't;
> By Cock they are to blame.

[61] Curiously enough Brahms had also composed a group of *Ophelia-Lieder* including some of the same passages. Strauss is unlikely to have known of these, however, as they were not published until Karl Geiringer rediscovered them in 1935. Unlike Strauss's settings they are intended to be sung unaccompanied as required by the drama, the piano parts being included only for study purposes.

Strauss's excerpts by no means constitute the whole of Ophelia's ramb-
lings, nor do they run consecutively in the original scene. The first lines
of the three passages are:

(1) 'How should I your true love know
     From another one?'
(2) 'Tomorrow is Saint Valentine's day
     All in the morning betime'
(3) 'They bore him bare fac'd on the bier;
     Hey non nonny, nonny, hey nonny'

Yet dashed off as no doubt they were, these sketches are far from
perfunctory. The craftsman in Strauss was nothing if not fluent and
moreover, as we know from the operas, madness and the grotesque
never failed to stimulate his imagination.

The first song suggests perfectly the demented Ophelia with its
hopeless wandering motif, which the voice echoes in augmentation,
above a blank unresolving dissonance:

Ex. 89

There is a tiny arpeggiando figure and a momentary tightening of
the heart for 'tot und hin, Fräulein' (Shakespeare's 'Dead and gone,
Lady'):

Ex. 90

In the end the pitiful little song dies away with repetitions of its initial figure (Ex. 89), the syncopated dissonance becoming ever more hesitant but never resolving. With vacant expression Ophelia has simply stopped.

The second song is even more senseless. From addressing Queen Gertrude, Ophelia has now turned to the King who having just entered is appalled by what he sees before him. Strauss's setting chatters away with some mad harmonies and constant flapping alternations between major and minor. Like the first song it also breaks up before stopping in its tracks open-mouthed.

Strauss's last excerpt comes from later in the scene when Ophelia's brother Laertes has burst in and is also made an agonized witness to her doleful ravings. Although the most considerable of the three Ophelia Lieder it is also the most conventionally Straussian with its momentary lapses into waltz tempo and snatches of broad melody. At the same time, with its deeper musical substance and greater finality in its closing bars, it well rounds off a set which, slender as it may be, has an unforgettable quality. Songs of the insane have an estimable tradition from as far back as Purcell's *Mad Bess*.

The three bad-tempered songs which form the second part of the op. 67 collection with which Strauss discharged his liability are more problematical. The words are selected from the *Buch des Unmuts* ('Book of ill-humour')[62] from Goethe's curious product of later life, the *Westöstlicher Divan*. The very title of the work requires a little unravelling.

In 1814, tired from a recent illness and disillusioned by the state of war-torn Europe, the sixty-five year old Goethe turned for comfort to oriental literature. Coming across a translation by the Viennese orientalist Joseph von Hammer-Purgstall of the great thirteenth-century Persian poet Shams-ud-din Mohammed, known as Hafiz, Goethe immersed himself in his works. The principal of these is the *Divan*, an originally Persian word signifying in addition to its numerous other and more familiar meanings a collection of short poems.

[62] Not *Bücher* (books) as given in Strauss's heading.

It so happened that in that same year Goethe fell in love with a young one-time dancer Marie Anne (Marianne) Jung and, although she had only just married her protector and an old friend of Goethe's, a Frankfurt banker called Willemer, a passionate liaison sprang up between them.

Under the influence of his Oriental studies he now began to see Eastern manifestations everywhere, even amidst the most normal scenes of everyday life in German towns and villages. He called Marianne his Suleika and took to carrying out in their intimate life together a pantomime of oriental behaviour, including the wearing of a turban and Turkish slippers, to which his new young partner contributed enthusiastically.

Carried away by the old man's romance, in which everything from his white woolly dressing-gown to various aspects of his coddling by the adoring Marianne was deeply symbolical, Goethe began to pour out a series of verses after the models of different Eastern poets. And strange to say Marianne herself was able to play her part here too, developing into a considerable poet in her own right. Indeed many of the verses in the final collection, which took over five years to compile and publish, may very well be her work.

At first Goethe entitled this new creation *Deutscher Divan*, but as the years passed and it assumed considerable proportions he renamed it *Westöstlicher Divan*, as if recognizing its particular character in bridging the Western and Oriental ways of thinking, in themselves basically so far apart.

Although remaining one of Goethe's most controversial works on grounds of sheer merit, the *Westöstlicher Divan* exerted an enormous influence on the subsequent generations of German romantic poets. Bodenstedt's *Mirza Schaffy*, and especially Rückert's *Persische Vierzeiler*, both of which we have met above (see pp. 268 and 331) were directly inspired by Goethe's example, and these are only isolated instances of a whole literary movement to which the *Divan* gave rise.

The collection is divided into twelve books with such varied titles as: Book of the Singers, of Love, of Hafi, of Proverbs, of Timur (a fifteenth-century Mongolian chieftain), of Suleika, the Gift Book (Das Schenkenbuch, many poems of which—as of the previous book— Schumann and Hugo Wolf among others, set to music) and so on, ending with the Book of Paradise. Each book cites at the head its title in Persian—*Moganni Nameh, Uschk Nameh, Hafis Nameh*, etc., so that the

Buch des Unmuts (which comes fifth in order) is also entitled *Rendsch Nameh*, which Strauss seems to mistake for the name of the original poet.

The three selected poems appear consecutively (though Strauss places the last of them first) in the latter part of the *Buch des Unmuts*, and reflect different aspects of the author's dissatisfaction with life. *Wer wird von der Welt verlangen* berates those who expect to be given what the world itself only dreams of. In constantly looking askance at it, they miss the day of days when it comes.

This little shaft of cynicism Strauss sets to music of greater warmth than was to be anticipated. The ill-humour is mostly to be found in the shifting, restless tonalities of the outer sections and especially the end where Strauss makes an apparently haphazard choice in the matter of which of several depressing minor chords finally to settle upon. But it is the richer middle passage which gives the song its thematic basis:

Ex. 91

This phrase—especially the group ⌈ x ⌉—recalls a passage at the beginning of the second act of *Die Frau ohne Schatten*, during which the Amme tries to allay the Färberin's gnawing discontent with visions of the boy of her dreams. In many of the songs such apparent connexions with similar motifs from Strauss's other works could be thought far-fetched, but here one is encouraged not only by the aptness of the allusion but by Strauss's use of direct quotations in the following song.

Hab' ich euch denn je geraten is a peevish outburst of the typical Oriental philosopher against fools who always think they know better than the sage. Whilst they make war or peace, he has quietly sat there accumulating wisdom from the simple ways of life, from Nature itself. All right, he says, if you think you are so sure, get on with it. But you should still look at my works and so learn 'that is how *he* does it'.

It has been necessary to paraphrase the latter part of the poem partly because its meaning is not immediately obvious, but also because the musical treatment is whimsical to say the least. After an opening of impetuous irritability followed by a gentle flowing passage to depict the simple life (the fisherman with his nets, the carpenter, etc.) Strauss identifies himself with the fakir. When the old man speaks of Nature working for him Strauss illustrates the thought with the 'meadows' section from *Alpensinfonie*, quoted at considerable length and combined with the climbing motif from the same work (Vol. II, pp. 108 and 113, Exx. 4 and 12). Furthermore the proud reference to 'my works' is heralded by the Kaiser's theme from *Die Frau ohne Schatten* which was only just completed and had not yet received its first performance at the time this song was written.

Lastly comes *Wanderers Gemütsruhe* ('Wanderer's peace of mind') Goethe's own ironical title to another savage thrust. Don't, he says, complain about the filth of the world, for filth is power and it is evil which gets to the top and changes things to its own way of thinking. Whatever is the use of fighting? 'Whirlwind and dry dung—leave them alone'.

This is the *non plus ultra* of disillusionment and might seem too radical for Strauss's purpose. However, his setting hardly reflects the bitterness of the words which are largely thrown off in a brilliant scherzo-like song taking its mood from the reference to the whirlwind and ending in mid-air with an inconclusive upward wisp of arpeggio, alternately major and minor.

They are not perhaps the most grateful songs for a fine vocalist to choose from amongst Strauss's vast Lieder *oeuvre*, but they are very far from inconsiderable. That Asow should have chosen to quote Strauss's remarks about some songs being made, not born, in respect of just these was all too ingenuous.[63] It was not when Strauss had an axe to grind that inspiration deserted him, but rather when he was composing for the sheer sake of routine music-making. The six songs Bote & Bock finally received may not have been of the kind they had expected or would have chosen for preference, but they are in their own way quite remarkable and well worth reviving.

Strauss was to return five times to the *Westöstlicher Divan* during the years to come but in each case only for an isolated song. This sporadic production was to some extent of an occasional nature as we shall see, and Strauss did not take sufficient interest in what was at best a haphazard group to consider any idea of publication in his lifetime. They will be found below listed as Nos. 190, 194, 195 and 206.

[63] See p. 248 above and Asow's *Thematisches Verzeichnis*, p. 730.

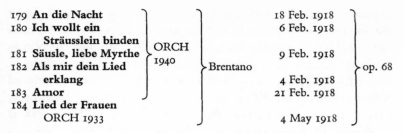

179 **An die Nacht**
180 **Ich wollt ein**
       Sträusslein binden
181 **Säusle, liebe Myrthe**
182 **Als mir dein Lied**
       erklang
183 **Amor**
184 **Lied der Frauen**
       ORCH 1933

ORCH
1940

Brentano

18 Feb. 1918
6 Feb. 1918

9 Feb. 1918

4 Feb. 1918
21 Feb. 1918

4 May 1918

op. 68

Although eighteen years had passed since Strauss had last composed a *Knaben Wunderhorn* song he still retained the liveliest affection for that great collection as well as interest in its joint authors Brentano and Arnim.

When, therefore, he re-addressed himself to the Lied after his long abstention, rather than trying to rival his now dead colleague Mahler's great success with the *Wunderhorn* poems, he conceived the idea of setting some of its authors' own individual work, beginning with six well-chosen and cleverly contrasted verses by Brentano.

Clemens Brentano was the romantic poet *par excellence*. He was the son of an Italian merchant and Maximiliane Laroche, the 'Maxe' of Goethe's *Werther* days, who was well known in literary circles through her own authoress mother Sophie Laroche.

After a stormy childhood Brentano went to one university after another where he enthusiastically joined the important circle of young Romanticists who followed and reacted against the *Sturm und Drang* of Goethe and Schiller. Unconventional and restless by nature, for some years he wandered about the country-side with a guitar on his back like a medieval minstrel.

His best work began after he formed his close and life-long friendship with Arnim who also married one of his sisters, the famous Bettina. Brentano endlessly failed to find happiness even when after untold troubles and tribulations he married the love of his life, only to experience the despair of her death on bearing the last of three still-born children. Yet while she was alive he had left her much alone, following Arnim from Heidelberg to Berlin in an admittedly successful search for poetic inspiration.

Much of Brentano's best writing was subsequent to his and Arnim's combined work on *Des Knaben Wunderhorn*. It includes *Märchen* (Fairy tales) and short stories, the best of the poems and especially the romantic drama *Die Gründung Prags* which stemmed from a visit to Prague in

1811 and a reference to which is contained in the first of the verses Strauss chose for his Brentano Lieder.

This is an impressive poem entitled *An die Nacht*, an apostrophe to Night full of poetic and mythical symbolism, the latter derived from Bohemian legend in its reference to 'Bjelbogs Speer', Bjelbog being the god of heavenly light in Czech mythology.

Strauss's treatment gives it something of the quality of a Bardic Hymn, with its formalized Naturthema of a principal motif:

Ex. 92

while its highly sophisticated chromatic modulations indicate the unmistakable approach of Strauss's late style. The composer is reputed to have stopped once when playing the accompaniment saying , 'What a modulation! Can this really be right?'

Ex. 93

A secondary motif is developed towards the end into an impassioned instrumental peroration suggesting that the orchestral treatment, which was to follow after no less than twenty-two years, must have been in Strauss's mind from the first. This is moreover by no means an isolated instance in what is one of Strauss's biggest and most important groups:

Ex. 94

The title of the next poem *Ich wollt ein Sträusslein binden,* must have presented itself to Strauss as *ben trovato.* It is a gentle enough love song with more than a tinge of melancholy as the lover tells of his unsuccessful attempt to produce a bouquet (Sträusslein) for his sweetheart, either because there are no flowers to be found or when, with tears streaming down his cheeks, he eventually lights on one and it begs him not to pick it.[64] So the beloved leaves him in the lurch for, as the poet philosophically reflects, love must always have its sad side.

Strauss takes his cue from this wistful, half regretful half smiling view of the little tragedy, which is sketched in with the lightest of hands. There is a touch of coloratura in the voice as it announces in the opening phrase the first of the two principal motifs:

Ex. 95

Ex. 96

[64] The romantic idea of the flower addressing its would-be destroyer is in line with the many other flowers of German poetry which speak up sharply when threatened with picking, such as the Blümchen in Goethe's *Gefunden,* a poem which Strauss had set as his op. 56 No. 1 (No. 155). The most famous of all is of course *Heidenröslein* which has for all intents and purposes become a folk-song in Schubert's unforgettable setting.

[65] The similarity of Ex. 96 to the theme of *Nichts* (No. 44) provides an interesting view of the composer's different treatment of such a figure some forty years later in life.

The other (Ex. 96), which remains throughout in the accompaniment, is equally light-hearted; it is in the mock pathetic chromatic harmonies and tearful episodes that the drama emerges. The whole song is entirely captivating and vividly recalls the art of that enchanting singer Elisabeth Schumann, for whom Strauss is known to have composed these songs.

Whereas not all six would by any means have suited her voice equally well, the next song, *Säusle, liebe Myrthe*, was once again perfectly composed for Madame Schumann. It is the most delicate lullaby full of nature sounds; the rustling of trees (hence the title), cooing of turtle-doves, the murmuring brook and so on, are all faithfully reflected in the music. But instead of the mother rocking her child, it is the lover whom the girl is tenderly singing to sleep.

Once again the song is based on two musical ideas, the opening phrase (which is quoted here in its later decorated form):

Ex. 97

Säusle,— lie - be— Myr - th!

and the refrain which also plays a substantial part in the development of the latter part of the song. This too is shown in one of its last appearances to indicate the range and beauty of the vocal line:

Ex. 98

With *Als mir dein Lied erklang* the mood changes and we are in one of Strauss's surging, passionate effusions. The bustling arpeggiando accompaniment, the intricate harmonies with excited plunges into one new key after another, all contrive to reflect the restless exuberance of the lover now that he has heard his beloved's song resounding amidst all the beauties of nature. The words 'dein Lied erklang' recur constantly through the poem and Strauss uses them for his similarly recurring motto theme which incidentally has the contours of the opening of a familiar tune from Weber's *Oberon*.

Ex. 99

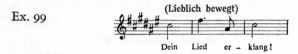

Amor is an out and out coloratura song treating Love with piquant flippancy as the traditional little blind child-god, his wings fanning the flames. But his wings themselves catch fire and he rushes crying for help into the lap of the shepherdess who little realizes the danger she is in through harbouring the 'sly, naughty child'. Here Strauss summons up his best Zerbinetta manner, alternating a warmly lyrical phrase for the shepherdess with spicy dissonances depicting the 'schlaues Kind', the whole clothed in trills and roulades for voice and accompaniment alike. The orchestral version, which is for a chamber ensemble of woodwind and strings without double basses, adds an extra bar at the beginning, allowing the oboe to anticipate the voice's first phrase.

The last song is the *pièce de résistance* of the whole set. Brentano's full title is *Lied der Frauen wenn die Männer im Kriege sind*. It is a powerful and tragic tribute to the wives of men who daily look death in the face whether they be seamen, shepherds, miners or warriors—thus goes the sequence in the successive verses of Brentano's poem. And with the soldier's death there may come to his wife the cruelly cold comfort of a joyful peace on the horizon, and glory, and the laurels of victory. At the end all she seeks is the total dark of a starless night. Her heartbreak is mixed with a pathetic touch of pride at her sacrifice for the fatherland, her words adapted from that desperate verse from the Book of Job:

> Dann sternlose Nacht sei willkommen
> Der Herr hat gegeben den Stern
> Der Herr hat genommen, genommen, genommen,
> Gelobt sei der Wille des Herrn![66]

an adaptation which Strauss intensified by changing 'Wille' to 'Name'.

Strauss's inspired setting is symphonic in style and proportion, and must stand as one of the finest in his entire Lieder opus. It opens in storm and turmoil and only gradually do the principal motifs emerge from

[66]   'Then welcome, starless night
             The Lord gave the star
             The Lord hath taken away
             Blessed be the will (name) of the Lord.'
Brentano's title translates: 'Song of women whose men are at war'.

the raging, turbulent textures although ⌐ x ⌐ has been implicit since
the very beginning, whereas ⌐ y ⌐ was introduced thunderously
during the verse about the miner's perils underground. At the climax of
the song, however, they come vividly to the foreground:

Ex. 100

The call of the lark ('Tireli, Tireli') hailing the victorious peace adds to her agony, and a mighty cadence brings the song to an extended though still swiftly flowing elegiac coda in C major. The music swells to an almost unbearable poignancy as the closing lines are approached and finally burst out on a high chromatically descending extended version of Ex. 100(x). At the words 'gelobt sei der Name des Herrn' it suddenly subsides, however, to the most beautiful calm ending with spaced-out, broken repetitions of the word 'Gelobt!'.

This was, naturally enough, the first song to be orchestrated, being one of the four Strauss so arranged in 1933 for Viorica Ursuleac. It is undoubtedly composed for a powerful lyric soprano both in its range and in its cruelly heavy accompaniment which in the orchestral version threatens at times to overwhelm the partially low lying voice.

Yet when in 1940 Strauss completed the orchestral settings which deserve to become the definitive form of the songs, he thought of them as a unit, and rightly, as they make a magnificent whole even though the outer Lieder seem at first sight to need an entirely different voice from the lighter central ones. But Strauss did not necessarily see them so, for at the time they were composed he was used to voices of a far greater range and versatility of technique than is commonly found to-day. One need only recall that his original Marschallin was also the first Zerbinetta, and that Strauss had written the role of the Kaiserin in *Die Frau ohne Schatten* for precisely the voice which could take this complete group in its stride.

One must however recognize that it is their unusual scale and difficulty which have militated against the popularity of the Brentano Lieder. It is not even sure that Elisabeth Schumann herself ever performed them; she certainly never sang them all. Nevertheless each of the six is a masterpiece in its own genre not only in freshness of invention but in the wealth of fascinating and advanced harmonic detail, whilst in *Lied der Frauen* Strauss showed yet again his true greatness in human insight and compassion; it was to be the last time in the Lieder until just before the end of his life.

185 **Der Stern**	⎫		June/July 1918	⎫ Fünf
186 **Der Pokal**	⎬ Arnim		June/July 1918	kleine
187 **Einerlei**	⎭		25 June 1918	⎬ Lieder
188 **Waldesfahrt**	⎱ Heine		26 June 1918	op. 69
189 **Schlechtes Wetter**	⎰		21 June 1918	⎭
190 **Sinnspruch**		Goethe	24 June 1919	

From the one author of *Des Knaben Wunderhorn* Strauss now turned to the other, Arnim, who was also a member of the Heidelberg Jüngere Romantik group. Ludwig Achim von Arnim was, as his name suggests, of an old and noble family. With his aristocratic Prussian connexions Arnim was deeply concerned at the disgrace of Prussia's military disasters in the early years of the nineteenth century and his poem *Der Stern* celebrates the appearance in 1811 of the great comet which the people of his homeland hailed as an encouraging omen.

> Die Haare im Fliegen
> Er eilet mir zu
> Das Volk träumt von Siegen
> Ich träume von Ruh'.[67]

It is thus to some extent a political poem although it comes in the collection rather loosely entitled *Liebe und Freundschaft*, which Arnim dedicated to Bettina, his wife and Brentano's sister.

This may have influenced Strauss, who set the poem in a gentle, 'friendly' (as he described it) folk-song manner. It could almost be a love song, but Strauss who was in a comfortable mood for Lieder composition did not really consider the matter too deeply. Just after he had completed *Der Stern* he had a visit from a friend, Max Marschalk, who asked him how he set about writing songs. Strauss answered, much to the same effect as in his letter to Hausegger twenty-five years before[63] but with interesting relevance to the music he had that moment put on paper:

> Well, you know, that isn't the sort of question one can answer on the spot and in a few words. Sometimes it is a very laborious process while at other times inspiration comes in a flash, and afterwards I can hardly account for how I came across a theme, a melody or a song. Just now when I was waiting for you I took up my copy of Achim von Arnim and read the little poem 'Stern' and, as I read, the musical inspiration came to me. I wrote the song down on the spot; if you like I'll play it to you.

—which he did, to the delight of Herr Marschalk who commented that in its simplicity and its noble, genuine folk-song quality the Lied would take its place amongst the composer's happiest creations.

[67] 'With hair flying' (i.e. the tail of the comet, one German word for 'comet' is 'Haarstern') 'it hurries towards me; the people dream of victory but I of rest.'
[68] See above, p. 248.

This now appears something of an over-estimation and the question arises whether it is necessarily that work of art which has come to its creator all of a piece, in a single moment of perception, which ultimately has the profoundest message. In a later, wiser discussion with Max Marschalk Strauss added:

> I work for a very long time on melodies: there is a great distance between the first sudden idea and the final melodic form . . . most people content themselves with the idea, whereas it is in the development of the idea that true art is shown . . . a melody which seems to have been born in an instant is almost always the result of painstaking work . . .

At the same time he revealed, however, that amongst the exceptions was *Traum durch die Dämmerung*, which like *Der Stern* was born on the spur of the moment but is one of Strauss's greatest and most beautiful songs.

The second Arnim Lied *Der Pokal* is purely and simply an infectious burst of high spirits. The poem is the first of a later collection entitled *Leben und Natur* and is an invitation to world-wide comradeship, Strauss working hard in a swinging $\frac{6}{4}$ to match the enthusiasm of the words.

Whether or not it was his original intention to match the Brentano Lieder with a similar Arnim set, Strauss only found one more text which captured his imagination and that a curious little fragment of verse, the closing refrain of which tickled his fancy:

Ex. 101

O du liebes Einerlei,   wie wird aus dir so mancherlei!

(lit. 'Oh, beloved sameness, how much diversity comes from you')

Here indeed is a case where the musical phrase must have fitted itself instantly to the lilt of the catchy couplet, though the song itself is the product of the most ingenious craftsmanship. The melody, for example, makes its appearance in the piano's preluding, long before we hear the words from which it sprang. Moreover Strauss readily solved the difficult problem of matching so insidiously memorable a phrase with a companion theme worthy to open the song and to which the first lines of the voice are then effortlessly fitted:

Ex. 102

(Gemächlich heiter, ziemlich lebhaft)

Particularly captivating is the device, used repeatedly, of an implied modulation which only sometimes comes off though it keeps going back and trying again.

This well-known Lied, although the purest artifice, certainly deserves the affection it has earned amongst singers. Strauss dedicated it to the parents of his future daughter-in-law, Alice Grab (who had recently become his secretary), on the occasion of their silver wedding.

To complete the group of 'kleine Lieder' (as Strauss called them, although they are no smaller than a great number in his earlier output) the composer turned back to Heine, with whom he had been preoccupied when in 1906 his quarrel with the publishing world had caused him to abandon song-writing.

The first of the two Heine poems with which he concludes this group comes again from the famous *Lyrisches Intermezzo* in which it immediately precedes *Ich hab' im Traum geweinet*, another familiar part of Schumann's *Dichterliebe*. Schumann also set *Mein Wagen rollet langsam*—*Waldesfahrt* is Strauss's not very helpful title.

It is a very peculiar poem and one has to admit that Strauss brings out its weirdness more vividly than Schumann's rather pale and uncharacteristic version. The lover is driving quietly along through colourful woods and valleys thinking and dreaming of his sweetheart, when he is suddenly beset by three phantoms who grimace and hop up and down around him.

We are told no more; the poem just stops at this point. But both Schumann and Strauss assume that the lover comes to no actual harm and allow him to continue his interrupted sentimental journey, Schumann by implication in a long piano postlude, Strauss with the repetition of the lines in which he sits and dreams of his beloved.

Strauss, unlike Schumann however, varies the tempo and texture of the music with wild contrast between the slow dreamy F sharp major melody of the lover in his coach and the darting ⁶/₈ dance-fragments of the cavorting spectres linked by crazy scales and arpeggios. It is clear from the sudden surges of passionate intensity that there are times when it understandably requires all the lover's concentration to preserve his sang-froid.

The last song is the best known of the five and one of the most popular of all the later Lieder. The poem *Das ist ein schlechtes Wetter* comes from *Die Heimkehr* from which Strauss also drew *Die Heil'gen drei Kön'ge aus Morgenland* and which contains the evergreen Lorelei poem *Ich weiss nicht, was soll es bedeuten.*

The subject of the poem changes gradually from the dreadful weather (*Schlechtes Wetter*), by way of the mother out in the dark street shopping, to the golden-haired daughter for whom she is going to bake a cake.

The continual use of diminutives ('Lichtchen', 'Mütterchen', 'Laternchen' etc.) gives the poem an atmosphere of mock whimsy which Strauss echoes in his featherweight setting. Particularly entertaining is the way the piano figuration describing the rain, hail, snow or whatever gradually becomes identified with the waves of the maiden's golden hair by the time the whole song has turned into an elegant Straussian waltz. The little *Frau ohne Schatten* Falke-like chirrups which pervade the song in every register of the piano also indicate that not a bar is to be taken seriously. But it is all delightful and Strauss's vocal line lies, as ever, beautifully for the voice.

A year later, in June 1919, Strauss dashed off another song from the *Westöstlicher Divan* at the desire of a publisher friend, Rudolf Mosse, to be included in the *Mosse Almanach* for 1920. The poem is taken this time from *Mathal Nameh*, that is to say the *Book of Parables*. It attacks the self-importance of human beings who in every walk of life resent interference and at the first signs of being disturbed think the world has come to an end. The analogy is made with spiders sitting in their webs threatened by the traditional clean sweep, and Strauss sets it to a light criss-cross of alternate hands brushed aside every so often with impatient little broom-strokes. If not a song of any great consequence it has many a characteristic touch and Herr Mosse would have had reason to be well satisfied with the result of his request.

16

191 **Hymne an die Liebe**		6 Apr. 1921	Drei Hymnen für eine
192 **Rückkehr in die**	Hölderlin		hohe Singstimme und
Heimat		2 Jan. 1921	grosses Orchester
193 **Die Liebe**		20 Jan. 1921	op. 71

Two more years passed during which, the war over, Strauss had been concerning himself with the long delayed first production of *Die Frau ohne Schatten* and the complicated turbulent affairs of the Vienna State Opera. In the midst of all this the collaboration with Hofmannsthal had temporarily languished, and in so far as time allowed in the disquieting post-war atmosphere, Strauss was occupying himself with *Schlagobers* and *Intermezzo*.

Feeling the need for something more immediate in the line of orchestral composition he turned again to the specifically orchestral Lied, and casting around for some larger poems for the purpose his eye lit on Hölderlin, who is revered by many as one of Germany's greatest poets.

Friedrich Hölderlin belongs to the post *Sturm und Drang* period in German literature immediately preceding the young Romantic school of Brentano and Arnim. An ardent lover of Greece, much of his work has an epic if remote classicism which has put it outside the scope of most Lieder writers. Probably the most famous Hölderlin setting is Brahms' *Schicksalslied* for Chorus and orchestra, and in modern times Britten has written a remarkable cycle to his words.

Strauss chose three extensive panegyrics on love and, taking his cue from *Hymne an die Liebe* (which although the last to be composed he placed first in the group), entitled the set *Drei Hymnen*. Hölderlin's Hymn of Praise to Love is one of a series of such *Hymnen*, dedicated to the Genius of Greece, to Freedom, Friendship and so on. The one addressed to Liebe is a eulogy on the abstract concept of love rather than a reflection on a great emotional experience. In some ways it could almost be considered as the counterpart to Freude ('Joy') as portrayed in Schiller's famous Ode immortalized in Beethoven's Choral Symphony, and indeed 'Freude' itself is strongly featured in the opening section of the poem. Moreover, all people are exhorted to join hands like so many brothers and sisters in appreciation and honour to the all-enveloping figure of winged Love.

It was not to be anticipated that this idealized but decidedly impersonal aspect of a subject which had been in the most vivid forefront of so many of Strauss's erotic compositions would stimulate him and one cannot but think the choice of text a strange one for this particular composer. Nevertheless it served well enough as a framework for a piece of glowing orchestral colour supporting a soaring cantilena, and in this respect the song stands as the prototype for the many such effusions to be found in the later operas from *Die Aegyptische Helena* to *Die Liebe der Danae*.

The bulk of the musical material is heard in the first bars, the melodic phrase ⌐ x ⌐ accounting for most of the argument though ⌐ y ⌐ and ⌐ z ⌐ receive their share of motivic treatment.

Ex. 103

During the tirelessly flowing course of the movement Ex. 103(x) is combined, sometimes in rather gauche counterpoint, with a long strand of melody:

Ex. 104

Appearing first unobtrusively in the bass, Ex. 104 recurs at various points and at different levels giving rise to some extremely strange harmonies. But whenever matters seem to become too obscure Strauss plunges with aplomb into some dramatic new key and the music surges forward with unabating flow.

Reference to the peaceful ocean brings a gently rocking water-music, while allusion to mountain crags calls up the opening motif from the *Alpensinfonie* on horns and trumpets. Eventually overlapping entries of Ex. 104 guide the music towards its long coda in the key of F, which we have understood to be the home tonality from the key signature and from the first entry of the voice, but from little else in the course of this harmonically kaleidoscopic, symphonic Lied.

Rückkehr in die Heimat is concerned with a different sort of love, affection for the fatherland together with nostalgia for the beauties of nature so much loved and enjoyed during years of youthful wanderings in far-off parts.

Of the three poems this is clearly the least hymn-like and Strauss sets it more in the manner of a mood and nature idyll. The atmospheric opening, which also makes a formal return to accompany the poet's apostrophe to his homeland coupled with his farewell to youth, is made up of the delicate orchestral filigree of the Färberin's transformation in the first act of *Die Frau ohne Schatten*. This gradually gives way to a more cantabile texture as the memory of beloved Italian landscapes evokes yearning and heartache. Even the sharp outline of the song's principal Naturmotif, so characteristic of the composer of *Heldenleben*:

Ex. 105

is softened and becomes a gentle woodwind ostinato.

The poet's melancholy reflection on the irrevocable passing of childhood's peace of mind brings from Strauss another self-quotation, this time of the childhood theme from *Tod und Verklärung* (Vol. I, p. 79, Ex. 18). The end brings the tranquillity of resignation amid tones which as in the first song set the pattern for much of Strauss's later work.

The last song is once more specifically entitled *Die Liebe* and is an exhortation on behalf of love and lovers. The admonition heard near the opening, after a brief recitative-like passage, to 'honour the souls of lovers' provides Strauss with the first of his two principal motifs:

Ex. 106

See – le der Lie – benden!

while a discourse on the rejuvenating power of love after the barrenness of winter provides the other, heard first on a solo oboe amidst birdcalls but quickly growing in scope and intensity.

Ex. 107

The particular virtue of this high-flown poem to end the cycle lies in its own built-in crescendo ending in an outright plea that 'the language of lovers be the tongue of the country itself':

> Sprache der Liebenden sei die Sprache des Landes
> Ihre Seele der Laut des Volks.

Such a motto-like phrase forms a natural climax which Strauss treats as a magniloquent coda introduced, after a tremendous orchestral surge, by the voice entirely unaccompanied for three bars, with these words, perhaps (if possible) even more idealistic in conception:

> Wachs' und werde zum Wald,
> eine beseeltere vollentblühende Welt![69]

The motto itself Strauss not only sets as the apotheosis of Exx. 106 and 107 combined, but after an extended orchestral peroration which subsides into what seem like the final cadences, repeats it *in toto*, this time in an ecstatic pianissimo.

It would be idle to pretend that these Hymnen represent the great or inspired composer in Strauss, and yet they contain much of his special vein of flamboyant lyricism, and are so grateful to perform for orchestra and soloist alike that they would justify far more frequent revivals than they have enjoyed in recent years. They were to be Strauss's last specifically orchestral Lieder until his great swan-song for which in some measure they paved the way, the *Vier letzte Lieder*.

194	**Erschaffen und Beleben**	Goethe	25 Dec. 1922[70]	
195	**Durch allen Schall und Klang**	Goethe	11 June 1925	
196	**Ihre Augen**	⎫	14 Aug. 1928	⎫ Gesänge
197	**Schwung**	⎪	15 Aug. 1928	⎪ des
198	**Liebesgeschenke**	⎬ Bethge	14 Aug. 1928	⎬ Orients
199	**Die Allmächtige**	⎪	15 Aug. 1928	⎪ op. 77
200	**Huldigung**	⎭	24 Sept. 1928	⎭

Unexpectedly the renewed burst of song writing faded and seven years were to elapse before Strauss once more turned to the Lied, except for two more isolated *Westöstlicher Divan* settings, which were again composed three years apart. The first was intended as a vehicle for one of the singers in the Berlin Opera, the bass Michael Bohnen, and not only was it dedicated to him in glowing terms, but the vocal line being of exceptional scope and virtuosity, was intended to show off his artistry. Strauss seems, however, to have been subsequently disen-

[69]   'May a spiritual, blossoming world
        grow and be transformed into woodland!'
[70] Described as 'op. 87 No. 2' in the Complete Edition. See p. 388.

chanted with Bohnen's work (in any case Bohnen soon after abandoned his career in Germany in favour of America) for he deleted the expressions of admiration in the dedicatory heading and ultimately re-dedicated the song altogether, inscribing it (as late as 1945) to Hans Hotter.

The title *Erschaffen und Beleben* (lit: 'Creation and Animation') is taken from the *Moganni Nameh*, the *Buch des Sängers*, but the song was first published under the opening words 'Hans Adam war ein Erdenkloss', which was also how Strauss himself had originally headed it.

A rumbustious drinking song, it is a characteristic example of at least one type of the 'ghazals' (kinds of ode or sonnet) with which, as was customary at the time, Hafiz made up his Divan. It paints old 'Hans Adam'—as the father of all mankind is irreverently called—as a brutish lump of clay who had emerged still very uncouth from his mother's womb and who really only became a tolerable being after imbibing quantities of liquor from the tankard which it took that notorious toper Noah to invent and put to use.

The poem ends with a paean of praise to Hafiz himself (whose real name, it may be recalled, was Shams-ud-din Mohammed), this use of his nom-de-plume in the concluding lines of his own poems being a matter of tradition.

'Hafiz' actually means 'one who remembers' and was given to the poet because, having at one time belonged to the order of dervishes, he could recite the entire Koran from memory. But as this song shows, he was very far from an ascetic, and indeed was at one time thought to be thoroughly dissolute. He enjoyed a long and active life and died in 1388.

This poem, another of the very few Strauss songs to texts previously set by other composers, forms one of Hugo Wolf's Lieder from the *Westöstlicher Divan*. Unlike Wolf's march-like treatment Strauss's setting begins somewhat in the manner of Hans Sachs' *Schusterlied* from *Meistersinger* though without comparable melodic distinction. Dr Willi Schuh is surely right in regarding the song as having been improvised (it goes off at a tangent in the closing bars and ends in quite the wrong key with extraordinary effect). But it is full of fun whether in the grotesque gawkiness of the vocal line at the beginning, in the elaborate sneezes in the piano part (as Wolf also gives, descriptive of poor Adam's reaction when the Almighty blew the best of spirits up his nose) or the unthinkable vocal description of Adam's ultimate animation through liquor which is compared with the rising and frothing of yeast in ferment.

If a palpable show-piece for any bass with the necessary range

it is musically somewhat slender and lingered unpublished until 1951, two years after the composer's death; nor was it
performed for a further six years. One can understand Strauss's initial
lack of concern for the song's fate better than his sudden whim in 1935
of surrounding it with three new Rückert songs which he wrote during
these later years. Together with them it would, he thought, make up a
nice set of four posthumous songs for bass which, now that his work
(what with one one thing and another) was likely to be at an end, might
just as well bear the opus number 81—op. 80 being significantly his ill-
fated opera with Stefan Zweig.

But his work proved very far from over and op. 81 was reclaimed
for *Friedenstag. Hans Adam* was eventually published by itself and only
in the Collected Edition is Strauss's 1935 idea honoured, with perhaps
rather doubtful wisdom, and the song sandwiched between the Rückert
Lieder under the fictitious opus number '87', Strauss having abandoned
enumeration in 1942 after the publication of the Couperin *Divertimento*
op. 86.

Durch allen Schall und Klang is even more of a *pièce d'occasion* and
certainly far less of a valid and performable example of Strauss's art.
It was composed in June 1935 for insertion in a book of offerings by
Romain Rolland's friends in celebration of the much beloved author's
sixtieth birthday early the following year.

The purely laudatory little verse comes this time from the *Tefkir
Nameh*, the *Buch der Betrachtungen* ('Reflections') where it is headed
'Schach Sedschan und seinesgleichen'. Shah Sedschan (or Sedschaa) was
Hafiz' protector and the original recipient of this eulogy. It is generally
assumed that Goethe, in making his adaptation of the poem, was referring (as witness the 'seinesgleichen'—'his like'—of the title) to his own
protector Herzog Karl August. So Strauss was paying his old friend
Rolland a pretty compliment and it is only a shame that he was not able
to make the music a little more interesting. Perhaps the dedicatory inscription was compensation:

> Romain Rolland
> to the great poet and highly honoured friend
> to the heroic fighter against all evil powers working for the
> downfall of Europe,
> with expressions of truest sympathy and sincerest admira-
> tion
> Richard Strauss 29 January 1926

Rolland's letter of thanks and appreciation is characteristically touching:

> My very dear friend,
> How can I thank you enough for the joy you have given me, with your regal gift of friendship—to the *Liber Amicorum*—the triumphal song of this 'Westöstlicher Divan' (which is one of my favourite books) and the magnificent dedication! The lustre of your music lights up the whole volume, as it has enveloped my life since the first day—(it will soon be thirty years ago!)—when the jubilant fanfares of *Heldenleben* made my heart dance.
> To have your friendship has been one of the greatest gifts vouchsafed to me by destiny. And that across so many ruins of empires—and friendships—our own should remain pure and steadfast I am proud, and I embrace you with brotherly affection.

Although, as with Hofmannsthal, Strauss and Rolland actually met so rarely, the composer had few such devoted friends.

17

Strauss's interest in quasi-oriental poetry was neither exhausted nor confined to Goethe's adaptions. The specific reference to Hafiz in *Erschaffen und Beleben* had reminded him of a possible source of inspiration well worth tapping. It so happened that a collection of *Nachdichtungen* (free poetic renderings) from Hafiz' writings had been made by Hans Bethge, a minor poet who had achieved considerable success with his publication in 1908 of a volume entitled *Die Chinesische Flöte*. This was a similar oriental anthology but with verses taken from a number of Chinese authors, some of considerable antiquity. It is particularly familiar to musicians in connexion with Mahler's masterpiece *Das Lied von der Erde*, but both Schönberg and Webern made settings of some of its poems.

So when in 1928 *Die Aegyptische Helena* lay behind him and it seemed high time to turn again to the Lied, Strauss thumbed through the Bethge volumes and picked out four of the Hafiz poems which, together with one from *Die Chinesische Flöte* (by—as it happens—an anonymous author), he grouped together to make a set of *Gesänge des Orients*.

They consist mostly of love poems, though one is a drinking song. As befits the title Gesänge they are on a markedly large scale but it will have been their extreme difficulty as well as sophistication of idiom which have made them amongst the least known of all Strauss's Lieder. Asow lists no performances at all, and while it is hardly likely that they have in truth never been sung this is an indication of their virtually complete neglect. While they may well be less immediately captivating than the best of Strauss songs they contain many beautiful and unusual features.

The first, *Ihre Augen* is a delicate love-song extolling the beauty of the loved one's eyes beneath their arching brows, an idea to which Strauss responds with curving melodic phrases supported sometimes by exotic and even gauche harmonies. Arpeggiando figurations and spread chords also help to create a serenade-like impression as if the poet were accompanying his song with some oriental lute or harp. Although restrained in character, the voice lies for the greater part very high and builds to a substantial climax requiring the most accomplished control and sustaining power in the upper tessitura.

Schwung, which follows, is the drinking song and the tersest of the group. Hafiz' verses certainly bear out his dissolute reputation with the blasphemous assertion that 'every sura of the Koran I steep in wine'. Strauss sets it as an outburst of good humour, the three verses if not actually treated strophically being at least musically parallel, with different assortments of kaleidoscopic harmonies and a certain freedom in the interplay of thematic motifs in order to bring out the effervescent expression of the words.

The central song of the group *Liebesgeschenke* is the single *Chinesische Flöte* setting and the text has just the delicate scented imagery one would expect from this source with its peach-blossom, slender swallow's wings and distant blue-tinted mountains. There is more than a touch of the exquisite about the music with which Strauss clothed this typical product of Oriental artificiality though he avoided any hint of the Chinoiserie which Mahler allowed himself in *Das Lied von der Erde*. At the same time Strauss somehow failed to find any pronounced stylistic substitute and the song leaves behind a disappointingly insipid memory. Admittedly even Mahler's more mannered settings, those of Li-tai-po's *Der Pavillon aus Porzellan* and *Am Ufer*,[71] are on a totally different symphonic scale, but it is worrying to realize how far removed from their level of inspiration is Strauss's easy-going effusion. Mahler's symphony certainly made *Die Chinesische Flöte* treacherous ground for his suc-

[71] These are the poems of Mahler's third and fourth movements re-titled *Von der Jugend* and *Von der Schönheit* respectively.

cessors and Schönberg and Webern were shrewd to make their few settings either choral or, in Webern's case, poles apart in style and content.

With *Die Allmächtige* Strauss returns to Hafiz, choosing a curious poem which acknowledges the evil deeds of the loved one but excuses them all on account of her matchless beauty. The title refers to the absolute power she wields through her irresistible charms and the verses end by granting her sway over the enraptured recording angels themselves.

The music, more typically Straussian once more, recalls ideas from *Die Tageszeiten* and *Intermezzo* which are worked together with their composer's ever-ready fluency and craftsmanship. Particularly interesting is the development of the sequential motif which arises out of the opening phrase of the voice, and which undergoes many changes of character as the true nature of the beautiful girl is revealed:

Ex. 108

f (cf Vol. II, p. 246, Ex. 25)

The last song, *Huldigung* ('Homage') is a combination of five short stanzas by Hafiz, the title being Strauss's own. These are clothed in an ebullient Scherzo-like movement based once again on motifs strongly reminiscent of *Intermezzo*—this time of the Interlude during which Robert Storch returns to Christine shortly before the closing scene.

Many of the harmonies are, however, far more astringent so that the flamboyant piano part needs to be played with great conviction if it is not to sound a mere splashing out of wrong notes. The voice line too is virtuoso and wide-ranged as the singer outlines the countless ways he has been ill-treated by his beloved, who nevertheless cannot in the least damp his ardour. The last stanza is flamboyantly adulatory and sends the voice flying up to a top C.

Like several of the earlier songs of the set *Huldigung* is best suited for a tenor, and it is with a little surprise that one observes the dedication to Elisabeth Schumann together with her conductor-husband, one of Strauss's best colleague friends, Karl Alwin. Elisabeth Schumann was above all things an outstanding interpreter of Strauss Lieder and yet neither the Brentano group written for her voice nor this one specifically dedicated to her was in fact well enough suited to be included in her wide repertoire.

With the *Gesänge des Orients* we reach the end of the Lieder to which Strauss designated opus numbers although he was still to live another twenty-one years. His intention was to eke out the time which remained to him exclusively with the composition of operas. But in the event neither the world nor his own inclination allowed him to be so single minded.

All the same, he stubbornly regarded the heterogeneous collection of odd songs which he penned from time to time as posthumous works, though we shall soon see that this can in no way suggest they are uniformly unimportant.

18

201	**Vom künftigen Alter**	⎫Rückert	early 1929[72]
202	**Und dann nicht mehr**	⎬	11 Feb. 1929[72]
203	**Wie etwas sei leicht**	Goethe	9 Jan. 1930
204	**Das Bächlein** ORCH 1933	? Goethe	3 Dec. 1933[73]
205	**Im Sonnenschein**	Rückert	24 Feb. 1935[72]
206	**Zugemessne Rhythmen**	Goethe	25 Feb. 1935
207	**Sankt Michael**	⎫Weinheber	3 Feb. 1942[73]
208	**Blick vom oberen Belvedere**	⎬	11 Feb. 1942[73]
209	**Xenion**	Goethe	20 Sept. 1942

Strauss had had no marked success hitherto with his settings of Rückert (with the possible exception of the lurid *Nächtlicher Gang* No. 126) and it is thus the more surprising to see him returning in his old age to that deeply romantic poet, composing three substantial Lieder and a further assortment of choral pieces.[74] Two of the Gesänge (as Strauss again justly designated them) derive from the gestation period of *Arabella* but, after enjoying working on the 8-part *a cappella* choral setting of Rückert's *Die Göttin im Putzzimmer* six years later in February 1935, Strauss added a third Gesang, all three being for bass voice.

It may well have been his advancing years which directed Strauss to *Vom künftigen Alter*, yet one more poem already set—this time a particularly fine Schubert Lied entitled *Greisengesang*. The poem is

[72] Described as 'op. 87 Nos. 1, 3 and 4' respectively in the Complete Edition (see above, p. 388).

[73] Described as 'op. 88 Nos. 1, 3 and 2' respectively in the Complete Edition (see below, p. 397).

[74] The choruses are briefly discussed in Chapter XIX (see p. 117).

actually about the winter of old age, and this is certainly music of the
ageing Strauss, anticipating the mood of Jupiter's renunciation in the
closing scene of *Die Liebe der Danae*. Many features, in fact, of this long
and rather diffuse Gesang suggest an operatic draft and the piano part
with its extended cantilenas and rows of octaves in either hand brings
to mind Strauss's rich sweeps of violin tone or heavy brass chording.

There is a semi-operatic flavour too about the voice line which suits
to perfection the style and quality of dramatic bass-baritones such as Hans
Hotter to whom Strauss later dedicated *Vom künftigen Alter* when
simultaneously arranging for the rededication of the comic *Hans Adam*
(No. 194, see above p. 387).

Moreover, the quality of regret is very typical of late Strauss in its
alternation of bitter harmonies to depict the frost and desolation of
winter, which melt into warmer colouring as the words pass to the
spring and youthfulness which still linger in the old man's breast.

Like *Vom künftigen Alter*, *Und dann nicht mehr* comes from a group of
poems forming one of the books from Rückert's *Wanderungen* entitled
Östliche Rosen; the fact that this begins with an acknowledgement to
Goethe's *Westöstlicher Divan* may indeed have been instrumental in
attracting Strauss's attention.

Here is another of those poems which make their effect through the
repetition of a catch phrase, legitimate enough in itself, but becoming
unduly emphasized when set to a recurring musical motif. As often
before, it is the words of the title which recur in every line so that 'Und
dann nicht mehr' appears no less than fifteen times during the course of
the song (including a few gratuitous repetitions of Strauss's own).

The motif which alternates with this textural refrain is one of
Strauss's most characteristic confections:

Ex. 109

while the melancholy 'and then no more' provides a contrast in more
sombre harmonies. The theme of the poem is a brief dazzling glimpse
of a beautiful but short-lived maiden, a sad enough notion, but one
might have thought hardly worthy of the sweetly self-indulgent despair

with which Strauss's quixotically effusive treatment imbues it. It is perhaps an irony of fate that the final cadence should actually be reminiscent of *Don Quixote*.

It would seem convenient and sensible to discuss here, out of strict chronological order, the third and last of these Rückert Gesänge. *Im Sonnenschein* is another of those great arches of Straussian *melos* which, from the treatment of voice and piano alike, might well have been some discarded extract from one of the operas which were the composer's chief pre-occupation during these last difficult decades of his long life. Strauss even added to the opening tempo indication of 'Sehr schnell' ('very fast') the words 'ganze Takte' ('whole bars'), normally an instruction to the conductor to beat the music 'one in a bar'.

Here again the title ('In the Sunshine') represents a recurring refrain though it is wisely treated with greater melodic freedom and the music in any case carries one along with its irresistible *élan*. But a magical surprise awaits: the song, and with it the group, ends with a deeply poetic coda so contrived, by making its slow bars correspond in effect to four of the previously surging bars, that the music remains a single unified movement while yet quietly reflecting the sentiment which must have exactly matched Strauss's state of mind, however prematurely:

> Ich geh, die süsse Müdigkeit des Lebens
> nun auszuruhn,
> die Lust, den Gram der Erde nun auszuheilen
> im Sonnenschein.[75]

19

To include *Wie etwas sei leicht* amongst the Lieder is really stretching a point, for the little Gedicht is only five bars long. Yet the poem of which it is a setting is given complete—tiny as it is—and belongs to the varied assortment of Strauss's compositions to words taken from Goethe's *Westöstlicher Divan*, on this occasion from the *Hiklet Nameh*, the 'Book of Proverbs'. This pearl of wisdom propounds the idea that 'how easy something may be, only he knows who has invented it and he who has attained it'. Strauss's jotting, which could hardly have been simpler, was his contribution to the Ladies of the Wiener Concordia on the occasion of their 1930 Carnival Ball.

[75] 'I go, now to take my rest from the sweet tiredness of Life, to find healing now from the passion and sorrow of the world, in the sunshine.'

Das Bächlein, however, also avowedly to words by Goethe although no one has yet succeeded in tracing them, is a different matter altogether. It was written at a time of Strauss's life which continues to arouse the sharpest controversy.

In the early months after Hitler's accession to power the Nazi rulers sought to allay wide-spread anxieties over the theatre and the arts. Few were deceived but all too naturally there were people who allowed themselves to be swayed into believing that perhaps after all there was some good in the dreaded Third Reich, and that by taking the promises in good faith much might be saved or protected. Amongst the many self-deluders was the politically naïve septuagenarian Strauss who, on waking up one November day in 1933, discovered that he had been appointed President of the Reichsmusikkammer, but allowed the unsought honour to stand on the grounds that 'through the goodwill of the new German government to support music and the theatre something really good can be accomplished and I also in fact have already been able to get several beneficial things done and prevent several misfortunes . . .' as he wrote to Zweig a little shamefacedly.

Hopefully he took the creation of a Reichsmusikkammer as an indication, he said in a public address, that 'the new Germany is unwilling to let artistic matters slide, as was done more or less up to now, but that ways and means are being systematically sought to bring to our musical life a new upsurge'.

As an early test of the sincerity of his new masters Strauss tried to revive some of his efforts on behalf of composers' performing rights with even some modicum of success, although he found the Ministry of Propaganda with whom he had to deal unexpectedly slippery.

It is clear that he could hardly pursue his endeavours while maintaining a cold front to the powers he hoped to propitiate and accordingly in those early misguided months he allowed a certain cordiality to enter into his relationships with Hitler and Goebbels, as some photographs eagerly reproduced by would-be counsels for the prosecution all too readily testify.

Moreover he could scarcely withhold some kind of musical gesture and it is to this obligation that *Das Bächlein* owes its origin. It was composed in December 1933 and dedicated to 'Herrn Reichsminister Dr Joseph Goebbels' in acknowledgement of the Reichsmusikkammer appointment. It thus amounts to a courtesy which in sheer politeness he could not evade. Yet one looks with distaste at the mystery poem, for

the concluding lines—without doubt the reason for Strauss's choice—
read:

> Der mich gerufen aus dem Stein
> der, denk ich, wird mein Führer sein![76]

an allusion to Hitler's self-appointed role which Strauss's setting emphasized with a three-fold repetition of 'mein Führer'.

The whole episode is both dubious and extremely dangerous for the
ammunition it provides for Strauss's enemies—and to this day they are
many. Yet if one can overlook the implications of its last line *Das
Bächlein* is a most attractive song. It belongs to that genre of Strauss
Lied, more familiar in bygone years, which couples a Schubertian
Volkslied melodic style with an enchanting sophistication of detail.
Even the offending closing words are clothed and disguised in music
with the freshness and innocence of Strauss's most youthful periods:

Ex. 110

Strauss clearly thought *Das Bächlein* to be worth more than its unfortunate *raison d'être* might have presaged, for in April 1935 he fulfilled
a long-standing promise to Viorica Ursuleac by making an orchestral

[76]   'He who has summoned me from the stone
            he, I believe, will be my leader.'

version which brings out to the full the implicit beauty of the original piano setting.

Like all the late songs this was intended to be a posthumous work and when during the war Kurt Soldan undertook the preparation of an ultimately abortive complete edition of the songs Strauss instructed him that the dedication was to be suppressed and that it was not to carry an opus number. Accordingly it was published by itself in 1951,[77] but was later grouped together with the two Weinheber songs (Nos. 207 and 208) when these were first published in the 1964 Boosey & Hawkes Complete Edition. The three were then given the opus number 88, but this is of course no more authentic than the op. 87 of the three Rückert Lieder and the Goethe *Erschaffen und Beleben*.

Whatever illusions Strauss might have had about the Nazis were to be quickly shattered. Within a year of his appointment, the Reichsmusikkammer, without reference to him as its titular head, was rapidly indulging in actions which provoked violent indignation from artists all over the world. By the autumn of 1934 he was no longer attending the meetings, writing to the conductor Julius Kopsch:

> I hear that the paragraph on Aryans is to be tightened up . . . I do not wish to take part in any more of this kind of rubbish. My extensive and serious reform proposals have been turned down by the Minister. . . .

and he performed the few duties which came his way as perfunctorily as possible. His only assignment of any consequence was the Olympic Hymn for the 1935 Games which he dashed off just before Christmas 1934, comforting himself perhaps that it was more for Germany than for the Nazis, much as they might be twisting the occasion for their own ends.

Early in 1935 a pro-Nazi music critic Walther Abendroth published a biography of Hans Pfitzner who, as Strauss progressively declined in favour, was being raised up by the authorities as a rival pope, a role to which the relatively neglected Pfitzner—who had always bitterly regarded himself as having been slighted by Mahler and Strauss in turn— was far from averse.

The official Nazi cultural party line was strongly opposed to

---

[77] For the first time after so many years, the publishers were Universal Edition of Vienna, who also copyrighted the last Rückert and Weinheber songs. Inexplicably, however, *Das Bächlein* was printed a tone too low (F) even in the 'high voice' copy, and this error is preserved in the Complete Edition. The original key of G is also that of the orchestral version.

'modernistic' trends of any kind and in the chapter on Pfitzner's *Palestrina* Abendroth had written:

> Whoever feels this exalted virility of Hans Pfitzner's musical language to be ascetic thereby only proves one thing: that his own corrupted ears seek here in vain the feminine voluptuousness and torpor of sounds padded with fat ('Feminine Schwelgen und Duseln in besagten klanglichen Fettpolstern') to which they are accustomed from other influences.

This revolting attack was widely recognized to be unmistakably directed against Strauss and was quoted in the Leipzig musical journal *Allgemeinen Musikzeitung* by Peter Raabe who although himself securely in the Nazi fold (later the very same year he took over the presidency of the Reichsmusikkammer from Strauss) on this occasion saw fit to take Strauss's part.

The effect of Raabe's championship was, however, to direct Strauss's attention to Abendroth's venomous tirade which also included a condemnation of the entire school of modern German composers with especial emphasis on the development of programme music.

In appreciation of Raabe's support Strauss found yet one more last fragment from the *Westöstlicher Divan* which he set satirically and dedicated to Raabe with the sardonic inscription:

> Garmisch, 25 Februar 1935. Ein im Abendrot des femininen 19. Jahrhunderts auf klanglichen Fettpolstern duselnder Programmusiker.[78]

The little appendage of a poem in the *Hafiz Nameh* ('the Book of Hafiz') *Zugemessne Rhythmen* seemed to Strauss to express to a nicety all that he felt and had always represented with respect to new musical wine in old bottles. So, although in his position he had no need to reply publicly to Abendroth's libel, it amused him to write down these few bars of retort filling them with quotations to underline the relevance of the words.

What Goethe was saying, after having struggled with one of Hafiz' ghazals, was that whereas the talented writer may well enjoy established forms and rhythms, these soon become abhorrent—hollow masks without blood or meaning—and he cannot remain content but must create new forms in their place.

---

[78] Allowing for Strauss's literal incorporation of the critic's own name ('in the *sunset* of the feminine nineteenth century') this needs no further translation to add to that of Abendroth's own words above.

In making his setting Strauss ironically uses Brahms to symbolize 'Das Talent' with that most famous melody from the finale of the C minor Symphony. Strauss himself takes the role of the dissatisfied spirit seeking for the new forms. The music passes on to self-quotations, the 'Richtige' theme from *Arabella* (Vol. II, p. 405, Ex. 14a), which Dr Willi Schuh takes to be further illustrative of the 'rightness' for a developing artist to be alive to new ideas (as Strauss himself was at one time), and the Ideology theme from *Tod und Verklärung* (Vol. I, p. 81, Ex. 22). Here too Dr Schuh finds a point in that the entry of this theme was in itself 'neue Form' coming first only at the central climax of the tone-poem and thus playing an important part in the killing off of the old dead forms.

At the end of the song the piano has a brief postlude in which the basic fanfare motif (which is the only even semi-original theme in the whole composition) is transformed into the opening phrase of Wagner's *Meistersinger*, Wagner being the arch-rebel against moribund tradition and *Meistersinger* the work in which above all he portrayed the all-important victory of new ideas over pedantry.

Zugemessne Rhythmen remained unknown until it was published as part of the *Richard Strauss Jahrbuch* for 1954 in which it appeared with an explanatory introduction by Dr Schuh to whom all subsequent biographers are constantly indebted. There is no record of the sketch ever having been performed.

At the time of its writing the storm clouds were gathering fast about Strauss's head and only four months later they broke. On 6th July 1935 he was expelled from the Reichsmusikkammer and thereafter treated with ostentatious disfavour.[79]

20

For seven years no further songs were added to the great life-work and it seemed improbable that there would be any more. Yet with Strauss's indefatigable mind, regardless of his first instinct never to compose another note now that he was publicly disgraced, he had been steadily writing vocal music in the shape of one opera after another.

At last in August 1941 he formally rounded off his operatic output with the last notes of *Capriccio* in which the whole problem of word-

---

[79] This unpleasant affair, arising principally out of Strauss's relations with Stefan Zweig and the first performance of *Die Schweigsame Frau*, is described at the end of Chapter XVIII, see p. 50.

setting was paraded and thrashed out. Once again he was without work on hand, and still death spared him. Germany was in the throes of a gruelling war which although it had not put an end to musical life, threatened a serious curtailment at any time.

Strauss's disfavour with the Nazis had made his Garmisch existence a burden and by the end of 1941 the Strauss family had moved to the Belvedere Villa in Vienna where they were sheltered by the patronage of Baldur von Schirach (see above p. 241 et. seq.).

It so happened that on the 9th March 1942 the Austrian poet Josef Weinheber celebrated his fiftieth birthday, and Strauss thought it a nice idea to compose for him two 'hübsche Lieder', as he described them in a letter to Clemens Krauss.

Weinheber is hardly remembered today outside Austria, but for a short period he enjoyed a spectacular rise to fame sparked by the award of the Mozart Prize in 1935 which spurred him to some of his best work. It was his misfortune that he became committed to the Third Reich and at its collapse in 1945 he took his own life. His memory has undoubtedly been clouded by these circumstances and by his disagreeable personality, the result of a wretched childhood divided between a poverty-stricken home (he was the son of a horse-butcher) and an orphanage. Yet much of his poetry is still very highly regarded in literary circles.

Strauss, however, used the less serious side of Weinheber's writings, first choosing one from a collection of verses published in 1937 entitled *O Mensch, gib acht,* a whimsical allusion to Nietzsche's famous lines. Jethro Bithell has neatly summed up the work as 'a species of calendar, dialectically coloured; the months with their appropriate poems, the legends of the zodiac and of the saints'. *Sankt Michael* is duly to be found amongst the verses for September (the month of Michaelmas). It consists of a prayer to the Saint of attractive medieval flavour, as the opening lines (repeated in the last verse) will show:

> Ein Mahl für uns und ein Licht für dich
> die Toten schlafen ewiglich
> der Acker, der liegt bloss.[80]

and each verse ends with the Latin phrase: 'Salva nos!'

[80] This translates roughly as:
> A meal for us and a light for you
> The dead sleep eternally
> The field lies bare.

If in a light, patriotic Landsknecht style, it is stimulating poetry and Strauss's pleasure in working with it comes across in every phrase though he makes no attempt at catching its mock-archaic flavour. Rather he amuses himself—and us—by making graphic play with the wind brought from the West and the plague from the East, while the passage in which the Archangel is asked for guidance in fighting dragons is particularly engaging:

Ex. 111

During the course of the song the arpeggiando figure ⌐ x ¬ seems more and more to depict Saint Michael in his heroic aspect (Strauss is also in his heroic key of E flat) while the two appearances of the gaily florid ⌐ y ¬ show the Archangel in all his beauty.

Blick vom Oberen Belvedere, the other Weinheber poem, is entirely different. It comes from a collection of verses published two years earlier in 1935, descriptive of every facet of Vienna and Viennese life. Entitled *Wien wörtlich*, its many poems are extremely varied and are often in the broadest dialect, though this happens not to be the case with the poem Strauss chose.

The reason for his choice is not hard to find, for the composer's Viennese villa was situated adjacent to the Belvedere Botanical Gardens.

The Belvedere district was so called from the Baroque palaces of Unteres and Oberes Belvedere which had been built in beautifully designed grounds on a site distinguished by its splendid view over the city. Created by the great architect Johann Lucas von Hildebrandt, this majestic achievement was the subject of a well-known picture painted in 1895 by the Viennese artist Carl Moll the title of which, *Blick vom oberen Belvedere*, was taken by Weinheber for his description in poetry of the scene shown on Moll's canvas.

By comparison with many of its companion poems, however, this seems very artificial and stilted in manner with its evocations of past glory, hooped petticoats, cavaliers and such-like, though the peculiar nature of its construction may be to blame for any absence of spontaneity.

For there is more to Weinheber's poem than meets the eye at a cursory glance. The first editions of *Wien wörtlich* were illustrated by a certain Marie Grengg, and *Blick vom oberen Belvedere* is designed as a dedicatory acrostic, the first letters of each line spelling vertically the words, 'Für Marie Grengg'.

Such word games are clearly untranslatable into music and Strauss, ignoring the purposeful line beginnings, strings the phrases together in long arches of cantilena accompanied by an elaborately decorated piano part and most of the motivic strands are presented before the voice enters.

One further motif is nevertheless added soon after the vocal line is superimposed upon the rich textures and this is of interest for its strong identification with Mandryka's Croatian theme from *Arabella* (Vol. II, p. 411, Ex. 19). In the opera this excitable folk-tune forms the background to Mandryka's description to Waldner of his decision to visit Vienna and in the circumstances it is quite possible that its appearance here, in moreover its original key of E major, constitutes a deliberate allusion.

Having no unified plan in mind, Strauss wrote *Sankt Michael* for a baritone voice and *Blick vom oberen Belvedere* for soprano and they were first performed at a birthday celebration concert for Weinheber in the Lobkowitz Palace in Vienna by Alfred Poell and Hilde Konetzni.[81]

Two years later Weinheber duly paid Strauss a return compliment in the shape of a dedicatory poem written for the composer's eightieth

[81] Nevertheless, *Blick vom oberen Belvedere* was dedicated to Viorica Ursuleac. See also p. 407.

birthday for inclusion in the Vienna Philharmonic's festival programme on 11th June 1944. Weinheber had sent Strauss in the meantime some of his latest poems in the hope that more songs would materialize, but this was not to be.

Both Weinheber and Strauss had been contributors to another eightieth birthday celebration which took place on 15th November 1942, that of the highly distinguished poet Gerhart Hauptmann. For this occasion Strauss turned once more to Goethe for a suitable text though not this time to the *Westöstlicher Divan*.

Instead he picked out a 'Xenion', or epigram, from the enormous collection which Goethe—together with Schiller—published in their *Museum Almanach* during the years around the turn of the century.

A large proportion of these little poetic shafts were distichs which were often highly satirical and caused considerable controversy amongst the current literary circles against whom they were directed.

But in addition Goethe wrote no less than nine sets of wise, thoughtful verses which he entitled *Zahme Xenien* ('peaceable epigrams'), no longer in distich form and in deliberate contrast to the others. It is in the first set of these that occur the famous lines, containing Goethe's own Credo, which Strauss selected for his tribute to Hauptmann. They constitute a declaration of faith in the eternal, and their choice reflects Strauss's share in the widespread acknowledgement of the great Silesian author's dominant position in contemporary drama, even though he never set a word of Hauptmann to music. The miniature, no more than six bars long, is inscribed to 'Gerhart Hauptmann, dem grossen Dichter und hochverehrten Freunde mit herzlichen Glückwünschen'.

With this fragment we reach the end of a life-long output of over two hundred Lieder which began seventy-three years before—the end, that is to say, apart from those four greatest products of Strauss's reawakened genius with which he ended not only his Lieder output but his whole life-work and which will accordingly be left over until the closing pages of this survey.

It is by any standards a remarkable accomplishment even with so great a disparity between the best, which are amongst the most famous in the entire range of German Lieder, and the least good which are utterly unknown and sometimes worthless. But as we have seen, there are a considerable number which do not in the least deserve the neglect they continue to suffer.

In fact, barely a dozen out of the two-hundred odd songs are popularly recognized and few people indeed are familiar with many more. There are books on the German Lied which scarcely mention Strauss, if at all, the view being held that he is outside the mainstream of true Lieder composers, Schubert—Schumann—Brahms—Wolf—Mahler.

It is a challenge hard to refute without coming to terms with what qualities are considered to make up the pure classical Lied and which, in some way hard to define, Strauss's songs lack.

Certainly the Lieder as a whole are not his chief claim to immortality, as they are Schubert's or Wolf's, even though they form a steady background of lyricism from which his larger works all spring, in the same way as—for example—Brahms. And like Brahms, whose output of Lieder was nearly half as large again, Strauss rarely set great poetry to music. Yet at those times of inspired genius which recurred during his long life he was able to imbue the writings of lesser authors with a touching intensity of feeling and human sympathy.

Where Strauss suffers in comparison with Brahms is in his greater sophistication, a doubtful quality in so delicate and intimate a medium, while a tendency towards the grand manner when he was not being casual or flippant also throws him into the lap of orchestral gesture or the operatic Scena. The necessary fluency Strauss the born song-writer could always command, but despite his natural, easy 'response to situation', to recall Tippett's dictum, his periodic fallibility of insight is perhaps the fault least forgivable in the world of the Lied. And as a result a very great deal of fine and fascinating music remains buried in a special limbo from which it takes the enthusiastic admirer of Strauss's instinctive music-making to rescue it.

CHAPTER XXIII

THE INDIAN SUMMER (II);
A LAST UPSURGE OF GENIUS

DURING the early days of 1942, *Capriccio* and thus his operatic work behind him, Strauss was composing Weinheber's verses with a view to a birthday offering for the poet, when another festivity appeared on the horizon for which it seemed a good idea to write a piece culminating in a further Weinheber setting.

Strauss had never been able to compose successfully to order, but the occasion was the centenary jubilee of the Vienna Philharmonic Orchestra, and being domiciled in Vienna as he now was, the least he could do was to try and sketch out a work for this great orchestra with which he had often enough been associated.

Casting about in his mind for some suitable plan, he remembered Smetana's *Vltava*. This popular symphonic poem traces the course of the river with musical portrayals of the different scenes along its length until it flows proudly into the capital city of Prague. Some similar tone poem might be concocted out of the Danube[1] making an analogous climax as it reaches Vienna, at which point a chorus could sing Weinheber's verses:

> Wie sing ich dich, du vielgeliebte Stadt?
> Wie bänd'ge ich das Herz, nicht aufzuweinen
> Vor einem Bild, das so viel Schönheit hat? . . .[2]

---

[1] Janacek had also planned a symphonic work on the subject of the Danube shortly before his death, but he too left it unfinished. Strauss is, however, unlikely to have known of this.

[2] 'How should I sing of thee, thou much-loved city?
How control my heart not to burst out weeping [continued on next page]

As for the scenes to be depicted en route, there was no shortage of these, and idly Strauss outlined a few possibilities: first an introductory wind section in C major descriptive of the castle at Donaueschingen which would link to some rippling passage-work for the source of the river much like Smetana's description of the sources of the Vltava in the opening bars of his tone poem. The theme of the Danube in full flow Strauss envisaged in G major, keys always coming first to his imagination even before the actual music itself. Gorges, rapids, woods, cornfields, everything would be there just as no item of mountain scenery was omitted from *Alpensinfonie*. At Ingolstadt, Pauline's birthplace, her theme from the *Sinfonia Domestica* was to be incorporated. The Nibelungen on the Danube, a vintage festival at Wachau (the latter a $\frac{6}{8}$ scherzo in D major)—Strauss filled four note-books with drafts and sketches as well as several pages with indications of instrumentation.

But it was no good. Nearly thirty years had passed since he had entertained himself in this sort of way and even then the pleasure was, as he had openly acknowledged at the time, only half-hearted. Now the ideas simply would not come and all that he had jotted down left him flat and discouraged.

Admitting defeat he wrote to the orchestra:

> Vienna 18 February 1942
>
> My dear Philharmonic!
> For your fine festivities I can today only send my congratulations in heartfelt words. The gift in sound which I had thought to offer my dear friends and artistic colleagues on so unique a jubilee I unfortunately cannot have ready for the desired date, however assiduously I struggle with it. Feeling does not turn itself into melodies as quickly as it did with the great old masters. I therefore ask you to have patience until my present is worthy of its recipients so that it will remain in your memories as a living expression of my love and admiration . . . I should like to put my words of praise today into one short sentence: 'Only he who has *conducted* the Vienna Philharmonic players knows what they —are!'
> But that will remain our very own secret!
> You understand me well enough: here—as at the desk!

Before a picture of so much beauty? . . .'
These rather commonplace lines are not, incidentally, amongst the far superior cycle of poems *Wien wörtlich* from which Strauss took the song *Blick vom oberen Belvedere*.

The implication that the tone poem *Die Donau* would one day be finished was scarcely to be taken seriously. When seven years later the orchestra sent the conductor their return congratulations on his eighty-fifth birthday he presented them with a page of the sketches with the despondent inscription: 'A few drops from the dried-up source of the Danube'.

2

But if the inspiration for this particular orchestral work had failed, it had been the means of setting Strauss's imagination working in a direction that had not been followed since he was a youth of nineteen. If a massive tone poem for large orchestra, organ and chorus was now beyond his power to pursue that did not mean instrumental composition itself was out of the question. After all these years a return to the smaller forms of absolute music might keep his mind occupied in those mornings at work which were a habit too deeply rooted to be broken. Although he had long been saying that only the setting of words would start his musical thought, he might try his hand at another Horn Concerto such as he had written for his father nearly sixty years ago. Perhaps ideas would come in connexion with the horn which had ever been his most favourite of all instruments.

This was quite a different story from *Die Donau* and on 12th November 1942, writing to Viorica Ursuleac to thank her for her part in the première of *Capriccio* (which had taken place in Munich on 28th October), he began his letter by saying, 'With *Blick vom oberen Belvedere* I have just completed a little horn concerto, the third movement of which—a $\frac{6}{8}$ Rondo—has come out particularly well . . .'

Strauss was actually being over-modest; the truth was that the piece had turned into a singular success from first to last. It is indeed hard to credit that this is the work of a depressed old man living in fear and disgrace from the authorities of a war-beleaguered country, so light and care-free a style did he recapture.

It is the freedom and originality of form, especially in the opening Allegro which reveals the experienced master as compared with the early concerto. Again he chose the key of E flat though he exactly reverses the relative crooks of his solo and orchestral horns, putting the former in E flat and the latter in F (cf. Vol. I, p. 21).

As in the first concerto the solo horn begins by itself with the principal *Naturthema*, though here it is a much terser motif, which Strauss follows up—the strings of the orchestra having joined in—with an array of further ideas all of which play an essential part in the construction of the movement:

Ex. 1

For all of fifty-four bars the horn rhapsodizes around these motifs accompanied only by the strings. At one point it seems to have led into what could be a classical first subject, but the cantabile flow of melody surges onwards through extended developments of Ex. 1(y) until, the music becoming more dramatic, the quicker figurations ⌐ v ¬ and ⌐ w ¬ reappear. As the horn phrases become increasingly declamatory, the first tutti is triumphantly heralded and all that has been heard so far reveals itself in retrospect to have been in the nature of a lengthy virtuoso introduction for the soloist, an inspired and highly unconventional elaboration of concerto form.

The tutti begins by enthusiastically playing the themes of Ex. 1 together, ⌐ x ¬ and ⌐ y ¬ in the bass instruments, ⌐ z ¬, ⌐ v ¬ and ⌐ w ¬ in the violins and flutes, and then doing it again the other way about, an idea Strauss may well have taken from a famous section of double counterpoint in the opening of Mendelssohn's Violin Concerto.

The semi-quaver figures ⌐ v ¬ and ⌐ w ¬ now take on a grazioso character by means of which the soloist's re-entry is prepared, at first in bold tones and then, as the tempo relaxes, leading to a kind of concertante section. Solo members of the woodwind, solo cello and the first violins all join the solo horn in a conversation piece based initially on ⌐ w ¬ but soon introducing the ingeniously amiable second subject which is uncommonly reminiscent of some of the Skat music from *Intermezzo*.

Ex. 2

The second violins also contribute a strand of melody suspiciously like the counter-theme from the finale of *Aus Italien*. But the most important facet of this section is its overall derivation from the neo-classic conversational music Strauss wrote for such scenes as the Ochs/Sophie betrothal ensemble in the second act of *Der Rosenkavalier* (see Vol. I, p. 384).

Ex. 1(z) soon joins the discussion followed by the opening principal Naturthema Ex. 1(x), which has an increasingly vivacious dialogue with figures evolving from Ex. 2(x) and this leads to a second much shorter tutti heralding the tiny development section.

The recapitulation is also very much curtailed though Ex. 2 returns regularly enough in the home key of E flat. A horn then makes play with Ex. 1(z) while the violins take over the second subject, and it is a pleasurable surprise to realize that this was the orchestral first horn, for the solo horn re-enters immediately afterwards with answering phrases of Ex. 2.

The final tutti also brings a surprise though of the kind one has learnt to enjoy from precedents in the Bruch and Dvořák Violin Concertos. For instead of bringing the movement to an end, elegiac phrases change the character of the music and lead it gently, even regretfully, into the Andante. Where Strauss varies the procedure is in his handling of the solo horn who takes the foreground in the whole of the beautiful coda (except for the last six linking bars), which thus balances the long rhapsodic opening solo section.

The beginning of the wide-spanned Andante is now left to woodwind principals in unison, the soloist remaining silent until the phrases reach the crest of their curve. Only then does he join in, to re-enforce the already well-established wind colouring of the cantilena, to which the strings have been adding a gently lapping background.

A pair of Mendelssohnian cadential figures of the deceptively simple kind Strauss used in *Sinfonia Domestica* turns aside at the last moment and gives way to the strangely meandering middle section. Here it is the violins and cellos, or alternatively violas, which sustain the melodic interest in a to-and-fro triplet movement. In spaced-out protests, how-

ever, the soloist succeeds in bringing back the Andante melody which
he keeps this time to himself, the violins continuing nevertheless with
the triplets of the middle section. The movement comes to an idyllic end
with the Mendelssohnian cadences in which the woodwind as before
play an essential part. The euphonious blend of sound is here supported
by pedal notes on the solo horn with enchanting effect. The whole
Andante is a beautifully-proportioned miniature and particularly well-
conceived as a relaxation for the soloist between the exacting outer
movements.

Certainly Strauss was not wrong in judging the Rondo to have turned
out well, although it has come to be regarded as notoriously tricky for
solo horn and orchestra alike. Again most of the material derives from
the superbly hornistic passages of the opening phrases:

Ex. 3

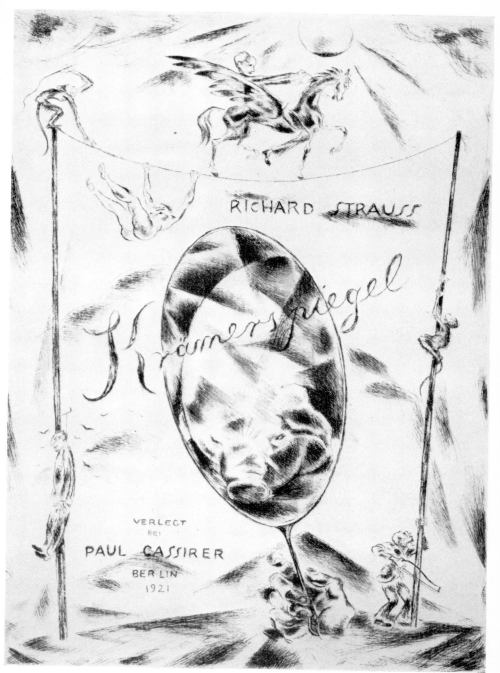

RICHARD STRAUSS

Krämerspiegel

VERLEGT
BEI
PAUL CASSIRER
BERLIN
1921

Title page of *Krämerspiegel*

Strauss with son Franz and grandsons Richard and Christian

Strauss's instinctive power of spinning melodies enables him to set the solo horn freely chanting away in long cantabile phrases while the violins perform scherzando acrobatics around ⌐ s ⌐ and ⌐ w ⌐ from Ex. 3c.

Bursts of tutti forte passages are excitedly devoted to the Rondo themes proper, ⌐ x ⌐, ⌐ y ⌐ and ⌐ z ⌐ but the second subject (or principal episodic theme) is given once again to the soloist:

Ex. 4

Graceful enough as it sounds at first, such a theme has splendid possibilities of climax building with its four strong repeated notes, as Schubert had already discovered in the finale of his Great C Major Symphony, and after a comical little subsidiary episode derived from ⌐ u ⌐ in Ex. 3a (more than a little reminiscent of Cornelius's *Barber of Bagdad* of which Strauss was particularly fond) it works up to a fine tutti.

The central episode is lyrical in character, the horn taking his cue for expanding melodies from the rising cello phrase ⌐ v ⌐ in Ex. 3b against woodwind repeated notes, much like the parallel episode in Strauss's First Horn Concerto.

It is this rising phrase, together with ⌐ w ⌐ and the second subject Ex. 4, which hesitantly introduces the rousing coda. Ex. 3 makes a great panoply of sound on three horns—the soloist is joined in a trio with the two in the orchestra—followed by Ex. 4 entering in cumulative imitation from various sections of strings and wind, while timpani are added for the first time to give still further panache. The end is a truly triumphant combination of the numerous motivic elements with the last word suitably given to the solo horn in a fanfare-like extension of the opening theme Ex. 3(x).

There is something positively flamboyant about the closing pages and yet the movement never exceeds the bounds of form and style laid out from the first. The concerto is a little masterpiece within self-imposed limits of size as well as depth of content, and an extraordinary product for a composer only two years short of eighty. In sheer youthfulness it is hardly less remarkable than Verdi's *Falstaff*.

But what is perhaps even more extraordinary, particularly in so successful a work, is that it reveals a mind wholly detached from the world as it had become; music of this kind had not been composed, except possibly as a stylistic exercise, for at least half a century. Nor was it even to be an isolated phenomenon. For, in proving to himself that he could actually summon up workable musical ideas without a programme, Strauss had also managed to sever all artistic connexion with a society he despised and to compose happily for himself alone music which belonged to the beloved world of his youth. And this he methodically continued to do since, as he remarked drily, 'One can't play Skat *all* the time'.

3

The winter and spring of 1942–3 were bad months for Strauss and Pauline. Already the previous August and September she had been afflicted with serious eye trouble and had been forbidden to read even the newspapers, for her the ultimate hardship. Then he fell victim to successive bouts of influenza after which she again spent most of April and May in bed, making this altogether a particularly trying time. The war was not going well and Vienna was beginning to come under bombardment so that it was not long before the Strauss family was forced to return to the comparative security of Garmisch.

As always Strauss continued to find relaxation in cards and work. The formal conferring upon him of the Beethoven Prize of the City of Vienna towards the end of 1942 required some gesture, which obligation he discharged by the completion on 14th January of a stirring *Festmusik*, for the Wiener Trompetercorps supported by trombones, tubas and timpani. This was given its ceremonial performance under Strauss himself the following April and pleased him well enough for him to agree to the Trompetercorps' request for a short version which they could put into their regular repertoire, the original lasting nearly a quarter of an hour. He was well advised to make the arrangement for whereas the *Festmusik* is something of a formidable *pièce d'occasion*, the material is most stirring and the shortened *Fanfare der Stadt Wien* must rate as one of the very best of Strauss's pieces of pageantry—infinitely more interesting than the two similar fanfares he had supplied (also for Vienna) in 1924 when he had more important matters on his mind.

But working with a wind group during these days of periodic illness in the New Year of 1943 had an important side effect. For it aroused in the old man certain other enjoyable memories of his early composing, of his preoccupation with wind instruments in the little Serenade op. 7 and the far more substantial Wind Suite, in connexion with which Bülow had given him his first frightening opportunity as conductor.

Since that time he had often felt that he had misjudged the effect of using only two-fold woodwind against four horns, and that given his time again he would correct the miscalculation. Now was clearly the opportunity and, although he knew well enough that he had nothing important to say (he even acknowledged this frankly in a letter to Willi Schuh) he could kill many a weary hour of his own and Pauline's convalescences by tackling the problems afresh.

With the confidence in his power once more to work on abstract forms given him by the recently completed Horn Concerto, he re-addressed himself patiently to the technique of a purely wind ensemble and on 21st February had drafted a Romanze und Menuett which were decidedly promising even though he had to some extent cheated by using only two horns while allowing himself the additional luxury of a basset horn and bass clarinet. But he had had fun putting each of the horns in a different crook like Mozart in the great G minor Symphony as well as Haydn in several of his earlier symphonies. (The fact that horn players had long since given up using different crooks and played all parts on a horn in F by means of a mental transposition had never in-fluenced Strauss's practice which was based on a sound understanding of horn players' psychology.)

Distinctly encouraged, Strauss now tackled the outer movements, the opening Allegro moderato being ready on 24th March and the Finale on 22nd July after the family's return to Garmisch. For these larger scale movements he restored the 3rd and 4th horns and also added a fifth clarinet, the clarinet in C which he had used in all his later operas to reinforce the upper woodwind in preference to the more universally recognized but shriller little E flat clarinet.

There is not the least doubt that Strauss had thoroughly enjoyed the task, for in his title to the work he showed that he had already made up his mind to embark on a further essay in the medium:

1 Sonatine für 16 Blasinstrumente
Aus der Werkstatt eines Invaliden.[3]

Touchingly, he arranged for the first performance to be given by the 'Tonkünstlerverein zu Dresden' at whose concerts the première of the Serenade op. 7 had been given in 1882. It did not, however, take place until 18th June 1944 when it was conducted by Karl Elmendorff.

4

To call the work a Sonatina might seem somewhat perverse as it is of quite weighty proportions. But Strauss will have been thinking of the substance rather than the length, and in this respect the title is well considered, for at no time is there any attempt to be profound. Here, if ever, Strauss was note-spinning for his own and his players' entertainment.

The Allegro moderato hardly corresponds to the normally accepted frame-work of a fully-fledged symphonic first movement, expansive as the constant development of the numerous ideas certainly is.

A sense of overall structure is, however, maintained by the opening bars, of which Ex. 5(x) is to become one of the primary motifs. This phrase recurs intact at the one clear division of the movement (though in quite another key) and again just before the end.

Ex. 5

---

[3] 'From the workshop of an Invalid.'

It would be impossible to guess from this that the work is actually in F major, and Ex. 5 has a strongly introductory character, leading rapidly by rising sequences to what is surely the first theme proper:

Ex. 6

A chattering figure with elaborate figurations for high woodwind marks a transition, while extended melodic phrases for in turn oboe, horn and C clarinet may be taken to represent the second subject. Exx. 7 and 8 show the easy-going workings of Strauss's mind when given untrammelled rein:

Ex. 7

Ex. 8

Shortly after a return of Ex. 5 has led the music off into the second half and a development section seems to be blossoming, an entirely new melody appears on the horn accompanied by delicate woodwind tracery:

Ex. 9

This now takes an equal part with the other themes in a section which combines the functions of development and reprise, the ebb and flow of ideas springing from Exx. 7–9 mingling with Exx. 5 and 6 in the un-tiring inventiveness of Strauss's *musizieren*.[4] At last a glowing fortissimo rounds off in a full tonic cadence to give way to the quietly descending

---

[4] 'Making music.' This is a term which used to be applied particularly to Hindemith: 'Er komponiert nicht, er musiziert'.

coda, in which Ex. 5(x), now transferred to the upper regions, comes into its own as a truly Straussian motif:

Ex. 10

Considering that it was Strauss's verdict about the impossibility of double wind against four horns which initiated the work in the first place, it is curious to find that there are still only two each of flutes and oboes. Hence, since the youthful wind works already boasted a contra-bassoon, it was only the greatly-inflated clarinet section which consti-tuted Strauss's rethinking after a lifetime of experience in the balancing of sonorities.

Moreover even in the Romanze und Menuett which as we have seen began his renewed application to the medium, he retained no fewer than four members of the clarinet family despite his decision to work with only two horns as a starting point. The Romanze is certainly the nearest in style to the early *Serenade* which Strauss will have had at his elbow, but it must be admitted that in his obsession with a rich palette of clarinet colour he sacrificed much of the variety of texture which had been so attractive a feature of the early pieces.

The Romanze is an extended Song Without Words in wide spans of melody arising from the figure:

Ex. 11

with which, enunciated four times by as many different instruments, the movement begins.

The Tempo di Menuetto is, for all its appropriate grace, less an in-dependent dance form than a brief middle section bringing a welcome change of mood, after which the Romanze returns with almost a com-plete restatement of its broad melodic arch.

With the finale one is reminded of Strauss's remark to Stefan Zweig that he could not get beyond short themes but that no one could match him in utilizing such a theme, in paraphrasing it and extracting every-thing that is in it.[5]

This is particularly applicable to the principal subject with its sly recollections of the 1885 *Burleske*:

Ex. 12

(cf Vol. 1, p. 39, Ex. 19)

Although at first gaily announced by oboe and C clarinet (the latter thus cockily proclaiming its return after remaining silent in the central movement) it is made up of figures palpably thought of for horns which before long, also restored to their four-fold status, revel in the possi-bilities offered by Ex. 12(x and y).

A broad transitional idea is used throughout the Finale as a massive tutti, as well as a means of building up impetus by way of its $\frac{3}{2}$ pulse across the bar-lines:

Ex. 13

The chattering figure of the first movement returns as part of a composite secondary group in which the tempo is eased a little. This time it is *Feuersnot* which is recalled, even the key being the same.

[5] See above, p. 7.

Ex. 14

(cf Vol. 1, p. 206, Ex. 2)

Strauss must have greatly relished reworking these memories of days long past as they flitted through his mind during the quiet mornings at his desk, the crazy world outside left to pursue its path of relentless destruction, ignored or forgotten. Exx. 12 and 13 jocularly interpose themselves from time to time, until the mood of temporary relaxation is briefly interrupted for the closing section of the exposition.

But instead of passing straight to the development, Strauss interpolates a further and entirely new episode in the form of a tranquil chordal passage alternating with languid curves of melody. It is not perhaps the most interesting theme he had constructed, being content to hover to and fro between its two ideas with some intriguing harmonies and a rather uniform, if mellifluous, thick instrumentation.

However, Strauss recognized that something of the kind was required to offset the virtuoso sprightliness of the main material, and after the development (which leads off with a fugato treatment of Ex. 12) has culminated in the varied and curtailed reprise, the episode reappears, though giving way to a closing section corresponding to that of the exposition. It then returns again before a gentle cadence at last hands over to the immense coda.

This is marked 'Presto' though there is in fact a distinct limit to how much faster Strauss's brilliant wind writing can be played; for the texture of the coda is the same as before, making no concessions to the fundamental change of pace prescribed by the new tempo indication. Motivically it is based almost entirely on Exx. 12 and 13 and with the latter it eventually (and with surprisingly little ceremony after such an extended build-up) reaches its jubilant end.

Yet it would be wrong to imply failure or disappointment. Rather the reverse; having indulged himself to the full in allowing the music to spin out for as long as he had permutations of key switch or thematic lay-out to hand (and the coda alone runs to 44 pages of score, or close on 300 bars) Strauss retains both the skill and the wit to stop at the appointed moment without fuss or bombast.

Interminable as the work looks to the score-reader thumbing through the fat volume, in performance Strauss's instinct for proportion is still an object for admiration.

Within its limits as a 'wrist exercise' (as Strauss called these workshop pieces) the work is an undoubted success and it is strange that it was the last to be published of the Indian Summer works (the score was still not printed when the first volume of this survey went to press in 1961).

Nor did Strauss feel that he had by any means written himself out in the medium. Without delay he embarked on another piece for wind in the form of an Introduction and Allegro. Much was to happen however before it was finished, let alone the second enormous *Sonatine* of which it was ultimately to form a part.

5

But the crazy world outside did not allow itself to be forgotten so easily. During the night of 2nd October 1943 the Munich Nationaltheater was destroyed in an air-raid. While not a personal tragedy, it came near enough to shake Strauss out of his ostrich-like obliviousness. He wrote to his sister Johanna:

> Garmisch, immediately after the destruction of the Hoftheater.
> Dear Hanna,
> Many thanks for your dear letter. I can't write any more today. I am beside myself.
> With heartfelt greetings. Richard.

And a few days later he wrote to Willi Schuh:

> . . . but the burning of the Munich Hoftheater, the place consecrated to the first Tristan and Meistersinger performances, in which 73 years ago I heard Freischütz for the first time, where my good father sat for 49 years in the orchestra as 1st horn—where at the end of my life I experienced the keenest sense of fulfilment of the dreams of authorship in 10 Strauss productions—this was the greatest catastrophe which has ever been brought into my life, for which there can be no consolation and in my old age, no hope. . . .

This was hardly the moment for Strauss to be bothered by interfering officialdom on however worthy a mission, but visited he was at the Garmisch villa by the local Nazi party leader with the demand that he relinquish a proportion of his nineteen living rooms to war victims. Reports vary over whether the prospective evacuees were bombed out civilians or wounded airmen but in either case Strauss's reply to the stern injunction that in wartime everyone had to make sacrifices was the same. Sourly he growled: 'I hat den Krieg net wollen. Wegen mir hätt keiner sterben brauchen!' ('I didn't want the war. On my account no one had to die!') and turned the official away.

Such actions were not without their repercussions and for all the excuse of his age and his work Strauss was quickly made to understand that he and his Jewish family were only safe for the moment thanks to the friendly intervention of Reichsminister Dr Hans Frank, the Nazi leader whose cruelties in Poland were to arouse world-wide horror.

Strauss's musical message of thanks to this sinister benefactor did him no good at all with post-war opinion but in actual fact it merely amounts to some half a dozen lines in comical near-limerick style and not even graced with a piano accompaniment.[6]

He was by no means out of the wood, however, where requisitioning of his living quarters was concerned. One of the more virulent of the Nazis, Martin Bormann (often referred to as 'Hitler's Shadow') was incensed enough to carry the matter to the Führer himself. Then, fortified by Hitler's anger, Bormann took it upon his own authority not only to sequester at least the servant's living quarters over the garage of Strauss's villa—this being as far as even he dared to go after Frank's intervention—but to send a directive to all Nazi authorities formally outlawing the composer with especial reference to his approaching eightieth birthday.

None of all this harrassment stopped Strauss's creative flow however. November saw the completion of the *Daphne* epilogue, the chorus *An den Baum Daphne* (described at the end of Chapter XIX). One might have thought that the débâcle of Gregor's removal from the *Capriccio* scene would have severed all contact between Strauss and the long-suffering historian. But to hold any such idea is to know Gregor badly, and Strauss himself had had to preserve diplomatic relations since at that time (1939) *Die Liebe der Danae* was not quite finished.

So, while simply ignoring pathetic complaints that the tone of his

---

[6] He had similarly bought protection once before with a handful of bars of unaccompanied vocal line when in February 1940 he had scribbled out a fragment into the album of another Reichsminister, Walter Funck.

letters seemed less cordial than before ('please do tell me in what way I have failed' wrote Gregor miserably) and at the same time turning aside suggestions for new ways of tackling *Semiramis*, or perhaps a new sister opera for *Daphne* ('*Nausikaa . . .* is a subject especially close to my heart') Strauss kept the door open so that when he needed something from Gregor there would be no ice to break.

That opportunity arose in June 1943 when Strauss was approached for an *a cappella* choral work by the Director of the Vienna State Opera Chorus Concerts Society, Viktor Maiwald. Gregor was delighted: 'I am overjoyed' he wrote 'to be able to work on something for you again'. Strauss specified the abandoned choral finale from *Daphne* and Gregor without delay resuscitated his sketches and tried to draft something on the lines Strauss had indicated.

Of course the old pattern of events repeated itself and Gregor had again and again to make fresh starts with Strauss writing to say 'thank you very much but it isn't exactly what I want'. But with a lesser work the composer was more easily satisfied and by the end of August Gregor received a picture postcard of the Garmisch villa with a note to say that the last version was fine and Strauss was sorry he hadn't thanked him for it before.

The composition was complete on 13th November but with the acceleration of disaster *An den Baum Daphne* was not performed until 5th January 1947, which became a suitable occasion, being the twentieth anniversary of the Society, to whom the work was also duly dedicated. It was not conducted by Clemens Krauss as originally proposed however, as for some years after the war Krauss was under a cloud on account of his Nazi affiliations.

6

Whilst finishing off this serene choral assignment Strauss was naturally unable to get out of his mind the destruction of his beloved Munich. Tentatively he jotted down a few bars of sketch for some still unformulated work of mourning:

Ex. 15

For the moment this got no further as Strauss had another idea. On 3rd January 1939 he had completed a little waltz for background music to a documentary film about Munich. But the way matters turned out the film was never publicly released as an interceptory telegram suddenly arrived—a decree from Hitler and Goebbels no less. It seems that the Nazi leaders had it in mind to erect in Munich some huge prestige 'Führerbauten' and until these were standing in all their glory the presentation of a film about the culture and architecture of the Bavarian capital which had been the scene of Hitler's first Putsch was simply not to be considered.

Yet the film had been the product of much thought and effort on the part of a great many people, and the Munich Oberbürgermeister Karl Fiehler decided on his own authority to permit at least a single showing at the UFA film studios followed by a reception for all who had contributed to its creation. The performance accordingly took place on 24th May 1939 and an augmented chamber orchestra was engaged under the conductorship of Carl Ehrenberg to perform Strauss's *Gelegenheitswalzer* ('Occasional Waltz').

Strauss himself, however, was not present. In some way he seems not to have heard of Fiehler's decision but only of the Nazi ban, for he later described the piece as having been 'neither published nor performed'. The manuscript he donated after the war to the Bayerische Staatsbibliothek at his 85th birthday celebration in the Garmisch Casino, saying that he hoped some little place might be found for it to slumber on.

But although he regarded *München* (as the waltz was called naturally enough) to be of no great consequence, Strauss had enjoyed writing it and had built it around themes from his opera about Munich, *Feuersnot*. In seeking a suitable memorial for the destruction of that great city of his birth—and of its opera house—he took another look at this fragment which had once been intended as a cheerful glorification. Changing the subtitle from *Gelegenheitswalzer* to *Gedächtniswalzer* he set about creating of it a self-sufficient concert piece by adding a middle section in the minor key to which he actually added the words 'Minore—In Memoriam'.

Nor was this too much out of keeping with the character of the original opening, preserved in the second version, in which a nostalgic 'München! München!' is added beneath the horns' initial motif:

Ex. 16

The elaboration of these two themes into an integrated waltz movement brings in its train a number of flowing violin passages akin to the music of Christine and her Baron in the Waltz Scene of *Intermezzo*.

A transition figure:

Ex. 17

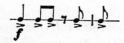

introduces the second waltz melody which is taken intact from Kunrad's address in *Feuersnot* (see Vol. I, p. 230, Ex. 35). In all these surging waltz melodies the little violin figure Ex. 16(x) persists though now generally transferred to the woodwind.

The tempo increases and another bustling transition theme carries the waltz headlong with immense vitality:

Ex. 18

It is after Ex. 18 has led to a jubilant restatement of the *Feuersnot* melody (though now in F sharp major—the key in which it appeared in the opera), that Strauss's mourning insertion begins. Ex. 16 is combined with Kunrad's waltz, both in the minor mode and with the addition of a wailing woodwind phrase. The music also rears at intervals to a sharply-anguished dissonance to which an extra edge is given by muted horns and trumpets. Exx. 16(x) and 17 are added and a development section follows including ideas which Strauss borrowed from his original coda.

A series of chromatically rising sequences alternating with the first waltz melody culminates in a wild, turbulent quotation of the 'Subendfeuer' motif from *Feuersnot* (Vol. I, p. 205, Ex. 1) combined with the theme of Diemut's surrender to Kunrad (Vol. I, p. 221, Ex. 29b). Even the flickering fire of the original orchestration is present in the upper wind although with the effect of air-raids strongly in Strauss's mind his purpose here is likely to have been more sinister than it had been in 1901. The whole effect of the stormy interlude, to which Ex. 17 adds a menacing undertone on the timpani, is one of tragedy in its metamorphosis of the gay material from an opera of almost complete good humour.

The turbulence subsides; gradually, even shyly at first, the waltzes recover and, although Ex. 17 is loath to relinquish its grip, a full reprise follows, to be duly succeeded by the original coda in which the themes (including the once menacing rhythm) combine in the build-up of a boisterous climax.

Whether because a *Gedächtniswalzer* seemed too trivial a memorial or because his first idea for a 'Trauermusik' (Ex. 15 above) was beginning to germinate into something altogether more important, the revised and extended *München* was not finished until 24th February 1945 by which time three movements of a second *Sonatine für Bläser* had long been ready as well as a dismal pot-pourri of waltzes from *Rosenkavalier*.[7] Nor did he ever hear this version of the Munich film-waltz, for it was not performed and published until two years after his death. There is some sadness in this, for within obvious limits of depth (apart perhaps for the 'In Memoriam' section which also enhances the structural balance) *München* is an excellent addition to the orchestral repertoire, the second version being both splendidly shaped and highly effective.

But the exceptional delay in the completion of so small a task was also symptomatic of a more general malaise. Between the by now disastrous pressure on Germany and such celebrations of his eightieth birthday as were able to penetrate the embargo of Nazi disfavour, 1944 had in fact been an unfruitful year for Strauss. After a wretched winter, the summer months had in particular been upset by the ultimately abortive preparations for the launching of *Die Liebe der Danae* despite Strauss's avowed wishes for its postponement until after the war. And when all the plans were disrupted by the fearful turn hostilities were

[7] See Vol. I, p. 417.

taking, which soon forced Goebbels's abrupt decree forbidding all theatrical performances in Germany (See chapter XX, p. 178) well may Strauss have felt that 'it was high time the gods summoned him to higher regions'. Yet typically while such of his beloved world as had survived one world war was crashing to ruins in the cataclysm of another, Strauss was still struggling to continue his work, and indeed he had much to say although for the last two or three years he had discounted any such possibility.

7

By the time *München* was finally laid aside it could have stood as a memorial for much more than just Munich. On the night of 12th February 1945 came the appalling raid which utterly devastated Dresden, the last German city to remain standing. On 2nd March he wrote to Gregor:

> . . . I too am in a mood of despair! The Goethehaus, the world's greatest sanctuary, destroyed! My beautiful Dresden —Weimar—Munich, all gone!

Every major opera house and concert hall throughout the land was now a mass of rubble, to speak only of that part of the universal holocaust which affected Strauss personally.

Considering that the full score of his true and greatest memorial work was already begun on 13th March 1945 and completed on 12th April, almost exactly within the space of a single month, one can only think that the ideas for it must have been gestating for some considerable time, most probably from as long ago as the penning of that fragment Ex. 15, when he had been so hard hit by the loss of the Munich Staatstheater. For *Metamorphosen*, as the work was ultimately to be, is far too complicated and profound to have been merely another product of his daily note-spinning.

As if, moreover, to accentuate the difference from, for example, the easy-going wind sonatinas, this heavy-hearted meditative piece is set for a purely string ensemble, although here too every player has his individual line. Strauss's subtitle in fact describes it as a 'Study for 23 Solo Strings' although this is applicable more in terms of responsibility than any thought of virtuoso display. There are ten violins, five each of violas and cellos, and three basses. Of these one might concede that the last two violins and the last player of violas, cellos and basses are largely doubling parts, but the remainder all have their moments of individual solo work, however much their lines mix and support each other.

The title *Metamorphosen* has generally been taken to signify the musical treatment of the themes, with particular reference to one which Strauss almost incidentally came to connect with Beethoven. But since within the work itself the themes never do undergo metamorphosis (a term which in its musical application is predominantly thought of in the Lisztian sense, as Strauss of all composers would have agreed) but rather a continuous symphonic development, it is not unreasonable to look for some deeper purpose behind Strauss's choice of title. And such a further meaning may perhaps be deduced from a literary source.

During these last terrifying months Strauss had been burying himself in a number of ways, such as—sad to say—trying to earn some ready cash by copying out the full scores of his earlier tone poems. But he also set himself the task of reading from cover to cover the entire works of Goethe, a study which linked itself sharply with his innermost self-probings when he came upon two of the later *Zahme Xenien*, from the seventh collection written when Goethe was himself a very old man:

> Niemand wird sich Selber kennen
> Sich von seinem Selbst-Ich trennen;
> Doch probier' er jeden Tag,
> Was nach aussen endlich, klar.
> Was er ist und was er war,
> Was er kann und was er mag.
>
> Wie's aber in der Welt zugeht,
> Eigentlich niemand recht versteht,
> Und auch bis auf den heutigen Tag
> Niemand gerne verstehen mag.
> Gehabe du dich mit Verstand,
> Wie dir eben der Tag zur Hand;
> Denk immer: 'Ist's gegangen bis jetzt,
> So wird es auch wohl gehen zuletzt'.[8]

---

[8] Freely rendered this might be translated:
'No one can really know himself, detach himself from his inner being; yet he must daily put to the test whatever he can see clearly from without—what he is and what he was, what he can do and what he cares for. . . . But what goes on in the world, no one really understands rightly, and also up to the present day no one gladly wishes to understand it. Conduct yourself with discernment, just as the day offers itself to you; always think: "It's gone all right till now, so it may well go on to the end".'

Strauss conducting in the Musikvereinsaal, Vienna

Strauss in London with Sir Thomas Beecham and the Royal Philharmonic orchestra, October 1947

These lines of searching introspection Strauss wrote out in full amongst the pages of sketches for *Metamorphosen*, the word 'metamorphosen' being itself a term Goethe used in old age to apply to his own mental development, especially with respect to works which had been conceived over a great period of time in the pursuit of ever more exalted thinking. Moreover Goethe took the word into the title of two poems of his later years: *Die Metamorphose der Pflanzen* and *Metamorphose der Tiere*. The former is an offshoot of Goethe's similarly named but considerable treatise on Natural History, while the poet's absorption in the general process of metamorphosis was such that he immediately embarked on a corresponding research into animal life. The latter poem is, however, all that emerged from this further study after some thirty years of contemplation on the subject.

Strauss always maintained that the musical phrase which associated itself ultimately with a famous theme from Beethoven, the Funeral March of the *Eroica* Symphony, had 'escaped from his pen'; it had been while working that he recognized it for what it was. Metamorphosis took place, in fact, as the composition grew out of the sketches. Throughout the completed work the phrase remains unchanged except that Strauss allows it to find its fulfilment in the very last bars of black despair where the whole Beethoven theme is quoted by the cellos and basses with the words IN MEMORIAM! (see below, Ex. 28).

It is first heard immediately after the tragic opening theme, a chordal subject not unlike the introductory phrase of the Wind Sonatina (see Ex. 5) yet immeasurably more intense.

Ex. 19

And here, then, is the melody from which the whole work may be said to have sprung, announced by the back two violas:

Ex. 20

It has travelled far from the 'Trauer um München' idea Ex. 15, but with the aid of the intermediary sketches it is possible to visualize how Strauss's invention developed the one from the germ of the other.

A projected restatement of Ex. 20, which can perhaps be described as the Motto theme, gets no further than the first figure of three repeated notes ⌐ x ⌐ before it turns aside and instead introduces another new theme:

Ex. 21

Out of Exx. 19–21 the huge arch of an introductory sentence is built with many a free modulation and alternating various groups with the tonal mass of the entire ensemble. At last a climax is reached in the sombre key of E flat minor at which point Ex. 21(x) is heard surging in the basses. The heavy sounds then subside and dissolve into the friendlier key of G as the tempo moves forward for yet a further subject:

Ex. 22

With the appearance of Ex. 22 not only is the main melodic material presented, but the work has embarked upon the extended journey of free fantasia which comprises its principal central section and in which little by little the pace and fluidity of the music is stepped up. One cannot but marvel at the endless range and resourcefulness of invention maintained without any of the props of classical form and within a single element of expression as well as of instrumental timbre.

Although Exx. 19–22 constitute the basic thematic structure, some smaller motifs enter from time to time adding to the richness of the symphonic flow. Ex. 23 appears simultaneously with Ex. 22 but the others are added at later more or less important turning-points of the argument:

Ex. 23

Ex. 24

Ex. 25

Ex. 26

Ex. 25, which marks another advance in the tempo, is introduced by a striking re-entry of the Motto Ex. 20, with which it is also frequently joined or alternated. Ex. 26 begins life as a concertante duo for solo violin and solo cello but it quickly combines with a more impassioned tutti thematic fragment:

Ex. 27

The music surges ever onward, now in huge sweeps of sound, now with returns to the concertante episodes. It is in one of these latter that against a florid violin solo the first viola has a pleading phrase derived initially from Ex. 22 which leads to a repetition of the descending seventh of Ex. 27, bringing to mind one of the most anguished motifs from

Tristan. Many commentators have noticed other apparent quotations in *Metamorphosen*; Ex. 21 has, for example, been said to have been drawn from King Mark's sorrowful address in the second act of the same opera. None of these similarities are close enough to support a claim of deliberate citation, in which Strauss showed himself perfectly prepared to indulge when the occasion seemed apposite. But in a work of mourning for the passing of German culture he would not have regretted, perhaps, some chance similarities with that most loved opera.

The Motto theme is redoubled in its intensity with almost savage canonic entries, the opening repeated notes jabbing upon each other at a semitone interval. There is a slight hesitation and the music suddenly streams forward at double speed, some of the passage work almost break-neck. Still a further accelerando and after an upward rush a high G is held fortissimo, poised for a moment. It then swoops down into a mighty return of the opening of the whole work, Ex. 19, once again in the original Adagio tempo. The long central fantasia is over.

After the expansive scale of all the foregoing, nothing could be terser than the reprise. The tremendous power with which Ex. 19 returns gradually crumbles as Ex. 20 gives way to Ex. 21. Ex. 22 tries to build up once more but is broken off in mid-phrase. After a breathless silence the opening (Ex. 19) thunders in with yet another massive return; but this time it is the great coda which it heralds with granite-like canonic pile-ups of the Motto Ex. 20, though here it is of four fortissimo superimposed entries twice reiterated, Ex. 25(x) being added as a partially submerged cadential figure. The tension then subsides into a threnody still based on the Motto, versions of which are played in duet by solo violin and solo viola against a gently-throbbing background in what we are soon to understand to be the tonic key of C minor.

When the cellos have joined in, however, the Motto is turned upside down so that the *Eroica* 'snaps' (Ex. 20(y)) ascend; against chromatically rising repetitions of the initial phrase from Ex. 19 other themes return, especially Exx. 21 and 22 in elegiac tones. These lead to a passionate statement of Ex. 25 which with the Motto still in attendance brings the coda to its final section.

Now it is Exx. 19 and 21, punctuated by the still prominent Ex. 25(x), which gradually—though in a constant mood of despairing resignation—form the last arch of modulations to arrive at the nadir of hopelessness where the Motto is given as bass the Beethoven theme itself:

Ex. 28

Recognized from the first as an outstanding work of the aged master, *Metamorphosen* has come to be held in affection and admiration as one of the most remarkable of all Strauss's works, proving that his genius so far from being spent had unexpectedly renewed itself in a third great curve, that of the Indian Summer.

8

The première was given on 25th January 1946 in the small hall of the Zurich Tonhalle under the direction of Paul Sacher, who could to some extent claim credit for the instigation of the work since he had for some time been pressing Strauss to accept a commission for his orchestra, the Collegium Musicum Zurich. It is to this enterprising conductor that we owe the creation of masterpieces by Bartók, Honegger, Frank Martin, Tippett, Britten and Stravinsky, to name only a few of the great composers from whom Sacher commissioned works.

Strauss treated Sacher with the utmost courtesy, writing to him in cordial terms to congratulate him on the quality of the orchestra and actually consenting to take up the baton at one of the rehearsals. By the time of the first performance the war was of course over and Strauss had been persuaded to abandon Germany and seek temporary asylum in Switzerland.

For the collapse of Germany had left him penniless. American soldiers had arrived on the doorstep of the Garmisch villa to be met by an irascible old man who curtly said: 'I am the composer of *Rosenkavalier*;

leave me alone'. And in peace they duly left him apart from requests for manuscripts, and for an oboe concerto by one soldier who happened to be John de Lancy, the principal oboe of the Philadelphia Symphony Orchestra.

But although life was very hard, Strauss and Pauline were deeply unwilling to leave Garmisch and it took his friends and Dr Roth, his publisher, many months before he could be induced to make the journey.

Moreover, the score of the second wind sonatina, the work known now as *Symphonie für Bläser*, was still growing. Two more sections—an Andantino and a Menuet which he placed second and third in the order of movements—were only completed on 10th and 22nd June 1945, a few weeks after peace was declared in Europe.

It would be impossible to guess Strauss's woeful circumstances from this care-free work which is even subtitled: 'Fröhliche Werkstatt' ('Cheerful workshop') and dedicated to 'the spirit of the immortal Mozart at the end of a life full of thankfulness'.

The only note of seriousness lies in the phrase forming the motto of the Einleitung, which, originally the beginning of a shorter self-contained composition,[9] was afterwards turned into the Finale of the four-movement Sonatina:

Ex. 29

This rather morbid passage Strauss also worked into an Allegro con brio which, completed in March 1944, three months after the Einleitung und Allegro, was to form the first movement of the eventual full-scale work.

In character the lively opening Allegro con brio takes up where the finale of the first Sonatina left off. The opening motif has more than a little in common with Ex. 12 above:

[9] See above, p. 419.

Ex. 30

And like the theme of the earlier work (the instrumentation of which is identical) Ex. 30 is a gift for the horns, as is also the secondary phrase which follows hard on its heels:

Ex. 31

More motifs follow, prominent amongst which is Ex. 29, now adapted to the prevailing rapid waltz measure. Other themes are strongly reminiscent of familiar passages from Strauss's operas such as Ex. 32 which recalls the idyll of Bichette and Quinquin's breakfast chocolate in *Rosenkavalier*, and Ex. 33—the second subject proper—which is very much akin to the Sonnet from *Capriccio*, as well as Sir Morosus' song of contentment 'wie schön ist die Musik' from the closing scene of *Die Schweigsame Frau*:

Ex. 32

Ex. 33

The arrival of Ex. 33 is prepared by an ascending sequence with an arched after-phrase which returns in richly glowing colours to round off the exposition. One further thematic element must be mentioned, a lightly tripping passage in staccato crotchets in which the oboes take the lead. This extra member of the second group provides valuable relief to the somewhat glutinous texture of the movement as a whole.

Development and reprise follow regularly enough although towards the end of the development a new derivative of Ex. 30 (by free retrograde) is subtly introduced:

Ex. 34

(ziemlich lebhaft)

At first linked to the end of Ex. 30 so casually as to suggest the merest after-thought, Ex. 34 becomes of primary importance in the coda. The reprise bursts in resolutely in its own key of E flat after the development has faded away with echoes of Ex. 33 and Ex. 31(x) in G minor, while the return of Ex. 33 as second subject is ingeniously compressed into a combined recapitulation with Ex. 32 appearing both in counterpoint and in alternation. The opening phrase of the first subject is also rarely absent for long, making shy little intrusions legato until it builds up courage when the ascending sequential theme (which had previously preceded the second subject as well as rounding it off) leads the music towards the coda.

Only the staccato tripping passage has been left out so far, and this is incorporated into the coda which is further marked by a two-tier stepping-up of the tempo. Both stages are introduced by Ex. 34, from the time of its first appearance during the development an essential influence in carrying forward the flow of music, especially by the use of urgent repetitions of its figure ⌈ x ⌉.

A significant moment is the reintroduction of Ex. 29 in sinister colouring (one of its returns during the reprise had been in the major, making it sound almost cheerful) but it is soon swept aside and the movement ends with jubilant repetitions of Ex. 30, the horns turning the rising figure ⌈ y ⌉ into positive whoops of delight.

It has been a long movement and the piece to which Strauss was already committed for the Finale is even longer. It was a wise decision therefore to hold back the work until a couple of short Serenade-like middle movements could find their way into the world. This they did, as we have seen, in June 1945 after the cataclysm had overwhelmed Germany; but at least there were no more horrors to await in dread and trembling. Nor need he any longer fear the Nazis. The Reign of Terror was over and Strauss sat down quietly to put on paper this untroubled

Andantino with its principal melody echoing long-remembered phrases from Mozart or Weber:

Ex. 35

An alternating section in easier tempo brings a gentle canon for oboe and basset horn, the oboe handing over to clarinet as the first return of Ex. 35 comes due, now to be accompanied by an assortment of sprightly figurations drawn from the middle passage.

The canon comes round a second time though no longer making any attempt at strictness and soon oboe, clarinet and basset horn combine in a little trio. The movement ends with a last statement of Ex. 35 relegated to the lower instruments (though the first horn cannot resist joining in) to form a bass to another perky figure only half-a-step removed from Mendelssohn's *Fingal's Cave*.

The other Serenade-like movement with which Strauss completed the Sonatina is a Minuet based on a jumpy theme very much in the style of that unusual Minuet in Mozart's Symphony No. 29 in A (K.201). There are two contrasted episodes, Trios perhaps in all but name, though neither is allowed much opportunity to develop before being either combined with or interrupted by the Minuet theme. One episode concerns a rather short-winded passage for horns while the other introduces a duet for two clarinets which can only have been suggested by one of Strauss's favourite movements from Mozart, the Trio for two clarinets in the E flat Symphony, No. 39.

So, for the finale we come back to the Einleitung und Allegro which begins with a full enunciation of Ex. 29. Suggestions of the Allegro theme also make their appearance during the latter part of the Einleitung. Ex. 36 shows the theme as it is given by the flute and basset horn after a hesitant oboe lead-in:

Ex. 36

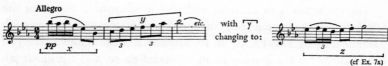

in the course of the lengthy opening sentence.

This is rounded off and the whole wind band takes a deep breath before launching a forte restatement with florid variants and punctuated by fanfare figures.

When the panache has subsided a grazioso little clarinet offshoot of Ex. 36 seems just about to carry the finale onwards as a conventional rondo or sonata movement when the running passage-work collapses abruptly into a repeat of the Einleitung music (Ex. 29) which temporarily usurps the position of second subject. There are even further returns of the doleful opening bars transformed by diminutions into the prevailing skittish mood of a scherzando section which follows the surprise interruption.

The entry of the true second subject Ex. 37 is thus delayed until after the series of sequential descending cadences with which Strauss seems to be concluding his exposition, until—in fact—the beginning of what should properly be the development, though the whole movement has by now taken the character of a continually developing improvisation around Exx. 29 and 36.

Ex. 37

Nor is Ex. 36 absent during the flow of this broad melodic line but keeps making impish reappearances in the background until the time comes for it to take over once again, in alternation (as ever) with Ex. 29, the main role of the discussion.

So homogeneous in texture and tonality is the effortless stream of music-making that it disguises the disciplined classicism of all that follows. In fact the outlines of development, reprise and coda can be traced, though in the reprise the events come in a different order. Ex. 37 is now restored to its rightful position and the forte statement of Ex. 36 with its attendant fanfare figures is reserved for a culminating moment near the close.

The coda too is in keeping with the inexhaustible nature of the whole movement, consisting of a collapse of the high spirits with pathetic lead-back to Ex. 29 in its original andante tempo, a revival of the allegro rising quickly to an expectant pause, and a brilliant più mosso full of running figures (which also make a bustling accompaniment to an adaptation of Ex. 37) and hilarious repetitions of the principal finale motif Ex. 36(x).

If this second 'Sonatina' is less successful than the first it is largely due to its extravagant dimensions, which also led to its being published under the title of *Symphonie für Bläser* though such a description never entered its creator's mind. As a 'workshop' piece—and Strauss claimed no more—one would be churlish to decry its mastery but whereas for the performer a constant joy, to the listener it is inclined to outstay its welcome. Perhaps however, its chief value lay in keeping Strauss's hand in, for it was followed directly by the most enchanting of all the Indian Summer instrumental works.

9

In the early autumn of 1945 Strauss and Pauline at last saw that they must accept the advice and help of friends and take refuge in Switzerland. All Strauss's ready funds, capital and the royalties from his works were blocked as long as he remained in Germany and he carried the additional burden that, on account of his period of office as President of the Reichsmusikkammer, his name remained associated with the Third Reich and he would in due course be required to submit to the indignity of a denazification inquiry before he could become *persona grata* once more.

In Switzerland, lonely and detached, he could at least remain in seclusion, totally withdrawn from the world, and it was in Baden, a little watering-place midway between Basle and Zurich, that he completed the score of the 'oboe piece', in fact a full-scale concerto, which was the result of the request made by 'that Chicago oboist' as Strauss was apt to miscall Philadelphia's solo oboe John de Lancy.

The short score was the last music to be completed in Garmisch and is dated 14 Sept. 1945, while the orchestration was ready barely six weeks later. Enforced emigration to life in hotel rooms abroad disturbed the old master's regular music-making no more than war or Nazi displeasure had done.

Moreover, with the perversity of genius, inspiration had truly been at Strauss's elbow enabling him to compose a work so immediately captivating that it at once became universally known and loved.

In the first bars Strauss at once established for one of the principal

motifs a little figure the origin of which can be traced back to the
Schlagobers Walzer (see Vol. II, p. 227, Ex. 7a):

Ex. 38

which is quickly extended to:

Ex. 38a

Over this, the oboe rhapsodizes in a long opening sentence very much
after the manner of the recent Horn Concerto, and in the same way
presents many of the melodic germs of the movement, such as:

Ex. 39

Ex. 40

And as with the horn's fifty-four introductory bars, so the oboe plays
without interruption for fifty-six, a considerable test of endurance and
breath-control. In addition to the background of strings, however, a
clarinet in due course adds an amiable line of counterpoint.

At last with an expansive cadence the soloist ushers in the tutti, a
chamber-orchestral ensemble with two each of flutes, clarinets, bassoons
and horns, though the oboe department is represented by a single cor
anglais.

When the little orchestra has briefly had its turn at looking through
Exx. 38–40 the oboe takes over the transition section which although
constantly interspersed with longer or shorter bits of Ex. 38 or Ex. 38a
contains a phrase which proves during the course of the concerto to
have an entity very much its own:

Ex. 41

This leads directly to the second subject which is in two parts, the first of which is a most affecting melody. The last of its three phrases is quoted to show the heart-warming curves as well as the enchantingly typical side-slip out of the prevailing harmony and then back again just in time:

Ex. 42

The oboe, which has played no part in the first presentation of Ex. 42 leads off with the other element of the second group:

Ex. 43

The canonic imitation illustrated in Ex. 43 is a feature of the theme, which causes some distinctly tricky moments when the first violins have later to take their turn with the figure ⌐ x ⌐. Both this jerky phrase with its shock tactics and the gentler ⌐ y ⌐ become important

independently, and the fact that they are once more connected by
Ex. 38 should not cause surprise when a glance at Ex. 42 shows that
Strauss manages to find a place for this primary motif in virtually any
context.

There are two extended statements of Ex. 43 linked by a two-bar
return of the transition theme Ex. 41, after which a slightly varied and
more masculine form of Ex. 43(y) becomes the subject of the ensuing
tutti's opening phrases. This central tutti and the dialogue of Ex. 40
between the first violins and the solo oboe which follows it constitute
the whole of the development section; yet although concise it is far
from uneventful with its fully instrumentated version of the spiky
Ex. 43(x) and conciliatory use of the second subject Ex. 42.

The recapitulation is varied but complete apart from the omission of
any further tuttis, even the elongated version of the melodious Ex. 42,
richly scored as it is, being largely reinforced by the oboe. This is, if
truth be told, a strange piece of writing and many of the most distinguished soloists tend to regard the passage as the natural opportunity for
a hard-earned rest, leaving matters to the orchestra, for the solo line is
doubled throughout by no less than two flutes and a clarinet.

There is, however, a further point of interest which lies in a new
figure of accompaniment interposed by a solo violin and solo viola:

Ex. 44

Although hardly noticed at this its first appearance, Ex. 44 is to become
one of the principal motifs in the closing movements of the concerto.

The opening Allegro ends with the oboe passing in review many of
the various themes ending with the little twisting figure ⎡ x ⎤ from
its opening melody Ex. 39 to which the wind instruments in turn add
the initial phrase from the second subject Ex. 42, the strings being occupied with the motif Ex. 38. By the time the oboe has reached its end on
a low D these last two elements have settled down to an ostinato which
is quite undisturbed by a change of tempo and time signature, though
the violins have taken over from the wind those three repeated notes
which are all that by now remains of the reiterations of Ex. 42.

We are in fact comfortably launched into the Andante, the melody
of which the oboe declaims:

Ex. 45

A subsidiary phrase, for which Strauss has an important role in store, begins:

Ex. 46

A central section brings reminiscences of melodies from the first movement, notably Exx. 39, 41 and 42, the latter at last allowed more than just its three repeated opening notes. Here again Strauss brings in the oboe as a mere additional colour in what is essentially a tutti passage, once for a period of four bars and at the climax for no more than two. Needless to say, like the parallel section in the first movement these are omitted by many soloists although Strauss's intention—here as there—is hardly in doubt, strange as it may seem. It is as if with his subtle ear for mixtures of timbre he regretted the lack of the oboe in his small orchestral ensemble and saw no reason why the solo instrument, granted a handful of bars to relax the lip, should not make shift to supply the deficiency.

The wide melodic arch of Exx. 45 and 46 returns in full, the last sentence being even further extended with glowing instrumentation after which the oboe rounds off the Andante with a reflective return of Ex. 41. Three gentle bars of the original doubly-motivic accompaniment figure (as shown in Ex. 45) seem to accept this idea when suddenly the whole orchestra declaims the first bar of Ex. 46 as if in protest. The oboe repeats it, answering the challenge, and then continues in a cadenza which is, however, punctuated from time to time with pizzicato chords.

Here then is the big moment for Ex. 46, which dominates the cadenza in the opening bars and then later, with ingenious twists, indicates its relationship to other themes past and future. Next there are the usual scales and trills, and abruptly the oboe plunges into the finale.

This is a sprightly rondo-like movement centring around a dual theme which gives Strauss every opportunity either to work it as a whole or to develop each of its figures separately:

Ex. 47

(It is an interesting reflection on Strauss's technique that one of the continuations of the running semi-quaver passage-work should—surely inadvertently—pass through a figure identical with one from the Second Horn Concerto, Ex. 2(y) above.)

Amongst the more striking subsidiary motifs Ex. 44, which we have already met, now comes into its own while another is rhythmically derived from Ex. 41(x):

Ex. 48

Both these motifs are integral to the organization of the movement. The first of the rondo episodes is however thematically independent, a long and meandering cantilena on strings reinforced by in turn bassoon, clarinet, horn and cor anglais, while the soloist winds around it arpeggiando arabesques. But the second episode is another fully-extended version in slightly altered melodic contours of the beautiful Ex. 42.

There is an attempted return, by way of reprise, of the first episode but it gets all mixed up in Exx. 44, 47 and 48, and the orchestra taking the foreground (much as it did, to Zerbinetta's despair, in the first version of her famous Rondo) quickly builds up to an expectant $\frac{6}{4}$ *fermata*.

The oboe obliges with a cadenza—unaccompanied this time—and leads the music not, as expected, to a standard coda, but to an entirely fresh allegro in a lilting $\frac{6}{8}$, a sort of *envoi* as it were.

Initially based on yet another derivative of Ex. 41, a particular feature is the elegantly-transformed return of Ex. 42 once on the oboe with its harmonic side-slips cunningly ironed out, and then restored in an orchestral repetition virtually as they were first heard, though allowing for the new swinging rhythm. Throughout the whole a similarly transformed version of the basic motif Ex. 38 maintains a series of flowing accompaniments whether in extended form or curtailed to a succession of little violin turns.

There is a jubilant tutti and a short coda in which the oboe engages in a dialogue with the orchestra in order first to share the $\frac{6}{8}$ versions of Ex. 38 and then to remind us briefly of Ex. 47 which was, after all, at one time the principal theme of the finale. But it is Ex. 38 which has the last word, albeit upside down.

10

Living only a handful of miles outside Zurich, it was perhaps natural for Strauss to allocate the first performance to the Tonhalle Orchestra, and with Marcel Saillet as soloist this took place on 26th February 1946. John de Lancy had to be content with a nice letter giving him permission to perform the work in America whenever he liked thereafter—before it was published, that is to say.

In the meantime a gramophone recording was made in London by that most distinguished of oboists, Leon Goossens, and this apart from its great intrinsic merits has become an important piece of documentation. For when in 1948 the concerto was prepared for the engraver, Strauss decided to alter and extend the closing pages. The amended coda originates on a separate piece of manuscript inscribed 'Montreux 1.Februar 1948' and adds eleven extra bars as well as rejuxtaposing and partially revising the original eighteen, all of which are however retained if in a different order.

Although one can with fascination follow the reasoning of Strauss's mind, one may perhaps regret the greater conciseness of the first version and wish that, as with Bartók's last works, both endings could have been perpetuated.

The address 'Montreux' on the manuscript slip gives another indication of the Strausses' more restless existence in Switzerland. For, as Pauline bitterly commented to Dr Roth on the occasion of one of his many solicitous visits, while Richard could happily sit at a desk and write music wherever he was,[10] what was she to do all day long? So, true to the character we know from *Intermezzo*, what she actually did was to complain, to create storms and scenes with members of the hotel staff. The food was uneatable, the rooms filthy (this in Switzerland, of all places).

Their memory is still green in Baden today, the tall spare figure of the famous old man setting off daily on his lonely constitutional while his termagant of a wife was throwing another of her hilarious tantrums in the room above. It is hardly surprising that one hotel after another found their continuing presence too great a strain.

But to do her justice life was hard for Pauline who, though like her Richard well into her eighties (she was after all slightly the elder of the two) was as active in mind as she had ever been and sorely missed her social rounds and position.

Yet when in October 1947 the possibility of diversion came in the form of a trip to London it was she who refused to entertain the idea and left Strauss to face the first air journey of his life without her. She was convinced that her nerves and health were in no way up to the discomforts and demands of such an adventure. It was the more astonishing that Strauss himself considered the undertaking feasible, as in April 1946 he had undergone an operation for appendicitis and although he had made a spectacular recovery it had taken its inevitable toll. But the manner of the invitation, as well as the opportunity the expedition offered for at last collecting some of his frozen assets, persuaded Strauss that he should accept these proposals made to him by his friends in England, and come he did.

Of this visit I have already written in the Preface to Vol. I, giving possibly what one commentator has called a 'grumpy' view of the veteran composer. The account was of course palpably subjective but no less real and the scenes are still as vividly before me as if they had happened twenty-three days, not twenty-three years ago.

If Strauss understandably presented an impatient and unforthcoming front amongst people he neither knew nor had any desire to know, he greatly enjoyed the company of his loyal friends in England, old and new. Whereas to the newspaper reporters who clamoured round him

[10] When he had nothing better to do Strauss occupied himself by making transcriptions of orchestral excerpts from *Die Frau ohne Schatten* and *Josephslegende* both of which date from the year following the completion of the Oboe Concerto. For details and discussions of these see Vol. II, pp. 148 and 217 respectively.

for his future plans he gruffly answered with the laconic words 'Na, sterben halt' ('well, to die') with Dr Roth and his other friends he elected to pass many a happy hour visiting amongst other things, the London picture galleries, this in itself an energetic occupation for a man of eighty-three. And he gave an endearing glimpse of the genial humorous fellow he had once been when before going on to the Albert Hall platform to conduct he said 'the old horse trundles out of the stables once more!'

Despite disturbing stomach upsets the trip was a success from every point of view[11] and was undertaken just in time, as the very next month came the first signs of the bladder infection of which he was ultimately to die. Yet even so his creativity continued unchecked. On his return from England he at once picked up some sketches which he had labelled 'Gute Skizze' and quickly carried them through until by 29th November he had before him the completed Particell (short score) of a *Duett-Concertino* for clarinet and bassoon with accompaniment for strings and harp. Addressing himself without delay to the full score, the whole work was intact just over a fortnight later, on 16th December 1947.

II

Although in style these Indian Summer works are all extremely closely related, each has distinctive features of form or setting, and this is especially true of the last of all Strauss's instrumental compositions, the *Duett-Concertino*. The unusual choice of the two wind soloists; the sparingly used addition of the harp; and the extraordinary devising of its continuous 3-movement form with the long sprawling Rondo entirely dominating and overshadowing the two fragmentary quasi-movements which precede it; these are all unique features proving that to the end Strauss never lost the sense of enjoyment in setting himself new problems.

Even the string writing has something of fascination being divided throughout into soli (the first player of each of the five normal groups) and tutti in the manner of the classical 'Concertino' and 'Concerto grosso'. And when the work opens with just the solo strings augmented

[11] A very detailed account of the whole visit can be found in Dr Roth's admirable book, *Musik als Kunst und Ware*, Atlantis Verlag, Zurich, 1966: pp. 200–208. The English version *The Business of Music*, Cassell, London, 1969, is, however, considerably curtailed.

by the temporary addition of a single extra solo viola, the similarity to
the string sextet Vorspiel of Strauss's last opera *Capriccio* is inescapable.

Ex. 49

Of the two figures bracketed in Ex. 49, ⌐ x ⌐ is to become the
principal motif of the work whereas ⌐ y ⌐ settles down into a gently
rocking figure of accompaniment in preparation for the entry of the
clarinet:

Ex. 50

So typical of all the Indian Summer works is this melodizing that it
seems as if we must have heard its various twists and turns in one or
other of the earlier pieces. The first arpeggiando is perhaps the most
individual, and this takes on something of the role of first subject.

When the clarinet has elaborated on Ex. 50 for a while, the bassoon
makes its appearance with an odd syncopated scale rising slowly from
the depths. At once the clarinet takes fright and breaks into wild cadenza-
like utterances punctuated by agitated outbursts of the full strings (now

also heard for the first time), ignoring the bassoon's attempts to get a word in edgeways. Eventually, however, the clarinet subsides exhausted and the bassoon is able to establish its presence, which it does with a doleful series of phrases, of which Ex. 51 is destined to take its place in the material of the closing Rondo:

Ex. 51

This by-play at the bassoon's first entry is a relic of an abortive idea in which, as Strauss told Clemens Krauss, there was to have been a programmatic connexion with Hans Andersen's story 'The Swineherd'. In Andersen's tale a prince woos a beautiful princess by taking the position of swineherd at her father's palace, and it is clear that the clarinet impersonating the princess is alarmed at the appearance of the bassoon-swineherd-prince. But the analogy stops here as Strauss found this kind of illustrative composition no longer interesting and pursued the work on a purely musical basis.

The clarinet joins the bassoon in the working out, alternating its own themes with Ex. 51 and thereby producing some interesting rhythmical juxtapositions as the bassoon's music has introduced a $\frac{6}{4}$ pulse. Strauss also varies the background by opposing the contrasted string groups, the movement building up to the first tutti section in which both are combined:

Ex. 52

This, after a short interruption by the two wind instruments, leads into a fully-scored restatement of the clarinet's opening melody Ex. 50, the clarinet now doubled by the solo first violin and the whole texture pointed at intervals by chords on the harp, which has curiously been entirely silent until this point.

The cursory reprise of the clarinet melody has no sooner run its course than it merges into the primary motif Ex. 49(x) with which the music then collapses. The fragmentary first section of the work is over and gives way to an even shorter Andante beginning with an extended bassoon solo over shimmering tremolos on high violins and harp.

Some of this cantilena centres round already familiar phrases but one new line emerges whose first rising figure is to have a role to play in the Rondo:

Ex. 53

Ex. 53 is repeated in varied forms though with the bassoon doubled by a solo cello while the clarinet adds counterpoints at first drawn from ⌐ y ⌐ which is itself related to an earlier melodic line from the opening melodizing.

The solo violin interjects the motif Ex. 49(x) and the clarinet and bassoon gather it up into a burst of flowing passage-work. This then subsides expectantly; the Andante too, has had its say and after a cadenza in which the two soloists experiment with different themes (Exx. 51, 50(x), 50(z), etc.) they agree upon the chief motif Ex. 49(x) and the work is ready to base upon it the one fully-developed and extended movement which accordingly follows without a break.

In its guise as Rondo subject, the motto theme is presented both upside down and the right way up, viz:

Ex. 54

The little bracketed afterphrase (which can reasonably claim origin from Ex. 53(y)) is also exploited upwards as well as downwards with very good-humoured effect.

A transition pair of figures which make their first entry together:

Ex. 55

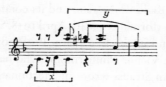

are followed shortly afterwards by the second subject proper, a wide-spanned melody for clarinet and bassoon in unison, whose phrases of $\frac{4}{4}$ straddle across two at a time of the Rondo's sprightly $\frac{6}{8}$ bars.

The Beethoven 7 rhythm of Ex. 55(x) gathers force until it becomes a salient feature with the tutti strings pounding away at it for two or even four bars, provoking indignant retorts of the Rondo motif (Ex. 49(x)) by the two wind players and the solo strings in a body.

The second subject itself brings a return of the harp which is indeed very sparingly used throughout the work. At the same time the solo strings persist with continual ostinatos of the Rondo figures from Ex. 54 as well as Ex. 55(x).

When this has died away the second half of the Rondo begins, its quasi-improvised character much like the first, though Ex. 55(x) is now strongly in evidence. In addition to Ex. 51, which has always re-appeared from time to time, other themes from earlier sections of the work are now brought back into the picture. The bassoon proposes Ex. 53, here extended in a way recalling a famous passage for the same instrument in *Heldenleben*. The arpeggiando Ex. 50(z) finds its way into the texture and leads to a return of the wider arpeggios of ⌐ x ⌐ from the same example in a short tutti passage for the full strings, the bassoon being given the option of doubling the allusion *ad lib.*, lest being in the lower instruments it should pass unnoticed.

After a full restatement of the wide-spanned second subject, still given in unison to the wind players though reinforced this time by the tutti violins, a tremendous outburst of the rhythmic Ex. 55(x) proves to be none other than a metamorphosis of the isolated fortissimo tutti from the first movement, Ex. 52.

From this point all is coda, Exx. 51 and 55(y) making strong con-tributions to the whirling crescendi, though the exuberant end is brought about with frenzied repetitions of the principal motif and the jumpy rhythm. The work, and Strauss's instrumental output, could hardly end in higher spirits.

The *Duett-Concertino* was written for the small orchestra ensemble of the Italian-Swiss Radio in Lugano and its conductor Otmar Nussio who gave the first performance on 4th April 1948. Strauss had, however, an old friend in mind in the first place, Professor Hugo Burghauser, the bassoonist of the Vienna Philharmonic who had since emigrated to New York.[12] To him Strauss wrote an affectionate dedication (though unaccountably this does not appear in the full score) and a letter alluding—in a slightly different way from the version so far recounted—to the original programmatic associations of the piece.

According to this a dancing princess was to be alarmed by the grotesque cavortings by a bear in imitation of her. At last she is won over by the creature and dances with it, upon which it turns into a prince. 'So in the end' he wrote to Burghauser, 'you too will turn into a prince and all live happily ever after . . .'

This version certainly corresponds more closely with the work as we have it than the Hans Andersen idea, and makes an attractive tribute to an old colleague to whom he had written already in October 1946:

> . . . I am even busy with an idea for a double concerto for clarinet and bassoon thinking especially of your beautiful tone—nevertheless apart from a few sketched out themes it still remains no more than an intention . . . Perhaps it would interest you; my father always used to say 'It was Mozart who wrote most beautifully for the bassoon'. But then he was also the one to have all the most beautiful thoughts, coming straight down from the skies!
>
> Please give Kapellmeister Szell my greetings! Does he still play my *Eulenspiegel* from memory?

Strauss's affection and loyalty towards his professional colleagues remained one of his most endearing traits.

12

A few months before the end of the war, on 14th January 1945, Strauss wrote to Gregor:

> I had a dream this morning: I was staying with some notable gentleman, though he wasn't present himself, and had just

[12] According to Marek, Burghauser helped Strauss in this time of financial trouble by finding suitable markets in America for the copies the composer had been making in his own hand of some of his earlier tone-poems.

had breakfast when Hofmannsthal came up to me with the words: 'I've got a one-act opera text for you: *very delicate*— with *nymphs*!'

He then went on to tell Gregor how he had searched through Greek mythology in an attempt to find a meaning for the dream. He even headed the letter with a quotation of verses from the third act of *Meistersinger* in which Sachs encourages Walther to turn his dream into poetic art.

Strauss ended rather wickedly by inviting Gregor to sketch out some masque-like entertainment centring around Diana and Endymion, or adding Venus and Adonis for good measure, with pantomime for the male characters and featuring a women's chorus—wickedly, because well he knew by now that he had only to lift a little finger for Gregor to shower him with drafts which he was unlikely to use.

Sure enough two weeks had hardly passed before Gregor was able to write and say that the first scene was ready. Certainly Strauss's replies give the impression that he was at least tempted to go back on the decision that *Capriccio* was to be his last word for the stage. After all, his mind needed more exercise than these occasional instrumental pieces supplied, and so he allowed himself the luxury of playing Gregor along. Moreover he was reading through Gregor's *Weltgeschichte des Theaters*, an impressive history of the world theatre for which he had long had a considerable admiration, whatever his views on Gregor as a librettist.

Indeed he took the trouble to send Gregor a lengthy set of notes on the book full of reminiscences, criticisms and suggestions (especially for the ending) which with its musical examples and actual quotations makes most stimulating reading.

Another basis for correspondence at this time arose from Gregor having undertaken to interest Strauss in the thematic catalogue of all his music being compiled by the musicologist Dr Erich H. Mueller von Asow. Begun already in 1942, this enormous undertaking was gathering pace; not unnaturally Asow wanted to refer his researches to the composer as much for encouragement as for documentation, otherwise in danger of being lost for ever.

But Strauss had no patience with such an enterprise even though he declared himself 'truly touched' by Dr Asow's painstaking labours. It was of course particularly unfortunate that at such a disrupted period of world affairs all Asow could refer to Strauss were questions about unpublished or youthful compositions, but in any case all this scholarship was to the composer the merest waste of so much good paper.[13]

Nor was Gregor, whom Strauss already saw as something of a pedant, the best advocate for such undiluted musicology. Just as in the days of *Daphne* or *Danae* Strauss minced no words either in his curt dismissal of Asow's efforts ('Philologenstaub', 'reiner Papierkorb')[14] or in his opinion of Gregor's own assiduous endeavours to meet his new demands. One thing after another was 'unmöglich' or 'unglücklich' ('impossible' or 'unhappy') and it is curious to see the man to whom the passions or perversions of real flesh and blood had once been the spring-board of all inspiration bothering with a puppet-like pantomime for the deities of classical mythology, yet never in all his life being drawn towards the Nordic gods and heroes which had sparked his idol Wagner.

It was in fact Strauss's fondness for great paintings which prompted a desire to bring classical figures to life on the stage. Again and again he referred Gregor to this or that work of, say, Titian, never coming to terms with Gregor's total lack of response in this field. Under the little historian's tireless hands *Die Rache der Aphrodite* grew and grew, regard-less of the fact that musically it remained a non-starter. Yet it must be said in Gregor's defence that Strauss filled many a page with really quite elaborate scenario details. Even the title was the composer's idea as was the surely discouraging conception of a 'Komödie ohne Worte'.

By October two extensive drafts were in Strauss's hands, upon which the composer took the trouble to sketch out a possible dialogue between Venus and Diana. There was to be a song and dance contest arising out of the goddesses' varying experiences of love. Their duet in the second act Strauss saw as a satirical confrontation and he even hazarded some verses himself to show Gregor the sort of stuff he wanted, incorporating his ideas into a letter dated 6th December 1945.

But between the disruption of communications and the Strausses' emigration to Switzerland, the letter was delayed for months and the next thing the poor librettist heard was of Strauss's operation for

---

[13] Ultimately the problems of assembling all the necessary information proved so formidable that it was 1954 before a start was made at publishing the catalogue by instalments; Dr Asow died ten years later during the centenary celebrations of Strauss's birth with the task still incomplete, and although two eminent Straussian scholars (Dr Alfons Ott and Dr Franz Trenner) have continued the project, at the time of writing—January 1971—the final section continues to be delayed and there seems to be no immediate prospect of the long-awaited conclusion.

[14] 'Dusty philology', 'pure waste-paper-basket stuff'.

appendicitis. Lastly in October 1946 came the bitterly disappointing verdict that such sporadic collaboration in these conditions was hopeless and would Gregor like to show the libretto, as far as it went, to Clemens Krauss? In vain Gregor protested that Krauss had already seen and approved the sketches and now had no notion what to do with them; in vain also the offer to visit Switzerland and try to continue the collaboration at closer quarters.

And yet Strauss would not let Gregor altogether off the hook; in January 1947 he suddenly wrote again setting the long-suffering poet onto an entirely new wild-goose chase.

13

Early in the new year of 1947 Strauss received a letter from Stephen Schaller, the monastic head of the Benedictine Gymnasium in Ettal to which Strauss had sent his son Franz and where since the previous year his grandson Christian was also now at school (Ettal being in the immediate vicinity of Garmisch). With the reconstruction of the educational system in Germany after the end of the war, Strauss had represented himself as strongly concerned about the place of music in Bavarian schools and in favour of a complete reform of the way music was taught there. To his mind graduation students should be as familiar with the scores of the Beethoven symphonies or *Tristan* as the works of Schiller or the *Iliad*.

Taking advantage of Strauss's avowed interest in educational affairs and his associations with the Ettal Gymnasium across two generations, Schaller took it upon himself to ask the composer to write a piece for the school stage, to be acted and played as far as possible by the boys themselves. Shrewdly he added that such a venture would provide the young people with a practical approach to the master's own greater works.

Strauss was quite captivated and passed on the proposition at once to Gregor, not considering for a moment how that worthy must still be feeling at the collapse of so much hard work on *Die Rache der Aphrodite*.

Nor did the good-natured historian even pause to think that yet another disappointing rebuff might be in store for him. Springing back again like a Jack-in-the-box he had before the end of February sent two new drafts to Strauss. Apologetically rejecting the composer's proposal for some Hans Sachs subject, he explained that he had during his recent travels been enjoying a browse through the old author Wieland, one of whose ideas seemed to him particularly happy in this context.

Christoph Martin Wieland was an important contemporary of Goethe although the classical, predominantly Greek background of much of his writings provided a strong contrast to the *Sturm und Drang* movement. One of his most attractive books, *Die Abderiten, eine sehr wahrscheinliche Geschichte*,[15] was published in 1774 and contains the episode that caught Gregor's fancy.

Although the home of two famous philosophers, Protagoras and Democritus, the ancient Thracian city Abdera was popularly supposed to be subject to breezes which caused universal stupidity. The proverbial foolishness of the Abderites provided Wieland with the material for an uproarious satire on contemporary German provincial life. A beautiful statue is mounted on a pedestal so high that no one can see it, a priceless fountain obtained but the water forgotten, and so on.

Many of the incidents are Wieland's own invention but perhaps the most amusing is of greater antiquity. This is the story of the dentist who makes an agreement with a donkey-drover to be carried to a neighbouring town. The day is scorching hot and the route provides no shelter from the pitiless sun. So the dentist dismounts and takes his ease in the donkey's shadow.

The drover, however, decides that this action constitutes an infringement of contract, on the grounds that it is the donkey and not its shadow which has been hired, and he knows no peace until he has brought his customer to court. The matter becomes a *cause célèbre*, the whole town taking up the cudgels and dividing into 'donkeys' and 'shadows'. The end is only brought about when discovery is made of the donkey's death of starvation through neglect during the interminable legal arguments.

Wieland's book ends with the Abderites being forced to evacuate their town which is overrun by frogs. It would have been a simple matter to kill them but being the sacred frogs of the town's patron goddess Latona (or Leto) this would have been impious, and abandonment of their homes remains their only alternative.

The tale of the donkey's shadow suited Strauss very nicely as long as it could be treated in the simplest way possible with little song-forms separated by a great deal of spoken dialogue in Singspiel manner, like

---

[15] 'The Abderites, a very probable story.'

Mozart's *Die Entführung aus dem Serail*. The closing scene in the court house with the full legal assemblage, to which could be added a chorus of frogs, all seemed highly appropriate for the schoolboy performers. The orchestra too, he wrote to Gregor, must be utterly unpretentious— a handful of strings supported by a good pianist would have to suffice. Strauss acknowledged that he was not used to the self-discipline such a primitive handling would impose, but it should not prove too hard a task.

And now the well-worn pattern of the Strauss/Gregor partnership began yet again, one sketch after another being rejected for being too wordy, too heavy-handed. Gregor had never had an instinct for the style Strauss demanded and it was too late for him to develop it now. At last, finding the composer's demands unbearably restricting—far closer adherance to Wieland, including all the original Greek names but compressed into pithy attractive couplets after the manner of the cartoonist and popular poetaster Wilhelm Busch—Gregor unwisely allowed himself the luxury of a protest. He had been unwell and the immediate post-war days were very hard (a food parcel from Franz Strauss's mother-in-law Frau von Grab had virtually saved his health); he found Wieland's style dull, old-fashioned and hard to hammer into dialogue form.

Admittedly Wieland was notorious for his complicated long-drawn-out sentences which Goethe and Schiller had caricatured in their *Xenien*, and yet after all he had been Gregor's own choice.

Then again Gregor complained on the one hand that he was over-burdened with work, and on the other that he had lost all sense of the purpose, even the length, of Strauss's requirements. Must it really be purely and simply an offering for Ettal? He, Gregor, had planned his first draft on lines which could have been suitable for the world-famous Vienna Boys' Choir. And the way it was developing it would last a minimum of two hours and a half without intervals. Strauss had written originally in terms of a school ceremony of not more than an hour at most. It was all very worrying and difficult.

Strauss's reply was automatic: he simply took the piece straight out of Gregor's hands. At the advice of the conductor and musicologist Bernard Paumgartner he enlisted the aid of another and lesser Viennese author, Hans Adler. Pitifully Gregor pleaded that the idea of *Des Esels Schatten* had been entirely his, quoting the full text of a telegram from Strauss in support of his claim. At the least his name must be retained in connexion with the published title,[16] at any rate until he could have a chance to see how Adler's work turned out.

But Strauss, who had been idly sketching out a few numbers before he had had a line of Gregor's drafts, was not interested. His enthusiasm for the piece itself was waning and although Adler was allowed to complete a two-act sketch it drew from Strauss little more than he had already done. At his death, of the nine projected scenes comprising eighteen musical numbers only the first few of Act I had been tackled, together with a brief idea for a chorus later in the drama. Certainly, as Stephen Schaller concedes, the removal of Christian Strauss to a Swiss boarding school did little to accelerate the work which remained essentially unwritten.

Nevertheless the enterprising Benedictine refused to admit total defeat. Having on his staff a music master of some qualifications as a Straussian in the person of one Karl Haussner, Schaller obtained from Strauss's family the sanction for an attempt at completing a performing version out of the eight sketch-books which had been found amongst Strauss's effects.

It was the end of the 1950's before the task of reconstruction was put in hand, by which time Adler too was dead. Yet even this additional blow did not deter Schaller and Haussner, although in view of the little music there was available the text had to be cut back to a single act. All in all Haussner managed to concoct some fifteen musical numbers which he orchestrated, often thickly, for a group rather larger than the *Ariadne* ensemble, taking his cue from one or two indications for wind instruments which he found in the sketch of the Vorspiel.

'In this form' wrote Schaller triumphantly, 'the work was publicly performed in the centenary week of Richard Strauss's 100th birthday on 7 and 14 June 1964 by the Humanistische Gymnasium der Benediktinerabtei Ettal', adding that its resounding success with public and critics alike proved what a shame it would have been to have allowed this last work of the great composer to remain buried in the archives as a mere torso.

But despite occasional performances since that time, including a London première in 1970, wrongly describing the piece as 'Strauss's last opera', Schaller's view of *Des Esels Schatten* savours of wishful

---

[16] Nor was this reasonable request honoured when the fragment was ultimately published in 1967 although Gregor's part in the genesis of the work is outlined in the preface.

thinking. Such music as Haussner was able to rescue is very slender, excepting possibly the Vorspiel, entitled 'Der Froschgraben' ('The Frog's Ditch'). Strauss seems to have wanted to make an especial feature of these creatures even though in Wieland's story they did not belong to the episode of the donkey's shadow. For this purpose Adler had, however, managed to find more than one excuse for their appearance.

The Vorspiel, then, is quite an interesting fragment with its croaks and clicks ('Klippern', Strauss scribbled over one passage), partly characteristic of and yet very different in style from the instrumental music of this last period:

Ex. 56

Over the colouristic figuration a broad melody in $\frac{12}{8}$ is eventually spread, after which the piece fades away ending rather abruptly.

The numbers which then follow are briefly:

No. 1—Duet for Antrax, the donkey drover, and Struthion the dentist, both complaining of the hardship the journey imposes.

No. 2—A second duet in which the two quarrel over the question of the shadow and decide to go to law. (Neither duet exceeds thirty-five bars though Haussner added postludes to both.)

No. 3—Song for Philippides, the town judge, to whose office the scene has now changed.

No. 4—Duet for Physignatus and Polyphonus, the respective lawyers of the two litigants.

No. 5—Song for Kenteterion, the local Hans Sachs, i.e. cobbler-philosopher and master-guildsman. The scene has changed again and is now in his workshop.

No. 6—Terzett for Kenteterion, the dentist Struthion and his lawyer Physignatus.

No. 7—Terzett for the donkey drover Antrax together with his wife and daughter, Krobyle and Gorgo.

So far Haussner was able to follow Strauss's own outline scheme but from this point he was on his own.

No. 8a—an Arietta for Gorgo and

   8b—a second Terzett for the Antrax family, are accordingly very terse as Haussner had no guide in his choice of musical fragments from the sketch-books. A facsimile of the excerpt employed in No. 8b (which contains no voice parts) is actually illustrated in the preface of the vocal score.

At this juncture, acting on the scribbled headings to two sketches, 'The procession to the frog's ditch' and 'the storks of Agathyrsus', Haussner introduced a quasi-balletic movement:

No. 9—'Pantomime of the frogs and storks', whose dramatic justification arises out of the influence each litigant tries to elicit in his favour from important town personages. To boil down the extremely cumbersome mesh of intrigue, hardly any aspects of which touch the music, it transpires that the rival high-priests of the opposing temples of Latona and Jason, Strobylus and Agathyrsus, have each been prevailed upon, the latter to support the 'donkeys', the former the 'shadows'. It also turns out that in defiance of the law Agathyrsus has been keeping storks in his garden who are menacing Strobylus' sacred frogs. The alarming omen of their cries of 'Feu, feu, eleleleleu!' replacing their previously cheerful 'Koax, koax, kekerekex' (cf. Aristophanes), forms the centrepoint of the pantomime in addition to influencing the subsequent action of the piece. Arising from a grotesque and petty incident the whole future of Abdera is at stake. The worshippers of Latona call for vengeance against Agathyrsus in:

No. 10—Chorus for men's voices, largely in unison. They decide to put the case to the people, and the scene changes from the frog pond to the market square.

No. 11—another chorus though this time for the assembled populace. This is the isolated movement which Strauss had sketched out of order and which would presumably have belonged to the originally-proposed second act.

No. 12—Philippides' address. The audience is here called upon to represent the town council of the 'Four Hundred' and is required by means of applause to indicate their approval at different points of the ensuing legal dispute. The tangled affair is brought to a halt when the donkey's corpse is brought in, and wise generous settlements are at last reached followed by universal reconciliations.

These mark the beginning of:

No. 13—Finale, consisting of a short quartet for Antrax, Struthion and their lawyers Physignatus and Polyphonus (the two latter singing in unison), which leads straight into an Allegro unison chorus for the whole gathering.

As so often with attempted reconstructions of this kind, the results produce agonizing conflicts. Movements like the opening duet No. 1, with its consecutive fourths and fifths, and sounds of the donkey's braying suggest that something extremely entertaining might have resulted had Strauss persevered:

Ex. 57

But Haussner's endings and transitions are lame, and some of the more serious songs, such as the Lied des Philippides No. 3, are surely duller than Strauss would have allowed them to remain.

Gorgo's Arietta No. 8a, with which she successfully seduces Agathyrsus, the high priest of the Jason temple, into putting his influence towards her father's cause, is an elegant Tempo di Menuetto somewhat in the style of the *Bourgeois Gentilhomme* incidental music of 1918, but suffers from its lack of an acceptable text[17] and suddenly comes—like so many of the numbers—to a premature and unpolished halt.

Unlike Strauss's normal practice, the sketches show little or no opportunity for motivic connexion between the numbers, except in the Pantomime No. 9, where a natural allusion existed to the Vorspiel which also refers to the frogs (Ex. 56).

The later movements become increasingly tantalizing as one intriguing idea follows another only to be clothed in unsophisticated and

---

[17] It is hard to understand how Schaller and Haussner thought that this would do:

> La, la, la, la, la, la, la!
> Eins zwei drei im Takt
> Als Sopran oder Alt
> da lass ich keinen Hörer kalt, etc.

ineffective forms, the Finale being particularly commonplace. One is left with the strongest reservations about the ethics of such patching-up which Strauss could surely never have condoned. To the many who will have hoped for an exciting new Strauss discovery *Des Esels Schatten* must remain a disappointment.

14

210 **Im Abendrot**	Eichendorff	6 May 1948	Vier letzte Lieder
211 **Frühling**		18 July 1948	für Sopran und
212 **Beim Schlafengehen**	Hesse	4 Aug. 1948	grosses Orchester
213 **September**		20 Sept. 1948	

However abortive Strauss's flirtations with this or that unsuitable text might have been, they had one miraculous side-effect in reviving his insatiable urge to write for the voice. And throughout his life from early childhood the Lied had been his one unfaltering stand-by save only for the gap caused by the GEMA quarrel.[18]

Yet in these last years his Lieder output had been sporadic indeed, with the Weinheber couple dating as far back as 1942. It was during the last months of 1946 that, having firmly put *Die Rache der Aphrodite* aside, Strauss's eye lit on a poem of Eichendorff whose mood fitted his own so exactly that it must have been irresistible.

Although Brahms, Wolf and especially Schumann had written many outstanding songs to Eichendorff poems, Strauss had only once before drawn on his work for inspiration and that was for his choral piece *Die Tageszeiten*;[19] even then the idea had not been his own.

A friend of Arnim and his group, Eichendorff was one of the contributors to the *Knaben Wunderhorn* volumes. He has been described as perhaps the greatest lyric poet of his age, especially with regard to the love poems *Frühling und Liebe* amongst which Strauss found *Im Abendrot*.

This is a deeply affecting poem conjuring up two old people who, having travelled through the joys and adversities of life, find themselves at the end of their wanderings and with tired eyes look to the sunset asking, as they prepare for their last sleep, 'Ist das etwa der Tod?' ('Is that perhaps death?')

It is written in the first person and Strauss touchingly took its

---

[18] See Chapter XXII, p. 357.
[19] This was discussed in Vol. II, p. 370, et seq.

message as a personal one for himself and Pauline. Changing the word 'Das' (that) to 'dies' (this) he illustrated his involvement by quoting a motif from *Tod und Verklärung*:

Ex. 58

[20] The lay-out of the accompaniment in this example is copied from the autograph Particell which has some interesting differences from the completed song as we know it.

So intense were the emotions aroused in him by the verses that he further decided on an accompaniment for large orchestra, the first time he had written for such forces in a new composition since the completion of *Capriccio* in 1941, and the song begins with a huge incandescent outburst of rich orchestral melody based on Ex. 58(y).

Very gradually the glow subsides into the pulsing background figure ⌐ x ⌐, over which the voice quietly enters while, taking their cue from the verse describing the flight of two larks high overhead, two trilling flutes (or, as they later become, piccolos) soar softly and delicately.

At length the closing lines approach and the music turns darker and more weary. Ex. 58 gives the full text of the song's kernel after which an ever gentler postlude leads by way of the melodic curve ⌐ y ⌐ to the velvety last cadences, the deepest atmosphere of absolute stillness only varied by the continued trillings of the larks. It is an end which leaves few dry eyes amongst listeners and performers alike.

There was no question but that this must reach the world as Strauss's *envoi*, and yet in such a case it could scarcely stand alone. During the aged composer's sojourn in Switzerland in 1948 an admirer had the happy idea of sending him a copy of the poetry of Hermann Hesse, with the hoped-for result that Strauss was stimulated to add some settings to *Im Abendrot* in order to make up a group.

His intention was to write a further four songs to texts by Hesse but in the end he completed only three. A few bars of a possible fourth were found on his desk after his death, and sketches for a choral work, *Besinnung* also to words by Hesse, lay abandoned as well—a fugal section in sixteen parts having, as Strauss told Dr Roth, become too complicated.

The philosophical author and poet Hermann Hesse, though actually born in Swabia, lived most of his life in his land of origin, Switzerland, where he died in 1962. His many beautiful poems range over half a century, from 1895 to 1946, the year in which he received the Nobel Prize for Literature. The three poems Strauss chose are all from different periods, the first *Frühling* belonging to a large collection written around the turn of the century when Hesse was still the traditional romantic. A simple ecstatic paean to the beauties of spring, it drew from the composer a flowing burst of melody set over a swaying undulating figure which pervades the Lied.

Mention of bird-song sets the flute trilling almost as if in recollection of the larks in Eichendorff's *Im Abendrot*, the score of which was only completed in May 1948, just before Strauss took up the Hesse poems. In its untrammelled lyricism the music reflects perfectly the joy and wonder of the poet, especially during the voice's soaring *vocalises* on single syllables, a particular feature of this song which carries all before it. At the same time the rich colour of both its harmonies and instrumentation is far nearer to the maturity of autumn.

Both the other Hesse poems, coming from later periods when the poet's life was overshadowed with suffering, express the weariness of spirit which struck so immediate a sympathetic response in the veteran composer. *Beim Schlafengehen* dates from the years of the first world war when Hesse, having witnessed the collapse of his wife's mind, himself passed through a grave emotional crisis. The verses tell of the soul's fatigue after the day and its desire for nothing more than to take wing in the magic circles of night; the analogy with the death-wish is clear enough and the beauty of Strauss's setting is indeed almost unearthly.

Arising out of the most profound depths a figure which is to become a central motif (see Ex. 59(x)) builds up in a series of imitations which soon usher in the voice. The settings of two of the three stanzas then follow in quick succession. The music of this portion of the song is now non-thematic and has, in fact, very much of a prefatory character even though it embodies the greater part of the poem. This is not to say, however, that it is insignificant and amongst the many striking ideas are the shimmering chords which ring out at the words 'die gestirnte Nacht' ('the starry night'). Introduced by little upward twisting phrases on the violins these gleaming blocks of sound are scored for celeste and a group of high wind with no less than four members of the flute family including two piccolos. This inspired piece of orchestration is a feature of the Lied and returns during the later sections even though the thematic background has entirely changed.

For with the end of the second verse the true material blossoms forth beginning with a long interlude for solo violin symbolizing the winged nocturnal journey of the soul which is to be described in the third verse when the vocal line is added to the floating cantilena.

Moreover, despite the sophistication of the composer's late style, the entry of the voice at the last descending phrase of the violin's solo with the words 'Und die Seele unbewacht . . .' calls to mind Strauss's earlier simpler use of this affecting device at 'Und Morgen wird die Sonne wieder scheinen . . .' in *Morgen!*, that evergreen favourite of Strauss's songs:

Ex. 59

The voice takes over the lovely curves of the violin's embroidery Ex. 59(y), after which the song is entirely built on the basic motif ⌐ x ⌐ whose characteristic rising sevenths soar over a top B before the cantilena sinks to rest with an augmented version of the same motif. The warm postlude is still concerned entirely with ⌐ x ⌐ apart from the shining chords, and it is with one of these that the music ends, the gloom of the opening bars left far behind.

Frühling and *Beim Schlafengehen* were finished in July and August respectively, upon which Strauss, on looking through his volume of Hesse for the next companion song, lighted most aptly on a poem actually entitled *September* in which summer 'slowly closes his weary eyes', just as Strauss himself was soon to do for the last time.

Here the spirit of autumn, so often and with reason applied to all these songs, finds its natural expression. Perhaps the most remarkable part of Strauss's achievement in this his counterpart to Schubert's *Schwanengesang* is the unity and unfaltering quality of the four songs, none of which is in any way less moving than the other three.

September is built on two musical ideas, the first—which opens the song—alternating a gentle undulation of chords with a wide melodic span:

Ex. 60

This is accompanied by a mass of intricate detail with the strings chirping, trilling and rustling in some thirteen parts. At the words 'Der Sommer schauert still seinem Ende entgegen' however, it opens out with a truly Straussian shifting cadence to the expansive second theme, one of its composer's most generous melodies although it never occurs twice the same, being a series of variants on the figure:

Ex. 61

Between the two themes contained in Ex. 60 and the endlessly fertile Ex. 61 a continuous web of melody unfolds adding richness upon richness, the orchestra taking advantage of the brief pauses in the vocal line to surge forward in glowing colours.

At length the phrases fall, Ex. 61 broadens into wider triplets, and as the violins curve over the figure Ex. 60(y) the voice reaches its ultimate cadence. But as in Strauss's last opera *Capriccio*, so in his last song, the horn has to have a final say. In quiet ruminative tones that best loved of instruments recapitulates one of the most beautiful melodic forms of Ex. 61, before subsiding under an assenting, immensely peaceful reminiscence of the undulations Ex. 60(x) with which the song began.

So, in tones of heart-breaking beauty, ends the life-work of a composer who for nearly half a century had clung to the pursuit of grateful sonorities, turning his back on the over-fast evolving contemporary tendencies of which he once had also formed a part.

This group of *Vier letzte Lieder* was never heard by Strauss himself, nor did he give a clear indication of the order in which they were to be presented, whereas there was never any doubt that they must be sung by a soprano. At the end only the memory of his Pauline's voice could be his companion on these farewell excursions through the music to which his whole existence had been dedicated.

The first performance was given on 22nd May 1950 by Kirsten Flagstad and the Philharmonia Orchestra under Furtwängler in the Royal Albert Hall, London, on which occasion they were sung not in chronological order, but with *Beim Schlafengehen* (No. 212) first and ending naturally with *Im Abendrot* (No. 210), *September* and *Frühling* taking the remaining places as second and third respectively.

But when during the same year they were published, the editor Dr Roth came wisely to the conclusion that a more satisfactory as well as more logical order was:

No. 211 Frühling
   213 September
   212 Beim Schlafengehen
   210 Im Abendrot

and in this form they have throughout the world become beloved above all Strauss's orchestral Lieder, and rank amongst his most admired works in any genre.

Nor is this out of sentimentality for their being Strauss's last pieces. In trying to understand the poignant feelings they arouse the word nostalgia comes to mind; but this is too superficial to cover music of the calibre of these songs, although their beauty undoubtedly contains a nostalgic element, as well as sadness. Yet the tiredness of great age in the presence of impending and welcome death is not really sad but something far deeper. It is the prerogative of great art that it arouses nameless emotions which can tear us apart. With his last utterances, as at intervals during his long life, Strauss showed himself such a genius of the highest rank.

EPILOGUE

ALTHOUGH he completed no more music Strauss lived for another year, a year which enabled him to return—as he so dearly longed to do—to his Garmisch villa, and to enjoy the tributes of the world on the occasion of his eighty-fifth birthday.

This happy rounding off to his life was made possible after a decision in his favour on the part of the Denazification Board at the urgent request of the Bavarian Secretary of State. Brief as it had been, Strauss's lip-service to the Presidency of the Reichsmusikkammer had automatically labelled him 'Class I—Guilty' and this rule-of-thumb categorization was not easily overridden, especially in view of testimony raised by people who resolutely held him to have been a genuine Hitler supporter. It is a fact that to this day Strauss's music is banned from the State of Israel on grounds which range from his superficial youthful anti-semitism when under the influence of the virulent Jew-hater Alexander Ritter to the clever photos taken by Nazis when the elderly Strauss sought to protect his interests and dependents by ingratiating himself with their leaders. He is often even accused of having 'sacked his Jewish librettist' whereas the exact opposite is nearer the truth—Zweig, in a sense, had sacked him.

However much Strauss's conduct could be ascribed to weakness or self-delusion, it at no time stemmed from malice. But for his enormous prestige he would himself have stood in danger from Nazi retaliation for many actions of obstinate defiance after his fall from grace in 1935, and he was not short of advocates at the tribunal even in the person of Nazi victims at home and foreign diplomats. Sad to say, there are those who still refuse to accept the findings of the Commission which in June

1948 after months of agonized indecision cleared Germany's Grand Old Man of Music of blame or participation in the misdeeds of the Third Reich.

Strauss was free to go home, and as soon as he and Pauline were well enough he did so. For in November 1948 his bladder infection had flared up and the following month he was obliged to undergo another operation in the Lausanne Hospital, from which again he recovered. Nor was Pauline free from health troubles. An irresistible tale is told of her being whisked off to hospital in the belief that her last hours were approaching and, as she was carried past her Richard, shaking her fist at him saying 'Now see how you'll get on without me'.

In May 1949, however, both were strong enough to travel and were soon once again installed in the Garmisch Landhaus surrounded by their devoted family.

Shortly after his arrival back home Strauss received a letter from Clemens Krauss. Krauss had been less fortunate in his treatment by the Denazification Tribunal and together with Furtwängler was still *persona non grata*. Unlike Strauss to whom the whole affair was so much water off a duck's back—never making the least effort to exculpate himself— Furtwängler was inconsolable. He had regarded himself as hardly less than a Crusader by remaining in the Third Reich to hold aloft the flag of German culture against the threat of debauchery by an evil régime. To be blamed and ostracized for being a collaborator was to him an intolerable injustice and he wrote letter after letter of protest to foreign ministers, press correspondents *et alia*, spinning his tale of woe to every friend and sympathizer.

Clemens Krauss was a more subtle character and made the best of his temporary exile from Germany (both conductors were cleared by 1950). He even managed by ingenious diplomacy to retain his position in Austria although his unquestionable opportunism was thought by many to have been far the more indictable of the two, despite the help he is reputed to have given to refugees from the Terror. Hence, when Strauss visited London in October 1947 Krauss was there with the Vienna State Opera and was able to greet him in person together with the great soprano Maria Cebotari.

It was from London that Clemens Krauss now wrote to Strauss congratulating him on his return to Garmisch, his restoration to health (this in itself a birthday present, as he put it) and on his anniversary.

With regard to the birthday wishes, he had the further idea, expounded at some length, of trying to tempt Strauss into turning the subject of Noah's Flood into an oratorio (thus anticipating Britten's and Stravinsky's handling of the subject by over a decade). As he wrote to Strauss:

> . . . Now that you are slowly approaching Noah's age the analogy lies near: you too have made an Ark with your music, in which we can save all the good spirits of our art from the flood of atonality. . . . So be it! Amen.

Krauss knew well enough Strauss would call out that his workshop was shut, but all the same . . .

The idea[1] was attractive and cleverly expounded with suggestions for an atonal deluge and a contrapuntal prayer of gratitude from all the animals near the end. But there was never the slightest chance that Strauss would take it up.

2

On 11th June Strauss celebrated his eighty-fifth birthday. In the Garmisch Casino there were speeches and presentations on behalf of the Bavarian Government and of the town itself which gave him the Honorary Freedom. He was created Doctor of Law by Munich University and a Strauss Foundation was formally established. In return Strauss made the gift to the Bavarian State Library of the score of *München* as has been told above (see p. 422).

The evening before, Strauss was unexpectedly prevailed upon to travel up to Munich where he attended the dress rehearsal of a new production of *Der Rosenkavalier*. To everyone's delight he expressed the wish to take the baton for two or three of the key passages in the opera and amidst enthusiastic demonstrations he took his old seat in the orchestra pit.

Cameras were hastily brought and he was filmed conducting the Waltz Finale to Act 2, a sequence which was subsequently made the centre-piece of a documentary film entitled *A Life for Music*. Shots were later taken of Strauss strolling round the garden of his villa and he furthermore agreed to sit at the piano and strum a few bars of *Daphne*. The film still exists and has been shown in many different countries.

---

[1] Clemens Krauss had cherished the plan since the days of *Capriccio* according to Walter Panofsky (*Richard Strauss Partitur eines Lebens*. R. Piper, Munich, 1965).

It was as if everyone wanted to make amends. The Bavarian authorities asked Strauss what he would best like to see performed during the Munich celebrations, and it is revealing that the work he chose from all his stage compositions was *Der Bürger als Edelmann*. The production accordingly took place as the climax to the festival a few days after the actual birthday and, amidst overwhelming crowds clamouring for a glimpse of him, was duly attended by Strauss. 'It is a long time', he said, 'since I have enjoyed any performance as much as this. It's a pity Hofmannsthal couldn't see it too.'

A month later, on 13th July, Strauss visited Munich for the last time, when he conducted for the Radio the *Krämerspiegel* melody in its setting as the moonlight interlude in *Capriccio*. This was the last music he ever conducted; shortly after, his health began ultimately to deteriorate. He had written no music since his return to Garmisch and he was to write no more; however, spurred by some newspaper reports, he jotted down some observations on music in general, including the retrospective view of the importance of *Feuersnot* outlined already in Vol. I, p. 233.

He had few visitors now but amongst the friends who were allowed to see him in bed was the producer Rudolf Hartmann. Already during the birthday celebrations Strauss had begun to suffer from bouts of giddiness and by the time of Hartmann's visit he had had a series of heart attacks which left him increasingly weak.

The meeting, which took place on 29th August, was at Strauss's request. Hartmann was greatly distressed by the deterioration in the great man's condition. Over a fortnight had passed since his most serious attack and he was now permanently bed-ridden. Hartmann wrote:

> . . . I enter the bedroom. In the room, which seems to be filled with light, the white bed stands with its head facing the doorway. Richard Strauss has turned his head a little, he reaches out his right hand to me and greets me: 'Good that you are here. Sit down beside me' . . . He replies only with a slight expressive gesture to my carefully groping question about his health. As he remains silent I want to say something comforting to him, but in the emotional tension of the moment I cannot find the right words—he gives me a long look, and I feel I must remain silent before the knowing expression of those bright, unclouded eyes. Then he says: 'Death has dealt me the first hard blow, has given me the

first sign'. Immediately after that he changes his tone however, and he asks about personal matters, showing his deep interest as always. His facial expression is scarcely altered, but one is not used to the deep pallor and tiredness of his features. His thoughts pass to matters which have always concerned him. He lies there calmly, propped up fairly high, and his hands glide over the blankets in brief, emphatic gestures. I hear the deep, rather hoarse voice speaking about his ever-recurring anxiety for the continuance of the European Theatre . . . 'So much for me to do still—but I believe that some of the things that I wanted and initiated have fallen on fruitful ground' . . . He is sad about the destruction of so many theatres . . . He mentions people he would like to see in particular positions, surveys the possibilities of the major opera organisations still functioning, and concludes, smiling: 'We would have divided the world quite well—our world' . . . After a while he goes on quietly, in a different tone of voice: 'Grüss mir die Welt' ('Greet the world for me'). He stops, asks 'Where does that come from?' I think of the similar words from *Walküre* and say so, but he shakes his head: 'No, no, it's not that, this occurs somewhere else'. . . He remains silent for a long time. I see that his face is showing signs of fatigue and that it is time to leave . . . I turn hesitantly away. He once more grasps my right hand in both of his and holds me back: 'Perhaps we'll see each other again; if not, you know everything.' A last vehement grip, his hands release me, and I quickly leave the room. On my way out I hear Richard Strauss give a suppressed sob, and then call loudly for his son.[2]

The quotation 'Grüss mir die Welt' is in fact Isolde's farewell to Brangäne from the first act of *Tristan*, the work he had always most enjoyed conducting, which, when in 1891 he had thought he might be going to die, he had wistfully hoped he could first conduct.

From this point the end came quickly. 'Funny thing, Alice', he remarked to his daughter-in-law, 'dying is just the way I composed it in *Tod und Verklärung*'. In the early afternoon of 8th September 1949 Richard Strauss died peacefully.

Four days later he was cremated in Munich to the sounds, at his express request, of the Trio from *Rosenkavalier*, and the urn was placed in the room of the Garmisch villa in which he had died, in sight of his garden and the beautiful mountains beyond.

[2] Rudolf Hartmann, 'Letzter Besuch bei Richard Strauss' in *Schweizerische Musikzeitung*. Jg 90. Vol. 8/9.

After he had gone Pauline's existence lost all purpose and within nine months she too followed the husband to whom, in her own unusual but dedicated way, she had entirely devoted her life. She died on 13th May 1950, nine days before the first performance of his last great legacy to the world, the ravishing *Vier letzte Lieder*.

3

When Strauss died his music suffered, as that of so many before and since, a temporary recession of favour in the critical world and even to some extent in public vogue. Yet the fact remains that this never affected his best works which continue to retain the unassailable position in the repertoire which they have enjoyed already for periods ranging up to well over three quarters of a century.

To say that Strauss outlived his own time is a truism: indeed he did so twice over and his place would have been simpler to determine had he conveniently joined Mahler or Debussy in death before the end of the first world war. He would then have seemed, like Mahler, one of the strongest links in a continuing tradition.

Death robbed Mahler of the logical outcome to the forward-looking tendencies shown in his maturest style. Strauss, by turning his back on changes with which he knew himself to be out of sympathy, came to take over the cloak of end-figure from Brahms, and the unusual circumstance that he continued to wear this cloak while still living on for some thirty years seemed at times to reduce it to a thread-bare condition.

Again and again critics pronounced Strauss's genius to have been mere precocity, never to return. Such a critic was, for example, Cecil Gray who, writing in 1924, after dismissing *Der Rosenkavalier* in bitterly scathing terms went on:

> It is unnecessary to devote much space to the consideration of Strauss's subsequent works. It is sufficient to say that they bear witness to the gradual degeneration and final extinction of his creative powers . . . From being a man of possibly unequal genius he has become a man of second-rate talent . . . The tragedy lies precisely in the fact that he might have been a very great artist. But as it is, one can only speculate as to which works, if any, stand a chance of surviving him . . . their manifest imperfections must inevitably tell against them

in the long run, and posterity will in all probability solve
the problem by performing none of them.[3]

Events have already amply shown how wrong this sweeping verdict
was, but with his usual sharpness of perception Gray caught the paradox
in Strauss's case even if he drew too hasty a conclusion.

Ten years later, in 1934, Eric Blom came nearer to the answer when
he wrote:

> . . . In a way, one has not nearly so much the feeling of the
> end of a career on his seventieth birthday as one had on his
> fiftieth . . . *The Rose Cavalier* with *Ariadne* as a sort of
> pleasant by-product, was Strauss's last great work. For the
> last three decades he has been, it must be said, in a decline,
> but a decline borne as bravely as the heroine in that most
> heart-searching opera bears the bitterness of ageing in body
> without losing the relish of life. But with him that relish
> was not quite great enough to induce him to strike out in
> new directions or to share the fresh adventures of those
> younger than himself . . . One would have liked to love
> those later works of his which at the best one could only
> respect. But there is one thing that stands out as remarkable.
> How was he able to stay the course so long without giving
> us anything really new? The answer is that he had an im-
> mense [musical] capital to live on for nearly a quarter of a
> century, a capital accumulated by sheer creative genius and
> yielding interest enough to last him a long time.[4]

For Strauss really was a very great artist, however much genius may
have deserted him over certain periods of his life; and his finest works
have shown themselves to contain precisely the durability only possessed
by those of the topmost rank. He actually lived to enjoy the rare
experience of seeing them become as much part of the standard repertoire as the Beethoven symphonies.

Musical fashions are notoriously unreliable, but the switchback
course of Strauss's position in the world of music remains perplexing.
It is clear that his was a composite, a double-sided character. Hence the
fact that this man who led so unromantic an existence and who presented
a disconcertingly uninterested façade to the world at large should have
come to write such emotional and extrovert music on the widest range
of the most adventurous themes. Literature from Cervantes and

[3] Cecil Gray, *A Survey of Contemporary Music*. O.U.P., London, 1924.
[4] Eric Blom, *A Musical Postbag*. Dent, London, 1941.

Shakespeare to Nietzsche, dramatic subjects from lurid Greek mythology to Molière, scenes of sun-baked Italy or the snow-covered Alps, all had been grist to his mill as he sat quietly day after day at his desk systematically filling the pages of score-paper with his thin immaculate manuscript.

Nevertheless his personality can scarcely be said to have been complex. In some ways indeed, it was disarmingly direct—even naïve—containing something of that peculiarly Bavarian jocular nature which the Germans term *Hanswurst*. This gave to one side of his creative work a lightness, a satirical quality which pulled it right out of that rut of heavy post-romantic music-making into which Strauss was born. In his early manhood and once again briefly at the outset of middle-age he had deliberately gone further, turning his genius towards a series of exotic, even erotic, subjects. In exploiting the love of the bizarre, of sharply-delineated caricature, he made his name and, many still maintain, his strongest contribution.

But there was the other side to his nature which, always present to a greater or lesser degree, was gradually to dominate his activities altogether. The smooth course of his life from a happy and successful childhood to a happy and successful adolescence and thence to the hardly less happy and successful career of his maturity, seems to have had few ripples of suffering or of complicated emotional situations.

To this may be attributed his *gemütlich*, easy-going nature, his basic love of comfort—mental as well as physical—his fundamental indifference to the world, its affairs and its inhabitants. Yet this very equanimity found valuable expression in a lyricism and warm harmonic colouring which served him faithfully all his life, even if it also sometimes resulted in too great a placidness in his work.

Bearing in mind his *Weltanschauung*, it becomes hardly surprising that he made no strong protest at anything that took place politically, whether he recognized the power in control as benevolent or otherwise. If he wrote banal military marches before the first world war at the behest of the Kaiser for whom he had no especial respect, so during the Hitler regime he was equally prepared to turn out some hack-work as a kind of insurance policy against interference.

Nor did he cut a very admirable figure during his brief period of responsibility in control of the Vienna Opera when he dictated a policy in which self-interest played a regrettable part.

Yet it would be ingenuous to see in this aspect of Strauss the reason for his periodic lapses from musical greatness. The course of history, which imposed upon him such extreme tests of character, does not seem to show in the case of other artists or musicians that their worldly conduct need have direct bearing upon the depth or originality of their output.

One may rather wonder in some later works what became of his sense of humour, his love of the grotesque, of that gaiety of spirit which at the times of inspiration so often fought successfully against the threat of Teutonic heaviness: or what at times became of that most valuable quality of all—the insight into the human heart and the power to express in music some of its most profound, most touching emotions. But to be convinced that Strauss did possess that quality one has only to recall the finale of *Don Quixote*, the great Trio from *Der Rosenkavalier* or the *Vier letzte Lieder*.

It is possible that Strauss's decision in 1924 to withdraw from regular and active participation in public musical life was, as Cecil Gray suggested, to some extent bound up with the increasing difficulty he experienced at summoning his former extraordinarily spontaneous freshness of musical invention. The world to which he really belonged had passed with the war. At sixty he was no longer in the foreground of musical style. He was wholly out of step with the artistic disillusionment of the twenties, with Hindemith, Stravinsky, Les Six, most of all with the mature Schönberg and the atonalists; he had no point of contact with such musicians. It is perhaps a little sad to think how dismayed the adventurous young composer of the *Burleske* of 1885, and of the deliberately provocative *Aus Italien* two years later, would have been had anyone suggested to him that he would one day be content to usurp Brahms's reactionary position as the Last of the Classics.

He remained, almost mummified as it were, in the pre-1914 musical world in which he knew himself at home, emerging from time to time to appear as uncrowned king at Strauss performances or festivals, whether to preside or to conduct.

Even the fast changing world of the 1930's made little impact upon him, or he on it. When he conducted—and his meticulous professionalism with the baton could arouse the most ardent devotion as Leo Wurmser has shown—everything would usually be pre-rehearsed for him, and all that was required was his presence on the podium, with stick or eyebrows moving a bare millimetre up and down. Meantime singers and players alike would naturally give of their utmost to the

Grand Old Man of German music who was already becoming a legend, a figure from the past, the last great Master of a bygone age.

Such occasions could scarcely be expected to provide any fresh outlook, any new creative stimulus to Strauss, sitting in the next train home to resume as soon as possible his too-long deferred game of Skat. Yet in between the rounds of cards he went on turning out of the same well-tried mould opera after opera,[5] until this was rendered purposeless by the cataclysm which engulfed Germany.

4

Strauss often gave the impression of being conceited; certainly he knew his worth, and in his behaviour or dealings with people he took their deference for granted even while despising it within himself. In Garmisch, where Pauline the General's daughter had sought to raise him above the bourgeois world of the professional musician by setting him up in style, he occupied a position not far removed from a country squire, revered, but to some extent feared also. For despite his geniality and disarmingly easy manner among friends, acquaintances were all too prone to see only his gruff side. At the same time he cherished no fond illusions about his place amongst the great, as we know from the remarks he let slip whether to Hofmannsthal, Zweig, or the Philharmonia Orchestra.

In one respect, however, he allowed himself justified credit in the midst of his amazingly clear-sighted self-assessment. His craftsmanship, built on the firm classical foundation of his youth, was always superb. Leaving aside the psychological content of works like *Don Juan, Till Eulenspiegel, Don Quixote,* or *Der Rosenkavalier* the detail of musical style and instrumental texture on every page is a joy in itself. This absolute mastery of technique had, of course, its own special dangers. He could scarcely look at a page of score without new counterpoints suggesting themselves instantly to him, a 'verdammte Begabung', as he described it, a damned gift which he was well aware prompted him too often to overfill his scores.

He was also a master of the cantilena. Even when he felt himself in

[5] A highly entertaining and well-informed parody of this aspect of Strauss's music-making was cast in the form of a science fiction short story. Entitled 'A Work of Art', the story appears in a collection *Galactic Cluster* by James Blish, Faber, London, 1960.

later life unable to invent longer melodies, he retained the art of spinning those soaring soprano lines. For this he had in part to thank his
wife, herself once a singer of distinction with just that warm quality
which never failed to conjure up in him ecstatic melodizings such as
abound in *Daphne*.

5

It is possible that the strain of softness in his make-up which prevented
him from maintaining an even quality over his whole *œuvre* also under-
mined the level of consistency in his largest conceptions. No doubt, one
can also discern in some of the acknowledged masterworks a lack of
substance, a deficiency of taste too at times, which became increasingly
marked in the periods when his inspiration was less strong. The very
lightness of style and character which had lifted him as a young man
head and shoulders above his contemporaries in Germany had to be
paid for later. His descent into C major banalities when he tried too
hard to portray the sublime, and his resort to the Viennese Waltz as the
symbol of the Dance, applicable equally to the Nietzschean Superman or
an exotic oriental princess, are only instances of a symptomatic un-
reliability in absorbing the deepest essence of philosophy and reflecting
it in his own work in the manner of his beloved Wagner.

But if *Tod und Verklärung*, *Heldenleben*, *Salome* and *Elektra* (to pick at
random) are to this extent imperfect masterpieces, masterpieces they
undoubtedly are: and so too Strauss himself was, if periodically, a
genius. The fact that his stature as an artist fluctuated, however widely,
cannot detract from those of his achievements which may fairly be
classed amongst the finest creations of our western civilization.

APPENDIX A

Youthful works catalogued by Strauss with Opus Numbers

op.	1	See op. 5	
	2 no. 5	Winterreise (Uhland)	(1871)
	3	Ouvertüre zum Singspiel, *Hochlands Treue* (short score only)	(1872–3)
	4	?	
	5 no. 1	Weihnachtslied (later changed to op. 1)	(1870)
	6	Panzenburg-Polka (pf.)	(1872)
	7 no. 1	Der müde Wanderer (Fallersleben)	(1873)
	2	Husarenlied (Fallersleben)	(1873)
	8	See op. 15 no. 2	
	9	Waldkonzert (Vogel) (See also op. 16)	(1871)
	10	Sonata no. 1 in E (pf.)	(1877)
	11	?	
	12 no. 1	Spielmann und Zither (Körner) (orig. op. 17)	(1878)
	2	Wiegenlied (Fallersleben)	(1878)
	12 (also)	Arie der Almaide (voice and orch.) (unfinished)	(1877)
	12 (also)	Kyrie, Sanctus and Agnus Dei (unacc. chorus)	(1877)
	13	Serenade in G for orchestra	(1877)
	14	Scherzo in B Minor (pf.)	(?1879)
	14 no. 1	Der Fischer (Goethe)	(1877)
	2	Die Drossel (Uhland)	(1877)
	3	Lass ruhn die Toten (Chamisso)	(1877)
	4	Lust und Qual (Goethe)	(1877)
	15	Trio no. 1 in A	(1877)
	15 no. 2	Der Spielmann und sein Kind (Fallersleben) (sop. and orch.) (later op. 8)	(1878)
	3	Alphorn (Kerner) (voice with horn and pf.)	(1878)
	16	Overture in E (orch.) (later changed to op. 9)	(1878)
	17	Introduction, Theme and Variations (horn and pf.)	(1878)
	17 no. 2	Overture in A Minor (orch.)	(1879)
	18 no. 1	Nebel (Lenau)	(1878)
	2	Soldatenlied (Fallersleben)	(1878)
	3	'Ein Röslein zog ich mir im Garten' (Fallersleben)	(1878)
	18 (also)	'Auf aus der Ruh' aus *Lila* (Goethe) (tenor solo and chorus)	(1878)
	19	See op. 25	
	20	Trio no. 2 in D	(1878)
	21	7 Lieder (4-part unacc. chorus)	(1880)
	22	Sonata no. 2 in C Minor (pf.)	(1879)
	23 no. 5	'O schneller, mein Ross' (Geibel)	(1879)
	24	5 kleine Klavierstücke (no. 5 also orchestrated)	(1879)

op. 25   Waldesgesang (Geibel) (orig. op. 19 and also later op. 23 no. 4)   (1879)
    25 (also) Introduction, Theme and Variations (flute and pf.)   (1879)
    26 no. 1 Das rote Laub (Geibel)   (1879)
           2 Frühlingsanfang (Geibel)   (1879)
    27   Romanze in E flat (clarinet and orchestra)   (1879)
    28   ?
    29   ?
    30 no. 1 Die drei Lieder (Uhland)   (1879)
           2 'In Vaters Garten heimlich steht ein Blümlein' (Heine)   (1879)
           3 Die erwachte Rose (Sallet)   (1880)
           4 Der Morgen (Sallet)   (1880)

APPENDIX B

Works published with Definitive Opus Numbers

op.			
1	Festmarsch	1876	Breitkopf (1881)
2	String Quartet in A	1879–80	Jos. Aibl
3	5 Klavierstücke	1881	Jos. Aibl
4	Suite in B Flat for 13 wind instr.	1883–4	Leuckart (1911)
5	Sonata in B Minor (pf.)	1880–1	Jos. Aibl
6	Cello Sonata in F	1882–3	Jos. Aibl
7	Serenade in E Flat for 13 wind instr.	1882	Jos. Aibl
8	Violin Concerto in D Minor	1881–2	Jos. Aibl
9	Stimmungsbilder (pf.)	1882	Jos. Aibl
10	8 Lieder aus 'Letzte Blätter' (Gilm)	1882–3	Jos. Aibl
11	Horn Concerto no. 1 in E Flat	1882–3	Jos. Aibl
12	Symphony in F Minor	1883–4	Jos. Aibl
13	Piano Quartet in C Minor	1884–5	Jos. Aibl
14	'Wanderers Sturmlied' (chor. and orch.)	1884	Jos. Aibl
15	5 Lieder	1884–6	Rahter
16	*Aus Italien*	1886	Jos. Aibl
17	6 Lieder von Schack	1887	Rahter
18	Violin Sonata in E Flat	1887–8	Jos. Aibl
19	6 Lieder aus 'Lotosblätter' (Schack)	1887–8	Jos. Aibl
20	*Don Juan*	1887–8	Jos. Aibl
21	5 Lieder 'Schlichte Weisen' (Dahn)	1888	Jos. Aibl
22	4 Lieder 'Mädchenblumen' (Dahn)	1888	Fürstner
23	*Macbeth*	1887–90	Jos. Aibl
24	*Tod und Verklärung*	1888–9	Jos. Aibl
25	*Guntram*	1887–93	Jos. Aibl
	(revised version)	1940	Fürstner
26	2 Lieder von Lenau	1891	Jos. Aibl
27	4 Lieder	1894	Jos. Aibl
28	*Till Eulenspiegel*	1894–5	Jos. Aibl
29	3 Lieder von Bierbaum	1895	Jos. Aibl
30	*Also sprach Zarathustra*	1894–5	Jos. Aibl
31	4 Lieder	1895–6	Fürstner
32	5 Lieder	1896	Jos. Aibl
33	4 Gesänge (voice and orch.)	1896–7	Bote & Bock
34	2 Gesänge (unacc. chor.)	1897	Jos. Aibl
35	*Don Quixote*	1897	Jos. Aibl
36	4 Lieder	1897–8	Jos. Aibl
37	6 Lieder	1896–8	Jos. Aibl

op. 38	*Enoch Arden* (melodrama for voice and pf.)	1897	Forberg
39	5 Lieder	1898	Forberg
40	*Ein Heldenleben*	1897–8	Leuckart
41	5 Lieder	1899	Leuckart
42	2 Männerchöre (from Herder's 'Stimmen der Völker')	1899	Leuckart
43	3 Lieder	1899	Challier
44	2 grössere Gesänge (bass and orch.)	1899	Forberg
45	3 Männerchöre (from Herder's 'Stimmen der Völker')	1899	Fürstner
46	5 Lieder von Rückert	1899–1900	Fürstner
47	5 Lieder von Uhland	1900	Fürstner
48	5 Lieder	1900	Fürstner
49	8 Lieder	1900–1	Fürstner
50	*Feuersnot*	1900–1	Fürstner
51	2 Gesänge (bass and orch.)	1902–6	Fürstner
52	'Taillefer' (Uhland) (chor. and orch.)	1902–3	Fürstner
53	*Symphonia Domestica*	1902–3	Bote & Bock
54	*Salome*	1903–5	Fürstner
55	'Bardengesang' (Klopstock) (male chor. and orch.)	1905	Fürstner
56	6 Lieder	1903–6	Bote & Bock
57	2 Military Marches (orch.)	1905	Peters
58	*Elektra*	1906–8	Fürstner
59	*Der Rosenkavalier*	1909–10	Fürstner
60	*Ariadne auf Naxos* ⎫		Fürstner
	Der Bürger als Edelmann ⎬ 1911–17		Fürstner
	Der Bürger als Edelmann Orchestersuite ⎭		Leuckart
61	Festliches Praeludium	1913	Fürstner
62	Deutsche Motette (unacc. chor.)	1913	Fürstner
63	*Josephslegende*	1912–4	Fürstner
64	*Eine Alpensinfonie*	1911–5	Leuckart
65	*Die Frau ohne Schatten*	1914–8	Fürstner
66	Krämerspiegel (12 Lieder von Kerr)	1918	Cassirer
67	6 Lieder	1918	Bote & Bock
68	6 Lieder von Brentano	1918	Fürstner
69	5 kleine Lieder	1918	Fürstner
70	*Schlagobers*	1920–1	Fürstner
71	3 Hymnen von Hölderlin (sop. and orch.)	1921	Fürstner
72	*Intermezzo*	1922–3	Fürstner
73	Parergon zur Sinfonia Domestica (pf. L.H. and orch.)	1924–5	Boosey & Hawkes (1964)
74	Panathenäenzug (pf. L.H. and orch.)	1926–7	Boosey & Hawkes (1953)
75	*Die Aegyptische Helena*	1924–7	Fürstner
76	*Die Tageszeiten* (male chor. and orch.)	1928	Leuckart
77	5 Gesänge des Orients (Bethge)	1928	Leuckart
78	*Austria* (male chor. and orch.)	1929	Bote & Bock
79	*Arabella*	1929–32	Fürstner
80	*Die Schweigsame Frau*	1932–5	Fürstner
81	*Friedenstag*	1935–6	Oertel

op. 82 *Daphne*   1936–7   Oertel
    83 *Die Liebe der Danae*   1938–40   Oertel
    84 Japanisches Festmusik   1940   Oertel
    85 *Capriccio*   1940–1   Oertel
    86 Divertimento nach Couperin   1940–1   Oertel

Two collections of Lieder have also been published posthumously under the op. nos. 87 and 88.

APPENDIX C

Works published without Opus Numbers

18 Jugendlieder	1870–9	Boosey & Hawkes (1964)
6 Jugendlieder	1871–80	Boosey & Hawkes (1968)
Chorus from *Elektra* (Sophocles) (with small orch.)	1880	Breitkopf & Härtel in 'Hilfsbuch für den Unterricht auf höheren Schulen' (1902)
3 Jugendlieder	1880–3	Peters (1958)
Fugue (from 14 Improvisations and Fugue) (pf.)	1885	Bruckmann in 'Das Klavier und seine Meister' (1889)
Burleske (pf. and orch.)	1885	Steingräber (1894)
'Schwäbische Erbschaft' (Loewe) (male chor. unacc.)	1885	Leuckart (1950)
Bühnenmusik zu 'Romeo und Julia'	1887	Boosey & Hawkes (1960)
Iphigenie auf Tauris (Gluck) 'arranged for the German stage'	1889	Fürstner
Festmusik—6th Tableau retitled *Kampf und Sieg* (orch.)	1892	Heinrichshofen (1930)
'Wir beide wollen springen' (Bierbaum)	1896	Boosey & Hawkes (1964)
Das Schloss am Meere (Uhland) (melodrama for voice and pf.)	1899	Fürstner (1911)
Weihnachtsgefühl (Greif)	1899	Boosey & Hawkes (1964)
2 Lieder aus Calderons 'Der Richter von Zalamea'	1904	Boosey & Hawkes (1954)
Instrumentationslehre (Berlioz) (translated and revised, 2 vols.)	1905	Peters
De Brandenburgsche Mars—Präsentiermarsch 2 Parade-Märsche Königsmarsch	1905–6	Fürstner
6 Volksliedbearbeitungen (male chor. unacc.)	1906	Peters
Feierlicher Einzug der Ritter des Johanniter-Ordens	1909	Lienau
Cantate (Hofmannsthal) (male chor. unacc.)	1914	Junker & Dünnhaupt
Sinnspruch (Goethe)	1919	Mosse
'Hans Adam war ein Erdenkloss' (Goethe)	1922	Oertel (1951)
Tanzsuite aus Klavierstücken von François Couperin (small orch.)	1922–3	Fürstner
Die Ruinen von Athen (Beethoven) (new version including mvts. from Beethoven's *Prometheus* by Strauss and Hofmannsthal)	1924	Fürstner
2 Fanfaren	1924	Boosey & Hawkes (1960)
'Durch allen Schall und Klang' (Goethe)	1925	Boosey & Hawkes (1959)

Militärmarsch in F (written for the *Rosenkavalier* film)	1925	Fürstner
Idomeneo (Mozart) (new version by Strauss and Wallerstein with many entirely new mvts.)	1930	Heinrichshofen
'Wie etwas sei leicht' (Goethe)	1930	Boosey & Hawkes (1968)
Das Bächlein (Goethe?)	1933	Universal (1951)
Olympische Hymne (chorus and orch.)	1934	Fürstner
Die Göttin im Putzzimmer (Rückert) (unacc. chor.)	1935	Boosey & Hawkes (1958)
3 Lieder von Rückert	1929–35	Universal (1964)
'Zugemessne Rhythmen' (Goethe)	1935	Boosey & Hawkes (1954)
3 Männerchöre von Rückert	1935	Boosey & Hawkes (1958)
2 Lieder von Weinheber	1942	Universal (1964)
Xenion (Goethe)	1942	Boosey & Hawkes (1964)
Horn Concerto no. 2 in E Flat	1942	Boosey & Hawkes (1950)
Sonatina no. 1 in F for wind instruments—'Aus der Werkstatt eines Invaliden'	1943	Boosey & Hawkes (1964)
An den Baum Daphne—Epilog zu *Daphne* (Gregor) (unacc. chor.)	1943	Boosey & Hawkes (1958)
München—Ein Gedächtniswalzer II Fassung (1st version 1939 unpublished)	1945	Boosey & Hawkes (1951)
Metamorphosen—Study for 23 solo strings	1944–5	Boosey & Hawkes (1946)
Sonatina no. 2 in E Flat for wind instruments—'Fröhliche Werkstatt'	1944–5	Boosey & Hawkes (1952)
Oboe Concerto	1945	Boosey & Hawkes (1948)
Duet-Concertino for Clarinet and Bassoon	1947	Boosey & Hawkes (1949)
Des Esels Schatten (completed Haussner)	1947–8	Boosey & Hawkes (1967)
4 letzte Lieder (voice and orch.)	1948	Boosey & Hawkes (1950)

APPENDIX D

Compositions arranged according to date of completion

DATE	TITLE	OPUS	DEDICATION	FIRST PERF.
1870	Weihnachtslied (Schubart)		Onkel Georg und Tante Johanna (Pschorr)	
	Schneider-Polka (pf.)		Peter Müller	
1871	Einkehr (Uhland)		Tante Johanna	
	Winterreise (Uhland)		Tante Johanna	
	Waldkonzert (Vogel)		Tante Auguste Schreiber	
	Der weisse Hirsch (Uhland)			
	Des Alpenhirten Abschied (Schiller)			(lost)
	Der Böhmische Musikant (Pletzsch)			
	Herz, mein Herz (Geibel)			
	Moderato in C (pf.)			
1872	Panzenburg-Polka (pf.)		August Pschorr	
	(Langsamer Satz) in G Minor (pf.)			
1873	2 Etuden für Horn			
	Der müde Wanderer (Fallersleben)		Tante Johanna	
	Husarenlied (Fallersleben)		Tante Johanna	
	2 Sonatinas (pf.)			(lost)
	Overture 'Hochlands Treue' (orch.)			
	5 kleine Stücke (pf.)			
1874	3 kleine Sonaten (pf.)			
	(Klavierstück) in C Minor (pf.)			
	Fantasie in C (pf.)		Papa	
1875	2 kleine Stücke (pf.)			
	2 4-part pieces in B Flat			
	Concertante for pf. 2 vls. and vc.		'Seinen Vettern Pschorr'	(lost)
1876	2 Lieder von Eichendorff (unacc. chor.)			
	2 4-part pieces (pf.)			
	4 Szenen zu einem Singspiel (voices and pf.)			
	Festmarsch (orch.)	op. 1	Onkel Georg Pschorr	26/3/81 'Wilde Gungl' Munich cond. Franz Strauss

DATE	TITLE	OPUS	DEDICATION	FIRST PERF.
	Concert Overture in B Minor (orch.)		Papa	
1877	Kyrie, Sanctus and Agnus Dei (unacc. chor.)		Papa	
	Serenade in G (orch.)		Friedrich Meyer	
	Der Fischer (Goethe)		Tante Johanna	
	Die Drossel (Uhland)		Tante Johanna	
	Lass ruhn die Toten (Chamisso)		Tante Johanna	
	Lust und Qual (Goethe)		Tante Johanna	
	Pf. Trio no. 1 in A		Anton Ritter von Knözinger	
	Sonata no. 1 in E (pf.)		Ludwig Thuille	
	Studies in Counterpoint			
1878	Spielmann und Zither (Körner)		Tante Johanna	
	Wiegenlied (Fallersleben)		Tante Johanna	
	Abend- und Morgenrot (Fallersleben)		Tante Johanna	
	Im Walde (Geibel)		Caroline v. Mangstl	
	Arie der Almaide 'Auf aus der Ruh' } aus *Lila* (Goethe) (for voices and orch.)			
	Der Spielmann und sein Kind (Fallersleben) (for sop. and orch.)		Caroline v. Mangstl	
	Nebel (Lenau)		Tante Johanna	
	Soldatenlied (Fallersleben)		August Pschorr	
	'Ein Röslein zog ich mir im Garten' (Fallersleben)		Tante Johanna	
	Thema con 12 Variazioni (pf.)		Pauline Nagiller	
	Overture in E (orch.)			
	Alphorn (Kerner) (for voice, horn and pf.)		Papa	
	Introduction, theme and variations (horn and pf.)		Papa	
	Pf. Trio no. 2 in D		Onkel Georg	
	Studies in Counterpoint (9 Fugues)			
1879	Für Musik (Geibel)		Sophie Diez	(lost)
	Waldesgesang (Geibel)		C. Meysenheym	16/3/81 Munich Museumsaal C. Meysenheym
	'O schneller, mein Ross' (Geibel)		C. Meysenheym	16/3/81 Munich Museumsaal C. Meysenheym (lost)
	'Die Lilien glühn in Düften' (Geibel)		C. Meysenheym	16/3/81 Munich Museumsaal C. Meysenheym (lost)

DATE	TITLE	OPUS	DEDICATION	FIRST PERF.
	Introduction, theme and variations (flute and pf.)			
	Gavotte 'aus alter Zeit' (pf.)			
	Andante in C Minor (pf.)			
	5 kleine Klavierstücke (pf.; no. 5 also orchestrated)			No. 5: 29/5/80 Munich 'Wilde Gungl' cond. Franz Strauss
	Das rote Laub (Geibel)		Tante Johanna	(lost)
	Frühlingsanfang (Geibel)		Tante Johanna	(lost)
	Sonata no. 2 in C Minor (pf.)		Karl Hörburger	
	Romanze (clar. and orch.)			
	Overture in A Minor (orch.)		Friedrich Meyer	
	Hochzeitsmusik (pf. and toy instr.)			(lost)
	Scherzo in B Minor (pf.)			
	Die drei Lieder (Uhland)		Tante Johanna	
	'In Vaters Garten heimlich steht ein Blümlein' (Heine)		Tante Johanna	
	Studies in Counterpoint (3 Fugues)			
1880	Der Morgen (Sallet)		Tante Johanna	(lost)
	Die erwachte Rose (Sallet)		Tante Johanna	30/11/58 New York Carnegie Hall Elisabeth Schwarzkopf
	7 Lieder (4 part unacc. chorus)		Papa	
	2 kleine Stücke (pf.)		Robert Pschorr	
	Ständchen for pf. quartet			(lost)
	Symphony in D Minor	(Orig. op. 4)		30/3/81 Munich Akademie Hoforch. cond. Levi
	String Quartet in A	op. 2	Benno Walter Quartet	14/3/81 Munich Museumsaal Walter Quartet
	Scherzando in G (pf.)			
	Fugue on 4 themes (pf.)	Papa		
	'Immer leiser wird mein Schlummer' (Lingg)		Tante Johanna	(lost)
	Begegnung (Gruppe)			30/11/58 New York Carnegie Hall Elisabeth Schwarzkopf
	'Mutter, O sing mich zur Ruh' (Hemans)		Tante Johanna	lost)
	'John Anderson mein Lieb' (Burns)		Tante Johanna	
1881	Chorus from Elektra (Sophocles) (male chor. and orch.)			

DATE	TITLE	OPUS	DEDICATION	FIRST PERF.
	Festchor (chor. and pf.)			(lost)
	5 Klavierstücke (pf.)	op. 3		
	Sonata in B Minor (pf.)	op. 5	Joseph Gierl	
	Geheiligte Stätte (Fischer)			(lost)
1882	Albumblatt (pf.)		Bertha Schüssel	(lost)
	Violin Concerto in D Minor	op. 8	Benno Walter	5/12/82 Vienna Bösendorfersaal Walter and Strauss (pf.)
	Serenade for wind instruments in E Flat	op. 7	Friedrich Meyer	27/11/82 Dresden Tonkünstler-verein cond. Wüllner
	Ballade (Becker)		Tante Johanna	(lost)
	Waldesgang (Stieler)		Tante Johanna	(lost)
1883	Cello Sonata in F	op. 6	Hans Wihan	8/12/83 Nuremberg Wihan and von Königsthal
	Overture in C Minor	(Orig. op. 10)	Hermann Levi	28/11/83 Munich Akademie Hoforch. cond. Levi
	8 Lieder aus 'Letzte Blätter' (Gilm)	op. 10	Heinrich Vogl	
	Horn Concerto no. 1 in E Flat	op. 11	Oscar Franz	4/3/85 (with orch.) Meiningen Leinhos and Hofkapelle cond. Bülow
	Romanze (cello and orch.)	(Orig. op. 13)		
	Rote Rosen (Stieler)		Lotti Speyer	30/11/58 New York Carnegie Hall Elisabeth Schwarzkopf
	Largo in A Minor (pf.)			
	Stiller Waldespfad (pf.)			
	Lied ohne Worte (orch.)			
	Variations for string quartet on a theme of Cesare Negri (1604)		August Pschorr	(lost)
1884	Stimmungsbilder (pf.)	op. 9		
	Symphony in F Minor	op. 12		13/12/84 New York Phil. Soc. cond. Thomas

DATE	TITLE	OPUS	DEDICATION	FIRST PERF.
	Suite in B Flat for 13 wind instruments	op. 4 (orig. op. 15)		18/11/84 Munich Odeon-saal. Meiningen Hofmusiker cond. Strauss
	Piano Quartet in C Minor	op. 13	Georg II Herzog v. Sachsen-Meiningen	8/12/85 Weimar Halir Quartet and Strauss (pf.)
	Improvisations and Fugue in A Minor (pf.)		Hans v. Bülow	10/6/85 Frankfurt a.M. Strauss (Improvisations lost)
	Der Zweikampf—Polonaise (Flute, Bassoon and orch.)			
	'Mein Geist ist trüb' aus den *Hebräischen Melodien* (Byron)		Tante Johanna	(lost)
	'Der Dorn ist Zeichen der Verneinung' aus *Mirza Schaffy* (Bodenstedt)		Tante Johanna	(lost)
	Festmarsch for pf. quartet			(lost)
	Schwäbische Erbschaft (Loewe) (male chor. unacc.)			7/10/50 Mönchen-Gladbach
	Wanderers Sturmlied (Goethe) (chor. and orch.)	op. 14	Franz Wüllner	8/3/87 Cologne Gürzenichsaal cond. Strauss
	Festmarsch in D (orch.)			8/1/85 Munich 'Wilde Gungl' cond. Franz Strauss
1885	Cadenzas to Mozart C Minor Piano Concerto K.491			20/10/85 Meiningen Hoftheater Strauss (pf.) cond. Bülow
1886	Bardengesang aus der *Hermanns-Schlacht* (Kleist) (male chor. and orch.)			Feb. 1886 Meiningen Hoftheater (lost)
	Burleske (pf. and orch.)		Eugen d'Albert	21/6/90 Eisenach Stadttheater d'Albert (pf.) cond. Strauss
	Aus Italien	op. 16	Hans von Bülow	2/3/87 Munich Odeonsaal Hofkapelle cond. Strauss
	5 Lieder	op. 15	Johanna Pschorr and Victoria Blank	

DATE	TITLE	OPUS	DEDICATION	FIRST PERF.
1887	6 Lieder von Schack	op. 17		
	Stage incidental music to *Romeo and Juliet*			23/10/87 Munich National-theater
	Violin Sonata in E Flat	op. 18	Robert Pschorr	3/10/88 Robert Heck-mann and Strauss
1888	6 Lieder aus 'Lotosblätter' (Schack)	op. 19	Emilie Herzog	
	'Schlichte Weisen'—5 Lieder von Dahn	op. 21	'Meiner lieben Schwester'	
	'Mädchenblumen'—4 Lieder von Dahn	op. 22	Hans Giessen	
	Don Juan	op. 20	Ludwig Thuille	11/11/89 Weimar Hofkapelle cond. Strauss
1889	Festmarsch in C (orch.)		'Wilde Gungl' for 25th Jubilee	1/2/89 Munich 'Wilde Gungl' cond. Franz Strauss
	Tod und Verklärung	op. 24	Friedrich Rösch	21/6/90 Eisenach Stadttheater cond. Strauss
	Scherzquartett 'Utan svafvel och Fosfer' (male chor. unacc.)			14/12/89 Weimar Künstlerverein
1890	*Iphigenie auf Tauris* (Gluck) (arranged with additional music)			(?)1890 Weimar Hoftheater cond. Strauss
	Macbeth	op. 23	Alexander Ritter	13/10/90 Weimar Hofkapelle cond. Strauss
1891	2 Lieder von Lenau	op. 26	Heinrich Zeller	
1892	Festmusik 'Lebende Bilder' (orch.) (comp. for Golden Wedding of Grand Duke and Duchess of Weimar)			8/10/92 Weimar Hofkapelle cond. Strauss
1893	*Guntram*	op. 25	'Meinen teuren Eltern'	10/5/94 Weimar Hoftheater cond. Strauss
	2 Stücke for pf. quartet (1) 'Arabischer Tanz' (2) 'Liebesliedchen'		Onkel Georg Pschorr zu Weihnachten 1893	(lost)
1894	4 Lieder	op. 27	'Meiner geliebten Pauline (de Ahna) zum 10 Sept. 1894'	
1895	*Till Eulenspiegels lustige Streiche*	op. 28	Arthur Seidl	5/11/95 Cologne Gürzenichsaal cond. Wüllner

DATE	TITLE	OPUS	DEDICATION	FIRST PERF.
	3 Lieder von Bierbaum	op. 29	Eugen Gura	
1896	4 Lieder	op. 31	Johanna Strauss and Marie Ritter	
	5 Lieder	op. 32	'Meiner geliebten Frau'	
	'Wir beide wollen springen' (Bierbaum)			
	Also sprach Zarathustra	op. 30		27/11/96 Frankfurt cond. Strauss
1897	4 Gesänge (voice and orch.)	op. 33		
	Enoch Arden (Tennyson) (melodrama for voice and pf.)	op. 38	Ernst von Possart	24/3/97 Munich Mathildensaal Possart and Strauss
	2 Gesänge (unacc. chor.)	op. 34	Julius Buths and Philipp Wolfrum	
	Hymne 'Licht, du ewiglich Eines' (female chor. wind band and orch.) (comp. for opening of art exhibition)			1/6/97 Munich Glaspalast Hoforchester cond. Strauss
	Don Quixote	op. 35	Joseph Dupont	8/3/98 Cologne Gürzenichsaal Grützmacher (cello) and Städtische Orch. cond. Wüllner
1898	4 Lieder	op. 36	Marie Riemer-schmid and Raoul Walter	
	6 Lieder	op. 37	'Meiner geliebten Frau zum 12 April'	
	5 Lieder	op. 39	Fritz Sieger	
	Ein Heldenleben	op. 40	Mengelberg and Concertgebouw Orchestra Amsterdam	3/3/99 Frankfurt cond. Strauss
1899	'Das Schloss am Meere' (Uhland) (melodrama for voice and pf.)			23/3/99 Berlin Possart and Strauss
	Soldatenlied (Kopisch) (male chor. unacc.)			
	5 Lieder	op. 41	Marie Rösch	
	2 Männerchöre aus 'Stimmen der Völker' (Herder)	op. 42		8/12/99 Vienna Schubertbund
	3 Lieder	op. 43	Ernestine Schumann-Heink	

DATE	TITLE	OPUS	DEDICATION	FIRST PERF.
	2 grössere Gesänge (bass and orch.)	op. 44	Anton van Rooy and Karl Scheidemantel	3/12/1900 Berlin B. Hoffmann cond. Strauss
	3 Männerchöre aus 'Stimmen der Völker' (Herder) Weihnachtsgefühl (Greif)	op. 45	'Meinem lieben Vater'	
1900	5 Lieder von Rückert	op. 46	'Meinen lieben Schwiegereltern'	
	5 Lieder von Uhland	op. 47	J. C. Pflüger	
	5 Lieder	op. 48		
1901	*Feuersnot*	op. 50	Friedrich Rösch	21/11/01 Dresden Hofoper cond. Schuch
	8 Lieder	op. 49	'Meiner lieben Frau', Ernst Kraus, Grete Kraus, Consul Simon Walter Ende and Baron A. von Stengel	
1903	*Taillefer* (Uhland) (soli, chor. and orch.)	op. 52	Faculty of Philosophy Heidelberg University	26/10/03 Heidelberg Festival cond. Strauss
	Kanon 'Hans Huber in Vitznau' (4 voices unacc.)			
	Symphonia Domestica	op. 53	'Meiner lieben Frau und unserm Jungen'	21/3/04 New York Carnegie Hall cond. Strauss
1904	2 Lieder aus *Der Richter von Zalamea* (Calderón) (voices with guitar and harps)			7/9/04 Berlin Lessing Theater
1905	Bardengesang aus der *Hermanns-Schlacht* (Klopstock) (male chor. and orch.)	op. 55	Gustav Wohlgemuth	6/2/06 Dresden Lehrergesang-verein cond. Brandes
	Salome	op. 54	Edgar Speyer	9/12/05 Dresden Hofoper cond. Schuch
1906	6 Volksliedbearbeitungen (male chor. unacc.)			
	Der Graf von Rom (voice without text and pf.)			
	2 Parade-Märsche (particell) *De Brandenburgsche Mars—* Präsentiermarsch (particell) Königsmarsch (particell) 2 Militärmärsche (orch.)	op. 57	Kaiser Wilhelm II	6/3/07 Berlin cond. Strauss

DATE	TITLE	OPUS	DEDICATION	FIRST PERF.
	2 Gesänge (bass and orch.)	op. 51	Paul Knüpfer	
	6 Lieder	op. 56	'Meiner lieben Pauline zum 8 August 1903' and 'Meiner lieben Mutter'	
1908	*Elektra*	op. 58	Natalie and Willy Levin	25/1/09 Dresden Hofoper cond. Schuch
1909	Feierlicher Einzug der Ritter des Johanniter-Ordens (brass and timpani)		Prinz Eitel Friedrich of Prussia	
1910	*Der Rosenkavalier*	op. 59	Pschorr family	26/1/11 Dresden Hofoper cond. Schuch
1912	*Ariadne auf Naxos* zu spielen nach dem *Bürger als Edelmann* des Molière	op. 60	Max Reinhardt	25/10/12 Stuttgart Hoftheater cond. Strauss
1913	Festliches Präludium (orch. and organ) (comp. for the dedication of the Vienna Konzerthaus)	op. 61		19/10/13 Vienna Konzertverein cond. Löwe
	Deutsche Motette (Rückert) (unacc. chor.)	op. 62	Hugo Rüdel and Berlin Hoftheater Singchor	2/12/13 Berlin Hoftheater Singchor. cond. Rüdel
1914	*Josephslegende*	op. 63	Edouard Hermann	14/5/14 Paris Opéra Ballets Russes Diaghilev cond. Strauss
	Cantata (Hofmannsthal) (male chor. unacc.)		Graf von Seebach	
1915	*Eine Alpensinfonie*	op. 64	Graf von Seebach and Dresden Hofkapelle	28/10/15 Berlin Philharmonie Dresden Hofkapelle cond. Strauss
1916	*Ariadne auf Naxos* (2nd version)	op. 60	Max Reinhardt	4/10/16 Vienna Hofoper cond. Schalk
1917	*Die Frau ohne Schatten*	op. 65		10/10/19 Vienna Staatsoper cond. Schalk
	Der Bürger als Edelmann (Molière-Hofmannsthal) incidental music	op. 60	Max Reinhardt	9/4/18 Berlin Deutsches Theater cond. Nilson
1918	*Krämerspiegel* (Kerr)	op. 66	Friedrich Rösch	

DATE	TITLE	OPUS	DEDICATION	FIRST PERF.
	6 Lieder (i) Songs of Ophelia (Shakespeare) (ii) Aus den Büchern des Unmuts (Goethe)	op. 67		
	6 Lieder von Brentano	op. 68		
	5 kleine Lieder	op. 69	Lori Nossal, Margit Steiner, Mizzi von Grab, Jenny Mauthner and Irene Hellmann	
1919	Sinnspruch (Goethe)		Rudolf Mosse	
	Der Bürger als Edelmann Suite (orch.)	op. 60		31/1/20 Vienna Wiener Philharmoniker cond. Strauss
1921	3 Hymnen von Hölderlin (sop. and orch.)	op. 71	Minnie Untermayr	9/11/21 Berlin Volksoper Barbara Kemp cond. Brecher
1922	*Schlagobers*	op. 70	Ludwig Karpath	9/5/24 Vienna Staatsoper cond. Strauss
	Hans Adam war ein Erdenkloss (Goethe)		Michael Bohnen	
1923	Tanzsuite aus Klavierstücken von François Couperin (small orch.)			17/2/23 Vienna Redoutensaal Hofberg cond. Krauss
	Intermezzo	op. 72	'Meinem lieben Sohne Franz'	4/11/24 Dresden Staatsoper cond. Busch
1924	Hochzeitspräludium (2 harmoniums) (comp. for the wedding of Franz and Alice Strauss)		'Meinem lieben Sohne Franz zum 15 Januar 1924'	15/1/24 Vienna Schottenkirche Karl Alwin and Rudolf Friedel
	Wiener Philharmoniker Fanfare (comp. for the Faschingsdienstag Ball) (brass and timps.)		Wiener Philharmoniker	4/3/24 Vienna
	Die Ruinen von Athen (Beethoven) (new version Hofmannsthal)			20/9/24 Vienna Staatsoper cond. Strauss
	Fanfare (brass and timps.) (comp. for opening of Vienna Musikwoche)			14/9/24 Vienna
1925	*Parergon zur Sinfonia Domestica* (pf. L.H. and orch.)	op. 73	Paul Wittgenstein	16/10/25 Dresden Wittgenstein and Sächsischen Staatskapelle cond. Busch

DATE	TITLE	OPUS	DEDICATION	FIRST PERF.
	'Durch allen Schall und Klang' (Goethe) (comp. for Liber Amicorum Romain Rolland)		'Romain Rolland zum 29 Januar 1926'	
	Militärmarsch in F (particell) (comp. for *Rosenkavalier* film)			10/1/26 Dresden Staatsoper cond. Strauss
	Hymne auf das Haus Kohorn (male voices unacc.)		Oscar Kohorn	
1927	*Panathenäenzug* (pf. L.H. and orch.)	op. 74		11/3/28 Vienna Wittgenstein and Wiener Philharmoniker cond. Schalk
	Die Aegyptische Helena	op. 75		6/6/28 Dresden Staatsoper cond. Busch
	Die Tageszeiten (Eichendorff) (male chor. and orch.)	op. 76	Viktor Keldorfer and Wiener Schubertbund	21/7/28 Vienna Schubertbund and orch. cond. Keldorfer
1928	5 Gesänge des Orients (Bethge)	op. 77	Elisabeth Schumann and Karl Alwin	
1929	Vom künftigen Alter (Rückert)		Hans Hotter	
	Und dann nicht mehr (Rückert)		Hans Hermann Nissen	
	Austria (Wildgans) (male chor. and orch.)	op. 78	Wiener Männergesangverein	10/1/30 Vienna cond. Strauss
1930	'Wie etwas sei leicht' (Goethe)		'Der Wiener Concordia zum 60. Jubiläum'	
	Idomeneo (Mozart) (new version Wallerstein)			16/4/31 Vienna Staatsoper cond. Strauss
1932	*Arabella*	op. 79	Alfred Reucker and Fritz Busch	1/7/33 Dresden Staatsoper cond. Krauss
1933	4 Sinfonische Zwischenspiele aus *Intermezzo*	op. 72		
	Das Bächlein (?Goethe)		'Dr Joseph Goebbels zur Erinnerung an den 15 Nov. 1933'	
1934	Olympische Hymne (Lubahn) (chor. and orch.) (comp. for 1936 Olympic Games)			1/8/36 Berlin Olympia Stadium Massed Chorus cond. Strauss
1935	*Die Schweigsame Frau*	op. 80		24/6/35 Dresden Staatsoper cond. Böhm

DATE	TITLE	OPUS	DEDICATION	FIRST PERF.
	Die Göttin im Putzzimmer (Rückert) (unacc. chor.)			2/3/52 Vienna Chor der Staatsoper cond. Krauss
	Im Sonnenschein (Rückert) 'Zugemessne Rhythmen reizen freilich' (Goethe)		Georg Hann Peter Raabe	
	3 Männerchöre von Rückert		Eugen Papst und Kölner Männergesangverein	29/3/36 Cologne Gürzenichsaal Kölner Männergesangverein cond. Papst
1936	Friedenstag	op. 81	Viorica Ursuleac and Clemens Krauss	24/7/38 Munich Nationaltheater cond. Krauss
1937	Daphne	op. 82	Karl Böhm	15/10/38 Dresden Staatsoper cond. Böhm
1938	'Durch Einsamkeiten' (Wildgans) (male chor. unacc.)		'Dem Wiener Schubertbund zum 50jährigen Jubiläum'	1/4/39 Vienna Wiener Schubertbund cond. Nurrer
1939	München (ein Gelegenheitswalzer) (1st version, comp. for film 'München')		'Der bayerischen Staatsbibliothek zur Erinnerung an den 11 Juni 1949' Anton Kippenberg	24/5/39 Munich Ufapalast cond. Ehrenberg
	'Hab dank, du gütger Weisheitsspender' (bass unacc.)			
1940	Notschrei aus den Gefilden Lapplands (voice unacc.)		Walter Funk	
	Japanische Festmusik (comp. for 2600th Ann. Empire of Japan)	op. 84		7/12/40 Tokyo cond. Felmer
	Die Liebe der Danae	op. 83	Heinz Tietjen	16/8/44 Salzburg Festspielhaus cond. Krauss
	Guntram (revised version)	op. 25		29/10/40 Weimar Nationaltheater cond. Sixt
	Verklungene Feste (nach Couperin)			5/4/41 Munich Nationaltheater cond. Krauss
1941	Capriccio	op. 85	'Meinem Freunde und Mitarbeiter Clemens Krauss'	28/10/42 Munich Staatsoper cond. Krauss
	Divertimento (Klavierstücke von Couperin) (small orch.)	op. 86		31/1/43 Vienna Wiener Philharmoniker cond. Krauss

DATE	TITLE	OPUS	DEDICATION	FIRST PERF.
1942	2 Lieder von Weinheber (comp. for Weinheber's 50th birthday)		Alfred Poell and Viorica Ursuleac	9/3/42 Vienna Palais Lobkowitz Poell and Hilde Konetzni
	Xenion (Goethe) (comp. for Hauptmann's 80th birthday)		Gerhart Hauptmann	
	Horn Concerto no. 2 in E Flat			11/8/43 Salzburg Freiberg and Wiener Philharmoniker cond. Böhm
1943	Festmusik der Stadt Wien (brass and timps.) (comp. for Wiener Trompeterchor)		'Dem Gemeinderat der Stadt'	9/4/43 Vienna Trompeterchor cond. Strauss
	Fanfare der Stadt Wien (brass and timps.) (2nd version of Festmusik above)			
	Sonatina no. 1 in F for wind instruments 'Aus der Werkstatt eines Invaliden'			18/6/44 Dresden Staatskapelle cond. Elmendorff
	'Wer tritt herein' (voice unacc.)		Hans Frank	
	An den Baum Daphne (Gregor) (unacc. chor.) (Epilogue to *Daphne*)		'Dem Wiener Staatsopernchor'	5/1/47 Vienna Staatsopernchor cond. Prohaska
1944	Suite aus *Capriccio* (harpsichord)		Isolde Ahlgrimm	7/11/46 Vienna Mozart-Saal Isolde Ahlgrimm
	Erste Walzerfolge aus *Der Rosenkavalier*		Ernst Roth	4/8/46 London Philharmonia Orch. cond. Leinsdorf
1945	*München* (ein Gedächtniswalzer) (2nd version)			31/3/51 Vienna Wiener Symphoniker cond. Lehmann
	Daphne-Etude (violin solo)		'meinem lieben Geigenschüler Christian zum 13 Geburtstag'	
	Metamorphosen		Paul Sacher and Collegium Musicum Zurich'	25/1/46 Zurich Tonhalle Collegium Musicum cond. Sacher
	Sonatina no. 2 in E Flat for wind instruments 'Fröhliche Werkstatt'		'Den Manen des unsterblichen Mozart an Ende eines dankerfüllten Lebens'	25/3/46 Winterthur Musikkollegium cond. Scherchen

DATE	TITLE	OPUS	DEDICATION	FIRST PERF.
1946	Oboe Concerto		Volkmar Andreae and Tonhalle orch. Zürich	26/2/46 Zurich Saillet and Tonhalle orch. cond. Andreae
	Symphonische Fantasie aus *Die Frau ohne Schatten*		Manfred von Mautner Markhof	26/6/47 Vienna Wiener Symphoniker cond. Böhm
1947	Symphonisches Fragment aus *Josephslegende*			?/3/49 Cincinnati Symph. Orch. cond. Reiner
	Duett-Concertino (clar. and bassoon with strings and harp)		'Hugo Burghauser, dem Getreuen'	4/4/48 Lugano Basile, Bergamaschi and Orch. della Radio Svizzera Italiana cond. Nussio
1948	Allegretto in E (vl. and pf.) (comp. for Christian Strauss) *Des Esels Schatten* (unfinished)			7/6/64 Ettal Gymnasium der Benediktinerabtei (in version completed by Haussner)
	Vier letzte Lieder		Ernst Roth, Willi Schuh, Adolf Jöhr and Maria Seery-Jeritza	22/5/50 London Royal Albert Hall Flagstad and Philharmonia Orch. cond. Furtwängler

APPENDIX E

Chronological list of Songs

1	Weihnachtslied	Schubart	Dec. 1870
2	Einkehr	Uhland	21 Aug. 1871
3	Winterreise	Uhland	1871
4	Waldkonzert	Vogel	1871
5	Der weisse Hirsch	Uhland	1871
6	Des Alpenhirten Abschied	Schiller	1871
7	Der Böhmische Musikant	Pletzsch	1871
8	Herz, mein Herz	Geibel	1871
9	Der müde Wanderer	Hoffmann v. Fallersleben	1873
10	Husarenlied	Hoffmann v. Fallersleben	1873
11	Der Fischer	Goethe	
12	Die Drossel	Uhland	1877
13	Lass ruhn die Toten	Chimasso	
14	Lust und Qual	Goethe	
15	Spielmann und Zither	Körner	Jan. 1878
16	Wiegenlied	Hoffmann v. Fallersleben	early 1878
17	Abend- und Morgenrot	Hoffmann v. Fallersleben	early 1878
18	Im Walde	Geibel	early 1878
19	Arie der Almaide (from 'Lila') ORCH	Goethe	early 1878
20	Der Spielmann und sein Kind ORCH	Hoffmann v. Fallersleben	28 Feb. 1878
21	Nebel	Lenau	1878
22	Soldatenlied	Hoffmann v. Fallersleben	1878
23	Ein Röslein zog ich mir im Garten	Hoffmann v. Fallersleben	1878
24	Alphorn (with horn obbligato)	Kerner	1878
25	Für Musik	Geibel	7 Apr. 1879
26	Waldesgesang	Geibel	9 Apr. 1879
27	O schneller mein Ross	Geibel	10 Apr. 1879
28	Die Lilien glühn in Düften	Geibel	12 Apr. 1879
29	Es rauscht das Laub zu meinen Füssen	Geibel	May 1879
30	Frühlingsanfang	Geibel	24 May 1879
31	Die drei Lieder	Uhland	18 Dec. 1879

32	In Vaters Garten heimlich steht	Heine	24 Dec. 1879	
33	Der Morgen	Sallet	10 Jan. 1880	
34	Die erwachte Rose	Sallet	12 Jan. 1880	
35	Immer leiser wird mein Schlummer	Lingg	17 Dec. 1880	
36	Begegnung	Gruppe	18 Dec. 1880	
37	Mutter, O sing mich zur Ruh	Hemans	29 Dec. 1880	
38	John Anderson, mein Lieb	Burns	31 Dec. 1880	
39	Geheiligte Stätte	Fischer	24 Dec. 1881	
40	Jung Friedel wallte am Rheinesstrand	Becker	Dec. 1882	
41	Waldesgang	Stieler	10 Dec. 1882	
42	Rote Rosen	Stieler	11 Sept. 1883	
43	Zueignung ORCH 1940 (also orch. Heger)			
44	Nichts			
45	Die Nacht			
46	Die Georgine	Gilm	1882–3	
47	Geduld	aus *Letzte Blätter*	Op. 10	
48	Die Verschwiegenen			
49	Die Zeitlose			
50	Allerseelen (orch. Heger)			
51	Mein Geist ist trüb	Byron	12 May 1884	
52	Der Dorn ist Zeichen der Verneinung	Bodenstedt	12 May 1884	
53	Madrigal	Michelangelo		
54	Winternacht		Nov/Dec. 1886	
55	Lob des Leidens	Schack	Op. 15	
56	Aus den Liedern der Trauer (no. 1)			
57	Heimkehr			
58	Seitdem dein Aug' in meines schaute			
59	Ständchen (orch. Mottl)			
60	Das Geheimnis	Schack	Summer 1887	
61	Aus den Liedern der Trauer (no. 2)		op. 17	
62	Nur Muth!			
63	Barkarole			
64	Wozu noch, Mädchen . .			
65	Breit' über mein Haupt . .			
66	Schön sind, doch kalt die Himmelssterne	Schack	Set completed 12 Jan. 1888	
67	Wie sollten wir geheim sie halten	aus *Lotosblätter*	op. 19	
68	Hoffen und wieder verzagen			
69	Mein Herz ist stumm . .			
70	All mein Gedanken . .			
71	Du meines Herzens Krönelein		1888	
72	Ach Lieb, ich muss nun scheiden!	Dahn	*Schlichte Weisen*	
73	Ach weh mir unglückhaftem Mann		op. 21	
74	Die Frauen sind oft fromm und still			
75	Kornblumen		28 Mar. 1888	*Mädchen-*
76	Mohnblumen	Dahn	29 Mar. 1888	*blumen*
77	Epheu		1888	op. 22
78	Wasserrose		1888	
79	Frühlingsgedränge	Lenau	2 Dec. 1891	op. 26
80	O wärst du mein			

81	Ruhe, meine Seele! ORCH 1948	Henckell	7 May 1894	
82	Cäcilie ORCH 1897	Hart	9 Sept. 1894	op. 27
83	Heimliche Aufforderung (orch. Heger)	Mackay	22 May 1894	
84	Morgen! ORCH 1897	Mackay	21 May 1894	
85	Traum durch die Dämmerung (orch. Heger)			
86	Schlagende Herzen	Bierbaum	7 June 1895	op. 29
87	Nachtgang			
88	Blauer Sommer		1 Jan. 1896	
89	Wenn . .	Busse	15 June 1895	op. 31
90	Weisser Jasmin		24 June 1895	
91	Stiller Gang (with viola obbligato)	Dehmel	30 Dec. 1895	op. 31 no. 4
92	Ich trage meine Minne (orch. Heger)	Henckell	26 Jan. 1896	
93	Sehnsucht	Liliencron	24 Jan. 1896	
94	Liebeshymnus ORCH 1897	Henckell	25 Feb. 1896	
95	O süsser Mai!	Henckell	28 Mar. 1896	op. 32
96	Himmelsboten	aus *Des Knaben Wunderhorn*	3 Jan. 1896	
97	Wir beide wollen springen	Bierbaum	7 June 1896	
98	Verführung	Mackay	5 July 1896	Vier Gesänge für eine Singstimme mit Orchesterbegleitung op. 33
99	Gesang der Apollopriesterin	Bodman	end Sept. 1896	
100	Hymnus	attr. Schiller	5 Jan. 1897	
101	Pilgers Morgenlied—An Lila	Goethe	25 Jan. 1897	
102	Das Rosenband ORCH 1897	Klopstock	22 Sept. 1897	
103	Für funfzehn Pfennige	aus *Des Knaben Wunderhorn*	2 Sept. 1897	op. 36
104	Hat gesagt—bleibt's nicht dabei		31 May 1898	
105	Anbetung	Rückert	24 Mar. 1898	
106	Glückes genug	Liliencron	8 Feb. 1898	
107	Ich liebe dich ORCH 1943	Liliencron	7 Feb. 1898	
108	Meinem Kinde ORCH 1897	Falke	8 Feb. 1897	
109	Mein Auge ORCH 1933	Dehmel	16 Apr. 1898	op. 37
110	Herr Lenz	Bodman	9 June 1896	
111	Hochzeitlich Lied	Lindner	30 Mar. 1898	
112	Leises Lied	Dehmel	2 July 1898	
113	Jung Hexenlied	Bierbaum	31 May 1898	
114	Der Arbeitsmann ORCH 1941		12 June 1898	
115	Befreit ORCH 1933	Dehmel	2 June 1898	op. 39
116	Lied an meinen Sohn		8 July 1898	
117	Wiegenlied ORCH 1900	Dehmel	22 Aug. 1899	
118	In der Campagna	Mackay	24 Aug. 1899	
119	Am Ufer	Dehmel	15 Aug. 1899	op. 41
120	Bruder Liederlich	Liliencron	16 Aug. 1899	
121	Leise Lieder	Morgenstern	4 June 1899	
122	An Sie	Klopstock	14 Aug. 1899	
123	Muttertändelei ORCH 1900	Bürger	15 Aug. 1899	op. 43
124	Die Ulme zu Hirsau	Uhland	4 Sept. 1899	

125	Notturno	Dehmel	16 Sept. 1899	Zwei grössere Gesänge für tiefe Stimme mit Orchester- begleitung op. 44
126	Nächtlicher Gang	Rückert	10 Nov. 1899	
127	Weihnachtsgefühl	Greif	8 Dec. 1899	
128	Ein Obdach gegen Sturm und Regen	Rückert	16 Jan. 1900	op. 46
129	Gestern war ich Atlas		21 Nov. 1899	
130	Die sieben Siegel		18 Nov. 1899	
131	Morgenrot		4 Feb. 1900	
132	Ich sehe wie in einem Spiegel		7 Feb. 1900	
133	Auf ein Kind	Uhland	5 May 1900	op. 47
134	Des Dichters Abendgang ORCH 1918		8 May 1900	
135	Rückleben		23 May 1900	
136	Einkehr		30 May 1900	
137	Von den sieben Zechbrüdern		11 June 1900	
138	Freundliche Vision ORCH 1918	Bierbaum	5 Oct. 1900	op. 48
139	Ich schwebe	Henckell	25 Sept. 1900	
140	Kling!		30 Sept. 1900	
141	Winterweihe ORCH 1918		23 Sept. 1900	
142	Winterliebe ORCH 1918		2 Oct. 1900	
143	Waldseligkeit ORCH 1918	Dehmel	21 Sept. 1901	op. 49
144	In goldener Fülle	Remer	13 Sept. 1901	
145	Wiegenliedchen	Dehmel	20 Sept. 1901	
146	Lied des Steinklopfers	Henckell	24 Sept. 1901	
147	Sie wissen's nicht	Panizza	14 Sept. 1901	
148	Junggesellenschwur	aus Des Knaben Wunderhorn	11 May 1900	
149	Wer lieben will, muss leiden	aus Elsässische Volkslieder	23 Sept. 1901	
150	Ach, was Kummer, Qual, und Schmerzen			
151	Das Thal	Uhland	11 Dec. 1902	Zwei Lieder für eine tiefe Bass- stimme mit Orchester- begleitung op. 51
152	Der Einsame	Heine	18 Feb. 1906	
153	Liebesliedchen	Zwei Lieder aus Der Richter von Zalamea	Calderón	16 Aug. 1904
154	Lied der Chispa			

155	Gefunden	Goethe	8 Aug. 1903	
156	Blindenklage	Henckell	1903	
157	Im Spätboot	Meyer	1903	
158	Mit deine blauen Augen		1906	op. 56
159	Frühlingsfeier ORCH 1933		1906	
160	Die heiligen drei Könige aus Morgenland ORCH 1906	Heine	7 Oct. 1906	
161 to 172	Es war einmal ein Bock . .		15 Mar. 1918	
	Einst kam der Bock als Bote . .		19 Mar. 1918	
	Es liebte einst ein Hase . .		16 Mar. 1918	
	Drei Masken sah ich am Himmel stehn . .		24 Mar. 1918	
	Hast du ein Tongedicht vollbracht . .		16 May 1918	Krämer-
	O lieber Künstler sei ermahnt . .	Kerr	25 May 1918	spiegel
	Unser Feind ist, grosser Gott . .		17 Mar. 1918	op. 66
	Von Händlern wird die Kunst bedroht . .		20 May 1918	
	Es war mal eine Wanze . .		21 May 1918	
	Die Künstler sind die Schöpfer . .		21 May 1918	
	Die Händler und die Macher . .		23 May 1918	
	O Schröpferschwarm, O Händlerkreis . .		23 May 1918	
173	Wie erkenn' ich mein Treulieb?	Drei Lieder		
174	Guten Morgen, 's ist Sankt Valentinstag	der Ophelia (aus *Hamlet*) Shakespeare		
175	Sie trugen ihn auf der Bahre bloss			
176	Wer wird von der Welt verlangen	Drei Lieder aus dem Büchern	1918	op. 67
177	Hab' ich euch denn je geraten	des Un- muts Goethe		
178	Wanderers Gemütsruhe	(West- östlicher Divan)		
179	An die Nacht		18 Feb. 1918	
180	Ich wollt ein Sträusslein binden	ORCH 1940	6 Feb. 1918	
181	Säusle, liebe Myrthe		9 Feb. 1918	op. 68
182	Als mir dein Lied erklang	Brentano	4 Feb. 1918	
183	Amor		21 Feb. 1918	
184	Lied der Frauen ORCH 1933		4 May 1918	
185	Der Stern		June/July 1918	Fünf
186	Der Pokal	Arnim	June/July 1918	kleine
187	Einerlei		25 June 1918	Lieder
188	Waldesfahrt		26 June 1918	op. 69
189	Schlechtes Wetter	Heine	21 June 1918	
190	Sinnspruch	Goethe	24 June 1919	

191	Hymne an die Liebe		6 Apr. 1921	Drei Hymnen für eine hohe Sing-stimme und grosses Orchester op. 71
191	Hymne an die Liebe	}Hölderlin	6 Apr. 1921	
192	Rückkehr in die Heimat		2 Jan. 1921	
193	Die Liebe		20 Jan. 1921	

194	Erschaffen und Beleben	Goethe	25 Dec. 1922	
195	Durch allen Schall und Klang	Goethe	11 June 1925	
196	Ihre Augen		14 Aug. 1928	Gesänge des Orients op. 77
197	Schwung		15 Aug. 1928	
198	Liebesgeschenke	}Bethge	14 Aug. 1928	
199	Die Allmächtige		15 Aug. 1928	
200	Huldigung		24 Sept. 1928	
201	Vom künftigen Alter	}Rückert	early 1929	
202	Und dann nicht mehr		11 Feb. 1929	
203	Wie etwas sei leicht	Goethe	9 Jan. 1930	
204	Das Bächlein ORCH 1933	?Goethe	3 Dec. 1933	
205	Im Sonnenschein	Rückert	24 Feb. 1935	
206	Zugemessne Rhythmen	Goethe	25 Feb. 1935	
207	Sankt Michael	}Weinheber	3 Feb. 1942	
208	Blick vom oberen Belvedere		11 Feb. 1942	
209	Xenion	Goethe	20 Sept. 1942	

210	Im Abendrot	Eichendorff	6 May 1948	Vier letzte Lieder für Sopran und grosses Orchester
211	Frühling		18 July 1948	
212	Beim Schlafengehen	}Hesse	4 Aug. 1948	
213	September		20 Sept. 1948	

APPENDIX F

Principal Events in Strauss's Life

1864	11th June. Richard Strauss born, Munich, Altheimer Eck 2
1867	9th June. Johanna Strauss born
1868	Starts piano lessons with Aug. Tombo
1870	First compositions
1872	Starts violin lessons with Benno Walter
1874–82	Attends Ludwigs-Gymnasium
1875	Begins lessons in theory and composition with F. W. Meyer
1881	First publication (*Festmarsch* op. 1)
1882–3	Attends Munich University
	First visit to Bayreuth
1883–4	Visits Leipzig, Dresden, and spends a period in Berlin
1884	First meets Bülow
	18th November. Conducting début. Wind Suite in Munich
1885	Accepts position in Meiningen. Assistant Court Director of Music under Bülow
	Meets Alexander Ritter
	November. Bülow resigns, leaving Strauss in full charge
1886	April. Leaves Meiningen, April–May. Travels to Italy
	August, until 1889, takes position as third conductor in Munich Court Opera
1887	Meets Pauline de Ahna at Feldafing
	Meets Mahler
1889	Summer. Musical assistant in Bayreuth
	July. Leaves Munich
	October. Takes up position as Conductor at Court Theatre, Weimar
1891	Summer. Falls ill with pneumonia and pleurisy
1892	June. Second illness
	November. Journey of convalescence to Greece, Egypt, and Italy
1894	June. Leaves Weimar
	September. Marries Pauline de Ahna
	October. Accepts position as Court Conductor in Munich with Levi
	Takes on Symphony Concerts of Berlin Philharmonic Orchestra owing to death of Bülow
1896	October. Levi leaves Munich. Strauss now Principal Conductor
1897	12th April. Birth of his son, Franz Strauss
1898	October. Leaves Munich
	November. Takes up position as Conductor at Berlin Court Opera (with Karl Muck and Leo Blech). (This position he held until 1908, when he was appointed General Music Director until 1924)
	Also Principal Conductor of Berlin Philharmonic Orchestra (until 1918)

	Founds Genossenschaft deutscher Tonsetzer (with Rösch)
1900	Meets Hofmannsthal for the first time, in Paris
1903	Receives Doctorate Heidelberg University
1904	Tours North America with Pauline
1905	31st May. Death of Strauss's father
1908	Completion of Villa at Garmisch
	Appointed General Music Director at Berlin Court Opera (until 1918, though beginning with a sabbatical year)
1909	Takes on Symphony Concerts of Berlin Court (Hofkapelle, later Staatskapelle) from Weingartner (until 1920)
1910	16th May. Death of Strauss's mother
1914	Receives Doctorate Oxford University
1918	Leaves Berlin Court Opera, and returns as Intendant of State Opera (during interregnum) for one year
1919	December. Becomes Director of Vienna State Opera (with Franz Schalk)
1920	Leaves Berlin Staatskapelle Concerts
	Tours South America
1922	Second tour of North America
1923	Second tour of South America
1924	15th January. Marriage of Franz and Alice Strauss
	October. Leaves Vienna State Opera
	Builds second villa at Belvedere in Vienna
	From now onwards no permanent position, but continues travelling extensively conducting opera and attending Festivals etc.
1929	15th July. Death of Hofmannsthal
1933	November. President of Reichsmusikkammer
1935	June. Disgraced by Nazi regime. Resigns position of President of Reichsmusikkammer
1936	November. Receives Gold Medal of Royal Philharmonic Society in London
1945	Takes asylum in Switzerland
1949	May. Returns to Garmisch
	85th birthday celebrations
	8th September. Death of Strauss in Garmisch
1950	13th May. Death of Pauline Strauss in Garmisch

APPENDIX G

Discography of Strauss as Performer[1]

a) As Conductor

1. Works by Strauss:

Alpensinfonie, Eine.	Bavarian State Orch.	Electrola HMV DB 5662–7
Ariadne auf Naxos, Overture.	(unspec. orch)	Polydor 040869
Bürger als Edelmann, Der.		
Overture, Vorspiel zum 2. Aufzug.	(unspec. orch.)	Polydor 040866/67
Auftritt und Tanz der Schneider.	(unspec. orch.)	Polydor 040868
Diner-Walzer	(unspec. orch.)	Polydor 040870–71
Menuet de Lully and Intermezzo Act 2	(unspec. orch.)	Brunswick 50017
Suite	Berlin State Opera Orch.	Polydor 95392–6
		Brunswick 90130–4
Suite	Vienna Phil. Orch.	Eurania URRS 7–8
Menuet & Der Fechtmeister (side 8 of Jupiter symph.)	Berlin State Opera Orch.	Polydor 66289
Don Juan	Berlin State Opera Orch.	Polydor 65856–7
	Berlin State Opera Orch.	Polydor 66902–3
		(also on Decca CA 8126–7)
	London Symph. Orch.	Columbia L 1419–20
Don Quixote (with Uhl)	Bavarian State Orch.	Polydor 67800–4
(with Mainardi)	Berlin Opera Orch.	Polydor 27320–4
		(also on Decca LY 6087–91)
Heldenleben, Ein	Berlin State Opera Orch.	Polydor 69840–4
	Bavarian State Orch.	Polydor 67756–60
Intermezzo:		
Interlude and Waltz Scene	Berlin State Opera Orch.	(pre-el) Polydor 69852–3
		(elec) Polydor 69867–8
Japanische Festmusik	Bavarian State Orch.	Polydor 67599–600
Rosenkavalier, Der.		
'Selected orchestral passages' (version for film presentation 1926)	Augmented Tivoli Orch.	HMV D 1094–7 (7 sides)

[1] Compiled in association with the British Institute of Recorded Sound and based on a discography by Francis F. Clough and G. J. Cuming.

Waltzes Act 2	Berlin State Opera Orch.	(pre-el) Polydor 65860
		(elec) Polydor 69854
	London Symph. Orch.	Columbia L 1421
	(unspec. orch.)	Electrola E 83389
Waltzes Act 3	Bavarian State Orch.	Polydor 67729
(2nd Waltz sequence)		
Salome: Dance of the Seven Veils	Berlin Phil. Orch.	Polydor 66827
		(also on Decca CA 8017)
	London Symph. Orch.	Columbia L 1422
Till Eulenspiegel	Berlin State Opera Orch.	(pre-el) Polydor 65858–9
		(elec) Polydor 66887–8
Tod und Verklärung	Berlin State Opera Orch.	Polydor 69849–51

2. Other works:

Beethoven:

| Symphony No. 5 | Berlin State Opera Orch. | Polydor 66814–7 |
| Symphony No. 7 | Berlin State Opera Orch. | Polydor 69836–9 |

Cornelius:

| Overture The Barber of Bagdad. | Berlin Phil. Orch. | Polydor 66936 |
| (in D—Liszt/Mottl version) | | |

Gluck:

| Overture Iphigénie en Aulide | Berlin Phil. Orch. | Polydor 66829 |

Mozart:

Overture Die Zauberflöte.	Berlin State Opera Orch.	Polydor 66826
		(also on Decca CA 8106)
Symphony No. 39 in E flat.	Berlin State Opera Orch.	Polydor 69833–5
Symphony No. 40 in G minor.	Berlin State Opera Orch.	Brunswick 90082–5
		(7 sides)
Symphony No. 41 in C 'Jupiter'.	Berlin State Opera Orch.	Polydor 66286–9
	(8th side see Bürger	69845–8
	als Edelmann)	

Wagner:

Overture Der Fliegende Holländer	Berlin Phil. Orch.	Polydor 66830
Prelude Tristan und Isolde		
(with Wagner's concert ending)	Berlin Phil. Orch.	Polydor 66832

Weber:

| Overture Euryanthe. | Berlin Phil. Orch. | Polydor 66828 |

Numerous works conducted by Strauss were recorded during actual performances and still exist in the German Radio archives, (Così fan Tutte, Beethoven Symphony No. 9, etc.). One such, of *Sinfonia Domestica*, has been issued on a LP disc in America and others may presumably follow in the course of time.

(b) As Pianist

1. As accompanist to his own songs:[1]

| Breit' über mein Haupt | } R. Hutt | Polydor 62363 |
| Morgen! | | |

[1] Two Odeon records of Tauber thought to have been accompanied by Strauss have since been discredited.

Ich liebe dich	} Schlusnus	Polydor 62364
Heimkehr		
Ruhe meine Seele	} Schlusnus	Polydor 62365
Zueignung		
Die Nacht	} Schlusnus	Polydor 62366
Geheimnis		

2. Numerous pianola rolls were issued shortly after the turn of the century of Strauss works or excerpts. The following have been established as played by Strauss himself. In recent years these have been transferred to various L.P. discs as being of historical interest.

An einsamer Quelle, from Stimmungsbilder op. 9 No. 2
Intermezzo, from Stimmungsbilder op. 9 No. 3
Reverie, from Stimmungsbilder op. 9 No. 4
Heldenleben, love scene
Feuersnot, love scene
Salome, Dance of the Seven Veils
Rosenkavalier, Waltzes
Heimliche Aufforderung (arr. by the composer for piano solo)

APPENDIX H

Select bibliography

Richard Strauss Bibliographie. Teil I 1882–1944. Bearbeitet von Oswald Ortner, aus dem Nach-
lass herausgegeben von Franz Grasberger (Vienna, 1964)
The above aims to be, when completed, the absolutely complete and definitive biblio-
graphy of all Strauss literature. At the time of writing only Vol. I has so far appeared.

In addition a list follows of some of the books consulted:

Richard Strauss Thematisches Verzeichnis. Mueller von Asow. Vols I and II. (Vienna, 1954–1962)
Vol. III edited posthumously by Alfons Ott and
Franz Trenner (Vienna, 1965–   )
Richard Strauss Gesamtverzeichnis. Schuh and Roth. (London, 1964)
Allgemeine Musikzeitung: Richard Strauss number. (Berlin-Leipzig, 1912)
Armstrong, Thomas: *Strauss's Tone Poems* (Oxford, 1931)
Baum, Gunther: *Richard Strauss und Hugo von Hofmannsthal* (Berlin, 1962)
Blom, Eric: *The Rose Cavalier of Strauss* (Oxford, 1930)
Böhm, Karl: *Begegnung mit Richard Strauss* (Vienna, 1964)
Brandl, Willi: *Richard Strauss, Leben und Werk* (Wiesbaden, 1949)
Busch, Fritz: *Aus dem Leben eines Musikers.* (Zurich, 1949)
Cardus, Neville: 'Richard Strauss', in *Ten Composers* (London, 1945)
Erhardt, Otto: *Richard Strauss, Leben, Wirken, Schaffen* (Olten and Freiburg, 1953)
Gehring, Egid: *Richard Strauss und seine Vaterstadt München* (Munich, 1934)
Gilman, Lawrence: 'Strauss and the Greeks' in *Nature and Music* (New York, 1914)
'Strauss's *Salome*: Its art, and its morals,' in *Aspects of Modern Opera* (New
York, 1909)
Grasberger, Franz: *Richard Strauss: Hohe Kunst, Erfülltes Leben* (Vienna, 1965)
Die Welt um Richard Strauss in Briefen (Tutzing, 1967)
Grasberger, Franz and Hadamovsky: *Richard Strauss Ausstellung zum 100 Geburtstag* (Vienna,
1964)
Gray, Cecil: 'Richard Strauss' in *A Survey of Contemporary Music* (Oxford, 1924)
Gregor, Josef: *Richard Strauss: Der Meister der Oper* (Munich, 1939)
Gysi, Fritz: *Richard Strauss* (Potsdam, 1934)
Jefferson, Alan: *The Operas of Richard Strauss in Britain* 1910–63. (London, 1963)
Kralik, H.: *Richard Strauss: Weltbürger der Musik* (Vienna, 1963)
Krause, Ernst: *Richard Strauss: Gestalt und Werk* (Leipzig, 1956)
Krüger, Karl-Joachim: *Hugo von Hofmannsthal und Richard Strauss* (Berlin, 1935)
Lehmann, Lotte: *Singing with Richard Strauss* (London, 1964)
Lindner, Dolf: *Die Liebe der Danae, Herkunft, Inhalt und Gestaltung* (Vienna, n.d.)
Mann, William: *Richard Strauss: A Critical Study of the Operas* (London, 1964)
Marek, George: *Richard Strauss: The Life of a Non-hero* (London, 1967)

Muschler, R. C.: *Richard Strauss* (Hildesheim, 1924)

Newman, Ernest: *Richard Strauss* (London, 1908)

Panovsky, Walter: *Richard Strauss: Partitur eines Lebens* (Munich, 1965)

Petzoldt and Crass: *Richard Strauss: Sein Leben in Bildern* (Leipzig, 1962)

Rolland, Romain: 'Richard Strauss' in *Musiciens d'aujourd'hui* (Paris, n.d.)
    Richard Strauss Correspondence et Fragments de Journal (Paris, 1951)

Rostand, Claude: *Richard Strauss: L'ambiance, les origines, la vie, l'oeuvre, l'esthétique et le style* (Paris, 1949)

Roth, Ernst: *Musik als Kunst und Ware* (Zurich, 1966)

Schlesinger: Meisterführer: No. 6 Strauss, Sinfonien und Tondichtungen (Berlin, n.d.)
    No. 9 Strauss, Musikdramen (Berlin, n.d.)

Schuch, Friedrich von: *Richard Strauss, Ernst von Schuch und Dresdens Oper* (Leipzig, 1953)

Schuh, Willi: Original version Act 2 *Rosenkavalier*⎱ in *Die Neue Rundschau* (Frankfurt, 1953/4)
    Original version Act 1 *Arabella* ⎰
    Über Opern von Richard Strauss (Zurich, 1947)
    'Die Entstehung des Rosenkavalier' in *Trivium* (Zurich, 1951)
    Hugo von Hofmannsthal und Richard Strauss: Legende und Wirklichkeit (Munich 1964)
   (editor): *Richard Strauss Jahrbuch 1954* (Bonn, 1953)
   (editor): *Richard Strauss Jahrbuch 1959–60* (Bonn, 1960)

Seidl, Arthur: *Straussiana* (Regensburg, 1913)

Specht, Richard: *Richard Strauss und sein Werk* (Leipzig, 1921)

Steinitzer, Max: *Richard Strauss* (4 editions) (Berlin-Leipzig, 1911–27)

Richard Strauss Woche München 1910, Festival Brochure. (Munich, 1910)

Strauss, Richard: *Briefe an die Eltern* (Zurich-Freiburg, 1954)
    Betrachtungen und Erinnerungen (ed. Willi Schuh) (Zurich, 1949)
    Briefwechsel mit Hans von Bülow (in *Jahrbuch 1954*)
    Briefwechsel mit Josef Gregor (Salzburg, 1955)
    Briefwechsel mit Hugo von Hofmannsthal (ed. Franz and Alice Strauss) (Zurich, 1952)
    Briefwechsel mit Anton Kippenburg (in *Jahrbuch 1959–60*)
    Briefwechsel mit Clemens Krauss (Munich, 1964)
    Briefwechsel mit Romain Rolland (see *Fragments de Journal*)
    Briefwechsel mit Willi Schuh (Zurich, 1969)
    Briefwechsel mit Franz Wüllner (Cologne, 1963)
    Briefwechsel mit Stefan Zweig (Frankfurt, 1957)
    'Anmerkung zur Aufführung von Beethoven Symphonien' in *Neue Zeitschrift für Musik* (6/1964)

Tenschert, Roland: *Anekdoten von Richard Strauss* (Vienna, 1945)
    3 x 7 *Variationen über das Thema Richard Strauss* (Vienna, 1944)
    Richard Strauss und Wien (Vienna, 1949)

Tenschert, Roland and Werba, Erik: *Musikblätter, Sondernummer Richard Strauss zum 85 Geburtstag* (Vienna, 1949)

Trenner, Franz: *Richard Strauss: Dokumente seines Lebens und Schaffens* (Munich, 1954)

Wellesz, Egon: 'Hofmannsthal and Strauss' in *Music and Letters*, XXXIII, (1952)

Wulf, Joseph: *Musik im Dritten Reich* (Gütersloh, 1963)

Wurmser, Leo: 'Richard Strauss as an opera conductor' in *Music and Letters* (Jan. 1964)

INDEX TO VOLUMES I–III

(Songs by Strauss are indicated by the enumeration used throughout Volume III)